Spies, Wiretaps, and Secret Operations

Spies, Wiretaps, and Secret Operations

An Encyclopedia of American Espionage

Glenn P. Hastedt, Editor

Volume 2: K–Z

ABC-CLIO

Santa Barbara, California • Denver, Colorado • Oxford, England

Copyright 2011 by ABC-CLIO, LLC

Library of Congress Cataloging-in-Publication Data

  Spies, wiretaps, and secret operations : an encyclopedia of American espionage / Glenn P. Hastedt,
editor.
     v. cm.
  Includes bibliographical references and index.
  Contents: v. 1 A–J — v. 2. K–Z.
  ISBN 978–1–85109–807–1 (hard copy : alk. paper) — ISBN 978–1–85109–808–8 (ebook)
1. Espionage—United States—Encyclopedias. 2. Espionage, American—Encyclopedias. 3. Intelligence
service—United States—Encyclopedias. 4. Spies—United States—Encyclopedias. 5. Wiretapping—
United States—Encyclopedias. 6. Secret service—United States—Encyclopedias. I. Hastedt, Glenn P.,
1950–
JK468.I6S68   2010
327.1273003—dc22   2010021639

ISBN: 978–1–85109–807–1
EISBN: 978–1–85109–808–8

15 14 13 12 11   1 2 3 4 5

This book is also available on the World Wide Web as an eBook.
Visit www.abc-clio.com for details.

ABC-CLIO, LLC
130 Cremona Drive, P.O. Box 1911
Santa Barbara, California 93116-1911

This book is printed on acid-free paper ∞

Manufactured in the United States of America

Contents

List of Entries

Contributors

Alan Allport

Shelley Allsop

Rolando Avila

Derek A. Bentley

Richard A. Best, Jr.

Cynthia A. Boyle

Kevin M. Brady

Dino E. Buenviaje

Pamela L. Bunker

Robert J. Bunker

Matthew C. Cain

Laura M. Calkins

David M. Carletta

Roger Chapman

Michael W. Cheek

Don M. Coerver

Peter F. Coogan

Justin Corfield

L. Sean Crowley

Phillip Deery

Paul W. Doerr

Nicholas Dujmovic

Richard M. "Rich" Edwards

Elizabeth B. Elliot-Meisel

James L. Erwin

Gregory C. Ference

Eric Fettmann

Richard M. Filipink Jr.

Daniele Ganser

Michael R. Hall

Arthur Holst

Charles F. Howlett

David Jimenez

A. Ross Johnson

Wendell G. Johnson

Peter C. Jones

Sean N. Kalic

Gregory Kellerman

Jonathan H. L'Hommedieu

Frode Lindgjerdet

Martin J. Manning

Steven F. Marin

Melissa A. Marsh

Terry M. Mays

Jefferson McCarty

James Brian McNabb

Richard M. Mickle

Alexander Mikaberidze

Donald K. Mitchener

Paul David Nelson

Contributors

Elizabeth M. Nuxoll

Naoki Ohno

Lazarus F. O'Sako

Charlene T. Overturf

Vernon L. Pedersen

Barbara Bennett Peterson

Richard W. Peuser

J. Peter Pham

Vincent Kelly Pollard

Matthew Plowman

Vanessa de los Reyes

Steve Roane

Peter Rollberg

Charles A. Rosenberg

Kathleen Ruppert

James G. Ryan

Tom Sakmyster

Nicholas M. Sambaluk

Jackson L. Sigler

Katie Simonton

Steven E. Siry

Douglas V. Smith

Cezar Stanciu

Arthur K. Steinberg

Samaya L. Sukha

William T. Thornhill

Rebecca Tolley-Stokes

Spencer C. Tucker

Thomas D. Veve

Andrew J. Waskey

Kristin Whitehair

Todd J. Wiebe

James H. Willbanks

Brett F. Woods

K

KADISH, BEN-AMI

In April 2008, 84-year-old Ben-Ami Kadish was arrested on charges of having spied for Israel from 1979 to 1985. He was charged with four counts of conspiracy including a charge that he disclosed national defense documents to Israel and that he was an unregistered agent of Israel. Kadish confessed to Federal bureau of Investigation agents that he had passed between 50 and 200 classified documents to Israel. Kadish stated that he did not receive financial compensation for the material, only small gifts and an occasional dinner.

Kadish was born in Connecticut and served in the British and American militaries in World War II. He grew up in the British Mandate of Palestine. Kadish was employed at the Armament Research, Development and Engineering Center at the Picatinny Arsenal from 1963 through 1990. During this time Kadish's Israeli handler provided him with lists of information that he should try and obtain. Information Kadish secured for Israel included that on the F-15 fighter, the Patriot missile, and nuclear weapons.

Kadish's Israeli handler, Yossi Yagur, appears to be the same individual who handled navy civilian analyst Jonathan Pollard who was also convicted of spying for Israel and is serving a life sentence. Yagur, along with Israeli embassy official Illan Ravid, were recalled by the Israeli government in 1985. Kadish was warned by Ravid in March 2008 that U.S. officials were investigating him for espionage and instructed Kadish to say nothing.

Kadish was defended by friends as a loyal American patriot who firmly believed that there should be a Jewish state where Jews could practice their religion without persecution.

See also: Pollard, Jonathan Jay

References and Further Reading

Black, Ian, and Benny Morris. *Israel's Secret Wars: The Untold Story of Israeli Intelligence*. London: Hamish Hamilton, 1991.

Raviv, Dan, and Yossi Melman. *Every Spy a Prince: The Complete History of Israel's Intelligence Community*. Boston: Houghton Mifflin, 1990.

Glenn P. Hastedt

KAHN, DAVID
(FEBRUARY 7, 1930–)

David Kahn, who was born on February 7, 1930, is a historian of communications intelligence specializing in code breaking. Kahn's groundbreaking work has provided critical insight into the history of military intelligence. As an author of numerous books, scholarly publications, and popular articles, Kahn is considered a leading scholar in the field of the use of codes in espionage. Kahn focuses on codes used in political and military intelligence activities.

Initially intrigued by codes as a young boy when reading *Secret and Urgent* (Fletcher Pratt, 1939), he decided to study cryptology. He attended Bucknell University and during his time as an undergraduate he pursued stories about the National Security Agency's code-making and code-breaking organization.

Kahn's most noted publication is *The Codebreakers* (1967). In 1968 it was nominated for the Pulitzer Prize for general nonfiction. After publication of *The Codebreakers* Kahn focused on World War II German military intelligence, which led to the publication of *Hitler's Spies* in 1978. In 1991 he published *Seizing the Enigma* that explores German naval code usage during the Battle of the Atlantic (1939–1945).

In 1995 Kahn served as a Scholar in Residence for the National Security Agency. Kahn is a founding coeditor for *Cryptologia*, a scholarly quarterly publication. He continues to actively write and currently serves on the board of the International Spy Museum in Washington, DC.

See also: Journalists, Espionage and

References and Further Reading

Abrams, Arnold. "The Man Behind 'The Codebreakers', How David Kahn Brought Cryptology in from the Cole," *Newsday* (September 19, 2004), G6.

Beckman, Bengt. *Codebreakers: Arne Beurling and the Swedish Crypto Program During World War II*. Stockholm: American Mathematical Society, 1996.

Kahn, David. "Biography," David Kahn: Official Website, http://david-kahn.com (accessed October 10, 2006).

Kahn, David. *Seizing the Enigma: The Race to Break the German U-Boat Codes, 1939-1943*. Boston: Houghton Mifflin, 1990.

Kristin Whitehair

KALB, BARON JOHANN DE
(JUNE 19, 1721–AUGUST 19, 1780)

Baron Johann de Kalb, a military officer in the Revolutionary army, was born on June 19, 1721, in Huettendorf, Bavaria. He was born into the peasantry, but was able to successfully master French and English, allowing him to take a position in the Lowendal regiment of the French army.

He fought valiantly throughout the War of Austrian Succession, receiving a significant military commission. He became a baron in 1763, after being awarded the Order of Military Merit award in the Battle of Wilhemstahl. De Kalb remained in the military and was asked by the French government to go on a mission to the American colonies in 1768. He was asked to investigate and evaluate the colonists' discontent with the British government.

When the Revolutionary War began, De Kalb returned with his friend, the Marquis de Lafayette, in 1777. Both joined the Continental army and quickly proved their worth to General George Washington. First, De Kalb served as a badly needed administrator for Washington, but received a field command in the spring of 1780.

De Kalb led his troops to Charleston, South Carolina, in an attempt to save the besieged city. At the resulting battle of Camden later in the season, he was mortally wounded and captured by the British, dying on August 18, 1780.

See also: American Revolution and Intelligence

References and Further Reading

O'Toole, George J. A. *Honorable Treachery. A History of U.S. Intelligence, Espionage, and Covert Action from the American Revolution to the CIA.* New York: Atlantic Monthly Press, 1991.

Arthur Holst

KALUGIN, OLEG DANILOVICH (SEPTEMBER 6, 1934–)

Arguably the most controversial Committee for State Security (KGB) officer during the late perestroika period, General Oleg Kalugin, a shooting star of the 1960s Soviet intelligence community, became a short-lived reformer of the intelligence system before resigning amidst scandal and persecution.

Born on September 6, 1934, in Leningrad as the son of an People's Commissariat for State Security (NKVD) guard, Kalugin graduated from high school in spring 1952, publicly announcing his intention to work for the secret police. From 1952 to 1956, he studied at the KGB-run Leningrad Foreign Language Institute and, after graduating from the KGB Advanced School in Moscow in 1958, was sent to the United States under the cover of a "Fulbright scholar" studying journalism at Columbia University. In August 1959, he recruited a Russian émigré chemist code-named "Cook" and delivered money to a Soviet mole, "UNSUB DICK," in the Federal Bureau of Investigation's (FBI) field office in New York. Kalugin joined the rezidentura (residency) of Vladimir Barkovskii under the code name "Felix" in New York in 1960, using the cover of a Radio Moscow correspondent. In July 1965, he joined the residency of Boris Solomatin in Washington, DC, where he delivered $50,000 to Soviet spies William (Vladimir) Weisband (1908–1967) and supervised the handling of John Anthony Walker. His cover was that of second secretary of the USSR embassy and press officer.

In March 1970, Kalugin was appointed KGB deputy chief of counterintelligence and later chief of counterintelligence (March 1973). He was promoted to the rank of major general—the youngest ever in the history of the KGB—in 1974. In December 1975, he was involved in the accidental death of defector and double agent Nikolai

Artamonov. In 1978, he played a major role in the assassination of Bulgarian dissident Georgi Markov. However, late in 1978, Kalugin had a fallout with his superiors over his first recruit, "Cook," now suspected of being a double agent. Kalugin was transferred to the Leningrad KGB office as first deputy chief under Daniil Nozyrev (1980–1987). Following a series of demotions, he was forced to retire in September 1989. A public supporter of perestroika and glasnost, Kalugin made sensational suggestions to reform the KGB. In September 1990, he was elected to the Soviet parliament, serving until December 1991. After the August 1991 coup attempt, President Gorbachev returned him his rank and awards which he had earlier revoked.

After the collapse of the USSR and a failed reelection attempt in 1993, Kalugin went into private business. While in the United States in 1995, the Russian government issued a warrant for his arrest, prompting Kalugin to request political asylum, which was granted. In 2002, he was sentenced in absentia to 15 years in prison for high treason. Kalugin now resides in New York and Washington, DC, as a consultant. In 2009 he published an updated version of his memoirs which provided more detailed information about many of the events he alludes to in the original.

See also: Cold War Intelligence; Federal Bureau of Investigation (FBI); KGB (Komitet Gosudarstvennoi Bezopasnosti); NKVD (Narodnyj Komissariat Vnutrennikh Del— Peoples Commissariat for Internal Affairs); Walker Spy Ring

References and Further Reading

Kalugin, Oleg (with Fen Montaigne). *The First Directorate: My 32 Years in Intelligence and Espionage Against the West.* New York: St. Martin's Press, 1994.

West, Nigel. *Historical Dictionary of Cold War Counterintelligence.* Lanham, MD: The Scarecrow Press, 2007.

Jefferson McCarty, Peter Rollberg

KAMPILES, WILLIAM
(1955–)

William Kampiles served as a watch officer at the Central Intelligence Agency (CIA) Operations Center from March to November 1977. In 1978, Kampiles was convicted on charges of espionage and sentenced to 40 years in prison. Kampiles received only $3,000 from a Soviet agent in Athens, Greece. The damage to U.S. national security cannot be estimated in monetary terms.

Kampiles became dissatisfied as a watch officer and wanted to become an intelligence operative. After seven months on the job, Kampiles had unlawfully removed a copy of the top-secret technical manual on the KH-11 ("Big Bird") reconnaissance satellite system, and then resigned. He then traveled to Greece, where he met with a Soviet agent, and sold the copy of the KH-11 manual.

According to Admiral Stansfield Turner, former Director of Central Intelligence and Director of CIA, the KH-11 manuals, each individually numbered, were not regularly inventoried, including the document Kampiles removed prior to resigning from the agency. The compromise of the KH-11 manual allowed the Soviets to implement countermeasures in order to negate U.S. space surveillance efforts.

Despite the fact that what Kampiles did was categorized as one of the most serious security breaches of the cold war, the U.S. satellite reconnaissance system, to this day, returns priceless intelligence against targets in North Korea, Iran, and numerous terrorist training camps throughout the world.

See also: Central Intelligence Agency; Cold War Intelligence; KEYHOLE—SIGINT Satellites

References and Further Reading

Bearden, Milt, and James Risen. *The Main Enemy: The Inside Story of the CIA's Final Showdown with the KGB*. New York: Random House, 2003.

Taubman, Philip. *Secret Empire: Eisenhower, the CIA, and the Hidden Story of America's Space Espionage*. New York: Simon & Schuster, 2003.

Trento, Joseph J. *The Secret History of the CIA*. Roseville, CA: Prima Publishing, 2001. (reprinted New York: Avalon, 2005)

Turner, Stansfield. *Secrecy and Democracy: The CIA in Transition*. Boston: Houghton Mifflin, 1985.

David Jimenez

KELLEY, CLARENCE
(OCTOBER 24, 1911–AUGUST 5, 1997)

Clarence Kelley was the sixth director of the Federal Bureau of Investigation (FBI). He assumed the position on July 9, 1973, and followed acting Directors L. Patrick Gray and William Ruckelshaus. Kelley was born in Kansas City, Missouri, and received his law degree from the University of Kansas City in 1940. Later that year he joined the FBI as a special agent. During his career with the FBI, Kelley was special agent in charge of the Birmingham and Memphis offices. He retired from the FBI in 1961 and became chief of police in Kansas City.

Following the highly controversial directorships of J. Edgar Hoover who died in office in 1972 and Gray, Kelley worked to improve the FBI's management and the morale of its agents. He is credited with opening up lines of communication between agents and senior administrators and shifting the FBI's focus away from short-term investigations that produced positive statistics about its performance level to more long-term investigations.

At the same time, Kelley continued to defend the FBI's programs of espionage directed at Americans. As justification for these programs, he cited both a 1939 Presidential Directive and a preventive law enforcement function. Shortly after taking office Kelley also spoke out in defense of the COINTELPRO program that had ended in 1971. Intended to target the activities of the American Communist Party, COINTELPRO quickly expanded to a general surveillance program of Americans. Kelley asserted it did more good than harm and called for legislation that would allow it to begin again in case of a national emergency. He also repeated the familiar refrain that the FBI was conducting its work because of its responsibilities to the American people.

See also: COINTELPRO; Federal Bureau of Investigation (FBI)

References and Further Reading

Glick, Brian. *War at Home: Covert Action Against American Activists and What We Can Do About It*. Boston: South End Press, 1989.
Kessler, Ronald. *The Bureau: The Secret History of the FBI*. New York: St. Martin's Press, 2002.

Glenn P. Hastedt

KEMPEI TAI

The Japanese Kempei Tai, a counterespionage unit, was a branch of the Japanese armed forces. Assigned tasks regarding Japan's security, including both internal and external threats, the Kempei Tai exerted influential power in Japan and in Japanese-occupied territories. The Kempei Tai's primary duties included counterintelligence; protecting military secrets and sensitive information; preserving peace by collecting information; enforcing discipline in the Japanese army; and conducting surveillance of depots, post offices, and civilian employers. Kempei Tai were distinguished by their white arm bands worn on the left arm.

The foundation of the Kempei Tai was developed by Toyotomi Kideyoshi (1536–1598) as part of an underground secret society later known as the Black Ocean Society that acted to protect the ruler's power. Kideyoshi is noted as a leader who unified Japan and a critical part of his unification efforts focused on espionage. The Kempei Tai was officially established by Japanese government officials in 1881 to preserve the emperor's power. The Kempei Tai are part of a long tradition of espionage and secret societies in Japanese culture.

As a semi-independent branch of the Japanese army, they worked closely with Japanese intelligence forces. The Kempei Tai developed training schools such as Nakaro Ku located in Tokyo. Students at these schools studied homeland defense, law, and thought control methods.

In Japan the Kempei Tai primarily focused on enforcing conformity and suppressing dissident individuals and organizations. Additionally, elite Kempei Tai worked with espionage and counterespionage operations. The Kempei Tai gathered information about enemies. For example the Kempei Tai investigated weapons used by potential enemies such as armaments used by Germany during World War I.

However, their primary focus was on movement of people in Japan to gauge the potential development of threats to the military and rulers. One method to limit expression of dissident opinions was arresting individuals on the charge of "dangerous thoughts." Dissident thoughts, as defined by the Kempei Tai, were ideas that advocated change. Individuals supporting decreasing the military's power were especially targeted. In Japan between 1933 and 1936 over 59,000 individuals were charged with "dangerous thoughts" and arrested. Although the majority of those arrested on this charge were released, approximately 5,000 were tried in a court. Those convicted in a trial were imprisoned.

The Kempei Tai also acted to implant key ideas in the Japanese populace through propaganda. The Kempei Tai were particularly active in the campaign to the Greater East Asia Prosperity Plan. Educating the public about potential threats identified by the Japanese military was a major task assigned to the Kempei Tai. The Kempei Tai sponsored antispy weeks when numerous posters were hung in public spaces.

During World War I and World War II the Kempei Tai became even more powerful in Japan in attempts to prevent liberalization. The influential Japanese military and political leader Hideki Tojo (1884–1948) is evidence of the power held by the Kempei Tai as he rose to power and essentially controlled the entire Japanese government through the Kempei Tai. In regard to size, the Kempei Tai also dramatically expanded. During World War II the Kempei Tai increased their numbers from an estimated 2,600 in the 1930s to 70,000 active and reservists in 1945.

Additionally, Nazi Germany influenced the Kempei Tai prior to the outbreak of World War II. Nazi leaders who oversaw Nazi prison and concentration camps visited Japan and consulted with the Kempei Tai. Nazi leaders offered advice pertaining to treatment of prisoners and general policies. Immediately after the Nazi visit the Kempei Tai were noted as being significantly more brutal.

In Japanese-occupied territories, Kempei Tai's primary goal was to ensure stability of Japanese rule. Often former rulers were placed in Kempei Tai camps. The strategic imprisoning of former leaders allowed the Japanese to more easily set up their own governing systems. Abroad, Kempei Tai were commonly assigned duties to suppress guerrilla movements. Communists were regularly targeted due to their tendency to be uncooperative with Japanese officials.

The Kempei Tai also attempted to create an atmosphere in the occupied territory that would create a friendly neighbor for Japan and promote a united greater East Asian economy. In Japanese-occupied territories where Kempei Tai were stationed, the Kempei Tai are often noted for their extreme torture tactics. Common tactics Kempei Tai used in Japanese-occupied territories between 1942 and 1945 include beatings, various forms of water torture, electrocution, starvation, and mental torture.

Kempei Tai commonly arrested individuals deemed dissident or suspected of espionage activities. Prisons where Kempei Tai captives were held commonly were overcrowded and dysentery was common among prisoners. Commonly prisoners were provided little food and water. As evidence of this it is estimated that at Fort Santiago, the Philippines, in December of 1944 more than 200 prisoners died due to overcrowding. Generally prisoners were confined approximately five months and then released or sent elsewhere.

The official Kempei Tai was dissolved during the Allied occupation of Japan. Additionally, 233 secret societies advocating rightist philosophies were disbanded by decrees issued by occupational forces including the secret society supporting the Kempei Tai. As the Japanese grew to trust the occupying Allied forces they grew more comfortable without a powerful espionage network as had existed before.

However, in 1954 Japanese Self Defense Forces were legalized. With the Japanese Self Defense Forces a Public Security Investigation Agency was established which engaged in limited espionage activities. As the Self Defense Forces continued to grow, other units were established that were charged with additional espionage activities.

See also: American Intelligence, World War I; American Intelligence, World War II

References and Further Reading

Allen, Louis. "Japanese Intelligence Systems," *Journal of Contemporary History* 22:4 (1987), 547–562.

Deacon, Richard. *Kempei Tai: A History of the Japanese Secret Service.* New York: Beaufort Books, 1983.

Norman, E. Herbert. "The Genyosha: A Study in the Origins of Japanese Imperialism," *Pacific Affairs* 17 (1944), 261–284.

Stargardt, A. W. "The Emergence of the Asian System of Powers," *Modern Asian Studies* 23:2 (1989), 561–595.

Syjuco, Ma. Felisa A. *The Kempei Tai in the Philippines, 1941-1945*. Quezon City: New Day Publishers, 1988.

Kristin Whitehair

KENNEDY ADMINISTRATION AND INTELLIGENCE

John F. Kennedy was president from 1961 to 1963. Allen Dulles and John McCone served as Directors of Central Intelligence during his presidency. Kennedy brought a military background to thinking about intelligence as had Dwight Eisenhower before him. He tended to think of human intelligence (HUMINT) in terms of paramilitary activity. He also shared Eisenhower's fascination with imagery intelligence (IMINT) but was far less taken with signals intelligence (SIGINT). Kennedy shared yet another link to Eisenhower. Both failed to ask hard questions of the Central Intelligence Agency (CIA) about its plan to overthrow Cuba's Fidel Castro by means of the Bay of Pigs invasion and when that failed through assassination. Both confused Richard Bissell's success in managing the development of the U-2 spy plane with a capacity to organize a successful covert operation. Eisenhower left office with the Bay of Pigs still in the planning stages. Kennedy dealt with the consequences of its failure. The price for the CIA was the dismissal of Allen Dulles and reduced influence with the president. One step it took to try and regain access was the product of a new morning intelligence report especially tailored to the president's interests, the "President's Intelligence Checklist." Kennedy also reactivated the President's Foreign Intelligence Advisory Board (PFIAB) in an attempt to upgrade the performance of the intelligence community and provide better oversight. James Killian, who during the Eisenhower administration had chaired the committee that recommended the development of the U-2 spy plane, and Clark Clifford, who would become secretary of defense in the Johnson administration, chaired the PFIAB under Kennedy. One of its many recommendations accepted by Kennedy was the creation of the Defense Intelligence Agency (DIA). It was to bring order to the competition among military service intelligence agencies without replacing them. During Vietnam it would emerge as a major competitor to the CIA within the intelligence community in construction of intelligence estimates.

Both HUMINT and IMINT played major roles in two of the Kennedy administrations most significant foreign policy successes. HUMINT, in the form of Soviet spy Colonel Oleg Penkovsky of Soviet military intelligence, provided valuable information regarding Soviet thinking during both the Berlin crises and the Cuban missile crisis. IMINT, in the form of U-2 photographs, provided the administration with concrete proof of Soviet actions in Cuba and time to formulate a response. Their public release helped galvanize American and world opinion behind the administration.

John Kennedy's relationship with the Federal Bureau of Investigation (FBI) was strained by the mutual hostility felt by FBI Director J. Edgar Hoover and Attorney

General Robert Kennedy toward one another. For political reasons Kennedy felt he had little choice but to allow Hoover to continue to serve as director and announced he would do so during the 1960 presidential campaign. Moreover, not only was Hoover widely respected by the American public but John Kennedy had been, and continued to be throughout his presidency, a prime target of Hoover's illicit domestic espionage activities. At the same time both John and Robert Kennedy were consumers of Hoover's intelligence on other political figures.

See also: Bay of Pigs; Bissell, Richard Mervin, Jr.; Castro, Fidel; Central Intelligence Agency; Cold War Intelligence; Cuban Missile Crisis; Dulles, Allen Welsh; McCone, John A.; Penkovsky, Oleg Vladimirovich; President's Foreign Intelligence Advisory Board

References and Further Reading

Andrew, Christopher. *For the President's Eyes Only: Secret Intelligence and the American Presidency from Washington to Bush*. New York: HarperCollins, 1995.

Donner, Frank. *The Age of Surveillance: The Aims and Methods of America's Political Intelligence System*. New York: Vintage, 1981.

Kessler, Ronald. *The Bureau: The Secret History of the FBI*. New York: St. Martin's Press, 2002.

Ranelagh, John. *The Rise and Decline of the CIA*. Revised and updated. New York: Touchstone, 1987.

Glenn P. Hastedt

KENNEDY ASSASSINATION

President John F. Kennedy was assassinated on November 22, 1963, in Dallas, Texas. Lee Harvey Oswald was arrested for murdering the president later that day. On November 23, Oswald was killed by Jack Ruby while he was in the custody of the Dallas police. Since that time controversy has surrounded the Central Intelligence Agency's (CIA) support of plans for assassinating Cuban leader Fidel Castro and the extent of the Federal Bureau of Investigation' s (FBI) knowledge of and handling of Oswald, prior to Kennedy's assassination.

Following a June 1963 decision by the Special Group of the National Security Council to increase covert actions against Cuba, the CIA had contact with a high-level Cuban official given the code name AMLASH, who proposed the overthrow of the Cuban government, an act he anticipated would require Castro's assassination. The United States had earlier made contact with and used underworld crime leaders to plot Castro's assassination. Not long after this June 1963 meeting Castro announced that the United States had met with terrorist leaders who wished to kill Cuban officials. He promised to retaliate in kind. Additional meetings were held between AMLASH and the CIA right before and on the day of Kennedy's assassination in which support for an overthrow of Castro was given.

Oswald provided a link to Cuba that has been at the center of conspiracy theories because of his contact with pro-Castro Cubans in the United States. Born on October 18, 1939, in Slidell, Louisiana, Oswald became a self-pronounced Marxist while a teenager. Nonetheless, he enlisted in the marines prior to graduating from high school and served

U.S. President John F. Kennedy, Governor John Connally of Texas, and First Lady
Jacqueline Kennedy ride through Dallas, Texas, on November 22, 1963, moments before
the president is killed by an assassin. (Library of Congress)

as a radar operator. Oswald defected to the Soviet Union in 1959 and told the American
embassy in Moscow he wanted to renounce his American citizenship and that he intended
to provide the Russians with radar secrets. At that point the Federal Bureau of Investigation (FBI) opened a file on Oswald. It concluded he did not have the information he
promised to deliver to the Russians but warned that someone might try and return to
the United States using Oswald's identity. This warning was apparently lost in the
bureaucracy.

Oswald returned to the United States on June 13, 1962, with a Russian wife, Marina
Prusakova. He was interrogated twice by the FBI and denied having threatened to
defect or turn over secrets to Russia. The FBI closed his case on August 20, 1962. It
was not opened again until March 26, 1963. Shortly after the case was reopened the
FBI's New York Field Office reported that Oswald had made contact with the Fair
Play for Cuba Committee, a pro-Castro organization. This information, along with
information that he had subscribed to a Communist newspaper, were not given to the
Dallas office until September 1963.

In August 1963 Oswald was arrested in New Orleans for his activities on behalf of
the Fair Play for Cuba Committee. At his request he also met with an FBI agent and
repeatedly lied to him. Soon thereafter, from September 27 to October 2, Oswald went
to Mexico City. While there he met with Soviet Embassy Vice Council Kostikov who
was known to work for the KGB and be involved in assassination and sabotage operations. Information on this meeting was slow to be sent to the Dallas and New Orleans
FBI offices and when uncovered did not produce any increased coverage of Oswald.
Upon his return to the United States, Oswald moved from New Orleans to Irving,

Texas. He also visited the FBI's Dallas office and left a note for FBI Special Agent James P. Hosty, Jr., that was subsequently destroyed. After Oswald's death an informer approached the U.S. embassy in Mexico City and stated that he was in the Cuban Consulate on September 18 and saw Cubans pay Oswald a sum of money and talk about assassination.

In reviewing the evidence, the Church Committee, officially the Select Committee to Study Government Operations with respect to Intelligence Activities, did not find evidence of a conspiracy to assassinate President Kennedy. It identified many instances of bureaucratic ineptitude in the handling of Oswald's case before the assassination. The Church Committee also concluded that there were serious deficiencies in how the FBI and CIA investigated the assassination, including efforts to prevent the Warren Commission from receiving potentially important information that reflected poorly on these agencies. The Church Committee also found that pressures were placed on the FBI by Director J. Edgar Hoover and higher government officials to conclude its investigation quickly.

See also: Castro, Fidel; Central Intelligence Agency; Church Committee; Federal Bureau of Investigation (FBI); Paisley, John

References and Further Reading

Garrison, Jim. *On the Trail of the Assassins: My Investigation and Prosecution of the Murder of President Kennedy*. New York: Sheridan Square Press, 1988.

Hinckle, Warren, and William Turner. *Deadly Secrets: The CIA-Mafia War Against Castro and the Assassination of J.F.K.* New York: Thunder's Mouth Press, 1992.

Posner, Gerald. *Case Closed: Lee Harvey Oswald and the Assassination of JFK*. New York: Random House, 1993.

Report of the President's Commission on the Assassination of President John F. Kennedy. [The Warren Commission Report]. Washington, DC: United States Government Printing Office, 1964.

Sample, Robert (ed.). *Four Days in November: The Original Coverage [by the New York Times] of the John F. Kennedy Assassination*. New York: St. Martins, 2003.

United States Senate, Select Committee to Study Governmental Operations with respect to Intelligence Activities. *Final Report, Book V: The Investigation of the Assassination of President John F. Kennedy: Performance of the Intelligence Agencies*. Washington, DC: Government Printing Office, April 23, 1976.

Glenn P. Hastedt

KENT, SHERMAN
(DECEMBER 6, 1903–MARCH 11, 1986)

Sherman Kent was an intelligence analyst at the Office of the Coordinator of Information (COI), the Office of Strategic Services (OSS), and the Department of State; director of the Office of National Estimates and chairman; of the Board of National Estimates of the Central Intelligence Agency (CIA). Born on December 1, 1903, in Chicago, Sherman Kent received his undergraduate and doctoral degrees in 1926 and 1933, respectively, from Yale University where, as a professor, he taught modern European history from 1935 to 1941.

In 1941, he joined the COI and became chief of the Africa section of its Research and Analysis Branch. From 1943 he served as chief of the Europe-Africa Division of the same branch of the OSS. After the OSS was abolished and the branch was transferred to the Department of State, he became the acting director of the Office of Research and Intelligence of the department.

He returned to Yale in 1947 and published a book in 1949, *Strategic Intelligence for American World Policy*. This is one of the earliest and most highly regarded writings on strategic intelligence. In 1950 he joined the CIA and became deputy director of the Office of National Estimates and vice chairman of the Board of National Estimates. Two years later he became their director and chairman, respectively, and remained in those positions until his retirement in 1967. He died on March 11, 1986, at his home in Washington, DC.

See also: Board of National Estimates; Central Intelligence Agency; Coordinator of Information; National Intelligence Estimates; Office of Strategic Services

References and Further Reading

Davis, Jack. "Sherman Kent and the Profession of Intelligence Analysis," Washington, D.C.: Central Intelligence Agency, The Sherman Kent Center for Intelligence Analysis Occasional Papers 1, (2002). https://www.cia.gov/library/kent-center-occasional-papers/ (accessed January 17, 2006).

Kent, Sherman. *Strategic Intelligence for American World Policy*. Princeton, NJ: Princeton University Press, 1949.

Winks, Robin W. *Cloak and Gown: Scholars in the Secret War, 1939–1961*, 2nd ed. New Haven, CT: Yale University Press, 1996.

Naoki Ohno

KEYHOLE—SIGINT SATELLITES

KEYHOLE, also referred to in the past as KH and TALENT-KEYHOLE is the previously classified top-secret codeword term, now unclassified, used to describe a series of U.S. communication and imagery satellites, the first of which was placed into orbit as early on December 19, 1976. The National Security Agency (NSA) had used the term *Keyhole*, whereas *Talent* belonged to the Central Intelligence Agency. The earlier versions of the KH satellite itself were described as about half the size of a football field. Subsequent generations of KH satellites, such as the cylindrical-shaped KH-11, measured 64 feet in length, 10 feet in diameter, and weighed in at around 30,000 pounds. Some of the KH satellites reached orbits of at least 300 miles from earth.

KEYHOLE satellites were used in 1968 to monitor and photograph various areas of Czechoslovakia (specifically activities at airfields, massing of troops near the border, and other logistical indicators), which revealed no indications of Soviet preparations for an invasion. Other subsequent satellite coverage (CORONA) did reveal the above indications, but was too late for the United States, as the invasion had already taken place.

The KH-11 satellite system, also referenced by the code names Crystal and Kennan, was also commonly known as "Big Bird." It was the first American spy satellite to utilize electro-optical digital imaging and create a real-time optical observation capability. Though the KH-11 provided near real-time digitized imagery, it was designated as an Electronic Intelligence (ELINT) type of satellite since it was also capable of transmitting signals intelligence (SIGINT) information. KEYHOLE results, particularly for the KH series satellites, were eventually classified Top Secret Umbra, an overall codeword used to describe high-level SIGINT information. Some of the names used to also describe the KH series included Kennan and Crystal.

On April 28, 1984, a KH-11 imagery satellite, an electro-optical satellite not requiring film, and already in orbit, was used to monitor the nuclear incident disaster in Chernobyl, Soviet Union, several days after the explosion. The KH-11 satellite was able to obtain such high-quality images of the disaster that photo interpreters at the National Photographic Interpretation Center (NPIC, now part of National Imagery & Mapping Agency) were able to observe that the roof of the nuclear power plant had literally blown off, and the walls of the facility pushed outward. The United States continued to monitor the Chernobyl disaster well into May 1984, providing updates to the U.S. intelligence community and government officials. The KH-11 reportedly provided imagery resolution down to four to six inches across, though subsequent generations and variations of the KH series satellites today provide much better resolution.

Also noteworthy is the fact that several of the KH series satellites could actually operate at stationary locations over 22,000 miles out from the earth, focused on the former Soviet Union and also China. Both telemetry tests and even microwave telephone calls were collected simultaneously by such platforms.

The KH-11 satellite was among the first generation of KEYHOLE satellites that were referred to as "real-time imagery." These KH series satellites did not require film. All imagery was processed into a digitized format which was then relayed to a ground station where the images were then "reassembled" within a relatively short period of time. The KH-11 series was also used to obtain very high-quality, near real-time images of the American embassy in Tehran, during the takeover by Iranian militants on November 4, 1979, and made available to then President Jimmy Carter.

During the mid-1980s, the average cost of an individual satellite was estimated to be anywhere from 60 to 70 million dollars. This does not reflect the cost of associated equipment and relay terminals on the ground. One such location, 600 miles southeast of Alice Springs in Australia, and code-named "Casino," processed information downloaded from KEYHOLE satellites after they passed over China. In the United States, Fort Belvoir, Virginia, about 20 miles south of Washington, DC, was another ground station.

KEYHOLE satellites came under the direct oversight of what was then the highly classified National Reconnaissance Office, or NRO. The designation NRO became public in 1995. Keyhole derived intelligence was shared with U.S. allies around the globe, most notably Australia, Canada, and the UK, sometimes referred to in correspondence as CANUKUS.

See also: National Photographic Interpretation Center (NPIC); National Reconnaissance Office; National Security Agency; Satellites

References and Further Reading

Bamford, James. *The Puzzle Palace: Inside the National Security Agency, America's Most Secret Intelligence Organization.* Boston, MA: Houghton Mifflin, 1982.

Bearden, Milt, and James Risen. *The Main Enemy: The Inside Story of the CIA's Final Showdown with the KGB.* New York: Random House, 2003.

Burrows, William E. E. *By Any Means Necessary: America's Secret Air War in the Cold War.* New York: Farrar, Strauss, and Giroux, 2001.

Frost, Mike, and Michael Gratton. *Spyworld: Inside the Canadian and American Intelligence Establishments.* Toronto: Doubleday Canada Limited, 1994.

Richelson, Jeffrey. *A Century of Spies: Intelligence in the Twentieth Century.* New York: Oxford University Press, 1995.

Richelson, Jeffrey. *The Wizards of Langley: Inside the CIA's Directorate of Science and Technology.* Boulder, CO: Westview Press, 2002.

RST. "Technical and Historical Perspectives of Remote Sensing," http://rst.gsfc.nasa.gov/Intro/Part2_26e.html (accessed January 12).

Schecter, Jerrold, and Leona. *Sacred Secrets: How Soviet Intelligence Operations Changed American History.* Washington, DC: Brassey's Inc, 2002.

Space.com. "Secret Satellite Photos To Be Unveiled," http://www.space.com/news/secret_sat_020906.html (accessed January 12).

David Jimenez

KEYSER, DONALD
(JULY 17, 1943–)

A career foreign service officer, Donald Keyser, then 63, was arrested on September 15, 2004, only days before retirement from the State Department and a few months after he submitted his resignation. He was sentenced on January 23, 2007, to one year and one day in jail, fined $25,000, and placed on three years of supervised release for (1) admitting that he was in unauthorized possession of 3,659 classified documents; (2) that he lied to State Department investigators about a relationship with Isabelle Cheng, then 37, and a Taiwanese intelligence officer, that made him vulnerable to coercion and exploitation by a foreign government; and (3) that he lied on a U.S. Customs form in September 2003 about not having visited Taiwan. In return for his cooperation U.S. authorities agreed not to prosecute Keyser for espionage. They later reversed this decision when it appeared that Keyser was not cooperating fully with investigators but then reaffirmed their original decision when his level of cooperation increased.

Keyser joined the foreign service in 1972. At the time of his arrest Keyser was the principal deputy assistant secretary of state for East Asian and pacific affairs. Prior to holding this position, Keyser had served as special negotiator for Nagorno-Karabakh and New Independent States Regional Conflicts, senior inspector in the Office of Inspector General, and office director in the Bureau of Narcotics and Law Enforcement Affairs. He had served three tours in the U.S. embassy in Beijing, two times in the U.S. embassy in Tokyo, and three times in the State Department's Office of Chinese and Mongolian Affairs. President Bill Clinton appointed Keyser to the rank of ambassador in 1999.

Keyser is known to have met with Cheng on his September 2003 trip to Taiwan, and again in May and July 2004. He often communicated with her through e-mail on such topics as his conversations with Chinese President Jiang and a possible target working for the Heritage Foundation Asia that Keyser said was "ripe for recruitment." He was stopped by FBI agents leaving an Alexandria, Virginia, restaurant on September 2, 2004. Cheng returned to Taiwan for "family reasons" after the FBI questioned her about her relationship with Keyser. Keyser's fourth wife was senior intelligence officer in the CIA who was working in the Office of the Director of National Intelligence and reportedly knew that Keyser had some classified material on his home computer.

Keyser was highly regarded by his colleagues for his expertise in Asian affairs but he had already encountered security problems once. In December 2000 he was one of several State Department officials disciplined for the disappearance of a laptop computer with secret information about weapons of mass destruction proliferation from Secretary of State Madeline Albright's office.

See also: Post–Cold War Intelligence

References and Further Reading

Herbig, Katherine. *Changes in Espionage by Americans.* Monterey, CA: Defense Personnel Research Center, 2008.
Lefebrve, Stephane. "The Case of Donald Keyser and Taiwan's National Security Bureau," *International Journal of Intelligence and CounterIntelligence* 20 (2007), 512–526.

Glenn P. Hastedt

KGB (KOMITET GOSUDARSTVENNOI BEZOPASNOSTI)

The main Soviet security and intelligence agency from March 13, 1954, to November 6, 1991. During this period, the Komitet Gosudarstvennoi Bezopasnosti (KGB, Committee for State Security) operated as an agency and even a ministry. Its tasks included external espionage, counterespionage, and the liquidation of anti-Soviet and counterrevolutionary forces within the Soviet Union. The KGB also guarded the borders and investigated and prosecuted those who committed political or economic crimes.

Soviet security forces have a long history, dating back to the pre-1917 czarist period. Communist predecessors of the KGB were the All-Russian Extraordinary Commissary against the Counterrevolution and Sabotage (also known by its Russian acronym, Cheka), the Main Political Department (GPU), and the Joint Main Political Department (OGPU) headed by Felix Dzerzhinsky, the "Knight of the Revolution," from 1917 to 1926. The name "Cheka" suggested that it was to be only a temporary body, but the agency became one of the principal pillars of the Soviet system. In 1934, the OGPU merged into the People's Commissariat of Internal Affairs (NKVD), with Genrikh Yagoda (1934–1936), Nikolai Yezhov (1936–1938), and Lavrenty Beria (1938–1945) as its chiefs. Under Yezhov and Beria, the NKVD carried out brutal purges within the Communist Party of the Soviet Union (CPSU). NKVD officers, for example, murdered Leon Trotsky in Mexico in 1940.

During the rule of Soviet dictator Josef Stalin, the security apparatus had achieved almost unrestricted powers to harass, arrest, and detain those who were perceived as class enemies. The Soviet Union thus became a police state in which millions of innocent victims suffered arbitrary and brutal terror. Official figures suggest that between January 1935 and June 1941, some 19.8 million people were arrested by the NKVD and an estimated 7 million were subsequently executed.

Following World War II, in 1946 the NKVD was raised to a state ministry under Beria, who became a member of the Politburo. After the deaths of Stalin (March 1953) and Beria (December 1953), the security services were again reorganized, and on

March 13, 1954, the secret police was renamed the KGB. There were a half dozen principal directorates.

The First Directorate was responsible for foreign operations and intelligence-gathering activities. The Second Directorate carried out internal political control of citizens and had responsibility for the internal security of the Soviet Union. The Third Directorate was occupied with military counterintelligence and political control of the armed forces. The Fifth Directorate also dealt with internal security, especially with religious bodies, the artistic community, and censorship. The Ninth Directorate, which employed 40,000 persons, provided (among other things) uniformed guards for principal CPSU leaders and their families. The Border Guards Directorate was a 245,000-person force that oversaw border control. Total KGB manpower estimates range from 490,000 in 1973 to 700,000 in 1986.

The KGB helped and trained the security and intelligence agencies in other Communist countries. It was also heavily involved in supporting wars of national liberation in the developing world, especially in Africa. The Soviet Union also maintained a close alliance with the Palestine Liberation Organization (PLO), providing it with arms, funds, and paramilitary training. The KGB mostly avoided direct involvement with terrorist operations, but it played an important role in directing aid to these groups and producing intelligence reports on their activities. Scandals concerning defectors and moles plagued the KGB throughout its existence, but the agency also scored notable successes such as, for example, the recruitment of the Cambridge Five in Great Britain; atomic scientist Klaus Fuchs; and Aldrich Ames, a KGB mole within the U.S. Central Intelligence Agency (CIA).

Under Stalin's successor, Nikita Khrushchev, the terror lessened considerably. Both the security police and the regular police were subjected to a new legal code, and the KGB was made subordinate to the Council of Ministers. Nevertheless, it was allowed to circumvent the law when combating political dissent. Indeed, in the 1960s and 1970s, the KGB waged a campaign against dissidents such as Aleksandr Solzhenitsyn and Andrei Sakharov, who became worldwide symbolic figures of communist repression. In July 1978 the head of the KGB received a seat on the Council of Ministers.

The KGB had a considerable impact on Soviet domestic and foreign policy making. Its chief, Yuri Andropov, became CPSU leader in 1982. Under Mikhail Gorbachev's reform policies from 1985 to 1990, Soviet citizens' fears of the KGB diminished, which signaled the erosion of the Soviet system. The KGB was dissolved in November 1991 following the August coup attempt against Gorbachev, which was engineered by KGB chief Colonel General Vladimir Kryuchkov. Its successor organization, the Federalnaya Sluzhba Bezopasnosti (FSB, Federal Security Service), bears great resemblance to the old security apparatus.

See also: Ames, Aldrich; Atomic Spy Ring; Beria, Laventry Pavlovich; Cold War Intelligence; FSB Russian Federal Security Service; Fuchs, Emil Julius Klaus; GRU (Main Intelligence Directorate); NKVD (Narodnyj Komissariat Vnutrennikh Del—Peoples Commissariat for Internal Affairs)

References and Further Reading

Bittman, Ladislav. *The KGB and Soviet Disinformation: An Insider's View*. London: Pergamon, 1972.

Ebron, Martin. *KGB: Death and Rebirth*. New York: Praeger, 1990.

Epstein, Edward, J. *Deception: The Invisible War Between the KGB and the CIA*. New York: Allen, 1989.

Kalugin, Oleg (with Fen Montaigne). *The First Directorate: My 32 Years in Intelligence and Espionage Against the West*. New York: St. Martin's Press, 1994 & 2007.

Kazichkin, Valdimir. *Inside the KGB: My Life in Soviet Espionage*. London: Andre Deutsch, 1990.

Glenn P. Hastedt

KILLIAN, DR. JAMES R., JR.
(JULY 24, 1904–JANUARY 29, 1988)

Dr. James Rhyne Killian, Jr., served as President Dwight Eisenhower's special assistant for science and technology from 1957 to 1959 and was responsible for recommending and overseeing the development of the U-2 spy plane and the Corona surveillance satellite, as well as the creation of NASA. He served as chairman of the President's Foreign Intelligence Advisory Board (PFIAB) under President John F. Kennedy from 1961 to 1963.

Killian was born July 24, 1904, in Blacksburg, South Carolina. After earning a BS in engineering and business from the Massachusetts Institute of Technology (MIT) in 1926, Killian remained at the school in a variety of positions over the next three decades, including the presidency of MIT from 1948 to 1959. Killian also served in a number of science and intelligence related posts in the 1950s and 1960s.

From 1954 to 1955, he served as chairman of the Technological Capabilities Panel in the Office of Defense Mobilization, which recommended the development of the U-2. Eisenhower appointed him special assistant for science and technology in 1957. Responding to Sputnik's launch, Killian chaired the President's Scientific Advisory Committee and recommended the creation of NASA and development of CORONA intelligence satellites. After the Bay of Pigs, President Kennedy appointed Killian chairman of the PFIAB. Killian died on January 29, 1988, in Cambridge.

See also: Bay of Pigs; CORONA; President's Foreign Intelligence Advisory Board; Satellites; U-2 Incident

References and Further Reading

Killian, James R., Jr. *Sputnik, Scientists, and Eisenhower: A Memoir of the First Special Assistant to the President for Science and Technology*. Cambridge, MA: The MIT Press, 1977.

Wenger, Andreas. *Living with Peril: Eisenhower, Kennedy, and Nuclear Weapons*. Lanham, MD: Rowman & Littlefield, 1997.

Richard M. Filipink Jr.

KIRKPATRICK, LYMAN BICKFORD, JR.
(JULY 15, 1916–MARCH 3, 1995)

Lyman B. Kirkpatrick, Jr., played a prominent role in the early formation of the U.S. intelligence structure. Kirkpatrick was born on July 15, 1916, in Rochester, New York. He graduated from Princeton University's School of Public and International Affairs in

1938. In 1942, Kirkpatrick relinquished his position on the editorial board of U.S. News and World Report in Washington, DC, to enlist in the Office of the Coordinator of Information, which later evolved into the Office of Strategic Services (OSS).

Based in London, Kirkpatrick served as a liaison to Allied intelligence services during World War II. In 1943, he was commissioned as a lieutenant in the U.S. Army and made responsible for briefing General Omar Bradley on intelligence matters. He retained this position until the end of the war. In January 1947, Kirkpatrick was recruited into the newly formed Central Intelligence Group. He continued his responsibilities with the Central Intelligence Agency (CIA) after its establishment in September 1947.

Kirkpatrick worked as a division chief and later as the Deputy Assistant Director for Operations under Director of Central Intelligence (DCI) Roscoe Hillenkoetter. In December 1950, DCI Walter Bedell Smith made Kirkpatrick his executive assistant. In July 1952, Kirkpatrick contracted polio while in Asia on CIA business. Paralyzed from the waist down, he spent the rest of his life in a wheelchair.

In 1953, Kirkpatrick returned to the CIA as inspector general under Director Allen Dulles. As inspector general, he chaired a joint study group on foreign intelligence whose findings led to the creation of the Defense Intelligence Agency in 1961. Following the failed Bay of Pigs invasion of 1961, Kirkpatrick compiled an internal report on the CIA's handling of the operation. The report, which was critical of the agency's management of the operation, incited controversy within the CIA and remained classified until 1998. In April 1962, DCI John McCone appointed Kirkpatrick to the newly created position of executive director. Kirkpatrick retired from the CIA in 1965 and assumed a professorship at Brown University.

While at Brown, Kirkpatrick published a number of books and articles on intelligence. He retired from teaching in 1982 and moved to Middleburg, Virginia, with his wife, Rita Kirkpatrick, in 1983. Kirkpatrick died in Middleburg on March 3, 1995.

See also: Bay of Pigs; Central Intelligence Agency; Office of Strategic Services; Smith, General Walter Bedell

References and Further Reading

Kirkpatrick, Lyman B., Jr. *The Real CIA: An Insider's View of the Strengths and Weaknesses of Our Government's Most Important Agency*. New York: Macmillan, 1968.

Montague, Ludwell Lee. *General Walter Bedell Smith as Director of Central Intelligence, October 1950– February 1953*. University Park, PA: The Pennsylvania State University Press, 1992.

Weber, Ralph E. *Spymasters: Ten CIA Officers in Their Own Words*. Wilmington, DE: Scholarly Resources, 1999.

Derek A. Bentley

KISSINGER, HENRY ALFRED
(MAY 27, 1923–)

Henry Alfred Kissinger was secretary of state of the United States from 1973 to 1977 and received the Nobel Peace Prize in 1973. As scholar and politician, Kissinger contributed to the elaboration of the American realpolitik and détente in the cold war.

President Richard Nixon in deep discussion with adviser Henry Kissinger. Kissinger was the principal architect of U.S. foreign policy during the administrations of Republican presidents Richard Nixon and Gerald Ford, serving as national security adviser during the first Nixon administration and secretary of state from 1972 until the end of the Ford administration. (National Archives)

He was born in Germany on May 27, 1923, and was naturalized in the United States after his family fled from Germany due to Nazi persecutions. Kissinger attended Harvard College and received a BA in 1950, MA in 1952, and PhD in 1954. Between 1954 and 1971 he worked as a member of the faculty in the Department of Government and at the Center for International Affairs. At the same time, he occupied different positions as a consultant within the National Security Council and the Council of Foreign Relations.

As a scholar, Henry Kissinger conducted extensive researches and studies on American foreign and security policy, international relations, and diplomacy. His books and articles in these fields brought him numerous awards and distinctions: the Woodrow Wilson Prize (1958), the American Institute for Public Service Award (1973), the International Platform Association Theodore Roosevelt Award (1973).

After Richard Nixon was elected president he appointed Henry Kissinger as national security advisor, a position in which he served until 1975. Later on in 1973, Kissinger became secretary of state. He held this office until 1977, under President Gerald Ford as well.

A convinced supporter of realpolitik, Kissinger played a dominant role upon the U.S. foreign policy during his years at the White House. His belief was that American national interest should prevail upon the idealistic principles pursued traditionally by American foreign policy makers since Woodrow Wilson. Kissinger sought a policy of détente between Washington and Moscow. He encouraged the negotiation of the Strategic Arms Limitation talks (SALT I Treaty) and the Anti-Ballistic Missile Treaty. His strategy towards the Soviet Union was dual: détente by negotiations in arms control were accompanied by an unusual turn in American foreign policy towards China. Given the conflict between China and the Soviet Union, Kissinger successfully tried to apply pressure on the Soviet Union and expand the American options in foreign affairs by a rapprochement with Red China. In 1971 Kissinger conducted the American talks with Chinese Prime Minister Zhou Enlai, which marked the beginning of a historical reconciliation between the two countries. This way, Kissinger managed to create a new Sino-American alliance directed against Moscow.

In order to counter the Communist menace, Kissinger was in favor of close political relations with anti-Communist military dictatorships in Latin America. Later on, he was to be accused of being responsible for the atrocities committed by the Argentine military Junta. Also, in the Indo-Pakistani War of 1971, Kissinger granted support to the Pakistani forces in spite of the massacres they committed. His purpose was to discourage the alliance between India and the Soviet Union. Henry Kissinger played an important part in the cease-fire that concluded the Vietnam War and made possible the American military withdrawal. For this contribution especially, Kissinger was awarded the Nobel Peace Prize in 1973. In 1977 he also received the Presidential Medal of Freedom.

Kissinger's stay in the White House was highly controversial for several reasons. For one, the Vietnam War was a highly divisive undertaking and the Nixon-Kissinger strategy to end it through large-scale bombings of the North and invading Cambodia produced large protests. His championing of détente as a foreign policy strategy to replace containment also alienated many conservative Republicans who would break with the party and support Ronald Reagan's candidacy for president over that of Gerald Ford. Finally, his support for covert action and tolerance of human rights abuses as part of a strategy for securing American national interest in the Third World drew the opposition of liberal internationalists. Nowhere was this more apparent than in their opposition to the Nixon-Kissinger policy of bringing down the government of Salvadore Allende in Chile. Kissinger's association with this policy and the repressive regime of General Augusto Pinochet would later lead to calls for bringing Kissinger before international and national courts for human rights violations.

See also: Chile, CIA Operations in; National Security Council; Nixon Administration and Intelligence

References and Further Reading

Isaacson, Walter. *Kissinger. A Biography.* London: Faber and Faber, 1992.
Kissinger, Henry. *The White House Years.* Boston: Little, Brown, 1979.
Kissinger, Henry. *Years of Upheaval.* Boston: Little, Brown, 1982.

Cezar Stanciu

KMSOURDOUGH, OPERATION

KMSOURDOUGH was a clandestine and illegal Central Intelligence Agency (CIA) mail opening operation run in the late 1960s and early 1970s. Unlike HTLINGUAL, which also operated at the time, KMSOURDOUGH did not involve gathering information for purposes of counterintelligence or domestic intelligence.

KMSOURDOUGH was run out of San Francisco and was targeted on mail entering the United States from East Asia. It consisted of four different episodes. The first took place in September 1960 and only involved the examination of exterior envelopes. Approximately 1,600 pieces of mail were examined. Mail was opened in the remaining three episodes which occurred in February 1970, May 1970 and October 1971. The second episode lasted one week. Between 5 and 80 pieces of mail were examined each day. The third episode lasted three weeks with 2,800 letters being screened. The fourth trip lasted two weeks and examined 4,500 letters. As was the case with HTLINGUAL, a Watch List of names of interest existed to govern the selection of letters for examination during KMSOURDOUGH. The locations of the mailings and possible signs of censorship also prompted letter inspection.

The foreign intelligence collected by KMSOURDOUGH involved such matters as a risk assessment of letter drops as a means of communicating with agents and as a basis for recruiting agents. It also was said to provide information on the health and activities of Asian leaders. No evidence exists that the Federal Bureau of Investigation (FBI) placed any collection requirements on the CIA in KMSOURDOUGH. One reason suggested is poor relations between the CIA and FBI which may have led the CIA not to reveal the existence of KMSOURDOUGH to the FBI.

No firm evidence exists as to when or why KMSOURDOUGH was terminated. An internal CIA memo of December 1974 does speak of its termination but admits to not having information on when that decision was made. A June 1973 memo suggests that the reason was largely political with a fear of the political fallout from its disclosure being seen as outweighing the intelligence benefits of its continued operation.

See also: Central Intelligence Agency; Federal Bureau of Investigation (FBI); HTLINGUAL

References and Further Reading

Corson, William. *Armies of Ignorance. The Rise of the American Intelligence Empire.* New York: Dial, 1977.

Donner, Frank. *The Age of Surveillance: The Aims and Methods of America's Political Intelligence System.* New York: Vintage, 1981.

Glenn P. Hastedt

KNIGHTS OF THE GOLDEN CIRCLE

The Knights of the Golden Circle was an organization founded in 1854 by George Bickley which hoped to conquer Mexico and the Caribbean and create a Southern slaveholding empire. During the Civil War, the Knights of the Golden Circle reinvented themselves as a pro-Confederate secret society.

Before the Civil War, a number of attempts were made to conquer or annex parts of Latin America. These filibusters (from the Dutch "vrijbuiter," or pirate) were almost entirely a Southern phenomenon. The first filibusters were aimed at Spanish possessions in North America; the most famous early filibuster attempt is that of Aaron Burr in 1805. After the Mexican War, filibusters focused on annexing Mexico or extending American influence into Central America. The most notable of these filibusters was William Walker, who briefly ruled Nicaragua in 1855.

George Bickley founded the Knights of the Golden Circle in 1854. A newspaper editor, self-styled doctor, and inveterate self-promoter, Bickley organized the group to capitalize on filibustering interest in the wake of Walker's expedition. The "Golden Circle" that Bickley conceived was a slavery-based empire, centered on Cuba that would encompass the islands of the Caribbean, the American South, Mexico, and parts of South America. This empire would ensure the survival of slavery and Southern ideals despite the growing political power and population of the industrial North and the West.

The Knights were a national organization, although most of its membership was based in Texas. It first came to wide attention in 1860, when Governor Sam Houston sparked a confrontation with Mexican troops and threatened to invade. Bickley summoned the Knights to the border to assist in the invasion, and several hundred actually made the journey. Governor Houston, alarmed at this, defused the crisis and ordered the Knights to leave. They did, although some did remain in the region as cattle rustlers. Anger over the failed invasion led to a leadership challenge in May of 1860, which Bickley managed to overcome.

After the start of the secession crisis which led to the Civil War, Bickley left Texas to drum up support for secession in Tennessee and Kentucky. The Texas Knights transformed themselves into a prosecession militia, which threatened and intimidated voters before Texas held a referendum on secession. Most joined the Confederate army.

Bickley, still in the North, became the focus of suspicion. The Knights in the North were the subject of nearly hysterical newspaper stories and rumors, which asserted that they were the nucleus of a vast pro-Southern conspiracy. Although the Knights of the Golden Circle were undoubtedly pro-Southern, they had neither the organization nor numbers to seriously threaten the United States. Bickley was arrested in July of 1863 and charged with espionage. He was released in October of 1865 and died in 1867.

See also: Civil War Intelligence

References and Further Reading

Crenshaw, Ollinger. "The Knights of the Golden Circle: The Career of George Bickley," *American Historical Review* 47 (1941), 23–50.

May, Robert E. *Manifest Destiny's Underworld: Filibustering in Antebellum America*. Chapel Hill, NC: University of North Carolina Press, 2002.

May, Robert E. *The Southern Dream of a Caribbean Empire, 1854–1861*. Baton Rouge, LA: Louisiana State University Press, 1973.

James L. Erwin

KOECHER, KARL
(1934–)

Karl Koecher is considered to be the only mole known to have infiltrated the Central Intelligence Agency (CIA). Born in Czechoslovakia in 1934, he joined the Czechoslovak intelligence service in 1962. In 1965 he and his wife staged a defect and moved to the United States where Koecher became a U.S. citizen in 1970. In reality they were positioning themselves as "sleepers" who would later be activated into espionage activities. This took place beginning in 1973 when Koecher joined the CIA as a translator/analyst tasked with analyzing wiretaps and documents provided by CIA agents. He, in turn, provided this information to Soviet intelligence. One of those whose identity Koecher compromised was Aleksandr Ogorodnik, who worked in the Soviet Ministry of Foreign Affairs. Henry Kissinger stated his intelligence was among the most important he read as secretary of state. Beyond engaging in espionage, Koecher and his wife were frequent participants in sex orgies with members of the White House, CIA, and Pentagon from whom they obtained intelligence.

Koecher would retire from the CIA only to be reactivated as a spy by the Soviets during the Reagan administration when he returned to the CIA as a part-time employee. Shortly after returning to work, he was arrested by the Federal Bureau of Investigation (FBI) as a spy and agreed to become a double agent, although his value and reliability as a double agent was soon called into doubt. On November 24, 1984, one day before the Koechers were to leave the United States they were arrested. Prosecuting Koecher proved difficult because the FBI was promised him immunity and his wife had been denied access to a lawyer. Ultimately a prisoner exchange was arranged in which the Koechers were released for nine dissidents held in the Soviet Union, including Natan Sharansky.

See also: Central Intelligence Agency; Cold War Intelligence; Federal Bureau of Investigation (FBI)

References and Further Reading

Epstein, Edward, J. *Deception: The Invisible War Between the KGB and the CIA*. New York: Allen, 1989.

Jeffrey-Jones, Rhodri. *Cloak and Dollar: A History of American Secret Intelligence*. New Haven, CT: Yale University Press, 2002.

Glenn P. Hastedt

KOLBE, FRITZ
(SEPTEMBER 25, 1900–FEBRUARY 16, 1971)

Fritz Kolbe was a German diplomat who provided the United States with information against the Nazi government during World War II. Born on September 25, 1900, Fritz Kolbe joined the diplomatic corps and worked as a junior diplomat posted to Madrid, Spain, and Cape Town, South Africa. As he refused to join the Nazi Party, he was not promoted and did not have access to any secret information. In 1941 he became influenced by the surgeon Ferdinand Sauerbruch who was keen on Germans doing something practical against the Nazis, and two years later Kolbe had his opportunity. On August 19, 1943, he was asked to take a diplomatic bag from Germany to Berne, Switzerland. There he offered the British some of the secret documents, but they turned him away, and so he turned to the Americans.

Allen Dulles was involved in the handling of Kolbe, who went by the code name "George Wood." Over the next two years Kolbe provided Dulles with 2,600 documents, including some highly sensitive ones such as the German plans for countering the D-Day landings, plans for the Messerschmitt Me 262 jet fighter, details on the V-1 and V-2 rocket programs, and some details about Japanese plans for the Pacific. He also managed to provide information which would lead to the identification of the Albanian Elyesa Bazna who was working as a cleaner at the British embassy in Turkey. His information was of such a high quality that the Americans initially felt it was false. Indeed Sir Claude Dansey was critical of the Americans falling for such an obvious double agent as Kolbe.

After World War II, Kolbe tried to settle in the United States, but, unable to find work, applied to the German Foreign Ministry which rejected him. He worked as a representative for an American manufacturing company and died on February 16, 1971. In 2004 a conference room at the German Foreign Ministry was named after him to commemorate his efforts against the Nazis during the war.

See also: American Intelligence, World War II; Dulles, Allen Welsh

References and Further Reading

Delattre, Lucas. *Betraying Hitler; the Story of Fritz Kolbe: The Most Important Spy of the Second World War*. London: Atlantic Monthly Press, 2005.

Grose, Peter. *Gentleman Spy: The Life of Allen Dulles*. Boston: Houghton Mifflin, 1994.

Justin Corfield

KOVAL, GEORGE
(1913–JANUARY 31, 2006)

George (Zhorzh) Koval's family was from the Byelorussian *shtetl* of Telekhany (near Minsk) and immigrated to the United States in the early twentieth century. George Koval was born on a Christmas Day in 1913 in Sioux City and graduated with honors from the local Central High School in 1929. After graduation, Koval enrolled in the University of Iowa where he studied electrical engineering. However, the Great Depression soon forced his family to move to Chicago where young Koval began to work as a secretary at the Association for Jewish Colonization in the Soviet Union (ICOR), a Yiddish organization that opposed the Zionist movement. In 1932, the Kovals traveled to the Soviet Union, seeking to return to Byelorussia but were instead compelled by the Soviet authorities to settle in Birobidzhan, administrative center of the newly established Jewish Autonomous Region. The family became involved in collective farming and Koval enrolled in the Dmitri Mendeleev Institute of Chemical Technology in Moscow in 1934. In 1939, he completed his studies with honors and, receiving Soviet citizenship, he was also recruited by the GRU (KGB's predecessor). In 1940, he returned to the United States and settled in New York City, where he worked at the Raven Electric Company, a cover for the GRU station where Koval served as a deputy chief and went under code name *Delmar*. With the start of World War II, Koval enlisted in the U.S. army in NYC and was assigned to the Army Specialized Training Program (ASTP) 1943. As part of this program, Koval, who scored particularly high on intelligence tests administered by the army, studied electrical engineering at the City College of New York and, in 1944, he was assigned to the Special Engineer Detachment (SED), a research laboratory based in Oak Ridge, Tennessee, which was part of the Manhattan Project. At the laboratory, Koval served as an officer, monitoring radiation levels and had almost unlimited access to various parts of the building. He used this access to transmit valuable research information to the Soviet intelligence. In 1946, he was transferred to a top-secret research laboratory in Dayton, Ohio, where, as a radiation officer, he was again given free access to the installation. While serving there, Koval passed crucial information on the design of nuclear bombs, particularly the makeup of the initiator, which, in combination with information provided by other spies, allowed the Soviet Union to detonate its first atomic bomb in the summer of 1949. By then, Koval left the United States after being discharged from the army and completing his bachelor's degree at City College of New York in 1948. He immigrated to the Soviet Union where he resided until his death in 2006. Koval was highly successful in infiltrating U.S. installations and passing highly sensitive information to the Soviets, which caused one scholar to describe him as a spy, who, with the exception of the British scientist Klaus Fuchs, may have done more than any other spy to help the USSR to develop nuclear parity with the United States. In November 2007, Russian President Vladimir Putin recognized Koval's contribution by posthumously awarding him a gold star of the Hero of the Russian Federation and publicly revealing him to be the agent Delmar.

See also: Cold War Intelligence; Fuchs, Emil Julius Klaus; GRU (Main Intelligence Directorate); KGB (Komitet Gosudarstvennoi Bezopasnosti); VENONA

References and Further Reading

Lota, Vladimir. GRU i atomnaja bomba: neizvestnaja istorija o tom, kak voennaja razvedka dobyvala svedenija ob atomnych proektach Velikobritanii, Germanii, SSHA i Japonii. Moscow: Olma-Press, 2002.

Walsh, Miechael, "George Koval: Atomic Spy Unmasked," *Smithsonian Magazine*, May 2009. http://www.smithsonianmag.com/history-archaeology/Iowa-Born-Soviet-Trained.html.

Alexander Mikaberidze

KRIVITSKY, WALTER
(1899–FEBRUARY 10, 1941)

Walter Krivitsky was an undercover Soviet intelligence officer who defected to the West in order to escape becoming a victim of Soviet leader Joseph Stalin's Great Purge of 1936. On February 10, 1941, Krivitsky was found shot to death in his room at the Bellevue Hotel in Washington, DC, along with suicide notes. Officially termed a suicide, many others believe he was murdered by Soviet agents who had uncovered his identity and whereabouts.

Krivitsky was born Samuel Ginsberg in the western Ukraine in 1899. He adopted the name Krivitsky when he joined the Red Army as an intelligent agent during the Russian Revolution. Fluent in many West European languages, his career in intelligence took him to Germany, Austria, Italy, and Hungary where he became a control officer running Soviet agents. In 1933 he was sent to Holland and was placed in charge of Soviet military intelligence for all of Western Europe. There he started to become disenchanted with Stalin's regime abandonment of socialist ideals. In September 1937 a close friend, Ignace Reiss, was assassinated after he defected and spoke out against Stalin. The following month, Krivitsky defected. After several attempts on his life in Paris, Krivitsky fled to Canada and became Walter Thomas.

Now in exile across the Atlantic Ocean, he penned a critical account of Stalin that first ran as a series of articles in *The Saturday Evening Post* and then as a book, *Stalin's Secret Service*, in which he predicted a nonaggression pact between Nazi Germany and the Soviet Union. Krivitsky provided both U.S. and British officials with information about Soviet espionage activities. In London he met with British intelligence officials identifying spies operating in Great Britain. By some accounts he gave descriptions of two individuals closely matching Kim Philby and Donald MacLean. In the United States he met with anti-Soviet journalist Isaac Don Levine and passed along information about Alger Hiss and a Washington, DC, spy ring. Krivitsky also appeared before the Dies Committee, a special investigations committee established under the House Un-American Activities Committee. Krivitsky's interpretation of Stalin as a threat to the West was not universally well received in the United States. Critics labeled him an opportunist, coward, gangster, and traitor. The information he gave the British Security Service (MI-5) and the Dies Committee was published in Walter G. Krivitsky, *MI5 Debriefing*.

See also: Hiss, Alger; MacLean, Donald Duart; Philby, Harold Adrian Russell "Kim"

References and Further Reading

Kern, Gary. *A Death in Washington: Walter G. Krivitsky and the Stalin Terror*. New York: Enigma Books, 2004.

Krivitsky, Walter. *In Stalin's Secret Service*. New York: Enigma, 2000.

Glenn P. Hastedt

L

LA RED AVISPA (THE WASP NETWORK)

La Red Avispa was a Cuban spy ring operating in south Florida. It was the subject of a major 1998 foreign counterintelligence investigation that led to the arrests of 10 individuals on September 12. Principal targets for La Red Avispa included U.S. military installations, including the U.S. Southern Command, and the Cuban-American émigré community.

For more than 30 years the FBI and other security and law enforcement organizations monitored the activities of suspected Cuban spies. Few arrests were made, however. The decision to pursue La Red Avispa more aggressively followed the February 1996 Cuban MIG shooting down of two planes operated by the anti-Cuban Brothers to the Rescue organization that resulted in the deaths of four members of that organization.

Five of the 10 arrested pled guilty, receiving prison terms of 42 months to seven years. The others, all Cuban nationals, asserted their innocence but were convicted of conspiracy to commit espionage and sentenced from 15 years to life imprisonment. One of them was also convicted of conspiracy to commit murder. The charge stemmed from his providing information to Cuban authorities that led to the February 1996 shoot-down incident. Known as the Cuban Five, they are the subject of an international protest movement.

Following the 1998 action against La Red Avispa, three Cuban diplomats accredited to the United Nations and the Cuban Interests Section in Washington, DC, were expelled. Two other diplomats suspected of involvement in the spy ring had already left the United States.

In 2001 two additional members of La Red Avispa were arrested in Florida as agents of the Cuban Directorate of Intelligence. George Gari and Marisol Gari entered into plea agreements with prosecutors and on January 4, 2002, they received sentences of 7 years and 42 months, respectively. They were charged with checking out the security system in place at the Cuban American National Foundation (CANF) headquarters and managing another agent who sought to obtain employment at the Southern Command. Marisol Gari was also charged with using her position at the U.S. Postal Service to try and intercept (CANF) mail.

See also: Post–Cold War Intelligence

References and Further Reading

Adams, James. *The New Spies: Exploring the Frontiers of Espionage.* New York: Hutchinson, 1994.

Herbig, Katherine. *Changes in Espionage by Americans.* Monterey, CA: Defense Personnel Research Center, 2008.

Glenn P. Hastedt

LAFITTE, JEAN AND PIERRE (JEAN, CA. 1776–1823; PIERRE, 1770–1821)

Jean and Pierre Lafitte were French-born smugglers and pirates based first in New Orleans and then at Galveston Island. They were involved in several filibusters against Mexico and were double agents in the pay of Spain.

Born in France, the Lafitte brothers immigrated with their father to the United States in 1803. Pierre established himself as a merchant, while Jean Lafitte found work as a privateer and smuggler. By 1809, both brothers had moved to New Orleans. They established a base outside the city and became leaders in the city's thriving black market. As their operations expanded, they relocated to the island of Barataria outside New Orleans, where they established a virtually independent enclave. Several hundred men were employed by the Lafitte operation.

The War of 1812 disrupted the Lafittes' preparations. Their success was attracting unwelcome attention as the war continued. The Lafittes began consorting with revolutionaries and filibusters, hoping to relocate their operations. Instead, Pierre Lafitte was arrested. Jean Lafitte was approached by British agents, who hoped to gain the Lafittes' assistance in an invasion. Instead, Jean Lafitte informed Louisiana's Governor Claiborne. Unable to trust the Lafittes, Claiborne responded by destroying the smugglers' base at Barataria. The Lafittes went into hiding, but their offer of help was accepted by the newly arrived General Andrew Jackson.

The Baratarians fought bravely at the Battle of New Orleans a few weeks later, and were given a presidential pardon. For several months, the Lafittes quietly prepared to leave New Orleans. In late 1815, the Lafittes secretly agreed to spy for Spain. The various filibustering schemes against Spain seemed unlikely to succeed, and the Lafittes needed any source of income they could find. The Lafittes, in return for payment, forwarded information on filibuster plans and even sounded Louisiana creoles on their willingness to rejoin the Spanish empire.

In 1817, much of the filibuster activity removed itself to Galveston Island in Texas, and the Lafittes followed the crowd. They also continued reporting to the Spanish on the activities there. Soon, the Lafittes had engineered a coup and taken control of the pirate kingdom. While profiting from control over the privateers of the Caribbean, they also milked them for information and gave the Spanish information. In turn, the

Spanish promised payment, but not enough to allow the Lafittes to build up a truly menacing power.

This state of affairs continued for several years, until Spain and the United States signed an 1819 treaty settling their border disputes. Although the treaty's ratification was uncertain, the Lafittes attempted to betray Spanish positions to the United States to preserve their own skins. This attempt failed, and the Lafittes were driven to outright piracy. Their base at Galveston was abandoned, and they turned to a series of temporary refuges. Pierre Lafitte died of disease after escaping Spanish custody in late 1821. Jean Lafitte, who obtained a legitimate privateering commission from Bolivar's Colombia, died in battle in 1823.

See also: Early Republic and Espionage; Jackson, Andrew

References and Further Reading

Davis, William C. *The Pirates Laffite: The Treacherous World of the Corsairs of the Gulf.* Orlando, FL: Harcourt, 2005.

Owsley, Frank Jr., and Gene A. Smith. *Filibusters and Expansionists: Jeffersonian Manifest Destiny, 1800–1821.* Tuscaloosa, AL: University of Alabama Press, 1997.

Warren, Harris Gaylord. *The Sword Was Their Passport: A History of American Filibustering in the Mexican Revolution.* Baton Rouge, LA: Louisiana State University Press, 1943.

James L. Erwin

LAMPHERE, ROBERT J. (FEBRUARY 14, 1918–JANUARY 7, 2002)

Robert Lamphere was a Federal Bureau of Investigations (FBI) agent who supervised some of the most important espionage cases of the early cold war, including Karl Fuchs, the Rosenbergs, and Kim Philby.

Robert Joseph Lamphere was born on February 14, 1918, in Wardner, Idaho. He graduated from the University of Idaho and attended the National Law School in Washington. Lamphere joined the FBI and worked on criminal cases before being transferred to the Soviet espionage squad. From 1943 until 1945 he worked on deciphering Soviet cables in order to identify spies. FBI director J. Edgar Hoover began such investigations because of the reports regarding Soviet infiltrations in the Manhattan Project.

Since 1948, Lamphere devoted his time to these activities and was the FBI liaison with the VENONA project. He was involved in almost all major investigations on Soviet espionage in the late 1940s and the early 1950s due to his previous experience in the field. Robert Lamphere had a major contribution in the discovering of the Soviet atomic espionage network. Some of the documents he deciphered pointed to Klaus Fuchs and Harry Gold. Further investigations revealed Julius and Ethel Rosenberg's involvement. These led to their arrest and subsequent execution in 1953. Although familiar with the vastness of the Soviet espionage in the United States, Lamphere was very critical of Joseph McCarthy's anti-Communist crusade.

Robert Lamphere left the FBI in 1955 and held positions in the Veterans Administration and in a large insurance company. After retirement, he published a book about the espionage cases of the 1950s and his experience with the FBI. Lamphere died on January 7, 2002, in Tucson.

See also: Federal Bureau of Investigation (FBI); Fuchs, Emil Julius Klaus; Gold, Harry; Philby, Harold Adrian Russell "Kim"; Rosenberg, Julius and Ethel; VENONA

References and Further Reading

Lamphere, Robert J., and Tom Shachtman. *The FBI-KGB War: A Special Agent's Story*. New York: Random House, 1986.

Romerstein, Herbert, and Eric Breindel. *The VENONA Secrets. Exposing Soviet Espionage and America's Traitors*. Washington, DC: Regnery Publishing, 2001.

Cezar Stanciu

LANG, HERMANN W.
(1902–)

Hermann Lang was a German agent during World War II who was responsible for acquiring the Norden bombsight plans. Hermann W. Lang was born in 1902, and had settled in the United States in 1927, living in New York where he was an inspector at the factory on Lafayette Street, Manhattan, where Carl L. Norden was producing a bombsight that was believed to be the most accurate way of guiding a bomb from the airplane onto its target. In the fall of 1937, while Lang was still working through his naturalization, he was approached by Major Nikolaus Ritter of German intelligence, the Abwehr. Lang, who retained a loyalty for Germany, told Ritter of his work, including the fact that he was supposed to leave the blueprints at work, but had taken them home. He then copied the blueprints over his kitchen table while his wife was asleep.

When Lang gave them to Ritter, the Abwehr major, who had only been in the United States for a fortnight, offered to pay Lang for the secrets. Lang refused, saying that he wanted Germany to have the bombsights and if he was given any money he would throw it away. On November 30, 1937, a steward from the *Reliance*, a passenger ship from the Hamburg-Amerika line, and who also worked for the Abwehr, smuggled the plans on board within an umbrella. Lang continued to copy other plans and get them to Ritter.

Days before Britain went to war with Germany in 1939, British Prime Minister Neville Chamberlain asked Roosevelt for the Norden bombsight plans but the Americans refused, wanting to remain neutral, unaware the Germans already had the plans and these were being used by the Luftwaffe. It later emerged that $3,000 was placed in a bank account in Lang's name in Germany.

See also: Abwehr; American Intelligence, World War II

References and Further Reading

Kahn, David. *Hitler's Spies: Germany's Military Intelligence in World War II*. London: Macmillan, 1978.

Persico, Joseph. *Roosevelt's Secret War: FDR and World War II Espionage*. New York: Random House, 2001.

Justin Corfield

LANGER, WILLIAM L.
(MARCH 16, 1896–DECEMBER 26, 1977)

William L. Langer was an American historian and intelligence analyst. Born March 16, 1896, in Boston, Langer received his BA from Harvard in 1916, before serving with the Chemical Warfare Service in World War I. He returned to Harvard to complete his PhD in 1923, with a specialty in the diplomacy of the Near East. He joined the faculty at Harvard in 1928.

In July 1941 Langer joined James Phinney Baxter III in establishing a research branch for the Organization for Strategic Services (OSS). With Baxter's retirement in October 1942, Langer became the head of the Research and Analysis Branch (R&A). In that capacity, Langer directed the work of hundreds of scholars studying international political, economic, social, and cultural issues affecting the U.S. war effort.

With the abolition of OSS at the end of the war, Langer moved with R&A to the State Department with the title of special assistant for research and intelligence. But when the staff was divided among the Department's regional desks, Langer resigned in the summer of 1946.

In November 1950, Langer joined the Central Intelligence Agency as the first director of the Office of National Estimates. He took personal responsibility for the content of all National Intelligence Estimates (NIE) until passing the directorship to Sherman Kent in early 1952. He returned briefly to the world of intelligence in 1962 as a member of John Kennedy's Board of Consultants on Foreign Intelligence Activities. In both the OSS R&A and the ONE, Langer sought to impose academic standards of integrity, unaffected by politics, on all written intelligence reports.

See also: Board of National Estimates; Central Intelligence Agency; National Intelligence Estimates; Office of National Estimates

References and Further Reading

Katz, Barry. *Foreign Intelligence: Research and Analysis in the Office of Strategic Services, 1942–1945.* Cambridge, MA: Harvard University Press, 1989.

Kent, Sherman. "The First Year of the Office of National Estimates: The Directorship of William L. Langer," in Donald Steury (ed.), *Sherman Kent and the Board of National Estimates,* pp. 143–156. Washington, DC: Center for the Study of Intelligence, 1994.

Langer, William L. *In and Out of the Ivory Tower.* New York: N. Watson Academic Publications, 1977.

Winks, Robin. *Cloak and Gown: Scholars in the Secret War, 1939–1961,* 2nd ed. New Haven, CT: Yale University Press, 1996.

Peter F. Coogan

LANGLEY, VIRGINIA

Langley, Virginia, located in Fairfax County of northern Virginia and combined with the unincorporated town of McLean, Virginia, in 1910, is one of the richest Washington, DC, suburbs and home of the Central Intelligence Agency.

Historically, Fairfax County was created out of a northern section of Prince William County and was named after the region's proprietor at that time, 6th Lord Fairfax of Cameron, Thomas Fairfax. Soon after, roughly two-thirds of what was then Fairfax County were used to create Loudoun County. The establishment of the District of Columbia, as well as the Civil War, further contributed to the diminishing size of the county from its larger original dimensions.

Thomas Lee, proprietor of the land where Langley is located, named his tract after his hometown in England in 1719. It was later divided among relatively wealthy plantation owners. Interestingly, President James Madison and his wife sought refuge in Langley, fleeing the British capture of Washington, DC, during the War of 1812. During the Civil War, Langley was home to significant Union forces, even though it was within Confederate territory. The arrival of the Great Falls & Old Dominion Railroad in 1906, following three years of construction, made Langley a suburb of Washington, DC, as well as a weekend and vacation getaway.

For Langley, as well as Fairfax County, the expansion of the federal government following the Great Depression and during World War II resulted in significant growth throughout the town and the county. In these years, the once rather rural region began to become more and more suburbanized.

In 1959, the federal government, notably President Dwight Eisenhower, began construction of the CIA's headquarters, which was completed in 1961. Although Langley had been combined with McLean in 1910, the building was located in Langley even though it was and still is simply a neighborhood of McLean, Virginia.

Following the arrival of the CIA, the area became even more suburbanized, especially after the opening of Tysons Corner Center. It was one of the first U.S. mega-malls and remains a top shopping attraction throughout the DC region. Today, the town of McLean, Langley included, has a population of roughly 40,000 and a per capita income of $62,000, well above the American average.

See also: Central Intelligence Agency

References and Further Reading

The CIA Online. "Frequently Asked Questions," https://www.cia.gov/cia/public_affairs/faq.html#11 (accessed January 12, 2006).

Fairfax County Online. "Visitors," http://www.co.fairfax.va.us/visitors/ (accessed January 11, 2006).

Kessler, Ronald. *Inside the CIA: Revealing the Secrets of the World's Most Powerful Agency.* New York: Simon & Schuster, 1992.

Arthur Holst

LANSDALE, EDWARD GEARY (FEBRUARY 6, 1908–FEBRUARY 23, 1987)

Born in Detroit on February 6, 1908, Edward Geary Lansdale spent a military career involved in counterinsurgency, overseeing clandestine activities in the Philippines (1946–1948, 1950–1954), Vietnam (1954–1957, 1965–1968), and Cuba (Operation MONGOOSE, 1961–1962). A shadowy figure of the cold war, much of his work was connected with the Central Intelligence Agency. After retiring from the U.S. Air Force as a major general in 1963, he briefly headed the Food for Peace program and afterwards served as a senior liaison officer at the American embassy in Saigon.

An innovator of counterinsurgency doctrines and tactics for countering the spread of Communism, Lansdale championed "democratic revolutions" that emphasized winning the hearts and minds of the people. His legacy influenced a generation of special operatives, including Colonel Oliver North.

Lansdale attended the University of California at Los Angeles, where he majored in English and participated in ROTC. Unfortunately, he never completed his degree due to his failure to learn a foreign language. Afterwards he joined the Army Reserve as a second lieutenant while working as an advertising copy editor. Following the attack on Pearl Harbor he was put on active duty and worked for the Office of Strategic Services, assigned to the San Francisco office of Army Military Intelligence. During the war he may have made some clandestine trips to New Zealand and China. After the Japanese surrender, he was sent to the Philippines, where he served as the deputy chief of staff for intelligence and later as the head public information officer. While studying Filipino culture, he worked to promote a positive American image and at the same time he monitored the Communist-inspired Hukbalahap (Huk) rebellion.

After transferring to the air force in September 1947, Lansdale taught strategic studies for the Department of Air Intelligence Training at Lowry Air Force Base in Denver. Afterwards, as a lieutenant colonel, he was assigned as an intelligence officer to the Office of Policy Coordination under the Central Control Group in Washington, DC. In September 1950 he returned to the Philippines and became a confidant of Ramón Magsaysay, the Filipino congressman whom he arranged to have appointed as secretary of the defense. Together the two directed a counterinsurgency campaign against the Huk rebels. In 1954, with Lansdale's behind-the-scenes involvement, Magsaysay was elected the country's president by an overwhelming margin, prompting one foreign ambassador to dub the American operative "Colonel Landslide."

In 1954 Lansdale joined the Saigon Military Mission and became a key adviser to Ngo Dinh Diem, the premier of South Vietnam. He was soon appointed the CIA station chief. Lansdale oversaw the training of Diem's army, worked at uniting the different military sects, and thwarted coup plots. Clandestine activities in the north included disinformation campaigns, sabotage, and the planting of deep-cover operatives. Lansdale utilized a network of Filipinos with experience against the Huks. Also, a Filipino-based company, Freedom Company (later the Eastern Construction Company), was a CIA front that enabled operatives disguised as technicians to be deployed in Vietnam as well as other parts of the Far East. Lansdale's time in Vietnam inspired novelistic portrayals, including "Alden Pyle" in Graham Greene's *The Quiet American* (1955) and "Homer Atkins" in William Lederer and Eugene Burdick's *The Ugly American* (1956).

He worked at the Pentagon in March 1957 through to his retirement in October 1963. In Washington he served in various planning roles involving strategic services and special operations. He warned that the Bay of Pigs invasion would fail due to its small force and lack of a political base of support on the ground. He also advised against sending troops to Vietnam, yet at the same time he inspired President John F. Kennedy to allocate more resources to Special Forces.

During the Kennedy administration, Lansdale was put in charge of Operation MONGOOSE for the purposes of orchestrating an anti-Castro rebellion. Years afterwards, appearing before the Church Committee, he denied any knowledge of the CIA attempts to assassinate Castro. However, Lansdale was found to have agreed with plans calling for the "liquidation" of Cuban leaders.

In retirement, Lansdale wrote his memoirs, *In the Midst of Wars*. On February 23, 1987, he died in his sleep at his home in McLean, Virginia. He was buried at Arlington National Cemetery.

See also: Central Intelligence Agency; Greene, Graham; MONGOOSE, Operation; Vietnam War and Intelligence Operations

References and Further Reading

Currey, Cecil B. *Edward Lansdale: The Unquiet American*. Boston: Houghton Mifflin, 1988.

Lansdale, Edward. *In the Midst of Wars: An American's Mission to Southeast Asia*. New York: Harper & Row, 1972.

McClintock, Michael. *Instruments of Statecraft: U.S. Guerilla Warfare, Counterinsurgency, and Counterterrorism, 1940–1990*. New York: Pantheon Books, 1990.

Roger Chapman

LAURENS, HENRY
(MARCH 6, 1724–FEBRUARY 24, 1792)

Henry Laurens was an American planter and merchant born in Charleston, South Carolina. Although originally favoring reconciliation with Britain, Laurens supported the United States in the conflict with the British by 1775. He was elected to South Carolina's first provincial Congress in 1775, and became president of the Committee of Safety in the same year. By March 1776, South Carolina had formed an independent government and chose him as vice president.

In 1779, the Continental Congress chose Laurens as minister to Holland. He was to travel to Holland in an effort to negotiate a treaty that would include Dutch support for the American Revolution, and to secure a $10,000,000 loan. Britain captured the *Mercury*, the ship carrying Laurens, off the coast of Newfoundland during his return voyage in 1780. In an attempt to keep the alliance between Holland and the United States secret, Laurens threw his official papers overboard; the British navy recovered the papers and the draft of the treaty. Britain used these documents to justify their declaration of war on Holland; Laurens was charged with treason and imprisoned in the Tower of London.

On December 31, 1781, Great Britain released Laurens in a prisoner exchange for General Lord Cornwallis, and Laurens returned to South Carolina. In 1783, Laurens helped negotiate the Treaty of Paris that ended the Revolutionary War. Once back in the United States, Laurens retired to private life. He served in the state convention that ratified the Constitution in 1788, before passing away at his home in Mepkin, South Carolina, on December 8, 1792.

See also: American Revolution and Intelligence

References and Further Reading

Boatner, Mark M. *Encyclopedia of the American Revolution*. Mechanicsburg, PA: Stackpole Books, 1966.

Lefkowitz, Arthur S. *George Washington's Indispensable Men: The 32 Aides-de-Camp Who Helped Win American Independence*. Mechanicsburg, PA: Stackpole Books, 2003.

Russell, David Lee. *The American Revolution in the Southern Colonies*. Jefferson, NC: McFarland & Co., 2000.

Gregory Kellerman

LE CARRE, JOHN (DAVID JOHN MOORE CORNWELL) (OCTOBER 19, 1931)

Born in Poole in County Dorset, the son of confidence man and political schemer Ronnie Cornwell, lightly fictionalized as the father of Magnus Pym in *The Perfect Spy*, David Cornwell had an irregular childhood marred by the desertion of his mother and his father's jailing on charges of fraud. Cornwell attended Bern University in Switzerland and studied modern languages at Oxford graduating in 1956. In 1958 he joined the British Foreign Service, a cover for his real work with the British Security Service (MI-5), the agency responsible for counterintelligence. After transferring to the Security Intelligence Service (MI-6), Britain's counterpart to the Central Intelligence Agency Cornwell became an eyewitness to such early cold war events as the construction of the Berlin Wall. One of the most famous Soviet agents, Kim Philby, a rising star in MI-6 and the most famous member of "Cambridge Five," a group of upper-class Britons recruited as Soviet agents in the 1930s while students at Cambridge, gave Cornwell's name, among many others, to the Soviet Union. Philby's treachery ended Cornwell's career in intelligence work and, coupled with his mother's abandonment of her family, inspired a lifelong fascination with the theme of betrayal. In 1954 Cornwell married Alyson Ann Veronica Sharp, the couple had three children, and for a time in the 1960s lived in Greece. Their divorce inspired his autobiographical novel *The Naïve and Sentimental Lover* (1971). Cornwell remarried in 1972 to Valérie Jane Eustace.

Cornwell adopted the pseudonym John le Carre and began writing while still in the Secret Service, publishing his first book, *A Call for the Dead*, in 1961. Written to counter the glamorous image of espionage in James Bond novels, the book introduces le Carre's greatest character, George Smiley, a chubby, unassuming anti-Bond in rumpled clothing. Le Carre's third novel, *The Spy Who Came in from the Cold*, published in 1963, established his reputation as a master of the grimly realistic espionage novel and won him the prestigious Somerset Maugham award. In his subsequent novels, le Carre perfected his depiction of a shadowy world held together by personal connections while simultaneously being torn apart by lies and betrayal. Although his novels are regarded by some as virtual handbooks on the practice of espionage, le Carre freely admits that most of it is made up for literary effect. His most famous three novels *Tinker, Tailor, Soldier, Spy* (1974); *The Honorable School Boy* (1977); and *Smiley's People* (1980) revolve around the hunt for "Karla," an austere spymaster resembling real-life East German intelligence chief Marcus Wolf. Another real-life character, Kim Philby, appears as the mole, Gerald, in *Tinker, Tailor, Soldier, Spy*. The end of the cold war left le Carre adrift and he experimented with plots involving drug dealers, *The Night Manager* (1993); American colonialism, *The Tailor of Panama* (1996); and post-Soviet regional conflicts such as *Our Game* (1995). Recent works such as *The Constant Gardener* (2000) and *Mission Song* (2006) take place in Africa and feature befuddled diplomats; heroic, doomed idealists; brutal security squads; and callous international corporations.

See also: Fiction—Spy Novels; MI-6 (Secret Intelligence Service); Philby, Harold Adrian Russell "Kim"

References and Further Reading

Aronoff, Myron Joel. *The Spy Novels of John Le Carre: Balancing Ethics and Politics*. London: Palgrave Macmillan, 1998.
Hoffman, Tod. *Le Carre's Landscape*. Montreal, Canada: McGill-Queens University Press, 2001.

Vernon L. Pedersen

LEE, ANDREW DAULTON
(1952–)

Andrew Daulton Lee, a drug dealer and spy, was born in Los Angeles, California, in 1952. He was the son of a well-established physician who had built a successful career in the Los Angeles area. He grew up in the Palos Verdes Peninsula section of the city, one of Los Angeles' more wealthy neighborhoods at that time.

Lee took to the streets during his childhood and became a relatively successful drug dealer in the area, avoiding arrest and making significant money. He began his illegal career while in high school and started to increase his supply and customers. Thanks to his abundant sales of heroin and cocaine, Lee became known as the "snowman" in Los Angeles and throughout California.

Along with his childhood friend, Christopher Boyce, who had received a top-secret position with a U.S. defense communications center located in Redondo Beach thanks to his father's connections with the FBI, the two began to intercept and to accumulate CIA messages that they hoped to eventually sell to the Russians for cash. Soon after, they decided upon the Soviet embassy in Mexico City as their transfer point.

Beginning in the early 1970s, Lee traveled to Mexico City and delivered the stolen documents to Soviet officials at the embassy in microfiche format. Most of the documents permitted the Soviets to better understand how to decode encoded messages from the CIA and FBI. Additionally, they gave the Soviets top-secret descriptions of the latest U.S. satellites.

For roughly two years and a couple trips, the scheme worked and Lee was able to deliver the secrets for cash that he then shared with Boyce. It came to an end however, in December 1976, when Lee was arrested by Mexican police in front of the Soviet embassy on suspicion that he was involved in the recent murder of a Mexican police officer. Once searched, the police found the microfiches and he was quickly extradited to the United States.

Once in the United States, Lee was found guilty of espionage and was sentenced to life in prison. He also told the police about his connection with Boyce, who was also convicted and sentenced to life in prison. Interestingly, Lee was released on parole in 1998 and was soon after hired by Sean Penn, who acted as Lee in a movie based on his life, titled *The Falcon and the Snowman*.

See also: Boyce, Christopher John; Falcon and the Snowman

References and Further Reading

Lindsey, Robert. *The Falcon and the Snowman: A True Story of Friendship and Espionage*. New York: Simon & Schuster, 1979.

San Francisco Chronicle Online. "U.S. Spy freed after 25 years in prison," http://www.sfgate.com/cgi-bin/article.cgi?file=/c/a/2003/03/15/MN205136.DTL (accessed December 2, 2005).

Andrew Holst

LEE, ARTHUR
(DECEMBER 20, 1740–DECEMBER 12, 1792)

Arthur Lee was an American agent and diplomat during the War of American Independence. Lee was born on December 20, 1740, in Stratford Hall, Westmoreland County, Virginia. He was educated at Eton (1751–1757), the University of Edinburgh (1761–1764), and the Inns of Court (1770–1774). He achieved degrees in medicine and law, proficiency in Greek and Roman history, and a deep respect for English Whig politics. Living in England in the 1760s and 1770s, he was a pro-American polemicist, cultivating a wide circle of influential acquaintances, among which was Benjamin Franklin. He became an intelligence agent for Congress in 1775. In 1777, he joined Franklin and Silas Deane in Paris as part of the U.S. fledgling diplomatic corps.

Restlessly practicing militia diplomacy, Lee antagonized his colleagues while seeking aid for his new country. He visited Spain and Prussia, and he infuriated Pierre Augustin Caron de Beaumarchais, a French agent, by arguing that French military assistance was a gift to the United States rather than a sale. In early 1778, he angered Franklin and Deane during negotiations leading to a French-American alliance. Also, he claimed that his colleagues were colluding with Dr. Edward Bancroft, a secretary in the embassy whom he knew to be a British spy. In 1778 Lee attempted without success to have Franklin recalled. He was himself recalled in 1779. He died on December 12, 1792, at Landsdowne, near Urbanna, Virginia.

See also: American Revolution and Intelligence; Bancroft, Dr. Edward; Deane, Silas; Franklin, Benjamin

References and Further Reading

Bemis, Samuel Flagg. *The Diplomacy of the American Revolution*. Bloomington, IN: Indiana University Press, 1961.

Potts, Louis W. *Arthur Lee: A Virtuous Revolutionary*. Baton Rouge, LA: Louisiana State University Press, 1981.

Riggs, Alvin R. *The Nine Lives of Arthur Lee, Virginia Patriot*. Edited by Edward M. Jones. Williamsburg, VA: Independence Bicentennial Commission, 1976.

Paul David Nelson

LEE, PETER H.
(1939–)

Peter Lee was a nuclear physicist who worked at the Los Alamos Laboratory from 1985 to 1991. Prior to that, he worked for almost a decade, from 1976 to 1984, at the Livermore Labs. On December 7, 1997, Lee pled guilty to having provided China with secret information in 1985 about using lasers to simulate a nuclear detonation. According to Lee, he passed on this information both to help the Chinese scientists and improve his reputation in China. Under terms of the agreement, Lee did not have to spend any time in prison. He was fined $20,000 and ordered to perform 3,000 hours of community service.

Lee was born in China in 1939. His father was strongly anti-Communist and the family moved to Taiwan in 1951. Later they moved to the United States where Lee became a naturalized citizen in 1975. He earned a PhD in aeronautics from the California Institute of Technology. As a result of his work on lasers and nuclear reactions, Lee came into contact with Chinese scientists. In 1985 he traveled to China where he was approached about providing Chinese scientists with help. He admitted to attending a meeting where he provided detailed answers on questions related to laser fusion research. This information was declassified in 1993 by the Department of Energy.

An investigation into Lee, code-named "Royal Tourist," was begun in 1991 by Federal Bureau of Investigation (FBI) agents James J. Smith and William Cleveland, Jr., and ran until 1997. After leaving Los Alamos, Lee went to work for TRW where he worked on a radar imaging program that is vital to the security of U.S. submarines. He sought to return to Los Alamos but was turned down for a job due to security concerns raised by the FBI. In 1997 he again when to China where he gave a lecture on radar imaging to Chinese scientists and answered questions about its relevance to antisubmarine warfare. Lee had told TRW his trip was for pleasure and did not reveal he planned to present a lecture.

The failure to charge Lee with espionage, his general lack of cooperation with government officials, and the light sentence imposed created a great deal of controversy. Singled out for blame for the failure to prosecute the case more vigorously was a prolonged period of miscommunication between the prosecutors, defense officials, and FBI. Adding further confusion to the case was the fact that FBI agents Smith and Cleveland, who investigated Lee, were handlers of Katrina Leung, who was reportedly a double agent for China but was never convicted of espionage. She also had an affair with both Smith and Cleveland.

See also: China, Intelligence Operations of; Federal Bureau of Investigation (FBI); Leung, Katrina; Los Alamos; Post–Cold War Intelligence

References and Further Reading

Eftimiades, Nicholas. *Chinese Intelligence Operations*. New York: Taylor Francis, 1994.

Richelson, Jeffrey. *A Century of Spies: Intelligence in the Twentieth Century*. New York: Oxford University Press, 1995.

Glenn P. Hastedt

LEE, WEN HO
(DECEMBER 21, 1939–)

Wen Ho Lee, a University of California at Los Angeles (UCLA) scientist at the Los Alamos National Laboratory, was accused of providing China with secret information about the W88, a U.S. nuclear warhead. Lee was born in Taiwan on December 21, 1939, and came to the United States to study. He received a PhD from Texas A&M and became a naturalized U.S. citizen in the 1970s. He was arrested in December 1999 and held without bail in solitary confinement for 278 days. This charge was dropped but in its place the government charged Lee with the improper handling of restricted data. On September 13, 2000, Lee pled guilty to one count as part of a plea bargain arrangement with the other 58 counts being dropped. Later, Lee brought suit against the U.S. government and five news organizations (the *Washington Post*, *New York Times*, *Los Angeles Times*, ABC News, and the Associated Press) for leaking information that violated his privacy. On August 18, 2004, a U.S. district judge held reporters from four manor news organizations in contempt for not revealing the source that identified Lee as a spy. On June 3, 2006, they agreed to pay Lee $1.6 million to settle the suit, with the government paying $900,000 in legal fees and taxes and the news organizations paying $750,000 saying it was the best way to protect their source and journalists.

Information from an intelligence source in China revealed that China had obtained details of the W88. The Federal Bureau of Investigation's (FBI's) examination of the case (Operation Kindred Spirit) led them to focus on Lee. He had traveled to China twice in the 1980s to meet with scientists. During his questioning by the FBI, Lee admitted that he had been asked by them to supply information that would help China develop a nuclear missile force. Lee took a polygraph test and it indicated he was not always being truthful in his responses. An examination of his computer revealed that he had transferred classified documents to an unsecured network and in the process deleted the security classification on the material. This information was accessed over 40 times on a computer at the UCLA student union by an unknown individual(s).

As the investigation in Lee's alleged espionage began, he was fired from his job at Los Alamos by UCLA on March 8, 1990, under pressure from the Energy Department which oversees the laboratory. His firing was leaked to the media that same day by an unidentified source and was widely reported. While his alleged espionage was making news, the FBI had determined that Lee could not have been the source of information on the W88 to China. Still the FBI continued with its investigation.

Lee's case raised a number of troubling issues. The first was the possibility of racial profiling. Lee and his supporters argued that he was unfairly singled out for investigation because of his Chinese heritage. Some have likened it to the Dreyfus affair in interwar France. A second issue relates to the state of security at national research labs where classified work is being done and more broadly the relationship between the culture of scientific research that values openness and the culture of national security that does not.

See also: China, Intelligence Operations of; Federal Bureau of Investigation (FBI); Los Alamos; Post–Cold War Intelligence

References and Further Reading

Lee, Wen Ho, and Helen Zia. *My Country Versus Me: The First-Hand Account by the Los Alamos Scientist Who Was Falsely Accused of Being a Spy.* New York: Hyperion, 2003.

Stober, Dan, and Ian Hoffman. *A Convenient Spy: Wen Ho Lee and the Politics of Nuclear Espionage.* New York: Simon & Shuster, 2002.

Trulock, Notra. *Code Name Kindred Spirit: Inside the Chinese Nuclear Espionage Scandal.* New York: Encounter Books, 2002.

Glenn P. Hastedt

LEUNG, KATRINA
(MAY 1, 1954–)

Katrina Leung was a naturalized U.S. citizen who was born in Canton, China, in 1954. On April 9, 2003, she was indicted for the "unauthorized copying of national defense information with the intent to injure or benefit a foreign nation." Although not charged with espionage, apparently for lack of evidence, she is regarded as having been a double agent for China for at least 20 years. Her case was dismissed on January 6, 2005, when a district judge ruled that prosecutors had acted improperly in and denied Leung her constitutional right to a witness for her defense by the terms of the plea agreement it reached with James J. Smith, a Federal Bureau of Investigation (FBI) agent who was her lover and handler, that prohibited him from sharing information on the case with Leung or her attorney. In December 2005 she would plead guilty to one count of lying to the FBI and one count of filing a false federal tax return for which she was required to cooperate with the government in debriefings, fined $10,000, required to do community service, and placed on three years' probation.

Leung first came to the attention of the FBI in 1980 as part of an investigation into illegal technology transfers to China. At that time she was not under suspicion but in February 1981 the FBI began an investigation into her activities, believing that while working at an export-import company she was engaged in clandestine intelligence collection for China. When Leung left the firm, the investigation was dropped. It was reopened by Smith in 1982 in pursuit of information on another. Smith soon recruited Leung as a spy for the FBI under the code name "Parlor Maid" and then began an affair with her. Smith worked for the FBI from 1970 to 2000 when he retired. By the time of her arrest, Leung had been paid over $1.7 million.

In 1984, with the FBI's help, Leung was recruited as a spy by China's Ministry of State Security. In 1990 the FBI discovered that Leung had been providing China with classified information about the FBI's counterintelligence program. As part of his plea agreement with the FBI, Smith later admitted to bringing top-secret material to her which he left in an open briefcase. In April 1991 a conversation between Leung and her Chinese handler was caught on tape by the FBI. Special Agent William Cleveland, Jr., who listened to the tape, recognized Leung's voice, and informed Smith that she might be a double agent. He too had become involved in an affair with her in the late 1980s. The FBI determined that she should not be terminated and allowed to continue to function as an FBI spy even though she was providing China with unauthorized information.

Leung's case attracted notoriety for two reasons. First, she was a prominent socialite who was regularly identified as a Republican fundraiser and activist. By one account she gave about $27,000 to the Republican Party. Second, her case highlighted the FBI's lax internal roles and procedures for handling agents. Smith was not closely watched nor was his judgment challenged by superiors when presented evidence that Leung was engaged in espionage for China. For example, information about her past activities and suspicions was not made available to an internal investigation that judged she should be allowed to continue to function as a spy for the FBI.

See also: China, Intelligence Operations of; Federal Bureau of Investigation (FBI); Lee, Peter H.; Los Alamos

References and Further Reading

Eftimiades, Nicholas. *Chinese Intelligence Operations*. New York: Taylor Francis, 1994.
Richelson, Jeffrey. *A Century of Spies: Intelligence in the Twentieth Century*. New York: Oxford University Press, 1995.

Glenn P. Hastedt

LEWIS, MERIWETHER (AUGUST 18, 1774–OCTOBER 11, 1809)

Meriwether Lewis was a leader, with William Clark, of the Corps of Discovery's exploring expedition through the Louisiana Territory and the Oregon Country from 1804 to 1806. The expedition was the first to navigate the Missouri River to its source, cross the Continental Divide, and descend the Columbia River to the Pacific Ocean. Lewis and Clark discovered and recorded many plant and animal species new to science, established relations with several Native American tribes, and helped the United States establish a claim to the Oregon Country—the present states of Oregon, Washington, and Idaho.

The son of William and Lucy Meriwether Lewis, Meriwether was born on August 18, 1774, near Charlottesville, Albemarle County, Virginia. In 1794, he volunteered as a private in the Virginia militia and participated in putting down the Whiskey Rebellion. Later that same year, he received a commission as an ensign in the regular U.S. Army. Serving in the army under Gen. Anthony Wayne, he first met William Clark in 1795.

After his election in 1800, President Thomas Jefferson—long a friend of Lewis' family—selected Lewis to serve as his private secretary. Jefferson, who held Lewis in high regard, described him as "Brave, prudent, habituated to the woods, and familiar with Indian manners and character." In 1803, when Congress appropriated funding for an expedition to explore the new Louisiana Territory, Jefferson chose Lewis to lead the Corps of Discovery. Lewis invited Clark to share command as a co-leader. On May 22, 1804, the party of 25 soldiers and voyageurs launched their boats up the Missouri River. One of factors motivating Jefferson's interest in the Pacific Northwest was French interest in the region. King Louis XVI couched French interest in terms of promoting scientific research but Jefferson doubted this was the case, seeing in it instead a political purpose.

Jefferson had instructed Lewis to follow the Missouri River to its source and find the best passage through the Rocky Mountains to the headwaters of the Columbia River and the Pacific Ocean. He also directed him to make detailed maps of the terrain through which they passed; to contact and establish relations with the Native American peoples through whose lands he traveled, and to make ethnographic observations of them; to investigate soils and the productive capacity of the land for agriculture; to identify and collect specimens of plant and animal species as yet unknown to science; to survey the territory's mineral resources and geological features; and to record detailed observations of the region's weather and climate.

Lewis and Clark constructed Fort Mandan on the Missouri River near present-day Bismarck, North Dakota, where they spent the winter of 1804–1805. In April 1805, they resumed their trek west. In August, they crossed the Continental Divide at Lemhi Pass, in the Bitterroot Mountains of present-day Idaho and Montana. Once in the Columbia River drainage, they made their way by foot and horseback to the Clearwater River, where they constructed dugout canoes. They arrived at the Pacific Ocean in November 1805 and erected Fort Clatsop near present-day Astoria, Oregon. In March 1806, they began the return trip eastward. At Traveler's Rest, in the Bitterroot Valley of present-day Montana, Lewis and Clark divided the party. While Clark went south to explore the Yellowstone Valley, Lewis went north to explore the Marias River country. On August 12, Lewis and Clark reunited their expedition on the Missouri River and continued downstream, reaching St. Louis on September 23, 1806.

As a naturalist, Lewis had kept detailed scientific records and specimens for the expedition. He described approximately 100 new animal species and 70 new plant species. The expedition also established relations with several Native American tribes and recorded ethnographic information that remains valuable to researchers to this day. Lewis shared his discoveries with Jefferson when he reached Washington, DC, in December 1806.

The expedition was the high point of Lewis' short life. Deepening depression, debt, and alcoholism consumed him and he committed suicide on October 11, 1809.

See also: Early Republic and Espionage

References and Further Reading

Fritz, Harry. *The Lewis and Clark Expedition*. Westport, CT: Greenwood Press, 2004.
Slaughter, Thomas. *Exploring Lewis and Clark*. New York: Knopf, 2003.

Glenn P. Hastedt

LIBERTY, USS

The USS *Liberty* was a U.S. Navy intelligence ship attacked by the Israeli military on June 8, 1967, during the 1967 Arab-Israeli Six Day War. The USS *Liberty*, with a crew of 294 sailors, was a modernized version of the World War II–era Victory ship. Loosely identified as an "Auxiliary General Technical Research Ship," the *Liberty* was a signals intelligence ship, equipped with modern listening devices. It carried an array of antennas and radars, and was lightly armed, with four .50-caliber machines guns. The *Liberty* was en route from Virginia to the Ivory Coast in mid-May 1967, when the Middle East crisis intensified, and the Joint Chiefs of Staff (JCS) ordered the ship to the eastern Mediterranean. Though technically under control of the Sixth Fleet, the *Liberty* was directed by the JCS and the National Security Agency. Although its mission still remains classified, because the crew included Arab and Russian linguists, the mission probably involved eavesdropping on the Egyptian army, with its Russian advisors.

The *Liberty* arrived on station in the predawn hours of June 8, 1967, four days after the Six Day War had begun, and assumed a patrolling position 12 miles off the coast of the Gaza Strip. This placement allowed the ship to maintain it was in international waters at the time of the attack, but also placed the ship in close proximity to the Sinai war zone. Poor communications within the U.S. Navy prevented the ship from receiving new orders issued by the JCS to move one hundred miles off the Egyptian coast, orders which were issued prior to the *Liberty*'s arrival off Gaza. Poor communications played a major role in the episode, as the Israelis were quite concerned about the lack of naval liaison with the American Sixth Fleet, which they would later claim caused, in part, the attack on the *Liberty*.

The Israelis acknowledge that their aircraft properly identified the *Liberty* as an American naval ship at least twice on the morning of June 8. The *Liberty*'s crew claimed proper recognition was made at least an additional six times that morning. When a morning explosion rocked the city of El Arish on the Sinai coast, the Israelis believed that an Egyptian naval attack was underway. The "fog of war" appeared to have caused the Israelis to change the *Liberty*'s status from friendly to possible enemy combatant, largely because the ship had changed direction as part of its patrolling procedure, and because the Israelis misjudged its forward speed. The Israelis later claimed that they believed the *Liberty* to be an Egyptian freighter, possibly the *El-Quseir*.

A harsh Israeli air attack was launched against the *Liberty* around 2 P.M., and was followed up with attacks from motor torpedo boats. The attack lasted well over an hour. Israeli pilots claimed that the ship did not display the American flag, a charge flatly rejected by the U.S. Navy and by the ship's crew. The Israeli attack ended when American aircraft launched by the carrier USS *Saratoga* were en route to the attack site. The spy ship was left a burning hulk, with heavy casualties: 34 dead, with another 173 wounded.

The attack on the *Liberty* remains a source of American unhappiness with Israel. The Israelis have long been condemned in many American quarters, from government officials to former military leaders to the press, most of whom believe the attack was deliberate and reject the Israeli claim of mistaken identity. The crew members of the *Liberty* still believe that their story was never truly told, thanks to a government cover-up. If the attack was deliberate, one important question remains unanswered: What information had the *Liberty* gathered which Israel absolutely wanted protected? The Israeli government continues to maintain that the attack was an unfortunate incident of poor liaison and misidentification. Formal inquiries conducted by both the United States and Israel all concluded that no proof existed that the Israeli military deliberately attacked the vessel. The Israeli government apologized for the attack and paid over $12 million in compensation to the victims and their families and to the American government. The United States later awarded the commander of the ship, Captain William L. McConagle, the Medal of Honor.

See also: National Security Agency; Naval Intelligence

References and Further Reading

Ennes, James M., Jr. *Assault on the Liberty: The True Story of the Israeli Attack on an American Intelligence Ship*. New York: Random House, 1979.

Oren, Michael B. "The USS Liberty: Case Closed," *Azure* (2000), 74–98.

Thomas D. Veve

LINCOLN ADMINISTRATION AND INTELLIGENCE

Abraham Lincoln and his administration started the Civil War with several disadvantages in the field of military and political intelligence. Washington, DC, and the federal bureaucracy were full of Southern sympathizers who could be tapped for espionage by the confederacy. Comparable federal agents did not exist in the confederate government, newly formed by the most dedicated secessionists. Prewar federal army strength was only around 16,000, with no department devoted to intelligence. Lincoln had to obtain intelligence where he could get it, and make the best of it.

The primary sources the Lincoln administration came to rely on were: (1) Allan Pinkerton, a private detective before and after the war who provided military intelligence services of mixed value; (2) scouting and intelligence networks established by generals in the field, which varied in scope and reliability; (3) telegraphic communication to the War Department; (4) civilian sympathizers in the confederate states, who organized their own networks; (5) Lincoln's personally recruited secret agent, William A. Lloyd, reporting directly and solely to the president.

Pinkerton detected a plot to kill the president-elect in Baltimore, on his way to Washington, and was successful in placing agents in the confederate capital. His best agent, Timothy Webster, was detected and hung as a spy, after penetrating the Richmond office that eventually became the War Department's secret service operation. Pinkerton became intelligence chief for General George McClellan, reinforcing the general's cautious nature with estimates inflating the actual strength of Confederate forces by a factor of two or three. The Army of the Potomac probably refrained from several opportunities for battlefield success against the Army of Northern Virginia as a result. General Joseph Hooker established a Bureau of Military Intelligence during his brief command of the Army of the Potomac, headed by Colonel George H. Sharpe, who continued in that capacity until the end of the war. One of the most accurate and comprehensive intelligence networks was developed by Grenville M. Dodge, the chief intelligence officer for General Ulysses S. Grant in the western theater of combat. Dodge organized over 120 operatives whose identities were known to him alone.

Elizabeth Van Lew, a Richmond resident who openly expressed sympathy with the Union, visiting imprisoned Union soldiers, was known as "Crazy Bet"—an excellent cover for her spy ring. Operatives included an educated former slave, Mary Elizabeth Bowser, whom she placed as a domestic in the Confederate White House, and Samuel Ruth, superintendent of the Richmond, Fredericksburg and Potomac Railroad, who was able to slow down, and provide reports on, the rail movement of troops and supplies for Confederate forces in Virginia. Van Lew, reporting to Colonel Sharpe, was particularly useful during the 1864 to 1865 campaigns around Richmond and Petersburg.

President Lincoln got most of his information on the many military fronts in the telegraph office at the War Department, walking over from the White House several times a day to keep up to date. Lincoln spent several hours a day reading incoming telegrams, writing responses to commanders in the field. David Homer Bates, one of the "Sacred Three" telegraph and cipher operators at the War Department, recorded that it was common for Lincoln to send 10 to 12 telegraph dispatches a day to various generals, after reading all incoming telegrams. Lincoln drafted the Emancipation Proclamation there, after the Seven Days battles. During the Second Battle of Bull Run, Lincoln kept up a running exchange of messages with a Colonel Haupt, who provided more detailed and timely information on federal positions than either General Pope or General McClellan.

In the early summer of 1861, Lincoln recruited William A. Lloyd as his personal secret agent for the duration of the war. Intelligence Lloyd collected went directly to President Lincoln, and was not shared with military commanders. The president seemingly used him as an independent measure of intelligence coming through military chains of command and the cabinet. His reports included maps of military camps and forts in various parts of the Confederacy, data on artillery and forts of Richmond in July 1862, and the strength of General Robert E. Lee's army in March 1865. Lloyd, a publisher of schedules for railroads and steamboats in Southern states, originally came to Lincoln's attention by applying for a passport to travel in the Confederacy to keep his information up to date. Lincoln made the espionage work a condition of issuing the passport, offering a salary of $200 a month. Ironically, he was never paid, having destroyed his contract when arrested by Confederate authorities, so after Lincoln's assassination, he had no proof. He did obtain $2,380 in expense reimbursements from Secretary of War Edwin Stanton.

See also: Baker, Lafayette; Civil War Intelligence; Pinkerton, Allan; Sanford, Henry; Van Lew, Elizabeth; Webster, Timothy

References and Further Reading

Bates, David Homer. *Lincoln in the Telegraph Office: Recollections of the United States Military Telegraph Corps During the Civil War*. New York: The Century Co., 1907.

Feis, William B. *Grant's Secret Service: The Intelligence War from Belmont to Appomattox*. Lincoln, NE: University of Nebraska Press, 2002.

Fishel, Edwin C. *The Secret War for the Union: The Untold Story of Military Intelligence in the Civil War*. New York: Houghton Mifflin Company, 1988.

Wheeler, Tom. *Mr. Lincoln's t-mails: The Untold Story of How Abraham Lincoln Used the Telegraph to Win the Civil War*. New York: Collins, 2006.

Charles A. Rosenberg

LONETREE, SERGEANT CLAYTON J.

Marine Sergeant Clayton J. Lonetree, who had served as a security guard at the U.S. embassy in Moscow was arrested for spying in December 1986 after he told a Central Intelligence Agency (CIA) official at an embassy Christmas party in Vienna what he had done. After his arrest he quickly confessed to having passed an old embassy phonebook, blueprints of the embassy building including the location of alarm systems, photographs of embassy employees, and other documents to his Soviet handler who he knew as "Uncle Sasha," believed to have been Alexei Yefimov. Lonetree was convicted of spying in August 1987 and received a 30-year sentence, reduced to the rank of private, fined $5,000, and given a dishonorable discharge. His sentence was reduced to 15 years in July 1994 by a Marine Corps general on the grounds that his lawyers, who included noted defense attorney William Kunstler, may have been incompetent. In October 1993 his sentence had already been reduced to 20 years because of his cooperation with U.S. authorities. Lonetree was released from prison on February 26, 1996. He was the first marine convicted of espionage.

Lonetree, a Navajo, is described as being not very bright and an alcoholic. He was also very lonely in Moscow and became infatuated with Violetta, a Russian translator/receptionist at the embassy in 1985. She introduced him to Yefimov. When his tour of duty in Moscow was up, Lonetree was able to get a position as a security guard at the U.S. embassy in Vienna, Austria. There he was visited by Yefimov who brought pictures and a letter from Violetta as well as a proposal that Lonetree should return to Russia to obtain KGB training. At this point Lonetree reportedly began to have second thoughts about what he was doing, began drinking even more heavily, and approached the CIA official with his story.

Lonetree received some $3,600 from Yefimov for the material he delivered. At first it was thought that Lonetree's espionage was responsible for the deaths of as many as 20 CIA agents. It was later determined that the source of the information that cost these individuals their lives was Aldrich Ames.

See also: Ames, Aldrich; Central Intelligence Agency; Cold War Intelligence; KGB (Komitet Gosudarstvennoi Bezopasnosti)

References and Further Reading

Andrew, Christopher, and Oleg Gordievsky. *KGB: The Inside Story of Its Foreign Operations from Lenin to Gorbachev*. London: Hodder & Staughton, 1990.

Barker, Rodney. *Dancing with the Devil: Sex, Espionage and the U.S. Marines: The Clayton Lonestreet Story*. New York: Simon & Shuster, 1996.

Kessler, Ronald. *Moscow Station: How the KGB Penetrated the American Embassy*. New York: Schribner's, 1989.

Zak, William, Jr. "Sixth Amendment Issues Posed by the Court-Martial of Clayton Lonetree," *American Criminal Law Review* 30 (1992), 187–214.

Glenn P. Hastedt

LONSDALE, GORDON ARNOLD
(JANUARY 17, 1922–SEPTEMBER 9, 1970)

Gordon Arnold Lonsdale was a Russian spy whose real name was Konon Trofimovich Molody. Gordon set up spy networks in Britain and continental Europe. In 1961, British police arrested a man who appeared to be a Canadian-born businessman named Gordon Lonsdale on charges of espionage. In 1964, he was exchanged for the British agent Greville Wynne who was convicted for espionage by the Soviets in 1962. The Soviets revealed Lonsdale's true identity as Konon Trofimovich Molody. The real Lonsdale was indeed Canadian born, but in 1931, at the age of seven, his mother had taken him back to her native Finland. Here, he fought and died in World War II, whereupon the Soviets stole his identity and used it in 1954 to plant Molody as an agent in the West. Molody had spent part of his childhood and youth in California, but went home to fight for the Soviet Union in World War II, probably serving in the Red Navy. Molody himself maintained that Lonsdale was his real name until his death.

Molody's cover was selling gambling machines and jukeboxes, under which he could travel across Western Europe to organize espionage activity. He was also the contact point of the so-called Portland Spy Ring, whose other members were Harry Houghton, Ethel Gee, and Peter and Helen Kroger (Morris and Lona Cohen). The group was named after their base in Portland Dorset, England. It was in relation to the uncovering of their activity that Molody was arrested by the Special Branch of the Scotland Yard. Upon apprehension, they held classified material originating from the British Admiralty in their possession.

See also: Cohen, Lona (Leontina) and Morris, aka Helen and Peter Kroger; Cold War Intelligence; Wynne, Greville

References and Further Reading

Bulloch, John, and Henry Miller. *Spy Ring: The Full Story of the Naval Secrets Case.* London: Secker & Warburg, 1961.

Clarke, Comer. *The War Within.* London: World Distributors, 1961.

Lonsdale, Gordon. *Spy: The Memoirs of Gordon Lonsdale.* London: Mayflower-Dell, 1966.

Frode Lindgjerdet

LOS ALAMOS

Los Alamos is the secure facility located on an isolated mesa in northern New Mexico that researched, developed, and constructed the first atomic bomb. It was part of the Manhattan Engineer District (the Manhattan Project), a U.S. Army Corps of Engineers program begun (1942) in the belief that Nazi Germany had a two-year lead in the development of nuclear weapons. The isolation facilitated both the scientific interaction of the American and British scientists and technicians as well as security. Though all of the personnel were vetted and stringent security enforced, at least three people are known to have engaged in espionage that sped the development of the Soviet Union's atomic weapons programs: Klaus Fuchs, Theodore Hall, and David Greenglass. Though these spies worked at Los Alamos at the same time, they were unaware of the others' activities. Evidence gleaned (1990s) from the Soviet Union's intelligence and security (KGB) archives and the VENONA files allude to a possible fourth spy code-named Perseus.

Klaus Fuchs, a German communist and theoretical physicist, fled Nazi Germany (1933) for Britain and was interned in Canada as an enemy alien (1940) before being assigned (1943) to the British scientific team working on implosion problems. Fuchs had earlier spied for the Soviets in Britain and that contact was reestablished (1944) through the American chemist, Harry Gold, who served as a Soviet courier in the 1940s after intermittently spying for them beginning in 1935. Fuchs passed details of implosion and bomb design to Gold in two meetings (Boston and Santa Fe) in February 1945. Fuchs spied again for the Soviets (1947) while head (1946) of the Theoretical Physics Division of Britain's Harwell nuclear facility. British intelligence and the Federal Bureau of Investigation were alerted (1949) to Fuchs' espionage by Soviet intelligence cables decrypted by the joint American and British VENONA project. Fuchs confessed (1950), was convicted of espionage, spent 14 years in prison, and moved to East Germany upon his release.

Theodore Hall, a Harvard-educated American physicist involved in the radioactive Lanthanum (RaLa) test instrumentation, volunteered to spy for the Soviets (November 1944) and passed supplemental information confirming Fuchs' espionage. VENONA uncovered (early 1950s) Hall's espionage, but he did not confess at the time; though he did confess later, he was never tried.

David Greenglass, a U.S. Army draftee (April 1943) and Special Engineering Detachment machinist, was initially assigned (July 1944) to Oak Ridge and then Los Alamos (August 1944) where he worked on the shaped charges for the Fat Man implosion bomb. He passed sketches of the implosion lens to Harry Gold (1945) and later claimed to have been recruited into espionage by his brother-in-law, Julius Rosenberg, to whom he also passed information. His plea-bargained testimony led to the Rosenbergs' execution (June 19, 1953).

See also: Atomic Spy Ring; Fuchs, Emil Julius Klaus; Gold, Harry; Greenglass, David; Hall, Theodore Alvin; Nunn May, Allan; Rosenberg, Julius and Ethel; VENONA

References and Further Reading

Joint Committee on Atomic Energy. *Soviet Atomic Espionage.* Amsterdam: Fredonia Books, 2001.

Kunetka, James W. *City of Fire: Los Alamos and the Birth of the Atomic Age, 1943-1945.* Englewood Cliffs, NJ: Prentice-Hall, 1978.

Melzer, Richard. *Breakdown: How the Secret of the Atomic Bomb Was Stolen.* Santa Fe, NM: Sunstone Press, 1999.

Richard M. "Rich" Edwards

LOVELL, JAMES
(OCTOBER 31, 1737–JULY 14, 1814)

James Lovell was a cryptanalyst during the war of American independence, credited with the invention of ciphers for encoding official dispatches. Born on October 31, 1737, in Boston, Massachusetts, Lovell was tutored by his father and received a degree from Harvard College in 1756. After a year's extra work in the classics, he joined his father in teaching Latin in Boston. He became an orator, and joined the American rebels in 1775. Arrested by the British for spying, he languished in jail until exchanged in November 1776. Immediately, he was elected to Congress, and spent five continuous years in that body. With his scholarly attributes, he became a key member of various committees. He quickly emerged as an advocate of independence from Britain, identifying with radicals such as Samuel Adams and Richard Henry Lee.

Among his many responsibilities, Lovell was a regular member of the Committee for Foreign Affairs. He corresponded with diplomats in Europe, sending and receiving official congressional correspondence. As part of his duties, he developed a system of ciphers for encoding official documents and provided recipients in Europe with keys to use in reading and encoding their own messages. In factional congressional disputes, he became a partisan of Arthur Lee, John Adams, and John Jay; he did not trust Benjamin Franklin and Silas Deane. He also supported General Horatio Gates in controversies over army command, particularly in 1777. He died in Windham, Maine, on July 14, 1814.

See also: Deane, Silas; Franklin, Benjamin; Jay, John; Lee, Arthur

References and Further Reading

Shipton, Clifford K. *Sibley's Harvard Graduates*. vol. 14. Boston: Massachusetts Historical Society, 1968.

Wharton, Francis (ed.). *The Revolutionary Diplomatic Correspondence of the United States*. 6 vols. Washington, DC: Government Printing Office, 1889.

Paul David Nelson

LOWE, THADDEUS
(AUGUST 20, 1832–JANUARY 16, 1913)

Thaddeus Lowe was chief of Army Aeronautics during the Civil War from October 1, 1861, until his resignation on May 8, 1863, due to differences with Union Major General Joseph Hooker. Lowe later became an inventor of numerous patents.

Born Thaddeus Sobieski Constantine Lowe in Jefferson Mills, New Hampshire, on August 20, 1832, Lowe achieved recognition for "designing, manufacturing and deploying gas-filled balloons and portable gas generators for the purpose of gathering intelligence" for the Union army. Though serving in a civilian capacity, Lowe was named Chief of Army Aeronautics where he supervised several aeronauts in the use of ballooning and handling gas generators he built.

A self-educated person, he completed only grammar school, Lowe was deeply interested in science. He built his first balloon in 1858. The following year he built a large balloon, the *City of New York*, which he had hoped could cross the Atlantic Ocean. Several trials proved unsuccessful, so he changed the name of his balloon to the *Great Western*. At the same time he continued to seek funds to underwrite his experiment. But he soon realized that the *Great Western* was incapable of flight. With the advice of the secretary of the Smithsonian Institution, Dr. Joseph Henry, Lowe went to Cincinnati, Ohio, with a new balloon named *Enterprise*. On April 19, 1861, he ascended for a flight to the East Coast. Due to unexpected southerly air currents, he ended up near Unionville, South Carolina. Though setting a distance record of more than 900 miles in nine hours, he was promptly arrested by Carolinians who thought he was a Yankee spy. Receiving help from some local academic supporters, Lowe was released and sent back to Ohio.

The outbreak of the Civil War in America led Lowe to offer his services to the Lincoln administration. He believed that aeronautics could be used to gather intelligence by aboveground observation. On June 18, 1861, to prove his point, Lowe lifted off from the Columbian Armory in Washington, DC. The balloon made a number of flights from the armory, the Smithsonian grounds, and the south lawn of the White House. Equipped with a telegraph, he sent Lincoln the following message: "I have pleasure in sending you this first dispatch ever telegraphed from an aerial station . . ." The responsibility for aeronautics as a military intelligence gathering unit was promptly given to the Topographical Engineers.

Despite competition from fellow aeronauts, John Wise and John La Mountain, Lowe emerged as the leading figure for the program. Ordered to produce several balloons, Lowe constructed two large ones, the *Union* and the *Intrepid*, and two smaller ones, the *Constitution* and the *Washington*. Sent to Fort Monroe in support of the Army of the Potomac, Lowe and his trained aeronauts served effectively during Major General McClellan's Peninsula Campaign. What enabled Lowe to assist the Union troops was the ability to telegraph the positions of the Confederates. During his many flights for gathering information, Lowe discovered the evacuation of Yorktown and made important observations during the battle of Fair Oaks in which he was able to distinguish the main attacks from false ones. After contacting malaria on the peninsula, his Balloon Corps lost favor with the army commanders who came after McClellan. After a disagreement with his new supervisor, Captain C. E. Comstock of the Corps of Engineers, one involving a reduction in pay and dismissal of his father from the corps, Lowe resigned on May 8, 1863. In July the Balloon corps was officially disbanded, yet the contributions Lowe made in gathering and relaying information proved valuable to commanders in the field.

After the war Lowe became a successful businessman and inventor. He developed numerous designs for refrigerated shipping and one patent, particularly, was for carbureted water gas. In 1887, Lowe moved to California where he devoted his remaining years to airship design and astronomy. He died on January 16, 1913, a year prior to the outbreak of world war in Europe.

See also: Balloons; Civil War Intelligence; Confederate Signal and Secret Service Bureau

References and Further Reading

Cameron, William. "Thaddeus S. C. Lowe," in David & Jeanne Heidler (eds.), *Encyclopedia of the American Civil War*, vol. III, pp. 127–28. Santa Barbara, CA: ABC-CLIO, 2000.

Evans, Charles M. *War of the Aeronauts: The History of Ballooning in the Civil War*. Mechanicsburg, PA: Stackpole Books, 2002.

Haydon, F. Stansbury. *Aeronautics in the Union and Confederate Armies with a Survey of Military Aeronautics Prior to 1861*. Baltimore: The Johns Hopkins University Press, 1941.

Raines, Rebecca Robbins. *Getting the Message Through, a Branch History of the U.S. Army Signal Corps*. Washington, DC: Center of Military History, 1996.

"Thaddeus Sobieski Lowe." http://www.civilwarhome.com (accessed August 24, 2005).

Charles F. Howlett

LUCY SPY RING

The Lucy Spy Ring was an anti-German operation focused on preventing the spread of Fascism during World War II. It provided vital information to the Union of Soviet Socialist Republics (USSR) leaders. The name Lucy Spy Ring is derived from the code name "Lucy" that the leader Rudolf Roessler used for his espionage activities.

Directed by Rudolf Roessler, the Lucy Spy Ring collected information about German operations and strategies. The Lucy Spy Ring consisted of a complex network of contacts and agents including individuals in USSR, British, and Swiss intelligence agencies.

The Lucy Spy Ring consisted of three primary spy networks, and Rudolf Roessler was the key contact connecting these spy networks. Roessler was born on November 22, 1897, in Kaufbeuren, Germany. Before entering the field of espionage Roessler served as manager of a German association of popular theater. While in this position he developed relationships with individuals both liberal and conservative throughout Germany. Additionally, he had contacts in the German military who were sympathetic to the anti-Fascism cause and provided Roessler with critical information.

One network was headed by Sandor Rado who was known by the code name "Alex." He was a Hungarian geographer, born in Budapest in 1899. He joined the Hungarian Red Army when the revolution collapsed and he was forced to flee. While studying geography at a university, he created a highly accurate atlas of the USSR that provided critical information for the Lucy Spy Ring and Allied forces. In 1935 Rado joined the Red Army and moved to Switzerland. His business contacts in the United States and geographical knowledge made him a valuable asset to the Lucy Spy Ring. While serving as an agent in the Lucy Spy Ring, Rado used the cover of running a press specializing in geographic publications. This provided an excellent cover for his travels throughout Europe and the Soviet Union.

Allan Foote headed the second network in the Lucy Spy Ring and first began his career in espionage in the summer of 1947. In the evenings he would then transmit information to his contacts to reach the Soviet government. Rado doubted Foote's loyalty and suspected that Foote was a double agent working for the British intelligence. However, the spy ring continued to heavily rely on him because he continued to provide valuable and reliable information. For Foote's service during World War II he earned the rank of major in the Soviet army and received four official honors.

The third branch was headed by renowned Communist Rachel Dubendorfer. She was motivated by her Communist ideology to prevent the spread of Fascism.

Using existing networks, Roessler contacted Alexander Rado to use contacts in Switzerland by Soviet intelligence. Rado Roessler then passed information to the Soviets. This information was provided to the Soviets on the condition that they would not attempt to identify his sources of information. This was a key condition that protected Lucy Spy Ring agents and their informants. The Lucy Spy Ring communicated with the Soviet Centre, which was the central agency for collecting information and distributing the information to appropriate leaders in Soviet intelligence. In addition to information discovered by Lucy Spy Ring agents sent to Moscow, at times the Soviets requested specific information from the Lucy Spy Ring about their enemy, such as specific information about German military locations.

An example of the critical information the Lucy Spy Ring provided to Soviet leaders is a message provided by the agent Dora. In early August of 1941 Dora sent a message that informed Soviet leaders that Japan would not attack the Soviet Union. Japanese military leaders reached this decision because Germany had not successfully defeated the Soviet Union in any battles. This key information was the basis of the Soviet decision to move forces from areas closest to Japan to those nearer the western front and Moscow. Later these troops were vital to fighting German attacks. This single critical piece of information provided by the Lucy Spy Ring had a substantial impact on the outcome of World War II.

The Lucy Spy Ring commonly encountered problems transmitting information. They relied heavily on radios to transmit their messages to government contacts. During the transition of a crucial message in October of 1941 to Moscow the signal was abruptly cut off. The message was cut off because at this time Moscow was essentially under siege by the German army. It is likely that the contact in the Soviet government receiving the signal was forced to evacuate the building where receivers were located.

Following the military disaster in 1942 in Kharkov, Stalin blamed the USSR Intelligence Centre for misinformation. In response, the Centre blamed its informant the Lucy Spy Ring. With this situation the Lucy Spy Ring lost favor with Moscow. The likely cause of inaccurate information provided by the Lucy Spy Ring was lost contacts within British intelligence. Without these key contacts the Lucy Spy Ring agents were left to their field agents with limited information. Later the Lucy Spy Ring regained support by providing accurate information regarding German troop movements.

Aware of the threat of the Lucy Spy Ring, Germany diligently worked to destroy it. Recognized as a key agent, Foote was also targeted by Germans who repeatedly attempted to kidnap him. When the Swiss government located Lucy Spy Ring transmitters, the spy network was shut down. Several key agents were arrested, including Foote. After shortly being imprisoned, Foote was released after a vague confession.

See also: American Intelligence, World War II

References and Further Reading

Brown, Paul. "Report on the IRR File on the Red Orchestra," *The U.S. National Archives & Records Administration*. http://www.archives.gov/iwg/research-papers/red-orchestra-irr-file.html (accessed December 21, 2006).

Mulligan, Timothy P. "Spies, Ciphers and 'Zitadelle': Intelligence and the Battle of Kursk, 1943," *Journal of Contemporary History* 22 (1987), 235–260.

Read, Anthony. *Operation Lucy, Most Secret Spy Ring of the Second World War*. London: Hodder & Stoughton, 1980.

Kristin Whitehair

LUDWIG, KURT FREDERICK
(1903–)

Kurt Frederick Ludwig was the head of a German spy ring operating in the United States from 1940 to 1941. He was born in 1903 in Ohio, his parents having migrated to the United States in the 1850s. Soon after Kurt was born, the family moved to

Germany and the boy went to school there, and ended up in business in Munich. He was recruited by German intelligence and was arrested by the Austrians in February 1938 after being caught photographing bridges along the Austrian-German border. He was still being held when the Nazis occupied Austria, was immediately released, and then sent to the United States to run an important spy ring.

Trained in Berlin, Ludwig's reports were to be sent by transatlantic clipper to a fictitious couple, through Spain, and directly to Heinrich Himmler and Reinhard Heydrich using the code names "Manuel Alonzo" and "Lothar Fredreich." On arrival in New York, Ludwig, operating as a salesmen of leather goods, attended some meetings of the German-American Bund, and recruited a number of agents including Paul Theodore Borchardt-Battua, an ex-German army officer who gained the code name "Joe"; Rene Charles Froehlich, an American soldier stationed at Fort Jay, in the middle of New York harbor; Cark Schroetter, a Swiss businessman from Miami; and Karl Mueller, a naturalized American from Austria. Ludwig and Mueller were involved in many clandestine actions getting information from factories. They even walked into the U.S. Naval Academy at Annapolis, where they photographed the cadets and the facilities.

British agents in Bermuda intercepted mail from the United States to Spain and Portugal, and among these were letters from "Joe K," who, using invisible ink, reported on the British soldiers stationed in Iceland and the U.S. bombers sent to Britain. Soon afterwards, on March 18, 1941, a pedestrian was run down while crossing Times Square, New York. He held a Spanish passport with the name Don Julio Lopez Lido. When the FBI searched his room at the Taft Hotel, they found intelligence documents including a report on the defenses at Pearl Harbor. It was not long before the British censors in Bermuda came across a letter referring to the death of "Phil" in Times Square and, realizing that he was an important German agent, had the Americans close in on the spy ring which they quickly learned centered on Ludwig. Ludwig fled New York for Montana and was eventually arrested in Seattle. He was tried in March 1942 and sentenced to 20 years' imprisonment. In 1953 Ludwig was released and deported.

See also: American Intelligence, World War II

References and Further Reading

Andrew, Christopher, and Jeremy Noakes. *Intelligence and International Relations, 1900–1945.* Exeter, UK: University of Exeter, 1987.

Kahn, David. *Hitler's Spies: Germany Military Intelligence in World War II.* London: Macmillan, 1978.

Justin Corfield

M

MACLEAN, DONALD DUART
(MAY 25, 1913–MARCH 16, 1983)

Donald Maclean (coded-named "HOMER") was a member of the Cambridge Group and an active Committee for State Security (KGB) agent with Kim Philby. He was probably the most productive of all British KGB agents in terms of the volume and quality of the secrets he stole.

The Maclean family was Scottish. Donald's father was a barrister, a knight, a member of Parliament, and a very stern authoritarian person. He compelled Donald to attend a very strict boys' school. After graduating, he entered Cambridge and was initiated into the excesses of alcohol and homosexual practices by Anthony Blunt and Guy Burgess. He was also led into a naive form of Marxism that was exploited by the KGB.

During his Cambridge days, Maclean dreamed of becoming a peasant instructor of English in the Soviet Union. However, Theodore Maly, a KGB agent of Hungarian origins, persuaded him to abandon this dream. Instead he was to blend into the English bureaucratic system and spy.

In 1935 Maclean began working for the Foreign Office. In 1938 he was posted to the British embassy in Paris. In 1940 he was evacuated to London, having given the KGB secrets of both the French and the British. In London he was assigned to the Combined Policy Committee where he had access to some of the Manhattan Project secrets which he promptly gave to the KGB. In 1944 Maclean was transferred to Washington, DC, which provided an intelligence bonanza for the Soviets.

After World War II, the Americans and the British began to decode and translate the huge volume of Soviet intercepts they had accumulated. Soon they realized that HOMER was a major traitor. In 1948 he provided the Soviets with information that revealed American planes carried only conventional bombs and therefore without a full-scale war could not stop the building of the Iron Curtain. In 1950, as head of the

American sector of the British embassy in Washington, he learned that Truman was going to keep the war in Korea limited.

In 1951 Burgess and Maclean were warned by Philby that a code-breaking success was leading investigators to Maclean. Philby contacted their Soviet handlers for extraction. On Friday, May 25, Burgess went to Maclean's home. The two fled to the Soviet Union where they were welcomed, but soon found life unsatisfying.

Maclean was sent to live in the industrial city of Kuibyshev where he worked on an economic magazine. He was joined by his wife and three children; however, unhappy, he turned to alcohol, causing his marriage to be destroyed. He died alone behind the Iron Curtain, a man embittered by his idealistic devotion to a failed cause on March 16, 1983.

See also: Blunt, Anthony; Burgess, Guy Francis De Moncy; KGB (Komitet Gosudarstvennoi Bezopasnosti); Philby, Harold Adrian Russell "Kim"

References and Further Reading

Cecil, Robert. *A Divided Life: A Personal Portrait of the Spy Donald MacLean*. New York: HarperCollins, 1989.

Hamrick, S. J. *Deceiving the Deceivers: Kim Philby, Donald Maclean, and Guy Burgess*. New Haven, CT: Yale University Press, 2004.

West, Rebecca. *The New Meaning of Treason*. New York: Viking, 1964.

Andrew J. Waskey

MACLEISH, ARCHIBALD
(MAY 7, 1892–APRIL 20, 1982)

Archibald MacLeish was American scholar, poet, librarian of Congress, and intelligence analyst. Born May 7, 1892, in Glenco, Illinois, MacLeish graduated from Yale University in 1915. He enrolled in Harvard Law School in 1916 but interrupted his studies to join the Yale Mobile Hospital Unit in 1917. He later became an artillery officer, commanding a battery during the Second Battle of the Marne.

Following the war, MacLeish returned to Harvard Law, where he graduated first in his class in 1919. He briefly taught government at Harvard before practicing law until 1923, when he turned down an offered partnership to become a poet. MacLeish won his first of three Pulitzer Prizes in 1922 for his poem "Conquistador," about the Spanish conquest of the Aztecs.

During the 1930s MacLeish joined the staff of *Fortune Magazine*. His writing, both poetry and prose, increasingly condemned both Fascism and Communism. During the Depression, he also criticized the excesses of American capitalism and strongly endorsed Franklin Roosevelt's New Deal. In 1939 FDR nominated him to be the librarian of Congress.

When Roosevelt's Executive Order 8922 created the Office of Facts and Figures in October 1941, the president's first choice for director was Archibald MacLeish. MacLeish's responsibilities in this role emphasized the dissemination of "white" propaganda about the justice of the Allied cause. When the newly formed Office of War Information absorbed the Office of Facts and Figures in June 1942, MacLeish became assistant director of OWI. In 1944 he became assistant secretary of state for cultural and public affairs, eventually becoming the head of the U.S. delegation to UNESCO. He retired from government service in 1949 and returned to teaching poetry at Harvard.

See also: Office of Strategic Services

References and Further Reading

Donaldson, Scott, in collaboration with R. H. Winnik. *Archibald MacLeish: An American Life*. Boston: Houghton Mifflin, 1992.

Winkler, Allan. *The Politics of Propaganda: The Office of War Information, 1942–1945*. New Haven and London: Yale University Press, 1978.

Peter F. Coogan

MAGIC

MAGIC is the code name given to information obtained by breaking into PURPLE, the Japanese cipher machine carrying messages in its most important diplomatic code. PURPLE was broken in 1940 but because the Japanese navy used a different code, JN-25, PURPLE did not provide warning of the Japanese attack on Pearl Harbor. It did yield a diplomatic message that was sent to the Japanese embassy in Washington instructing the ambassador to break off diplomatic relations with the United States at 1:00 P.M., December 7, 1941.

The U.S. Army and Navy worked independently of one another in decoding the information from PURPLE intercepts. Each maintained a series of intercept stations and then sent those intercepts to Washington. A significant time lag often took place in transmitting these intercepts. The most common delivery method was by air but on occasion bad flying weather led to the use of ships. Once the messages arrived, the lack of translators again created a bottleneck that slowed the production of intelligence. The navy, for example, had six translators only three of whom were skilled enough in Japanese to work alone. Once translated, the distribution of MAGIC was tightly controlled. The distribution list in January 1941 consisted of nine individuals: the secretary of state, the president's military aide, the secretary of war, the chief of staff, the director of military intelligence, the secretary of the navy, the chief of naval operations, the director of naval intelligence, and the chief of the War Plans Division. The army was responsible for daily deliveries of selected MAGIC to the State Department, War Department, and White House, whereas the navy did likewise for the Navy Department and the White House. After they were read, the material was taken back by messengers.

This limited distribution of MAGIC would later come in for extensive criticism by those who argued a fuller distribution of MAGIC would have allowed for greater coordination in Washington and permitted U.S. officials to anticipate the attack on Pearl Harbor. Although not rejecting the argument that MAGIC was not distributed widely enough, others counter that MAGIC in and of itself would not have prevented or limited the consequences of the attack. They assert that although 20–20 hindsight does reveal information pointing to the attack, at the time there was information supporting many different interpretations of Japanese actions. It was only after the attack was it possible to separate out true signals from background noise and clutter.

MAGIC was not the only source of information on Japanese thinking available to military and civilian policy makers before Pearl Harbor. PURPLE was the transmission means used for the highest-ranking diplomatic messages. American cryptanalysts also had access to espionage messages sent in simpler J-19 or PA-K2. Deemed less urgent than PURPLE intercepts, these messages were given secondary priority.

See also: American Intelligence, World War II; Pearl Harbor; PURPLE

References and Further Reading

Ameringer, Charles. *U.S. Foreign Intelligence: The Secret Side of American History*. Lexington, MA: Lexington Books, 1990.

Farago, Ladislas. *The Broken Seal: 'Operation Magic' and the Secret Road to Pearl Harbor*. New York: Bantam, 1968.

Lewin, Ronald. *The American Magic: Codes, Ciphers, and the Defeat of Japan*. New York: Farrar, Straus and Giroux, 1982.

Prange, Gordon W. *At Dawn We Slept: The Untold Story of Pearl Harbor*. New York: McGraw-Hill, 1981.

Wohlstetter, Roberta. *Pearl Harbor: Warning and Decision*. Stanford: Stanford University Press, 1962.

Glenn P. Hastedt

MAGNUM

MAGNUM is the code name given to a class of signals intelligence (SIGINT) satellites launched into a geosynchronous orbit between 1985 and 1990 by the National Reconnaissance Office. MAGNUM satellites have a mass of nearly 6,000 pounds and a large 100-m diameter umbrella-like reflecting dish pointed at Earth to collect signals. There were believed to be three MAGNUM launchings, all by space shuttle missions: January 24, 1985, November 23, 1989, and November 15, 1990. Within the framework of their general SIGINT mission against the Soviet Union and China, MAGNUM satellites also obtained missile test telemetry intelligence (TELINT), radio communications intelligence (COMINT), and radar emissions intelligence (RADINT).

MAGNUM satellites replaced the RHYOLITE/AQUADE and CHALET series of SIGINT satellites. The name of the program itself was changed to ORION by the time of the first launch by the Discovery Space shuttle and the entire program is often referred to by the joint designation MAGNUM/ORION satellites. In turn this program was replaced by MENTOR/Advanced ORION satellites. Three MENTOR launchings took place on Titan IV and Titan IVB rockets from Cape Canaveral between 1995 and 2003: May 14, 1995, May 9, 1998, and September 9, 2003.

It is believed that at least one of the MAGNUM satellites launched in the 1980s is still functioning. With the end of the cold war, the mission for the MAGNUM/ORION and MENTOR satellites has changed. ORION satellites downloaded information directly to receivers in Saudi Arabia during the Persian Gulf War. The Australia-based Nautilus Institute, which examined the involvement of Australian forces and facilities such as the Pine Gap Radar station in supporting the war in Afghanistan and Iraq, reported the use of MENTOR satellites in those conflicts.

See also: CHALET; Cold War Intelligence

References and Further Reading

Nautilus Institute in Australia. http://www.globalcollab.org/Nautilus/australia (accessed July 17, 2008).

Richelson, Jeffrey. *The U.S. Intelligence Community*, 5th ed. Boulder, CO: Westview, 2008.

Glenn P. Hastedt

MAK, CHI

Chi Mak, who was born in the People's Republic of China (PRC) in 1940 and became a naturalized citizen of the United States in June 1985, was sentenced in March 2008 to 24 ½ years in jail on charges that he did not register as an agent of a foreign government (the PRC), conspired to violate export control laws, and made false statements to federal investigators. He was arrested at his home in Downey, California, on October 28, 2005. The same day, his brother, Tai Wang Mak, was arrested at the Los Angeles International Airport.

Mak was employed as an electrical engineer by Power Paragon where he worked on more than 200 U.S. defense and military contracts during his career. Included among them was the navy's highly sensitive Quiet Electric Drive (QED) propulsion system. Mak was charged with taking computer disks home where his wife copied them and delivered the disks to his brother who encrypted them in preparation for a flight to Hong Kong. Mak is also charged with e-mailing photos and reports on the QED system to his home computer.

Mak obtained a secret level security clearance in 1996. Mak was identified as a "sleeper" agent. He admitted to having been sent to the United States more than 20 years before his arrest for the purpose of gaining entry into the defense-industrial establishment in order to steal secrets. Mak had been under investigation for 18 months. Court-ordered wiretaps were obtained to follow his activities. Secret property searches and the clandestine installation of a video camera inside his home were also used to obtain information. Among the shredded documents found in a search of the trash at his residence were two documents urging him to join more professional organizations on topics of particular concern to China. Included among them were space-based electromagnetic intercept systems; space-launched magnetic levitation platforms; submarine torpedoes; aircraft carrier electronic systems; water jet propulsion systems; early warning technologies; and high-frequency, self-linking satellite communications.

In his defense, Mak argued that all of the information he copied was available from nonclassified sources on the Internet and that it therefore was in the public domain. The prosecution argued that the information was export-controlled and could not be shared with foreign nationals without explicit permission.

Other members of Chi Mak's espionage ring included his wife, Rebecca Lai-wah Chiu Mak; his brother, Tai Wang Mak; his brother's wife, Fuk-heung Li; and Tai and Fuk Li's son, Yui "Billy" Mak. Tai Mak was sentenced to 10 years in prison, Fuk Li was sentenced to three years of probation, and Yui Mak was sentenced to time served. All three members of the family were deported. Rebecca Mak received the same 24-year jail sentence as her husband.

The investigation of Mak's home also revealed the identity of another person engaged in espionage for the PRC, Dongfan Chung, who was arrested on February 12, 2008.

See also: China, Intelligence Operations of; Post–Cold War Intelligence

References and Further Reading

Eftimiades, Nicholas. *Chinese Intelligence Operations*. New York: Taylor Francis, 1994.
Richelson, Jeffrey. *A Century of Spies: Intelligence in the Twentieth Century*. New York: Oxford University Press, 1995.

Glenn. P. Hastedt

MARINE CORPS INTELLIGENCE

The twenty-first-century U.S. Marine Corps emphasizes the generation of tactical intelligence that facilitates the planning and execution of marine air-ground task force (MAGTF) operations. This downward focus, toward the point where marines are in contact with the enemy, ensures that commanders of marine ground and air units have the maximum amount of relevant intelligence at their fingertips when they are called upon to make informed decisions as to the best use of the assets under their control. The development of Marine Corps intelligence operations during the twentieth and twenty-first centuries has led to the integration of the corps' collection and dissemination assets with those of the broader intelligence community, but not at the expense of commanders in the field.

The Marine Corps' appreciation of the importance of intelligence has evolved over time. The nineteenth-century Corps did not have a need for sophisticated intelligence capabilities until the expansion of American interests in the Pacific and its participation in the Spanish-American War led to an increase in the Corps' size and its range of activities. As an adjunct of the "New Navy," the Marine Corps acted as colonial infantry, providing muscle for the imperialistic American foreign policy of the early twentieth century. With this mission in mind, marine and navy planners developed the Advanced Base Concept. It was in the development of this concept that the most famous Marine Corps covert operative, Major Earl "Pete" Ellis, made his name. Ellis' prescience was not typical of Marine Corps intelligence analysis, however. Insertion ashore to develop and defend advanced bases for the navy did call for the development of better intelligence capabilities, but the Corps developed a rudimentary intelligence structure for itself that emphasized the production of tactical intelligence for use by lower-level commanders in the field, relying on the navy for the generation of intelligence above the battalion level. This low-level tactical focus, joined to a reliance on the swift application of massive firepower to make up for any shortfalls in overall intelligence coverage, remained the Marine Corps mind-set concerning the generation and use of intelligence products until the late 1980s.

General Alfred M. Gray, Jr., began to change this mind-set after assuming the office of commandant on July 1, 1987. Gray brought a combination to the job of commandant that was rare in the Marine Corps: he considered himself a "warrior" in the best traditions of the Corps, but he believed in fighting smarter rather than just ratcheting up the level of combat power in the field. His emphasis on brains as well as brawn was most evident in his attitude toward intelligence. Gray had served in an intelligence capacity several times during his career. His experience in the gathering and use of intelligence and his interest in helping the Corps recover its self-confidence and sense of importance after the difficulties of the 1980s led him to establish the USMC Intelligence Center. In a "White Letter" to senior marine officers dated July 27, 1991, Gray explained his intentions: "When I established the . . . Center almost four years ago, I had a clear vision of the need for a Service intelligence center and the functions it would perform . . . [It] is the institutional vehicle by which our Service exploits and augments existing defense intelligence capabilities in order to obtain the all-source tailored intelligence required to make sound decisions about our force structure for the future. . . . I urge each of you to visit the Center, gain an understanding of its capabilities, and return to your command or parent activity prepared to task and exploit this precious Service asset. . . . We have made a substantial investment. Use it!" Gray's work became the foundation upon which the present Marine Corps intelligence structure is built.

Even with all the strides made by Gray, however, the test of combat showed that further improvements were warranted. After the first Persian Gulf War, Carl E. Mundy, Jr., Gray's successor, issued a directive detailing solutions to problems uncovered by an analysis of Marine Corps intelligence during Desert Storm. Six fundamental deficiencies were identified: inadequate doctrinal foundation; no defined career progression for intelligence officers; insufficient tactical intelligence support; insufficient joint manning; insufficient language capability; and inadequate imagery capability. The solution for doctrinal deficiencies addressed more than one problem area. Concerning doctrine, the directive stated that the mission of Marine Corps intelligence was "[to p]rovide commanders, at every level, with tailored, timely, minimum essential intelligence, and ensure that this intelligence is integrated into the operational planning process." It then laid down seven principles considered essential in ensuring effective intelligence support of operations. These principles, modified by further thought and experience, are listed in the 2003 publication *Intelligence Operations*: the focus is on tactical intelligence; intelligence is focused downward to tactical commanders; intelligence drives operations; intelligence activities require centralized management; the G-2/S-2 (staff intelligence officer) facilitates use of intelligence; intelligence must be tailored to the requirements of the user and delivered in a timely fashion; and, finally, utilization, not dissemination, is the final step of the intelligence cycle.

The connection between Marine Corps intelligence and the national security intelligence structure was finally solidified on April 27, 2000, when Commandant General J. L. Jones announced the establishment at Marine Corps Headquarters of an Intelligence Department. Jones stated in his announcement that "the emblematic and practical significance of the Commandant having a 'G2' who can serve as both a proponent of intelligence, surveillance, and reconnaissance inside the combat development process and as the focal point for leveraging intelligence community support for our warfighting capability." With the elevation of intelligence to the level of USMC Headquarters staff, General Gray's ultimate goal of fighting smarter was realized and the evolution of Marine Corps intelligence was brought full circle. The Marine Corps could now reach out to the intelligence assets of the world and pass the benefits of those assets to tactical commanders in the field.

See also: Air Force Intelligence; Army Intelligence; Code Talkers; Intelligence Community; Office of Naval Intelligence

References and Further Reading

Millett, Allan R. *Semper Fidelis: The History of the United States Marine Corps*, rev. ed. New York: The Free Press, 1991.

Richelson, Jeffrey T. *The United States Intelligence Community*, 5th ed. Boulder, CO: Westview Press, 2008.

United States Marine Corps. ALMAR 100/95. March 24, 1995.

United States Marine Corps. ALMAR 021/00. April 27, 2000.

United States Marine Corps. *Marine Corps Doctrine Publication 2 (MCDP-2): Intelligence*. Washington, DC: Headquarters Marine Corps, 1997.

United States Marine Corps. *Marine Corps Warfighting Publication 2–1 (MCWP 2–1): Intelligence Operations*. Washington, DC: Headquarters Marine Corps, 2003.

United States Navy. *Naval Doctrine Publication 2 (NDP-2): Naval Intelligence*. Washington, DC: Department of the Navy, 1994.

Donald K. Mitchener

MARQUAND, JOHN P.
(APRIL 10, 1893–JULY 16, 1960)

A prominent American novelist, Marquand wrote a number of spy novels about a fictional "Mr. Moto," some of which were turned into films. John Phillips Marquand was born in Massachusetts and won a scholarship to Harvard University. He served in World War I and then started writing fiction for the *Saturday Evening Post* and other magazines, as well as novels, his most famous being *The Late George Apley* (1937) which won the Pulitzer Prize for fiction in 1938.

Marquand traveled extensively, including to Malaya, Indochina, Mongolia, and Japan, and in 1935 started writing his "Mr. Moto" spy novels. The first was *Your Turn, Mr. Moto*, and the others were: *Thank You, Mr. Moto* (1936), *Think Fast, Mr. Moto* (1937), *Mr. Moto Is So Sorry* (1938), *Last Laugh, Mr. Moto* (1942), and *Right You Are, Mr. Moto* (1957). This led to eight films, the first being *Think Fast, Mr. Moto* (1937) starring Peter Lorre, only loosely based on the novels. The books and films do not have Mr. Moto as the main character—not meant to be a Japanese agent—but as the man who helps the American hero escape from the entanglement with others. The last film had the Moto character removed from the story. Marquand died on July 16, 1960. There was an attempt to revive the character in the film *The Return of Mr. Moto* (1965).

See also: Fiction—Spy Novels; Movies, Spies in

References and Further Reading

Koga, James S. "The Mr. Moto Novels of John P. Marquand," http://www.csupomona.edu/~jskoga/moto/.

Wires, Richard. *John P. Marquand and Mr. Moto: Spy Adventures and Detective Films*. Muncie, IN: Ball State University, 1990.

Justin Corfield

MARSHALL, GENERAL GEORGE CATLETT (DECEMBER 31, 1880–OCTOBER 16, 1959)

George Catlett Marshall was army chief of staff during World War II, secretary of state (1947–1949), secretary of defense at the start of the Korean War, architect of European Recovery Plan named after him, key shaper of U.S. cold war policies, and first professional soldier honored with the Nobel Peace Prize.

Although George C. Marshall is best remembered as the architect of the European Recovery Program (Marshall Plan), he is considered, first and foremost, the creator of the World War II army and the primary organizer of the Allied victory over the Axis powers. Born into a well-to-do family in Uniontown, Pennsylvania, Marshall graduated from Virginia Military Institute in 1902, where he served as first captain of the Corps of Cadets. Upon receiving his commission as a second lieutenant of infantry, Marshall served one year in the Philippines and later graduated with honors from the Infantry-Cavalry School at Fort Leavenworth.

Throughout his early years in the military, Marshall demonstrated extraordinary ability as a staff officer. His organizing abilities earned him the praises of his superiors to the extent that he was given numerous responsibilities well beyond his rank. In World War I he was deployed with First Division Units to France. A favorite of the AEF (American Expeditionary Forces) commander, General John J. Pershing, Marshall was assigned to his staff. During the war Marshall played a major role in planning the St. Mihiel and Meuse-Argonne offensives. Developing a unique reputation for organizing and operating within Allied commands, he served as First Army's chief of operations in the final weeks of the war.

During the interwar period Marshall served as head of the Infantry School at Fort Benning from 1927 to 1932, training many of the key officers who would compose the U.S. High Command during World War II. In July 1938, Marshall accepted a post with the General Staff in Washington, DC. In September 1939, Marshall was named chief of staff and accorded the rank of general by President Franklin D. Roosevelt. He was selected for the post over numerous senior officers.

With the start of World War II, Marshall began focusing all his energies on the creation of a large, modern army. Due to his efforts, he reorganized the nation's fighting capacity as well as its intelligence-gathering capabilities. The U.S. military expanded from 175,000 in 1939 to 1.4 million in 1941. After the Japanese attack on Pearl Harbor on December 7, 1941, Marshall was responsible for "the building, supplying, and, in part, the deploying of over eight million soldiers." Overseeing highly secretive intelligence and logistic matters, Marshall became the leading figure in the newly formed U.S. Joint and Anglo-American Combined Chiefs of Staff and later became Roosevelt's chief military adviser.

Involved with top-secret intelligence information, Marshall attended all the Allied wartime summit conferences from Argentina in the summer of 1941 to Potsdam in 1945. Under his guidance he created "the joint and combined chiefs and in the application of the unity of command principle to all U.S. and British ground, naval, and air forces." His most secretive assignment was his participation as a member of the policy committee, the Top Policy Group, which supervised the atomic studies engaged in by American and British scientists. Along with Secretary of War Henry Stimson, Marshall obtained significant funding from Congress—which was told very little about where the money was going—for the top-secret project.

One of Marshall's greatest strategic and planning achievements was his securing approval for the 1944 cross-channel assault culminating in the decisive invasion of Normandy. Roosevelt refused to send him overseas to carry out the invasion. Instead, that assignment fell into the hands of General Eisenhower. So effective was Marshall's efforts in training, planning, and supplying the Allies that British Prime Minister Winston Churchill referred to him as the "true organizer of victory." He became only one of a handful of five-star generals when Congress established such rank in 1944.

From 1947 to 1949, Marshall served as secretary of state. In this position he was responsible for "defining, implementing, and winning bipartisan support for an activist cold war policy of containing Soviet expansionism." The European Recovery Program, named after him, saw Congress earmark more than $13 billion for the reconstruction and rebuilding of the devastated countries in Europe. He also played a major role in the formation of West Germany. When the Korean War broke out, despite some health issues, he acceded to President Truman's wishes and assumed the post of secretary of defense from 1950 to 1951. In this capacity he rebuilt U.S. military forces; played a key role in the controversial relief of General Douglas MacArthur, accused of being soft on Communism by followers of Senator Joe McCarthy; pushed a plan for universal military training; and helped establish a military alliance, the North Atlantic Treaty Organization (NATO).

Marshall was a strong defender of U.S. military interests, but his diplomatic savvy encouraged him to seek peaceful solutions despite cold war hostilities. In 1953, for his efforts in this regard, he was awarded the Nobel Peace Prize, the only professional soldier to receive such distinction. Considered by most one of the world's greatest soldier-statesmen, Marshall was "one of the foremost defenders of civilian control of the military" and a major policy maker regarding the army's proper role in a democratic society. He is buried in Arlington National Cemetery.

See also: American Intelligence; Office of Policy Coordination; Office of Strategic Services

References and Further Reading

Cray, Edward. *General of the Army: George C. Marshall, Soldier and Statesman.* New York: Cooper Square Press, 1990.

Frye, William. *Marshall: Citizen Soldier.* Indianapolis, IN: Bobbs-Merrill, 1947.

Marshall, George C. *General Marshall's Report—The Winning of the War in Europe and the Pacific.* Washington, DC: War Department, 1945.

Payne, Robert. *The Marshall Story*. New York: Prentice-Hall, 1951.

Pogue, Forrest C. *George C. Marshall*. 4 vols. New York: Viking Press, 1963–1987.

Stoler, Mark A. *George C. Marshall: Soldier-Statesman of the American Century*. New York: Twayne Publishers, 1989.

Charles F. Howlett

MARTIN, RICHARD H., AND BERNON MITCHELL

Richard H. Martin was an employee of the National Security Agency (NSA) who, along with his colleague Bernon F. Mitchell, defected to the Soviet Union in 1960. At a Moscow press conference on September 6, 1960, they revealed information about the mission, workings, and operations of the NSA that had not been known publicly before.

Martin and Mitchell first met at the Naval Security Group in Alaska in the early 1950s. They remained friends after their tour of duty ended and both joined the NSA in September 1957. Martin and Mitchell showed few signs of disaffection with their jobs until 1959 when they became aware of U.S. electronic intelligence over fights over Soviet territory. They were sufficiently disturbed by what they saw as reckless behavior by the Untied States that they arranged to talk with Representative Wilbur Mills about their concerns. Mills listened but did little with the information. At that point the two apparently began to consider defecting to the Soviet Union as a means of highlighting their concerns.

On June 25, 1960, the two of them flew from Washington, DC, to Mexico City. From there they made their way to Havana and on to Moscow where they held a press conference revealing to the existence of NSA. Beyond the highly unfavorable publicity generated by their defection and the light it shined on the NSA, it is uncertain how much information of significance they were able to pass on to the Soviet Union since by all accounts they did not have access to highly classified information.

Their defection became the subject of a House Committee on Un-American Activities investigation as well as internal NSA inquiries. The explanation that became popularized in the media was that Martin and Mitchell were homosexuals. Consistent with this explanation, NSA soon dismissed some 26 employees suspected of being security risks because of their sexual orientation. Later studies suggested that evidence against Martin and Mitchell on this point was weak. This explanation, it is argued, was seized upon as a way of casting doubts on them as individuals and keeping the image of the intelligence community intact.

Reportedly both considered their defections to have been a mistake and began exploring ways of returning to the United States. They were unsuccessful in this. Mitchell died in Moscow on November 12, 2001. Martin died in Mexico on January 17, 1987.

See also: Cold War Intelligence; National Security Agency

References and Further Reading

Bamford, James. *The Puzzle Palace: Inside the National Security Agency, America's Most Secret Intelligence Organization*. New York: Penguin, 1982.

Glenn P. Hastedt

MARTIN, ROBERT M.

Robert M. Martin was a Confederate agent who coordinated a plot to terrorize and then capture New York City by setting fires throughout the city in 1864. The plot was devised by Jacob Thompson, a Confederate sympathizer based in Canada and supported by Judah P. Benjamin, the Confederate secretary of state. A small team of Confederate agents, led by Colonel Martin, was to set fire to the city's hotels as a signal to Confederate sympathizers to rise up and seize New York City before the elections. Martin arrived in New York but found that a mole had revealed the plot to U.S. authorities and that soldiers were stationed throughout the city. As a result, the plotters had to postpone their attack until after the elections.

Martin faced reluctance on the part of Confederate sympathizers in New York, and therefore did not execute his plan until November 25, when he received word of the burning of Atlanta. That evening, he and his men set around 30 buildings and several ships on fire. The federal authorities, helped by informants, closed in rapidly. Although Martin and nearly all of his men escaped, several of their collaborators were arrested and one member of his team, Robert Kennedy, was captured and later hung.

Martin made his way from Canada through the United States after his escape, and attempted, without success, to abduct Vice President Andrew Johnson in Louisville. He was captured near the war's end, but never charged with a crime. He became a tobacco merchant and lived until 1900, dying in a New York hospital.

See also: Civil War Intelligence

References and Further Reading

Ellis, Edward Robb. *The Epic of New York City*. New York: Carroll and Graf, 2005.
Schultz, Duane P. *The Dahlgren Affair: Terror and Conspiracy in the Civil War*. New York: W.W. Norton and Company, 1999.

James L. Erwin

MASTERMAN, SIR JOHN (JANUARY 12, 1891–JUNE 6, 1977)

Sir John Cecil Masterman was the chairman of the Twenty Committee during World War II, which ran the "Double-Cross System"—German spies captured in Britain were given the choice of either being executed or turning into double agents.

John Masterman was educated at the Royal Naval Colleges of Osborne and Dartmouth, and then studied Modern History at Worcester University. When World War I broke out, he was working at the University of Freiburg in Germany on an exchange, and spent four years in a prisoner-of-war camp where he became fluent in German. Returning to England, Masterman was a tutor of modern history at Christ Church, Oxford, and also a keen cricketer, and played tennis and field hockey.

In 1933 Masterman wrote a novel called *An Oxford Tragedy*, in which an Oxford University tutor is found murdered and the crime is solved by a Viennese lawyer and his assistant, an Oxford don. The book is seen as the first of the Oxford-based crime novels which gained popularity under Michael Innes.

When World War II broke out, Masterman became chairman of the Twenty ("XX") Committee which had the task of dealing with German agents captured in Britain. As such, it was responsible for feeding false information to the Germans, initially on air bases. This caused the Germans to divert their attacks from important bases to others which had few or no supplies. The main effort, later in the war, was in Operation Fortitude, persuading the Germans that the main attack on D-Day in 1944 would be on the region around the Pas de Calais, not Normandy. That was regarded as the greatest success of the committee's work.

After the war, Masterman returned to academia as provost of Worcester College from 1946 until 1961 and vice chancellor of Oxford University from 1957 to 1958. In 1957 he wrote his second novel, *The Case of the Four Friends*, in which a crime is "pre-constructed," an approach which was novel. Masterman was knighted in 1959. He wanted to write about the Double-Cross System and when he asked Roger Hollis in 1961, permission was refused. After the unveiling of the Cambridge Spy Ring in the 1960s, Masterman again asked whether he could publish about his wartime exploits in order to increase the morale in British intelligence. This was again rejected, and in 1970 he approached Yale University Press to publish in the United States. Norman Holmes Pearson of Yale University, who had served with the Twenty Committee as the wartime head of the counterintelligence division of the OSS, although not as a member of the committee itself, was keen on the book which was finally published in 1972 with several passages deleted. Masterman died on June 6, 1977.

See also: Double-Cross System; Fiction—Spy Novels; Office of Strategic Services

References and Further Reading

Hinsley, F. H., and Simpkins, C. A. G. *British Intelligence in the Second World War, Volume 4, Security and Counter-Intelligence*. London: H.M. Stationery Office, 1990.

Masterman, John C. *The Double-Cross System: The Incredible True Story of How Nazi Spies were Turned into Double Agents*. New Haven, CT: Yale University Press, 1972.

Glenn P. Hastedt

MATA HARI (MARGARETHA ZELLE MACLEOD) (AUGUST 7, 1876–OCTOBER 15, 1917)

Falsely known as a spy for the Germans in World War I, Mata Hari was born Margaretta Gertrude Zelle on August 7, 1876, in Leeuwarden, Netherlands. "Mata Hari" (the sun at dawn) was her stage name. In 1905, when she took Paris by storm as an exotic dancer, Mata Hari claimed to have been born in the Dutch East Indies and raised as a sacred dancer in a Hindu temple. In reality she had married at age 18 to Captain Rudolph (John) MacLeod of the Netherlands Colonial army, 20 years her senior, and moved with him to the Indies. The marriage ended badly, and they separated. With no other means of livelihood, she went to Paris, became a dancer and courtesan, and invented the striptease.

Never a good dancer, Mata Hari was, however, an extraordinary courtesan. One of her biographers claimed that she slept with lovers "on an almost industrial scale." Reportedly her conquests included both French diplomat Jules Cambon and Crown Prince Wilhelm of Germany.

During World War I, Mata Hari was brought to trial in Paris, accused of spying for the Germans, and was convicted on little real evidence and executed in 1917. (Library of Congress)

Mata Hari was in Berlin when World War I began, but was not recruited there as a German agent as later charged. Indeed, the Germans seized her possessions, and she returned to Amsterdam penniless. Traveling to Paris, she came under immediate suspicion as a German agent. Confronted in 1916 by Georges Ladoux, the chief of French counterintelligence, she agreed to work for the French for money, so that she might marry the love of her life, Vladimir de Masloff, a young Russian officer whom she met in France. De Masloff was 21; Mata Hari had just reached 40.

The British knew nothing about her dealings with French officials, and mistakenly confused her with a real German spy, taking her off a Channel ship when she tried to reach Germany by sea. Ladoux took the British mix-up as proof of her guilt. Mata Hari ended up in Spain where she endeavored to win over a German diplomat who was in charge of a spy network in Barcelona. He saw through her efforts and fed her stale information. He also hatched a plan to deal with her, sending a message to be intercepted by the French, implicating her as a German agent.

Mata Hari returned to France to report to Ladoux. She was arrested on February 13, 1917. Incompetence and duplicity on the part of French and British counterintelligence officers, and the situation in France (1917 was the low point in the war for the Entente), were the chief factors in her conviction of July 25, 1917, as a German agent. Mata Hari protested her innocence and died bravely before a French firing squad at Vincennes on October 15, 1917.

See also: American Intelligence, World War I

References and Further Reading

Howe, Russell Warren. *Mata Hari: The True Story*. New York: Dodd, Mead, 1986.

Keay, Julia. *The Spy Who Never Was: The Life and Loves of Mata Hari*. London: Michael Joseph, 1987.

Wagenaar, Sam. *Mata Hari: A Biography*. New York: Appleton, 1966.

Spencer C. Tucker

McCARTHY, JOSEPH
(NOVEMBER 14, 1908–MAY 2, 1957)

In 1952 Senator Joseph McCarthy became chairman of the Senate Committee on Government Operations and headed its subcommittee on Investigations. He used those positions to launch what is commonly described as a witch hunt for Communist sympathizers within the government. He was known for his bullying tactics, deceit, and loose use of facts. McCarthy left the Senate in disgrace. McCarthy was born in Wisconsin. His first foray into politics was an unsuccessful bid for district attorney as a Democrat. In his next attempt he was elected as a circuit judge. The election was nonpartisan. McCarthy won handily in an election in which he misrepresented facts about the incumbent. McCarthy joined the military in 1942 in hopes of laying a foundation that would advance his postwar political career. For most of the war he served as an intelligence officer and saw minimum combat duty. In his political campaigns he would embellish this record to make it appear he was a war hero. In 1946 McCarthy pulled off a stunning upset of Republican Senator Robert La Follette, Jr., in the primary and went on to win election to the Senate. Both campaigns were marked by innuendo and falsehoods on McCarthy's part. McCarthy accomplished little his first term.

With his reelection campaign in the offing, McCarthy made his most famous speech on February 7, 1950, in Wheeling, West Virginia. He boldly announced that he had in his possession the names of 205 known Communists in the State Department. The allegations were not new; they had first been raised in 1946 and were investigated with some 79 people being fired. Spies were known to exist in and outside of the State Department. Alger Hiss had recently been convicted for perjury and Klaus Fuchs confessed to sending atomic secrets to the Soviet Union. Moreover, McCarthy did not have such a list nor was he an expert on espionage. His allegations created a sensation due to their timing. China had "fallen" to the Communists; Russia had exploded an atomic bomb; and the Korean War was on the horizon. The country was looking for answers as to why U.S. security was threatened and the specter of spies from within provided a comforting answer.

Emboldened by the positive public response to his charges, McCarthy went on the offensive. He referred to Secretary of State Dean Acheson as the "Red Dean of Fashion" and called Secretary of Defense George Marshall a traitor. Republican senators who had once shunned him now urged him on, hoping to weaken the Truman administration. McCarthy's first series of public hearings into Communist influence within the government were held in 1953 and produced little that was newsworthy. Hearings held in the fall of that year would accomplish all that McCarthy hoped. He now targeted the army for harboring a spy ring at Fort Monmouth, New Jersey, and for coddling Communists. Army officials were constantly on the defensive and McCarthy pressed his case.

By spring 1954, however, the political tide had turned against McCarthy. Republican leaders expressed concern about the impact of "McCarthyism" on what was now a Republican foreign policy bureaucracy and President Dwight Eisenhower who had resisted engaging in "politics" with McCarthy was now angry with McCarthy and wished to see him stopped. In April 1954 the Senate held 36 days of televised hearings into McCarthy's conflict with the army. They proved to be McCarthy's undoing as he came across to the American public not as a defender of freedom but a bully. In December 1954 the Senate censured McCarthy for bringing "dishonor and disrepute" to that body by a vote of 67–22. Just as rising cold war tensions had earlier helped McCarthy, they now conspired against him. The Korean War had ended, Joseph Stalin had died, and European postwar economic recovery was under way. The world no longer appeared to be quite as threatening. McCarthy was now politically isolated within the Senate and died on May 2, 1957, in a Bethesda, Maryland, military hospital of hepatitis reportedly brought on by alcoholism.

See also: Chambers, Whittaker; Cold War Intelligence; Fuchs, Emil Julius Klaus; Hiss, Alger

References and Further Reading

Doherty, Thomas. *Cold War, Cool Medium: Television, McCarthyism and American Culture.* New York: Columbia University Press, 2005.

Fried, Albert. *McCarthyism, the Great American Red Scare: A Documentary History.* New York: Oxford University Press, 1997.

Griffith, Robert. *The Politics of Feat: Joseph R. McCarthy and the Senate*. University of Amherst: Massachusetts Press, 1970.

Glenn P. Hastedt

McCONE, JOHN A.
(JANUARY 4, 1902–FEBRUARY 14, 1991)

John Alex McCone was the sixth Director of Central Intelligence (DCI) serving under Presidents John Kennedy and Lyndon Johnson from November 19, 1961 to April 28, 1965. Born in San Francisco, he received a BS degree from the University of California–Berkeley in 1922. An engineer, McCone went into the steel and construction businesses. He founded the Bechtel-McCone construction company and the California Shipbuilding Corporation, enterprises which made him a millionaire. McCone first entered government service in 1947 as a member of the President's Air Policy Commission. From there he went on to become deputy secretary of defense, undersecretary of the air force, and chairman of the Atomic Energy Commission. Kennedy appointed McCone to succeed DCI Allen Dulles, whose career had become tarnished by the failed Bay of Pigs operation. The choice was largely political. McCone was known to be a hard-line anti-Communist and a Republican. He was also an outsider to intelligence.

McCone was far more interested in intelligence analysis and technical intelligence collection than was Dulles, who considered himself the classic "spymaster." He was also a skilled manager both inside the Central Intelligence Agency (CIA) and within the broader intelligence community. Among his most significant administrative moves in the area of espionage was to create the CIA's Directorate of Science and Technology and to increase CIA decision-making power with regard to the operation of the National Reconnaissance Office.

Two episodes in intelligence analysis marked McCone's tenure as DCI. The first was the Cuban Missile Crisis where McCone correctly asserted that the Soviet Union was trying to build up a missile presence in Cuba. Photographic intelligence obtained by U-2 overflights of Cuba played a key role in supporting McCone's argument and guiding U.S. decision making during the crisis. The second episode involved Vietnam estimates. Here McCone was less optimistic than Johnson over the prospects for victory. Conflicts with Johnson in the form of unsupportive intelligence estimates caused him to be seen as a naysayer and would lead to his removal in favor of Admiral William Rayborn. In fact, virtually from the outset McCone and Johnson had failed to connect personally. Where he had easy access to Kennedy, McCone was now kept at a distance and excluded from key Vietnam decision-making bodies.

After resigning, McCone returned to private business. He would go on to serve on the Board of Directors of International Telephone and Telegraph (ITT). From this post in May 1970 he approached DCI Richard Helms about the possibility of a joint CIA-ITT venture to prevent the election of Socialist Party candidate Salvadore Allende to the Chilean presidency. ITT was one of many American firms who had major investments in Chile and were distressed by the possibility of an Allende victory. McCone offered Helms $1 million to carry out a covert action to stop Allende.

Anaconda Copper had already offered $500,000 for this purpose. Uncertain of the prospects for success of such an operation, Helms declined the money but provided them with contacts in Chile to help them in their cause. This did not mean an end to the CIA's involvement, as President Richard Nixon and National Security Advisor Henry Kissinger had formulated their own plans for accomplishing this same end and Helms was carrying that plan out.

See also: Central Intelligence Agency; Chile, CIA Operations in; Cuban Missile Crisis; Director of Central Intelligence; Helms, Richard McGarrah; Johnson Administration and Intelligence; Kennedy Administration and Intelligence; U-2 Incident

References and Suggested Reading

Andrew, Christopher. *For the President's Eyes Only: Secret Intelligence and the American Presidency from Washington to Bush*. New York: HarperCollins, 1995.

Garthoff, Douglas. *Directors of Central Intelligence as Leaders of the U.S. Intelligence Community, 1946–2005*. Washington, DC: Center for the Study of Intelligence, Central Intelligence Agency, 2005.

Ranelagh, John. *The Rise and Decline of the CIA*. Revised and updated. New York: Touchstone, 1987.

Glenn P. Hastedt

McCONNELL, VICE ADMIRAL JOHN
(JULY 26, 1943–)

Retired Vice Admiral John Michael McConnell was the second Director of National Intelligence (DNI) holding that position under President George W. Bush from February 20, 2007, and into the first seven days of the Obama administration. McConnell previously served as director of the National Security Agency from 1992 to 1996 and before that as the intelligence officer for the chairman of the Joint Chiefs of Staff.

McConnell's tenure as DNI was marked by the promulgation of two major initiatives for improving cooperation among the members of the intelligence community. The first, the 100 Day Plan, established six priorities: (1) creating a culture of collaboration, (2) fostering collection and analytical transformation within the intelligence community, (3) building acquisition excellence and technology leadership, (4) modernizing business practices, (5) accelerating information sharing, and 6) clarifying and aligning the DNI's authorities. The 100 Day Plan was declared a success.

It was followed by the announcement of a second, 500 Day Plan. Whereas the 100 Day Plan was meant to jump-start progress in the above areas, the 500 Day Plan was designed to sustain the gains made and broaden the collaborative process now under way. It contained nine initiatives. They were (1) treat diversity as a strategic mission imperative, (2) implement a civilian intelligence community joint duty program, (3) enhance information-sharing practices, (4) create a collaborative environment for intelligence analysis, (5) establish National Intelligence Coordination Centers, (6) implement an acquisition improvement plan, (7) modernize the security clearance process, (8) better align budget and capabilities through an enhanced management system, and (9) update policy documents pertaining to authority within the intelligence community. McConnell left the position of DNI before the 500 days had been reached.

McConnell also worked on Vision 2015 as DNI. This plan sought to lay the foundation for a new twenty-first-century intelligence enterprise for the U.S. government based on the principles of integration, collaboration, and innovation. It was made public in July 2008.

See also: Director of National Intelligence; Intelligence Community; Post–Cold War Intelligence

References and Further Reading

Bamford, James. *Body of Secrets: Anatomy of the Ultra Secret National Security Agency*. New York: Anchor, 2002.

Hastedt, Glenn. "Washington Politics, Intelligence, and the Struggle Against global Terrorism," in Loch K. Johnson (ed.), *Strategic Intelligence: Counterintelligence and Counterterrorism*, volume 4. Westport, CT: Praeger, 2007.

Glenn P. Hastedt

MEHALBA, AHMED FATHY
(1973–)

On January 10, 2005, Ahmed Fathy Mehalba pled guilty to lying to government agents and removing classified documents. Initially Mehalba denied having stolen classified material but in January 2005 he changed his plea to guilty. On February 20, 2005, Mehalba was sentenced to 20 months in prison and given time off for the 17 months he already served. Mehalba was released from prison on March 10, 2005.

Mehalba was born in Egypt, immigrated to the United States in 1992, and became an American citizen in 1999. After holding a variety of jobs, having a marriage end in divorce, and filing for bankruptcy, Mehalba joined the army military intelligence program as an interrogator. He received a medical discharge due to depression in May 2001. In 2002 Mehalba was hired as a translator by Titan Corporation that provides "comprehensive information and communication products, solutions, and services for national Security." He was sent to Guantanamo Bay. After-the-fact analysis indicated that major security breaches occurred at Guantanamo Bay as regular checks of contract employees did not occur.

On September 29, 2003, upon returning from visiting his family in Egypt, one of whom, an uncle, worked for Egyptian intelligence, Mehalba was detained by U.S. customs agents at Logan Airport, Boston. In his possession they found over 100 computer disks in his possession. One of them contained 725 documents, 368 of which were classified FBI, CIA, Justice Department, and Defense Department documents classified as SECRET or SECRET/NOFORN. Mehalba indicated that he had no idea how these documents got onto the disk. Later he would assert it was an innocent mistake brought about by being overly zealous about his job, wanting to do work at home. Additionally Mehalba sold a personal computer used at Guantanamo Bay. It was recovered and found to contain classified documents on the hard drive.

See also: Post–Cold War Intelligence

References and Further Reading

Adams, James. *The New Spies: Exploring the Frontiers of Espionage.* New York: Hutchinson, 1994.
Herbig, Katherine. *Changes in Espionage by Americans.* Monterey, CA: Defense Personnel Research Center, 2008.

Glenn P. Hastedt

MENDEZ, ANTONIO J.
(1940–)

Antonio J. Mendez became a pioneer of disguise in espionage during his career with the U.S. Central Intelligence Agency (CIA). At the CIA he developed new disguise techniques that were used in numerous CIA operations during the cold war.

In 1940 Mendez was born in Eureka, Nevada. He briefly attended the University Colorado at Boulder and then married Karen Smith. In 1965 Mendez was recruited by Richard Ryman to duplicate documents from foreign countries after responding to a newspaper advertisement.

In this position he developed his skills duplicating documents and eagerly pursued foreign assignments. In 1967 his first overseas assignment stationed him in Okinawa, Japan. During his time in Okinawa, Mendez met "Jacob Jordan" who was known as an expert disguise artist in the CIA. While working with Jordan, Mendez further developed his artistic skills creating disguises.

In 1974 he returned to the United States as the CIA chief of disguise. Motivated by the conviction that realistic disguises allowed for critical face-to-face meetings between informers and agents, Mendez lobbied for increased support of his projects. Mendez used disguise techniques and materials originally developed for use in motion pictures in his CIA operations.

In February of 1976 Mendez arrived in Moscow for the first of his repeated visits. While in Moscow he collected information about KGB surveillance practices and developed tactics to evade their watch, primarily using disguises that could easily and quickly be applied and removed. This information was critical to the development of standard procedures for U.S. agents in the USSR.

In 1979 he was promoted to the CIA deputy of authentication. In recognition of Mendez's significant contributions to the CIA, Mendez received the Intelligence Star, the second-highest CIA valorous declaration, in May of 1980. In November of 1990, ending a career of 25 years at the CIA, Mendez retired. After retirement, Mendez acted as an advisor to the International Spy Museum located in Washington, DC.

See also: Central Intelligence Agency; Cold War Intelligence; KGB (Komitet Gosudarstvennoi Bezopasnosti)

References and Further Reading

Mendez, Antonio. *The Master of Disguise: My Secret Life in the CIA.* New York: William Morrow & Co., 1999.

———. *Spy Dust: Two Masters of Disguise Reveal the Tools and Operations that Helped Win the Cold War*. New York: Atria, 2002.

Owen, David, and Mendez, Antonio J. *Hidden Secrets: The Complete History of Espionage and the Technology Used to Support It*. Toronto: Firefly Books, 2002.

Kristin Whitehair

MERRY, ANTHONY
(AUGUST 2, 1756–JUNE 14, 1835)

British minister to the United States during Thomas Jefferson's presidency, Anthony Merry supported Aaron Burr's western conspiracy by requesting British assistance from 1804 to 1806. Merry, born in London, keenly watched American politics and the possibility that the United States might divide along sectional lines. Others too were waiting to pounce, including Vice President Aaron Burr, who asked Merry for British assistance in 1804. Burr's conspiracy was to separate the Trans-Appalachian west from the United States, and lead a filibustering expedition against Spanish Mexico. Burr told Merry that many western citizens desired independence and would welcome the British. He recommended the British send him two or three frigates to protect New Orleans and he asked for a 100,000-pound loan.

However, the British never responded to Aaron Burr's requests. Soon the conspiracy had leaked, and the press questioned Burr's western activities. In December 1805, Jefferson received an anonymous letter warning of Burr's activities and the possible involvement of Merry. In June 1806, Burr called on Merry again, but by this point it was too late. Merry realized the British would not help Burr. Although Merry's involvement was not deemed inappropriate, later Jefferson partially blamed Merry for the deterioration in American-British relations. By the end of 1806 Merry returned to England. He continued to serve the Foreign Office and died in 1835 in Dedham, England.

See also: Early Republic and Espionage

References and Further Reading

Abernethy, Thomas Perkins. *The Burr Conspiracy*. New York: Oxford University Press, 1954.

Lester, Malcolm. *Anthony Merry Redivivus, a Reappraisal of the British Minister to the United States, 1803–6*. Charlottesville: University Press of Virginia, 1978.

Wheelan, Joseph. *Jefferson's Vendetta, the Pursuit of Aaron Burr and the Judiciary*. New York: Carroll & Graf Publishers, 2005.

Cynthia A. Boyle

MEXICAN SPY COMPANY

The Mexican Spy Company was an organization of disaffected Mexicans who served the U.S. Army as scouts, translators, and antiguerrilla forces during the Mexican-American War. After the war, many of the Spy Company's members took refuge in the United States. The Mexican Spy Company was largely the work of one man,

Manuel Domínguez. Domínguez started in life as a weaver, but joined a bandit gang after his goods were stolen on the road by a Mexican officer. Domínguez soon rose to lead the band. In the years before the Mexican-American War, Domínguez's men dominated the road between Puebla and Mexico City. They lived by robbing travelers on the road and exacting tolls for safe passage.

When American forces arrived in Puebla during their invasion of Mexico, Domínguez was arrested. He offered his services to the U.S. Army, and was given his first assignment as a courier on June 5, 1847. After the Americans gained confidence in his skill and reliability, Domínguez was allowed to recruit men from the Puebla jail and form the Mexican Spy Company. The Company's original mission was to act as couriers and scouts. Much of the American invasion route from Puebla to Mexico City was reconnoitered by the Spy Company. Soon, Domínguez was tasked with suppressing guerrilla resistance to the U.S. Army.

In September of 1847, Mexico's President Santa Anna offered a pardon and a substantial reward to Domínguez and his men. The pardon was on the condition that they use their position of trust to sabotage the American offensive. Domínguez instead handed the pardon to his commanding officer, Colonel Ethan Allen Hitchcock.

Domínguez acted under the direct supervision of a Virginian officer named Spooner, who had also run an outlaw group in Mexico before the war and who had volunteered to join the U.S. Army. The Spy Company was extremely efficient at discovering and capturing anti-American guerrillas, as they had an unmatched knowledge of the countryside around Puebla.

Captured guerrillas and Mexican troops were sometimes given the choice of joining Domínguez, but others were summarily executed. Domínguez gained an infamous reputation from one instance when he captured a Mexican detachment and prepared to execute his 50 prisoners. An American observer, Dr. Elisha Kane, prevented the execution but received several sword wounds in the process. The attack erased any goodwill the Spy Company had earned.

At the conclusion of the war, Domínguez and his men were removed from Mexico. Domínguez, who ended the war as a colonel, arrived at New Orleans and was soon living in abject poverty. Despite appeals by Domínguez and Hitchcock, Congress refused to take up the cause of compensating the Spy Company for their services. In 1856, Congress passed a law granting homestead lands to veterans of the Mexican War, but Domínguez and his men were not recognized as veterans. Most of the Spy Company ended up settling in southern Texas, where they lived out their lives in anonymity.

See also: Early Republic and Espionage; Hitchcock, Ethan Allen

References and Further Reading

Caruso, A. Brooke. *The Mexican Spy Company: United States Covert Operations in Mexico, 1845–1848*. Jefferson, NC: McFarland & Co., 1991.

Hitchcock, Ethan Allen. W. A. Croffut, editor. *Fifty Years in Camp and Field: Diary of Major-General Ethan Allen Hitchcock, U.S.A.* New York: G.P. Putnam's Sons, 1909.

James L. Erwin

MEYER, CORD, JR.
(NOVEMBER 10, 1920–MARCH 13, 2001)

Cord Meyer, Jr., was a career Central Intelligence Agency (CIA) officer who spent most of his career involved in covert operations. Meyer came to intelligence work in 1949 when he joined the Office of Policy Coordination. By that time he has established himself as a supporter of world federalism but was now becoming disillusioned with the promises of world government although he continued to be involved in its causes, founding the Committee to Frame a World Constitution. In 1951 he joined the CIA and became active in counterintelligence operations. One of those he was linked to was Operation MOCKINGBIRD, an effort by the CIA to influence reporting on it by the U.S. news and motion picture industries.

Another important part of Meyer's early CIA career was his work as head of the International Organizations Division which was the clandestine point of contact with left-wing academic, trade, and political organizations in Western Europe. Later he would supervise Radio Free Europe and Radio Liberty. Closer to home, Meyer's area of expertise put him in contact with such groups as the National Student Organization, the National Education Association, and the Congress of Cultural Freedom. It was not long, however, before Meyer's earlier political views and CIA operations drew the attention of Federal Bureau of Investigation Director J. Edgar Hoover and Senator Joseph McCarthy, who accused him of being a Communist. These allegations were effectively rebuffed by Meyer and the CIA. Progressing through the ranks, Meyer would serve as head of the Covert Action Staff of the directorate of plans, assistant deputy director of plans, and CIA station chief in London before retiring in 1977 for a career as a syndicated columnist.

Meyer's career at the CIA has also become a source of controversy due to events in his personal life. His first wife, Mary Pincohet Meyer, had an affair with President John Kennedy and was shot to death on October 12, 1964, in a crime that was never solved. After the tragedy, James Jesus Angleton, head of the CIA's counterintelligence operations, was discovered in her home looking for her diary. These events have given rise to rumors that Meyer was involved in Kennedy's assassination.

See also: Central Intelligence Agency; Kennedy Assassination; MOCKINGBIRD, Operation; Office of Policy Coordination

References and Further Reading

Fried, Albert. *McCarthyism, the Great American Red Scare: A Documentary History*. New York: Oxford University Press, 1997.

Meyer, Cord. *Facing Reality: From World Federalism to the CIA*. New York: Harper & Row, 1980.

Glenn P. Hastedt

MI-5 (THE SECURITY SERVICE)

MI-5, also known as the Security Service, is the United Kingdom's counterintelligence and security agency. Responsible for protecting the United Kingdom from threats against national security, MI-5, along with the Secret Intelligence Service (SIS or MI-6), and the Government Communications Headquarters (GCHQ) are all under the direction of the Joint Intelligence Committee. MI-5 and British intelligence have long had a close relationship with the United States in intelligence gathering from World War II and the cold war to the war on terrorism after the events of September 11, 2001.

MI-5 came into existence in 1909 and was first known as the Secret Service Bureau. It was created to help combat Imperial Germany's espionage operations in the United Kingdom on the eve of World War I. Under the leadership of Major Vernon Kell, MI-5 successfully identified and arrested several German spies, including Frederick Gould, and destroyed a German spy ring. During the war, MI-5 continued to identify and detain German spies in the United Kingdom. After the war, the growing threat of Nazism, Fascism, Communism, and Irish nationalism posed a different threat to the United Kingdom. Several British citizens became Fascists and Communists and MI-5 monitored them before and during World War II.

During World War II, MI-5, under the umbrella of the British Security Coordination, had a presence in the United States even before the United States joined the war with its base in New York City. The American Office of Strategic Services (OSS), the precursor to the CIA, and MI-5 pooled together their intelligence gathering, helping to uncover spies, collaborating on different operations, and, in one instance, thwarting a Nazi kidnapping plot in the United States. British and American intelligence's biggest collaboration was Operation Fortitude, part of Operation Bodyguard, which was the deception surrounding the Normandy invasion in 1944. MI-5 supplied a double agent named Juan Pujol, code-named "Garbo," who deceived the German High Command by misleading them into believing the invasion would occur at areas other than Normandy. MI-5 also enacted a unique program called the Double-Cross System, which turned captured German agents into British double agents. This highly successful operation played a major role in the victorious deception surrounding the Normandy invasion.

After the war, MI-5 focused its attention on the Soviet Union and the Cold war. In 1947 or 1948, the UK and U.S. intelligence organizations, along with Australia, New Zealand, and Canada, formed the highly secret UKUSA agreement. Called ECHELON and still in effect today, this alliance enables each country's intelligence organization to have shared satellite technology access or SIGINT. Secrecy still surrounds this agreement, with many countries refusing to acknowledge their participation.

In 1952, during his second term as prime minister, Winston Churchill undertook significant internal reforms within MI-5. Personal responsibility for the organization went to Home Secretary Sir David Maxwell-Fyfe, who placed MI-5 on a statutory footing until 1989.

During the postwar years, the relationship between the American and British intelligence services and the British evolved into one of necessity rather than sentiment. The Soviet Union's penetration into MI-5 and other British intelligence services combined with the massive amount of defections contributed to an already tense relationship.

In particular, the Cambridge Spy Ring delivered a crushing blow to British and American intelligence. Before World War II, the Soviet Union recruited five affluent students from Cambridge with the intention of placing them in prestigious civil service jobs in an effort to infiltrate British intelligence.

One of the "Magnificent Five," as they were dubbed, Harold "Kim" Philby was part of a British-American intelligence cooperative operation. In 1949, he was stationed in Washington, DC, and gained access to CIA and FBI files. He also was privy to the VENONA project intercepts, allowing him to tell the Soviets of the U.S. efforts to break their codes. He also monitored how much the United States knew of the Soviet spy networks in the United States and passed on this information, as well.

For some time, another of the five, Donald Maclean, had been under MI-5 surveillance, but they acted too late. He worked at the British embassy in Washington, DC, and was able to tell the Soviet Union about Anglo-America policy. He was also privy to highly classified atomic secrets which he passed on to the Soviet Union.

MI-5 and the CIA continued to battle Soviet espionage, especially in terms of atomic secrets. The Cambridge Five caused remarkable damage to both the United Kingdom and the United States not only in terms of classified information lost, but also to their relationship. After Philby's defection to the Soviet Union in 1965, Great Britain and the United States only shared limited information with each other for the next decade.

The Suez Crisis in 1956 only exacerbated the relationship between the United Kingdom and the United States, exposing the holes in the British and American policy machine. But the crisis served to show the balance of power shifting from Europe and Great Britain to the United States and the USSR. This signaled a significant decline in the British Empire and reduced the United Kingdom and United States' already rocky relationship to strictly business.

After the collapse of the Soviet Union and the end of the cold war, MI-5 and American intelligence began to focus on counterterrorism. Middle Eastern terrorist groups continued to plague MI-5 and the United States, but MI-5 also had to worry about Northern Ireland and the IRA.

After the terrorist attacks in the United States on September 11, 2001, the United States opened an ongoing discussion of forming an intelligence agency very similar to MI-5. Due to the large-scale attack of 9/11, government funding for MI-5 was substantially increased. The Joint Terrorism Analysis Centre was created to analyze and assess international terrorism, and the two countries have continued their business relationship. MI-5 continues to work closely with the American CIA and the FBI in the fight against terrorism.

See also: Bletchley Park; Blunt, Anthony; Burgess, Guy Francis De Moncy; ECHELON; Government Communications Headquarters; MacLean, Donald Duart; MI-6 (Secret Intelligence Service); MI-8 (British Radio Service); Philby, Harold Adrian Russell "Kim"; UKUSA; VENONA

References and Further Reading

Aldrich, Richard J. *The Hidden Hand: Britain, America, and Cold War Secret Intelligence.* New York: The Overlook Press, 2002.

Burnes, John P. *MI5.* London: Pocket Essentials, 2007.

MI-5 Official Website, "History of MI5," http://www.mi5.gov.uk/ (accessed January 15, 2007).

West, Nigel. *The Circus: MI5 Operations, 1945–1972.* New York: Stein and Day, 1983.

West, Nigel. *MI5: British Security Service Operations, 1909–1945.* London: The Bodley Head, 1981.

Melissa A. Marsh

MI-6 (SECRET INTELLIGENCE SERVICE)

The Secret Service Bureau was founded in 1909 as Britain's prime intelligence agency under the leadership of Commander (later Captain) Mansfield Cumming. The Foreign Section of the Bureau, responsible for gathering intelligence outside Britain, expanded steadily and in 1920 became known as Secret Intelligence Service (SIS), or MI-6 (MI referring to military intelligence). The SIS today is an essential component of Britain's national intelligence machinery.

The rise of German naval and military power in the years leading up to World War I proved worrisome to British leaders who needed accurate intelligence on German strengths and weaknesses. The Foreign Section of the Secret Service Bureau was created in 1909 to provide accurate intelligence from foreign sources to the British government. During World War I the Foreign Section, increasingly known as the Secret Intelligence Service, developed networks of agents in German-occupied areas of France and Belgium, making an invaluable contribution to the war effort.

After the war ended Captain Mansfield Cumming made sure that the SIS would not be dismantled. During the 1920s the SIS focused on the activities of the USSR and the Communist International (Comintern), which were believed to pose a major threat to Britain and the empire. However, the rise of Nazi Germany in the 1930s forced the SIS to refocus on Germany once again. The Nazi conquest of Western Europe in 1940 meant that the SIS lost most of its sources of human intelligence. SIS intelligence networks had to be painfully rebuilt from the ground up during the years of Nazi occupation in Europe. The SIS also supervised the work of the Government Code and Cypher School at Bletchley Park during World War II. At the Bletchley Park location Allied code breakers decrypted intercepts from the German Enigma enciphering machine. The decrypts, known as Ultra, were distributed to Allied commanders during the war.

During the years of the cold war the SIS focused on the threat posed by the USSR. The SIS was challenged with providing accurate intelligence during the many crises of that long conflict. More controversially, the SIS was also involved in a range of covert activities, ranging from an early, clumsy attempt to overthrow the Bolsheviks in Russia to a more successful role in overthrowing the government of Iran in 1953 (Operation Boot). Since the end of the cold war, the SIS has dealt with a variety of issues including terrorism, international crime, and regional instability. The SIS has most recently been the subject of criticism for its part that led up to the 2003 invasion of Iraq.

The role of the SIS was formally defined by the Intelligence Services Act of 1994. SIS headquarters are located at Vauxhall Cross, central London.

See also: Bletchely Park; MI-5 (The Security Service)

References and Further Reading

Andrew, Christopher. Her Majesty's *Secret Service: The Making of the British Intelligence Community*. New York: Viking, 1985.

Hinsley, F. H., et al. *British Intelligence in the Second World War*, 5 vols. London: Cambridge University Press, 1993.

Wark, Wesley. *The Ultimate Enemy: British Intelligence and Nazi Germany, 1933–1939*. Ithaca, NY: Cornell University Press, 1985.

Paul W. Doerr

MI-8 (BRITISH RADIO SERVICE)

Military Intelligence, Section 8 (MI-8) was the label attached to the British Radio Security Service (RSS) during World War II. It was set up in 1939 as a department within the Directorate of Military Intelligence within the War Department. The need for MI-8 stemmed from the need to identify German agents in Great Britain who were communicating with German intelligence officials through illegal wireless stations.

In order to accomplish its mission Major J. P. G. Worlledge recruited voluntary interceptors throughout Great Britain who scanned the airwaves for evidence of such communications. Within three months a staff of 50 voluntary interceptors had identified over 600 transmitters, none of which originated in Great Britain.

MI-8 continued to intercept communications even after its initial mission of identifying possible Germany spies in Great Britain had passed. So successful was it at gathering this information and even at breaking its codes that control over MI-8 was transferred to MI-6 in 1941. Up until this time MI-6 had lacked its own communication interception ability. The merger of these two organizations is seen has having contributed greatly to Great Britain's decoding of the Enigma cipher in December 1941.

See also: Bletchley Park; MI-5 (The Security Service); MI-6 (Secret Intelligence Service)

References and Further Reading

Aldrich, Richard J. *The Hidden Hand: Britain, America, and Cold War Secret Intelligence*. New York: The Overlook Press, 2002.

Andrew, Christopher. Her Majesty's *Secret Service: The Making of the British Intelligence Community*. New York: Viking, 1985.

Glenn P. Hastedt

MI-8 (U.S., CIPHER BUREAU)

More popularly known today as the Black Chamber, MI-8 was the Cables and Telegraph unit within the Military Intelligence Division. It was created shortly after the United States entered World War I. Organizationally it was a successor to the Military Information Division but conceptually it was closer to the British Secret Intelligence Service. Where the Military Information Division served largely as a central reference service, the Military Intelligence Division also supervised the army's positive and negative intelligence activities. MI-8 was located within the positive branch of intelligence work, along with other units engaged in such activities as foreign intelligence gathering, mapping, photography, and field training but it also had a strong negative intelligence component. As the army's cryptological unit, MI-8 was responsible for setting the codes to be used in army communications, ensuring the security of those codes and intercepting and decrypting foreign ciphers. Herbert Yardley was placed in charge of MI-8.

A reorganization of the Military Intelligence Division came about following the conclusion of World War I, resulting in establishment of MI-8 as a standalone unit funded by both the War and State Departments. The navy had its own communications intelligence service located within the Office of Naval Intelligence. The existence of MI-8 was hidden from the public by the use of a false flag operation. MI-8 operated from New York City under the name of the Code Compilation Company, which produced codes from private businesses.

One of Yardley's major early successes was breaking the Japanese diplomatic code in 1919. This allowed the United States to read Japanese communications during the Washington Naval Conference (1921–1922). At the end of the decade MI-8 was closed as a result of a loss of funding from the State Department due to Secretary of State Henry Stimson's objection to the practice of communication intercepts. By the time it ceased operations, MI-8 had read more than 45,000 communications from over 20 countries.

See also: Army Intelligence; Black Chamber; Yardley, Herbert

References and Further Reading

Khan, David. *The Reader of Gentlemen's Mail: Herbert O. Yardley and the Birth of American Codebreaking*. New Haven, CT: Yale University Press, 2004.

Wrixon, Fred B. *Codes Cyphers & Other Cryptic & Clandestine Communications*. New York: Black Dog & Leventhal Publishers, Inc., 1998.

Yardley, Herbert O. *The American Black Chamber*. Annapolis, MD: Naval Institute Press, 1931.

Glenn P. Hastedt

MIDWAY, BATTLE OF

Allied cryptographers, composed of the American Combat Intelligence (COMINT) Units in Philippines (Station Cast) and Pearl Harbor (Station Hypo under Commander Joseph J. Rochefort's command since 1941), Washington's Office of Naval Intelligence's (OIC) OP-20-G, and British cryptographers, first in Hong Kong and then later in Singapore, along with Dutch cryptographers (Dutch East Indies), combined their expertise to break (1942) the Imperial Japanese Navy's (JN) JN-25 code following the Pearl Harbor attack (December 7, 1941). The information derived from this intelligence coup (1942) led Commander in Chief Admiral Chester W. Nimitz, Pacific Fleet, to commit the U.S. aircraft carriers *Lexington* and *Yorktown* to the Battle of the Coral Sea (May 7–8, 1942) and uncovered an impending target designated by the Japanese simply as AF, posited by Rochefort's staff as Midway Island and by the OP-20-G and Station Cast as the Aleutian Islands.

During May 1942 the staff of Hypo worked 36-hour shifts decoding, translating, and analyzing up to 140 JN messages daily and passing them onto Nimitz's intelligence officer, Lieutenant Commander Edwin Layton. Knowing in early May that the Japanese First, Second, and Fifth Fleets were being assembled to attack AF between May 20 and June 20, Hypo's Jasper Holmes suggested that Midway report a broken freshwater condenser in a compromised cipher hoping the Japanese would report the problem in their Daily Intelligence Reports in the decrypted code, thereby confirming or disproving Midway as the target of the planned attack. The message was sent somewhere between May 14 and 16. The Japanese reported "AF is short of water" and on May 16 ordered its AF attack force to load additional water desalinization equipment and to position itself 50 miles northwest of AF.

Nimitz ordered Admiral Bull Halsey's task force with the carriers *Enterprise* and *Hornet* to Pearl Harbor the same day (May 17) that COMINT had determined the JN task force included the carriers *Kaga, Akagi, Soryu, Hiryu, Zuikaku*, and *Junyo*, and the positioning of the JN submarines prior to the attack, 150 miles east of A1 (a presumed garbled AF). COMINT noted the change (May 20) of code designator from AF to MI (Midway Island) and determined (May 25), based on the JN task force element departure dates, that the attack would commence on approximately June 4 with occupation planned for June 6. Halsey's task force arrived on May 26, followed on May 27 by the *Yorktown* badly in need of repair from the damage sustained in the Coral Sea engagement. The JN changed (May 28) to an as-of-then undecrypted code the same day Nimitz set the Battle of Midway (June 3–6, 1942) ambush when he ordered the *Enterprise* and *Hornet* (Task Force 17) to sortie for a position 350 miles northeast of Midway to be followed by the miraculously repaired *Yorktown* (Task Force 16) on May 30.

U.S. Navy long-range reconnaissance PBYs (Catalina Flying Boats) found the JN task force of 185 ships 600 miles from Midway and the ensuing battle (June 4 and 5) saw the American carrier aircraft sink four Japanese carriers to the U.S. one (*Yorktown*). The JN also lost 275 aircraft, substantially more than the 115 total American aircraft committed to the battle, and some of their best pilots. The Battle of Midway brought the opposing naval forces into rough parity in the Pacific and established the importance of Comint in modern warfare.

Though Rochefort's intelligence changed the course of the war, infighting between the director of naval intelligence and the director of naval communications led to his eventual transfer to the Pacific Strategic Intelligence Group in Washington (1942–1946). However, the contribution of COMINT to the success of Midway was never disputed and resulted in increased funding, more and better trained personnel, more and better equipment, and more direct communications between COMINT units bypassing the Washington bottleneck. Commanders increasingly incorporated COMINT into their battle plans and by 1943 the army, navy, and marine COMINT units were colocated in the field under the Joint Intelligence Committee, Pacific Ocean Area, which more efficiently coordinated local and theater-wide operations.

See also: American Intelligence, World War II

References and Further Reading

Layton, Rear Admiral Edwin T. *And I Was There: Breaking the Secrets—Pearl Harbor and Midway*. Old Saybrook, CT: William S. Konecky Associates, Inc., 2001.

Prange, Gordon W., Donald M. Goldstein, and Katherine V. Dillon. *Miracle at Midway*, reprint ed. New York: Penguin, 1983.

Richard M. "Rich" Edwards

MILITARY INFORMATION, BUREAU OF

During the American Civil War (1861–1865), the Bureau of Military Information (BMI) was the Union's most effective intelligence-gathering organization. The BMI was not given any counterintelligence duties. Instead, under the direction of Colonel

George H. Sharpe, the BMI's main function was collecting intelligence from all sources on the Confederacy. It was the all-source intelligence approach that distinguished the BMI from all previous Civil War intelligence ventures, and earned it the distinction of being the first modern intelligence service. The BMI provided Union generals valuable information that greatly benefited the Union cause and ultimately aided Union victory.

In 1861, at the beginning of the war, both the South and North were ill-equipped for intelligence gathering. Union General George B. McClellan, who was in command of the Army of the Potomac, enlisted the help of Allan Pinkerton, John C. Badcock, and a team of agents to secure intelligence. For the first two years of the war, Pinkerton's team took on the huge tasks of disguising themselves as Confederate troops and infiltrating the Confederate army; interrogating captured soldiers, deserters, and runaway slaves; rooting out spy rings from Washington, DC; and reporting on enemy troop movements, strength, and morale. Pinkerton had some successes, but his chief shortcoming was that he often overestimated the Confederate troop strength in his reports to McClellan. As a consequence, this contributed to McClellan's reoccurring reluctance of moving on the enemy with haste.

In November 1862 President Abraham Lincoln relieved McClellan of command of the Army of the Potomac and replaced him with General Ambrose Burnside. McClellan's dismissal also terminated Pinkerton's employment, who departed taking his team with him. In fact, only Badcock remained to aid Burnside with intelligence as a one-man agency. General Joseph Hooker replaced Burnside in January 1863 and appointed Sharpe as deputy provost marshal with the primary duty of creating an effective intelligence service for the Army of the Potomac. Sharpe retained Badcock as his deputy and took Captain John McEntee as his assistant, and together they built up the BMI with government payroll to 70 scouts and agents from the military ranks.

In contrast to Pinkerton's endeavors, the BMI spent a negligible amount of effort on counterintelligence. Instead, Sharpe made intelligence gathering the primary mission of the BMI. Also, compared to the earlier endeavor, the BMI used a much greater variety of sources to collect information, which included the earlier sources plus cavalry reconnaissance, captured documents, intercepted mail, intercepted telegraph messages, newspapers, balloonist's observations, signal corps stations of observation, and others. The increased number of information sources resulted in a much greater accuracy of intelligence than ever before. Furthermore, the BMI collected, analyzed, and summarized fairly reliable information in detailed reports.

In 1863, no comparable intelligence organization existed in the South or North. The Confederacy's intelligence efforts paled in comparison. Even the Union's Army of Northern Virginia's information service was a far smaller organization to merit fair comparison. Hooker soon came to trust and rely on the information supplied to him by the BMI. During the Chancellorsville Campaign (April–May 1863), for example, BMI intelligence convinced Hooker to order troops to the rear of Confederate General Robert E. Lee's army. Consequently, Hooker was able to surround Lee's army at Fredericksburg. In June, the BMI was able to provide General George Mead, who replaced Hooker, with accurate and detailed information about the size and direction of Lee's army right before the largest battle of the war at Gettysburg (July 1–3). The foreknowledge of Lee's direction enabled Mead to secure the best ground for the three-day battle in which Lee's forces were repulsed.

The BMI's work soon impressed other Union generals in the field. For example, General William S. Rosecrans, who was in command of the Army of the Cumberland, asked Mead to direct the BMI to also keep him informed of Confederate troop movements in Tennessee. Mead agreed and Sharpe directed activities as he was ordered. In 1864, Lincoln appointed General Ulysses S. Grant commander of the entire Union army. Soon after, Grant placed Sharpe on his staff and left Badcock with Mead, while the BMI continued to work as a solitary unit. By this point, the BMI had become so adroit in its craft that Sharpe boasted that he could provide Grant with any specific accurate information about the enemy that he desired.

Like generals before him, Grant came to trust and rely on BMI intelligence. In fact, Grant kept Sharpe close at hand during his sieges of Petersburg and Richmond. After the fall of Richmond, the BMI took over the activities of the "Richmond Underground," a pro-Union group who lived in the Confederate capital. Headed by Elizabeth Van Lew (an abolitionist) and Samuel Ruth (a member of the BMI) the group had reported on morale, living conditions, and any other information that could be gleaned from the residents of the city.

Grant was so impressed with the BMI that, in December 1864, Sharpe was promoted to Brigadier General, and, just three months later, he was again promoted to Major General. On April 6, 1865, Sharpe managed paperwork in Lee's surrender to Grant at Appomattox Court House. Soon after, the BMI, the first modern intelligence organization, was dissolved.

See also: Civil War Intelligence; Pinkerton, Allan; Van Lew, Elizabeth

References and Further Reading

Feis, William B. "Intelligence Activities," in Steven E. Woodworth (ed.), *The American Civil War: A Handbook of Literature and Research*, pp. 419–432. Westport, CT: Greenwood Press, 1996.

Feis, William B. *Grant's Secret Service: The Intelligence War from Belmont to Appomattox*. Lincoln, NE: University of Nebraska Press, 2002.

Feis, William B. "'Lee's Army Is Really Whipped': Grant and Intelligence Assessment from the Wilderness to Cold Harbor," *North & South* 7:4 (2004), 28–37

Fishel, Edwin C. "The Mythology of Civil War Intelligence," *Civil War History* 10 (1964), 344–367.

Fishel, Edwin C. "Myths That Never Die," *International Journal of Intelligence and Counterintelligence* 2 (1988), 27–58.

Fishel, Edwin C. *The Secret War for Union: The Untold Story of Military Intelligence in the Civil War*. Boston: Houghton Mifflin, 1996.

Rolando Avila

MILLER, RICHARD W.

Richard Miller was a Federal Bureau of Investigation (FBI) agent who was arrested for espionage in 1984. The case is noteworthy not so much for the information which Miller provided as it is for the FBI's handling of the matter. Miller was the first FBI agent indicted for espionage. His first trial ended in a mistrial after 11 weeks of testimony. He was found guilty of espionage and bribery in his second trial. On

July 14, 1986, Miller was sentenced to two consecutive life terms for espionage and 50 years on other charges. His conviction was overturned by a higher court on the grounds that the presiding judge in Miller's trial had made a mistake in allowing polygraph evidence be used against him. A third trial took place in 1990 and on October 9, 1990, once again he was convicted on all counts and sentenced to 20 years' imprisonment. On May 6, 1994, Miller was released from prison after having his sentence reduced to 13 years.

Miller was a 20-year veteran of the FBI when he committed espionage. He is described as inefficient and a blunderer who was once suspended for using his government car to sell Amway products. Miller also had significant financial problems. In 1982 Miller was transferred to the counterintelligence unit. In May 1984 Miller became romantically involved with Svetlana Ogorodnikov who was a low-level KGB agent and well known to the FBI. She and her husband had come to the United States in 1973. Both Richard Miller and Svetlana were soon placed under surveillance. In August Svetlana went to the KGB and told them about Miller and her plan to turn him into a Soviet mole within the FBI. She then revealed her KGB identity to Miller and asked him to sell her information. He agreed and sought $50,000 in gold for his information. Among the items Miller gave her was a 1983 FBI handbook detailing U.S. counterintelligence activities and techniques.

The FBI now became interested in the possibility of turning Miller into a double agent. Wiretaps revealed that Miller was going to fly to leave the United States with Svetlana and possibly defect. Miller failed a lie detector test given to him on September 28, 1984, and a search of his Los Angeles home produced Svetlana's original FBI file and classified documents. At this time Miller offered to become a double agent. The FBI did not take the offer seriously, seeing it as an attempt by Miller to protect himself from prosecution. Instead, the FBI fired Miller and then arrested him as a former agent in order to protect the FBI's reputation.

See also: Cold War Intelligence; Federal Bureau of Intelligence (FBI); KGB (Komitet Gosudarstvennoi Bezopasnosti)

References and Further Reading

Allen, Thomas, and Norman Polmar. *Merchants of Treason, America's Secrets for Sale.* New York: Delacorte Press, 1988.
Pincher, Chapman. *Traitors: The Anatomy of Treason.* New York: St. Martins, 1987.

Glenn P. Hastedt

MINARET, PROJECT

Project MINARET was a series of watch lists of Americans deemed by intelligence agencies to be engaged in subversive activities. In one form or another Project MINARET ran from 1965 to 1973 and is closely associated with the longer running secret electronic surveillance program known as Project SHAMROCK. In the period from 1967 to 1973 the Federal Bureau of Investigation (FBI) provided the names of 950 Americans to these lists, the Central Intelligence Agency provided 30 names, the Secret Service provided 180 names, the Defense Intelligence Agency provided 20 names, and the National

Security Agency provided between 50 to 75 names. Found on those lists were Black power advocate and civil rights leader Malcolm X, actress Jane Fonda, singer Joan Baez, pediatrician Dr. Benjamin Spock, and minister and civil rights leader Dr. Martin Luther King. All told over 5,925 foreigners and 1,690 organizations and U.S. citizens were found on Project MINARET's lists. From 1969 to 1973 the NSA distributed approximately 2,000 reports based on Project MINARET to other government agencies. Additionally, from 1972 to 1974 NSA's Office of Security Services had on file reports on over 75,000 Americans. The name of anyone mentioned in an NSA-intercepted message was included in that report list.

Project MINARET moved from an informal set of watch lists to a more formal program in July 1969. Construction of the watch lists as well as the secret operation of the program was a self-authorized action. No such authority was given by Congress. And in fact, after 1969 NSA placed an even greater veil of secrecy surrounding this program than it did its other intelligence-gathering activities. That blanket of secrecy was partially lifted by the 1972 *Keith* case in which the Supreme Court ruled that warrants were needed to place wiretaps on Americans who did not have a clear connection with a dangerous foreign power.

Subsequent to that verdict and with the political storm over the Watergate break-ins gathering steam, Assistant Attorney General Henry Peterson inquired as to the FBI's involvement in Project MINARET. FBI Director Clarence Kelley minimized the FBI's involvement and challenged the applicability of the Supreme Court's ruling in the *Keith* case to NSA domestic electronic surveillance programs. Nevertheless, in October Peterson and Acting Attorney General Elliot Richardson informed the NSA that they considered Project MINARET to be of questionable legality. Like the FBI, the NSA challenged this view but they too failed to change Richardson's position and in the fall of 1973 Project MINARET was terminated.

See also: Central Intelligence Agency; Defense Intelligence Agency; Federal Bureau of Investigation (FBI); SHAMROCK, Project

References and Further Reading

Corson, William. *Armies of Ignorance. The Rise of the American Intelligence Empire.* New York: Dial, 1977.

United States Senate, Select Committee to Study Government Operations with respect to Intelligence Activities. *Final Report, Book II, Intelligence Activities and the Rights of Americans.* Washington, DC: U.S. Government Printing Office, April 26, 1976.

Glenn P. Hastedt

MITROKHIN, VASILI NIKITICH (MARCH 3, 1922–JANUARY 23, 2004)

Vasili Mitrokhin was a Committee for State Security (KGB) agent who became famous for his defection in the West in the early 1990s. Mitrokhin left Russia in 1992 with a large number of classified documents from the former KGB archives. The documents were published in a large collection called the Mitrokhin Archives, revealing important information regarding secret KGB operations abroad during the Soviet era.

Vasili Nikitich Mitrokhin was born on March 3, 1922, in Yurasovo, in the central region of the Russian Soviet Federated Socialist Republic. He graduated from an artillery school after which he attended university courses in the former Soviet and Socialist Republic of Kazakhstan. He obtained degrees in history and law. Mitrokhin started a military career in Kharkov but soon after World War II entered the KGB (Ministry of State Security) in 1948, where he served as a foreign intelligence officer.

Since 1952, when he received his first assignment abroad, Mitrokhin served on numerous undercover missions in foreign countries. In 1956 he was removed from the operational field due to apparent failures in mission and became an archivist at the KGB's First Chief Directorate. He would serve there for the rest of his career. From 1972 until 1984 he was in charge of a large transfer of KGB archives from the Lubyanka headquarters to the new building at Yasenevo. It was during this move that he stole or made copies of a series of classified KGB documents which he deposited at his home. Mitrokhin retired in 1985 and only came to attention after the fall of the Soviet Union.

Vasili Mitrokhin fled with these documents in the west in 1992. During the Soviet era he had no contact with Western intelligence services. He would claim that even from the 1950s he was disillusioned with the Soviet system, especially after the Khrushchev secret report. In 1992 Mitrokhin traveled to Estonia with copies of the documents and turned them over to MI-6 at the British embassy in Tallinn, after being refused by the CIA. Mitrokhin and his family moved to Britain.

The *Mitrokhin Archives* were published by Vasili Mitrokhin in collaboration with historian Christopher Andrew, expert in espionage. The documents reveal important information regarding: weapon designs stolen from the United States, Western politicians who worked with KGB in France or West Germany, political parties in Western countries infiltrated with KGB agents, sabotage operations prepared in the United States, attempts to incite racial hatred in the United States, etc. Also, the documents disclosed information about preparations for the assassination of certain personalities like Third World leaders or Russian anti-Communist dissidents. The names of KGB agents or informers in other countries, including major political leaders, were published as well.

The book determined judicial and parliamentary inquiries in countries such as Italy, India, and Great Britain. Although its significance for Western intelligence had been confirmed by American and British officials, there are still historians who doubt the originality of the documents. Vasili Mitrokhin published two other books with Christopher Andrew on related issues. He died on January 23, 2004.

See also: Andrew, Christopher; KGB ((Komitet Gosudarstvennoi Bezopasnosti)

References and Further Reading

Andrew, Christopher, and Vasili Mitrokhin. *The Mitrokhin Archive: The KGB in Europe and the West.* London: Penguin Press, 1999.

Andrew, Christopher, and Vasili Mitrokhin. *The Sword and the Shield: The Mitrokhin Archive and the Secret History of the KGB.* London: Basic Books, 1999.

Andrew, Christopher, and Vasili Mitrokhin. *The World Going Our Way: The KGB and the Battle for the Third World.* New York: Basic Books, 2005.

Cezar Stanciu

MOCKINGBIRD, OPERATION

Beginning in the 1950s the Central Intelligence Agency sought to control and shape both the extent to which the existence of intelligence activities and organizations were reported on in the media and the manner in which they were depicted when discussed. Operation MOCKINGBIRD was the code name given to this set of activities. Attention was given to periodic film and book accounts as well as day-to-day reporting and commentary in major U.S. newspapers and weekly magazines.

Operation MOCKINGBIRD was set in motion in 1948 by Frank Wisner when he was placed in charge of the CIA's Office of Special Programs was tasked with engaging in propaganda efforts, among other activities. Cord Meyer would join the CIA in 1951 and become Operation MOCKINGBIRD's principal guiding force.

The scale of Operation MOCKINGBIRD's undertakings remains debated. Published accounts place the number of American journalists participating in it reaching as high as 400. Reportedly 25 newspapers and wire agencies were under its influence in the early 1950s. Among those journalists linked to it are Joseph Alsop, Ben Bradlee, James Reston, and Walter Pincus. Executives similarly identified are Henry Luce of *Time* and *Newsweek*, Arthur Hays Sulzberger of the *New York Times*, and Phillip Graham of the *Washington Post*. Other assets identified include ABC, NBC, and CBS television networks along with the Associated Press and United Press International news wire services. Operation MOCKINGBIRD activities here ranged from suppressing news stories such as on the operation to unseat Jacobo Arbenz in Guatemala to writing favorable stories and commentaries and using newspapers and media outlets as cover for stationing agents abroad.

U.S. journalists were not the only ones whose cooperation was sought out or paid for by the CIA. According to the Church Committee's 1976 investigation of CIA activities, it maintained a network of several hundred foreign contacts in press services, publishing houses, periodicals, newspapers, television, and radio who would use their positions to author and propagate support of stories about the CIA and U.S. foreign policy. That same year Director of Central Intelligence George H. W. Bush announced that the CIA would no longer enter into any paid or contractual relationship with full-time or part-time news correspondents accredited by any U.S. news service, newspaper, periodical, radio, or television network or station. He did, however, indicate that the CIA would continue to enter into a voluntary, unpaid relationship with journalists.

Beyond influencing journalist's accounts of the CIA, the agency also sought to stop the publication of periodical articles and books that portrayed the CIA in a negative light. Particularly notable in this regard was a 1966 article in *Ramparts* and a 1963 book, *The Invisible Government*, by David Wise and Thomas Ross. The CIA entered into a failed covert campaign aimed at undermining its financial stability to block *Ramparts* from publishing the article. Failing to get Wise and Ross to agree not to publish the book, the CIA reportedly considered buying the entire production run. The CIA also secretly helped support the publication of books that were favorable to it such as the *Penkovsky Papers* and financially supported Hollywood filmmaking efforts of movie projects that it favored.

See also: Bush, George Herbert Walker; Central Intelligence Agency; Meyer, Cord, Jr.; Penkovsky, Oleg Vladimirovich; Wisner, Frank Gardiner

References and Further Reading

Mackenzie, Angus. *Secrets: The CIA War at Home.* Berkeley, CA: University of California Press, 1997.

Saunders, Frank Stonor. *The Cultural Cold War.* New York: Norton, 2000.

Thomas, Evan. *The Very Best Men: Four Who Dared: The Early Years of the CIA.* New York: Simon & Schuster, 1995.

Wilford, Hugh. *The Mighty Wurlitzer: How the CIA Played America.* Cambridge, MA: Harvard University Press, 2008.

Glenn P. Hastedt

MONGOOSE, OPERATION

Operation MONGOOSE was a program of covert activities—political, economic, psychological, and sabotage—conceived by the administration of John F. Kennedy to destabilize the regime of Fidel Castro of Cuba and promote an internal rebellion that would lead to Castro's overthrow. The U.S. failure at the Bay of Pigs in April 1961 provided the immediate background for the formation of MONGOOSE. President Kennedy appointed a commission headed by General Maxwell Taylor, former army chief of staff, to investigate the Bay of Pigs and to make recommendations for future Cuban policy. Among the recommendations of the commission was a new program of covert activities against Cuba.

On November 30, 1961, President Kennedy authorized a new program of covert action against Castro, code-named Operation MONGOOSE. The president selected as "chief of operations" for the program Brigadier General Edward G. Lansdale, who had earned his reputation as a successful counterinsurgency fighter in the Philippines in the 1950s. Oversight of MONGOOSE lay with the "Special Group," made up of top-level representatives of the Department of State, the Department of Defense, the Central Intelligence Agency (CIA), the White House, and the Joint Chiefs of Staff. When this group was joined by Attorney General Robert Kennedy and General Maxwell Taylor, a special advisor to the president, it was referred to as the Special Group Augmented. It was clear from the outset that the real person in charge was Robert Kennedy.

Lansdale energetically developed plans for the operation, a difficult task given the number of different agencies involved. In particular the CIA took a dim view of both Lansdale and MONGOOSE. Although the CIA had a leading role to play in the operation, it had only 28 agents in Cuba in late 1961. On January 18, 1962, Lansdale issued a program review of MONGOOSE which established 32 tasks that needed to be accomplished including intelligence gathering, political action, economic activities, and sabotage efforts. Two days later in a discussion with Robert Kennedy, CIA Director John McCone questioned whether many of the 32 tasks could be completed as scheduled—if at all.

The early months of the project were spent planning, discussing, and increasing intelligence assets in South Florida and Cuba rather than carrying out exile raids and sabotage. On March 14, 1962, the Special Group Augmented approved "guidelines" for Operation MONGOOSE. The guidelines stressed the need for more hard intelligence and the use of indigenous resources. At the same time the guidelines put forward the contradictory view that decisive use of U.S. military force would be needed to achieve final success.

The slow pace of MONGOOSE activities, especially sabotage, came under official scrutiny. By the end of July 1962, the CIA had infiltrated 11 teams into Cuba but had aborted 19 maritime operations. On July 25, 1962, Lansdale reported to the Special Group Augmented that possible targets for sabotage were still being reviewed.

As the United States lurched toward the missile crisis, Robert Kennedy at a meeting of the Special Group Augmented on October 4, 1962, expressed the president's concern over the lack of progress of MONGOOSE, operations, especially sabotage activities. The group decided to put more emphasis on sabotage, including the possibility of mining Cuban harbors. As late as October 16, Robert Kennedy was still urging an acceleration of activities under MONGOOSE. Fearful that MONGOOSE might be interfering with a settlement of the missile crisis, the Kennedy administration ordered an end to all MONGOOSE, operations on October 30.

For much of its history, Operation MONGOOSE activities mainly centered on organization, planning, and building up an intelligence capability. Sabotage activities received increasing emphasis, but few were undertaken, and fewer succeeded. Ironically, one of the few successful sabotage activities—the blowing up of a Cuban industrial facility—took place on November 8, 1962, after operations were supposed to have been suspended. Not all covert activities between November 1961 and November 1962 took place under the auspices of Operation MONGOOSE. Cuban exiles engaged in some covert activities independent of MONGOOSE and of the U.S. government. Not all U.S. activities fell under the MONGOOSE program. A plan to drop propaganda leaflets over Cuba developed outside of MONGOOSE. The highly controversial assassination plans promoted by the U.S. government were not a part of Operation MONGOOSE. Although Operation MONGOOSE was dismantled in early 1963, the Kennedy administration continued its covert activities against the Castro regime, including the planning of sabotage efforts.

See also: Castro, Fidel; JMWAVE; Kennedy Administration and Intelligence; Shackley, Theodore; G. Jr.; Special Group

References and Further Reading

Bohning, Don. *The Castro Obsession: U.S. Covert Operations against Cuba, 1959–1965.* Washington, DC, Potomac Books, Inc., 2005.

Chang, Laurence, and Peter Kornbluh (eds.). *The Cuban Missile Crisis, 1962.* New York: New Press, 1998.

White, Mark J. (ed.). *The Kennedys and Cuba: The Declassified Documentary History.* Chicago: Ivan R. Dee, 1999.

Don M. Coerver

MOORE, EDWIN G., II
(1921–)

Edwin Gibbons Moore II was a retired Central Intelligence Agency (CIA) Supply Officer who attempted to sell classified information to the Soviet Union in 1976. Moore began working with the CIA in 1951 but was suspended in 1961 following allegations of intentionally setting fire to a motel he owned in North Carolina. He was reinstated in 1967 after his arson conviction was overturned. He was sent to Vietnam by the agency, but returned after being diagnosed as suffering from paranoia. He retired from the CIA in 1973 on a disability pension. Moore was on a list of five individuals suspected of writing a letter to Director William Colby in 1975 that threatened to compromise the names of 5,000 agency employees unless staff, including retirees, were retroactively promoted. On December 21, 1976, Moore threw a package over the gate of a Soviet residence, containing sensitive information and an offer for additional information in return for $200,000. The offer instructed the Soviet Resident to drop the money in front of Moore's. The package contained pages from the CIA's internal telephone directory, which identified approximately 300 agency employees. The Soviets, thinking the package was a bomb, contacted U.S. officials. Upon inspecting the package, the Federal Bureau of Investigation (FBI) developed a plan to arrest Moore after he took possession of what he believed to be payment for the compromised documents. In Moore's home, the FBI found eight boxes containing thousands of sensitive pieces of information. The FBI also discovered portions of the 1975 letter to Colby. Moore pled guilty by reason of insanity during his trial in 1977, while also claiming that he had been recruited to work on behalf of the agency on a special project. He was found guilty and sentenced to 15 years in prison. He received parole in 1979.

See also: Central Intelligence Agency; Colby, William Egan; Cold War Intelligence; Federal Bureau of Investigation (FBI)

References and Further Reading

Meyers, Robert. "Attorney Says man Accused of Espionage Thought He Was on Assignment for the CIA," *Washington Post* (April 13, 1977), A7.

Meyers, Robert. "Moore Guilty of Trying to Sell CIA Files," *Washington Post* (May 6,1977), B1.

Meyers, Robert. "Trial of Ex-Agent Leads to Deeper CIA Problems," *Washington Post* (April 25, 1977), A1.

William T. Thornhill

MORRISON, SAMUEL LORING (OCTOBER 30, 1944–)

Samuel Loring Morrison was not a spy in a traditional sense. He did not provide a foreign power with secret information. Rather, he provided classified photos to the press. For this he was charged with "the willful release of secret government documents to a person not entitled to receive them." Federal Bureau of Investigation (FBI) officials and naval investigators agreed that Morrison did not intend to provide information to a hostile intelligence service. Arrested on October 1, 1984, Morrison was convicted on October 17, 1985, and sentenced to two years in prison on December 4, 1985. President Bill Clinton pardoned Morrison on January 20, 2001.

Morrison was an American citizen born in London on October 30, 1944. He followed in his grandfather's footsteps and joined the U.S. Navy after graduating from the University of Louisville in 1967. Beginning in 1974, he went to work for the Naval Intelligence Support Center (NISC) and remained employed there until his arrest. While working for the NISC, Morrison was also employed as a part-time contributor to the London-based *Jane's Fighting Ships*. This was a position he hoped to turn into a full-time job.

In July 1984 Morrison sent *Jane's Defense Weekly* three photographs classified secret. They were pictures taken of a Soviet naval shipbuilding facility taken by the KH-11 surveillance satellite. Morrison had cut off the top-secret control marking. He also planned to provide them with a summary of a report that he did on an explosion at Severomorsk, a Soviet naval base on the Kola Peninsula. A search of his residence revealed several hundred classified government documents.

Morrison justified his actions on the ground that the public had a right to know what the Soviet Union was doing. The photos showed the construction of a nuclear-powered aircraft carrier. Morrison believed this changed the naval balance of power between the United States and Soviet Union. Armed with this information, he hoped the American public would support an increase in the defense budget. It was also argued in his defense that similar photos had already appeared in *Aviation Weekly* and other press outlets, thereby casting doubt upon their secret status and that spy William Kampiles had already provided the Soviet Union with information on the KH-11.

See also: Clinton Administration and Intelligence; Cold War Intelligence; Federal Bureau of Investigation (FBI); Kampiles, William

References and Further Reading

Bearden, Milt, and James Risen. *The Main Enemy: The Inside Story of the CIA's Final Showdown with the KGB*. New York: Random House, 2003.

Kessler, Ronald. *Spy vs. Spy: Stalking Soviet Spies in America*. New York: Scribner's, 1988.

Glenn P. Hastedt

MOSSAD

Prior to the creation of the State of Israel, underground Jewish groups engaged in numerous intelligence operations against hostile Arabs and against the British. These groups, including the Hagganah, were abolished and replaced by new Israeli organizations almost immediately after independence was declared on May 14, 1948.

In 1948 the creation of the new state of Israel, which was almost immediately at war, demonstrated the need for an Israeli intelligence community. Three organizations were created: military intelligence, domestic counterintelligence, and foreign intelligence. In 1951 these were refined with the emergence of the Mossad, called the Institute of the Mossad. It is Israel's foreign intelligence agency which is more far reaching in its activities than the Central Intelligence Agency.

The chief officer of the Mossad reports to the Israeli prime minister alone. Its budget is secret, but its work ultimately includes protecting every Jew in the world. It is organized into eight departments. The Collections Department is the largest and operated to gather intelligence data globally. Its agents operate under both diplomatic cover or without it. Its overseas stations run agents in every country with a Mossad presence.

The Political Action and Liaison Department conducts both political activities and engages in liaisons with the intelligence services of friendly foreign countries. The Special Operations Division (Metsada) conducts covert black operations. These include

One of the hostages injured aboard a hijacked Air France flight is transported by Israeli military to Tel Aviv on July 7, 1976. The plane had been hijacked by pro-Palestinian terrorists on June 27 and landed at Entebbe in Uganda. Non-Jewish passengers were released, but 103 Jewish people were held captive until a daring rescue raid by the Israeli Defence Force on July 4. The IDF acted on intelligence provided by Israeli secret agency Mossad. (AFP/Getty Images)

assassinations, sabotage, psychological warfare, and paramilitary operations. The Lohama Psichlogit Department (LPD) is in charge of the conduction of psychological warfare through deceptions, disinformation campaigns, and propaganda operations.

The Mossad Research Department is organized into 15 geographically specialized departments. These are called sections, or desks, for Canada, the United States, and Western Europe; Latin America; the former Soviet Union; China; Africa; the Maghreb (Morocco, Algeria, and Tunisia); Libya, Iraq, Jordan, Syria, Saudi Arabia, the United Arab Republic, and Iran. In addition it has a WMD intelligence desk.

The Research Department is responsible for intelligence analysis and production. The intelligence products include the daily report, the weekly summaries, and the monthly reports.

The Technology Department develops advanced technological equipment for the Mossad's agents. It also evaluates all technology considered for Mossad agent use.

The directors of the Mossad have been Reuven Shiloah (1951–9852), Isser Harel (1952–1963), Meir Amit (1963–1968), Zvi Zzmir (1968–1974), Yitzhak Hofi (1974–1982), Nahum Admoni (1982–1989), Shabtai Shavil (1989–1996), Danny Yatom (1996–1998), Efraim Halevy (1998–2002), and Meir Dagan (2002). The individuals have been recognized as people of high achievement and integrity. It has been the goal of the Mossad to recruit the "princes of the people."

The success of Mossad in generating a steady stream of intelligence on Arabic countries and Islamic terrorists is due to dedicated quality agents such as Shula Cohen who was a housewife with a large family and a flower shop in Beirut or Wolfgang Lotz the "champagne spy" in Cairo produced volumes of high-quality intelligence data.

Most of the achievements of the Mossad will never be known; some of its successes are known. The Mossad's successes have included kidnapping and assassination. Its most famous kidnapping was of Adolph Eichmanm in Buenos Aires, Argentina. Eichmann was taken to Jerusalem, put on trial, and eventually hanged.

Mossad agents have been very good at infiltrating both Arab and Communist organizations. Eli Cohen, in the 1960s, infiltrated the top ranks of the Syrian government. After two years he was caught and publicly hanged in Damascus.

One of those alleged to have been assassinated by the Mossad was Canadian artillery expert Gerald Bull, who was developing a long-range cannon that could fire a round for hundreds of miles. His last sponsor was Saddam Hussein. However, Bull was killed at this apartment in Brussels. This relieved Israel of the threat he posed.

Other assassinations have included all of those responsible for the killing of Israeli athletes at the 1972 Olympics. In addition, the leaders of violence in the Intifada who make bombs, launch rocket attacks, or engage in other violent practices have been assassinated.

Another very important success was Operation Thunderbolt. The Operation's mission was to conduct a raid on the Entebbe, Uganda, airport at night to free hostages on Air France Flight 139. The hostages were being held at the Entebbe Airport in Entebbe, Uganda. Idi Amin, the strongman ruler of Uganda at the time supported the PLO hijackers. The raid's commander was Colonel Yonatan "Yoni" Netanyahu, brother of Benjamin Netanyahu. Colonel was the only Israeli killed on the raid. Also killed were 3 hostages, 40 Ugandan soldiers, and 6 hijackers. One hundred hostages were freed.

A major blow against the Palestinian Liberation Organization came in April 1988. The Mossad send an assassination team on a small but very fast naval craft from Israel to Tunisia. The target was Abu Jihad, the deputy of Yasser Arafat. Abu Jihad was the PLO's chief military and terrorism planner. His seaside home was assaulted, Jihad was killed, and the team was extracted successfully.

In 1966 the Mossad aided the defection of a Christian Iraqi pilot to Israel. The pilot flew a MiG-21, the top Russian fighter, to Israel in what looked like a defection. At the same time Mossad also exfiltrated his family.

A major intelligence failure of Mossad came on July 21, 1973, when Admad Boushiki was murdered in Lillehammer, Norway, in the presence of his pregnant wife. He was an Algerian with a Moroccan passport who had the misfortune to be a dead-ringer for Ali Hassan Salameh, the head of PLO security. The five operatives were caught and convicted; however, their sentences were light. Salameh was killed in a car bombing in 1979.

See also: Cold War Intelligence; Eitan, Rafael; Pollard, Jonathan Jay; Terrorist Groups and Intelligence

References and Further Reading

Halevy, Efraim. *Man in the Shadows: Inside the Middle East Crisis with a Man Who Led the Mossad.* New York: St. Martin's Press, 2006.

Payne, Ronald. *Mossad: Israel's Most Secret Service.* New York: Bantam, 1990.

Raviv, Dan, and Yossi Melman. *Every Spy a Prince: The Complete History of Israel's Intelligence Community.* Boston: Houghton Mifflin, 1990.

Thomas, Gordon. *Gideon's Spies: The Secret History of the Mossad.* New York: St. Martin's Press, 1999.

Andrew J. Waskey

MOVIES, SPIES IN

The movie industry had made movies about spies from virtually the beginning of Hollywood. One constant in spy movies is that there has to be an antagonist. The enemy may be rogues, criminals, Nazis, the KGB, the Japanese, Islamists, or others. In more recent times the enemy may be rogue elements in American and British intelligence agencies. What is essential is that there is a melodramatic or a cosmic struggle between the forces of good and evil. Some spy movies during the latter part of the cold war tried to put the work of espionage into the category of keeping potential friends from misunderstanding or expressed a cynical attitude toward the cold war and espionage.

In the silent movies about Confederates and Union supporters it was common for there to be girl spies such as *The Girl Spy* (1909). Spies, male and female, for both sides made profitable film themes. In other cases a romantic female spy from North of the Border who spies for one side in Mexico was a theme. In Westerns a detective or a cowboy would go undercover to expose outlaw gangs. John Wayne played the role of secret agent in several Westerns.

The outbreak of World War I made the German spy the agent of evil. After the October Revolution (1917), until the Soviets became allies in World War II they were depicted as evil in films such as *Siberia* (1926), *Mockery* (1927), *Tovarich* (1937), and *Ninotchka* (1939). Whether as Bolsheviks or as Stalinists, the godless communists were defeated by American know-how and moral superiority.

Nazis are frequent villains in spy movies such as *The House on 92nd Street* (1945) or *North by Northwest* (1959). Two of the Indiana Jones series, *Raiders of the Lost Ark* (1981) and *The Last Crusade* (1989) have Nazis as bete noirs. Quite often the locations in which the Nazis were operating were exotic places such as Shanghai or Morocco, *Casablanca* (1943) with Humphrey Bogart and Ingrid Bergman, or North Africa, *Sundown* (1941). Nazis, powerful agents of evil have figured even in post–World War II movies as conspirators. In the *Lucifer Complex* (1978) the star, Robert Vaughn, an intelligence agent, discovers that Nazi scientists are cloning world leaders to get loyal leaders.

American spies, operating behind enemy lines in World War II, were a common theme in many movies. *Cloak and Dagger* (1946) portrays Gary Cooper as an American spy who parachutes into Nazi-occupied Europe to gain scientific information. Or in *Submarine Alert* (1946) the FBI uses a loyal American, who is a naturalized citizen, as bait to catch a Nazi spy ring operation in the United States.

In some movies such as *The Adventures of Tartu* (1943) the spy may be British but he or she has deep foreign connections and secretly works for the Allies as an undercover agent in Nazi-occupied Europe. Some World War II movies exhibited great daring, as did Rex Harrison in *Night Train to Munich* (1940).

In other spy movies of the era, exotic locations of intrigue were used. Prior to the Communist takeover of China, Shanghai was a favorite location for espionage.

Tom Cruise stars in Brian De Palma's 1996 film, *Mission Impossible*. (Photofest)

However, in *Blood on the Sun* (1945), Jimmy Cagney is living in Tokyo and links up with spies working for the Chinese intelligence against Japanese intelligence prior to the invasion of Manchuria. Cagney also starred in *13 Rue Madeleine* (1947) as an OSS agent who dies heroically fighting against the Nazis in occupied Europe.

Many real spy stories were told after World War II such as *Triple Cross* (1967), which tells the story of Eddie Chapman who was a triple agent for the Nazis and the British. Others such as *Operation Crossbow* (1994), staring Sophia Loren, George Peppard, and Trevor Howard mixed fact and fiction. Others such as *The Man Who Never Was* (1956), which tells the true story of the British World War II Operation Mincemeat, mixes some fiction with fantasy to increase the drama of the story.

Spy movies with Soviet agents as the evil agents were made during the early days of the cold war. In *Captain Scarface* (1953) several American civilians defeat Soviet agents operating a ship loaded with an atomic bomb they intend to use to destroy the Panama Canal.

In some espionage movies agents are forced out of retirement in order to deal with some problem. In *Beyond Justice* (1992) a former CIA officer seeks to free a young boy from Arab kidnappers. In *The Sell Out* (1976) a retired CIA officer is forced to return to action.

Sometimes the lives of actors and espionage mix in deadly ways. Trevor Howard, who played in the *Scarlet Pimpernel*, was shot down in World War II because of intelligence inaction.

Documentary movies about spies have had educational benefits in their day. The 1982 documentary *The KGB Connections* describes the operations of the KGB in North America and the Caribbean as well as how it made use of the intelligence services of the Eastern Bloc countries it dominated. In 1998 Roger Moore narrated a 150-minute documentary called *Spy Tek*. The "Q" branch (quartermaster) developed numerous "Bond" devices. These were more than matched by the spy devices developed during the cold war by both the Eastern Bloc and the West. Other documentaries include a series narrated by Charlton Heston (*Secrets of War: Intelligence*) that includes coverage of subjects such as *The Ultra Enigma*, and *Women Spies of World War II*, *Spy Games of World War II*, and *German Intelligence in World War II*.

Many of the film noirs of the 1930s, 1940s, and 1950s involved spies such as *Ministry of Fear* and *British Intelligence* (1940). Women have also played important roles in spy movies *British Intelligence*, *The Forbidden Woman* (1927), and *Mata Hari* (1931).

Some movies used spies to portray the lives and adventures of spies. *5 Fingers* portrayed a spy code-named "Cicero" by the Nazis who stole British secrets from the British Ambassador to Turkey in World War II. *A Family of Spies* (1990) portrays traitors who spied for the Soviet Union and against the West during the cold war.

Some movies are virtually docudramas of historic espionage operations. In some cases, such as *The Uranium Conspiracy* (1978), the story is about a successful operation of Israeli intelligence to capture some significant quantities of uranium. The operation was an intelligence semisuccess story which gained the uranium and left others wondering what had happened.

In others the agents are engaged in a military operation behind enemy lines. In some cases such as *Five Graves to Cairo* (1943) and *Desert Commandos* the agents are Nazis spies. In other cases such as *The Guns of Navarone* (1961), *Tobruk* (1966), *Raid on Rommel* (1971), *Force 10 from Navarone* (1978), and *Where Eagles Dare* (1968) the agents are inventive soldiers working to achieve some destructive objective.

James Bond, 007, the world's most famous spy, is licensed to kill as an agent of MI-6. He engages in covert operations that are usually very black operations. However, all of his opponents are rogues or criminals and not the agencies of sovereign nations. Although Bond is a MI-6 officer, he often works closely with the CIA and visits the United States in the conduction of his operations.

Because of the decades over which the Bond series has been produced, there have been numerous contemporary events depicted in each of the films. Some of those that were the least successful were those that sought to portray Bond as having a tender side in response to the peak of the feminist movement.

Cities often used as a setting for espionage include New York, Washington, DC, and San Francisco. Other American cities are used but not as often. Las Vegas and New Orleans were two others used in two of the James Bond movies. Other cities that have been frequently depicted have been London, Paris, Berlin, Cairo, Jerusalem, Rio de Janeiro, or Casablanca. Exotic locations synonymous with espionage and intrigue were Tokyo and Shanghai especially in the 1930s. Charlie Chan, a mysterious Chinese man who was also westernized, played the role of a man who could bring spies to justice.

The Spy Who Came In from the Cold has been hailed as signaling a change in attitudes in the West about spies. The movie portrayed a cold war spy played by Richard Burton as jaded and sickened by the whole deceitful game. Critics have used it and other similar negative portrayals as the basis for attacking intelligence agencies. In other films such as *The Looking Glass Wars* (1970) cynicism over the spy game leads to death.

In the more recent productions of Hollywood, the CIA is at times portrayed as the victim of rogues who carry out their own agenda. In films such as *Volunteers* (1985) starring Tom Hanks and the late John Candy as Peace Corps volunteers, the CIA operative they encounter is pictured as insane. In the film *The Company Man* (2000) the whole theme is to picture the CIA as extremely inept and ludicrous. The movie is like Graham Green's attack on the British intelligence in his book, rather than a spoof as in *The Fat Spy* (1966).

Some films have portrayed intelligence agencies negatively. In *Conspiracy Theory* (1998) and *Enemy of the State* (1998) the National Security Agency is portrayed as an evil doer. However, secret agencies have figured in the *Mission Impossible* series on television and in movies. And some spies have been depicted as action heroes in movies such as *I Spy* (2002) with Eddie Murphy and Owen Wilson, *The Detonator* (2006) with Wesley Snipes, *Sneakers* (1992) with Robert Redford, *True Lies* (1994) with Arnold Schwarzenegger, and *The Foreigner* (2003) with Steven Seagal. What is common is that all of these actors play agents who are interpreted as positive persons in a dark world.

In contemporary movies some have portrayed viral outbreaks to be the result of biological weapons made by the American government, but used by rogues to attack Americans. Or the virus falls into the hands of terrorists, especially Islamic terrorists who seek to use it to do harm. In *Outbreak* (1995) and in *Covert One: The Hades Factor* (2006) a super secret agency of the United States is portrayed as responsible for a biological weapon that is being used to kill Americans.

In the *Bourne Identity* (2002) and the *Bourne Supremacy* (2004) the CIA officers in charge of project "Tread Stone" are actually running a rogue black operation that Bourne is trying to escape. The CIA is portrayed as unable to control some of its assets. A similar theme occurs in *Silent Partner* (2005) when a young CIA officer is used as a pawn by sinister forces in his own agency. *The Good Shepherd* (2006) portrays a career American agent with the CIA; however, the individual's life is portrayed as one of personal failure and even of betrayal.

See also: Fiction—Spy Novels; MOCKINGBIRD, Operation

References and Further Reading

Abel, Richard. *Americanizing the Movies and "Movie-Mad" Audience: 1910–1914*. Berkeley, CA: University of California Press, 2006.

Booth, Alan R. "The Development of the Espionage Film," in Wesley K. Wark (ed.), *Spy Fiction, Spy Films, and Real Intelligence*. Portland, OR: Frank Cass & Co., 1991.

Bouzereau, Laurent. *The Art of Bond: From Storyboard to Screen: The Creative Process Behind the James Bond Phenomenon*. New York: Abrams, 2006.

Britton, Wesley. *Onscreen and Undercover: The Ultimate Book of Movie Espionage*. Westport, CT: Praeger, 2006.

Gresh, Lois H., and Robert Weinberg. *The Science of James Bond: From Bullets to Bowler Hat to Boat Jumps, the Real Technology Behind 007's Fabulous Films*. New York: John Wiley & Sons, 2006.

Melvin, David Skene, and Ann Skene Melvin. *Crime, Detective, Espionage, Mystery and Thriller Fiction and Film: A Comprehensive Bibliography of Critical Writing through 1979*. Westport, CT: Greenwood Press, 1980.

Strada, Michael J., and Harold R. Troper. *Friend or Foe?: Russians in American Film and Foreign Policy, 1933–1991*. Lanham, MD: Rowman & Littlefield Publishers, 1997.

Andrew J. Waskey

MUELLER, ROBERT S.
(AUGUST 7, 1944–)

Robert Swan Mueller, current Director of the Federal Bureau of Investigation (FBI) nominated by President George W. Bush, was born on August 7, 1944, in New York City. He spent most of his youth in the Philadelphia suburbs, but went to boarding school at St. Paul's, located in Concord, New Hampshire. He received his undergraduate degree from Princeton University in 1966, going on to study at New York University, where he earned a masters in international relations in 1967.

Following his studies, Mueller signed up with the U.S. Marine Corps, going on to become an officer for a rifle platoon in the Third Marine Division. He saw extensive service in the Vietnam War, during which he received the Bronze Star, the PURPLE Heart, and the Vietnamese Cross of Gallantry, as well as two commendation medals. Returning to the United States, Mueller studied at the University of Virginia, receiving a Juris Doctor degree in 1973.

Professionally, Mueller started working as a lawyer in San Francisco, before moving on to the U.S. attorney's offices. He stayed in San Francisco and became the chief of the branch's criminal division. In 1982, he moved to Boston, where he was recruited to be an assistant U.S. attorney, dealing primarily with cases of fraud and corruption.

In 1989, Mueller joined the U.S. Department of Justice as an employee of Attorney General Richard L. Thornburgh. Soon after, he took charge of the Department's criminal branch, notably prosecuting Panamanian dictator Manuel Noriega and the Lockerbie bombing. For his work, the American College of Trial Lawyers selected him to join their ranks.

After a stint in the private sector, he joined the homicide division of the District of Columbia's U.S. Attorney's Office in 1995, before going back to San Francisco as U.S. attorney in 1998. Called back to Washington to fill a vacancy in 2001 as acting deputy attorney general of the Department of Justice, President Bush nominated him to be FBI director on July 5, 2001. He assumed the post on September 4, 2001, only a couple days before the terrorist attacks. In the aftermath of September 11, he came out against the creation of a new domestic intelligence agency, preferring to reform current structures.

See also: Bush, George W., Administration and Intelligence; Federal Bureau of Investigation (FBI)

References and Further Reading

Jeffrey-Jones, Rhodri. *The FBI: A History*. New Haven, CT: Yale University Press, 2007.

Kessler, Ronald. *The Bureau: The Secret History of the FBI*. New York: St. Martin's Press, 2002.

Zegart, Amy B. *Spying Blind: The CIA, the FBI and the Origins of 9/11*. Princeton, NJ: Princeton University Press, 2007.

Arthur Holst

MURPHY COMMISSION

The Murphy Commission was established by Congress on July 13, 1972. It was one of a series of presidential commissions that have been established to examine the performance of the intelligence community and make recommendations for improvement. The Murphy Commission reported its findings on June 27, 1975. The overall tenor of its report was supportive of the intelligence community. Unlike previous studies, the Murphy Commission concluded that "it was neither possible nor desirable to give the Director of Central Intelligence (DCI) line authority over that very large fraction of the intelligence community which lies outside the CIA." Instead it recommended increasing the DCI's political clout by placing this office "in close proximity to the White House and be accorded regular and direct contact with the President."

The Murphy Commission was highly politicized from the outset. Appointed by the president were Anne Armstrong, council to the president, and William J. Casey, president and chairman of the Export-Import Bank. When Armstrong resigned she was replaced by Vice President Nelson Rockefeller. Congressional members included Senator Mike Mansfield, Representative Clement Zablocki, and later as a replacement Representative William Broomfield.

A difference of opinion on the part of the authors of the Murphy Commission Report existed over its founding conditions. In the preface to its report the Commission spoke of an increasingly pluralistic world characterized by interdependence and rapid technological change that was blurring the boundaries between domestic and foreign policy. As a consequence of these trends, it stated that the United States needed to consider "a fresh organization of the government for the conduct of foreign policy." Mansfield dissented, asserting that "the Commission paid little attention to the circumstances in which the legislative mandate for the Commission was created." He identified the most prominent feature of the period in which the Commission was set up as "a time of intense confrontation between the executive and legislative branches of the U.S. Government." Rather than addressing these issues, he characterized the Commission's study as being "a sort of elaborate management study."

Mansfield was especially upset with one of the Commission's major new proposals, the creation of a Joint Congressional Committee on National Security. He asserted that over time the new joint committee would become a barrier to the dissemination of sensitive material to other committees. Mansfield was most concerned that it would become an instrument of executive domination over Congress.

The Murphy Commission did not have a substantial impact. Before its investigation was completed, Washington politics increasingly became focused on Watergate and the CIA's role in the break-in and covert action. These concerns spawned a series of investigations by Congress and the president. On January 4, 1975, President Gerald Ford appointed Vice President Nelson Rockefeller to head a Commission on CIA Activities within the United States. It reported out the same month as did the Murphy Commission. Ford had hoped this inquiry would forestall action by Congress. That was not to be the case as both the Senate (the Church Committee) and the House (the Pike Committee) began their own broader investigations into allegations of CIA wrongdoing.

See also: Church Committee; Clark Report (Second Hoover Commission); Eberstadt Report; Hoover Commission (First); Intelligence Community; Pike Committee; Rockefeller Commission

References and Further Reading

Olmsted, Kathryn S. *Challenging the Secret Government.* Chapel Hill, NC: University of North Carolina Press, 1996.

Oseth, John. *Regulating U.S. Intelligence Operations.* Lexington, KY: University of Kentucky Press, 1985.

Rockefeller Commission. Report to the President by the Commission on CIA Activities Within the United States, June 1975 History-Matters http://history-matters.com/archive/church/rockcomm/contents.htm (accessed September 2007)

Glenn P. Hastedt

N

NASSIRI, GENERAL NEMATOLLAH
(1911–FEBRUARY 16, 1979)

An Iranian intelligence chief, Nematollah was director of SAVAK, the intelligence service of Shah Mohammad Reza Pahlavi, to whom he remained loyal until his execution. Nematollah Nassiri was born in 1911, the son of Amidol Mamalek, a former deputy in the Persian *Majilis* (parliament). He grew up serving the Shah and in 1953 was the man who personally delivered the *firman* (edict) to Iranian Prime Minister Mohammed Mossadegh, by which the Shah ordered the arrest of the politician. Following the assassination of Prime Minister Hassan Ali Mansur on January 21, 1965, Nassiri was appointed as head of SAVAK, replacing General Hassan Pakravan, who was sacked. Nassiri rapidly became one of the most feared men in the country, although some writers have suggested that he was more interested in real estate and only the nominal head of SAVAK, with the real power held by Parviz Sabeti. Certainly Nassiri was identified heavily, in the public eye, as the man responsible for crackdowns on opponents of the Shah during the late 1960s and early 1970s.

At the urging of the Iranian ambassador to the United States, Ardeshit Zahedi, and Martial Law Chief General Ali Oveissi, Nassiri was arrested along with his predecessor Pakravan, and Amir Abbas Hoveida (prime minister 1965–1977). It seems that these were to be made scapegoats for the excesses of the Shah's government, and all three men remained in prison when the Shah left Iran on January 16, 1979. Following the fall of the government of Shahpour Bakhtiar on February 11, Nassiri and his colleagues were arraigned before a tribunal, presided over by Ayatollah Khalkhali. Nassiri appeared briefly on television at the trial, his face and neck showing signs of torture. He was sentenced to death and executed by firing squad on February 16, 1979.

See also: Central Intelligence Agency; Cold War Intelligence

References and Further Reading

Hoveyda, Fereydoun. *The Fall of the Shah*. Translated by Roger Liddell. New York: Wyndham Books, 1980.

Shawcross, William. *The Shah's Last Ride*. London: Chatto & Windus, 1989.

The 1974 Iran Who's Who. Tehran: Echo of Iran, 1974.

Justin Corfield

NATIONAL COMMISSION ON TERRORIST ATTACKS ON THE UNITED STATES (THE 9/11 COMMISSION)

On November 27, 2002, more than a year after the terrorist attacks of September 11, 2001, Bush and Congress created the National Commission on Terrorist Attacks on the United States. The 10-person bipartisan commission received testimony from 160 witnesses and held 12 public hearings. After 19 months of investigation the Commission released its 567-page report on July 22, 2004. The 9/11 Commission issued its report on July 22, 2004.

It identified four kinds of failures that contributed to the 9/11 terrorist attacks and made 41 recommendations. The failures were those of imagination, policy, capabilities, and management. In turning to specific recommendations for reform, the Commission asserted that U.S. national security institutions had been constructed to fight the cold war and that today's global setting required a different structure. It recommended creating the position of Director of National Intelligence (DNI). This individual would oversee all-source national intelligence centers, serve as the president's principal intelligence advisor, manage the national intelligence program, and oversee the component agencies of the intelligence community. Included in this power would be responsibility for submitting a unified intelligence budget appropriating funds to intelligence agencies, and set personnel policies for the intelligence community. The DNI's office would be in the White House.

Political pressure for creating a bipartisan commission had been slow to build. With U.S. forces engaged in a war against al-Qaeda and the Taliban in Afghanistan, there was little interest in Washington into an investigation into the causes of 9/11 and Republicans easily defeated efforts by Democrats to establish an independent commission of inquiry. With victory in Afghanistan in hand in December 2001 Senators Joseph Lieberman (D-CT) and John McCain (R-AZ) introduced legislation to bring such a commission into existence The administration objected citing a February 2002 decision by the House and Senate to establish their own investigation.

Pressure for an independent inquiry, however, continued to mount as families of the 9/11 victims pressed forward. They found the terms of reference and degree of access to intelligence materials for the House-Senate Joint Committee to be too restrictive and the time frame for the inquiry too short. In July 2002 the House succumbed to their lobbying efforts and voted to endorse the creation of a bipartisan commission. The Senate and White House still resisted, although by October the White House publicly supported the concept. Among the White House's major concerns was the fear that blame would be laid at the door of the Bush administration and that the report would be issued in the midst of the 2004 presidential campaign.

Cover of *The 9/11 Commission Report: Final Report of the National Commission on Terrorist Attacks upon the United States*. The report, issued on July 22, 2004, provides the findings and recommendations of the 9/11 Commission in its investigation into the terrorist attacks on the World Trade Center and Pentagon on September 11, 2001. (National Commission on Terrorist Attacks)

The 9/11 Commission got off to a rocky star and frequently found itself at odds with the Bush administration. Both of its co-chairs, former Secretary of State Henry Kissinger (Republican) and former Senator George Mitchell (Democrat), withdrew due to conflict of interest charges. They were replaced by former New Jersey Governor Thomas Kean and former congressperson Lee Hamilton, respectively. The Commission held its first hearing in late January 2004 and by July was publicly complaining of a lack of cooperation by the White House and Justice Department in making documents and personnel available to it. By October, Kean was threatening to issue subpoenas. Another major point of contention between it and the White House was the Commission's expiration date of May 27, 2004. Any extension was opposed by the Bush administration, but once again a vigorous lobbying campaign from the families of victims of the 9/11 terrorist attacks forced it to accede to public pressure. In February 2004 it agreed to extend the Commission's life for an additional 60 days. In a final reversal, the administration reluctantly agreed to allow Condoleezza Rice to testify in public and under oath. It had argued against such testimony on executive privilege grounds, seeking to have her testimony carried out in secret as was the case with Bush and Vice President Dick Cheney.

The Commission's reform proposals met with different responses on Capitol Hill and from the White House. Where congressional leaders promised to move quickly on overhauling the intelligence community's structure, the White House urged caution. Acting CIA Director John McLaughlin, Secretary of Defense Donald Rumsfeld, and Homeland Security Secretary Tom Ridge all spoke out against creating a national intelligence director. With democratic presidential candidate John Kerry endorsing the Commission's report, the Bush administration came under political pressure to do the same. It came out in favor of a national intelligence director but with authority only to coordinate intelligence. Lieberman criticized Bush for wanting a "Potemkin national intelligence director," whereas republican Senator Arlen Specter (Pa.) referred to it as a shell game.

On October 8, 2004, the House voted 282–134 to create a new national director of intelligence. The Senate had voted in favor of such a move the week before. Their bills differed on the power to be given to that individual. For example, according to the Senate bill, the CIA director "shall be under the authority, direction, and control" of the national intelligence director. In the House version, the CIA director would only "report" to the national intelligence director. By the end of October the House and Senate were dead-locked, with some House Republicans led by Rep. Duncan Hunter (Calif.), chair of the House Armed Services Committee, being adamant that the Pentagon not lose control over its intelligence budget and that the overall budget remain secret. Family members of the victims of the 9/11 attacks called upon President Bush to break the stalemate in favor of the Senate's version of the bill. He did not. Republican opposition in the House remained firm, forcing Speaker J. Dennis Hastert (R-Ill) to pull the bill from the docket in late November. Behind-the-scenes negotiations produced a compromise acceptable to House Republicans and the White House. President George W. Bush signed The Intelligence Reform and Terrorism Prevention Act of 2004 on December 17, calling it "the most dramatic reform of our Nation's intelligence capabilities since Harry S. Truman signed the National Security Act of 1947. Under this new law, our vast intelligence enterprise will become more unified, coordinated, and effective."

The legacy left by the 9/11 Commission has been subject to much debate. Critics have raised four broad areas of concern with the ability of the 9/11 Commission's recommendations to prevent future 9/11s or Pearl Harbors. Even Commission members have raised doubts, although their criticisms have been directed at Congress and the Bush administration. This was most notably the case in December 2005 when members of the 9/11 Commission, acting as the Public Discourse Project, issued a report card on the degree of progress of the Bush administration's implementation of their 41 recommendations. Overall it gave more Fs than it did As. The administration received a B for creating a DNI but a D for intelligence in general.

One line of criticism is that although numerous shortcomings were identified in U.S. intelligence policy by the 9/11 Commission, the structure of the intelligence community was not one of them. The identified problems fell more accurately under the heading of managerial shortcomings. The two are not identical. Management is process oriented. It is concerned with such matters as how individuals approach their work, coordinate their efforts, and are rewarded. Organization is concerned with structure. It deals with the establishment of bureaucratic units and their placement. Where managerial problems frequently are identified as contributing factors to instances of strategic surprise, organization is not. No intelligence organization is immune to being caught unaware.

A second and related criticism is that if the 9/11 Commission was concerned with organizational aspects of intelligence failures, it made the problem worse. Creating a DNI has added an additional layer to the intelligence community and it is a heavy layer. Rather than a powerful staff and lean office with agency heads reporting to one of three deputy directors as put into place, the Office of the DNI contained 1 principal deputy, 4 deputies, 3 associate deputies, and more than 19 assistant deputies. A second move was to establish a National Counterterrorism Center. Establishing joint centers is also no guarantee of success. In the case of the National Counterterrorism Center, a major factor inhibiting its success is the nature of its database. Although analysts at the Center have access to 26 different information networks spanning the intelligence community no single database unites all 26 and no search engine combs all 26. Finally, in this regard, for many the ultimate test of organizational authority is control over the budget. The DNI emerged with budgetary powers less than those envisioned by the 9/11 Commission. Actions taken by intelligence organizations effectively have further reduced the DNI's budgetary power. Not long after the 9/11 Commission's report was released, Secretary of Defense Donald Rumsfeld, who had spoken out against creating a powerful DNI, announced he would create an Undersecretary of Defense for Intelligence who would have authority over all of the Defense Department's intelligence units and control their budgets. The FBI moved 96 percent of its intelligence budget into units not under the jurisdiction of the DNI.

Third, there is continued concern that the culture of intelligence on which the analytical process rests has not changed. Press reports spoke of an atmosphere in the intelligence community that did not encourage skepticism. Studies of how intelligence analysts approached their work documented the pull of the past on current analysis. When given a request, analysts first checked to see what previous intelligence products by that unit had said about the problem and then talked with others to ascertain their views. With these inputs in place the analyst then begins to formulate a response. To break through the stifling influence of status quo thinking observers, including the 9/11 Commission, have called for increasing the diversity of views brought to bear on intelligence matters and hold analysts more accountable for their intelligence products. Evidence on this point is not encouraging. Director of Central Intelligence Porter Goss publicly stated that he would not reprimand any CIA analyst for mistakes made leading up to the Iraq War for fear of further damaging agency morale.

Finally, some maintain that the creation of the 9/11 Commission and its recommendations signified the triumph of domestic politics over intelligence policy. Presidential commissions have become a readily recognizable feature of the American political landscape and the 9/11 Commission was neither the first nor the last presidential commission to examine the analytic and estimating performance of the intelligence community and make recommendations for improvement. Among the core functions commonly identified for presidential commissions is to provide symbolic assurance to the public that the government is aware of the problem and taking steps to deal with it. The history of the 9/11 Commission showed that President Bush resisted its creation and his administration displayed little interest in cooperating with its inquiry, fearing that the Commission would be critical of its pre-9/11 policies. In its immediate response to the release of the Commission's report, the administration was decidedly noncommittal about the merits of its recommendations, although Bush did characterize the report as "an important tool in mapping future strategies against terrorism." He went on to note that many of the actions called for by the Commission had already been taken by his administration.

See also: Bush, George W., Administration and Intelligence; Director of National Intelligence; Homeland Security Act; Intelligence Community; September 11, 2001; Terrorist Groups and Intelligence

References and Further Reading

9/11 Commission Report: The Final Report of the National Commission on the Terrorist Attacks Upon the United States. New York: Norton, 2004.

Strasser, Steven. *The 9/11 Investigations.* New York: Public Affairs Reports, 2004.

Glenn P. Hastedt

NATIONAL DETECTIVE POLICE

The National Detective Police (NDP) was an intelligence organization directed by Lafayette Baker, which pursued Confederate spies and extracted information from them. The NDP's greatest success was the arrest or shooting of the conspirators in the Lincoln assassination.

Lafayette Baker first entered the intelligence world when he walked into the office of Winfield Scott and volunteered to head his espionage division. Scott's embryonic intelligence apparatus was in poor shape—a double agent had penetrated the operation, and ruined efforts to uncover a mole in the U.S. War Department. Scott sent Baker into Virginia, where he gathered some intelligence and, according to Baker's memoirs, bluffed his way past Jefferson Davis. After returning, Baker took on a new assignment. Appointed as provost marshal of the War Department, Baker moved quickly to promote his reputation and to crack down on Confederate intelligence in Washington, DC. Pushing aside the Pinkerton Agency, Baker established the National Detective Police. The grandiose name referred to an organization of 30 men, with responsibilities that focused almost entirely on the capital. In his pursuit of Southern spies, Baker arrested and detained people without charges or trial. His interrogations usually lasted for days, and included questionable tactics such as the use of sleep deprivation, false witnesses, and blank confessions. It must be noted, however, that the usual condition for release was merely taking an oath of allegiance to the United States.

In November of 1861, Baker led a cavalry raid through southern Maryland in order to capture Southern sympathizers and disrupt the communication lines of Confederate intelligence. The raid, meant largely for the benefit of newspaper reporters, accomplished little except angering the residents of the area.

Throughout the war, Baker continued to pressure the Southern sympathizers in the Washington area. One of his greatest coups was the arrest of the Confederate spy Belle Boyd. It was not until the last days of the Civil War, though, that the National Detective Police took on their most important case.

On April 14, 1865, John Wilkes Booth shot and killed President Lincoln. On the same day, co-conspirators shot Secretary of State Seward and stalked Vice President Andrew Johnson, although they made no attempt on his life. The conspirators fled, and remained at large for almost two weeks. Baker took charge of the manhunt, and led the contingent of soldiers that finally cornered Booth. Baker's men set fire to the barn where Booth was hiding, and shot him as he attempted to flee. In the wake of Booth's killing, Baker was promoted to brigadier general.

After the end of the Civil War, Baker's National Detective Police invented new functions for itself. Baker monitored the post office and tracked former Confederate agents. He monitored the activities of Confederate diehards in Canada and Latin America.

Baker also investigated allegations of war profiteering and abuse, which is ironic given lingering questions about his own veracity and accounting. President Johnson discovered that Baker was spying on him, and demanded his resignation in 1867. Baker resigned, but published a book hinting that Booth had been part of a wider conspiracy involving Union officials. He died of meningitis the following year. The National Detective Police was disbanded, although Baker's favored name—the Secret Service—was adopted by the later organization tasked with protecting the president.

See also: Baker, Lafayette; Boyd, Belle; Civil War Intelligence; Confederate Signal and Secret Service Bureau

References and Further Reading

Axelrod, Alan. *The War Between the Spies: A History of Espionage During the American Civil War*. New York: Atlantic Monthly Press, 1992.

Central Intelligence Agency. "Intelligence in the Civil War," 2005 https://www.cia.gov/cia/publications/civilwar/docs/Civil_War.htm.

Fishel, Edwin C. *The Secret War for the Union: The Untold Story of Military Intelligence in the Civil War*. Boston: Houghton Mifflin, 1996.

Steers, Edward. *Blood on the Moon: The Assassination of Abraham Lincoln*. Lexington, KY: University Press of Kentucky, 2001.

James L. Erwin

NATIONAL FOREIGN INTELLIGENCE BOARD

The National Foreign Intelligence Board, an important advisory body which reports to the Director of Central Intelligence, was created on January 14, 1997, pursuant to a directive by the DCI. The NFIB, although established by the DCI, was also formed in accordance with the National Security Act of 1947 as amended at that time and Executive Order 12333.

The NFIB was created to serve and to better inform the DCI on the various issues and aspects of national intelligence and the intelligence community. It is responsible for advising the DCI on the gathering, analyzing, and dissemination of national and foreign intelligence; sharing between government branches and agencies; coordinating with foreign governments; protection of sources, agents, and procurement practices; and new intelligence policies and initiatives.

The NFIB is composed of highly ranking intelligence officials who are intricately involved in intelligence gathering, analysis, and dissemination at their respective posts. It is chaired by the DCI or by the Deputy DCI in the case of the latter's absence. The organizations represented included the CIA, the U.S. military, the State Department, the Defense Intelligence Agency, the National Security Agency, the National Imagery and Mapping Agency, the FBI, the Department of Energy, the Treasury Department, and the National Intelligence Council. On certain occasions, other relevant officials may be invited to attend specific NFIB meetings, either as active participants or simply as observers. For example, a representative of the Department of Commerce and Drug Enforcement Administration is often invited when programs or information within its range of interest are discussed.

See also: Director of Central Intelligence; Executive Orders; Intelligence Community

References and Further Reading

Federation of American Scientists Online. "National Foreign Intelligence Board," http://www.fas.org/irp/offdocs/dcid3-1.html (accessed January 2, 2006)

Kessler, Ronald. *The CIA at War: Inside the Secret Campaign Against Terror.* New York: St Martin's Press, 2004.

U.S. Intelligence Community Online. "Intelligence Terms and Definitions," http://www.gpoaccess.gov/serialset/creports/pdf/glossary.pdf (accessed January 2, 2006)

Arthur Holst

NATIONAL GEOSPATIAL-INTELLIGENCE AGENCY

The National Geospatial-Intelligence Agency (GSA) came into existence on November 24, 2003, with the signing of the 2004 Defense Authorization Bill which contained a provision mandating that the National Imagery and Mapping Agency (NIMA) change its name to the National Geospatial-Intelligence Agency.

As was the case with NIMA, GSA is a major combat support agency of the Defense Department. It is headquartered in Bethesda, Maryland, and operates major facilities in the northern Virginia; Washington, DC; and St. Louis areas and employs cartographers, imagery analysts, computer and telecommunications engineers, photogrammetrists, geodesists, and geospatial analysts.

The GSA is organized into four major directorates. The first is the Analysis and Production Directorate. It provides policy makers, both civilian and military, with the geospatial intelligence they need to make decisions and plans. The Acquisition Directorate focuses on both preacquisition studies as well as obtaining needed systems, engineering, technology, and infrastructure programs. The InnoVision Directorate forecasts future operating environments and defines future needs. Finally, the Source Operations and Management Directorate provides end-to-end support for the production and management of geospatial intelligence requirements.

Although the GSA is among the newest members of the intelligence community, U.S.-government-sponsored research into geospatial intelligence dates as far back as 1803 when President Thomas Jefferson sent Meriwether Lewis and William Clark on an expedition to explore and map the just-acquired Louisiana Territory. A few decades later, in 1830, the U.S. Navy would establish the Depot of Charts and Instruments as it began to map the oceans.

The GSA provides geospatial intelligence for a wide range of needs that extend beyond the boundaries of national security policy. For example the NGA supported Hurricane Katrina relief efforts by providing information to the Federal Emergency Management Agency on affected areas from U.S. government satellites, commercial satellites, and airborne reconnaissance platforms. It also partners with commercial providers of geospatial intelligence to supplement that obtained from U.S. geospatial-intelligence gathering platforms.

See also: Lewis, Meriwether; National Imagery and Mapping Agency

References and Further Reading

Lowenthal, Mark. *Intelligence: From Secrets to Policy*, 4th ed. Washington, DC: Congressional Quarterly Press, 2008.

Richelson, Jeffrey. *The U.S. Intelligence Community*, 5th ed. Boulder, CO: Westview, 2008.

Glenn P. Hastedt

NATIONAL IMAGERY AND MAPPING AGENCY

The National Imagery and Mapping Agency (NIMA) had a relatively short live span, coming into existence in on October 1, 1996, through the passage of the National Imagery and Mapping Agency Act of 1996 and officially passing out of existence in 2004 with the passage of the Defense Authorization Bill. At that time it became known as the Geospatial-Intelligence Agency.

NIMA was responsible for managing imagery and geospatial analysis and production in order to meet national intelligence requirements. Broken down into separate tasks, this meant that among other assignments NIMA was responsible for supporting the intelligence requirements of the State Department and other non–Defense Department intelligence agencies, tasking Defense Department imagery collection agencies to meet the requirements and priorities established by the Director of Central Intelligence, establishing and consolidating Defense Department geographical information data collection requirements, providing advisory tasking for theater and tactical intelligence consumers, and disseminating imagery intelligence and geospatial information in the most efficient and expeditious means that were consistent with security requirements.

This lengthy and complex set of assignments reflected the political conflict that led to its creation and the agencies that were combined to bring it into existence. Indications that problems existed in the collection of imagery intelligence surfaced publicly in the early 1990s as a result of the perceived inability to provide timely imagery intelligence to combat troops during the Persian Gulf War and the general sense that this would be a key mission that imagery intelligence would have to fulfill in the future. A House Armed Services Committee report on intelligence success and failures in Operations Desert Storm and Desert Shield found that collection was generally good and that new imagery intelligence collection platforms proved to be outstanding; substantial shortcomings existed in the distribution of intelligence within the theater especially from the point of view of the air force as only 4 of 12 secondary imagery distribution systems could interact with one another and that the record of analysis efforts was mixed.

In 1992 Director of Central Intelligence (DCI) Robert Gates noted in testimony before the House and Senate intelligence committees in April that he had put together an Imagery Task Force. It had recommended establishing a National Imagery Agency that would bring together the Central Intelligence Agency's (CIA) National Photographic Interpretation Center (NPIC) and the Defense Mapping Agency. Gates went on to reveal that he opposed the plan. He also opposed congressional calls for a more thorough reform of imagery intelligence, one that would have created a single agency with broad control over all means of imagery collection, satellite, and aircraft, from research and development through tasking and analysis of the information obtained.

In spite of Gates' opposition on the next month, on May 6, 1992, a Central Imagery Office was created in the Department of Defense as a combat support agency through simultaneous CIA and Defense Department directives. This office did not absorb any existing imagery intelligence agencies but existed alongside of them. This peaceful coexistence did not last long. During his confirmation hearings to become DCI, John Deutch stated his preference for consolidating all imagery collection, analysis, and distribution duties within a single organization, much like the National Security Agency did for signal intelligence. Once in office Deutch established a National Imagery Agency Steering Committee to look into the matter. A task force put forward 11 different options. In November 1995 Deutch and Secretary of Defense William Perry indicated that they would proceed with the establishment of NIMA.

Unlike the Central Imagery Office, they saw NIMA as absorbing other imagery agencies. Scheduled for inclusion were NPIC, the Defense Mapping Agency, the Central Imagery Office, and portions of the Defense Intelligence Agency, the National Reconnaissance Agency, and the Defense Airborne Reconnaissance Office. When it finally came into existence, NIMA included these organizations along with the CIA's Office of Imagery Analysis and the Defense Dissemination Program Office. All together about 9,000 individuals were moved into NIMA from other agencies.

The move to establish NIMA was not without controversy. Some in Congress feared that while creating NIMA would result in stronger tactical intelligence for military commanders it might also have the effect of diluting the quality of national imagery intelligence that would otherwise be provided by the CIA through NPIC. To lessen this likelihood, the legislation establishing NIMA contained language that ensured the DCI would have a strong voice in the selection of its head and in tasking imagery collection. According to some observers, however, this fear was realized when the United States was caught off guard by the 1998 Indian nuclear explosion.

In addition to its traditional national security missions NIMA was tasked to provide support to the 2002 Winter Olympics in Utah and the Summer 2004 Olympic Games in Greece and surveyed the World Trade Center site after the 9/11 terrorist attacks. It reportedly offered to provide images to the Space Shuttle Columbia while it was in orbit in order to try an determine the extent of damage done during takeoff NASA declined this offer but has since entered into a partnership with the National Geospatial-Intelligence Agency to collect imagery on future shuttle flights.

See also: Central Imagery Office; Defense Intelligence Agency; Deutsch, John Mark; Gates, Robert Michael; National Photographic Interpretation Center (NPIC); National Reconnaissance Office

References and Further Reading

Dreyfuss, Robert. "TECHINT: The NSA, the NRO, and NIMA," in Craig Eisendrath (ed.), *National InSecurity: U.S. Intelligence After the Cold War*, pp. 149–171. Philadelphia: Temple University Press, 2000.

Lowenthal, Mark. *Intelligence: From Secrets to Policy*, 4th ed. Washington, DC: Congressional Quarterly Press, 2008.

Glenn P. Hastedt

NATIONAL INTELLIGENCE AUTHORITY

The National Intelligence Authority was a supervisory body for the Central Intelligence Group (CIG). On January 22, 1946, President Harry S. Truman issued a directive that established the National Intelligence Authority (NIA). The NIA consisted of the secretaries of state, war, and navy, and the president's personal representative. Its task was to plan, develop, and coordinate all federal intelligence activities.

In order to substantiate NIA's decisions, the directive also created the post of Director of Central intelligence (DCI) and the CIG. The DCI, designated by the president and responsible for the NIA, was a nonvoting member of the NIA and directed the CIG, the immediate predecessor organization of the Central Intelligence Agency (CIA), whose budget and personnel were furnished by the Departments of State, War, and Navy.

When the National Security Act was signed by President Trumann on July 26, 1947, and became effective on September 18, NIA and CIG were replaced by the National Security Council and the CIA, respectively.

See also: Central Intelligence Group; Director of Central Intelligence; Intelligence Community

References and Further Reading

Darling, Arthur B. *The Central Intelligence Agency: An Instrument of Government, to 1950.* University Park, PA: The Pennsylvania State University Press, 1990.

Rudgers, David F. *Creating the Secret State: The Origins of the Central Intelligence Agency, 1943–1947.* Lawrence, KS: University Press of Kansas, 2000.

Troy, Thomas F. *Donovan and the CIA: A History of the Establishment of the Central Intelligence Agency.* Frederick, MD: University Publications of America, 1981.

Naoki Ohno

NATIONAL INTELLIGENCE COUNCIL

In 1973 the Board of National Estimates and the Office of National Estimates were replaced by a National Intelligence Officer system that became responsible for producing National Intelligence Estimates (NIEs). In 1979 Director of Central Intelligence Admiral Stansfield Turner set up the National Intelligence Council (NIC) to provide a corporate sense of identity for the National Intelligence Officers, along with a supporting staff structure. It came into being on January 1, 1980.

In the mid-1980s there were three at-large NIOs and NIOs with specific responsibility for Africa, East Asia, Europe, the Near East, South Asia, Latin America, the Soviet Union, Counterterrorism, Science and Technology, Economics, General Purpose Forces, Strategic Programs, Warning, Foreign Denial and Intelligence Activities, and Narcotics.

At the time the move to National Intelligence Officers and the elimination of the Board of National Estimates is generally seen as reflecting the diminished importance that NIEs have had in the policy-making process. Where once presidents and their advisors relied upon the intelligence community to provide analysis of information collected by covert or overt means, they now were relying upon their own interpretations of events.

The NIC has had a number of different organizational homes, existing both as part of the Central Intelligence Agency and as an independent operation. Today it reports directly to the Director of National Intelligence. Its principal includes providing a focal point for policy makers in tasking the intelligence community regarding midterm and long-term strategic issues, and helping the intelligence community better allocate its resources in response to policy makers' changing needs.

To accomplish this task, the NIC currently is led by a chairperson who is assisted by a vice chair; a vice chair for evaluation; and two directors, one for strategic plans and outreach and another who is in charge of analysis and production. For analytic purposes the NIC in 2006 was composed of 13 National Intelligence Officers: Africa, East Asia, Economic and Global Issues, Europe, Military Issues, the Near East, Russia and Eurasia, Science and Technology, South Asia, Transnational Threats, Warning, Weapons of Mass Destruction and Proliferation, and the Western Hemisphere. Each NIO is charged with (1) becoming knowledgeable about substantive intelligence problems of interest to policy makers, (2) drawing up concept papers and terms for reference for NIEs, (3) participating in the drafting of NIEs, (4) chairing sessions where substantive issues are debated, and (5) ensuring that the final draft accurately reflects the judgment of the Director of National Intelligence.

See also: Board of National Estimates; Central Intelligence Agency; Office of National Estimates; Turner, Admiral Stansfield

References and Further Reading

Lowenthal, Mark. *Intelligence: From Secrets to Policy*, 4th ed. Washington, DC: Congressional Quarterly Press, 2009.
Richelson, Jeffrey. *The U.S. Intelligence Community*, 5th ed. Boulder, CO: Westview, 2008.

Glenn P. Hastedt

NATIONAL INTELLIGENCE DAILY

The National Intelligence Daily served as the intelligence community's main current intelligence product from its introduction under Director of Central Intelligence William Colby until it was renamed the Senior Executive Intelligence Brief. Colby, a career intelligence officer, had long recommended that the CIA's National Intelligence Digest should be recast from a magazine to a document that took on the appearance of a daily newspaper. That manner of presentation he argued more effectively conveyed the relative importance of items to readers and better allowed them to determine what issues they wished to read more about. Experience with the National Intelligence Daily as a newspaper showed that this format was too inflexible and it returned to a magazine-style publication.

The National Intelligence Daily was one of several different current intelligence products produced by the intelligence community on a daily basis, including the President's Daily Brief (CIA), the National Intelligence Daily (CIA with IC-wide input), the Secretary's Morning Summary (Department of State), National Military Joint Intelligence Center Daily (Defense Intelligence Agency [DIA] with input from other IC members), and the SIGINT Digest (National Security Agency). As a product of the CIA, the National Intelligence Daily bore the CIA seal on its masthead. Under DCI William Webster the seals of all members of the intelligence community were placed there at the urging of another intelligence agency.

The National Intelligence Daily and its successor, the Senior Executive Intelligence Brief, contain six to eight relatively short articles that address events which have occurred over the last day or two or which are expected to take place in the near future. It is made available to several hundred senior officials in the executive branch as well to members of the Congressional Oversight Committees. Coverage is said to approximate that of the President's Daily Brief but excludes sensitive information and information that would identify sources and methods.

One example of a National Intelligence Daily is a declassified report issued on June 20, 1981, "USSR-Poland: Polish Military Attitudes." It takes up the question of the reaction of the Polish military to a possible Soviet invasion of Poland. The report concluded that most of the Polish military command is alienated from the Soviet Union and likely to resist an invasion. A second example is a 1987 two-page story on the situation in Lebanon that surfaced as a result of a photo of an issue of the National Intelligence Daily that was inadvertently placed on the cover of the Foreign Service Journal.

Criticism about the National Intelligence Daily and similar intelligence community publications have come from two very different directions. Some argue that there is too much duplication in the material being presented and that the Intelligence Community should eliminate some products. Others argue that these products overwhelm policy makers with more intelligence than they need or can process. The solution here is not necessarily to eliminate products but to better differentiate among audiences and platforms for the dispersal of intelligence.

See also: National Intelligence Estimates; National Intelligence Survey

References and Further Reading

CIA National Intelligence Daily. "USSR-Poland," www.gwu.edu/~nsarchiv/NSAEBB/NSAEBB211/doc03.pdf (accessed September 23, 2008).

Lowenthal, Mark. *From Secrets to Policy*, 4th ed. Washington, DC: Congressional Quarterly Press, 2008.

Glenn P. Hastedt

NATIONAL INTELLIGENCE ESTIMATES

Information gathered through espionage and open sources is not self-interpreting. To be of value it must first be analyzed and interpreted. After that it must be communicated to policy makers. In addition to oral briefings, five different written means have been employed by the intelligence community for this purpose. They are background or encyclopedic type reports, current intelligence documents that summarize the contemporary situation, warning intelligence documents that highlight and pinpoint unfolding dangerous situation that may require an American response, daily briefs to presidents and other key policy makers that present the latest intelligence on subjects of interest and estimates that project a current military, political, or economic situation or problem into the future.

The most authoritative estimates are known as National Intelligence Estimates (NIEs). They represent the consensus assessment of the intelligence community as to how a situation containing national security implications is likely to unfold. As such, an NIE is not a prediction of a specific event occurring at a specific time and place. Rather, it is a net assessment of probable future courses of action and developments. Not surprisingly, the content of NIEs are often highly contested as by their very nature they often deal with topics around which great controversy exists and where the consequences of being wrong can be momentous.

In the cold war years the great majority of NIEs focused on the Soviet Union and its allies. Of particular note were the questions of the projected strength of Soviet bombers and Soviet missile forces. In each case the intelligence community was internally divided, with the air force supporting more alarmist interpretations of a bomber gap and missile gap. Incomplete interpretation, organizational self-interest, and partisan political concerns were major contributing factors to these intelligence controversies. Intelligence obtained through aerial and later satellite surveillance helped bring an end to these controversies and the fears they engendered.

Improved intelligence did not, however, bring an end to disagreements over the aims, purposes, and composition of Soviet military power. The 1970s saw renewed controversy as the United States and Soviet Union entered into arms control negotiations. This intelligence debate culminated in the B Team exercise in which a group of outside experts holding far more hostile and ominous interpretations of Soviet policy was convened to challenge and reexamine the intelligence community's assessment. Controversial Soviet-oriented NIEs in the 1980s dealt with Nicaragua.

The pace of production of NIEs has been uneven, reflecting such factors as the foreign policy agenda of the administration, its receptivity to intelligence, and the degree of internal disagreement within the intelligence community. From 1960 to 1962 at least 14 NIEs were produced on various aspects of Soviet military and economic capabilities. In the last years of the Carter administration only about a dozen NIEs were written. Thirty-eight NIEs were written in 1981 and 60 were produced the following year. The number of NIEs in 1997 was down 60 percent from where it had been only a few years before. This decrease reflected the fact that there no longer existed a country with the military power capable of threatening the United States. It also reflected changes in technology which brought more and more information directly to the attention of policy makers and the desire of presidents and their aides to direct all aspects of American foreign policy from the White House. With the end of the cold war and the break-up of the Soviet Union, NIEs also began to address a wider array of foreign policy topics including the global energy situation, North Korea, terrorism, South Africa, Iraq, Zaire, France, the former Yugoslavia, global humanitarian emergencies, and France.

The end of the cold war has not made the content of NIEs any less controversial, as witnessed by the NIE produced just before the Iraq War. An NIE on Iraq was commissioned only after Senator Bob Graham, who was then chair of the Senate Intelligence Committee, asked Director of Central Intelligence George Tenet to produce one. The administration had not produced an NIE because according to Tenet "we had covered parts of all those programs over 10 years through NIEs and other reports, and we had a ton of community product on all these issues." Where normally NIEs may take months to produce, as the intelligence community comes to a judgment on a question, the Iraq NIE, some 90 pages long, was produced in three weeks. One senior intelligence official described it as a "cut and paste job." A draft NIE was sent to the CIA, Defense Intelligence Agency, State Department's Bureau of Intelligence and Research, the Department of Energy's intelligence unit, the National Image and Mapping Agency, and the National Security Agency on September 23. On September 25 mid- to senior-level officials from these agencies met on the draft. On September 26, the CIA produced a coordinated draft NIE. It was reviewed by Tenet and the heads of the above agencies on October 1. The next day Tenet briefed the Senate Intelligence Committee on its content. Compounding matters was the later admission that neither President George W. Bush nor National S Security Advisor Condoleezza Rice did not read the 90-page report in its entirety and failed to see the objections raised by the State Department to claims that aluminum purchased by Iraq was for nuclear weapons or that Iraq was seeking uranium in Africa. The State Department's dissent that Iraq was not reconstituting its nuclear weapons program came at the end of the first paragraph and in an 11-page annex.

See also: Cold War Intelligence; National Intelligence Daily; National Intelligence Survey

References and Further Reading

Estimative Products on Vietnam, 1948–19975. Washington, DC: National Intelligence Council, 2005.

Koch, Stuart (ed.). *Selected Estimates on the Soviet Union, 1950–1969*. Washington, DC: Center for the Study of Intelligence, Central Intelligence Agency, 1993.

Prados, John. *The Soviet Estimate: U.S. Intelligence Analysis and Soviet Strategic Forces*. Princeton, NJ: Princeton University Press, 1986.

Richelson, Jeffrey. *The U.S. Intelligence Community*, 5th ed. Boulder, CO: Westview, 2008.

Glenn P. Hastedt

NATIONAL INTELLIGENCE SURVEY

National Intelligence Surveys are classified encyclopedic treatment of countries that provide policy makers and analysts with basic information. Typical entries would include government, geography, economy, communications, transportation, science and technology, military, and intelligence.

Chronologically it followed the publication of the Joint Army-Navy Intelligence Studies (JANIS) during World War II. Beginning in 1943 and through 1947, 34 JANIS were produced that provided the military with basic information about countries in different theaters of operation. After the war it was determined that the need for this type of basic information still existed and National Security Council Intelligence Directive #3 of 13 January 1948 authorized the production of the National Intelligence Survey under the general direction of the Central intelligence Agency but with participation from all members of the intelligence community. Once produced, a volume in the National Intelligence Survey series would be periodically updated. For countries such as the Soviet Union and China, several volumes were needed to catalog all of the pertinent information, whereas for others one volume was sufficient.

By the mid-1960s the National Intelligence Survey series had, according to one Director of Central Intelligence, grown to be "10 times the size of the Encyclopedia Britannica." The series was terminated in 1974 largely because it was found to be less important for analysts and policy makers than other products. Increasingly policy makers favored current intelligence and estimates over basic intelligence. Analysts found that their own expertise plus working documents provided them with sufficient information to proceed with their tasks.

See also: National Intelligence Daily; National Intelligence Estimates

References and Further Reading

Breckinridge, Scott. *The CIA and the U.S. Intelligence System*. Boulder, CO: Westview Press,1986.

Ransom, Harry Howe. *The Intelligence Establishment*. Cambridge, MA: Harvard University Press, 1970.

Glenn P. Hastedt

NATIONAL PHOTOGRAPHIC INTERPRETATION CENTER (NPIC)

The National Photographic Interpretation Center (NPIC) was established within the Central Intelligence Agency (CIA) to be a community-wide asset in the interpretation of aerial photos. It grew out of the CIA's Photographic Intelligence Center and later was collapsed, along with several other imagery interpretation and production units, to form the National Imagery and Mapping Agency (NIMA). Today NIMA is known as the National Geospatial-Intelligence Agency.

The CIA's Photographic Intelligence Center was not the first unit with the agency tasked with the interpretation of aerial photographs. It was preceded by the Photographic Intelligence Division, which was established in 1953 with 13 photo interpreters under the direction of Arthur Lundahl. In 1958 it was merged with a statistical unit to form the Photographic Intelligence Center. A few years later, in 1961, in recognition of the increased volume of aerial and satellite photographs now being produced and their value to analysts throughout the intelligence community and not just the CIA, the Photographic Intelligence Center was made a "service of common concern."

The 1950s and early 1960s saw considerable disagreement between intelligence agencies over the state of Soviet military power and gave rise to such controversies as the bomber gap and the missile gap. Aerial photography did much to end these controversies but it not escape unscathed from the growing sense among policy makers that the intelligence community was in need of reform. In 1958 the Eisenhower administration planned to undertake a series of studies on the structure and organization of the government. Intelligence was one area recommended for study. Action was not forthcoming until after the U-2 incident in which an American aerial reconnaissance plane was shot down over Soviet territory in May 1960 on the eve of a U.S.-Soviet summit conference in Paris. The pilot, Francis Gary Powers, was captured alive.

After the U-2 incident, CIA Inspector General Lyman Kirkpatrick was placed in charge of intelligence with special attention to military intelligence. It produced a list of 42 recommendations one of which was the creation of a National Photographic Interpretation Center to better coordinate the production and dissemination of photographic intelligence. Secretary of Defense Robert McNamara acted on this recommendation and NPIC came into existence in 1961. For the early part of its existence, NPIC was part of the CIA's Intelligence Directorate. In the mid-1970s Director of Central Intelligence William Colby transferred it to the CIA's Science and Technology Directorate.

NPIC photo interpreters did not undertake an extensive analysis of the material they received. Rather, they did a quick and dirty analysis, often based on a list of items of interest such as Soviet missile silos. Within 48 hours after its receipt NPIC would provide a preliminary report and send photos that were of potential interest on for further analysis. Still, their initial analysis often was quite definitive. NPIC was able to document that Soviet bombers were being crated up for shipment back to the Soviet Union at the conclusion of the Cuban Missile Crisis and that intermediate range ballistic missile sites at San Critobal and Remedios had been abandoned.

NPIC was absorbed into NIMA in 1996 due to growing dissatisfaction with the production and dissemination of imagery intelligence during the Persian Gulf War. Some in Congress objected to incorporating NPIC into NIMA on the grounds that the new structure favored military tactical intelligence at the expense of national strategic intelligence. This argument did not, however, prevent the establishment of NIMA.

See also: Central Intelligence Agency; Colby, William Egan; National Geospatial-Intelligence Agency; National Imagery and Mapping Agency; U-2 Incident

References and Further Reading

Lowenthal, Mark. *Intelligence: From Secrets to Policy*, 4th ed. Washington, DC: Congressional Quarterly Press, 2008.
Richelson, Jeffrey. *The U.S. Intelligence Community*, 5th ed. Boulder, CO: Westview, 2008.

Glenn P. Hastedt

NATIONAL RECONNAISSANCE OFFICE

The National Reconnaissance Office (NRO) is formally responsible for managing and supervising the development of space reconnaissance systems and related intelligence activities needed to support global information superiority. Its emergence as a major force in the intelligence collection efforts of the United States is symbolic of the position of importance that technological intelligence collection has assumed. Espionage is no longer the exclusive province of human spies. It is an activity engaged in from great distances by expensive and highly sophisticated devices that listen to conversations; take pictures; and capture signals emitted from aircraft, missiles, and satellites.

The NRO was established by President Dwight Eisenhower by executive order in August 1960. It became operational on September 6, 1961, following an agreement between the Central Intelligence Agency (CIA) and the air force setting it up as a joint CIA-air force operation. Its existence did not become public until 1973 when a Senate report inadvertently failed to remove its name from a list of intelligence agencies whose budgets were to be made public. Its existence was not officially recognized until September 18, 1992.

The importance of moving beyond human intelligence in gathering scientific and technical information on Soviet missile developments was quickly recognized after World War II. The knowledge of captured scientists and technicians would soon become obsolete and gathering additional information through traditional means of espionage would be difficult. A 1946 RAND Corporation study, Preliminary Design for an Experimental World Circling Spaceship, suggested a long-term solution to the problem. Another RAND study pointed to the short-term solution, the development of an aircraft capable of penetrating Soviet airspace and taking pictures of missile installations and test facilities. This aircraft became the U-2. From the outset policy makers recognized that U-2 flights would produce a counter-response by the Soviet Union, which would limit its long-term utility. As such in March 1955 the air force issued General Operational Requirement #80 that set out the desired specifications of an advanced reconnaissance satellite.

Both the air force and Central Intelligence Agency (CIA) put forward competing concepts and satellite systems. The air force program was initially referred to as the Advanced Reconnaissance System. It was soon relabeled as the SENTRY system and then SAMOS. The CIA plan was known as CORONA. In February 1958 President Eisenhower gave his support to CORONA in large part out of concerns that the air force plan would not lead to an operational satellite quickly enough. These concerns became intensified in May 1960 when a U-2 plane was shot down over Soviet airspace and its pilot, Francis Gary Powers, was captured alive. These developments did not end the air force program. Instead it was reorganized in an effort to speed it up and improve the performance of its satellites. With competing satellite programs still under way, two of the principal movers behind the U-2 spy plane and satellites, James Killian and Edwin Land, called for a CIA-air force satellite partnership. The two intelligence organizations had worked together successfully on the U-2 and Killian and Land now urged the creation of a permanent joint venture.

Given this history, the NRO was not envisioned as a stand-alone unified organization. It was seen as a loose federation of those parts of the CIA and air force that were involved in the development and operation of satellites. Predictably, the result was repeated conflicts between the CIA and the air force over such matters as the selection of reconnaissance missions, launch schedules, and the technical specifications of the satellites being developed.

From its inception until 1992, NRO's programs tended to divide into three groups. Program A consisted of the Air Force Office of Special Projects which was in charge of developing reconnaissance satellites. Program B consisted of CIA reconnaissance projects including the CORONA satellite and the U-2, an A-12 reconnaissance aircraft. Program C was made up of the navy's signals intelligence satellite project known as GRAB (Galactic Radiation and Background). From 1963 through 1969 a second air force program was Project D. It was the air force's version of the CIA's aerial reconnaissance effort. In 1969 it was placed under the jurisdiction of the Strategic Air Command. It was terminated in 1970 or 1971.

In 1992 Director of Central Intelligence announced a major reorganization of the NRO. No longer would it be restructured around the three separate agency intelligence projects. Instead there would be three functional acquisitions and operations director-ates organized around IMINT (imagery intelligence), SIGINT (signals intelligence), and COMINT (communications intelligence). Five years later a fourth directorate was established. It grew out of a project that was investigating the potential utility of small reconnaissance satellites. Other offices include Management Services and Opera-tions, Plans and Analysis, Space Launch, and Operational Support. The NRO does not analyze the information it collects but distributes the pictures and signals intercepts to other intelligence agencies where the analysis takes place.

CORONA was the NRO's first photo reconnaissance satellite. Although its first test flight took place on February 28, 1959, the first successful mission did not take place until August 12, 1960. CORONA's pictures were jettisoned back to earth in film capsules, where they were caught in midair and then developed and dissemi-nated for analysis. The 145th and last CORONA mission was launched on May 25, 1972.

A second major photo reconnaissance satellite program was the Keyhole launch series that went by the designator KH. Particularly important in the series were the KH-11 launches, the first of which took place on December 19, 1976. The last launch in the original KH series took place on November 6, 1988, and remained in orbit for seven and one-half years. What made the KH-11 series so important was that they produced near real-time photographs. Among the missions it was used for were trying to find where in the U.S. embassy in Tehran the American hostages were being held in 1980. It also revealed the existence of Soviet programs to construct new super submarines and mini aircraft carriers and disproved reports of a new Soviet chemical-biological-warfare center.

Also of importance is the LACROSSE series, which initially was known as INDIGO and later as VEGA. Rather than take pictures, this satellite carries imaging radar that allows it to operate even when targets of interest are covered by clouds. Between 1991 and 1996 LACROSSE satellites were tasked with covering such diverse tasks as missile and nuclear activity in China, North Korea, Israel, Pakistan, Russia, and India as well as refugee movements in Rwanda and narcotics convoys in Laos.

With the end of the cold war the place of the NRO in the intelligence community is being reexamined. Many believe that technological intelligence collection has been emphasized to the detriment of human intelligence collection and that a better balance between the two needs to be restored. This is especially so in light of the emergence of terrorists as the prime national security threat to the United States. Additionally, the NRO has found itself being asked to provide more tactical information for the military. The first tactical use of NRO capabilities came in Bosnia in 1996.

See also: Air Force Intelligence; Central Intelligence Agency; Cold War Intelligence; CORONA; Director of Central Intelligence; Eisenhower Administration and Intelli-gence; Post–Cold War Intelligence; Powers, Francis Gary; U-2 Incident

References and Further Reading

Dreyfuss, Robert. "TECHINT: The NSA, the NRO, and NIMA," in Craig Eisendrath (ed.), *National InSecurity: U.S. Intelligence After the Cold War*, pp. 149–171. Philadelphia: Temple University Press, 2000.

Odom, William. *Fixing Intelligence: For a More Secure America*. New Haven, CT: Yale University Press, 2003.

Richelson, Jeffrey. *America's Space Sentinels: DSP Satellites and National Security*. Lawrence, KS: University of Kansas Press, 1999.

United States Senate, Select Committee to Study Government Operations with respect to Intelligence Activities. *Final Report, Book II, Intelligence Activities and the Rights of Americans*. Washington, DC: U.S. Government Printing Office, April 26, 1976.

Glenn P. Hastedt

NATIONAL SECURITY ACT OF 1947

Following the conclusion of World War II, American officials intended to reform the nation's military system in light of the wartime experiences. For instance, the war caused President Harry S. Truman, Joint Chiefs of Staff, and other civilian and military leaders to favor the unification of the armed services into an integrated system. Additionally, the developing cold war between the United States and the Soviet Union reinforced their decision to centralize defense and foreign policies. More importantly, federal planners believed that modernizing the U.S. national security programs through the establishment of new institutions to coordinate military and diplomatic strategies would reduce security threats and promote lasting world peace.

On July 26, 1947, President Truman signed the National Security Act of 1947, which realigned the U.S. armed forces; coordinated domestic, foreign, and military policies; and created new security agencies. The Act established the U.S. Air Force as an independent armed service, and it coordinated the navy, army, and air force under the National Military Establishment headed by the secretary of defense. Air force officials favored the plan because they believed that it would protect their interests against the army in regards to scarce funds. However, the navy opposed the unification of the armed forces because it feared that the air force and army would dominate the new military system. Despite the navy's misgivings, James Forrestal took office as the first secretary of defense on September 17, 1947.

The act solved the problems associated with interservice coordination by stipulating that the three military branches would be administered as individual executive departments, and had specific powers and duties. For example, each of the service secretaries had a right to appeal to the president regarding military policies.

According to the National Security Act, the secretary of defense, the three service secretaries, and the three service chiefs constituted the War Council. Additionally, the three service chiefs and a Chief of Staff comprised a Joint Chiefs of Staff organization.

The National Security Act of 1947 also created the National Security Council (NSC), which was a defense planning group designed to coordinate national security policy. Composed of the president, chairman of the National Security Resources Board, secretary of state, secretary of defense, secretary of the air force, secretary of the army, secretary of the navy, and other department and agency heads appointed by the president, the NSC discussed all problems relating to the defense of the nation. In 1949, an amendment to National Security Act dropped the military service secretaries from the NSC and added the vice president as a member of the group. The permanent staff of the NSC remained small during its initial years of operation, but its personnel increased to 70 by 1980.

Additionally, the Act established the Central Intelligence Agency (CIA) to coordinate intelligence-gathering activities of the various government agencies. Personnel in the CIA interpreted information relating to foreign and domestic actions deemed as vital to national security. The agency also provided facts and information to help the National Security Council and other federal institutions in making plans and decisions.

Other organizations established by the National Security Act of 1947 included the National Security Resources Board, which advised the president on issues relating to the coordination of military, industrial, and civilian mobilization for future war efforts; the Munitions Board, which coordinated the procurement activities of the three armed services; and the Research and Development Board, which coordinated military research and development.

In March 1949, President Truman amended the National Security Act to provide the secretary of defense with more authority. The amendment also changed the National Military Establishment into the U.S. Department of Defense. Thus, the three military branches were no longer administered as separate executive departments; instead they became military departments within the Department of Defense.

The National Security Act of 1947 represented a major component of the U.S. cold war strategy. The legislation established a variety of institutions that enabled the nation to cope effectively with threats to its security.

See also: Central Intelligence Agency; Intelligence Community; National Security Council; Office of Strategic Services

References and Further Reading

Hammond, Paul Y. *Organizing for Defense: The American Military Establishment in the Twentieth Century.* Princeton, NJ: Princeton University Press, 1961.

Weigley, Russell F. *The American Way of War: A History of the United States Military Strategy and Policy.* Bloomington, IN: Indiana University Press, 1973.

Zegart, Amy B. *Flawed by Design: The Evolution of the CIA, JCS, and NSC.* Stanford: Stanford University Press, 1999.

Kevin M. Brady

NATIONAL SECURITY ADVISOR

The national security advisor, also known as the assistant to the president for National Security Affairs, directs and oversees the work of the National Security Council. Over time the national security advisor has emerged as the president's principal advisor on national security affairs, although this individual's actual influence has varied from administration to administration. As an assistant to the president and not a cabinet secretary running a department such as the secretary of state or secretary of defense, the national security advisor is not subject to Senate confirmation.

The National Security Council came into existence as a result of the National Security Act of 1947. Under President Harry Truman, the National Security Council was directed by Sidney Souers who held the title of executive secretary. This position was transformed into that of the national security advisor by President Dwight Eisenhower in 1953. Robert Cutler was the first national security advisor. Initially the national security advisor served primarily as an impartial communication link between the national security bureaucracies and president as each distanced themselves from national security council decision making.

The national security advisor became a more visible and politically important figure in the Kennedy and Johnson administrations, and the growing American involvement in the Vietnam War. In part this was due to the greater role that the national security council staff began to play in decision making. It also reflected the change in orientation that Walt Rostow brought to the position under Johnson. He saw himself less as a facilitator and more as a policy advocate. Behind these changes lay a common refrain coming from presidents that the national security bureaucracies lacked an appreciation or understanding of the presidential perspective on foreign policy matters and instead were trying to advance their own particular bureaucratic and professional agendas.

Perhaps the most powerful national security advisor was Henry Kissinger who held that position under President's Richard Nixon and Gerald Ford. Kissinger and Nixon distrusted the national security bureaucracy in general and the Central Intelligence Agency in particular. Consequently they concentrated national security decision making in the White House and controlled the national security bureaucracies through an elaborate National Security Council committee system that he personally controlled. Also powerful was Zbigniew Brzezinski who held the post under President Jimmy Carter. However, unlike Kissinger who dominated over Secretary of State William Rogers, Brzezinski frequently clashed with Carter's Secretary of State Cyrus Vance. The result was that important foreign policy decisions made at the National Security Council, such as those pertaining to the Iranian Hostage Crisis, were not always effectively communicated to the State Department. Vance would resign in protest over the failure to inform him of the failed hostage rescue effort.

The influence of the national security advisor declined in the Reagan administration with the appointment of a series of weak individuals who were unable to mediate the conflicts between Secretary of State George Shultz, Secretary of Defense Caspar Weinberger, and Director of Central Intelligence William Casey. Only with the selection of Colin Powell late in the Reagan administration and the departure of these individuals did the National Security Council system begin to operate smoothly.

The trend since the Reagan administration has been to appoint relatively low-keyed and knowledgeable individuals to the position of national security advisor. As with early national security advisors, they have seen their task as primarily that of protecting the president and serving as a mediator among competing bureaucratic interests. They have not sought to invite conflict with the secretaries of state and defense or the head of the Central Intelligence Agency. Nor have they sought to inject themselves into the day-to-day operations of these agencies.

Neither the mediator nor policy advocate approach by the national security advisor guarantees the effective use of intelligence in the policy process. Problems of over selling intelligence obtained through espionage, competition among agencies, and the production of "intelligence to please" have occurred under both approaches as evidenced by the histories of the Vietnam and Iraq Wars.

See also: Kissinger, Henry Alfred; National Security Council

References and Further Reading

Destler, I. M. "National Security II: The Rise of the Assistant," in Hugh Heclo and Lester Salamon (eds.), *The Illusion of Presidential Government*, pp. 263–286. Boulder, CO: Westview, 1981.

Inderfurth, Karl, and Loch Johnson (eds.). *Decisions of the Highest Order: Perspectives on the National Security Council*. Pacific Grove, CA: Brooks/Cole, 1988.

Lord, Carnes. *The Presidency and the Management of National Security*. New York: Free Press, 1988.

Prados, John. *Keepers of the Keys: A History of the National Security Council from Truman to Bush*. New York: William Morrow & Co., 1991.

Shoemaker, Christopher. *The National Security Council Staff: Counseling the Council*. Boulder, CO: Westview, 1991.

Glenn P. Hastedt

NATIONAL SECURITY AGENCY

The National Security Agency (NSA) was established by a secret executive order, National Security Council Intelligence Directive (NSCID) No. 6 entitled "Communications Intelligence and Electronics Intelligence," on September 15, 1952. That directive remains secret. A version of NSCID No. 6 dated February 17, 1972, states the director of the NSA "shall exercise full control over all SIGINT (Signals Intelligence) collection and processing activities of the United States and to produce SIGINT in accordance with the objectives, requirements, and priorities established by the Director of Central Intelligence Board." It formally came into existence on November 4, 1952. So secret was the NSA that its existence was not even mentioned indirectly by U.S. government organizational manuals until 1957 when a reference appeared to an organization performing "highly specialized technical and coordinating functions relating to national security."

The NSA is the successor organization to the Armed Forces Security Agency. It was set up as the result of a Joint Chiefs of Staff Directive signed by Secretary of Defense Louis Johnson on May 20, 1949. Located within the Defense Department, the Armed Forces Security Agency was assigned responsibility for directing the communications intelligence and electronic intelligence of the three military services signals intelligence units. In spite of this broad mandate, the Armed Forces Security Agency had little power. For the most part its activities consisted of tasks not being performed by the Army Agency, the Naval Security Group, and the Air Force Security Service, the units whose work it was to direct.

Walter Bedell Smith, President Harry S. Truman's executive director of the National Security Council, found this state of affairs to be unsatisfactory. He wrote a memo in December 1951 calling for a review of communications intelligence activities, calling the current system for collecting and processing communications intelligence "ineffective." Three days later, on December 13, 1951, the National Security Council

Headquarters of the National Security Agency (NSA) at Fort George G. Meade, Maryland. Although the agency's budget and number of employees are classified, the NSA is the U.S. government's largest intelligence agency. (National Security Agency)

set up a committee commonly referred to as the Brownell Committee, after its chair Herbert Brownell, to examine the matter. The Brownell Committee recommended strengthening the national level coordination and direction of communications intelligence activities. The NSA was created as a result of these recommendations.

SIGINT is signals intelligence. It is typically used as an overarching term referring to three different types of intelligence-gathering efforts. First, it refers to intelligence obtained by intercepting communications. Second, it refers to intelligence gathered by monitoring data relayed during weapons testing. Third, it can refer to electronic emissions of weapons and tracking systems.

SIGINT is gathered by earth-based collectors such as ships, planes, or ground sites as well as by satellites. Key ground stations are located in Colorado, Great Britain, Australia, Turkey, Japan, and Germany. Protecting and securing NSA earth-based collection platforms has often presented significant challenges to U.S. foreign policy. In 1967 the USS *Liberty*, a signals collection ship, was bombed inadvertently by Israeli forces during the June 1967 Arab-Israeli War. Similarly, during the Vietnam War, the C Turner Joy and Maddox were reportedly attacked in 1964 by North Vietnamese forces in the Gulf of Tonkin in an action that provided the justification for a major escalation of the U.S. war effort. Both ships were on intelligence-gathering missions for the Navy Security Group. Turkey has repeatedly threatened to evict the United States from listening posts in retaliation either for U.S. support of Greece in conflicts over Cyprus or for American support of Armenian claims of Turkish genocide. NSA listening posts in Iran were a reason that the United States continued to support the Shah in Iran in the face of rising opposition.

One of the major challenges faced by the NSA is deciphering the raw information it obtains. Much of SIGINT is encrypted. The information is encased in a code that must be broken. Decoding information thus is a major component of NSA's work. Given the volume of information that must be studied and the time-sensitive nature of intelligence work, computers are an important tool for finding patterns within the flow of information and determining what it means. The high cost of its computer systems makes the NSA budget the largest of all members of the intelligence community. NSA's leading role in breaking codes has, on occasion, placed it at the center of controversy with private firms and organizations. In the 1970s it was accused of deliberately recommending changes in the creation of a Data Encryption Standard that would potentially make it easier for NSA to break commercial and governmental codes.

NSA was also involved in debates in the 1990s over exporting cryptography software and hardware.

NSA does not engage in analysis. It is a collector of raw information. The job of translating that information into intelligence falls upon the analytic agencies such as the Central Intelligence Agency (CIA) and the Defense Intelligence Agency (DIA). The line between collecting SIGINT and interpreting it is a fine one and in reality analysis does take place. Often this creates tension in the intelligence community when the results of NSA information gathering/analysis can be presented directly to policy makers and not filtered through other agencies. This occurred during the Carter administration when Admiral B. R. Inman, head of NSA, reported that it had found evidence of a previously unreported Russian "combat brigade" in Cuba. Director of Central Intelligence Admiral Stansfield Turner was angered by Inman's conclusion, feeling it crossed the line from collection to analysis. The report subsequently became public and created a serious problem for the administration. Secretary of State Cyrus Vance had denied the allegations in private. Now, satellite photos confirmed the presence of between 2,000 to 3,000 Russian troops in Cuba. For its part, the CIA and other elements of the intelligence community believed that those troops had been in Cuba for at least three years.

Beyond breaking foreign codes, the NSA is charged with the task of making and protecting U.S. codes. The highly sensitive nature of this work has made the NSA a target for penetration by foreign intelligence services. One of the more publicized cases of foreign penetration was the arrest of Richard Pelton in 1985. Pelton had worked for NSA from 1965 to 1979 and worked for the Soviet Union from 1980 until his arrest. Among the operations compromised was a project to tap Soviet underwater cables in the Sea of Okhostk off of the coast of Siberia.

The NSA has also become repeatedly embroiled in domestic controversy because of its involvement in espionage carried out in the United States and against Americans. Executive Order 12333 from 1981 allows NSA to collect foreign intelligence and counterintelligence but prohibits it from "acquiring information concerning the domestic activities of U.S. persons." Three secret NSA espionage programs directed against American citizens have received special notoriety.

NSA espionage against Americans is often identified as beginning with the Kennedy administration and its interest in Cuba. The target of these early NSA communication intercepts, begun in 1962, were American racketeers whose names were given to NSA officials by the Federal Bureau of Investigation (FBI). In the late 1960s the target list changed. An October 20, 1967, top-secret message sent by William Yarborough, the army's assistant chief of staff, to NSA Director Marshall Carter requested assistance in obtaining information about possible foreign influences on civil disturbances in the United States. Specially included here were peace groups and Black power organizations. The army, CIA, DIA, and FBI all began providing NSA with names. On July 1, 1969, this domestic surveillance program officially and secretly became christened Operation MINARET. Between 1967 and 1973 when it was terminated by Attorney General Elliot Richardson over 5,925 foreign and 1,690 organizations and U.S. citizens were included on this watch list. In 1975 NSA Director Lew Allen acknowledged that over 3,900 reports had been written on watch-listed Americans.

A second major secret NSA domestic communications intercept program was Operation SHAMROCK. Its origins precede NSA and date back to the closing days of World War II when in August 1945 Brigadier General W. Preston Corderman Chief of the Signal Security Agency, the predecessor of the Armed Forces Security Agency, launched an effort to persuade ITT, Western Union, and RCA to take part in a plan whereby incoming and outgoing cable traffic into the United States would be microfilmed. At one point 150,000 messages per month were being copied and analyzed. Operation SHAMROCK was terminated in 1975 by NSA Director Lew Allen.

The third major NSA program is ECHELON. It intercepts radio and satellite communications, telephone calls, faxes, and emails from almost anywhere in the world through a system of intercept stations operated by the UKUSA community. Under an agreement worked out among U.S. allies after World War II each member of the system is responsible for monitoring a different area. The information gathered is the analyzed through a series of supercomputers and made available to the intelligence agencies of member states (U.S., Great Britain, Canada, Australia). An estimated three billion communications are intercepted daily. NSA critics argue that ECHELON is used to get around prohibitions on spying on Americans. When the existence of these types of programs came to light they served as a major rationale for writing legislative charters for the members of the intelligence community. These efforts stalemated and no legislative charter for NSA was written.

Questions about the existence, legality, and effectiveness of NSA domestic surveillance program erupted again on December 16, 2005, when stories broke that in the aftermath of the 9/11 terrorist attacks the George W. Bush administration had authorized NSA to conduct warrantless phone taps on individuals inside the United States calling individuals outside the United States. The Bush administration claimed the program was limited and restricted in nature, focusing on legitimate national security issues. Further controversy erupted in May 2006 when it was reported that the NSA had been secretly collecting the phone records of Americans obtained from AT&T, Verizon, and Bell South. Qwest also was approached but declined to participate.

Where the Bush administration claimed the authority to conduct such programs on several grounds including inherent presidential commander and chief powers, critics argued that he had bypassed the Foreign Intelligence Surveillance Court set up by the Foreign Intelligence Surveillance Act of 1975 that was designed to provide presidents with a means for obtaining secret warrants while at the same time protecting American civil liberties. Critics also raised doubts about the effectiveness of these domestic surveillance programs, arguing that terrorists had long since abandoned any heavy reliance on telephones to reduce the likelihood of having their communications intercepted and identities uncovered.

See also: Armed Forces Security Agency; Bush, George W., Administration and Intelligence; ECHELON; Foreign Intelligence Surveillance Act of 1947; Foreign Intelligence Surveillance Court; Intelligence Community; MINARET, Project; SHAMROCK, Project; UKUSA

References and Further Reading

Bamford, James. *Body of Secrets: Anatomy of the Ultra Secret National Security Agency.* New York: Anchor, 2002.

Bamford, James. *The Puzzle Palace: Inside the National Security Agency, America's Most Secret Intelligence Organization.* Boston: Houghton Mifflin, 1982.

Dreyfuss, Robert. "TECHINT: The NSA, the NRO, and NIMA," in Craig Eisendrath (ed.), *National InSecurity: U.S. Intelligence After the Cold War*, pp. 149–171. Philadelphia: Temple University Press, 2000.

Richelson, Jeffrey. *America's Space Sentinels: DSP Satellites and National Security.* Lawrence, KS: University of Kansas Press, 1999.

Glenn P. Hastedt

NATIONAL SECURITY ARCHIVE

Founded in 1985 by Thomas Blanton, the National Security Archive is a private nonprofit organization that serves as a repository for declassified information obtained under Freedom of Information Act (FOIA) requests. Based at George Washington University, it "serves as a repository of government records on a wide range of topics pertaining to the national security, foreign, intelligence, and economic policies of the United States." Documents are also acquired through mandatory declassification, court records, congressional records, presidential libraries, and through diligent pursuit of information by the Archive's staff.

The Archive provides access to documents primarily through its Web site and at its reading room in George Washington University's Gelman Library. In addition, it publishes portions of its collections on microfiche, CD-ROMs, and books, as well as providing e-mail updates to subscribers.

The Archive has long emphasized the declassification of intelligence-related documents. Over the past 15 years, it has published documents collections from the Cuban Missile Crisis and the Iran-Contra affair, which drew heavily from previously unseen files from intelligence agencies. Additionally, it published a top-secret Central Intelligence Agency (CIA) study of the Bay of Pigs debacle in which the CIA's internal auditor blamed the CIA for the failure of the program. In 2006 it released documents on the CIA's activities during the Hungarian Revolution in 1956, Poland in the 1970s and 1980s, and war games on Iraq.

The Archive has clashed repeatedly with the CIA over its interpretation of the FOIA and of the Clinton administration's rules for declassification. In 2006, the Archive sued the CIA for illegally charging journalists copying fees for documents obtained under FOIA requests. Furthermore, the Archive uncovered a secret reclassification program that sought to remove from public circulation documents concerning U.S. nuclear weapons and intelligence programs from as early as the Truman administration. The ensuing public outcry forced a reexamination of the program.

See also: Bay of Pigs; Central Intelligence Agency; Cuban Missile Crisis; Iran-Contra Affair

References and Further Reading

Chang, Laurence, and Peter Kornbluh (eds.). *The Cuban Missile Crisis, 1962: A National Security Archive Documents Reader.* New York: The New Press, 1992.

Digital National Security Archive. http://nsarchive.chadwyck.com/marketing/index.jsp (accessed January 15, 2007).

Kornbluh, Peter (ed.). *Bay of Pigs Declassified: The Secret CIA Report*. New York: The New Press, 1998.

Richard M. Filipink Jr.

NATIONAL SECURITY COUNCIL

The National Security Council was established in 1947 as an interagency cabinet-level position responsible for advising the president and coordinating various forms of policy to developing and ratifying policy decisions related to the defense and security of the United States.

Post–World War II decisions over armed services unification were finally achieved through compromise in 1947. During World War II it became apparent that there existed certain inadequacies in civil-military policy coordination, between the various service branches, and means of intelligence gathering. The main concern was that if there was going to be a unified military force, civil-military coordination had to be improved. Such improvement in terms of policy coordination also required more coherent intelligence support. A combination of problems at the beginning of World War II, along with an emerging cold war with the Soviet Union, led to the enactment of the National Security Act. The bill was signed into law on July 26, 1947. It created a number of permanent structures within the government: a National Security Council (NSC) to coordinate policy, composed of the president, vice president, secretary of state, the newly created secretary of defense, a Department of Defense, a Joint Chiefs of Staff (JCS), and a Central Intelligence Agency (CIA). The act became a central document in cold war policy making. Although the act did not unify the armed services—the U.S. Air Force was now recognized as a separate branch and the marines were not absorbed by the army—it nonetheless increased the coordination of the national security establishment.

The council's creation as a mechanism to coordinate military and foreign policy was initially proposed in the 1946 Eberstadt Report. Ferdinand Eberstadt, a former business colleague of Navy Secretary James V. Forrestal, proposed an American version of the British Committee of Imperial Defense. Forrestal's worry about unifying the armed services led him to support the creation of a National Security Council as a way to guarantee "timely and unified action in time of crisis, avoid the organizational confusion of World War II, and check the authority of a president." More directly, Forrestal had little confidence in Truman and considered the council's creation as a way to offset a strong secretary of defense. His primary objective was to preserve the navy's autonomy. The navy failed in its attempts to block the creation of a secretary of defense but did manage to win support for the permanent establishment of a National Security Council.

In the 1947 act Congress declared that the NSC's purpose would be to "advise the President with respect to the integration of domestic, foreign, and military policies" in order to provide for more effective cooperation in national security policy making. The council was also given the authority to supervise the Central Intelligence Agency, recently created to monitor overseas intelligence gathering. At first, council members were the president, secretary of defense, secretary of state, the three service secretaries—army,

President Harry S. Truman with members of the National Security Council (NSC) on August 19, 1948. Truman was the first president to have an NSC. From left to right, clockwise around the table: Assistant Secretary of the Air Force Cornelius Vanderbilt Whitney, Secretary of the Army Kenneth Royall, Executive Secretary of the National Security Council Sidney Souers, National Security Resources Board Chairman Arthur M. Hill, Director of Central Intelligence Roscoe Hillenkoetter, Secretary of Defense James Forrestal, Secretary of State George C. Marshall, President Truman, Under Secretary of the Navy W. John Kenney.
(Harry S. Truman Presidential Library)

navy, and air force—chairman of the National Security Resources Board, and other such officials as the president chose to appoint. A 1949 amendment removed the service secretaries and the National Security Resources Board, and replaced them with the vice president and designated the director of Central Intelligence and chairman of the Joint Chiefs of Staff as statutory advisers.

With the outbreak of the Korean War (1950–1953), Truman elevated the NSC's status. He regularly presided over its meetings and designated a senior staff under the direction of the council's executive secretary. He also integrated it into the executive office of the presidency. In 1950, he appointed well-known democrat, W. Averill Harriman, as a special assistant, authorized to monitor the implementation of national security policy. During Truman's presidency one of the council's most comprehensive and ambitious memoranda was NSC 68. Issued on April 14, 1950, and titled, "United States Objectives and Programs for National Security," it called for massive increases in military spending to support the U.S. position in Europe and Asia. This document highlighted the U.S. policy of containment against the threat of Communist expansion.

Upon leaving the presidency of Columbia University to head the nation in 1953, Dwight D. Eisenhower made the most use of the NSC. Throughout his eight years in office, Eisenhower met the council on a weekly basis. He designated Robert Cutler, Dillon Anderson, and Gordon Gray to serve, at various times, as special assistant to the president for national security affairs. He relied heavily on his assistants and instituted auxiliary planning and coordinating boards to develop position papers offering guidelines for official state policy on many different issues. Among some of the more important papers the council issued were those on basic national security policy delineating foreign and military policy in Asia, Latin America, and Europe; concepts detailing strategic objectives; and standard requirements for foreign aid and military capabilities. Of all presidents during the cold war period, Eisenhower made the most of the council as an advisory body.

Unlike Eisenhower, President John F. Kennedy dismantled much of the complex structure of the NSC. During his brief tenure, Kennedy and the council rarely met. His chief national security assistant, McGeorge Bundy, was directed to turn the NSC staff "into an instrument that could work quickly and secretly at the president's command and develop a 'White House' perspective that was not restricted by the bureaucracy's recommendations." Burdened by the debacle in Vietnam, moreover, Kennedy's successor, Lyndon B. Johnson, did away with council meetings, opting, instead, for policy discussion and coordination over luncheon meetings on Tuesdays.

As a forum for policy discussion the council did not fare much better under Richard Nixon or Gerald Ford. Chief executives were now more inclined to pay lip service to the council. Nixon's national security advisor, Henry Kissinger, created new decision-making parties such as the Washington Special Action Group. Secrecy and limiting information to a select few guided his actions. When it came to arms control talks with the Soviet Union or normalizing relations with the People's Republic of China, Nixon and Kissinger avoided the council's input. Instead, they favored secret communications or "backchannels" with key allies and opponents.

In an effort to allay the fears of agency heads and chief negotiators who felt that they were being left out of the process, President Jimmy Carter and his national security advisor, Zbigniew Brzezinski, enabled the NSC staff to play central roles when it came to offering policy advice. The Carter administration did sustain the trend toward a strong national security advisor and an important role for the NSC, but also put in place certain structures and policies governing its actions. The revelations of the "Pentagon Papers" of the Vietnam era had made chief executives more cautious with respect to the dissemination of national security information.

The 1980 election of Ronald Reagan, following on the heels of the Iranian hostage crisis, witnessed the new president's desire for cabinet members, not national security advisors, to play a dominant role in policy making. Reagan did not have a major national security advisor, choosing rather to showcase the role of his secretary of state. Reagan was far more determined to reawaken the spirit of patriotism in the United States and devoted a good portion of his foreign policy to ending Communism in Eastern Europe through a massive U.S. military buildup. Yet the role of activism in policy making and implementation of programs by the NSC staff was clearly evident in the "Iran-Contra" roles played by national security advisors Robert McFarlane and John Poindexter as well as their assistant, Lt. Colonel Oliver North.

With the cold war at an end and the sour taste regarding Iran-Contra, subsequent presidents George H. W. Bush, Bill Clinton, and George W. Bush have relied less and less for council advice. They have turned to other advisory bodies such as the War Cabinet and allowed powerful individuals to dominate the advisory process. Also, since the 9/11 attacks more and more emphasis has been devoted to homeland security, while the secretary of defense has increased visibility due to the war on terrorism. The addition to the cabinet of the secretary for homeland security and the reorganization of government agencies to deal with the threat of terrorism has not diminished the importance of a national security advisor and NSC staff. The NSC remains in place to coordinate the various aspects of military, diplomatic, and intelligence policy as a necessary springboard for advice and implementation of significant initiatives. Yet the NSC's major historical contribution occurred during the early years of the cold war when certain strategic initiatives were undertaken to counter the threat of Communist expansion. For most of the cold war, national security policy was premised on the twin pillars of containment and deterrence. The National Security Council provided valuable input with respect to an overall strategy that alternated between arms buildups and deployment, nuclear doctrines and targeting, and rhetorical commitment to preserve democratic freedoms throughout the world.

See also: Eberstadt Report; Iran-Contra Affair; Kissinger, Henry Alfred; National Security Act of 1947; National Security Advisor

References and Further Reading

Inderfurth, Karl F., and Johnson, Loch K. (eds.). *Fateful Decisions: Inside the National Security Council.* New York: Oxford University Press, 2004.

Lowenthal, Mark. *Intelligence: From Secrets to Policy.* Washington, DC: Congressional Quarterly Press, 2003.

Lowenthal, Mark. *The National Security Council: Organizational History.* Washington, DC: Congressional Research Service, 1978.

Nelson, Anna K. "President Truman and the Evolution of the National Security Council," *Journal of American History* 71 (1985), 360–378.

Prados, John. *Keepers of the Keys: A History of the National Security Council from Truman to Bush.* New York: William Morrow & Co., 1991.

Shoemaker, Christopher. *The National Security Council Staff: Counseling the Council.* Boulder, CO: Westview Press, 1991.

Shoemaker, Christopher. *Structure, Function and the NSC Staff: An Officer's Guide to the National Security Council.* Washington, DC: Government Printing Office, 1989.

Charles F. Howlett

NAVAL INTELLIGENCE

Naval intelligence involves the synthesized or collated information that relates to an adversary's naval war-making intentions and capabilities. Naval intelligence has existed as long as there has been naval warfare. In its simplest form, it consists of the identification of an adversary's ships or strategic location.

During the age of sail, individual ship commanders were their own intelligence officers. Their main concern was to balance information provided by superiors, scout ships, and spies. Although this system could be quite sophisticated, the lack of institutional memory and lessons learned put a premium on the ability of an individual commander. Capture of enemy vessels and interrogation of their crews yielded intelligence information.

From the eighteenth through the mid-nineteenth centuries, naval intelligence was gathered primarily in nonclandestine ways. Naval officers with billets abroad (naval attachés) had access to information on the host country's military establishment. Newspapers provided a wide variety of information, including shipping news, commercial transactions, and government policy of a given country.

With the advent of the Industrial Revolution and the concomitant rise of technology and modern weapons, gathering intelligence became especially important. Countries closed off avenues of access, and information, once easily available, became harder to obtain. By the end of the nineteenth century, naval intelligence became more formalized and its operations more secretive.

In 1882 Britain and the United States established formal intelligence offices. These organizations, poorly staffed and without centralized planning or coordination, were chiefly interested in the increasingly dynamic and evolving world of technology, specifically ordnance and ship design. Such organizations were more technology assessment offices than naval intelligence organizations. In time, they addressed other subjects, including geographical, industrial, political, and social aspects of an adversary or potential adversary. In 1896 the U.S. Naval War College and the Office of Naval Intelligence (ONI) collated intelligence relating to Spain into a coherent (and successful) war plan. Germany, Great Britain, and Japan followed that same pattern and integrated war planning into their intelligence efforts.

By the eve of World War I, radio revolutionized communications. Ships could now communicate over vast distances. With radio waves bouncing from unit to unit, interception was inevitable, making radio transmissions a valuable target for intelligence collection. The capture by the Russians early in World War I of codebooks in the German cruiser Magdeburg was of great importance in enabling the British code-breakers of "Room 40 O.B." (Old Building, Admiralty) to read German signals traffic. Supported by Director of Naval Intelligence Admiral Sir William R. Hall, the British built up a comprehensive direction-finding system. German signals traffic led the Admiralty to commit the entire Grand Fleet to the North Sea before the May 31 to June 1, 1916, Battle of Jutland. Despite this, the Grand Fleet was at least partially surprised because of a misunderstanding by the Operations Division. Signals intelligence—the ability to locate, intercept, and translate radio transmissions and message traffic for tactical or strategic use—had become a crucial element at sea by the beginning of World War II.

Even before World War II, Germany sought to protect its message traffic by encoding it using the Enigma machine. Thanks to the initial work of the Poles, the Western Allies could ultimately read encoded German radio messages. The British set up a complex at Bletchley Park for this work, which came to be known as the Ultra secret. Ultimately, all German codes could be read, the Luftwaffe being the easiest to break and U-boat communications the most difficult. Ultra played a key role in the Battle of the Atlantic, for example. The Germans also had considerable success with their own code-breaking operation, B-Dienst, and were able to read Allied convoy codes.

Code-breaking also proved invaluable in the fight against the Imperial Japanese Navy in the Pacific. Beginning in 1939, British, Dutch, and American intelligence units were busy working to read the Japanese Navy operation codes (JN-25), but this proved a daunting task because the Japanese changed the already complex codes. After the Japanese attack on Pearl Harbor on December 7, 1941, the Allies stepped up this effort. The U.S. Navy's lead cryptographer, Commander Joseph R. Rochefort, had little success at breaking the JN-25 code and its variants, but by March 1942 he was able to provide sufficient information for Pacific Fleet Commander in Chief Admiral Chester Nimitz to send carriers to intercept a Japanese invasion force heading for Port Moresby. This resulted in the May 7–8 Battle of the Coral Sea. Naval intelligence also provided critical warning that the Japanese planned to attack Midway Island. This enabled Nimitz to position resources and win the pivotal battle in the Pacific war, the Battle of Midway on June 3–6, 1942.

Signals intelligence continues to be of great importance today, although it is only one part of a complicated system of intelligence collection. Such information must then be carefully analyzed and the proper conclusions drawn. Students of the cold war will have to wait until primary source material is declassified before a balanced conclusion can be made concerning the role naval intelligence played in the post–World War II era. We already know, however, that for years the United States was able to read highly sensitive communications of the Soviet military by tapping into submarine cables.

See also: Air Force Intelligence; American Intelligence, World War II; Army Intelligence; Fleet Intelligence Center; MAGIC; Marine Corps Intelligence; Midway, Battle of; Pearl Harbor; PURPLE; Room 40; Ultra

References and Further Reading

Deacon, Richard. *The Silent War: A History of Western Naval Intelligence.* New York: Hippocrene Books, 1978.

Kahn, David. *The Codebreakers: The Comprehensive History of Secret Communications from Ancient Times to the Internet.* New York: Charles Scribner & Sons, 1996.

Muffeo, Steven E. *Most Secret and Confidential: Intelligence in the Age of Nelson.* Annapolis, MD: Naval Institute Press, 2000.

Prados, John. *Combined Fleet Decoded: The Secret History of American Intelligence and the Japanese Navy in World War II.* New York: Random House, 1995.

Winton, John. *ULTRA at Sea: How Breaking the Nazi Code Affected Allied Naval Strategy during World War II.* New York: William Morrow, 1988.

Richard W. Peuser

NEGROPONTE, JOHN
(JULY 21, 1939–)

John Negroponte was sworn in as the first Director of National Intelligence (DNI) on April 21, 2005. Born in London, England, he graduated from Yale University and entered the Foreign Service. His career as a foreign service officer spanned three decades, from 1960 to 1997. Among the high-ranking positions he held were ambassadorships to Honduras, Mexico, and the Philippines. During the Vietnam era he served as a political officer in South Vietnam and as a liaison officer between the American and

North Vietnamese delegations at the Paris Peace Talks. Negroponte also served two tours of duty with the National Security Council. On September 14, 2001, just days after the 9/11 terrorist attacks on the World Trade Center and the Pentagon, the Senate approved Negroponte's nomination as U.S. ambassador to the United Nations. There he would argue unsuccessfully the U.S. case for war against Iraq.

Negroponte's nomination for the position of DNI was highly controversial for two reasons. The first had to do with his tour as ambassador to Honduras during the Reagan administration. As part of the administration's efforts to defeat Communism in Central America, U.S. military aid to Honduras rose from $3.9 million in 1980 to $77.4 million in 1984. A significant portion of this money went to train the Honduran military and intelligence units and the Contras, the Nicaraguan paramilitary force the United States was supporting against the Sandinista government in Nicaragua. Human rights agencies have concluded that large numbers of Honduran and Nicaraguan citizens were killed, kidnapped, and tortured by these U.S.-trained forces during that time period. Negroponte is accused of permitting these killings to occur and then suppressing information to this effect from appearing in official U.S. reports from Honduras. Negroponte maintains such accounts of his actions are no more than revisionist history.

The second reason Negroponte's nomination was controversial had to do with the position of DNI itself. Creating this position was one of the central recommendations of the 9/11 Commission Report. It found the significant problems facing the intelligence community and called for its restructuring. Among the problems it cited were lack of common standards, a weak capability to set priorities and allocate resources, and divided management authority. The DNI was to replace the Director of Central Intelligence (DCI) as head of the intelligence community. The DCI would retain his position as head of the Central Intelligence Agency. The George W. Bush administration initially resisted creating a DNI but reluctantly agreed to do so under mounting public and congressional pressure.

Legislation creating the position of DNI did not give this individual all of the authority proposed by the 9/11 Commission, especially in the area of budgetary control. Negroponte's first major decision regarding espionage capabilities came in 2005 when he made a recommendation to Congress on two new controversial spy satellite programs developed by the National Reconnaissance Office. Critics argued they were too expensive and ill suited to deal with terrorist groups, whereas supporters cited their technological potential and sophistication.

See also: Director of Central Intelligence; Director of National Intelligence; National Commission on Terrorist Attacks on the United States (The 9/11 Commission); National Security Council; Post–Cold War Intelligence

References and Further Reading

Lowenthal, Mark. *Intelligence: From Secrets to Policy*, 4th ed. Washington, DC: Congressional Quarterly Press, 2008.

9/11 Commission Report: The Final Report of the National Commission on Terrorist Attacks on the United States. New York: Norton, 2004.

Glenn P. Hastedt

NICHOLSON, HAROLD JAMES
(NOVEMBER 17, 1950–)

At the time of his arrest for espionage on November 16, 1996, at Dulles Airport in Washington, DC, awaiting a flight to Zurich, Switzerland, Harold Nicholson was the highest-ranking Central Intelligence Agency (CIA) official charged with espionage. He began spying for Russia in June 1994 while serving in Malaysia as deputy station chief. It is estimated that Nicholson received about $120,000 for the information he passed on to the Russian Federation Foreign Intelligence Service (SVRR). Following his arrest, Nicholson pled guilty to charges of espionage in March 1977 and cooperated with U.S. authorities in order to reduce his prison sentence from a possible life imprisonment to 20 years.

Nicholson began working for the CIA in 1980 following a tour of duty with the U.S. Army as an intelligence officer fulfilling his ROTC requirement. He was posted by the CIA to Manila, Bangkok, and Tokyo as a case officer from 1982 to 1989. He was then sent to Romania where he served as chief of station. From there he went to Malaysia as deputy chief of station. While there he had a number of authorized meetings with representatives of the SVRR. On June 30, 1994, after his last meeting he wired $12,000 to his U.S. bank account. This pattern was repeated in the following months. After a December 1994 trip to Kuala Lumpur he wired $9,000 to his account. He also made $6,000 cash payment on a credit card bill. In June 1995 a repeat trip to Kuala Lumpur was followed by a $23,815 deposit. In December 1995 and June 1996 Nicholson made deposits in his bank account of $26,900 and $20,000, respectively. The information Nicholson passed to the SVRR included the identities of recruits at the CIA's training facility where he was transferred to after leaving Malaysia. He also sought information at their request on Chechnyan terrorism.

Nicholson came under suspicion when in October 1995 he took a routine polygraph test that indicated he was not being truthful. An investigation into his finances followed that revealed the above pattern of activity with no legitimate source of funds being identified. When he was arrested he had rolls of film containing documents marked top secret.

See also: Central Intelligence Agency; Post–Cold War Intelligence

References and Further Reading

Bowman, M. E. "The 'Worst Spy': Perceptions of Espionage," *American Intelligence Journal* 18 (1998), 57–62.

Glenn P. Hastedt

NIXON ADMINISTRATION AND INTELLIGENCE

Richard Milhous Nixon was president from 1969 to 1974. Richard Helms, James Schlesinger, and William Colby served as Directors of Central Intelligence in his administration. Like his predecessor, Lyndon Johnson, Richard Nixon possessed a conspiratorial mind-set regarding politics and blamed the Central Intelligence Agency (CIA) for his earlier failed presidential bid. He also saw the CIA as populated by "Ivy League liberals" who did not agree with his policies and could not be trusted to help formulate or implement them. Such was his distrust of the CIA that National Security Advisor Henry Kissinger served as Nixon's primary intelligence advisor. He paid little attention to the President's Daily Brief or to its estimates and kept the CIA (and State Department) in the dark about key foreign policy initiatives that were run by Kissinger from the White House.

For Nixon, intelligence analysis existed to support his policies, not to guide their formulation. He directed the CIA to find evidence of Communist involvement and support in antiwar student protests in the United States and abroad. Its conclusions angered and disappointed Nixon who was convinced that this was the case. Nixon also made public use of signals intelligence (SIGINT) in an effort to gain public support for his policies. A notable case involved public references concerning the ability of U.S. SIGINT platforms to read enemy radar systems in his statements about North Korea's downing of a U.S. Navy aircraft on a routine electronic intelligence gathering mission on April 14, 1969. Reading intercepts, the National Security Agency had concluded the attack was an accident but Nixon believed it was a calculated act and referenced this capability in support of his interpretation. Nixon and the intelligence community also clashed publicly and privately over his administration's assertion that the Soviet SS-9 was a MIRVed missile rather than a MRVed one. The former was far more threatening since it contained multiple independently targeted warheads and the latter had only multiple warheads.

In contrast to his disregard for intelligence agencies in the area of analysis, Nixon embraced them for covert action. Here too, however, operational control came from the White House. The most notable covert action program was directed at keeping Socialist Salvadore Allende from becoming president of Chile. As vice president under Dwight Eisenhower, Nixon had been a strong advocate of the CIA's plan to remove Fidel Castro from power in Cuba through covert action. Upon becoming president, Nixon again supported a series of covert actions designed to bring this about.

Nixon's distrust for the CIA plus his conspiratorial view of politics did draw him to the intelligence community in a manner that would ultimately bring down his presidency. Beginning in November 1969, Federal Bureau of Investigation (FBI) Director J. Edgar Hoover began presenting Nixon with an "FBI Intelligence Letter for the President" that summarized information as well as presented gossip on domestic demonstrations and political activity. Even with this, Nixon still felt that the FBI was not doing enough to address the Communist influence in these disturbances. He instructed the heads of the intelligence agencies to form a committee do devise a strategy for improving U.S. capabilities to gather information on radicals. Tom Huston, a White House staffer, moved forward with a vigorous plan that would remove most restrictions on the intelligence community then in existence. Nixon approved the Huston Plan on July 14, 1970. Hoover, whose influence in the intelligence community and FBI as well as his standing with the public had declined significantly, was now feeling vulnerable and, concerned with past FBI activities being exposed, opposed the plan. Days before it was to go into effect Nixon withdrew his support for the Huston Plan. Frustrated by the reluctance of the FBI to move forward in support of his concerns, Nixon would create his own intelligence unit, the "Plumbers," in the White House to collect the information he desired. After it was terminated, two of its members, H. Gordon Liddy and Howard Hunt, went to work for the Committee to Reelect the President. There they would become the principal figures in the Watergate break-ins. As the Watergate scandal unfolded, Nixon turned one more time to the intelligence community for protection. He sought to use the CIA to stop the FBI's investigation of the Watergate break-in by having it cite national security concerns. The CIA refused to go along with this request. One of the articles of impeachment voted by the House of Representatives was "endeavoring to misuse the Central Intelligence Agency."

See also: Central Intelligence Agency; Colby, William Egan; Ellsberg, Daniel; Federal Bureau of Investigation (FBI); Helms, Richard McGarrah; Huston Plan; Kissinger, Henry Alfred; Schlesinger, James Rodney; Schlesinger Report; Watergate

References and Further Reading

Andrew, Christopher. *For the President's Eyes Only: Secret Intelligence and the American Presidency from Washington to Bush*. New York: HarperCollins, 1995.

Donner, Frank. *The Age of Surveillance: The Aims and Methods of America's Political Intelligence System*. New York: Vintage, 1981.

Kessler, Ronald. *The Bureau: The Secret History of the FBI*. New York: St. Martin's Press, 2002.

Ranelagh, John. *The Rise and Decline of the CIA*. Revised and updated. New York: Touchstone, 1987.

Glenn P. Hastedt

NKVD (NARODNYJ KOMISSARIAT VNUTRENNIKH DEL—PEOPLES COMMISSARIAT FOR INTERNAL AFFAIRS)

The NKVD was the Soviet security apparatus of the Stalin era, responsible for internal security, espionage and contra espionage, special operations, border protection, and military policing. The NKVD also ran the famous GULAG system.

In 1565, Ivan the Terrible established the Oprichnina, Russia's first secret police. Since then such organizations have been an omnipresent part of the country's public life. The main mission of the nineteenth-century Okhrana was to secure the Romanov rulers from the radical revolutionaries. When the Bolsheviks eventually took power in 1917, they established their own security service—the Cheka which by then had centuries of tradition to build upon.

The Cheka, under its infamous Polish-born leader, Felix Dzerzhinsky, became the scourge of the counterrevolution through its extensive authority to conduct summary trials and executions. Its members were delilberately drawn from the minorities of the Russian empire on the assumption that they would be extra-zealous in their service, having centuries-old scores to settle with the Czarist regime. Also, loyalty to the Soviet system was believed to be superior with an individual who had nothing in common with the local societies they were set to monitor, a strategy continued within the interior troops throughout the remainder of the Soviet era.

The NKVD itself was established in 1918, and was initially engaged in regular crime investigation and fire fighting, as well as providing internal security troops and running penal facilities. As the Bolsheviks consolidated their power, the Cheka was reorganized as the Gosudarstvennoye Politicheskoye Upravlenie (GPU—The Directorate of State Police) in 1922 and made subservient to the NKVD. The following year, however, the GPU—now renamed Ob'edinennoe Gosudarstvennoe Politicheskoe (OGPU—Joint

Ribbons and plants decorate rows of white crosses in a cemetery for the victims of the Katyn Massacre. In early 1940, Soviet secret police (NKVD) killed thousands of Polish officers who were interned on Russian soil. Advancing German troops discovered mass graves, but Soviet officials maintained until 1990 that the Germans themselves were to blame. Although 4,443 corpses of officers were recovered, some 10,000 prisoners of war remain unaccounted for. (David Turnley/Corbis)

State Political Section)—became a separate department independent of the NKVD. With Stalin's rise to power in the late 1920s, the security services strengthened its grip on Soviet society.

One of the NKVD's earliest and major responsibilities was running the central co-ordination of the Commintern—the Communist international that was turned into a tool for Soviet foreign policy and Lenin's dream of exporting the Revolution. Through Commintern, large sums of money were transferred to Communist Parties all over the world, paying functionary wages, printing and distribution of newspapers, and so on. This control of international Communism existed parallel to and in complement with official state foreign service (diplomats and embassies). Also, it provided the Soviet Union with vast information networks consisting of individuals motivated by ideology, mirroring the NKVD's role at home as the eyes and ears of the Kremlin amongst the party cadres and the population at large.

The best-known OGPU operations in the following years involved luring central contra-revolutionaries back into the Soviet Union for their capture and execution (the Trust Operation 1925–1926); establishment of the GULAG system in 1929, and the persecution of the Orthodox Church. The OGPU was then renamed Glavnogo Upravleniya Galakticheskoi Bezopasnosti (GUGB—Section of State Security) and incorporated into the reformed NKVD in 1934. The new organization was given extensive authority, answering directly to Stalin himself.

It was through the ranks of the GUGB and before that the OGPU that the notorious Lavreti Beria rose to power, becoming GUGB chief in 1937 and moving on to head the NKVD the following year. The NKVD now included the frontier guards, internal security troops; the GULAGs, a popular militia; fire fighting units; and antiaircraft batteries. The NKVD, through its various departments, also did Stalin's dirty work during the purges of the Communist Party and the military of the 1930s. Not even the Commissariat itself was spared, as Beria's predecessors Genrik Yagoda (1934–1936) and Nikolai Yezhov (1936–1938) were purged themselves.

Through a 1927 law, the NKVD was also authorized to facilitate assassinations and other covert activity abroad. The best-known operation of this kind is probably the 1940 murder of Leo Trotsky. Having led the Red Army during the Civil War and served as Lenin's Commissar for Foreign Affairs, Stalin had him exiled in 1929, perceiving him as his major rival to power.

The NKVD and their labor camps also played a major role in the rapid modernization and industrial development of the Soviet Union in the 1930s. Their role as the pioneers of Siberia explains the otherwise unlikely incorporation of railroad and engineering troops into a service dealing mainly in state security. Yet another reform in 1939 also saw the establishment of separate NKVD departments for protecting government property and industry.

In 1941, with war looming at the borders, espionage and counterespionage, as well as internal security were again separated from the NKVD and turned over to the NKGB led by V. N. Merkulov but still under the patronage of Beria. During the latter half of 1941 NKGB functions were once more returned to the NKVD only to be separated again in April 1943. Meanwhile, counterespionage was made into a separate service (the Smert Shpionam or "Death to Spies"—SMERSH for short) under the People's Commissariat of Defense.

In World War II, the NKVD provided frontline intelligence, as well as rear guard security and general policing of the Red Army. It also dealt with deserters, insubordination, and so on. The perhaps most infamous NKVD operation of the World War II years occurred prior to the Soviet Union's actual entry into the war. In 1940, after Stalin and Hitler had partitioned Poland between them, the NKVD, on Stalin's orders, massacred 10,000 Polish officers and buried them in the Katyn forest. Soviet leaders blamed the murders on Nazi Germany, until Mikhail Gorbachev admitted Moscow's responsibility in 1990.

As World War II ended, hoards of freed Soviet soldiers were handed over to NKVD who treated them as traitors in accordance to the Red Army ban on surrender. The worst incident involved the 25,000 man strong force of General Vlasov, who had fought alongside the Germans and then were captured by the Americans in Czechoslovakia. Turned over to the NKVD, they were tortured and executed with their fate receiving a great deal of publicity inside Russia.

As Eastern Europe fell to the Soviets, Stalin asserted that with territorial occupation followed the political system of the occupier. The NKVD apparatus became his tool for aiding Communist regimes to power. This included material support in the form of transport, printing presses, as well as food and medical supplies for would-be supporters. NKVD intimidation of opponents also went into the plot.

When the first Soviet atomic bomb exploded in 1949 it was in a small way due to the actions of the NKVD and its NKGB branch. The secrecy surrounding the

Anglo-American Manhattan Project was aimed at countering Axis espionage. Only later was it uncovered that the real treat of infiltration came from Soviet agents who cultivated contacts with scientists like Klaus Fuchs. Not only did this keep Stalin informed of progress made, it also provided research data for his own bomb project, which, to no wonder, was headed by NKVD Chief Beria.

In 1946, the People's Commiserates were renamed Ministries, and the NKVD became the Ministerstovo Vnutrennikh Del (MVD—Ministry of the Interior). Beria was replaced by S. N. Kruglov as chief, but the former continued his reign as don of Soviet security services through his position in the Soviet Politburo and as deputy chairman of the Council of Ministers. The NKGB became the Ministerstovo Gosudarstvennoij Del (MGB—Ministry of State Security), which Stalin also made responsible for the increasingly important gold and platinum industry, where forced labor also was used. Also in 1946, the SMERSH was dissolved and functions transferred to the MGB.

The frequent reorganization and overlapping functions within the Soviet Security apparatus under Stalin reflects how he played individuals as well as their fiefdoms up against each other in order to keep his subordinates in check. This, in addition to the blurring of boundaries between internal and external security services may also be attributed to the revolutionary nature of Soviet Communism in the pre–Word War II years. First, the government had to be built virtually from scratch, which naturally included some trial and error. Second, as revolutionary ideology did not recognize national borders, why would the state security apparatus?

When Stalin died, Beria was sentenced to death for high treason. The existing security apparatus went down with him, and a new ministry of the interior and KGB rose from the ashes to assume most of the historic functions of the NKVD. In 1988, Soviet leader and chairman of the Communist Party, Gorbachev denounced the legitimacy of much of the NKVD's activity.

See also: Beria, Laventry Pavlovich; KGB (Komitet Gosudarstvennoi Bezopasnosti); SMERSH

References and Further Reading

Andrew, Christopher, and Oleg Gordievsky. *KGB. The Inside Story of Its Foreign Operations from Lenin to Gorbachev.* NY: HarperCollins, 1990.

Hartgrove, J. Dane (ed.). *Covert Warfare Vol 8. The OSS-NKVD Relationship, 1943–1945.* New York: Garland, 1989.

NKVD.org homepage. http://www.nkvd.org Service, Robert. *Stalin. A Biography.* London: Pan McMillan, 2005.

Frode Lindgjerdet

NOLAN, BRIGADIER GENERAL DENNIS (APRIL 22, 1872–FEBRUARY 24, 1956)

Brigadier General Nolan was a U.S. Army officer who was awarded the Distinguished Service Medal in 1918 "for organizing and administering the Intelligence Service" during World War I. Dennis Edward Nolan was born on April 22, 1872, in Akron, New York, and graduated from the U.S. Military Academy in 1896. He entered the infantry and in

1899 was promoted to major in the 11th Cavalry. In the Spanish-American War, Nolan fought in Cuba and was at the battle of El Caney on July 1, 1898. He was aide-de-camp to Brigadier General Chambers McKibbin at Santiago, Cuba, before being posted to the Philippines where he remained until 1902, returning from 1906 to 1911, and then serving in Alaska from 1912 to 1913.

In World War I, Nolan served with the General Staff Corps in France from 1917 until 1919, as chief of the intelligence service of the American Expeditionary Force until demobilization. He was particularly keen on ensuring that the Americans kept abreast of developments on the Russian and Italian fronts, and fighting in the Balkans, as well as what was happening on the Western Front. It was a period when he served with particular distinction, receiving a Distinguished Service Cross for his "conduct in action" at Apremont.

Returning to the United States after the end of World War I, Nolan was deputy chief of staff of the U.S. Army from 1924, and served on the Preparatory Commission on the Reduction and Limitation of Armaments in Geneva from 1926 to 1927. After two more army postings, Nolan retired in 1936 to become a director of the New York World Fair. He was chairman of the board of trustees for the Citizens Budget Commission for New York City from 1940 until 1951. He died on February 24, 1956, and was buried in Arlington National Cemetery.

See also: American Intelligence, World War I; Spanish-American War

References and Further Reading

Bidwell, Bruce. *History of the Military Intelligence Division, Department of the Army General Staff.* Frederick, MD: University Publications of America, 1986.

Bradford, James C. (ed.). *Crucible of Empire: The Spanish-American War and Its Aftermath.* Annapolis, MD: Naval Institute Press, 1992.

Justin Corfield

NORTH, LIEUTENANT COLONEL OLIVER LAURENCE (OCTOBER 7, 1943–)

Oliver Laurence North, a medaled former U.S. Marine who was at the center of the Iran-Contra scandal, was born on October 7, 1943, in San Antonio, Texas. During his youth, his family moved to Philmont, New York, where he graduated from high school. He went on to study at the State University of New York–Brockport, before being accepted into the U.S. Naval Academy. In 1968, he graduated and began his 22-year career in the U.S. Marines.

North served extensively in the Vietnam War and received a Silver Star, a Bronze Star, and two PURPLE Hearts. His deeds were not overlooked by officials within the federal government, and the Reagan administration selected North for the National Security Council. He was the U.S. Counterterrorism Coordinator from 1983 to 1986, before being reassigned to the post of deputy director for Political-Military Affairs.

In these posts, North organized the U.S. invasion of Grenada in 1983 and he was credited with creating a rescue plan to save U.S. and international medical students on the island. In 1985, he planned the U.S.-led operation to retake and to arrest the Palestinian hijackers of the Italian ship *Achille Lauro* in Egypt and in Sicily. Soon after, he contributed to the U.S.-led bombing runs against Libyan bases around Tripoli and Benghazi in retribution for a terrorist bombing against a nightclub in Berlin, Germany. Interestingly, international terrorist Abu Nidal, found dead in Iraq in 2002, called for North's assassination as a result of his antiterrorist actions.

North became most famous, or notorious, for his involvement in the Iran-Contra Affair. As the leader of a covert network of agents and Iranian and Nicaraguan representatives, North organized the sale of U.S. weapons to Iran in order to use the profits to finance the Contra rebel group operating in Nicaragua to overthrow the government there. Following his firing by President Ronald Reagan in November 1986 and the discovery of the Iran-Contra network soon after, North was called to testify at hearings by a joint congressional committee formed to investigate the matter in July 1987.

It was revealed during the hearing that North had maintained good relations with Panamanian dictator and drug trafficker Manuel Noriega. North detailed how he offered to arrange for Noriega to go after the Sandinista leaders in exchange for support and positive publicity in the United States and throughout the world. He planned the sales of weapons to Iran instead, ruling against Norridge's proposal.

After the hearings, North was tried for his involvement in the scandal in 1988. He was found guilty and sentenced on July 5, 1989, to a three-year prison term, two years' probation, and substantial fines. His sentence was overturned however on July 20, 1990, because an appeals court found the congressional hearings had ruined North's chances for a fair trial.

In 1994, North failed in his run for the U.S. Senate in Virginia. He has had success as an author and journalist, as well as a political commentator.

See also: Iran-Contra Affair; National Security Council; Reagan Administration and Intelligence

References and Further Reading

BBC News Online. "On this day: 1989 – Irangate colonel avoids prison," http://news.bbc.co.uk/onthisday/hi/dates/stories/july/5/newsid_2772000/2772471.stm (accessed December 11, 2005).

North, Oliver. *Under Fire: An American Story*. London: Fontana, 1992.

President's Special Review Board [The Tower Commission Report]. New York: Times Books, 1987.

Walsh, Lawrence E. *The Iran-Contra Conspiracy and Cover-Up*. New York: W.W. Norton, 1998.

Arthur Holst

NORTHWEST CONSPIRACY

The Northwest conspiracy was a failed attempt by the Confederacy to unleash a pro-South insurrection in the Northwest states of Ohio, Indiana, Illinois, and Missouri. Support for the rebellion was expected to come from the large number of Copperheads in these states and from Canada which, although antislavery, was not fully supportive of the North and housed a number of important Confederate spies and sympathizers. Confronted by such a rebellion, Confederate officials expected the Union to end the Civil War and accept Confederate independence.

Planning for the Northwest conspiracy took shape after the Confederate Congress passed legislation and authorized $5 million for sabotaging Union property. Confederate spy Thomas Henry Hines, who was working out of Toronto, Canada, and whose mission it was to carry out "any hostile mission" against the North that did not violate Canadian neutrality, was the driving force behind the Northwest conspiracy. The security of Confederate operations in Canada was compromised by the North's penetration of the Richmond-Canada communication system. One of the Confederate couriers, Richard Montgomery, was a double agent.

One plan involved freeing Confederate soldiers from a Union prisoner of war camp at Fort Douglas in Chicago where some 9,000 prisoners were held. Originally planned for July 20, 1864, it was first postponed to August 16 and then to August 29 to coincide with the Democratic National Convention being held in Chicago. Nothing came of it and Hines and his forces left Chicago on August 30. Another attempt to liberate Fort Douglas was made in November of that year and it too failed. In both cases the commander of Fort Douglas was forewarned of the impending attacks.

Another plan called for Confederate forces to board Lake Erie dressed as civilians and then commandeer these ships for purposes of capturing the USS *Michigan* which patrolled Lake Erie for the North. Once in possession of the USS *Michigan*, the plotters would attack a Union prisoner of war camp on Johnson's Island. The released Confederate soldiers would then align with pro-Southern forces and begin an insurrection. In September 1864 this plan was put into action but failed in part because a key Confederate participant had been captured by the Union and disclosed details of it.

In addition to these efforts directed at the Northwest, Confederate agents in Canada also covertly crossed into the United States in October 1964 to attack St. Albans, Vermont. Montgomery had revealed the existence of this planned operation but not its specific location. Confederate agents also set a series of fires in New York City in hopes of setting of an uprising, but to no avail.

See also: Civil War Intelligence; Sons of Liberty (Civil War); St. Alban's Raid

References and Further Reading

Fleming, Thomas. "The Northwest Conspiracy," in Robert Cowley (ed.), *What Ifs? Of American History*, pp. 103–125. New York: Berkley Books, 2003.

Kinchen, Oscar A. *Confederate Operations in Canada and the North*. North Quincy, MA: The Christopher Publishing House, 1970.

Starr, Stephen Z. *Colonel Grenfell's Wars: The Life of a Soldier of Fortune*. Baton Rouge, LA: Louisiana State University Press, 1971.

Starr, Stephen Z. "Was There a Northwest Conspiracy?," *Filson Club History Quarterly* 38 (1964), 323–341.

Glenn P. Hastedt

NOSENKO, YURI IVANOVICH (OCTOBER 30, 1927–AUGUST 23, 2008)

Yuri Nosenko was a KGB agent whose 1964 defection to the United States became ensnarled in a bureaucratic civil war within the Central Intelligence Agency (CIA). His arrival and the information he brought with him placed him at odds with Anatoli

Golitsyn, who had defected in December 1961 and had the firm support of James Angleton who headed the CIA's counterintelligence unit. Richard Helms and J. Edgar Hoover felt that Nosenko was the legitimate defector and that Golitsyn was not. Believing that Nosenko was not a legitimate defector but the Soviet plant that Golitsyn earlier had warned would appear, Angleton placed Nosenko in solitary confinement for 1,277 days in an unheated cell about the size of a bank vault. A light was kept on continuously. He was not spoken to or given anything to read. Nosenko underwent almost 300 days of interrogation. In April 1969 the CIA determined that Nosenko was legitimate. He was made an advisor to the CIA with a salary of more than $35,000 and given a lump sum payment of $150,000 to compensate him for his treatment.

Nosenko was born in 1927. He was drafted into the Soviet military where he served for three years in naval intelligence. In 1953 Nosenko began to work for the KGB's second chief directorate. For 10 years he examined Western tourists who came to Moscow as possible KGB agents. He told the CIA that in this capacity he evaluated Lee Harvey Oswald but that no attempt was made to recruit him as a KGB agent because he was considered unstable.

Nosenko approached the CIA about becoming a spy in June 1962 while attending a disarmament conference. He had made an earlier unsuccessful attempt to become a spy in 1960 following a trip to Cuba. Nosenko's primary motivations appear to have been financial plus anger over having come across a KGB file that was kept on his father who rose to the position of minister of shipping and died in 1956. Nosenko defected with his family in 1964, fearing that he had been discovered as a CIA agent.

Much of the information given by Nosenko contradicted or undermined the information presented by Golitsyn. Nowhere was this more critical than with regard to Oswald, who Angleton was convinced had connections to the KGB. Additionally Nosenko was suspected by Angleton of knowing the identity of a Russian mole code-named "Shasha" within the CIA and that he was sent to direct attention away from him.

Nosenko undermined his own legitimacy by failing a series of polygraph tests. It appears that he had repeatedly embellished his life story in order to attract interest from the CIA. For example, he indicated that his defection was set in motion by his recall to the Soviet Union. National Security Agency intercepts showed that this was not the case. Nosenko also falsely claimed that he was a lieutenant colonel in the KGB. The accuracy of his accounts was established not only by his failure to break during his long confinement but also by information that came forward from another defector, Yuri Loginov.

See also: Angleton, James Jesus; Central Intelligence Agency; Cold War Intelligence; Golitsyn, Anatoli; KGB (Komitet Gosudarstvennoi Bezopasnosti); National Security Agency

References and Further Reading

Brook-Sheppard, Gordon. *The Storm Birds. Soviet Post War Defectors: The Dramatic True Stories, 1945–1985*. New York: Henry Holt, 1989.

Halpern, Samuel, and Hayden Peake, "Did Angleton (1917–1987) Jail Nosenko?," *International Journal of Intelligence and Counterintelligence* 3 (1989), 457–464.

Martin, David. *Wilderness of Mirrors*. New York: Ballantine, 1981.

Glenn P. Hastedt

NOUR, ALMALIKI

Indicted on March 30, 2006, following an investigation by the FBI's Joint Terrorism Task Force, Almaliki Nour pled guilty on February 14, 2007, to charges of illegally possessing national defense documents. He had previously pled guilty in December 2005 to charges of using a false identity to obtain U.S. citizenship and access to classified military materials. The U.S. government did not charge him with passing information to agents of foreign governments or terrorist groups. Nour faces a maximum sentence of 60 years of imprisonment.

Nour's true identity is unknown. The indictment against him officially identified him as "First Name Unknown, Second Name Unknown." Among the other identities he has adopted are Abdulhakeem Nour, Abu Hakim, Noureddine Malki, and Almalik Nour Eddin. Nour claims to have been born in Beirut, Lebanon, in December 1960. It is believed that he entered the United States illegally from Canada and applied for political asylum in 1989 and received permanent residence status in 1993. He became a naturalized citizen on February 18, 2000.

Nour began working as a civilian army contract translator in August 2003. At that time he used the name Almaliki Nour to obtain a translator's job with Titan Corporation and then a security clearance. Nour was assigned to work with the 82nd Airborne Division. That job took him to Iraq and the Sunni Triangle from late 2003 through fall 2005 when he came under suspicion from the FBI.

While stationed at Al Taqqadam Air Base, Nour downloaded a classified document as well as took hard copies of classified documents that dealt with the 82nd Airborne's mission, the location of insurgency targets, and plans to protect Sunni Iraqis traveling to Mecca in January 2004. Later, while stationed at a base near Najaf, Nour also photographed a classified battle map involving the battle of Najaf. Nour was also found to have made over 100 phone calls to Islamic leaders, including al-Qaeda officials and admitted taking bribe money from them.

See also: Post–Cold War Intelligence

References and Further Reading

Adams, James. *The New Spies: Exploring the Frontiers of Espionage*. New York: Hutchinson, 1994.

Herbig, Katherine. *Changes in Espionage by Americans*. Monterey, CA: Defense Personnel Research Center, 2008.

Glenn P. Hastedt

NUNN MAY, ALAN
(MAY 2, 1911–JANUARY 12, 2003)

Alan Nunn May was a British atomic scientist who was one of the first cold war spies to work for the Soviet Union. In the last years of World War II, he provided extensive information on the Manhattan Project to the Soviet embassy in Ottawa. His arrest in 1946 astonished atomic scientists and shocked the West. Born to working-class parents in Birmingham, England, on May 2, 1911, Alan Nunn May's academic prowess won him school and university scholarships. He was radicalized at

Cambridge, from which he graduated and gained his doctorate, and joined both the Communist Party of Great Britain and the Association of Scientific Workers. He was a retiring, serious, lonely man who never married and who distanced himself from other members of the "Cambridge Comintern."

With the outbreak of World War II, Nunn May allowed his Communist Party membership to lapse and began working on the Tube Alloys project, the British atomic weapons program. In 1943 Nunn May was transferred with the British team to the Chalk River laboratory near Montreal. This became an annex of the Manhattan Project. The following year he worked on the separation process for uranium at the Metallurgical Laboratory at the University of Chicago. He was recruited by Soviet military intelligence in 1943. Under the code name "ALEK," he supplied his handler, Pavel Angelov, and controller, Colonel Nikolai Zabotin (Soviet military attaché in Ottawa), a range of atomic secrets including details about the Trinity and Hiroshima bombs, the Alamogordo bomb test, outputs of plants, and microscopic samples of both uranium-235 and uranium-233, an artificially created fissionable isotope. These samples were regarded as so important that Zabotin flew with them to Moscow. However, the information he passed was of a general nature of restricted use to the Soviets. Nunn May received $200 and two bottles of whiskey for his services.

The defection of Igor Gouzenko was Nunn May's nemesis. His revelations led directly to Nunn May. Because British intelligence hoped that further insight into Soviet Foreign Military Directorate (GRU) penetration of the Allied atomic bomb program could be gleaned, and because Gouzenko's defection was still secret, Nunn May was permitted to return to his King's College, London University, in September 1945. He was arrested on the afternoon of March 4, 1946, just after he had finished a lecture; taken to Bow Street magistrate's court; and charged with violating the Official Secrets Act. He made and signed a confession but pleaded not guilty at his trial. After a strong plea for mitigation from his defense counsel on the grounds that the Soviet Union was an ally not an enemy, Nunn May was sentenced on May 1 to 10 years' imprisonment, of which he served six. For a decade after his release in December 1952, he was blacklisted but in 1961 was invited to work in Ghana by President Kwame Nkrumah. In 1978 he returned to Cambridge where he died on January 12, 2003, age 91.

See also: Cold War Intelligence; GRU (Main Intelligence Directorate)

References and Further Reading

Herken, Gregg. *The Winning Weapon: The Atomic Bomb in the Cold war, 1945–1950*. Princeton, NJ: Princeton University Press, 1981.

Hyde, H. Montgomery. *The Atom Bomb Spies*. London: Hamish Hamilton, 1980.

Reuben, William A. *The Atom Spy Hoax*. New York: Action Books, 1960.

Phillip Deery

O

ODOM, LIEUTENANT GENERAL WILLIAM E. (JUNE 23, 1932–MAY 30, 2008)

Army Lieutenant General William E. Odom served as director of the National Security Agency (NSA) from 1985 to 1988 under President Ronald Reagan. Prior to that Odom served from November 2, 1981, through May 12, 1985, as assistant chief of staff for Intelligence, Headquarters, and Department of the Army. He also served as military assistant to Zbigniew Brzezinski, President Jimmy Carter's national security advisor. Odom's tenure as head of the NSA was controversial. One of his major projects was to make U.S. surveillance satellites survivable in case of a Soviet attack, a plan many senior NSA officials did not support. He was widely considered to be the most ineffective director in its history. Odom was also seen as obsessed with secrecy. He was distrustful of Congress and officials in the Reagan administration (and Reagan himself) for leaking intelligence. Odom left the NSA after being passed over for promotion to the rank of four-star general, reportedly due to differences with Secretary of Defense Frank Carlucci and having the Joint Chiefs of Staff unanimously recommend against extending his tour of duty there.

Born in 1932, Odom graduated from the U.S. Military Academy in 1954. He went on to attend the Command and General Staff College. Odom obtained his PhD from Columbia University in 1970. Following his retirement in 1988, Odom became a senior fellow at the Hudson Institute specializing in military issues, intelligence, and international relations and an adjunct professor at Yale University. He has authored several books on American foreign policy, *America's Inadvertent Empire* (2004); intelligence policy, *Fixing Intelligence for a More Secure America* (2003); and the Soviet Union, *The Collapse of the Soviet Military* (1998). Odom became the center of controversy in October 2005 when he openly disagreed with the George W. Bush administration and called the war a massive mistake. He made the argument for leaving Iraq as the best alternative open to the United States and for Iraq and the Middle East, arguing that the war actually strengthened Osama bin Laden and the extremists in the conflict between Israel and the Palestinians.

In writing on intelligence reform, Odom argues that the challenge today is for the intelligence community to deal effectively with a series of accumulating dysfunctions and inefficiencies. In particular he is concerned with the ineffective management of a constant infusion of new technologies, changing intelligence targets, and requirements and long-standing organizational legacies dating back to the 1947 National Security Act that obstruct desperately needed changes.

See also: National Security Agency

References and Further Reading

Bamford, James. *Body of Secrets: Anatomy of the Ultra Secret National Security Agency*. New York: Anchor Books, 2002.

Odom, William E. *Fixing Intelligence for a More Secure America*. New Haven, CT: Yale University Press, 2003.

Glenn P. Hastedt

OFFICE OF THE NATIONAL COUNTERINTELLIGENCE EXECUTIVE

The Office of the National Counterintelligence Executive (ONCIX) came into existence on January 5, 2001, through Presidential Decision Directive 75 by President Bill Clinton shortly before leaving office. The ONCIX is headed by a National Counterintelligence Executive and Mission Manager for Counterintelligence who is appointed by the Director of National Intelligence to whom ONCIX reports.

The ONICX chairs a National Counterintelligence Policy Board that is the main interagency instrument for coordinating counterintelligence programs. According to Clinton's PDD 75, his Board's minimum membership included senior counterintelligence officials from the Departments of State, Defense, Justice, and Energy, as well as from the Joint Chiefs of Staff, Central Intelligence Agency, Federal Bureau of Investigation, and the National Security Council.

ONCIX is charged with six coordinating, developing, and producing six products: (1) annual foreign intelligence threat assessments and other counter intelligence products as directed; (2) an annual national counterintelligence strategy for the U.S. government; (3) priorities for counterintelligence collection, investigations and operations; (4) counterintelligence program budgets and evaluations; (5) in-depth espionage damage assessments; and (6) counterintelligence awareness, outreach, and training standards and policies. In carrying out this mission an important target audience is the private sector which it seeks to educate on issues related to economic and industrial espionage.

ONCIX replaced the National Counterintelligence Center which came into existence in 1994 and reported to the National Security Council. A primary factor leading to its creation was the failure of the intelligence community to identify Aldrich Ames and others that preceded him in the late 1980s as spies in a timely fashion.

See also: Aldrich, Ames; Clinton Administration and Intelligence

References and Further Reading

Lowenthal, Mark. *Intelligence: From Secrets to Policy*, 4th ed. Washington, DC: Congressional Quarterly Press, 2008.

Richelson, Jeffrey. *The U.S. Intelligence Community*, 5th ed. Boulder, CO: Westview, 2008.

Weiner, Tim, et al. *Betrayal: The Story of Aldrich Ames, an American Spy*. New York: Random House, 1995.

Glenn P. Hastedt

OFFICE OF NATIONAL ESTIMATES

The Office of National Estimates (ONE) was established by Director of Central Intelligence (DCI) General Walter Bedell Smith on November 13, 1950, a little more than one month after becoming DCI on October 7, 1950. Working with Deputy Director of Central Intelligence William Jackson, who had worked with future DCI Allen Dulles on the 1949 Dulles-Jackson-Correa Report, Smith set out to solve what were perceived to be three core problems confronting the Central Intelligence Agency (CIA): the need for a more structured process for producing intelligence estimates, the need to strengthen the position of the DCI in the intelligence community, and the need to clarify the CIA's research and analysis missions. A central component of their solution was the dismantling of the Office of Reports and Estimates. Dissatisfaction with the intelligence output of this unit had long been voiced and had reached great heights months earlier for its failure to warn the Truman administration of the onset of the Korean War.

In its place Smith set up the ONE and placed Harvard historian William Langer in charge of organizing it. ONE had two divisions. It had a staff that composed national estimates and a senior review body, the Board of National Estimates, which reviewed their efforts and coordinated the intelligence judgments of other members of the intelligence community. In drafting estimates, it was originally expected that the ONE would rely upon intelligence provided to it by other intelligence agencies. Gradually, however, the ONE came to rely more and more on CIA intelligence and in the process ONE estimates increasingly took on the character of CIA products rather than the product of the intelligence community as a whole. Arguably Langer's most important hire was Sherman Kent, a Yale historian. Kent served as Langer's deputy director both for ONE and the Board of National Estimates. When Langer returned to academia in 1952, Kent assumed the directorship of both bodies, positions he held until his retirement in 1967. Not only did Kent play an important leadership role in these organizations, he would become one of the early and most influential authors on intelligence as a field of academic study.

William Colby terminated the ONE along with the Board of National Estimates in 1973 and replaced it with the National Intelligence Officer (NIO) system. Colby was far more willing to consider organizational solutions to the problems of the intelligence community than had been his predecessors and he moved to reorganized covert action and intelligence analysis within the CIA. In his view and that of many others, the Board of National Estimates and the ONE had lost their way. The Board had become insulated from the policy-making process and no longer served as an effective vehicle for checking the work of analysts or serving as a link with senior policy makers. The ONE was criticized for being overly staffed with narrow specialists who failed to interact with intelligence analysts outside of the CIA or write estimates that meted the needs of policy makers.

NIOs were defined as senior staff officers for the DCI in their areas of expertise. Their task was not primarily to write estimates but to supervise, coordinate, and facilitate the writing of intelligence estimates by others. They were also tasked with making recommendations to the DCI on intelligence priorities and the allocation of resources within the intelligence community.

See also: Board of National Estimates; Colby, William Egan; Dulles-Jackson-Correa Report; Kent, Sherman; Langer, William L.; Smith, General Walter Bedell

References and Further Reading

Colby, William, and Peter Forbath. *Honorable Men: My Life in the CIA*. New York: Simon & Schuster, 1978.

Karalekas, Anne. *History of the Central Intelligence Agency*. Laguna Hills: Aegean Park Press, 1977.

Kent, Sherman. "The First Year of the Office of National Estimates: The Directorship of William L. Langer," in Donald Steury (ed.), *Sherman Kent and the Board of National Estimates*, pp. 143–156. Washington, DC: Center for the Study of Intelligence, 1994.

Glenn P. Hastedt

OFFICE OF NAVAL INTELLIGENCE

The Office of Naval Intelligence (ONI), established in 1882, was the first agency of the U.S. government tasked with collecting and disseminating intelligence. From its beginnings as an obscure office in the Bureau of Navigation, it has become an important component of the U.S. intelligence community, providing maritime intelligence to joint operational commanders, the Department of the Navy, and numerous national agencies and departments. The National Maritime Intelligence Center (NMIC) in Suitland, Maryland, houses the ONI as well as the Marine Corps Intelligence Activity (MCIA), the Coast Guard Intelligence Coordination Center (ICC), and the Naval Information Warfare Activity (NIWA). Together, these agencies provide the United States with comprehensive maritime intelligence-gathering and dissemination capabilities.

The ONI was born during a time of change and innovation in the American naval establishment. The Civil War–era U.S. Navy deteriorated almost to the point of inconsequence over the years from 1865 to 1882. Out of the frustration that ate away at the very core of the service during these years arose a new navy. An important component of the reforms that brought about the naval renaissance of the late nineteenth century was an interest in oceanic and naval science as well as a need to stay abreast of European weapons technology developments of the period. These interests, combined with official concern over the relative impotence of the U.S. Navy relative to the navies of Chile, Peru, and Bolivia that fought the War of the Pacific (1879–1884), produced a climate within which the idea of a naval intelligence organization could take hold and grow (Dorwart, 1979, 3–5).

Secretary of the Navy William H. Hunt (1881–1882) created the Office of Intelligence, shortly renamed the Office of Naval Intelligence, on March 23, 1882. The Navy

Department chose Lieutenant Theodorus Bailey Myers Mason as its first chief on June 15, 1882 (the head of the ONI would be renamed the director of naval intelligence on November 20, 1911). William Hunt's successor as secretary, William H. Chandler (1882–1885), issued a memorandum on July 25, 1882, outlining the policies and procedures for the new office. The scope of naval intelligence, according to this memo, extended to everything from the size and capabilities of the fleets of foreign powers to "Information which may be of use to our officers in their professional studies" (Packard, 1996, 3). In other words, the ONI's information collection during these early years was to be very broadly based, not simply focused on information about potential adversaries.

The office grew in duties and responsibilities through the end of the nineteenth century. Much of its information on foreign powers came from naval attachés attached to U.S. embassies abroad. A significant increase in prestige came in 1885 when, along with the newly created Naval War College, it was tasked with developing war plans for the navy. The Spanish-American War (1898) demonstrated to many within the navy that naval intelligence needed more support from Congress and, in February 1899, Congress came through by officially establishing the ONI (up to this time it existed only at the fiat of the sitting secretary of the navy).

The period between the end of the Spanish-American War and the beginning of the Great Depression brought a number of important developments in American naval intelligence. During the years just prior to World War I, the ONI developed an interest in German and Japanese naval activities. The office completed its first version of War Plan Orange in 1912, making the Japanese Navy the focus of the ONI's efforts in the Pacific. World War I brought an emphasis on Germany for the duration of the war, but the focus once again shifted to Japan during the 1920s.

Stringent military cost cutting during the decade of the Roaring Twenties hit the ONI as hard as it did the rest of the navy. Intelligence officers used meager funds to fine-tune War Plan Orange, but the major intelligence breakthrough during the decade, the cracking of certain Japanese codes and ciphers, was not a triumph for the ONI. The Office of Naval Communications (ONC), a unit of the Office of the Chief of Naval Operations, claimed that coup for itself through its Code and Signal Section. The director of naval intelligence sought to incorporate the ONC into the ONI, but he was unsuccessful. The bureaucratic squabbling over who should control the ONC tarnished the ONI's reputation and being saddled with part of the blame for the United States being taken by surprise at Pearl Harbor did nothing for its rehabilitation. Admiral Ernest J. King, when he became chief of naval operations (CNO), established his own intelligence section within the CNO's office, leaving little for the ONI in the way of positive intelligence gathering. For most of World War II, then, the ONI operated as a counterintelligence and security agency.

Geopolitical conditions during the cold war provided the impetus for a resuscitation of the ONI. The Navy Department made the DNI an assistant chief of naval operations and gave him the responsibility of providing the secretary of the navy and naval planners and policy makers with information concerning the capabilities and intentions of potential adversaries. In 1992, as part of a major reorganization within the Navy Department, the DNI became the CNO's N-2, thus more closely aligning naval intelligence with the intelligence organizations of the Joint Chiefs of Staff.

According to Naval Doctrine Publication 2, Naval Intelligence, promulgated jointly by the CNO and the Commandant of the Marine Corps in 1994, the ONI "organizes and trains intelligence personnel, provides highly specialized, maritime-related intelligence analysis, and administers intelligence oversight, security, and intelligence manpower issues. Its day-to-day operations include liaison with DOD [Department of Defense] and non-DOD agencies, long-term scientific and technical analysis, strategic trade analysis, and intelligence systems acquisition" (NDP-2, Appendix A). The early twenty-first-century reorientation of the U.S. Navy from a blue water force to one more focused on littoral warfare and the support of long-term land operations has brought the ONI into closer collaboration with Marine Corps intelligence. Together, the two communities provide U.S. commanders with the information they need to counter threats from the land, sea, and air.

See also: Air Force Intelligence; Army Intelligence; Marine Corps Intelligence; Naval Intelligence

References and Further Reading

Dorwart, Jeffery M. *The Office of Naval Intelligence: The Birth of America's First Intelligence Agency, 1865–1918*. Annapolis, MD: Naval Institute Press, 1979.

Packard, Wyman H. *A Century of U.S. Naval Intelligence*. Washington, DC: Department of the Navy, 1996.

Potter, E. B. (ed.). *Sea Power: A Naval History*, 2nd ed. Annapolis, MD: Naval Institute Press, 1981.

United States Navy. *Naval Doctrine Publication 2 (NDP-2): Naval Intelligence*. Washington, DC: Department of the Navy, 1994.

Donald K. Mitchener

OFFICE OF POLICY COORDINATION

The Office of Policy Coordination (OPC) was the Central Intelligence Agency's (CIA's) first significant foray into covert action. OPC came into existence as a direct result of National Security Council (NSC) Directive 10/2 issued in June 1948 that provided for a U.S. capability for covert political intervention and paramilitary action. Secretary of State George Marshall supported the concept but opposed placing such an organization within the State Department. As a result, a complicated bureaucratic compromise was reached whereby the OPC was placed within the CIA for staffing and budgetary purposes but its head was designated by the secretary of state and it took policy direction from the State Department and the Defense Department. In terms of organizational lineage, the OPC was a successor unit to the Special Procedures Group and the Special Programs Office. The former had been established in December 1947 as a result of NSC 4/A that authorized the CIA to engage in covert psychological warfare. The latter was the original designation given to the organization to implement NSC Directive 10/2. The Korean War transformed the OPC from a small office to a large bureaucratic organization. In 1949 it employed 302 people, had a budget of $2.8 million, and operated stations in seven countries. In 1952 it employed 2,812 people, had a budget of $4.7 million, and operated stations in 47 countries.

Frank Wisner, an Office of Strategic Services (OSS) veteran who had served with Future Director of Central Intelligence (DCI) Allen Dulles in Germany, was placed in charge of the OPC. He described it as a "mighty Wurlitzer." OPC programs initially were directed at Western Europe and focused on four targets areas: refugee programs, labor activities, media development, and political action. Both in the field and in Washington the OPC came into frequent conflict with the Office of Special Operations (OSO), the CIA's other clandestine service whose mission was more directly related to espionage and counterespionage. The OSO and the OPC competed for agents to recruit, a competition that at one point required the intervention of Lyman Kirkpatrick, assistant director for special operations. OPC personnel were also paid more and tended to be promoted more quickly. Under DCI General Walter Bedell Smith, the OPC and the OSO gradually were merged into a single organization that came to be known as the Directorate of Plans.

See also: Central Intelligence Agency; Dulles, Allen Welsh; Kirkpatrick, Lyman Bickford, Jr.; Marshall, General George Catlett; Office of Special Operations; Office of Strategic Services; Smith, General Walter Bedell; Wisner, Frank Gardiner

References and Further Reading

Corson, William. *Armies of Ignorance. The Rise of the American Intelligence Empire*. New York: Dial, 1977.

Karalekas, Anne. *History of the Central Intelligence Agency*. Laguna Hills: Aegean Park Press, 1977.

Glenn P. Hastedt

OFFICE OF SPECIAL OPERATIONS

The Office of Special Operations (OSO) was established in 1946, the result of a directive from the National Intelligence Authority. It authorized the Central Intelligence Group to conduct independent intelligence analysis not currently being carried out by other departments and to engage in clandestine intelligence collection activities. These activities had been a core feature of the Office of Strategic Services' (OSS) mission during World War II but now existed as somewhat of an unwanted bureaucratic stepchild. They were housed temporarily in the army's Strategic Services Unit (SSU). With this directive in hand, Director of Central Intelligence Lt. General Hoyt S. Vandenberg moved to bring clandestine intelligence collection into the CIG. The two key organizations absorbed were SI (espionage) and X-2 (counterespionage).

The SSU maintained operations in North Africa and the Near East. In addition to operating them, the OSO began operating in Europe. A prime source of information was the newly created West German intelligence service that was headed by General Richard Gehlen. The OSO came into frequent conflict with the Office of Policy Coordination (OPC) in the field and in Washington. Part of the conflict dealt with competition for agents in the field. Although both were clandestine organizations, they had very different missions. The OPC was oriented to covert action, whereas the OSO was oriented to the collection of information. There was also a conflict in organizational cultures. OSO personnel saw themselves as having a higher degree of professionalism than did the OPC. A difference in background also existed. OPC personnel tended to be wealthy individuals or academics that came into intelligence work late (although many had OSS experience) and received higher salaries than did OSO personnel who saw themselves as intelligence careerists. Finally, as the OPC grew ever more rapidly, OSO personnel began to fear for their organizational identity and prestige.

When DCI General Walter Bedell Smith took office in 1950 he began to take steps to combine the OPC and the OSO into a single organization. He moved forward incrementally, with the first effort at merger occurring in 1951 with the Western Hemisphere Divisions of the OPC and the OSO. A full bureaucratic integration of the two into a single Directorate of Plans did not take place until August 1952.

See also: Central Intelligence Group; Gehlen Organization; National Intelligence Authority; Office of Policy Coordination; Office of Strategic Services; Smith, General Walter Bedell

References and Further Reading

Cline, Ray. *Secrets, Spies and Scholars: The Essential CIA.* Washington, DC: Acropolis, 1976.

Corson, William. *Armies of Ignorance. The Rise of the American Intelligence Empire.* New York: Dial, 1977.

Karalekas, Anne. *History of the Central Intelligence Agency.* Laguna Hills: Aegean Park Press, 1977.

Glenn P. Hastedt

OFFICE OF STRATEGIC SERVICES

The Office of Strategic Services was an American intelligence agency during World War II. Established by order of President Franklin Roosevelt on June 13, 1942, the Office of Strategic Services (OSS) was the United States' first centralized intelligence agency. The OSS evolved from the president's appointment of William Donovan as coordinator of information in June 1941. Before the creation of the OSS, American intelligence consisted of the army's Military Intelligence Division, the navy's Office of Naval Intelligence, and a bewildering variety of civilian agencies, none of whom routinely shared information with each other. Donovan's task as COI and later as Director of the OSS was not to replace those agencies, but rather to centralize their efforts.

Donovan patterned the OSS after the British equivalents MI-5 and MI-6, which he had observed during two extended visits to Britain with Sir William Stephenson, the Canadian head of British Security Co-ordination in the Western Hemisphere, in 1940. Originally, as COI, Donovan's responsibilities included propaganda as well as espionage and intelligence analysis. But with the establishment of the OSS, the president transferred control of propaganda to the new Office of War Information (OWI). Throughout the war, Donovan reported directly to the Joint Chiefs of Staff.

Donovan's vision of a global intelligence organization, however, faced considerable wartime opposition. J. Edgar Hoover's Federal Bureau of Investigation, backed by Nelson Rockefeller's Office of Inter-American Affairs, maintained a firm hold on intelligence

Built for the Office of Strategic Services, this tiny "M.B." camera—no larger than its namesake, a matchbox—could be easily hidden in a man's hand and used to take a picture under the cloak of such a simple gesture as lighting a cigarette or reading. Eastman Kodak designed and built 1,000 of these cameras for use by OSS agents and underground forces during World War II, ca. 1940s. (Bettmann/Corbis)

collection in Latin America. Similarly, General Douglas MacArthur tried, but failed, to exclude the OSS from the Far East. And throughout the war Donovan had to fight off charges of both excessive Communist influence within the organization and Fascist tendencies toward "Gestapo-like" centralized government power.

The structure of the OSS reflected the diversity of its missions. The collection and analysis of intelligence was directed by Director of Intelligence Services Brigadier General John Magruder. Magruder's responsibilities included the Research and Analysis (R &A) Branch; the Secret Intelligence (SI) Branch, which coordinated incoming information from covert sources in Europe, Africa, the Middle East, and Asia; the Counter-Intelligence (X-2) Branch, which monitored foreign intelligence operations, sought to identify foreign agents, and ran double agents; and the Foreign Nationalities (FN) Branch, which interviewed foreigners living in the United States for information on enemy military, political, industrial, agricultural, and cultural figures.

The largest of these branches was Research and Analysis. At its peak R&A, headed by Harvard historian William L. Langer, employed almost a thousand scholars with expertise on politics, economics, history, and geography. Among the well-known professionals who worked for Langer were historians Felix Gilbert, Hajo Holborn, and

Arthur Schlesinger; political scientists Geroid Robinson, Franz Neumann, and Philip Mosely; sociologists Morris Janowitz, Edward Shils, and Barrington Moore; social theorists Herbert Marcuse and Otto Kirchheimer; geographers Richard Hartshorne and John Morrison; and economists Walt Rostow, Charles Kindleberger, and Carl Kaysen. R&A specialists produced reports ranging from the future of the British empire to the character of individual foreign leaders to the growth potential of foreign agriculture and industry. Long-term strategy and postwar planning were specific areas in which R&A produced significant work.

The Special Intelligence Branch, directed by New York businessman Whitney Shepardson, maintained agents around the globe to provide secret intelligence to Washington. SI agents in Spain kept close watch on Francisco Franco's government. From Madrid and Lisbon, American observers reported on military and economic collaboration between Spain and Germany. SI personnel in Switzerland, including Allen Dulles, conveyed critical information from sources within the German Foreign Ministry, and eventually played a critical role in relaying intelligence about the Nazi "Final Solution." SI operatives in Scandinavia provided highly classified data on Nazi efforts to secure heavy water for nuclear experiments. SI also quickly moved into liberated areas in Italy and France to coordinate the flood of information from captured documents and enemy personnel. SI agents, including future Central Intelligence Agency Director William Casey, maintained communications with French resistance groups and played significant roles in linking intelligence and military operations in German-occupied France.

Perhaps the most successful OSS operations involved Germany. Throughout the war the OSS tried to establish contact with any viable anti-Nazi opposition. One of those assets, German Foreign Ministry official Fritz Kolbe, smuggled over 2,000 documents to OSS representatives in Switzerland. OSS agents also negotiated the surrender of German forces in Italy under the command of SS General Karl Wolff.

The responsibility for protecting OSS operations around the globe from foreign infiltration fell to the Counter-Intelligence Branch. X-2, led by Norman Holmes Pearson, cooperated closely with British Intelligence and the Federal Bureau of Investigation in identifying and tracking potential security risks. The unit actively vetted both new OSS employees and intelligence sources recruited by SI operatives. By the end of hostilities, X-2 operated over 600 employees and maintained a card file of approximately 400,000 names.

The final branch of the intelligence directorate, the Foreign Nationalities Branch, headed by DeWitt Poole, was perhaps the most controversial of OSS activities. FN provided translations of foreign news stories, worked with foreign national groups inside the United States, and sought to identify potential sources of contact with foreigners in occupied areas. FN was most successful in its gathering of information on nationalist groups in Eastern Europe. But those same contacts also led to frequent accusations that FN relied too heavily on ethnic workers who had contacts with Eastern European Communists, and was, as a result, riddled with Communist sympathizers.

The second directorate of the OSS organization was the Special Operations Branch (SO), headed initially by Lt. Col. Robert Solborg, and after February 1942 by Maj. Preston Goodfellow. The men and women of SO carried out missions of subversion and sabotage in enemy-controlled areas. The most famous of these operations were the Jedburgh missions into occupied France. Jedburgh teams consisted of one OSS member, plus one member of the British Special Operations Executive and a representative of the French Underground. These teams parachuted into France and coordinated resistance activities in support of Allied military operations after the Normandy landings in June 1944.

SO also played a significant role in preparing for the TORCH landings in North Africa in November 1942. Agents operating from Oran and Tangiers sabotaged French defenses and established communications between Allied forces and French underground units. The success of SO operations in identifying and contacting potential French supporters in that zone of operations helped convince General Dwight Eisenhower to permit an expanded role for the OSS in future operations in the Sicily and Normandy landings.

OSS operations were less successful in other theaters. In the Balkans, for example, SO agents tried to work with both Tito's Communist partisans and the Serbian nationalist Chetniks of Draza Mihailovich in coordinating anti-Nazi activities. But Americans, as they would at the end of the twentieth century, underestimated the depth of ethnic animosities in Yugoslavia. That misjudgment resulted in occasional military victories, but eventual political failure.

Similarly in China, OSS operatives struggled to define a role amidst three constituencies who lacked trust in the organization: the Chinese Communist Party of Mao Zedong, the Kuomintang of Chiang Kai-shek, and the American military commanders in the Pacific, General Douglas MacArthur and Admiral Chester Nimitz. Although OSS units in China reported few successes, operations in Thailand and Burma made significant contributions to the war effort in those theaters. In Burma, OSS agents formed Detachment 101, commanded by Col. Carl Eifler, which recruited and trained Kachin tribesmen into a combat unit over 10,000 strong which engaged in extensive combat operations along the Burma Road. One OSS mission in Asia, which later resulted in controversy, involved contacts with Ho Chi Minh's forces fighting the Japanese in Indochina. OSS agents supplied Ho's Viet Minh with small arms and explosives in return for intelligence and assistance extricating downed American flyers. In fact, the first American casualty of the Vietnam War is usually listed as Major Peter Dewey, the OSS station chief in Indochina.

Another branch of the operations directorate, the Morale Operations (MO) unit, commanded by Frederick Oechsner and after 1943 by Col. K. D. Mann, controlled "black" propaganda. Although "white" propaganda, control of information at home, had been transferred to the OWI in 1942, the OSS continued to employ propaganda abroad as a method of subversion. MO propaganda sought to discredit Nazi leaders by disseminating false information about anti-Hitler activities. Other operations used German film and music stars, including Marlene Dietrich, to broadcast into Germany. One station, Soldatensender West, particularly targeted German military units with American music interspersed with negative news stories about the Nazi leadership. Other efforts targeted German industrialists with tales of phony Nazi economic plans for state-run industries. Operation SAUERKRAUT, run by the MO office in Rome, infiltrated captured German POWs back behind enemy lines to distribute counterfeit pamphlets and letters and spread dissention among German troops. The same office originated Operation CORNFLAKES, which issued counterfeit Nazi stamps with Hitler's image as a death's head.

A third significant element of the OSS was its technical branch. This section developed and provided communications equipment to agents in the field, created its own code ciphers, pioneered miniaturized photography techniques, produced counterfeit documents, and coordinated communications with all of the organization's far-flung outposts. The research and development office created a number of specialized weapons for sabotage, including new limpet mines, types of explosives, and silencing devices. Elsewhere in technical services, OSS geographers produced some of the most sophisticated maps drawn anywhere in the world, while others designed and produced creative presentation materials.

By the end of the war, the OSS had established major bases of operations in London, Berne, Stockholm, Rome, Caserta, Paris, Wiesbaden, Salzburg, Rome, Cairo, Istanbul, Chungking, and New Delhi. OSS personnel eventually exceeded 13,000 men and women before cuts started near the end of the war.

The existence of the OSS was terminated by Harry Truman's presidential order on September 20, 1945. Truman not only distrusted the Republican Donovan, but he also apparently accepted the advice of those around him who warned against the potential dangers of an enormous secret intelligence agency in a democracy. Although only R&A was maintained reasonably intact and transferred to the State Department, many other OSS operatives joined the War Department's new Strategic Services Unit until the creation of the Central Intelligence Agency in 1947. OSS alumni who went on to significant careers in intelligence or national security included Frank Wisner, William Casey, Allen Dulles, David K. E. Bruce, Sherman Kent, Lyman Kirkpatrick, Edward Lansdale, Henry Cord Meyer, Richard Helms, E. Howard Hunt, and William Colby. Other famous OSS members who went on to fame in other fields included Supreme Court Justice Arthur Goldberg, actor Sterling Hayden, director John Ford, baseball player Morris "Moe" Berg, missionary and anti-Communist symbol John Birch, chef Julia Child, and diplomat Ralph Bunche.

See also: Berg, Morris (Moe); Birch, John; Casey, William; Child, Julia McWilliams; Colby, William Egan; Donovan, Major General William Joseph; Dulles, Allen Welsh; Goldberg, Arthur Joseph; Hayden, Sterling; Hoover, J. Edgar; Kent, Sherman; Kirkpatrick, Lyman Bickford, Jr.; Langer, William L.; Lansdale, Edward Geary; Meyer, Cord, Jr.; Special Operations Forces; Stephenson, Sir William Samuel

References and Further Reading

Chalou, George (ed.). *The Secrets War: The Office of Strategic Services in World War II.* Washington, DC: National Archives and Records Administration, 1992.

Ford, Kirk. *OSS and the Yugoslav Resistance, 1943–1945.* College Station, TX: Texas A&M University Press, 1992.

Katz, Barry. *Foreign Intelligence: Research and Analysis in the Office of Strategic Services, 1942–1945.* Cambridge, MA: Harvard University Press, 1989.

Mauch, Christof. *The Shadow War against Hitler: The Covert Operations of America's Wartime Secret Intelligence Service.* Translated by Jeremiah Riemer. New York: Columbia University Press, 2002.

McIntosh, Elizabeth. *Sisterhood of Spies: The Women of the OSS.* Annapolis, MD: Naval Institute Press, 1998.

O'Donnell, Patrick K. *Operatives, Spies, and Saboteurs: The Unknown Story of the Men and Women of World War II's OSS.* New York: Free Press, 2004.

Smith, Bradley F. *The Shadow Warriors: OSS and the Origins of the CIA.* New York: Basic Books, 1983.

Troy, Thomas. *Wild Bill and Intrepid: Donovan, Stephenson and the Origin of the CIA.* New Haven, CT: Yale University Press, 1996.

United States. War Department. Strategic Services Unit. History Project. *War Report of the OSS.* New York: Walker, 1976.

Yu, Maochun. *OSS in China: Prelude to Cold War.* New Haven, CT: Yale University Press, 1996.

Peter F. Coogan

OFFICIAL SECRETS ACT (1889; NEW 1911; AMENDED 1920, 1939, 1989)

The Official Secrets Act (OSA) is a piece of British legislation aimed at protecting the United Kingdom from espionage and the unauthorized disclosure of official information. The original OSA, enacted in 1889, targeted unauthorized leaks by Crown servants and government contractors but did little in practice to combat threats of espionage. In 1911, the 1889 act was replaced with a more extensive law making it illegal to approach or enter a prohibited place "for any purpose prejudicial to the safety or interests of the State" or to obtain or communicate information that might be useful to an enemy. Section 1 of the Act dealt specifically with espionage, while Section 2 covered unauthorized disclosure of official information. Amendments to the OSA in 1920 introduced a number of new ancillary crimes connected with espionage, as well as new powers of enforcement and stiffer penalties. Section 6 of the 1920 law, which made it a misdemeanor to fail to provide information relating to any suspected offense under the OSA, was revised in 1939 to apply only to espionage offences. Finally, in 1989, Section 2 of the OSA was amended to cover only limited classes of official information deemed essential to national security.

The difficulty of obtaining espionage convictions under the existing legislation—together with high-profile leaks of official documents in the 1880s—provided the impetus for the passage of the first Official Secrets Act in 1889. The legislation, which covered both espionage and unauthorized disclosure, was beset with several shortcomings. In addition to its limited scope (the Act applied only to servants of the Crown and certain classes of government contractors), the first OSA was difficult to enforce. Although it was the norm in British law to assign the burden of proof to the prosecution, such a requirement in cases of espionage—for example, the requirement to prove *intent* to obtain information illegally—made convictions under the OSA (1889) difficult to obtain and rendered the Act largely unworkable.

As rumors of German spy rings and invasion plots circulated throughout Britain on the eve of World War I, the British public became increasingly receptive to tighter security measures. The House of Lords approved a new Official Secrets Bill in July 1911. The following month the bill passed its second and third readings in the House of Commons in less than an hour. The new law, which replaced the 1889 legislation, extended the ambit of the Official Secrets Act and strengthened the powers of enforcement. Additions were made to the list of "prohibited places," and the legal burden of proof in espionage cases shifted from the prosecution to the accused. Under the 1911 legislation, all crimes of espionage (covered by Section 1 of the OSA) were classified as felonies, whereas information leaks (Section 2) were considered misdemeanors. Section 2 of the Act was extended to cover anyone—including the press—who knowingly received or communicated official information without prior authorization.

The OSA was once again revised at the close of World War I in order to make permanent certain antiespionage provisions found in the wartime Defense of the Realm Act. Amendments in 1920 included the introduction of ancillary crimes related to espionage such as impersonating a government employee or tampering with a passport. The maximum penalty for espionage was increased from seven years, as stipulated by the 1911 Act, to 14 years. Changes to the rules governing evidence also made it possible to prosecute an espionage case under a lesser Section 2 (unauthorized disclosure) charge if there was insufficient evidence for a Section 1 (espionage) conviction. Section 6 of the 1920 amendments made it a misdemeanor to withhold information about a suspected breach of the OSA.

Initially Section 6 of the 1920 Act applied to any breach of the OSA, including unauthorized disclosure. After sufficient public outcry about the rights of journalists to protect their sources, however, a further amending Act was passed in 1939 limiting Section 6 to cases of espionage. Finally, in 1989—one hundred years after the passage of the original Official Secrets Act—Section 2 of the OSA was amended to cover only limited classes of official information deemed essential to national security. Despite public pressure, however, there continues to be no Freedom of Information Act in the United Kingdom comparable to the U.S. legislation allowing for the eventual disclosure of classified material.

See also: MI-5 (The Security Service); MI-6 (Secret Intelligence Service)

References and Further Reading

Griffith, John. "The Official Secrets Act, 1989," *Journal of Law and Society* 16.2 (1989), 273–290.

Hooper, David. *Official Secrets: The Use and Abuse of the Act.* London: Secker & Warburg, 1987.

Rogers, Ann. *Secrecy and Power in the British State: A History of the Official Secrets Act.* London: Pluto Press, 1997.

Thomas, Rosamund M. *Espionage and Secrecy: The Official Secrets Acts 1911–1989 of the United Kingdom.* London: Routledge, 1991.

Kathleen Ruppert

OLSON, DR. FRANK R.
(JULY 17, 1910–NOVEMBER 28, 1953)

Dr. Frank Rudolph Olson was a U.S. Army biochemist who died under mysterious circumstances after being unwittingly dosed with LSD by Central Intelligence Agency scientist Dr. Sidney Gottlieb as part of the agency's MKULTRA experiments. Prior to his death on November 28, 1953, Olson worked in the Special Operations Division at Fort Detrick in Frederick, Maryland, where he was involved in biological weapons research. Although his death was officially ruled a suicide, evidence exists that contradicts the U.S. government's version of events.

According to information uncovered in 1975 by the Rockefeller Commission, Olson jumped through a closed window on the tenth floor of the Hotel Statler in New York City to his death after suffering a mental breakdown as a result of LSD consumption. Olson's widow, Alice Olson, accepted a settlement of $750,000 in compensation for government complicity under the condition that she could not pursue the case in civil court. In 1994, however, Olson's son, Eric Olson had his father's body exhumed to undergo an autopsy at the George Washington University.

Professor James E. Starrs, the forensic scientist in charge of the examination, found no evidence of cuts or abrasions consistent with a fall through a closed glass window. Starrs also determined that Olson had suffered a blunt force trauma to the head prior to falling and concluded that Olson had been immobilized by a blow to the head and then thrown to his death. Although the evidence revealed by Eric Olson's inquiry convinced the Manhattan district attorney to open a homicide investigation into Olson's death in 1996, he did not acquire enough evidence to bring specific charges.

See also: Gottlieb, Dr. Sidney; Rockefeller Commission

References and Further Reading

Marchetti, Victor, and Marks, John D. *The CIA and the Cult of Intelligence*. New York: Dell, 1974.

Regis, Ed. *The Biology of Doom: America's Secret Germ Warfare Project*. New York: Owl Books, 2000.

Thomas, Gordon. *Journey Into Madness: The True Story of Secret CIA Mind Control and Medical Abuse*. New York: Bantam Books, 1989.

Derek A. Bentley

OPEN SKIES PROPOSAL

A personal initiative of President Dwight Eisenhower and presented at a July 1955 Geneva Summit Conference with the Soviet Union, the Open Skies Proposal would have legalized overhead reconnaissance and aerial photography. It called for (1) exchanging "blueprints" on all military forces and installations, (2) permitting verification through aerial reconnaissance, and (3) reinforcing aerial reconnaissance with a system of on-site inspection. Nikita Khrushchev, general secretary of the Communist Party of the Soviet Union, rejected the proposal as "nothing more than a bald espionage plot." The Soviets also objected to the plan because it did not include provisions for aerial reconnaissance over other countries, it did not provide for arms reductions, and it would not prevent the concealment of military forces.

The Open Skies Proposal was linked to two ongoing technological national security initiatives. The first involved military competition and the development of new weapons technologies. At this time the development of intercontinental ballistic missiles (ICBMs) had introduced a new element into the strategic equation. First-generation ICBMs were highly vulnerable and slow-reacting weapons that were incapable of being recalled. They created a "reciprocal fear of surprise attack."

The second involved the development of the U-2 spy plane which offered the promise of providing the United States with valuable information about the state of Soviet military programs, especially in the nuclear area, that could otherwise not be obtained. Eisenhower made his proposal the same month as the U-2 spy plane flew its first test flight. The Soviet Union was expected to take military countermeasures once the U-2 began its espionage missions and the long-term success of the U-2 would best be ensured by establishing its legitimacy. Once the U-2 program became public, Eisenhower sought to justify it by noting that although spying was a distasteful business it was necessary in order to lessen the chances of being surprised and experiencing another Pearl Harbor.

Analysts are uncertain as to Eisenhower's true intent. Some see it largely as an exercise in cold war propaganda because there was little doubt that the Soviet Union would reject the proposal. As recently as May 1955 the Soviet Union had made it clear that in their view American disarmament had to precede any verification system. A second interpretation asserts that Eisenhower was personally committed to reducing the dangers of nuclear war through arms control and that he had become worried about the specter of an arms race between the two countries. He made the proposal over the objections of his Secretary of State John Foster Dulles who was extremely skeptical over any plans for cooperation with the Soviet Union.

Over the next few years events overtook the Open Skies Proposal. In 1957 the Soviet Union launched Sputnik into orbit around the earth. This added an entirely new dimension to the question of national control over air-space and the manner in which espionage was conducted. In 1960, the Soviet Union shot down a U-2 spy plane over its territory. This act and the revelations of U.S. over-flights changed the debate from a theoretical question of the limits of sovereignty to one that had a real politico-military dimension.

See also: Powers, Francis Gary; U-2 Incident

References and Further Reading

Ambrose, Stephen. *Ike's Spies: Eisenhower and the Espionage Establishment*. Garden City, NY: Doubleday, 1981.

Krepon, Michael, and Amy Smithson (eds.). *Open Skies, Arms Control, and Cooperative Security*. New York: St. Martins, 1992.

Glenn P. Hastedt

ORLOV, ALEXANDER MIKHAILOVICH
(AUGUST 21, 1895–APRIL 7, 1973)

A master spy of the Soviet Union during the interwar years and a recipient of the Order of Lenin, Major Alexander Mikhailovich Orlov was the primary professional pseudonym for Leiba Lazarevich Feldbin, who was born on August 21, 1895, in Bobruisk, Byelorussia. In July 1938, after coming under suspicion of being part of an assassination conspiracy against Stalin, he fled with his wife and teenage daughter to the United States. The most senior Soviet intelligence officer to defect to the West, Orlov died in Cleveland on April 7, 1973, after being hospitalized for cardiac complications.

During the early 1930s this NKVD operative was on assignment throughout Western Europe, establishing a network of deep-cover agents in Germany, France, Czechoslovakia, Austria, and Switzerland. In 1934 and 1935 he lived in London and had some connection with the Cambridge spy ring. Afterwards he ran the NKVD operation in Spain during the Spanish Civil War, conducting a purge against Trotskyites, establishing a secret police network, and diverting the Spanish gold reserves to Moscow.

Orlov, who had joined the Communist Party in 1920 and had fought with the Red Army in the Russian Civil War, may have maintained a lifetime allegiance to the Bolshevik Revolution. His writing of *The Secret History of Stalin's Crimes* (1953), which was serialized in *Life* magazine, is not necessarily a repudiation of Communism. Despite debriefings with American intelligence officials and even presenting testimony before Congress, he died taking many Soviet secrets to the grave.

Twice, on November 14, 1969, and August 10, 1971, Orlov was paid a visit by the KGB agent Dimitri Petrovich Feoktistov, who worked undercover as a Soviet employee of the UN Secretariat in New York. There are conflicting reports about the nature of those meetings and what the two men discussed.

See also: KGB (Komitet Gosudarstvennoi Bezopasnosti); NKVD (Narodnyj Komissariat Vnutrennikh Del—Peoples Commissariat for Internal Affairs)

References and Further Reading

Brook-Shepherd, Gordon. *The Storm Petrels: The Flight of the First Soviet Defectors*. New York and London: Harcourt Brace Jovanovich, 1977.

Costello, John, and Oleg Tsarev. *Deadly Illusions: The KGB Orlov Dossier Reveals Stalin's Master Spy*. New York: Crown Books, 1993.

Gazur, Edward P. *Alexander Orlov: The FBI's KGB General*. New York: Caroll & Graf Publishers, 2002.

Roger Chapman

ORTIZ, COLONEL PETER JULIEN (JULY 5, 1913–MAY 16, 1988)

One of the most decorated and well-known OSS agents during World War II, he later became a Hollywood legend. Peter Julien Ortiz was born on July 5, 1913, in Arizona, his father being from Mexico. He grew up in Yavapai, Arizona, and then in France, becoming fluent in French. In 1932 at the age of 19 he joined the French Foreign Legion and fought the Germans in the Battle for France in 1940. Interned as a prisoner of war by the Germans, Ortiz managed to escape and managed to get to the United States where he joined the U.S. Marines. Given a commission, he was appointed as assistant naval attaché in Tangier, Morocco. There he was involved in intelligence work getting tribesmen to fight against the Germans in preparation for the Allied landing in Operation Torch.

With OSS, in 1943 Ortiz was parachuted into France to work with the Free French Resistance. In France, he helped organize the rescue of four Royal Air Force pilots who had been shot down over the country. This continued until 1944 when Ortiz was forced to hand himself in to the Germans in order to prevent reprisals against some villagers, spending the rest of the war as a German internee. For his efforts, he was awarded two Navy Crosses, the Legion of Merit, the Order of the British Empire, and five Croix de Guerre, also being made a Chevalier of the (French) Legion of Honor. The legend for one of his navy crosses noted: "The story of self-sacrifice of Major Ortiz and his marines has become a brilliant legend in that section of France where acts of bravery were considered commonplace."

Returning to civilian life in 1955, Ortiz became the subject of two films produced in Hollywood. The first, *13 Rue Madeleine* (1946) by TCF, starred James Cagney, and the second, by Warner Brothers was *Operation Secret* (1952), produced by Henry Blanke and directed by Lewis Seiler, starring Cornell Wilde. Ortiz retired to Prescott, Arizona, and died on May 16, 1988, in Prescott. He was buried at the Arlington National Cemetery.

See also: Movies, Spies in; Office of Strategic Services

References and Further Reading

Booth, Alan R. "The Development of the Espionage Film," in Wesley K. Wark (ed.), *Spy Fiction, Spy Films, and Real Intelligence*. Portland, OR: Frank Cass & Co., 1991.
Smith, R. Harris. *OSS: The Secret History of America's First Central Intelligence Agency*. Berkeley, CA: University of California, Press 1972.

Justin Corfield

OSHIMA, HIROSHI
(APRIL 19, 1886–JUNE 6, 1975)

Hiroshi Oshima was a Japanese soldier and diplomat who unknowingly provided the Western Allies with much useful intelligence during World War II. Born in Gifu Prefecture, Japan, on April 19, 1886, Oshima Hiroshi came from a prominent family. He graduated from the Military Academy in 1905 and, as a major in the army in the early 1920s, served as a military attaché in Germany, Austria, and Hungary.

In 1934 Colonel Oshima, who spoke excellent German, secured appointment as the senior military attaché in Berlin. A strong supporter of Adolf Hitler and the National Socialists, Oshima secured direct access to the upper governmental echelons, including Hitler himself. By 1938 Oshima had risen to both lieutenant general and ambassador to Germany.

Oshima worked hard to bring about the 1936 Anti-Comintern Pact that led to the 1940 Tripartite Pact of Germany, Italy, and Japan. Shortly after the beginning of World War II, Oshima was recalled to Tokyo but Japanese leaders were sufficiently impressed with German military successes during 1939 and 1940 that he returned to Berlin in his former post in early 1941. Because the two men were in near complete agreement on policies, Hitler confided much to Oshima.

By this time, however, the U.S. Army Signal Intelligence Service (SIS) had broken the Japanese diplomatic cipher, identified as PURPLE. SIS was thus able to read more than 2,000 of Oshima's communications to Tokyo sent by supposedly secure cipher. These provided invaluable information to the Allies on German attitudes, intentions, and strategic dispositions. Oshima, for example, provided information on the German military buildup in North Africa and the German reluctance to conclude a separate peace with the Soviet Union. Oshima also assisted D-Day planners seeking to determine German defensive dispositions. Oshima was, however, unaware of Japanese attentions to attack Pearl Harbor and thus did not provide any information on it to the Americans.

Oshima escaped from Berlin in April 1945 but surrendered to U.S. forces. Interned in the United States, after the war he was taken to Japan to be tried as a war criminal by the International Military Tribunal for the Far East. Found guilty in November 1948 of conspiracy against peace, he was sentenced to life imprisonment but was paroled in December 1955. Oshima died in Chigasaki, Japan, on June 6, 1975, shortly before the declassification of SIS successes in solving Japanese World War II ciphers.

See also: American Intelligence, World War II

References and Further Reading

Boyd, Carl. *The Extraordinary Envoy: General Hiroshi Oshima and Diplomacy in the Third Reich, 1934–1939.* Washington, DC: University Press of America, 1982.

Boyd, Carl. *Hitler's Japanese Confidant: General Oshima Hiroshi and MAGIC Intelligence, 1941–1945.* Lawrence, KS: University Press of Kansas, 1993.

Spencer C. Tucker

OVERFLIGHT, OPERATION

After the Soviet Union successfully tested an atomic bomb in 1949, abruptly ending the American nuclear monopoly, officials in Washington desperately sought a means to obtain intelligence information on the military capability behind the Iron Curtain. American concerns were increased after the Soviets successfully detonated a nuclear bomb in an air-burst test in 1951 and exploded a thermonuclear weapon in 1953. The fear of the unknown in the atomic age, coupled with a "Pearl Harbor" complex prompted President Dwight D. Eisenhower to approve Operation OVERFLIGHT, for conducting covert reconnaissance flights over Communist territory. From 1956 to 1960 this CIA program flew 24 missions over the USSR.

During the Geneva Summit in July 1955 Eisenhower proposed Open Skies, a plan in which the United States and the Soviet Union could openly conduct reconnaissance flights over each other's territory. Predictably, Soviet Premier Nikita Khrushchev dismissed the plan as simply another Western espionage scheme. His pessimism was based on the harsh realities of the cold war, events beginning with the Truman administration.

In a futile effort code-named "Redsox," the United States parachuted behind the Iron Curtain specially trained agents who were nationals of the new territories under Soviet control. In 1946 the Western Allies started conducting flights along the Red borders as part of the Peacetime Airborne Reconnaissance Program. In 1949 the U.S. Air Force began deliberate over-flights of the Soviet Far East, using specially modified RF-80A aircraft. The British utilized CIA-owned RB-45C Tornado as well as RAF English Electra Canberra aircraft to fly over Communist territory. Even Sweden participated in surveillance missions, flying CIA-supplied DC-3 aircraft and forwarding to Washington reports on Soviet radar chains along the Baltic. The

Americans also experimented with unmanned balloons equipped with cameras (Project GENETRIX) for traversing the Soviet Union.

After Open Skies was rejected, Eisenhower proceeded with the U-2 program, a Central Intelligence Agency project that was well underway. The year prior the first U-2, a high-altitude reconnaissance aircraft, called the Dragon Lady, rolled out of its Skunk Works hangar in Burbank, California. This single-seat, single-engine spy plane, capable of flying at an altitude of 80,000 feet, was practically a glider. It was designed to collect signals and imagery intelligence. Operated by a single pilot wearing a pressurized suit and breathing liquid oxygen, the U-2 was capable of flying beyond the range of missiles and fighter jets. Engineers believed that the aircraft would fly undetected by ground radar. U-2 pilots did not wear military uniforms because Eisenhower thought that would otherwise represent an act of war. Having the CIA run the program had the advantage of keeping the gathering and interpreting of intelligence out of the hands of air force officials, the same who proposed budgets based upon perceived Soviet threats.

On April 29, 1956, Detachment A, consisting of four U-2 planes, was deployed in Lakenheath, England. It was soon, however, transferred to Wiesbaden and later Giebelstadt, both in West Germany, due to Great Britain's refusal to grant permission for surveillance flights to originate from its territory. Beginning in late August of that same year Detachment B was stationed at Incerlik Air Base near Adana, Turkey. Detachment C moved to Eieslon Air Force Base in Alaska during summer of 1957. At different times U-2 planes used bases in Norway, Pakistan, and Japan.

In June 1956 the first U-2 over-flights of East Germany began. On July 4 of that year the first U-2 surveillance of the Soviet Union was conducted. Flown by Harvey Stockman, the plane photographed the bomber bases in the Baltic and the submarine base at Leningrad. To the surprise of the Americans, the spy plane was tracked by Soviet radar and pursued by MiG-17 fighters. The second flight over the USSR, piloted by Carmine Vito, occurred the following day and covered Moscow and the flight test and research center at Ramenskoye. Four additional missions over Soviet territory took place on July 9 and 10. After Moscow issued a protest note on July 10, U-2 flights over Russia were temporarily suspended.

The intelligence gathered from these flights disproved the speculation that there was a "bomber gap" with the Reds ahead of the Americans. The film developed afterwards clearly showed that the Soviets did not have near the number of Bison bombers Pentagon strategists had supposed. In its first 17 months Operation OVERFLIGHT conducted 23 missions, including six flights over the USSR and five over Eastern Europe. Eisenhower reluctantly approved additional missions when analysts convinced him that data from a specific site was needed. But between March 1958 and July 1959 there were no U-2 flights over the USSR.

The U-2 program was not the only flight espionage the Americans were conducting against the Soviets during this period. Operation HOME RUN, which was approved by Eisenhower, was designed to determine the best flight entry points along the northern, 3,500-mile-long Soviet border, from the Bering Strait to the Kola Peninsula in Eastern Europe. Approximately 50 converted American bombers were used for this task. In one dramatic episode on May 6, 1956, six bombers flying abreast, as if in attack mode, crossed the North Pole and penetrated Soviet air space during daylight hours. The purpose was to activate Soviet radar to ascertain its capabilities.

On May 1, 1960, with the Soviets shooting down a U-2 over Sverdlovsk, a serious cold war crisis erupted. Although the pilot Lieutenant Francis Gary Powers was photographing intercontinental ballistic missile test sites near the Urals, the State Department initially denied that the flight was a spy mission. The May 1960 Paris summit abruptly ended on its first day after Khrushchev walked out, angry over Eisenhower's refusal to issue an apology for violating Soviet airspace. He also cancelled Eisenhower's upcoming visit to the Soviet Union.

The Soviet downing of the U-2 prompted the CIA to develop a faster-flying reconnaissance plane, capable of higher altitudes, producing the SR-71 Blackbird. Also, spy satellites, beginning with Corona in 1960, offered improved photography and electronic eavesdropping. Even so, heading into the twenty-first century the U.S. military maintained nearly three dozen U-2 aircraft in its inventory.

See also: Eisenhower Administration and Intelligence; Open Skies Proposal; Pearl Harbor; Powers, Francis Gary; U-2 Incident

References and Further Reading

Beschloss, Michael R. *MAYDAY: Eisenhower, Khrushchev, and the U-2 Affair.* New York: Harper & Row, 1986.

Lashmar, Paul. *Spy Flights of the Cold War.* Annapolis, MD: Naval Institute Press, 1996.

Pocock, Chris. *The U-2 Spyplane: Toward the Unknown: A New History of the Early Years.* Atglen, PA: Schiffer Military History, 2000.

Polmar, Norman. *Spyplane: The U-2 History Declassified.* Osceola, WI: MBI Publishing Company, 2001.

Powers, Francis Gary, and Curt Gentry. *Operation Overflight: A Memory of the U-2 Incident.* New York: Holt, Rinehart and Winston, 1970.

Prouty, L. Fletcher. *The Secret Team: The CIA and Its Allies in Control of the United States and the World.* Englewood Cliffs, NJ: Prentice Hall, 1973.

Roger Chapman

OVERLORD, OPERATION

Operation Overlord was the cover name for the D-Day operation on June 6, 1944, during which Allied forces landed on the beaches of Normandy to begin the Liberation of France.

Because of the difficulties with a seaborne landing, and the vulnerability of the troop-carriers, before the operation, the Allies were involved in a mass deception plan to get the Germans to believe that the Allies were actually landing in the Pas-de-Calais rather than at Normandy. This deception became known as Operation Fortitude, and included Operation Zeppelin, whereby the Allies pretended that they were going to attack in the Balkans rather than in France.

The origins of Operation Overlord go back to the Casablanca Conference in January 1943 after which there was a massive buildup in U.S. and Canadian forces in the British Isles. The first aim was to find a place where the beaches were suitable for landing, and which was within range of Allied aircraft based in England. There was also the need to have a rapid buildup of Allied forces to establish a massive beachhead. The raid at Dieppe on August 19, 1942, had been a disaster and Operation Overlord involved planning a landing between Cherbourg and Le Havre—the former, it was hoped, would be captured early in the campaign to allow for large ships to bring supplies which, until then, would have to be landed on the beaches of Normandy.

The Quebec Conference of August 1943 confirmed the feasibility study but the British prime minister wanted an increase of 25 percent in the soldiers being used. The main problem was the massive shortage of landing craft and a decision on whether or not this was possible was delayed. In February 1944 U.S. General Eisenhower was made supreme commander of the Allied Expeditionary Force, with British General Montgomery in charge of land forces.

The Allies succeeded in deceiving the Germans as to the place of the invasion, and then also after the actual attack whether or not it was the full assault or just a diversionary operation. Part of this relied on the structure of the German command, with Hitler and Field Marshal Rommel, commander of Army Group B, wanting to use maximum force to prevent any Allied landing, and Field Marshal von Runstedt, commander-in-chief west, wanting a large reserve to attack the Allies after they had landed.

The attack was originally scheduled for June 4, June 5, or June 6, owing to the tides, and started on the morning of June 5, but had to be delayed until the very early hours of June 6 because of bad weather in the English Channel. Just after midnight of June 5/6, Operation Neptune saw 23,400 British and U.S. paratroopers landed on the flanks of the invasion beaches to hold the areas and prevent any German reinforcements coming once the main beach assaults began. The first village to be liberated was Ste Me"ere Eglise, where the 82nd and 101st U.S. Airborne Divisions landed. Several hours afterwards the five main naval assault forces started landing on the beaches which were code-named "Utah," "Omaha," "Gold," "Juno," and "Sword." At the same time Allied ships bombarded German positions while the five Allied divisions landed and held the beaches which allowed two artificial harbors to be towed across the English Channel. Altogether 75,215 British and Canadian soldiers and 57,500 U.S. troops landed on D-Day, June 6, with 3,450 British casualties, 946 Canadian casualties (of whom only 35 were killed), and 6,603 U.S. casualties (1,465 killed, 3,184 wounded, 1,928 missing, and 26 captured)—high figures but far lower than were expected by the Allied High Command. there were 1,1213 naval warships involved in D-Day, of which 79 percent were British and Canadian, 16.5 percent were American, and the remainder were Dutch, French, Greek, Norwegian, and Polish. Some 195,701 naval personnel took part, with some of these, and also some of the Allied Expeditionary Air Force, being involved in operations against Calais to confuse the Germans as to the actual place of the assault. It has been estimated that German casualties ran to between 4,000 and 9,000 on D-Day itself, with by the end of June, Rommel being able to report that he had lost 28 generals, 354 commanders, and some 250,000 men, killed, injured, captured, or missing.

See also: American Intelligence, World War II

References and Further Reading

Brown, Anthony Cave. *Bodyguard of Lies*. London: HarperCollins, 1975.
Ryan, Cornelius. *The Longest Day: June 6th, 1944. D-Day*. London: Victor Gollancz, 1960.

Justin Corfield

P

PAISLEY, JOHN
(AUGUST 25, 1923–SEPTEMBER 24, 1978)

John Paisley was a Central Intelligence Agency (CIA) employee who died on September 24, 1978, under circumstances that have clouded his career in debate and made him the subject of conspiracy theories regarding the assassination of President John F. Kennedy. Two days after Kennedy's death, Paisley was found floating in the Patuxent River. His boat was found anchored to a mooring. He was strapped down with two 19-pound diving weights and had a single gunshot wound to the left side of his head. The coroner ruled his death a suicide.

Paisley was born on August 25, 1923, in Sand Springs, Oklahoma. In 1941 he joined the marines. In 1948 he started work at the United Nations as a radio operator, a position he had held in the marines. In December 1953 Paisley joined the CIA. There he was responsible for monitoring the development of electronics in the Soviet Union. In 1955 he was posted to the National Security Agency (NSA) where he analyzed information obtained from a listening post secretly established by the CIA in a tunnel under the Soviet embassy in Berlin. He returned to work for the CIA in 1957 and would eventually reach the position of deputy director of the Office of Strategic Research. In that position he interviewed Soviet defectors including Oleg Penkovsky, Anatoli Golitsyn, and Yuri Nosenko. At the time of Paisley's death, Nosenko was making claims that as a member of the KGB he had evaluated Lee Harvey Oswald, Kennedy's assassin, as a potential agent.

In 1971 Paisley was made the CIA's liaison to the White House Special Investigations Unit, "the Plumbers," whose job it was to identify sources of leaks in the Nixon administration. Their first target was Daniel Ellsberg. His relationship with the Plumbers did not become a major point of investigation by the Senate Watergate Committee. Paisley ostensibly retired in 1974 but in fact kept working for the CIA.

The day of his death Paisley had gone out sailing on the Chesapeake Bay. He told a friend that he had an important report to write. Found in the boat were an attaché case filled with classified documents. Some argue that he was a Soviet spy and did not die but rather escaped to the Soviet Union. Others claim he was executed perhaps because he had identified a Soviet mole in the CIA or knew something about the Kennedy assassination.

See also: Central Intelligence Agency; Ellsberg, Daniel; Kennedy Assassination; National Security Agency; Nosenko, Yuri Ivanovich; Watergate

References and Further Reading

Corson, William, Susan B. Trento, and Joseph Trento. *Widows: The Explosive Truth Behind 25 Years of Western Intelligence Disasters*. London: MacDonald and Company, 1989.
Hougan, Jim. *Secret Agenda*. New York: Random House, 1984.
Russell, Dick. *The Man Who Knew Too Much*. New York: Avalon Books, 2003.

Glenn P. Hastedt

PALMER RAIDS

A. Mitchell Palmer had a tumultuous political career that reached its most controversial point during his service as President Woodrow Wilson's attorney general from 1919 to 1921. Palmer worked his way quickly up the ranks of the Democratic Party in Pennsylvania. Loyal to the party, elected to Congress, and a gifted speaker, he served as Woodrow Wilson's floor manager in the 1912 democratic presidential convention. Wilson offered Palmer the position of secretary of war following his election as president, but Palmer declined sighting his Quaker background and beliefs. Remaining in Congress, Palmer established himself as a champion of workers' rights. In 1914 he failed to obtain a seat in the Senate and his candidacy was opposed by organized labor. In 1919 Wilson appointed Palmer to be attorney general.

With Wilson largely incapacitated by a stroke and World War I not yet officially over, Palmer moved vigorously to end strikes by miners and railroad workers by invoking wartime powers. Allied with J. Edgar Hoover, director of the Federal Bureau of Investigation, Palmer also unleashed a campaign against political radicals claiming to have uncovered a worldwide Communist conspiracy. Palmer's legal justification for acting was the Immigration Act of 1917, which as amended to allow for the deportation of alien anarchists and those who supported organizations that advocated violence. In excess of 3,000 suspected anarchists and members of the Communist Party were arrested, often without warrants. Among those arrested was notable anarchist Emma Goldman.

The Palmer Raids are widely considered to be among the most widespread violation of civil liberties and few of his arrests were later upheld. Politics figured prominently in Palmer's thinking. Having helped create the "Red Scare," he had no choice but to take forceful action. This was especially the case since he was an active candidate for the 1920 democratic presidential nomination. He failed to get the nomination in part because party leaders feared that labor would not support the ticket in the general election. Palmer continued to be active in Democratic Party politics in his later life. At Franklin Roosevelt's invitation, he played a central role in writing the party's 1932 platform and died while working on the 1936 platform.

See also: American Communist Party; Federal Bureau of Investigation (FBI); Hoover, J. (John) Edgar

References and Further Reading

Feuerlicht, Roberta. *America's Reign of Terror: World War I, the Red Scare and the Palmer Raids.* New York: Random House, 1971.

Finan, Christopher. *From the Palmer Raids to the Patriot Act: A History of the Fight for Free Speech in America.* Boston: Beacon Press, 2007.

Glenn P. Hastedt

PANETTA, LEON
(JUNE 28, 1938–)

Leon E. Panetta is the 19th director of the Central Intelligence Agency (CIA). He assumed that position on February 13, 2009, after having been nominated for the post by President Barak Obama and approved by the Senate. His prior executive branch service consisted of being President Bill Clinton's chief of staff and director of the Office of Management and Budget. Panetta also served in the House of Representatives for California from 1977 to 1993.

Panetta's appointment came as somewhat of a surprise since he had no prior experience in intelligence work or the broader field of national security policy. His was the last major initial appointment made by Obama. The new administration had run into difficulty in finding a nominee who was not somehow tainted by the Guantanamo Bay prisoner interrogation controversy. Panetta's nomination was characterized as a testament to his managerial skills and bipartisan standing in Washington. It is thought that his standing in Democratic Party circles would provide him with access to President Obama and provide the Obama administration with tighter control over the CIA than if an intelligence insider had been appointed. Skeptics pointed out that the CIA historically had not proven to be an inviting place for those with little experience in intelligence.

Prior to his nomination, Panetta openly criticized the CIA for its interrogation practices which he termed to be torture. After assuming office, Panetta sent an e-mail to agency employees reassuring them that no one who engaged in torture would be held personally accountable so long as they were following orders.

See also: Central Intelligence Agency; Waterboarding

References and Further Reading

Clinton, Bill. *My Life.* New York: Vintage, 2005.

Ignatious, David. "A Surprise for Langley," *Washington Post* (January 7, 2009), A15.

Glenn P. Hastedt

PEARL HARBOR

The Japanese attack on Pearl Harbor on December 7, 1941, came as a complete surprise to the U.S. military and public, but had been the result of many years of preparation by the Japanese, including the use of some of their best spies.

The idea of attacking Pearl Harbor was to destroy the U.S. Pacific fleet and thus give the Japanese dominance at sea for their invasion of Southeast Asia. The idea was similar to the Japanese actions in the Russo-Japanese War when they had successfully destroyed the Russian fleet in Port Arthur, buying them enough time to build up their land forces. Curiously, the idea of attacking Pearl Harbor had been envisaged by a British World War I spy, Hector Bywater, who had been born in London but had spent some of his childhood in Cambridge, Massachusetts, his father having served with the secret service section of the Union forces, later himself working in New York before becoming a British spy. Becoming the British naval attaché in Washington, Bywater wrote his book *The Great Pacific War* (1925) in which he showed that a Japanese attack on the U.S. Pacific fleet could give them victory in a Pacific War. The importance of the book was quickly realized by Japanese intelligence, and Admiral Yamamoto later credited the work with providing the basis for his plans. U.S. General Billy Mitchell also warned of a possible Japanese attack but his advice was ignored.

In 1932 the U.S. Admiral Yarnell embarked on a joint army-navy exercise which was to deal with a hypothetical situation in which the United States had to retake Hawaii. To this end, he planned to have aircraft carriers, and use planes from them to attack. It was a military exercise that was earnestly followed by Japan.

The Japanese sent some of their best agents to Hawaii where some members of the large Japanese population were called on for assistance, often unwittingly. Although the basic intelligence about Pearl Harbor was easy to gain, the Japanese were keen to know the exact disposition of the U.S. naval vessels on any particular day, their antiaircraft positions, and similar information. The U.S. authorities had broken the Japanese code and there are theories that either they, or British intelligence, with access to German decoded messages, knew about the attack on Pearl Harbor in advance, but did not reveal this because an attack would have forced the United States to enter the war. However it seems that the Japanese had anticipated that some of their codes might have been compromised and for this reason sent one of their best spies, Takeo Yoshikawa, to Hawaii as the vice consul, using the name Ito Morimura.

When he arrived in Hawaii in August 1941, three German agents had been collecting information for several years. They were the Keuhns—Dr. Bernard Keuhn, his wife, and another woman who they claimed was their daughter, but was actually unrelated. The three were members of the German Secret Service who had settled in Honolulu, their interest in the prehistory of the Hawaiian islands allowing them to travel around easily. Although the Keuhns had established a good network, with the "daughter" running a beauty parlor where she listened to the U.S. officers' wives gossip, the Japanese felt that they needed their own agent, and this was why Yoshikawa was dispatched. There were already some 200 Japanese consular agents and staff on the Hawaiian islands, mainly because of the large Japanese population, but many would also have been involved in spying.

Yoshikawa quickly collected the information that was needed, and clearly suspected that the Americans knew that he was a spy, although they never realized how important

Aftermath of the Japanese attack on Pearl Harbor, December 7, 1941. The battleship *West Virginia* is in the background. (Library of Congress).

his role was in the Japanese operations on Hawaii. Yoshikawa worked out two ways of deceiving the Americans. He increased the number of messages he sent through normal consular channels, thereby creating a backlog in translating by a short-staffed FBI, and sent all important information using a different route. The Americans followed him around Hawaii and reported in detail on his social engagements.

On December 5, only two days before the actual Japanese attack on Pearl Harbor, Yoshikawa was able to continue to send messages to Tokyo recording that three battleships had arrived in the port, but inaccurately named one of them as the *Wyoming* whereas it was actually the *Utah*. He also did not spot the arrival of two heavy cruisers. On the night before the Japanese attack, Yoshikawa, clearly expecting the Japanese planes at any time, destroyed all his code books and records. The Keuhns were less well prepared and Bernard Keuhn was sending signals from his house to the Japanese Consul Otojiro Okuda during the attack. Noticed by an alert U.S. intelligence officer, the FBI arrested the Keuhns and sentenced Dr. Keuhn to death, later commuted to life imprisonment. For his cooperation with the authorities, he was released in 1946, but his wife and "daughter" were both deported at the end of the war. Yoshikawa, working under consular cover, was repatriated to Japan in the exchange of diplomatic and consular staff which took place, and he spent the rest of the war working in Japanese naval intelligence.

Straight after the attack on Pearl Harbor, following worries about the possible disloyalty of Japanese-Americans, President Roosevelt signed an order for the internment of all Japanese-American civilians. Some residents on Hawaii were already thought to have been spies and one, Dr. Motokazu Mori (1890–1958), a dentist, was repeatedly questioned over a recent telephone call he had made to Tokyo in which he had described some flowers in bloom, the FBI believing that it was a coded message for something far more sinister.

See also: MAGIC; PURPLE; Yoshikawa, Takeo

References and Further Reading

Andrew, Christopher. *For the President's Eyes Only: Secret Intelligence and the American Presidency from Washington to Bush.* New York: HarperCollins, 1995.

Deacon, Richard. *A History of the Japanese Secret Service.* London: Frederick Muller Limited, 1982.

Honan, William H. *Bywater: The Man Who Invented the Pacific War.* London: Futura Publications, 1991.

Prange, Gordon. *At Dawn We Slept: the Untold Story of Pearl Harbor.* New York: McGraw-Hill, 1981.

Justin Corfield

PEARSON, NORMAN HOLMES (APRIL 13, 1909–NOVEMBER 6, 1975)

Norman H. Pearson, a professor of American literature, was the OSS counterintelligence director during World War II. Norman Holmes Pearson was born on April 13, 1909, in Gardner, Massachusetts, the son of Chester Page Pearson and Fanny Holmes (née Kittredge). He was educated at Phillips Academy, Yale University, and Magdalen College, Oxford, gaining a doctorate from Yale University in 1941. He had also completed some graduate study at Berlin University in 1933. From 1941 until 1975 he was a member of the faculty at Yale University, attached to the OSS from 1942 until 1946.

Going to Britain, Pearson's role was to liaise with British intelligence, some of whom he had known from his time at Oxford. He found working with the Double Cross Committee extremely difficult and full of moral contradictions, but acquitted himself well, earning the respect of his British counterparts. Pearson worked alongside many of the major figures in British intelligence, including Kim Philby. He was also responsible for recruiting poet James Angleton into the OSS. Pearson was awarded the American Medal of Freedom and made Chevalier of the Legion of Honor for his wartime work. After World War II, he returned to Yale and remained there until his death. During that time he held several important fellowships and wrote extensively on American literature, specializing in Nathaniel Hawthorne and Henry David Thoreau. From a young age he had been crippled by polio, and required leg braces to walk. He died on November 6, 1975.

See also: Office of Strategic Services; Philby, Harold Adrian Russell "Kim"

References and Further Reading

Brown, Anthony Cave. *Wild Bill Donovan: The Last Hero*. London: Michael Joseph, 1982.
Chalou, George (ed.). *The Secrets War: The Office of Strategic Services in World War II.*
    Washington, DC: National Archives and Records Administration, 1992.

Justin Corfield

PELTON, RONALD W.
(1942–)

Ronald Pelton joined the National Security Agency (NSA) in 1965 after having served in air force intelligence in Pakistan. He worked at NSA for 14 years as a communications specialist and had top security clearance, although he did not rise very high in the organization. Pelton left NSA in 1979 under the clouds of a growing personal debt that he feared would cost him his security clearance and lead him to declare bankruptcy. Pelton was a classic "walk-in." Soon after leaving NSC, in January 1980, Pelton contacted the Soviet embassy with an offer of information for cash. His phone call was recorded by the Federal Bureau of Investigation (FBI) as was his subsequent visit to the Soviet embassy. But his identity was not established. At the embassy he talked with Vitaly Yurchenko, a security officer at the embassy. Pelton was not able to provide Soviet intelligence officers with any secret documents but he was able to recount from memory key pieces of information that were of value to the Soviet Union.

Twice between 1980 and 1983, Pelton flew to Vienna where he was debriefed by a Soviet intelligence officer. For his information he was paid $35,000. The most valuable pieces of information that Pelton revealed involved Project Ivy Bells. This was a NSA-navy intelligence operation run by the Central Intelligence Agency that intercepted messages from a Soviet communications cable in the Sea of Okhotsk that linked Soviet naval bases at Vladovostok and Petrapavlovsk. The unencrypted communications seized in this operation provided the United States with an important window into Soviet military procedures and planning. Disclosing the existence of Project Ivy Bells also undermined a planned expansion of the program to replace recorders with an on-line system that would provide early warning of any change in the deployment of Soviet naval forces. Other possible disclosures include Operation Chalet/Vortex and a joint American-British signals and communication intercept operation.

Pelton's espionage was revealed in 1985 when Yurchenko briefly defected and told the Central Intelligence Agency (CIA) of the visit by a "Mr. Long." Although they had little firm evidence to go on, a process of elimination led the FBI to identify Pelton as Mr. Long. He was arrested on November 25, 1985. By this time he had left his wife and was living with a girlfriend, Ann Berry, and was heavily involved in drugs. Pelton admitted to the FBI that he had spied for the Soviet Union, apparently in the expectation that he might stay free and become a double agent.

Few details of Pelton's espionage career surfaced at his trial given the sensitivity of Project Ivy Bells. On June 5, 1986, he was convicted of two counts of espionage, one count of disclosing classified information, and one count of disclosing classified communications intelligence. He was sentenced to three consecutive life terms in prison plus 10 years.

See also: Central Intelligence Agency; Federal Bureau of Investigation (FBI); IVY BELLS, Project; National Security Agency

References and Further Reading

Allen, Thomas, and Norman Polmar. *Merchants of Treason, America's Secrets for Sale.* New York: Delacorte Press, 1988.

Richelson, Jeffrey. *A Century of Spies: Intelligence in the Twentieth Century.* New York: Oxford University Press, 1995.

Glenn P. Hastedt

PENKOVSKY, OLEG VLADIMIROVICH (APRIL 23, 1919–MAY 15, 1963)

Born in the period following the Russian Revolution, Oleg Penkovsky's family had strong connections with the old Tsarist regime. He never knew his father, who was an engineer and lieutenant in the tsar's army and who died fighting the Bolsheviks in the last phases of the civil war. As a youth, Penkovsky joined the Komsomol, the Communist youth league, and graduated from Kiev Military School. In 1937 he enlisted in the army and would later join the Communist Party. After World War II Penkovsky enrolled in the Frunze Military Academy and in 1949 he joined the GRU, the Soviet military intelligence organization. Penkovsky became arguably the most important known spy the United States had in the Soviet Union during the cold war.

His first overseas assignment was to be in Turkey in 1955 but after a dispute with a supervisor he was sent back to Moscow and began studying missile technology at the Dzershinky Military Artillery Engineering Academy. He was scheduled to return to intelligence work as a military attaché in India in 1957 when his father's background was uncovered. He was kept in Moscow where he secured a position as a senior officer in the GRU's Third Division, which was responsible for collecting scientific and technical intelligence from the West.

It was from this position the Penkovsky approached the West about spying. His initial attempts to volunteer his services as a spy were directed at the United States and took place in 1960. They met with failure. Following closely on the heels of captured U-2 pilot Francis Gary Powers' public trial, his offers were met with skepticism and provoked fears that he might act as a double agent spying on the West. Penkovsky was more successful in his approach to Great Britain through British businessperson Greville Wynne. Some two weeks after providing Wynne with secret information that established his legitimacy, Penkovsky was part of a Soviet trade mission to London. There he met with British and American intelligence officials, supplying them with documents and information about Soviet missiles. One estimate suggests that he passed along 5,000 photographs of key documents before his arrest on October 22, 1962, during the Cuban Missile Crisis. In addition he provided "gossip" intelligence on high-ranking GRU conversations he heard and participated in as well as the identities of key GRU personnel in India, Egypt, Paris, London, and Ceylon (Sri Lanka) as well as hundreds of GRU and KGB officers. Penkovsky had warned Wynne at one of their meetings in July 1962 that he thought he was being watched by the KGB. In fact, in

January 1962 the KGB photographed him meeting with the wife of a British intelligence officer to whom he regularly gave information. His last act of espionage came in August 1962. Evidence points to two double agents working in Washington, William Whalen and Jack Dulap, who revealed Penkovsky's identity to the KGB.

The information provided to the United States by Penkovsky is widely credited with having played a major role in American decision making during the Cuban Missile Crisis. He provided the United States with the operating manual for the SS-4, which the Soviet Union was placing in Cuba as well as information regarding problems with the Soviet missile guidance system and warheads. Additionally he provided important information on Soviet military doctrine, bureaucratic behavior and patterns of decision making, and Soviet command and control problems.

Controversy surrounds Penkovsky's espionage career on three counts. The first centers on whether or not (and for how long) the Soviet Union knew he was spying but allowed him to continue to feed information to the West. The possibility also has been raised that Penkovsky was in fact a triple agent. The second controversy centers on the timing of his arrest and execution. Some suggest that it was an attempt by the Soviet Union at crisis management, signaling to the United States that the information he had given them was accurate. The third questions the significance of Penkovsky's intelligence during the Cuban Missile Crisis. Here it is argued that the lack of archival documents and the political and personal agendas of those writing on Penkovsky have led to a sensationalization of his role and in the process distorted his true influence.

Penkovsky was tried along with Wynne, who was arrested in Hungary, for espionage in May 1963. Both were found guilty. Penkovsky was shot five days after the verdict was rendered. Wynne was sentenced to eight years in prison and exchanged in April 1964 for Soviet spy Gordon Lonsdale who was operating in Great Britain.

See also: Cuban Missile Crisis; GRU (Main Intelligence Directorate); KGB (Komitet Gosudarstvennoi Bezopasnosti); Lonsdale, Gordon Arnold; Powers, Francis Gary; U-2 Incident; Wynne, Greville

References and Further Reading

Andrew, Christopher, and Oleg Gordievsky. *KGB: The Inside Story of Its Foreign Operations from Lenin to Gorbachev*. London: Hodder & Stoughton, 1990.

Gibney, Frank (ed.). *The Penkovsky Papers: The Russian Who Spied for the West*. London: Collins, 1965.

Richelson, Jeffrey. *American Espionage and the Soviet Target*. New York: Quill, 1987.

Scott, Len. "Espionage and the Cold War: Oleg Penkovsky and the Cuban Missile Crisis," *Intelligence and National Security* 14 (1999), 23–47.

Glenn P. Hastedt

PERSIAN GULF WAR

The Persian Gulf War was the first major international conflict of the post–cold war era. The first stage of the conflict began in early 1990 and ended with Iraq's August 2 invasion of Kuwait. It was dominated by raising tension between the United States and Iraq, and Iraq and its Arab neighbors. On February 15, 1990, Iraq protested a Voice of

America broadcast on global democratization that characterized Iraq as a state where "secret police were widely present." Iraqi President Saddam Hussein repeated his attacks on the United States in a late February meeting of the Arab Cooperation Council where he also stated that Arab states needed to provide Iraq with $30 billion in aid for its war effort against Iran in the 1980 to 1988 Iran-Iraq War. Failure to do so, he threatened, would cause Iraq to "take steps to retaliate." That war had cost Iraq over $500 billion. Oil sales were the key to Iraq's recovery but the price of oil was steadily dropping.

A flurry of diplomatic activity followed. Jordan's King Hussein tried and failed to broker an agreement between Iraq and the other Middle East oil-producing states. Saddam Hussein continued his verbal attacks on the United States and the George H. W. Bush administration responded by labeling them as "inflammatory" and "irresponsible." At a May summit meeting of Arab states he charged that Kuwait and other quota-busting oil-producing states were "virtually waging an economic war" against Iraq. He then charged Kuwait with being part of a "Zionist plot aid by imperialists." Low oil prices were termed a "dagger" pointed at Iraq. These outbursts set off a new round of diplomatic activity to defuse the growing crisis. On July 31 a high-ranking State Department spokesperson told Congress the United States had "no defense treaty relationship with any Gulf country."

Accompanying this hostile rhetoric were troop movements by key units of Iraq's Republican guard toward the Kuwaiti border. The United States was disturbed by this action but concluded that their purpose was to intimidate rather than invade. The United States continued to hold to this interpretation right up until the invasion, although on July 31 elements of the intelligence community concluded that war was now imminent given the scale and direction of recent Iraqi troop movements. Within 11 days Saddam Hussein had moved eight divisions to within 300 to 400 miles of the Kuwait border. Given that the United States only had 10,000 military personnel in the region and that most of them were naval forces, there was little that the United States could do to prevent the invasion.

A second period of the Persian Gulf War encompasses the period between the invasion of Kuwait and the beginning of the bombing campaign in January 1991. On August 2, 1990, Kuwait was invaded by Iraqi troops that took control of most of the country within a matter of hours. Caught off guard by the Iraqi attack, the George H. W. Bush administration's first priority became protecting Saudi Arabia and its vast oil reserves from Iraqi forces that were massing along the Iraq-Saudi border. To accomplish this objective Operation Desert Shield was launched. An unprecedented aspect of this operation, one that would be objected to strongly by Osama bin Laden, was Saudi Arabia's unprecedented willingness to allow U.S. soldiers to be stationed on its soil.

It was the third week of August before the international coalition of forces, assembled under U.S. leadership, was able to be confident that an Iraqi attack against Saudi Arabia could not succeed. The United States was the major contributor with 430,000 troops. Great Britain (35,000), Egypt (30,000), and France (17,000) were significant contributors of military personnel. Saudi Arabia provided 66,000 front line troops. In addition to organizing army troops, Operation Desert Shield also put in place a naval force to protect Saudi Arabia. The core of the naval force was provided by the United States. It sent more than 100 ships, including six aircraft carriers. Great

Britain and France sent 18 and 14 ships, respectively. This coalition of forces would come to provide the foundation for Operation Desert Storm in January 1991. Japan and Germany provided funding rather than troops. The largest financial contributors were Saudi Arabia and Kuwait. Each gave more than $16 billion. All totaled, foreign states gave some $54 billion to the effort.

On November 8, 1990, just after the midterm elections, the Bush administration announced that it was sending reinforcements to the region. This move signaled a shift in U.S. thinking away from the use of economic sanctions as a means of forcing Iraq out of Kuwait. Instead, a large military force would be assembled that would try to intimidate Saddam Hussein into withdrawing from Kuwait and failing that could undertake an offensive military operation. On November 29, the Security Council voted 12–2, with China abstaining, to set January 15, 1991, as the deadline for Iraq's peaceful exit from Kuwait. It authorized member states to "use all means necessary" to bring about Iraq's complete and unconditional withdrawal. That same month Congress took up the question of whether to support the use of military force as requested by Bush. On January 12, the House of Representatives voted 250–183 to support the president's use of military force against Iraq. The Senate did so by a 52–47 margin. When the compliance deadline established by UN Resolution 678 went unmet, the Persian Gulf War entered its offensive phase with the launching of Operation Desert Storm.

On January 16, 1991, Operation Desert Storm began. Coalition aircraft took off from Saudi Arabia to begin the air campaign against Iraq. Coalition air forces would fly over 109,000 sorties, drop 88,500 tons of bombs, and shoot down 35 Iraqi planes. On January 17, Iraq responded by launching Scud missile attacks on Saudi Arabia and Israel. One of the major concerns U.S. war planners had was Israel's response to these attacks. The fear was that if Israel retaliated, the Arab members of the coalition would defect. Israel did not retaliate and the coalition held together. On September 23, after a failed Soviet-Iraqi peace initiative and the refusal of Iraq to begin a large-scale withdrawal of its forces from Kuwait, coalition forces launched a ground assault into Iraq.

The ground phase of Operation Desert Storm began on February 24. It lasted exactly 100 hours. Approximately 700,000 troops were assembled in and around Saudi Arabia for the attack but fewer than 400,000 actually participated in it. Great uncertainty surrounded the beginning of the campaign due to the uncertainty over the abilities of Iraq's army and Saddam Hussein's strategy. American, British, and French forces led a blitzkrieg operation deep into Iraq when the fighting began. With his forces defeated and surrounded, Saddam Hussein announced that Iraq had withdrawn from Kuwait on February 26. Fighting continued until February 28 when President Bush announced that the coalition's military objectives had been met. American war casualties were listed as 125 combat deaths. Approximately 63,000 Iraqi soldiers were taken as prisoners of war and 25,000 to 100,000 were killed. As many as 30 percent of Kuwaiti forces in Kuwait deserted. British estimates place the number of Iraqi tanks destroyed at 3,500 out of 4,200.

On February 28, Iraq announced a cease-fire and agreed to a meeting of military commanders to discuss terms for ending the war. The UN Security Council approved Resolution 686, setting out the terms for ending hostilities on March 2. The following day Iraq agreed to these terms. On April 3 the UN Security Council approved Resolution 687, which established a permanent cease-fire in the Persian Gulf War and ended international sanctions against Iraq. Iraq accepted these terms on April 6, formally ending the war.

The performance of the intelligence community during Operations Desert Shield and Desert Storm was found to range from very good and deserving of praise to very poor, depending upon which facet is analyzed. Intelligence collection came in for the highest praise. Still, several problems were identified. One problem was that in the buildup to Operation Desert Shield intelligence capabilities were intentionally restricted, with the emphasis instead being placed on building up U.S. forces in the region as quickly as possible. As a result, military commanders in the theater of combat were forced to rely primarily upon national collection systems for much of their intelligence. A further complicating factor is that the Central Command (CENTCOM) was unprepared to handle the surge of intelligence it began to receive once war appeared imminent. When CENCOM/J-2 was first deployed to the theater on August 7 it had a staff of less than 10. It was described as being an empty shell to which people and resources would be attached should it become necessary. As such, no intelligence architecture or structure was in place to guide the buildup of theater intelligence resources. Over time the number of individuals assigned to CENTCOM/J-2 rose to almost 700.

An additional complicating factor was that some national intelligence organizations appeared to be unfamiliar with or unresponsive to the needs of wartime commanders. The Central Intelligence Agency (CIA) was singled out for criticism in this regard. In its defense, the CIA noted it responded to over 1,000 information inquiries from CENTCOM. Additionally it appears that some combat commanders did not have a full appreciation of the capabilities and limitations of the U.S. intelligence system. As a consequence, all of the information potentially available to commanders was not used to its maximum potential.

On a more positive note, although some tactical imagery and signals intelligence systems were not able to provide a high degree of support to field commanders, other collection systems performed admirably. The air force-army Joint Surveillance Target Radar System (JSTARS) provided combat commanders with near real-time intelligence on a wide range of targets in all weather conditions. Working in tandem with JSTARS, the air force's U-2 reconnaissance aircraft provided high-resolution images tracking the movement of vehicles during all weather conditions and during night and day. Also, the Pioneer unmanned aerial vehicle (UAV) provided considerable imagery support to army, navy, and marine units.

Dissemination of intelligence was rated as very poor. Here again the absence of an intelligence structure to ensure that commanders received intelligence, especially imagery intelligence, in a timely fashion was a major problem. No fewer than one dozen different secondary imagery dissemination systems were delivered in theater. Each of the services brought their own systems with them. Operating independently, they often performed admirably but only four of them were able to send pictures from one system to another. No service was willing to give up its system and at the same time no service was capable of forcing others to adopt its system. Moreover, the timely dissemination of tactical intelligence within the combat theater was hindered by bottlenecks created by communication problems within CENTCOM. Problems arose from junior officers having insatiable intelligence appetites and more senior officers removing intelligence from distribution channels without adequately consulting others about its potential value. These problems were largely found in the air force, although they also existed to some extent in army units.

The quality of intelligence analysis was judged to be mixed. The central analytical weakness involved tactical battlefield damage assessments. This task was given to the army rather than the air force in part because of the well-established tendency for pilots to overstate the success of their missions. Unfortunately, the army had little idea of how to do this. In the brief period of combat, great doubts were expressed in Washington about the rapidly mounting number of kills reported. After-the-fact analysis of selected engagements found that CENTCOM counts of Republican guard tank units destroyed was exaggerated by 100 percent. Another combat analysis found the margin of error in estimating tank kills to be above 134 percent. An additional dimension to the analytical problem was the manner in which intelligence was reported. For example, stating that a bridge was 52 percent destroyed did not inform commanders if a truck could cross the bridge, which is the key operational question from their point of view.

Finally, intelligence controversies encompassing collection, dissemination, and analysis arose in two areas. The first was the hunt for SCUD mobile missile launchers. Observers described it as a double military loser. It diverted resources from more pressing ground battle targets and no evidence emerged that even a single SCUD missile or mobile launcher was destroyed. The second intelligence controversy surrounded the search for Iraq's nuclear, biological, or chemical weapons capability. The absence of definitive intelligence on this matter would return to haunt U.S. policy in Iraq years later when George W. Bush would use an Iraqi weapons of mass destruction capability as a major reason for going to war.

See also: Iraq War; Post–Cold War Intelligence

References and Further Reading

Freedman, Lawrence, and Efraim Karsh (eds.). *The Gulf Conflict, 1990–1991.* Princeton, NJ: Princeton University Press, 1993.

Mazarr, Michael, et al. *Desert Storm: The Gulf War and What We Learned.* Boulder, CO: Westview, 1993.

United States Congress, Committee on Armed Forces, House of Representatives. *Intelligence Success and Failures in Operations Desert Shield/Storm.* Washington, DC: Government Printing Office, August 18, 1993.

Woodward, Bob. *The Commanders.* New York: Simon & Schuster, 1991.

Glenn P. Hastedt

PETERS, J.
(1894–1990)

J. Peters was an alias used by a Hungarian Communist, Sándor Goldberger, who played a prominent role in the American Communist Party (CPUSA) during his 25-year residence (1924–1949) in the United States. His major accomplishment was the establishment in the mid-1930s of a spy apparatus that was one of the earliest and most successful Soviet beachheads in the Roosevelt administration.

Born in Hungary to Jewish parents in 1894, Sándor Goldberger received an excellent secondary school education. He enrolled in a law college but his studies were interrupted by World War I, in which he served as an infantry officer. Traumatized by the war and the rise of political anti-Semitism, he became a Communist and emigrated to the United States in 1924. In 1931 he was sent by the CPUSA to Moscow where he received special training in conspiratorial work. In 1932 he took the name J. Peters and was appointed director of the CPUSA's secret apparatus. His most important project was the creation of an underground Party unit in Washington, DC, consisting of middle- and high-level government workers, some of whom he recruited for espionage work. Peters was the handler of Whittaker Chambers, who actively coordinated the work of Peters' spy ring. Its greatest success was penetration of the State Department, where Alger Hiss was a principal source. In late 1936 Peters handed over control of the spy apparatus to Col. Boris Bykov, a Soviet military intelligence agent. When Whittaker Chambers defected in 1938, Peters withdrew from his Washington underground activities but continued to cooperate with Soviet intelligence agencies by providing the names of government employees willing to carry out espionage work.

Peters, who had never become an American citizen, was deported in 1949 and returned to Hungary. Adhering to the code of silence expected of Communists who had engaged in conspiratorial work, he insisted in the rare interviews he gave to historians or journalists that he had never been involved in underground or espionage work. However, in an unpublished memoir that he wrote for the Hungarian Communist Party archive, he admitted for the first time that he had indeed engaged in what he euphemistically called "special work" for the CPUSA. He died in 1990, one year after the collapse of the Communist regimes in Eastern Europe.

See also: Chambers, Whittaker; Hiss, Alger

References and Further Reading

Klehr, Harvey, John Earl Haynes, and Fridrikh Igorevich Firsov (eds.). *The Secret World of American Communism*. New Haven, CT: Yale University Press, 1995.

Schmidt, Mária. *Battle of Wits*. Budapest, Hungary: Század Intézet, 2007.

Weinstein, Allen, and Alexander Vassiliev. *The Haunted Wood*. New York: Random House, 1999.

Tom Sakmyster

PETROV, VLADIMIR M.
(FEBRUARY 7, 1907–JUNE 14, 1991)

Vladimir Petrov was the most senior Soviet spy to defect to the West since the 1930s. His defection was a coup for the Australian Security Intelligence Organisation, aroused the intense interest of the Western counterintelligence community, and threw fresh light on the "missing diplomats," Anthony Burgess and Donald McLean. Of peasant origin, Vladimir Mikhailovich Petrov was born in the Siberian village of Larikha on February 15, 1907. He established a local Komsomol cell in 1923, became a full-time organizer and Communist Party member in 1927, and was recruited by the People's Commissariat for State Security (NKVD) in 1933. He survived Stalin's purges, was posted to Stockholm during World War II, and arrived in Australia on February 5, 1951. Ostensibly third secretary to the Soviet embassy in Canberra, Petrov was actually a colonel in the Ministry of State Security (MGB) and directly responsible to Beria.

On April 3, 1954, Petrov defected. Two weeks later his wife, Evdokia, an embassy cipher clerk and MGB officer, also defected, after dramatically being freed from armed Soviet couriers by Australian police at Darwin airport. This resulted in the dual withdrawal of the Soviet embassy from Canberra and the Australian embassy from Moscow. Prime Minister Robert Menzies promptly established the Royal Commission on Espionage, which sat for 126 days, examined 119 witnesses, and received over 500 exhibits. The latter included the controversial "Petrov Papers," documents handed over at the time of defection. Although many on the Left alleged these to be forgeries, the declassified VENONA decrypts confirmed their authenticity in 1996. The Royal Commission exposed Soviet espionage in Australia between 1945 and 1948, but prosecutions could not be initiated without compromising the VENONA operation. Petrov's revelations also caused a sensation in Great Britain, for he provided new material, leaked to the British press by Security Service (MI-5) officers, concerning the escape and whereabouts of Burgess and Maclean. Petrov was given a new identity, Sven Allyson; lived in a "safe house" in East Bentleigh, Melbourne; and thereafter in a nursing home in Parkville, Melbourne, where he died, aged 84, on June 14, 1991.

See also: Australian Security Intelligence Organisation; MI-5 (The Security Service); NKVD (Narodnyj Komissariat Vnutrennikh Del—Peoples Commissariat for Internal Affairs)

References and Further Reading

Bialoguski, Michael. *The Petrov Story*. Melbourne, Australia: William Heinemann, 1955.
Manne, Robert. *The Petrov Affair: Politics and Espionage*. Sydney, Australia: Pergamon, 1987.
Thwaites, Michael. *Truth Will Out: ASIO and the Petrovs*. Sydney, Australia: Collins, 1980.
Whitlam, Nicholas, and John Stubbs. *Nest of Traitors: The Petrov Affair*. Brisbane, Australia: Jacaranda, 1974.

Phillip Deery

PHILBY, HAROLD ADRIAN RUSSELL "KIM" (JANUARY 1, 1912–MAY 11, 1988)

Harold "Kim" Philby was a member of the Cambridge Group of spies. His betrayals cost the lives of hundreds of agents and provided the Soviets with an enormous number of American and British secrets. Philby was born on January 1, 1912, in Ambala, India, the son of Harry St. John Philby. He was nicknamed "Kim" after Rudyard Kipling's famous fictional character.

In 1929 he entered Cambridge University. With the Great Depression growing he was drawn into socialist politics and joined the Cambridge University Socialist Society. In 1933 "Kim" completed his studies at Cambridge and moved to Vienna where he joined underground Communists. While in Vienna, Philby married Alice "Litzi" Friedman, a Communist on the run from the police. In 1934 he returned to Great Britain with her. Not long afterward he was recruited as a Soviet spy and given the long-term assignment

Kim Philby in 1955, the time he was cleared of being the "hired man" in the Maclean Burgess Affair. Philby later defected to the Soviet Union. (AP/Wide World Photos)

of getting into the British secret service. His short-term assignment was to go the Spain where Civil War raged between Fascists and Communists.

Philby was a reporter for the *Times* of London and went to Spain where he pretended to be a supporter of General Francisco Franco's nationalists. He was given the Red Cross of Military Merit by the nationalists. He also cut all visible ties to his former Communists associations and separated from "Litizi." With his right-wing cover, Philby successfully joined the Secret Intelligence Service (SIS), also known as MI-6, with the aid of Guy Burgess who was also a KGB agent.

During World War II Philby was head of a subsection of SIS which directed resistance groups in Nazi-occupied Europe. His work was viewed as excellent so in 1944 he was put in charge of a new section of British counterintelligence, a unit (Section Nine) tasked with uncovering Communist moles within British intelligence.

Section Nine was small at first but Philby built it into an organization which was in charge of all intelligence, counterintelligence, and covert operations against the Soviet Union and other Communists. He was thus able to protect the Committee for State Security's (KGB) important assets and himself. However, all would have been lost with the defection to the British of KGB agent Konstantin Volkov in Turkey because Volkov knew the names of numerous British agents serving the Communists. Philby was able to delay Volkov's debriefing, which gave the KGB time to murder Volkov, thus eliminating the threat of exposure.

In 1946 Philby married Aileen Furse. The marriage however, required a divorce from Litzi. At the time she was living in East Berlin with a Soviet agent known to British intelligence. The divorce and her association with Philby should have rendered him a security risk; however, an investigation that might have exposed him did not occur.

In 1947 Philby was posted to Istanbul. There he was able to betray several anti-Communist groups, which were subsequently exterminated. In 1949 he was assigned to the British embassy in Washington, DC, as the liaison officer between SIS and the Central Intelligence Agency (CIA). With his CIA connection, Philby was able to give the Soviets numerous American secrets about its military intensions, relations with allies, atomic research, and covert operations against Communists.

In late 1950 Philby learned that David Maclean, another KGB agent and an old friend of Philby's from Cambridge days, was about to be exposed. Philby used Guy Burgess to alert Maclean. Together the two escaped to Moscow. Because Burgess went to Moscow with Maclean, he brought suspicion on Philby who had been an active friend of Burgess'. After a long investigation British intelligence was convinced, but unable to prove, Philby was a KGB agent. However, Philby stoutly denied that he was a spy. In the end his reputation was undone and he was asked to resign.

Philby then went to work again as a journalist for *The Observer* and *The Economist*. And then to the surprise of many he was rehired by SIS of which he remained a member until 1963. He also continued to provide the KGB with intelligence, only mostly overt political information at this time.

In 1957 Philby was stationed in Beirut, Lebanon, where his wife, Aileen, died of heart problems. In 1958 he married Eleanor Brewer, ex-wife of a *New York Times* correspondent. In 1961, Anatoli Golitsyn, a KGB officer, defected to the West where he provided proof of Philby's espionage activities. Golitsyn's information stimulated a new investigation of Philby. In late 1962 he was confronted with the evidence against him and seemed to be prepared to give a complete confession. However, on January 23, 1963, he fled Beirut on a cargo ship bound for Russia.

In the Soviet Union Philby learned Russian, became a Soviet citizen, and eventually was promoted to the rank of KGB general. He gave the Soviets every detail of every agent he had ever met, the organizational structure and function of the British and American intelligence organizations, the physical layouts of every facility where he had worked, and every detail he could remember no matter how trivial. The secrets that he gave were very damaging and took years to assess.

In 1963 Eleanor Philby joined him in the Soviet Union, but she never adjusted. She left in 1965 after Philby began an affair with David Maclean's wife. Eleanor died in 1968. Philby then married in 1971 his fourth wife, Rufina Ivanova, a Russian 20 years younger.

Philby worked for Soviet intelligence after his defection. In 1965 he received the Order of Lenin. He died on May 11, 1988. He was buried with full military honors in Kuntsevo Cemetery in Moscow.

See also: Blunt, Anthony; Burgess, Guy Francis De Moncy; Central Intelligence Agency; Golytsin, Anatoli; KGB (Komitet Gosudarstvennoi Bezopasnosti); Maclean, Donald Duart; MI-6 (Secret Intelligence Service)

References and Further Reading

Borovik, Genrikh Avitezerovich, and Phillip Knightley. *Philby Files: The Secret Life of a Master Spy*. Boston: Little, Brown & Co., 1994.

Knightly, Philip. *Master Spy: The Story of Kim Philby*. New York: Knopf, 1989.

Philby, Kim. *My Silent War: The Autobiography of a Spy.* New York: Random House, 2002.

Philby (Filbi), Rufina, Mikhail Lybimov, and Hayden B. Peake. *The Private Life of Kim Philby: The Moscow Years.* New York: Fromm International, 2000.

Andrew J. Waskey

PHILLIPS, DAVID ATLEE (OCTOBER 31, 1922–JULY 7, 1988)

David Atlee Phillips was a career Central Intelligence Agency (CIA) officer who specialized in covert action. He joined the CIA as a part-time agent in Chile in 1950 where he was editing an English-language newspaper. Phillips joined the CIA full-time in 1954. That same year he participated in PBSUCCESS the CIA covert action plan targeted at removing Guatemalan President Jacobo Arbenz from power. The propaganda campaign he ran was a major reason for its success. Phillips worked in Cuba around the time that Castro came into power. Returning to Washington from the posting, he participated in the planning of the failed Bay of Pigs invasion that was intended to topple Fidel Castro as well as assassination plots directed against him.

These later sets of covert operation plans found Phillips working out of Mexico. It is here that he came into contact with Gilberto Alvarado, a Nicaraguan youth that contacted the U.S. embassy in Mexico City with information about Lee Harvey Oswald and an upcoming murder. The failure to act on this information, along with his reported contacts with anti-Castro Cuban refugee groups, has fueled conspiracy theories involving Phillips and President John Kennedy's assassination.

Phillips retired from the CIA in 1975 and helped found the Association of Former Intelligence Officers (AFIO). Phillips successfully sued for libel against those making these accusations, donating the money he was awarded to the AFIO for use as a defense fund for other intelligence officers who felt they were being libeled.

See also: Association of Former Intelligence Officers; Central Intelligence Agency

References and Further Reading

Corson, William. *Armies of Ignorance. The Rise of the American Intelligence Empire.* New York: Dial, 1977.

Phillips, David Atlee. *The Night Watch: 25 Years of Peculiar Service.* New York: Antheneum, 1977.

Glenn P. Hastedt

PIGEONS

The United States first used homing pigeons extensively in military service during World War I. European countries had hundreds of thousands of pigeons in service during World War I. The United States had none upon entering the war in 1917. General John J. Pershing saw how successful the birds were for communication on the battlefields in France and insisted that the United States had to incorporate pigeons into its strategy as well. Until this time pigeons were seen as impractical for military value according to a U.S. Army Signal Corps report released in 1882.

Pigeons were used primarily as a means of last-resort communication in World War I; however, in World War II they took on another role: spy. American pigeons were trained predominantly in Fort Monmouth, New Jersey, by the Pigeon Service of the U.S. Army Corps, whose motto was "Get the message through!" In those days birds were trained to fly at night. A flock of pigeons was equipped with cameras attached to their breasts. These cameras were about two inches and took snapshots "at regular intervals when the rush of air through a tiny ball released the lever and clicked the shutter" (Cothren 1944, 14). When the Germans gained knowledge of possible espionage, "they ordered every pigeon in the occupied countries put to death by the Gestapo" (Cothren 1944, 11).

Signal Corps' Pigeon Service became official in 1917 and ended on May 1, 1957. Pigeons were used in the Korean War and made a brief comeback during the Vietnam War, which proved unsuccessful. Technology was the demise of the Pigeon Service; pigeons could not compete with the advancements in technology. Pigeons were also used in the navy, Marine Corps, and Coast Guard.

See also: American Intelligence, World War I; American Intelligence, World War II

References and Further Reading

Cothren, Marion B. *Pigeon Heroes: Birds of War and Messengers of Peace*. New York: Coward-McCann, 1944.

Marshall, Max (ed.). *The Story of the U.S. Army Signal Corps*. New York: Franklin Watts, 1965.

Office of the Chief Signal Officer, Information Circular: Homing Pigeons. Washington, DC: War Department, 1934.

Raines, Rebecca Robbins. *Getting the Message Through, a Branch History of the U.S. Army Signal Corps*. Washington, DC: Center of Military History, 1996.

Vanessa de los Reyes

PIKE COMMITTEE

Formally known as the House Select Intelligence Committee, the Pike Committee, so named after its chair Congressperson Otis Pike (D-NY), was initially created on February 19, 1975, to investigate the operation of the Central Intelligence Agency (CIA) and the Intelligence Community. It was created shortly after the Ford administration created the Rockefeller Commission and the Senate created the Church Committee for the same purpose. From the very outset, the Pike Committee's activities were surrounded in controversy and its final report was never officially released.

The House established the House Select Intelligence Committee by an overwhelming vote of 286–120. Pike was the second person to chair this committee. The first chair was Congressperson Lucien Nedzi (D-Ohio), who chaired the House Armed Services Subcommittee on Intelligence and was known to be a strong supporter of the CIA but otherwise had solidly liberal foreign policy credentials opposing the Vietnam War and the development of the B-1 bomber. Nedzi's Committee had 10 members, seven Democrats and three Republicans, and was highly partisan in nature with all Democrats being hostile to the CIA and all Republicans being supporters of it. Nedzi identified the CIA's own internal study of wrongdoings, the "Family Jewels" report, as the focal point for the committee's work. However, before the committee held its first meeting, a *New York Times* article showed that Nedzi had been briefed on its contents two years earlier. This revelation angered Democrats on the committee and led to Nedzi's resignation. The full House refused to accept his resignation by a vote of 290–64. Nedzi refused to reconsider his decision and on July 17 the House formally abolished his committee and established a new one under Pike's leadership.

Pike was first elected to Congress in 1960 and served until January 1979 when he retired after choosing not to seek reelection. Pike's Committee had 13 members but the partisan split remained. This divide, along with Pike's perceived political ambitions, and a young and aggressive staff that was seen by the CIA and Ford administration to be hostile and naïve—often demanding that significant amounts of sensitive intelligence information be turned over to it the next day—prevented it from ever achieving a solid working relationship with the CIA or White House in its quest to gather information.

Where the Church Committee focused largely on questions of domestic abuses by the CIA and the intelligence community, Pike directed his committee's attention to three areas that were broadly concerned with the effective management and operation of intelligence. The first area was intelligence budgets. Pike hoped to determine how much money was being spent, on what, and whether or not waste existed. These budgets had been secret and Director of Central Intelligence (DCI) William Colby refused to testify in open sessions regarding CIA expenditures. He did, however, testify on the budget when the committee went into executive session. In its final report the Pike Committee concluded that the intelligence budget was three to four times higher than Congress was led to believe.

The Pike Committee's second area of inquiry was with intelligence failures. It wanted all documents relating to the 1973 Mideast War, the 1974 Cyprus crisis, the 1974 coup in Portugal, the 1974 Indian nuclear explosion, the 1968 Tet offensive in Vietnam, the declaration of martial law in the Philippines and South Korea in 1972, and the 1968 Soviet invasion of Czechoslovakia. The committee found fault with the CIA's intelligence work in several of these cases, an assessment often shared by the CIA's own internal postmortems. Singled out for criticism were its predictive efforts in the 1973 Mideast War, the 1968 Tet Offensive, the 1974 coups in Cyprus and Portugal and the Indian nuclear explosion of the same year, and the 1968 Czech invasion.

The final area it examined was CIA covert action. Among the operations highlighted were the 1972 Italian elections, aid to the Kurds, and activities in Angola. In its conclusions, the Pike Committee rejected the charge that the CIA was out of control. Instead it concluded that covert actions were often sloppily implemented and irregularly approved. It did not recommend doing away with covert action except for assassinations.

The first draft of the committee's Final Report was rejected by Pike. A second draft was found to be acceptable. The CIA then was given one day to review it. Over its objections the Pike Committee voted along party lines to release the report without any substantial changes. DCI Colby then made a preemptive public attack on the not-yet-released report, calling it a threat to U.S. national security. At this point the full House stepped in and voted 246–124 to direct the Pike Committee not to release the report. Pike refused to accept this decision. As the political battle raged over whether or not to release the report, how much, and to whom, Daniel Schorr gave a copy of the report to *The Village Voice*, which published it in its entirety on February 16, 1976.

See also: Central Intelligence Committee; Church Committee; Colby, William Egan; Family Jewels; House Permanent Select Committee on Intelligence (HPSCI); Senate Select Committee on Intelligence

References and Further Reading

Pike Committee Report. *The Village Voice* (February 16, 1975), 1.
Smist, Frank. *Congress Oversees the United States Intelligence Community, 1947–1989*, 2nd ed. Knoxville, TN: University of Tennessee Press, 1990.

Glenn P. Hastedt

PINCHER, HENRY CHAPMAN (MARCH 29, 1914–)

A British journalist and author, Chapman has written extensively on the intelligence services, including *Their Trade is Treachery*, published in 1981 which claimed that Sir Roger Hollis, former director general of MI-5 had been a Soviet spy. He also named Sir Anthony Blunt, using a code name "Maurice," as having confessed to being a Soviet spy.

Henry Chapman Pincher was born on March 29, 1914, in Ambala, India, the son of a British army officer. He was educated at Darlington Grammar School and King's College, London, where he studied botany and zoology. In 1940 Pincher joined the Royal Armoured Corps and then worked as a technician at the Rocket Division of the Ministry of Supply, resigning in 1946 to became a defense, science, and medical writer at the *Daily Express*, a position he held until 1972 when he was appointed the assistant editor of the paper and chief defense correspondent of the Beaverbrook newspapers.

Pincher's first two books were on farm animals and fishes, but he rapidly became interested in security matters and was the author of *Inside Story* (1978), *Their Trade is Treachery* (joint author, 1981), *Too Secret Too Long* (1984), *Traitors—The Labyrinths of Treason* (1987), *The Web of Deception* (1987), and *The Truth about Dirty Tricks* (1991). Several other books followed, as well as a number of novels. Pincher was taken into confidence by many senior government officials and members of the British security services. At the heart of many of Pincher's work during the 1980s, including his collaboration with Peter Wright, author of *Spycatcher* (1987), was his belief that Roger Hollis was a Soviet spy and that the Wilson Labour government in Britain in the 1970s included many Soviet agents.

See also: Journalists, Espionage and; MI-5 (The Security Service)

References and Further Reading

Pincher, Chapman. *Too Secret Too Long*. New York: St. Martin's Press, 1984.
Wright, Peter. *Spycatcher*. New York: Viking, 1987.

Justin Corfield

PINKERTON, ALLAN
(AUGUST 21, 1819–JULY 1, 1884)

Allan Pinkerton founded one of the United States' most famous detective agencies and served as director of intelligence for the Union during the Civil War. His success in that role was limited, however; the intelligence he provided was often inaccurate, and his key agent was captured and executed by Confederate forces.

Pinkerton was born in Glasgow, Scotland. Due to police persecution for his involvement in a workers' protest movement, he fled Scotland in 1842, going first to Canada and then to the United States. Ultimately settling in Chicago in 1850, he became that city's first detective, setting up the North West Police Agency, which later became Pinkerton's National Detective Agency. Pinkerton had entered the detective business accidentally when in 1847 Pinkerton had helped break up a rural counterfeiting ring and in the process earned a reputation as a detective.

Railroads provided the main source of employment for Pinkerton's firm. Railroad companies had dramatically increased the miles of track laid in the 1850s to the point that they could no longer police or secure the property themselves. Pinkerton focused his efforts on dishonest employees and set up an espionage system to uncover corrupt behavior. Not only was he successful, his successes were also highly publicized and contributed to rising labor tensions within the railroad industry. In early 1861 while he was investigating the possibility of Confederate sabotage against the Philadelphia, Wilmington, and Baltimore Railroad, Pinkerton claimed to have uncovered a plot to assassinate president-elect Abraham Lincoln. He met with Lincoln's advisors and organized a plan to get Lincoln safely to Washington for his inauguration.

Pinkerton met with newly elected President Lincoln about the establishment of a federal secret service, but nothing came of the discussions. In May 1861 Pinkerton was asked by General George McClellan to set up a spy ring that could be used to gain information from the Confederacy. Pinkerton's successes were well publicized but not extensive. In the area of counterespionage he did succeed in capturing Confederate spy Rose O'Neal Greenhow, but his own espionage efforts provided little intelligence of value and were restricted in scope. When McClellan was relieved of command in 1862, Pinkerton returned to his detective business. Railroad companies continued to provide an important segment of his business. He now expanded the scope of his efforts from policing employee honesty to pursuing railroad robbers and bank robbers such as the Dalton gang and the James brothers.

See also: Civil War Intelligence

References and Further Reading

Lavine, Sigmund. *Allan Pinkerton: Amercia's First Private Eye*. New York: Dodd Mead, 1963.

Mackay, James. *Allan Pinkerton: the First Private Eye*. New York: Wiley, 1997.

Glenn P. Hastedt

PITTS, EARL E.
(SEPTEMBER 23, 1953–)

Earl Pitts was a Federal Bureau of Investigation (FBI) supervisory special agent who was arrested for conspiracy to commit espionage on December 18, 1996. Pitts had spied for the Soviet Union from 1987 to 1992 and received $224,000 for the information he provided. This included information on recruitment operations involving Russian intelligence officers, double agent operations, operations targeting Russian intelligence officers, the true identities of human assets in Russia, operations against Russian illegals, and procedures concerning surveillance of Russian intelligence officers in the New York area. Pitts was arrested after being lured into a trap by FBI agents in 1995 who posed as Russian intelligence officers wishing to reactivate him in a "false flag" operation. The purpose of this operation was to confirm his espionage in the 1987 to 1992 period.

Pitts was a 13-year veteran of the FBI, having begun work there in 1983. He went to work in the New York office in 1987 where he soon wrote to the Soviet mission at the United Nations asking to be put in contact with a KGB agent. This individual put Pitts in touch with Alesandr Karpov. They first met at the New York Public Library. They would meet nine times between 1988 and 1992, with Pitts exchanging information for money that was deposited in various bank accounts. With his 1992 transfer to the FBI's Legal Counsel Division, Pitts' espionage came to an end.

The individual who received Pitts' letter in 1987 later became a double agent who recalled its contents. Armed with this information, the FBI determined that Pitts was the likely spy. The false flag operation began in August 1995 when this individual contacted Pitts and informed him that there were visitors from Moscow who wished to see him. In reality, they were FBI agents. During the 16 months that the false flag operation was in place, Pitts provided information on 22 occasions and received $65,000 for his efforts. Pitts also revealed information from his previous activity as a spy and about an individual who was passing top-secret military information to the Soviet Union. It is believed that this individual was Robert Hanssen.

Pitts had been transferred to the FBI's Quantico Training Academy, and it was there that he was arrested. The charges against him carried a possible sentence of life imprisonment. Pitts pled guilty to the charges of espionage on April 30, 1997. He was sentenced to a 27-year prison term. Pitts explained his spying for the Soviet Union/Russia by saying that he did so in revenge for the many grievances he held against the FBI.

See also: Cold War Intelligence; Federal Bureau of Investigation (FBI)

References and Further Reading

Bowman, M. E. "The 'Worst Spy': Perceptions of Espionage," *American Intelligence Journal* 18 (1998), 57–62.

Kessler, Ronald. *The Bureau: The Secret History of the FBI*. New York: St. Martin's Press, 2002.

Glenn P. Hastedt

PLAME, VALERIE ELISE
(APRIL 19, 1963–)

Valerie Elise Plame Wilson, a U.S. Central Intelligence Agency (CIA) officer at the center of a political scandal starting in 2003, was born in Anchorage, Alaska, on April 19, 1963. She went to high school in Lower Moreland, Pennsylvania, going on to receive her BA in journalism from Pennsylvania State University in 1984.

Following her graduation, she was recruited by the CIA, although not many details of her career are known. She most likely worked as a CIA agent in Europe, where she was also able to complete two masters programs, the first at the London School of Economics and the second at the College of Europe in Bruges, Brussels.

Her superiors were pleased with her performance in Europe. She had agreed to work in Europe, oftentimes without her passport, which could have resulted in life in prison if she was caught spying. For these actions, she received a promotion and a new position.

Back in the United States, she worked for a "private company," essentially a CIA-front organization, known as "Brewster Jennings & Associates." While working as an "energy analyst" for the front company, Plame was able to perform certain classified investigations.

Plame married Joseph C. Wilson IV, former U.S. ambassador to Gabon and Sao Tome and Principe, on April 3, 1998. They had met while at a social function in Washington, DC, one year earlier. Early in the relationship, Plame was able to reveal her CIA status since Wilson had security clearance.

Although some have debated whether or not she was actually a secret agent at the time, as a result of her family situation with Wilson and their two young children, Plame's cover was blown by an article written by political analyst Robert Novak in the *Washington Post* on July 14, 2003. This information leak, which Novak claims came from a senior U.S. official in the Bush administration, was printed just days after Wilson had criticized President's Bush position on Iraq's attempts to purchase uranium in Niger.

A Justice Department investigation followed, looking into potential violations of the Intelligence Identities Protection Act of 1982. Vice President Cheney's top advisor, Lewis Libby, was indicted as a result of this investigation and convicted of obstruction of justice and perjury. He was sentenced to 30 months in jail and fined $250,000. He was also sentenced to community service and placed under supervisory parole. President George W. Bush commuted Libby's prison term but let the other parts of the sentence stand.

See also: Agee, Philip; Bush, George W., Administration and Intelligence; Intelligence Identities Protection Act of 1982

References and Further Reading

Plame, Valerie. *Fair Game*. New York: Simon & Schuster, 2007.
Source Watch Online. "Covert Agent Identity Protection Act," http://www.sourcewatch.org/wiki.phtml?title=Covert_Agent_Identity_Protection_Act (accessed January 12, 2006)

Arthur Holst

POINDEXTER, ADMIRAL JOHN
(AUGUST 12, 1936–)

Admiral John Poindexter, born August 12, 1936, was national security advisor under Ronald Reagan from December 1985 to November 1986. He was deeply involved in the Iran-Contra scandal. He worked for 20 months as head of Defense Advanced Research Projects Agency (DARPA) under George W. Bush, stepping down in 2003. Poindexter graduated first in the class of 1958 at Annapolis and earned a doctorate in nuclear physics from the California Institute of Technology. His naval career included service as assistant naval secretary from 1966 to 1974.

In September 1986, the mutual release by the Soviets of journalist Nicholas S. Daniloff and by the Americans of science student Gennadi Zakharov ended an international tension. Although neither man was a true espionage agent (Daniloff had been implicated by Central Intelligence Agency correspondence intercepted by the KGB), both had been held as spies. Reagan insisted that the two had not been traded. Poindexter, apparently not comprehending the danger Daniloff was in, urged during the crisis that the United States expel Soviet diplomats.

Poindexter was surprised at Reagan's interest in the imminent Reykjavik summit shortly after the Daniloff affair. Poindexter recognized that the United States would lose credibility if it simply rejected Soviet offers to reduce strategic arms, but he also believed that the American public would not accept the elimination of all nuclear arms.

National security policy was compromised by a conflict between Defense Secretary Casper Weinberger and Secretary of State George Shultz. Shultz conceded oversight of Central America and the Middle East to Director of Central Intelligence William Casey.

Casey, Poindexter, and Colonel Oliver North organized a covert program to sell missiles to Iran at inflated prices. Iran would then use its influence to help secure the release of American hostages held in Lebanon. Proceeds from the arms sales would be provided to the Contras, an anti-Communist rebel group in Nicaragua. Congress had forbidden aid to the Contras, and the administration itself had called for Operation Staunch, a worldwide arms embargo against Iran to facilitate an end to the Iran-Iraq war; the covert operation would undercut both of these policies.

In October 1986 a C-123 carrying arms bound for the Contras was shot down, and the following month the Lebanese newspaper *Al Shiraa* broke the story of covert U.S. operations. Casey died several months later from a brain tumor. Poindexter and North were each prosecuted for lying to Congress.

Poindexter returned to government in 2002 when George W. Bush named him head of DARPA. His controversial projects under Bush, Total Information Awareness (TIA) and especially the Futures Markets Applied to Predictions (Futures MAP), became known in the summer of 2003 and prompted his resignation. TIA would track personal information and commercial transactions, and Futures MAP would allow individuals to wager on terrorist acts.

See also: Bush, George W., Administration and Intelligence; Daniloff, Nicholas; Iran-Contra Affair; North, Lieutenant Colonel Oliver Laurence; Reagan Administration and Intelligence

References and Further Reading

Fitzgerald, Frances. *Way Out There in the Blue: Reagan, Star Wars, and the End of the Cold War.* New York: Simon & Schuster, 2000.

Pemberton, William E. *Exit with Honor: The Life and Presidency of Ronald Reagan.* New York: M.E. Sharpe, 1997.

Nicholas M. Sambaluk

POLGAR, THOMAS C.
(JULY 24, 1922–)

CIA station chief in Saigon at the end of the Vietnam War, Polgar was born in southern Hungary on July 24, 1922, to Jewish parents, who fled to the United States in 1938 to escape the Nazi oppression in Europe. He earned a BA degree from the Gaines School in New York City in 1942 and became a naturalized citizen in 1943. He was subsequently drafted into the U.S. Army and, because of his fluency in several languages, trained to be a counterintelligence agent in the Office of Strategic Services (OSS), the predecessor to the CIA. Later, he parachuted behind enemy lines with a false Nazi Party ID card, and operated as a spy in Berlin during the closing days of the war. After the war, he remained with the OSS and with its subsequent incarnations, the Strategic Services Unit, the Central Intelligence Group and, finally, the Central Intelligence Agency. He became a principal assistant to General Lucian Truscott, chief of the CIA's station in West Germany, where he served until 1954. He was assigned to the U.S. embassy in Vienna from 1961 to 1970.

In 1970, he became the CIA's station chief in Buenos Aires, Argentina. There, his successful handling of an airliner hijacking resulted in his assignment to the highly coveted station chief's job in Saigon. Polgar first arrived in Southeast Asia in 1971 for an area orientation in Laos and Vietnam before assuming his new job in January 1972. He was among the last Americans to be lifted by helicopter off the embassy rooftop on the morning of April 30, 1975, as Saigon fell to the North Vietnamese troops.

Much to his consternation on his return to Washington, top officials at the State Department and at CIA Headquarters in Langley, Virginia, threatened those who were in Saigon during the final days from talking, as though the debacle never happened. Polgar maintains that he knew about North Vietnamese plans months in advance of the final offensive that toppled Saigon, but he asserts that Washington refused to accept human resource reporting without corroborating evidence from radio or electronic intercepts, thereby willfully blinding itself to the reality of the situation until it was too late.

Polgar became chief of the Agency's Mexico City station in 1976. He retired from the CIA in 1981 and has since worked as a writer for the *Miami Herald* and as a consultant to the Department of Defense. In 1991, Polgar testified against the nomination of Robert Gates for CIA director, maintaining that Gates had been part of the Iran-Contra cover-up. Nevertheless, Gates was confirmed and served as CIA director until 1993.

See also: Central Intelligence Agency; Gates, Robert Michael; Office of Strategic Services

References and Further Reading

Dorland, Gil. *Legacy of Discord—Voices of the Vietnam War Era*. Washington, DC: Brassey's, 2001.

Engelmann, Larry. *Tears Before the Rain: An Oral History of the Fall of South Vietnam*. New York: Oxford University Press, 1990.

Miller, Nathan. *Spying for America: The Hidden History of U.S. Intelligence*. New York: Dell Publishing, 1990.

Murphy, David, Sergei A. Kondrashev, and George Bailey. *Battleground Berlin: CIA vs. KGB in the Cold War*. New Haven, CT: Yale University Press, 1999.

Snepp, Frank. *Decent Interval: An Insider's Account of Saigon's Indecent End Told by the CIA's Chief Strategy Analyst in Vietnam*. New York: Random House, 1977.

Sullivan, John F. *Of Spies and Lies: A CIA Lie Detector Remembers Vietnam*. Lawrence, KS: University Press of Kansas, 2002.

Trento, Joseph J. *The Secret History of the CIA*, reprint ed. New York: Avalon Publishing Group, 2005.

James H. Willbanks

POLLARD, JONATHAN JAY
(AUGUST 7, 1954–)

Jonathan Jay Pollard was born in Galveston, Texas, and grew up in South Bend, Indiana. He received his undergraduate degree from Stanford University in 1976 and went on to graduate work in law at Notre Dame and in international affairs at the Fletcher School of Diplomacy at Tufts University but did not receive an advanced degree at either institution. Pollard began working as a naval analyst in 1979. In November 1985 Pollard was arrested as an Israeli spy. He was sentenced to life in prison in March 1987.

Working in naval intelligence was not Pollard's first career choice. In 1977, while still in law school, Pollard applied for a position with the Central Intelligence Agency (CIA) and was rejected after a polygraph test pointed to drug use. Undeterred he applied for a job with the U.S. Navy in 1979 and was hired as an intelligence analyst in the navy's Filed Operational Intelligence Office (NFOIO). The navy did not know of his failed CIA polygraph test nor did it detect false information on his application for a government job.

Pollard's office was responsible for providing warning of hostile foreign naval activity. Although technically his access to intelligence was limited to his job requirements, Pollard found that in this position and others he would go on to hold that he could circumvent this compartmentalization and gain access to a far wider range of intelligence. While working for NFOIO Pollard constructed a fictionalized life history, claiming that he had lived in South Africa and that his father, a university professor, had been a CIA station chief there. Friends at Stanford had been told his father was a CIA station chief in Czechoslovakia and that he was a member of the Mossad, Israeli's intelligence organization. He also made contact with a South African military attaché. It is unclear whether Pollard passed any secrets to South Africa but its intelligence service was known to have been penetrated by Soviet spies. When this contact was discovered his superior reduced Pollard's security clearances in 1981. After his superior had moved on to another job

Pollard successfully appealed this reduction in his security clearance and his rights were restored and no damage was done to his career. This episode did not stop Pollard from talking freely with those who came in contact about the secrets he had access to.

In June 1984 Pollard began work in the navy's new Anti-Terrorism Alert Center. That same month he contacted Israeli officials about the possibility of spying for them. He had long told friends of his fervent support for Israel and, to the end, justified his spying in ideological terms rather than in monetary ones, although he would receive substantial compensation by Israel for the information he provided them. Pollard's initial contact was Col. Aviem Sella, to whom he would give information regarding the identity of Iraqi chemical weapons plants. Not long thereafter, Pollard and his fiancé were sent to Paris where Pollard met his handler. They were provided with $10,000 or $12,000 for the trip and Pollard was promised $1,500 per month. A similar amount would fund another trip to Europe in 1985, at which time Pollard's monthly retainer increased to $2,500. Pollard was also provided with an Israeli passport under the name of Danny Cohen and a Swiss bank account that reportedly contained $30,000 and would increase by that amount for each of the next 10 years.

Pollard's tradecraft was relatively straightforward. Several times a week he would take secret material from work. With his security clearance, his briefcase was not inspected. About every other week he would take this material to the Washington, DC, apartment of an Israeli intelligence official to be copied. On the last Saturday of each month he would meet with another Israeli intelligence officer to be paid, go over select documents, and receive guidance as to what material he should bring them. Pollard was told that terrorism intelligence was not needed. Among the secrets he provided Israel were U.S. military plans, maps, and reconnaissance photos of the Middle East; documents regarding Libyan, Syrian, and Saudi Arabian weapons systems; the identity of American agents in the Middle East; and U.S. military and diplomatic codes. Some of this intelligence was obtained by the Soviet Union and led to the capture of several agents.

Gradually Pollard's espionage began to impinge on his actions as an intelligence analyst and he came under suspicion. Hidden cameras at his workplace showed him stealing secrets. On November 18, 1985, Pollard was arrested. During a break in his interrogation, he and his wife sought refuge in the Israeli embassy where they were assured help awaited them. Instead, they were turned away. His handlers, whom he had alerted to his arrest, had already fled the United States. Pollard was sentenced to life in prison and his wife, Anne, received a five-year sentence.

Pollard's conviction has drawn strong protests from Jewish-American groups. Israeli officials have also intervened on Pollard's behalf, going so far as to return material to the United States that Pollard gave them. President Bill Clinton turned down Prime Minister Yitzhak Rabin's request that Pollard be pardoned. Although his supporters argue that his sentence was excessive, members of the intelligence community argue that was fully deserved given the information he provided Israel with. Underlying these different evaluations is the question of does the identity of the state spying on the United States matter?

See also: Central Intelligence Agency; Eitan, Rafael; Kadish, Ben-Ami

References and Further Reading

Allen, Thomas, and Norman Polmar. *Merchants of Treason, America's Secrets for Sale*. New York: Delacorte Press, 1988.

Black, Ian, and Benny Morris. *Israel's Secret Wars: The Untold Story of Israeli Intelligence*. London: Hamish Hamilton, 1991.

Raviv, Dan, and Yossi Melman. *Every Spy a Prince: The Complete History of Israel's Intelligence Community*. Boston: Houghton Mifflin, 1990.

Richelson, Jeffrey. *A Century of Spies: Intelligence in the Twentieth Century*. New York: Oxford University Press, 1995.

Glenn P. Hastedt

POLYAKOV, DIMITRI (JULY 6, 1921–MARCH 15, 1988)

Dimitri Polyakov was a Foreign Military Directorate (GRU) officer who reached the rank of general and who spied for the United States. Operating under the code name "Top Hat," he was one of America's most valuable cold war spies. Polyakov's identity was revealed to the Soviets first by Robert Hanssen in 1979 and then again by Aldrich Ames who was arrested for espionage in 1994. He is credited with having uncovered 19 Soviet spies and 150 foreigners acting as undercover agents. Polyakov was arrested on July 7, 1986, and subsequently sentenced to death in November 1978 on charges of espionage. He was reportedly executed on March 15, 1988.

Polyakov served in the Russian military during World War II as an artillery officer. After the war ended he received an appointment to the Frunze Military Academy where he graduated at the top of his class and was recruited by the GRU. His first overseas posting came at the United Nations in 1951. From there he moved to Berlin where he was in charge of sending illegal immigrants into Germany as agents.

Polyakov first offered his services as a spy to the United States in 1960. Then a colonel, he had come to the attention of U.S. intelligence officials the year before while stationed at the Soviet mission to the United Nations. Polyakov gave as his justification a sense of disillusionment with the Soviet system and a belief that it was broken and headed for disaster.

In his 25 years of espionage for the United States Polyakov provided U.S. intelligence with information on such Soviet spies as Jack E. Dunlap, who gave the Soviets National Security Agency documents; William Whalen, who provided them with air force operational plans; Nelson Drummond, who supplied weapons systems and cryptographic information from a navy communications center; and Herbert Bockenhaupt, who provided details of the air force's cryptographic system to the Soviet Union. Polyakov also provided the United States with important information on Soviet military matters and the Sino-Soviet split. All told, the information he provided the Federal Bureau of Investigation and Central Intelligence Agency are said to fill 25 filing cabinets. Polyakov was also used to send false information to the Soviet Union. One key area was with regard to chemical and biological warfare, where the United States wished the Soviet Union to believe it was engaging in a significant research and development program. Polyakov's efforts were seen as so successful that he was promoted to general.

The sudden loss of Central Intelligence Agency agents in the Soviet Union in 1985 signaled that the Committee for State Security (KGB) was in possession of an important intelligence source operating within the American intelligence community. It was later determined that this source was Aldrich Ames and that he provided the Soviet Union with Polyakov's name. In 2001 another Soviet spy, Robert Hanssen, claims to have alerted Soviet officials to Polyakov's identity in 1979. This raises the unanswered question of why the Soviet Union did not act on Hanssen's information and the possibility that Polyakov was being provided with false information to give to the United States from that time forward.

At a May 1988 summit conference between President Ronald Reagan and Soviet President Mikhail Gorbachev, Reagan reportedly offered to release a Soviet spy held by the United States for Polyakov. Gorbachev replied that Polyakov had been executed two months earlier.

See also: Ames, Aldrich; Boeckenhaupt, Herbert W.; Central Intelligence Agency; Drummond, Yeoman 1st Nelson C.; GRU (Main Intelligence Directorate); Hanssen, Robert Philip; KGB (Komitet Gosudarstvennoi Bezopasnosti); Whalen, William

References and Further Reading

Garthoff, Raymond. "Polyakov's Run," *The Bulletin of the Atomic Scientists* 56 (2000), 37–40.
Schiller, Lawrence. *Into the Mirror: The Life of Masterspy Robert Hanssen*. New York: Harper-Collins, 2001.

Glenn P. Hastedt

POPOV, PYOTR SEMYONOVICH (1922–1960)

Pyotr Popov was one of the Central Intelligence Agency's (CIA) first and most important cold war spies, providing the United States with information on Soviet military plans and capabilities. An officer in the Foreign Military Directorate (GRU), he volunteered to spy for the United States in 1953. Popov was arrested in October 1959 and tried on January 6–7, 1960. He was executed in June 1960.

Popov was born in 1922. He served in World War II and joined the Communist Party in 1943. Two years later he began his education at Frunze Military Academy. From there he went on to attend a military intelligence school from which he graduated in 1951. In 1952 he began a tour of duty in Vienna, Austria. In January 1953 Popov placed a note inside a car belonging to a U.S. Foreign Service officer. That act began his recruitment as a spy. Although he had financial problems, largely due to the need to support a family and a mistress, Popov's primary motivation for engaging in espionage against the Soviet Union was a deep-felt antipathy for the Soviet System. He also harbored a resentment for the manner in which his family had been treated when he was a child and the poverty that surrounded their existence.

Once he made the decision to become a spy, Popov was put in touch with George Kisevalter who was his CIA handler. Kisevalter, himself, was born in Russia to the son of a tsarist military officer. In the United States, when the Russian Revolution erupted, the family stayed here and became American citizens. Kisevalter would also be Colonel Oleg Penkovsky's handler when he became an American spy in 1961. Popov provided the United States with the identities of some 650 GRU officers and information that helped locate numerous Soviet agents.

Popov's exposure is linked to a March 29, 1957, report written by the CIA which he provided information for. The report contained information from a speech given that month by Soviet Minister of Defense Marshal Zhukov in East Berlin, which Popov attended. Though only a few copies of this report existed, one fell into the hands of the KGB and allowed it to track the information back to Popov.

See also: Central Intelligence Agency; Cold War Intelligence; KGB (Komitet Gosudarstvennoi Bezopasnosti)

References and Further Reading

Ashley, Clarence. *Spymaster*. Gretna, LA: Pelican Publishing Company, 2004.
Hood, William. *Mole: The True Story of the First Russian Intelligence Officer Recruited by the CIA*. New York: Norton, 1982.
Murphy, David, Sergei Kondrashev, and George Bailey. *Battleground Berlin: CIA vs. KGB in the Cold War*. New Haven, CT: Yale University Press, 1997.

Glenn P. Hastedt

POST–COLD WAR INTELLIGENCE

Just as the onset of the cold war did not mark the beginning of espionage by and against the United States, so its passing in 1989 did not mark the end of espionage. Evidence of the continued relevance of espionage regularly surfaces. President George W. Bush's first foreign policy crisis involved the downing of a spy plane over China on March 31, 2001. A U.S. Navy surveillance plane collided with a Chinese fighter pilot that had been "playing tag" with it in international airspace over the South China Sea. The plane and crew landed safely in China. China demanded an apology for the incident and the death of the pilot. The United States refused and demanded the return of the plane and crew. The crisis was ended peacefully but not until the U.S. aircraft had been subjected to careful analysis by Chinese authorities.

Soviet espionage has also not ended. In 1996 CIA officer Harold Nicholson was arrested and charged with spying for Russia. He pled guilty and is serving a 23-year sentence. In 1997 Edward Pitts, a 13-year FBI agent, was charged with spying for Russia. The FBI was tipped off to his case by a Russian double agent. Pitts is serving a 27-year prison term. In 1998 David Boone, an analyst with the National Security Agency, was arrested for spying for Russia. A walk-in, among the information he passed to the Russians was the list of Russian sites targeted by U.S. nuclear weapons. In 2000, Army Reserve Colonel George Trofimoff was arrested for spying for Russia for over 25 years. He is the highest-ranking military officer ever charged with espionage.

Still, if anything, espionage in the post–cold war era is a more complex phenomenon and therefore one more difficult to counter. During the cold war, the United States concentrated its national security resources on one enemy: the Soviet Union. Likewise, it had to protect its secrets from only one enemy. The end of the cold war reduced, but did not eliminate, the Russian security threat. At the same time, it elevated the challenges and threats posed by other states. As a consequence, the United States faces a

Equipment and parts from the Navy EP-3, a naval reconnaissance aircraft, are loaded onto an AN-124 cargo plane on July 2, 2001. (AP/Wide World Photos)

situation in which prudence suggests it must seek to obtain information about the policies and capabilities of many states and it must protect its own secrets from a larger number of states. Accused spies in the post–cold war era have worked for Cuba, China, Taiwan, and Israel.

In addition, the national security agenda of states has expanded. Where once questions of military capability and strategy sat atop this agenda and dominated all others, today we are as likely to find trade, monetary, scientific, and technology issues being contested at the highest levels of government. Just as espionage served to further the development of military policy in the cold war, it has the potential for advancing state policy in these areas as well. Industrial espionage, for example, is of increasing concern as states seek dual-use technologies and seek to better position themselves in a globalized economy.

Advances in technology also have not stopped and the game of spy and counterspy continues apace here. In 1999, for example, India knew when American spy satellites would be over their nuclear testing facilities and took countermeasures to ensure that their development of a nuclear weapon would go undetected. And although satellite technology remains very much an area in which the advanced industrial states of the north hold a comparative advantage over all others, the burgeoning commercial satellite industry is making satellite technology available to all. Cyber warfare, in which the Internet becomes the weapon of choice, is also coming into its own. Russia made effective use of it against Georgia in their 2008 border war.

Spy satellites also remain very much an important part of the U.S. espionage arsenal, especially in war or the preparation for war. Published accounts suggest that Keyhole and Lacrosse satellites (the former produces digital pictures and the latter radar images) flew over Baghdad 19 times in the first 18 hours of the land war against Iraq in the Persian Gulf War. More recently, in Afghanistan as part of the war against terrorism, the United States made use of Predator drone aircraft that provided long-term coverage. The Keyhole and Lacrosse satellites were over their targets for only a few minutes at a time, whereas the Predator could provide 24-hour coverage. Some suggest that perhaps the most significant long-term post–cold war development in the technology area was the decision of the Clinton administration to approve the export of advanced encryption software. This will greatly complicate the task of trying to intercept and break enemy codes and ciphers.

If all of this were not enough, the events of September 11, 2001, were a transformational event for the U.S. intelligence services. Both the Federal Bureau of Investigation and the Central Intelligence Agency came under public and congressional criticism for their failure to anticipate and provide warning of the terrorist attacks on the Pentagon and World Trade Center. The net result of these investigations was the creation of a Director of National Intelligence to oversee the intelligence community and the establishment of a Department of Homeland Security to better deal with the problem of terrorist attacks on the United States.

The declaration of a "Global War on Terrorism" has raised concerns in many quarters. Some within the intelligence community are concerned that it will lead to a neglect of spy satellites. In place is a program to develop a new generation of spy satellites, the Future Imagery Architecture program. One estimate suggests that from $625 to $900 million is needed to get the program back on track so that new satellites will be operational when needed to replace the existing inventory of KH-11 Keyhole satellite. Others inside and outside of the intelligence community voiced concerns about possible violations of civil rights and liberties that might accompany an overzealous or excessive interpretation of the mandate given to those charged with domestic spying. Among the programs which have drawn the most intense criticisms are those involving the warrantless wiretapping of Americans, the waterboarding of suspected terrorists and their sympathizers, and the policy of renditions. An overarching concern is that intelligence has become politicized to an unprecedented extent, as seen by the selective use and release of intelligence on the reasons for going to war with Iraq, most notably on the question of its possessing weapons of mass destruction.

See also: Bush, George W., Administration and Intelligence; Central Intelligence Agency; Clinton Administration and Intelligence; Director of National Intelligence; Federal Bureau of Investigation (FBI); Industrial Espionage; Homeland Security, Department of; Iraq, U.S. Operations In/Against; National Commission on Terrorist Attacks on the United States (The 9/11 Commission); National Security Agency; Persian Gulf War; Renditions; September 11, 2001; Terrorist Groups and Intelligence; Waterboarding

References and Further Reading

Adams, James. *The New Spies: Exploring the Frontiers of Espionage.* New York: Hutchinson, 1994.

Betts, Richard. *Enemies of Intelligence.* New York: Columbia University Press, 2007.

Coll, Steven. *Ghost Wars: The Secret History of the CIA, Afghanistan, and Bin Laden, from the Soviet Invasion to September 10, 2001*. New York: Penguin. 2004.

Cronin, Audrey, and James Lutes (eds.). *Attacking Terrorism: Elements of a Grand Strategy*. Washington, DC: Georgetown University Press, 2004.

Posner, Gerald. *Why America Slept: The Failure to Prevent 9/11*. New York: Random House, 2003.

U.S. Commission on the Intelligence Capabilities of the United States Regarding Weapons of Mass Destruction. *Report to the President of the United States*. Washington, DC: Government Printing Office. 2005.

U.S. National Commission on Terrorist Attacks Upon the United States. *The 9/11 Commission Report*. Washington, DC: Government Printing Office. 2004.

Glenn P. Hastedt

POWERS, FRANCIS GARY
(AUGUST 17, 1929–AUGUST 1, 1977)

Francis Gary Powers was a U-2 reconnaissance aircraft pilot whose spy plane was shot down over Russia in 1960. The United States first denied that it was involved in spying but when Russian authorities produced Powers they were forced to recant their story. Powers' failed mission led to the cancellation of a Paris summit conference between President Dwight Eisenhower and Soviet leader Nikita Khrushchev that was under way at the time. Powers was born in Kentucky and enlisted in the air force upon graduation from Milligan College. Commissioned in 1952, he was assigned to the Strategic Air Command. In January 1956, Powers and other pilots were recruited by the Central Intelligence Agency (CIA) to fly the new U-2 high-altitude reconnaissance aircraft on spy missions over the Soviet Union and other key sites. For example, in 1956 Powers flew missions over the Mediterranean Sea to provide information on the Suez Crisis. Powers' unit was based at Incerlik Air Force Base in Adana, Turkey, and operated under the cover of the Weather Observational Squadron of the National Advisory Committee for Aeronautics. This was the predecessor body to the National Aeronautics and Space Administration (NASA). Powers flew his first mission over the Soviet Union in November 1956. He would fly his last on May 1, 1960. On that date he was flying a mission that was to take him from Preshawar, Pakistan, to Bodo, Norway. As his plane approached Sverdlovsk, Soviet Union, it was hit by a surface-to-air-missile. The Soviets had known about the U-2 overflights from the beginning and protested against them to the United States. Initially they lacked the capacity to shoot down these planes due to the high altitude they flew at, some 80,000 feet. The CIA had provided Powers with suicide poison but he chose to eject from the aircraft. On the ground he was captured with documents identifying him as a CIA agent. Under interrogation he admitted to being a spy. Khrushchev made his confession public as well as some of the aerial photographs he was taking, thereby nullifying the American cover story that a weather plane was missing along the Soviet border. Powers was placed on trial by Soviet authorities in August 1960. He pled guilty to spying and sentenced to 10 years in prison.

Two years into his sentence he was exchanged for Soviet spy Rudolf Abel on February 10, 1962, at one of the checkpoints along the Berlin Wall. Powers died on August 1,

1977, when the helicopter he was piloting as part of his job as a traffic reporter for a radio station in Los Angeles crashed. With the permission of President Jimmy Carter, Powers was buried in Arlington National Cemetery.

See also: Eisenhower Administration and Intelligence; Open Skies Proposal; U-2 Incident

References and Further Reading

Ambrose, Stephen. *Ike's Spies: Eisenhower and the Espionage Establishment*. Garden City, NY: Doubleday, 1981.

Powers, Francis Gary, and Curt Gentry. *Operation Overflight: A Memory of the U-2 Incident*. New York: Holt, Rinehart and Winston, 1970.

James H. Willbanks

PRESIDENT'S FOREIGN INTELLIGENCE ADVISORY BOARD

The President's Foreign Intelligence Advisory Board (PFIAB) is a group of independent, nongovernmental experts who provide nonpartisan advice and analysis of the quality of intelligence being provided to the president. The board meets in secret with the heads of the intelligence agencies and with the president, providing both a limited amount of citizen oversight and an objective source of insight for the president.

President Dwight Eisenhower established the board as the President's Board of Consultants on Foreign Intelligence Activities in 1956 in response to questions about the Central Intelligence Agency (CIA) involvement in the overthrow of the governments of Iran and Guatemala. Under Eisenhower, the board played primarily a technological/scientific role by affirming the decision to maintain the secrecy of the U-2 program.

President John F. Kennedy gave the board its present name in May 1961 when he reconstituted the PFIAB in the aftermath of the Bay of Pigs. Kennedy blamed the intelligence community and the CIA for the failure, and asked the PFIAB to recommend changes in the way U.S. intelligence operated. Chaired by James Killian and with longtime presidential advisor Clark Clifford a key member, the PFIAB made 170 recommendations, including reassigning some of the CIA's military intelligence activities to the Defense Intelligence Agency and expanding the CIA's technological capabilities, emphasizing satellite and ultra-high-resolution photography. Clifford chaired the PFIAB from April 1963 until becoming secretary of defense in February 1968.

Under President Richard Nixon, the PFIAB became less important and less independent as Nixon appointed a number of political allies without any particular expertise to the board. President Gerald Ford expanded the PFIAB's scope in the aftermath of the Church and Otis Committees' investigations into the CIA's activities. Ford created the Intelligence Oversight Board as an addendum to the PFIAB to monitor the intelligence agencies for improprieties and abuses, which it could then report directly to the president.

President Jimmy Carter, responding to the advice of CIA Director Stansfield Turner, abolished the board in 1977, claiming it did not provide any unique or necessary functions. President Ronald Reagan revived the board in 1981, although neither he nor President George H. W. Bush appeared to utilize the PFIAB significantly.

Under President Bill Clinton the PFIAB again assumed an important oversight and analytical role. Clinton asked the PFIAB to analyze security and intelligence threats to the Energy Department's nuclear laboratories. The PFIAB's 1999 report suggested that China had acquired American technology to enhance its nuclear program through espionage. Under President George W. Bush the PFIAB once again diminished in importance.

See also: Bush, George W., Administration and Intelligence; Carter Administration and Intelligence; Clinton Administration and Intelligence; Eisenhower Administration and Intelligence; Ford Administration and Intelligence; Kennedy Administration and Intelligence; Reagan Administration and Intelligence

References and Further Reading

Clifford, Clark, with Richard Holbrooke. *Counsel to the President.* New York: Random House, 1991.
Executive Office of the President. "President's Foreign Intelligence Advisory Board," http://www.whitehouse.gov/administration/eop/piab/
Shapley, Deborah. "Foreign Intelligence Advisory Board: A Lesson in Citizen Oversight?," *Science* 191 (March 12, 1976), 1035–1036.

Richard M. Filipink Jr.

PRESIDENT'S INTELLIGENCE OVERSIGHT BOARD

The President's Intelligence Oversight Board (PIOB) was created by President Gerald Ford via Executive Order (EO) 12334 in 1976. Ford was responding to the many revelations of illegal CIA activity that surfaced as part of the Church Committee investigations and hoped that by creating such a committee he could lessen the growing interest in setting up permanent congressional oversight committees for the intelligence community. To this end, according to EO 12234, the purpose of the IOB was "to enhance the security of the United States by assuring the legality of activities of the Intelligence Community."

Composed of three private citizens, most of whom were members of the President's Foreign Intelligence Advisory Board that was charged with providing the president with advice on the quality and adequacy of intelligence collection, analysis, estimates, counterintelligence, and other intelligence activities, the PIOB was tasked with the responsibility of preparing reports on intelligence activities it considered to be "unlawful or contrary to Executive order or Presidential directive." It was empowered to refer these reports directly to the attorney general.

Perhaps the most highly publicized FIOB investigation took place in the mid-1990s when it was tasked by National Security Advisor Anthony Lake in April 1995 to investigate intelligence that related to the death, torture, and disappearance of any U.S. citizens in Guatemala since 1984. A public outcry had arisen around the 1990 torture of Sister Diana Ortiz, the 1990 death of Michael Devine, the 1992 disappearance of Effrain Bamaca Valasquez, the 1985 death of Griffith Davis, and the 1995 death of

Nicholas Blake. The PFIO report issued in June 1996 concluded that the CIA had failed to keep Congress informed about its operations in Guatemala and that it paid insufficient attention to human rights events there but that it did not find any complicity by CIA officers or any other U.S. government employees in the abuses referred to it for investigation.

In 1993 President Bill Clinton made the IOB a subcommittee of the President's Foreign Intelligence Advisory Board. This was not seen as a major structural change in oversight since as a matter of general practice the three IOB members had been drawn from the membership of the larger 16-person Foreign Intelligence Advisory Board.

A more controversial change took place as a result of an executive order issued by President George W. Bush in February 2008. Through it he ended the PIOB's authority to oversee the general councils and inspector generals of the intelligence community members, ended the requirement that inspector generals report to the PIOB every three months, and took away the PIOB authority to refer matters directly to the attorney general. Now, the PFIOB informs the president if it has found a problem but only if other officials are not adequately addressing the matter.

See also: Bush, George W., Administration and Intelligence; Clinton Administration and Intelligence; Ford Administration and Intelligence

References and Further Reading

Andrew, Christopher. *For the President's Eyes Only: Secret Intelligence and the American Presidency from Washington to Bush.* New York: HarperCollins, 1995.
Richelson, Jeffrey. *The U.S. Intelligence Community*, 5th ed. Boulder, CO: Westview, 2008.

Glenn P. Hastedt

PRIME, GEOFFREY
(1938–)

Geoffrey Prime was a Soviet spy who worked in Great Britain's cryptography agency. He confessed to being a spy on June 26, 1982. In November 1982 he was sentenced to 35 years in prison for espionage. He received an additional three-year term for assaulting three young girls. Prime was released from prison in March 2001.

Prime was drafted into the Royal Air Force in 1956. With a flair for learning foreign languages, Prime became an expert in Russian and in 1964 he was assigned to Berlin where his job involved monitoring Soviet voice transmissions. In January 1968, while traveling on a train, he threw a message out of a window to a Soviet guard in which he volunteered his services to the Soviet Union as a spy. His offer was taken up and he was trained in spycraft in Potsdam, East Germany, where he learned how to photograph sensitive documents, use one-time pads for communication, and microdots.

In September 1968, Prime, now retired from the Royal Air Force, began working as a civilian transcription specialist working on Russian transmissions. His Soviet handlers provided him with $400. He would later travel to Vienna, Dublin, and Rome to meet with his handlers and receive additional payments. On a 1972 trip to Cyprus to meet his controller, Prime lost his one-time pads. Informed of this, his handlers deactivated Prime and turned him into a "sleeper." He was reactivated in December 1974. By now he had been promoted to the point where he worked with information gathered by Rhyolite satellites. Prime resigned from General Communications Headquarters (GCHQ) on September 28, 1977, but not before taking numerous photographs and over 15 reels of film that he gave to his KGB handler in Vienna. Published estimates place the amount of money received by Prime from the Russians for the information he gave them at $6,200.

Prime was identified as a Soviet spy in 1981 after he went to the home of a 14-year-old girl and attempted to assault her. When she resisted and screamed he fled. His car was identified and the police visited his home to question him. He was later arrested and his home searched and an extensive amount of pedophile information, including 2,287 index cards with notes and pictures, was seized. The police would be summoned to his home again by his wife who had uncovered spycraft paraphernalia. The subsequent police search revealed additional material, including top-secret information that Prime had taken from GCHQ.

See also: Cold War Intelligence

References and Further Reading

Aldrich, Richard J. *The Hidden Hand: Britain, America, and Cold War Secret Intelligence*. New York: The Overlook Press, 2002.
Cole, D. J. *Geoffrey Prime: The Imperfect Spy*. London: Robert Hale Ltd., 1999.

Glenn P. Hastedt

PROJECT PAPERCLIP

Project Paperclip is the code name for a series of operations and plans, including Operation Paperclip and Operation Overcast, to acquire German scientists and war material for use by American forces. Its original purpose was to use the information and material against the Japanese, but quickly shifted focus to the Soviet Union with the end of World War II and the increase in cold war tensions. Throughout its history, Project Paperclip brought over 642 specialists between 1945 and 1952. The value of their work was estimated at $2 billion worth of intellectual and military property and saved defense agencies decades in researching man-hours. Nearly as important, the project also denied these same scientists to the Russians. However, it also brought hundreds of former Nazi scientists who had suspicious pasts in some of the more notorious German research and concentration camps.

Operation Paperclip began as Allied troops were overrunning German units following the invasion of Europe. American troops were instructed to interview the German scientists they met, and these were found to be so valuable that the Pentagon created a new program to harness this intellectual force. The Alsos Mission was created as a joint venture between the army, navy, and Office of Scientific Research and Development, with a focus on finding nuclear secrets. Teams of civilian scientists and technicians would enter active theaters of war to seize personnel, equipment, and documents alongside combat troops. Members of an Alsos team were among the first Americans to enter Paris in 1944 with French forces. Other navy and army groups under the Combined Intelligence Objectives Subcommittee (CIOS) and the Technical

Industrial Intelligence Committee (TIIC) would be operating by October of 1944. These groups justified themselves with the capture of many distinguished Germans including Dr. Herbert Wagner, inventor of the HS-293 glide bomb. Following the war, Operation Paperclip would come under the jurisdiction of the Office of the Military General United States (OMGUS) and then the Joint Intelligence Operations Agency (JIOA). It is important to note that intelligence groups were in charge of Paperclip because of the implications for espionage and the need for secrecy with such high-profile scientists.

One of the most well-known captures is Wernher von Braun and his team of rocket experts at Peenemunde. Besides the many surplus V-2 rockets and rocket parts found at Peenemunde, the Americans had over 400 of the world's top rocketry experts in their hands. Von Braun and his team would eventually become top rocket experts at government research installations in Huntsville, Alabama; White Sands Proving Ground, New Mexico; and Fort Bliss, Texas. Although the Russians got the laboratories and research facility at Peenemunde because it was in their zone of occupation, the Americans got the brains behind the German rocket superiority. Besides rocket experts, Americans also got top scientists in chemistry, space medicine, physics, communications, and other fields. In fact, denial of the specialists to the Soviets motivated Operation Paperclip as much as any gains the scientists could give the United States.

Americans also received intelligence information on the Soviet forces and terrain. Immediately following the war, the United States had little to no intelligence on the Russians. The scientists living in areas invaded by the Russians gave detailed reports on troop strengths, terrain, and other elements of the Russian military. This was some of the first intelligence received by the United States and helped allay fears that the Russians might continue their invasion Western Europe.

One of the most controversial aspects of Paperclip is the fact that former enemies were given access to top-secret American research facilities and information. The scientists went through a supposedly very thorough investigation of their backgrounds to ensure that no one who was an "ardent Nazi" be allowed into the country. It is clear now that the ideological background was less important in restricting potential specialists than their value to science and to the Russians. Several scientists were sent to the United States but bypassed the normal State Department channels because they would not pass State Department rules prohibiting former Nazis from entering the country. The government kept much of this information confidential as it could have created a huge public outcry. Paperclip scientists were also responsible for some ethically questionable behavior, including the MKULTRA project, extreme cold, and high-altitude experiments on U.S. soldiers and civilians. In 1946, dozens were arrested in Canada in connection to giving atomic secrets to the Russians. There was a great fear that Paperclip would cause similar security risks.

One of the most serious espionage breeches of Paperclip did not involve any German scientists, but one of its chief officers in the 1960s, Lieutenant Colonel William H. Whalen. In 1957, Whalen became head of the Joint Intelligence Operation Agency (JIOA), which at that time ran "National Interest." This program allowed the government to bring German scientists over to the United States and place them in governmental agencies and universities. Whalen's clearance as head of the JIOA gave him access to the offices of the Joint Chiefs of Staff and others. In 1959, Whalen, a near bankrupt alcoholic, began spying for the Russians after being recruited by Sergi Edemski, a Soviet Intelligence (GRU) agent. Whalen would eventually become the "highest placed American military officer ever convicted of espionage."

Although Paperclip had an auspicious end with several scandals in the 1960s to 1990s, its rewards were almost incalculable for American military research, not to mention the industrial technology and academia. Without Project Paperclip, many of the achievements in space travel, military weaponry, and pure science would not have occurred. Whether this is justification to allow former war criminals and Nazis into the country remains to be seen.

See also: American Intelligence; Cold War Intelligence; GRU (Main Intelligence Directorate); Whalen, Lieutenant Colonel William H.; World War II

References and Further Reading

Gimbel, John. "U.S. Policy and German Scientists: The Early Cold War," *Political Science Quarterly* 101 (1986), 433–451.
Hunt, Linda. *Secret Agenda: The United States Government, Nazi Scientists, and Project Paperclip, 1945–1990.* New York: St. Martin's Press, 1991.
Lasby, Clarence G. *Project Paperclip: German Scientists and the Cold War.* New York: Atheneum, 1971.
Naimack, Norman. *The Russians in Germany: A History of the Soviet Zone of Occupation, 1945–1949.* Cambridge, MA: Harvard University Press, 1995.

Peter C. Jones

PUEBLO, USS

The USS *Pueblo* was a U.S. Navy intelligence ship seized by the Democratic People's Republic of Korea (North Korea) in January 1968. In 1967, under a joint naval and National Security Agency (NSA) program, the *Pueblo*, a former cargo ship commissioned in 1944, was refitted with sensitive electronic and cryptographic gear and converted into an intelligence-gathering ship.

After training operations off the U.S. West Coast, the *Pueblo*, captained by Commander Lloyd Bucher, sailed for Japan in late 1967. In January 1968, the ship began conducting surveillance of Soviet naval activity in the Tsushima Straits to collect signal and electronic intelligence.

On January 23, the *Pueblo* was approached by a North Korean subchaser, which ordered her to stand down or be fired upon. The *Pueblo* attempted to maneuver away, but the subchaser was soon joined by four torpedo boats, another subchaser, and two MiG-21 fighters. The *Pueblo* was armed with only two .50-caliber machineguns, which were wrapped in cold-weather tarpaulins. The ammunition was below decks and the gun mounts were unarmored, so the crew made no attempt to man them.

The *Pueblo* at first tried to outmaneuver the North Korean vessels while her sailors attempted to destroy the great volume of classified equipment and material aboard. However, the quicker North Korean vessels opened fire and Bucher had no choice except to direct the *Pueblo* to follow the North Koreans as ordered. However he stopped the ship just outside North Korean waters; the North Koreans opened fire again, killing

Members of the USS *Pueblo* crew greet officers at the United Nations Advance Camp after almost a year in North Korean custody. (Naval Historical Center)

a U.S. sailor, Seaman Duane Hodges, and wounding several other crew members. North Korean sailors subsequently boarded the *Pueblo*, and tied up and blindfolded the crew.

The *Pueblo* was taken into port at Wonsan and the crew was moved to POW camps, where members of the crew later said they were starved and regularly tortured. During their imprisonment, they were forced to sign confessions that they had been spying.

Following negotiations between the United States and North Korea, the United States apologized and the North Korean government released the eight-two remaining crew members. On December 23, 1968, the crew was trucked to the DMZ between North and South Korea where they were ordered to walk south across the "Bridge of No Return" at Panmunjon.

A navy court of inquiry recommended the court-martial of Commander Bucher and two of his officers, but Secretary of the Navy John H. Chafee overruled the court, saying that the men had "suffered enough" in their 11 months of imprisonment. Bucher, however, did receive an official letter of reprimand. He died in San Diego on January 28, 2004, partly from complications caused by the injuries he had suffered during his time as a prisoner in North Korea. The *Pueblo* remains a commissioned ship in the U.S. Navy, but has never been released by the North Koreans. Today, it is a major tourist attraction in Pyongyang.

See also: Bucher, Commander Lloyd M.; Naval Intelligence

References and Further Reading

Brandt, Ed. *The Last Voyage of USS Pueblo*. New York: Norton, 1969.

Bucher, Lloyd M., with Mark Rascovich. *Bucher: My Story*. New York: Doubleday, 1970.

Lerner, Mitchell B. *The Pueblo Incident: A Spy Ship and the Failure of American Foreign Policy*. Lawrence, KS: University Press of Kansas, 2002.

Schumacher, Frederick Carl, Jr., and George C. Wilson. *Bridge of No Return: The Ordeal of the USS Pueblo*. New York: Harcourt, Brace, Jovanovich, 1970.

James H. Willbanks

PURPLE

PURPLE was the code name given to the cipher machine that broke the most important Japanese diplomatic code. Collectively, the products of this code-breaking operation were known as MAGIC. The term *PURPLE* was used because it identified the color of the binder used in the code-breaking process.

The most common cipher machine is an electrorotor machine used to send and receive secret messages. The heart of the machine consists of a keyboard for typing in the message, a set of rotating disks (rotors) which substitute a different letter for that being struck, and a system for turning the disks as a key is pressed. In the system, each press of a key results in a different substitution being made for the letter struck. Cipher machines came into existence at the end of World War I and were commercially available in the early 1920s. Enigma is the best known rotor machine. The PURPLE machine differed slightly from the Enigma machine because it did not use rotors but a set of telephonic switches connecting two typewriters, one of which input the message and the other which printed it out for transmission.

During the Washington Naval Conference that was held from November 1921 to February 1922 the United States succeeded in breaking the code used to transmit Japanese diplomatic communications. Having become aware that the Black Chamber had broken the secrecy surrounding their communications, Japan set out to construct a new machine. It was first used in prototype form at the London Naval Conference of 1930. The "Red" machine, as it was known, again for the color of the binder used to collect the information obtained from it, was formally put into place in 1931. It proved to be relatively unreliable and was replaced in 1937 by the PURPLE machine.

American cryptanalysts, led by William Friedman, broke the PURPLE machine in 1940. The U.S. possessed four PURPLE machines for cryptanalysis. The army and navy each had one in Washington, one was in the Philippines, and one was in Great Britain. The Japanese were informed that the United States had broken into PURPLE by their Russian allies. They reached this conclusion on the basis of comments made by Undersecretary of State Sumner Welles, close advisor to President Franklin Roosevelt. Japanese authorities, however, disregarded this warning and continued to use PURPLE, confident that it could not be broke.

Japanese military and diplomatic communications were sent by different machines, with the result that the information contained in these communications was often highly compartmentalized. PURPLE thus revealed little about the impending Japanese attack on Pearl Harbor. Later in the war, PURPLE provided important insights about

Germany's war plans because of messages sent by the Japanese ambassador in Berlin back to Tokyo. Evidence also points to the Soviet Union as having independently broken into PURPLE communications during World War II.

See also: MAGIC; Pearl Harbor; Ultra

References and Further Reading

Farago, Ladislas. *The Broken Seal: 'Operation Magic' and the Secret Road to Pearl Harbor*. New York: Bantam, 1968.

Lewin, Ronald. *The American Magic: Codes, Ciphers, and the Defeat of Japan*. New York: Farrar, Straus and Giroux, 1982.

Prange, Gordon W. *At Dawn We Slept: The Untold Story of Pearl Harbor*. New York: McGraw-Hill, 1981.

Glenn P. Hastedt

R

RABORN, VICE ADMIRAL WILLIAM FRANCIS, JR. (JUNE 8, 1905–MARCH 6, 1990)

Born in Decatur, Texas, William Francis Raborn, Jr., graduated from the Naval Academy in 1928. He served as Director of Central Intelligence (DCI) from April 28, 1965 to June 30, 1966. Raborn was retired from the navy and working for the aerospace industry at the time of his appointment to the post of DCI by President Lyndon Johnson. In his navy career Raborn reached the rank of vice admiral and held the position deputy chief of naval operations (development). Much of his career had been spent in the Special Projects Office where he directed work on developing the Polaris submarine.

Johnson appointed Raborn with the hope of making intelligence more responsive to the direction of the White House. Johnson had become increasingly frustrated with the intelligence community as the Vietnam War continued. Its analyses were often at odds with the desired policies of the administration. An example of what Johnson sought from the Central Intelligence Agency (CIA) and Raborn came in the Dominican Republic when Johnson sought intelligence to support his sending of troops and not about the situation itself or the wisdom of this course of action. Johnson's hopes for Raborn were not realized for at least two reasons. First, Raborn's managerial skills did not translate into control over the CIA. He came to the CIA with no background in intelligence and he had difficulty adapting himself to the internal operations of the CIA. Second, Raborn failed to establish a good working relationship with Congress, thus preventing him from obtaining important external support in any effort to redirect the CIA. Soon Johnson also began to distance himself from Raborn. Consequently, Raborn had only a minimal impact at the CIA and on intelligence. Critics cite his brief ineffective tenure as DCI and the political nature of his appointment as the beginning of a decline in the prestige of the CIA.

See also: Central Intelligence Agency; Director of Central Intelligence

References and Further Reading

Andrew, Christopher. *For the President's Eyes Only: Secret Intelligence and the American Presidency from Washington to Bush.* New York: HarperCollins, 1995.

Cline, Ray. *Secrets, Spies and Scholars: The Essential CIA.* Washington, DC: Acropolis, 1976.

Ranelagh, John. *The Rise and Decline of the CIA.* Revised and updated. New York: Touchstone, 1987.

Glenn P. Hastedt

RADIO FREE EUROPE AND RADIO LIBERTY

During the cold war, Radio Free Europe (RFE) and Radio Liberty (RL), U.S. government-sponsored international radio broadcasts transmitted to Communist nations and other authoritarian regimes, broadcast uncensored news and information to audiences in the Soviet bloc in an attempt to weaken Communist control over information and to foster internal opposition. RFE broadcast to Bulgaria, Czechoslovakia, Hungary, Poland, and Romania and, in the 1980s, to Estonia, Latvia, and Lithuania. RL transmitted in Russian and some 15 other national languages of the Soviet Union.

Unlike other Western broadcasters, RFE and RL concentrated on developments within and about their target countries not covered by state-controlled domestic media. They acted as surrogate home services, reporting on actions of the authorities and relaying views of dissidents and opposition movements. Notwithstanding repeated technical interference (jamming, for example), broadcasts generally reached their intended audiences. Evidence of the impact of the broadcasts on the eventual collapse of the Communist regimes has been corroborated in the testimony of leaders such as Czech President Václav Havel after 1989.

RFE and RL were conceived in 1949 by George F. Kennan of the U.S. Department of State and Frank G. Wisner, head of the Central Intelligence Agency (CIA) Office of Policy Coordination, as instruments to utilize Soviet and East European émigrés in support of U.S. foreign policy objectives. Founded as nonprofit corporations ostensibly supported with private funds, RFE and RL were in fact funded by the U.S. government through the CIA until 1972. The first official broadcast took place on July 4, 1950. RFE and RL initially adopted more confrontational editorial policies and used more aggressive language than other Western broadcasters. By the mid-1950s, however, as U.S. foreign policy toward the Soviet bloc became more conciliatory, the networks emphasized the need for liberalization and evolutionary system changes. In so doing, they broadcast news and information about domestic politics and economic issues as well as cultural and historical traditions normally suppressed by Communist authorities. Over time, the networks evolved into saturation home services, seeking large audiences by broadcasting almost around the clock and by incorporating programs on Western music, religion, science, sports, youth, and labor issues.

The networks faced the considerable challenge of operating as surrogate home services in information-poor environments. They carefully monitored state-controlled print and electronic media and frequently interviewed travelers and defectors in field bureaus around the world. The networks cultivated ties with Western journalists and other visitors to Communist countries and received information from regime opponents, often

President of the U.S. government-funded and Prague-based Radio Free Europe/Radio Liberty (RFE/RL), Thomas A. Dine addresses a news conference in Prague, 2002. The radio was established in 1949 to spread pro-Western news to countries behind the Iron Curtain and to promote democratic values and institutions. (AP/Wide World Photos)

at great personal risk to the informants, within their target countries. This information was gathered to support broadcasts, but RFE and RL research reports also served many Western observers as their major source of information about the Communist bloc.

RFE and RL programs were produced in Munich in the Federal Republic of Germany (FRG, West Germany) and were broadcast via shortwave transmitters operating on multiple frequencies and high power to overcome jamming and other frequency-disruption tactics. The networks enjoyed substantial operational autonomy and were highly decentralized in function. Émigré broadcast service directors with intimate knowledge of their audiences were responsible for most broadcast content, within broad policy guidelines and under U.S. management oversight.

The Communist authorities devoted major resources to countering RFE and RL broadcasts. In 1951, Soviet leader Josef Stalin personally ordered the establishment of local and long-distance jamming facilities to block Western broadcasts. Eastern bloc authorities also launched propaganda, diplomatic, and espionage campaigns intended to discredit the broadcasts. In addition, they jailed individuals providing information to either network. Ironically, the same authorities relied on secret transcripts of the broadcasts for information they could not obtain from local media that they themselves controlled.

After 1971, direct CIA involvement in the networks ended, and they were then openly funded by congressional appropriation through the Board for International Broadcasting. The network corporations were merged into a single entity, RFE/RL, Incorporated, in 1976.

The networks established intimate contact with their audiences during the 1970s and 1980s, when new waves of émigrés strengthened broadcast staffs and as dissidents and other regime opponents, emboldened by the Helsinki Final Act (1975), began to challenge the Communist system. RFE and RL provided a "megaphone" through which independent figures, denied normal access to local media, could reach millions of their countrymen via uncensored writings. RFE and RL were able to document large audiences and acted as the leading international broadcaster in many target countries. After the Velvet Revolution of 1989, many East European and Russian leaders testified to the importance of RFE and RL broadcasts in ending the cold war. Operating today from Prague in the Czech Republic, RFE/RL broadcasts to the southern Balkans, most of the former Soviet Union, Afghanistan, Iran, and Iraq in support of democratic institutions and a transition to democracy.

See also: Central Intelligence Agency; Radio Marti; Wisner, Frank Gardiner

References and Further Reading

Nelson, Michael. *War of the Black Heavens: The Battles of Western Broadcasting in the Cold War.* Syracuse: Syracuse University Press, 1997.

Soley, Lawrence C., and John S. Nichols. *Clandestine Radio Broadcasting.* New York: Praeger, 1987.

Urban, George. *Radio Free Europe and the Pursuit of Democracy: My War within the Cold War.* New Haven, CT: Yale University Press, 1997.

A. Ross Johnson

RADIO MARTI

Radio Marti is a U.S. broadcasting service to Cuba. Prior to the 1980s, the U.S. government tried its hand unsuccessfully at broadcasting to Cuba. Radio Swan was unveiled to support the 1961 Bay of Pigs invasion; it soon became Radio Americas and then disbanded. These stations lacked credibility and an effective audience to justify their funding. Then, in 1981, President Ronald Reagan declared that it was his administration's intention to establish a Radio Free Cuba that was modeled on Radio Free Europe/Radio Liberty, but there was initial opposition by other North American broadcasters who feared that Cuban President Fidel Castro would retaliate by jamming existing commercial medium-wave broadcasts from Florida.

The Office of Cuba Broadcasting, which operates Radio Marti and Television Marti, was created by the Radio Broadcasting to Cuba Act of 1983 (Public Law 98-111) to focus on Cuban domestic and international news and information that is not reported by the media controlled by the Cuban government. According to the legislation, Radio Marti programming, with its mixture of Spanish-language news, feature, cultural, and entertainment programming to its Cuban audience, must follow all Voice of America standards; programs must be objective, accurate, and well balanced.

Radio Marti went on the air May 20, 1985, which commemorated the anniversary of Cuba's independence from Spanish colonial rule, May 20, 1902. The new station, using a transmitter located in the Florida Keys, was named for Cuban writer Jose Marti who fought for Cuba's independence from Spain and against U.S. influence in Latin

America. Since its first broadcast, the Cuban government has continuously jammed its signals, especially those on medium wave, but the Cuban government's most effective interference has been to transmit alternate programs on the same AM frequency used by Radio Marti.

In 1994, Radio Marti introduced live coverage of special events in the United States and around the world that directly affect Cuba and its citizens, such as hearings held by Congressman Charles B. Rangel (D-NY) to lift the U.S. embargo against Cuba; speeches by Latin American heads of state at the Summit of the Americas in Miami; and reports from exiles, defectors, and former prisoners in Cuba.

The administration consolidated U.S. international broadcasting operations with Public Law 103-236 (April 30, 1994), under an International Broadcasting Bureau (IBB), and created a new Broadcasting Board of Governors (BBG), with oversight authority over all civilian U.S. government international broadcasting; this included the VOA and Radio and TV Marti.

In 1998, Radio Marti completed the move of its operations from Washington, DC, to Miami, Florida, under legislation passed by Congress and signed by President Clinton in April 1996. This move placed the radio station closer to its target audience. Today, Radio Marti, which broadcasts seven days a week, transmits over shortwave transmitters in Delano, California, and Greenville, North Carolina, with an AM-medium wave broadcast band in Florida.

See also: Castro, Fidel; JMWAVE; Radio Free Europe and Radio Free Liberty; Shackley, Theodore G., Jr.

References and Further Reading

Radio Marti. http://www.martinoticias.com/.

Soley, Lawrence C., and John S. Nichols. *Clandestine Radio Broadcasting*. New York: Praeger, 1987.

U.S. Congress. House. Committee on International Relations. Subcommittee on the Western Hemisphere. *Overview of Radio and Television Marti Hearings*, 108th Congress, 1st Session. Washington, DC: Government Printing Office, 2003.

U.S. Congress. Senate. Committee on Foreign Relations, *Radio Broadcasting to Cuba, Hearings*. 97th Congress, 2nd Session. Washington, DC: Government Printing Office, 1982–1983.

Youm, Kyu Ho. "The Radio and TV Marti Controversy: A Re-Examination," *Gazette* 48 (1991), 95–103.

Martin J. Manning

REAGAN ADMINISTRATION AND INTELLIGENCE

Ronald Reagan was president from 1980 to 1989. William Casey and William Webster served as Directors of Central Intelligence under him. Reagan campaigned as president on a platform of rebuilding U.S. military strength and conducting an aggressive foreign policy against the Soviet Union, which he once referred to as the "evil empire," holding it to be a national security threat to the United States and not a partner as had been the case under the détente policies of Richard Nixon, Gerald Ford, and Jimmy Carter. Reagan had unsuccessfully challenged Ford for the Republican nomination for the 1976 election. He won the party's 1980 nomination and, buoyed by the foreign policy setbacks of the

Carter administration, most notably the 1979 Iranian Revolution and the Soviet invasion of Afghanistan, Reagan was easily elected.

Upon entering office, Reagan made good on his promises. Following Jeanne Kirkpatrick's assertion that there was a fundamental difference between authoritarian regimes and Communist regimes, Reagan supported these governments as allies rather than criticize their human rights records. Second, in rejecting détente he did not move U.S. foreign policy back to containment. Instead, the Reagan doctrine not only called for containing existing Communist regimes but also for helping to remove them from power. The initial application of the Reagan Doctrine and the support for authoritarian governments was in Central America where El Salvador was identified as a threat, Grenada invaded, and the Contras were created to fight against the Sandinista government of Nicaragua. The Reagan Doctrine also provided the rationale for supporting mujahedin against the Soviet Union in Afghanistan. The spirit of the Reagan Doctrine also led to stepped-up action in the Middle East even though the enemy was not so much Communism as it was radical opposition to the United States. In 1984 Reagan sent marines to Lebanon where they became the target of a terrorist attack, killing 244. He also ordered a military raid on Libya, intended to kill Libya President Muammar Qaddafi for his role in the 1986 bombing of a Berlin Discotheque that killed U.S. soldiers. Earlier, in 1985, he had authorized a covert action program to destabilize his government. Under Reagan, the United States also supported Iranian exile groups who opposed the new regime there and as well as running an anti-Khomeini radio station out of Egypt. Finally, it led the administration to support Saddam Hussein against Iran in the Iran-Iraq War.

As these last examples illustrate, a central component of this new foreign policy was a change in direction of U.S. intelligence policy. Where Carter's executive order governing the policies of the intelligence community had stressed negatives, what not to do, Reagan's Executive Order 12333 adopted a more positive and supportive rhetoric. For example, it permitted the Central Intelligence Agency (CIA) to collect "significant foreign intelligence" within the United States so long as it did not involve gathering information on the domestic activities of U.S. persons. This executive order largely remains in place.

The person Reagan called upon to redirect U.S. intelligence was William Casey. A veteran of World War II and the Office of Strategic Services (OSS), Casey embraced covert action. He also treated intelligence estimates as his estimates and felt free to adjust them to this thinking. This attitude brought Casey, and thus intelligence policy, into frequent conflict with Congress. His selective use of CIA intelligence analysis was most pronounced with regard to Soviet estimates. It led to resignations in protest and public charges by intelligence analysts of politicizing intelligence. Casey's deputy, Robert Gates, was sufficiently tarred by these accusations that his 1987 nomination as Director of Central Intelligence had to be withdrawn.

Casey's stance on covert action led him to hold information back from Congress on the extent of U.S. covert action undertakings such as mining Nicaraguan harbors. This standoff ultimately resulted in the Boland Amendments that forbid the use of U.S. government funds to overthrow the Nicaraguan government. It was an attempt to circumvent this restriction that led the Reagan administration to embark on the Iran-Contra initiative in which arms intended for Israel would be sold to Iranian moderates (with Israel getting replacement weapons) in return for help in getting U.S. hostages in Lebanon released and with the money being deposited in foreign bank accounts and then sent on to the Contras. When discovered, it created a crisis for the administration from which it did not recover.

See also: Casey, William; Central Intelligence Agency; Cold War Intelligence; Iran-Contra Affair; Webster, William Hedgcock

References and Further Reading

Andrew, Christopher. *For the President's Eyes Only: Secret Intelligence and the American Presidency from Washington to Bush*. New York: HarperCollins, 1995.
Draper, Theodore. *A Very Thin Line: The Iran Contra Affairs*. New York: Touchstone, 1992.
Hersh. Seymour. *The Target Is Destroyed*. London: Farber, 1986.
Woodward, Bob. *VEIL: The Secret Wars of the CIA 1981–1987*. New York: Simon & Schuster, 1987.

Glenn P. Hastedt

RED ORCHESTRA

The Red Orchestra, or Rote Kapelle in German, was the name of a group of spies who gathered intelligence for the Soviet Union. Numbering around one to two hundred, they were discovered in 1942 and executed by the Abwehr. The Nazis called spy rings orchestras because they referred to the transmitters as "music boxes" and the radio operators as "musicians." Because the Red Orchestra operated in so many countries at once it was really a set of overlapping spy rings.

Prior to World War II the Soviets had organized a spy network in the countries around Germany. Belgium was the first country with spies in this ring. Later, Holland, Switzerland, and Germany were added as locations for spies being run by Leopold Trepper, who was chief of the European Red Orchestra.

After the beginning of Operation Barbarossa, Stalin was desperate for intelligence on the Nazi war machine, so he ordered that an ever-increasing amount of intelligence data be sent. For over a year the Red Orchestra was successful in passing large volumes of intelligence data to the Soviets. However, on December 13, 1941, the Abwehr got a break.

Directional finders were used to locate radio signals. The finders would first position a signal along a line. Then it would try to cross the line in one or two other places. The crossing would be a line drawn by other directional finders. This meant that "X" would mark the source of the radio signals.

The capture of the first of the Red Orchestra agents was due to a common espionage problem. The more successful a spy or a spy ring is at stealing intelligence the more information it has to transmit. The larger the volume of intelligence to transmit, the longer time it takes to transmit and thus the more vulnerable are the agents transmitting to detection. In the case of the Red Orchestra agents, coded messages had been sent for over five straight hours from three houses in Brussels located on the Rue des Attrebats.

Seized in the raid were code books, equipment, invisible inks, false papers, and other spy craft tools. While the raid was in progress, Leopold Trepper arrived. He however was able to lie his way to freedom with a claim that he was selling rabbits.

In June of 1942 the Nazis captured Johann Wenzel, a radio operator for a sector of the Red Orchestra. He gave information that led to the capture of the whole spy ring and to Leopold Trepper. For some months thereafter the Nazis ran the Red Orchestra as a disinformation operation against the Soviets. Eventually the Soviets became suspicious and demanded sensitive information the Nazis would not supply. This led to the end of the activities of the Red Orchestra.

Inside of Germany the original leaders of the Red Orchestra were Harro Schulze-Boysen and Arvid Harnack, nephew of a world-renowned theologian. Schulze-Boysen was a member of the Junker class. He was also an officer for the German Ministry of Air. He joined forces with Arvid Harnack and his U.S.-born wife, Mildred Harnack. The Harnacks were prominent prewar members of Berlin literary society. They also recruited Alexander Erdberg, Adam Kuckhoff, Holst Heilmann, Herbert Gollnow, Gunther Weisenborn, and Johann Graudenz as agents.

Harnack was a member of the German Ministry of Economics. Adam Kuckhoff was a theater producer, but his wife worked in Alfred Rosenberg's department of race policy. Heilmann was a cryptologist working in the coding department of the Wehrmacht signals group. Gollow worked for German counterintelligence. Graudenz had access to all German airfields because he sold brakes for airplanes to the German military. Weisenborn was an official with Joseph Goebbel's propaganda radio department.

Other spies working with the Red Orchestra were Rudolf von Scheliha, an aristocrat and a libertine. He at first sold German secrets to the British who then dropped him when they learned he was also selling the same secrets to the Soviets. Scheliha used the money from espionage to finance his hedonistic lifestyle. He was discovered when a message to Moscow was intercepted and decoded by Johann Wenzel, a former SOE operative who had gone over to the Nazis. Scheliha and his assistant Ise Stobe were executed by a firing squad on December 22, 1942.

The German portion of the Red Orchestra was destroyed by the treachery of Johann Wenzel. Arrested on August 30, 1942, were Schulze-Boysen and his wife. Harnack and his wife were arrested on September 3, 1942.

Fourteen of the leaders of the Red Orchestra were tried by the Nazis. Eleven were sentenced to death. Mildred Harnack and Ericka von Brockdorf were given life sentences. The men were sentenced to be hanged; however, Berlin did not have a gallows so meat hooks were thrust through their throats. They were then pulled up to be left dangling until dead.

Adolph Hitler took a deep personal interest in the trial of the Red Orchestra. He was so angry at the idea that Germans should spy on his Nazi regime that he complained to the Nazi court about those who were not executed. For Hitler their treason merited death and those who thought differently were of suspect loyalty. The Gestapo court changed its sentence for Mildred Harnack and Ericka von Brockdorf. Both were beheaded with a guillotine.

In neutral Switzerland the operating head of Red Orchestra was Sandor Rado. His ring was not shut down when the rings in Germany and in occupied Europe were arrested. However, traitors within his ring betrayed it to Swiss authorities.

See also: American Intelligence, World War II

References and Further Reading

Brysac, Shareen Blair. *Resisting Hitler: Mildred Harnack and the Red Orchestra.* Oxford: Oxford University Press, 2000.

Kesaris Paul (ed.). *The Rote Kapelle: The CIA's History of Soviet Intelligence and Espionage Networks in Western Europe, 1936–1945.* Westport, CT: Greenwood Publishing, 1979.

Perrault, Gilles. *Red Orchestra.* New York: Knopf Publishing Group, 1989.

Tarrant, V. E. *The Red Orchestra: The Soviet Spy Network inside Nazi Europe.* New York: John Wiley & Sons, 1960.

Andrew J. Waskey

REGAN, SERGEANT BRIAN PATRICK (OCTOBER 23, 1962–)

On August 23, 2001, Air Force Sergeant Brian Patrick Regan, age 38, was arrested at Dulles Airport in Washington, DC, on espionage charges as he was planning to board a flight to Zurich, Switzerland, via Frankfort, Germany. He carried with him a coded message and a list of names and addresses hidden in his shoe. Regan's clients were Iraq, China, and Libya. On April 19, 2002, the Justice Department announced that it would seek the death penalty for Regan even though it acknowledged that no information had been passed to these countries. This marked the first time that the death penalty had been sought since Ethel and Julius Rosenberg were executed in 1953. On February 20, 2003, a federal grand jury convicted Regan of three charges of attempted espionage. Four days later it rejected the death penalty. Less than one month later, on March 20, 2003, an agreement was reached between Regan and the government on a sentence of life imprisonment in return for his agreeing to tell the government about any classified information he may have given to others. In return, the government agreed not to prosecute his wife and allowed her to keep a portion of his military pension.

Regan retired from the air force on August 30, 2000, at which time he went to work for TRW, a defense contractor, where he was assigned to work at a National Reconnaissance Office (NRO) facility. Trained in cryptanalysis, Reagan last worked at the NRO where he managed a classified Intelink Web site that was accessible only to members of the intelligence community and held a top-secret security clearance. According to the government affidavit in fall 2000, U.S. government officials were told by a reliable source that someone had made contact with government "A" from a public library in an encrypted message offering to provide classified documents. The public library was near Regan's house and surveillance began in May 2001 and he was observed regularly using computers at the library. The computer used by Regan at NRO also was examined by the Federal Bureau of Investigation (FBI); it contained links to documents that the reliable source indicated were being offered to these states. They included electronic images from overhead surveillance platforms, statements about a foreign country's satellite capabilities, and pages from a Central Intelligence Agency newsletter. The day he was arrested the FBI observed Regan on a closed-circuit surveillance television examining and taking notes on a secret document on his computer. The primary motive appears to have been money. The affidavit indicates

The FBI displays various items during a news conference in 2003 to discuss the items recovered after being buried by Brian Regan, a former air force master sergeant serving a life sentence for attempting to sell U.S. secrets to Saddam Hussein and others. Officials said roughly 10,000 pages of documents, as well as videotapes and CD-ROMs, were taken and buried at undisclosed locations in the Washington area by Regan while he worked at the National Reconnaissance Office, which operates the nation's spy satellites. (AP/Wide World Photos)

that in February 2001 Regan had consumer debts of $53,000. Other accounts place his debt at almost $117,000. Regan requested a total of more than $13 million for the secrets he was offering.

See also: Federal Bureau of Investigation (FBI); National Reconnaissance Office; Post–Cold War Intelligence; Rosenberg, Julius and Ethel

References and Further Reading

Carmichael, Virginia. *Framing History: The Rosenberg Story and the Cold War*. Minneapolis: University of Minnesota Press, 1993.

Centre for CounterIntelligence and Security Studies. "Spy Cases," http://www.cicentre.com/ (accessed July 17, 2008).

Glenn P. Hastedt

REILLY, SIDNEY
(MARCH 24, 1874–NOVEMBER 5, 1925)

Born Salomon Sigmund Rosenblum on March 24, 1874, Sidney Reilly, considered by some to be the model for the fictional James Bond, was much more of a confidence man and opportunist than the intrepid secret agent portrayed by Sam Neil in the successful and well regarded 1980s mini-series *Reilly: Ace of Spies*. A youthful brush with radical politics brought Reilly to the attention of the Trazist secret police, the Okrana, who recruited him as an informant to spy on the exile community in Paris. In 1895 Reilly appeared in England, continued to work with the Okrana, and may have begun to cooperate with the British Secret Service as well, but mainly occupied himself with a series of dubious commercial ventures. On August 22, 1898, Reilly married Margaret Callahan Thomas, the widow of a wealthy English cleric and the first of several wives and mistresses. While married to Margaret he changed his name to Sidney George Reilly, acquired a passport identifying him as an Irish-born British citizen, and returned to Russia where he established himself as middleman bringing together Western businessmen with Russian officials.

Reilly's myriad connections made him very appealing to the British Secret Service during the Russian Revolution, especially after the seizure of power by the antiwar Bolsheviks. Commissioned a captain in the Royal Air Corps as a cover for his fieldwork, the Secret Service charged Reilly with keeping Russia engaged on the Eastern Front. Reilly's activities over the next year earned him his undying fame and reputation as the Ace of Spies. Reilly joined forces with anarchist and former Okrana agent Boris Savinkov and Robert Bruce Lockhart, a British diplomat, in the "Lockhart" or "Ambassador's Plot." Reilly infiltrated the Latvian guards assigned to protect top Bolshevik leaders in a plan to kidnap or kill them, topple the young Communist state, and replace it with a pro-Allied government possibly headed by Reilly himself. The scheme failed and the increase in security following an assassination attempt on Lenin forced Reilly to flee the country.

Reilly returned to England, where he continued to work for British intelligence advocating a gradualist approach to the Bolsheviks, who he believed would be forced by economic realities to abandon radicalism for a pragmatic approach to government. At the same time Reilly continued to involve himself in unsavory business ventures and political conspiracies, which in 1921 caused the Secret Service to sever all official ties with him. Reilly continued to independently pursue anti-Bolshevik activities and became involved with a monarchist group inside Russia known as the Trust. Unfortunately, the Trust had been created by the Unified State Political Agency (OGPU), precursor of the KGB, as part of its counterintelligence efforts to penetrate genuine opposition groups abroad. In 1925 members of the Trust lured Reilly into Russia where he was arrested, interrogated, and executed. Reports of Reilly's death contained numerous ambiguities, leading many to believe that he was still alive. Documents released after the fall of the Soviet Union, however, confirm his death on November 5, 1925.

See also: Fiction—Spy Novels

References and Further Reading

Andrew, Christopher, and Oleg Gordievsky. *KGB: The Inside Story of Its Foreign Operations from Lenin to Gorbachev*. New York: Harper Collins, 1990.

Reilly, Sidney. *Britain's Master Spy: The Adventures of Sidney Reilly, an Autobiography*. New York: Carroll & Graf, 1986.

Spence, Richard B. *Trust No One: The Secret Life of Sidney Reilly*. Los Angeles: Feral House, 2002.

Vernon L. Pedersen

RENDITIONS

In legal terms, rendition refers to the practice of handing over someone to another authority. In the context of intelligence work it has become associated with the Central Intelligence Agency's (CIA) abduction of individuals suspected of being involved in terrorist activities and handing them over to foreign intelligence agencies where they are held captive and interrogated. Often the program is referred to as "extraordinary renditions."

President Bill Clinton approved a renditions program that targeted returning suspected Islamic terrorists to foreign countries where they were wanted for criminal prosecution. In order to be in compliance with the International Convention Against Torture, the CIA obtained assurances that the suspects would not be tortured. The purpose of this renditions program, according to Clinton administration officials, was to disrupt terrorist attacks and not to obtain information as was the case with the George W. Bush administration's post–September 11, 2001 program.

This renditions program was the product of two different post-9/11 concerns. The first problem was what to do with high-ranking al-Qaeda leaders. One option was assassination. A second was to capture them and interrogate them. President Bush authorized both courses of action in a Presidential Finding signed six days after 9/11. On September 6, 2006, Bush acknowledged the existence of a covert action program in which suspected terrorists were kidnapped and taken to prisons located outside of the United States where they were subjected to what he referred to as "tough" but "safe and lawful and necessary" interrogation methods carried out by specially trained CIA officers.

Nearly 100 detainees were held in these prisons until they were shut down when Bush made his speech. Fourteen "high-value" terrorist suspects were moved to Guantanamo Bay. Whereas Bush characterized the interrogation methods as legitimate, others condemned them as torture. Interrogation techniques said to be used include feigned drowning, extreme isolation, slapping, sleep deprivation, reduced food intake, and light and sound bombardment. The first agreements on "black site" facilities were reached in mid-2002 with Thailand and an east European country. Publicity about the Thai site in June 2003 led to its closing and agreements were then signed with other countries. Public reports indicated that Egypt, Indonesia, Poland, and Romania were among the countries to which suspects were taken. A European Union investigation identified Germany, Sweden, Spain, Ireland, Greece, Cyprus, Denmark, Turkey, Macedonia, Bosnia, and Romania as all having participated in some fashion in the CIA flights that took terrorist suspects to their final destinations. In four cases the renditions took place in Europe (Sweden, Macedonia, and Italy) and in five instances European intelligence services were said to have provided direct assistance to the CIA.

In April 2009 Leon Panetta, the Director of Central Intelligence Agency, announced that the CIA was no longer holding anyone at any of their detention sites.

See also: Bush, George W., Administration and Intelligence; Clinton Administration and Intelligence; Panetta, Leon; Terrorist Groups and Intelligence

References and Further Reading

Gray, Stephen. *Ghost Plane.* New York: St. Martin's, 2006.

Paust, Jordan. *Beyond the Law: The Bush Administration's Unlawful Responses in the War on Terror.* Cambridge, MA: Cambridge University Press, 2007.

Glenn P. Hastedt

REVERE, PAUL
(JANUARY 1, 1735–MAY 10, 1818)

Paul Revere, a courier for patriot American Revolutionaries, was born in Boston in 1735, educated in metallurgy, and became a master silversmith and engraver. As an artisan, Revere became the leader of Boston's mechanic class of rebels, rising to political prominence through his participation in the North End Caucus that reported on British troop activities. His friendship with Samuel Adams, John Hancock, and Joseph Warren, and his anti-British engraving that made prints immortalizing the Boston Massacre in 1770, distinguished him as a political leader. Revere took an active part in the Boston Tea Party in 1773 and in its aftermath rode as courier to New York to advise patriots there of Boston's activities to resist the British Coercive Acts. In the spring of 1774 he completed a horseback circuit journey urging support from patriots in New York and Philadelphia for Boston's revolutionary measures opposing the Boston Port Bill that had closed Boston to trade. In September 1774 Revere rode as official courier for the Boston Committee of Safety, carrying the Suffolk Resolves to Philadelphia. Because of his trustworthiness and competence as an express rider, he was named the official courier for the Massachusetts Provincial Assembly to the Continental Congress. His daringly magnificent rides aroused patriotic fervor and bound the colonies together in common cause against British tyranny through his communications network.

On the evening of April 18–19, 1775, in an event immortalized by Longfellow, the "midnight ride of Paul Revere" occurred. Revere waited to receive the signal from the steeple of the Old North Church of how the British were moving—"one if by land, and two if by sea." Upon seeing two lanterns, Revere crossed the Charles River and rode from Charlestown to Lexington to warn Hancock and Adams that the British intended to arrest them for their revolutionary activities and to alert the minutemen of Middlesex County that the British were coming to seize their military stores. Revere reached Hancock and Adams, who escaped British capture. Revere then rode towards Concord but was halted, questioned by the British, and his horse taken. He returned to Boston and continued to work for independence by designing and printing the first Continental currency, making the first official seal used by the revolutionary government, and designing the state seal for Massachusetts. Revere served the Revolution as lieutenant colonel, commanding the defense of the fort, Castle William, in Boston Harbor. Post-Revolution, he developed a mill for rolling sheets of copper used in plating American ships including the Constitution. Revere died in Boston in 1818.

See also: American Revolution and Intelligence; Sons of Liberty (American Revolution)

References and Further Reading

Forbes, Esther. *Paul Revere and the World He Lived In*. Boston: Houghton Mifflin, 1988.

Revere, Paul. *Paul Revere's Three Accounts of His Famous Ride*. With an introduction by Edmund S. Morgan. Boston: Massachusetts Historical Society, 1976.

Triber, Jayne. *A True Republican: The Life of Paul Revere*. Amherst, MA: University of Massachusetts Press, 1998.

Barbara Bennett Peterson

RICHELSON, JEFFREY T.
(1949–)

One of the leading U.S. writers on the U.S. and foreign intelligence community, Jeffrey Richelson has written extensively on the field of intelligence collection and dissemination since the mid-1970s. Educated at the University of Rochester in Rhode Island with a masters in 1974 and a PhD in 1975, Richelson has taught at the University of Texas and American University. Richelson is currently a senior fellow at the National Security Archive in Washington, DC.

His books published between the middle 1980s until now cover a variety of intelligence topics. His *US Intelligence Community* is in its fourth edition and is a standard text for students studying the intelligence community.

At the archive, Richelson has directed projects examining U.S.-China relations, the organization and operation of the U.S. intelligence community, U.S. military space activities, and presidential national security directives. His February 1998 article in *Scientific American*, "Scientists in Black," examined the involvement of scientists in the use of intelligence community assets for nonintelligence research.

Richelson has published articles in the *Scientific American, Bulletin of the Atomic Scientists, International Journal of Intelligence and Counter Intelligence, International Security*, and *Intelligence and National Security*, as well as others. Richelson's books include *Ties that Bind: Intelligence Cooperation Between the UKUSA Countries; The UK, US, Canada, Australia, and New Zealand* (1985); *The US Intelligence Community 1–4th Editions* (1985, 1989, 1995, 1999); *Sword and Shield: the Soviet Intelligence and Security Apparatus* (1986); *American Espionage and the Soviet Target* (1987); *Foreign Intelligence Organizations* (1988); *A mericas Eyes in Space: The US Keyhole Spy Satellite Program* (1990); *Americas Space Sentinels: DSP Satellites and National Security* (1991); *A Century of Spies: Intelligence in the Twentieth Century* (1995); *The Wizards of Langley: Inside the CIA's Directorate of Science and Technology* (2001); and *Spying on the Bomb: American Nuclear Intelligence from Nazi Germany to Iran and North Korea* (2006).

See also: Cold War Intelligence; Post–Cold War Intelligence

References and Further Reading

Richelson, Jeffrey. *American Espionage and the Soviet Target*. New York: Quill, 1987.

Richelson, Jeffrey. *America's Space Sentinels: DSP Satellites and National Security*. Lawrence, KS: University of Kansas Press, 1999.

Richelson, Jeffrey. *A Century of Spies: Intelligence in the Twentieth Century*. New York: Oxford University Press, 1995.

Richelson, Jeffrey. *The U.S. Intelligence Community*, 5th ed. Boulder, CO: Westview, 2008.

Richelson, Jeffrey. *The Wizards of Langley: Inside the CIA's Directorate of Science and Technology.* Boulder, CO: Westview, 2002.

Steven F. Marin

RIDGE, TOM
(AUGUST 26, 1945–)

Tom Ridge was the first secretary of Homeland Security, serving in that position from October 8, 2001, to February 15, 2005. Ridge was born near Pittsburgh and received a law degree from Dickinson School of Law. Drafted into the military, he served as an infantry staff sergeant in Vietnam. Ridge entered government service as an assistant district attorney in Pennsylvania and then was elected to Congress in 1982. He was serving his second term as governor of Pennsylvania when he became secretary of Homeland Security. Ridge had strong personal ties to President George W. Bush, who described Ridge as a "trusted friend". He was reportedly considered as a possible vice presidential running mate from both Robert Dole in 1996 and Bush in 2000, and was also under consideration for secretary of defense by Bush. In each of these cases Ridge encountered opposition from the conservative wing of the Republican Party that objected to his Reagan-era opposition to U.S. policy in Nicaragua and to the MX missile and the Strategic Defense Initiative.

Ridge came to his position as a Washington outsider and with little experience in bureaucratic infighting. The task facing Ridge was daunting, combining 22 preexisting agencies and 180,000 employees into a single cohesive unit. By most accounts it remained only partly accomplished. Solidifying managerial control over the Department of Homeland Security was a top priority facing Ridge's successor, Michael Chertoff. Ridge also enjoyed only limited success in warding off challenges to its role in the intelligence community from the White House and existing intelligence organizations and addressing gaps in terrorism protection. Internal government reports cited the failure to secure U.S. ports and to effectively monitor cargo on commercial aircraft as areas in need of attention. It was also under Ridge that the Department of Homeland Security began issuing nationwide color-coded terrorist threat alerts. These alerts proved to be quite controversial since they provided little concrete information to the public about the nature or location of possible terrorist activity.

See also: Bush, George W., Administration and Intelligence; Homeland Security Department of; September 11, 2001; Terrorist Groups and Intelligence

References and Further Reading

Kettl, Donald. *System under Stress: Homeland Security and American Politics.* Washington, DC: CQ Press, 2004.

Lehrer, Eli. "The Homeland Security Bureaucracy," *The Public Interest* 156 (2004), 71–85.

Wise, Charles. "Organizing for Homeland Security," *Public Administration Review* 62 (March/ April 2002), 44–57.

Glenn P. Hastedt

RIVINGTON, JAMES
(AUGUST 14, 1724–JULY 4, 1802)

James Rivington was a journalist, newspaper editor, and possible double agent during the War of American Independence. Rivington was born on August 17, 1724, in London, England. He entered the family printing business, but was bankrupted in 1760 and moved to New York City. He opened bookstores in New York, Philadelphia, and Boston, but soon confined his business to the New York store. In 1766 he moved to Annapolis and dabbled in a land scheme, bankrupting himself for a second time. He returned to New York and in 1773 established a successful newspaper, *Rivington's New York Gazeteer*. At first, he published both British and American views on divisive issues between Britain and America, but soon evinced Tory convictions. In November 1775, his press was destroyed by the Sons of Liberty, led by Isaac Sears, and he fled with his family to England.

Rivington returned to New York in September 1777, after the British army occupied the city. He published a pro-Tory paper, *Rivington's New York Loyal Gazette* (later *Royal Gazette*), during the war, and remained in New York after the British were defeated. There is some evidence that he may have been a double agent, spying for the Americans during the conflict. In his later years, he returned to bookselling, but went bankrupt for a third time. He was in debtor's prison from 1797 to 1801, and died in poverty in New York on July 4, 1802.

See also: American Revolution and Intelligence

References and Further Reading

Crary, Catherine S. "The Tory and the Spy: The Double Life of James Rivington," *William and Mary Quarterly* 16 (1959), 61–72.

Lawson, John L. "The 'Remarkable Mystery' of James Rivington, 'Spy,'" *Journalism Quarterly* 35 (1958), 317–323, 394.

Paul David Nelson

ROBERTS, EDMUND
(1784–1836)

Edmund Roberts was Andrew Jackson's special agent responsible for initiating diplomatic relations and commercial treaties with the nations of Cochin China, Siam, and Muscat. Roberts was also tasked with spying on the operations of the British East India Company, which controlled commerce in and around India and coastal Africa, as well as reporting on U.S. commercial security interests in the Indian Ocean. The mission was kept secret to prevent British, French, and Dutch disruption of U.S. outreach in the region. For this reason, Jackson bypassed the Senate and designated Roberts as "special agent" rather than provide him with a diplomatic rank.

Roberts left for the Far East in March 1832 aboard the USS *Peacock*. Despite a failure in Cochin China, Roberts secured a Treaty of Amity and Commerce with Siam on March 30, 1833, and a commercial treaty with Muscat on September 21, 1833. Both treaties opened these nations to U.S. trade on most-favored-nation basis and were ratified by the Senate in June 1834.

Because of the mission's success, Jackson dispatched Roberts back to the area in April 1835. He was to renew talks with Cochin China and initiate negotiations with Japan. Roberts died en route on June 11, 1836, in Macao. The information Roberts obtained about commercial advantages in Asia prompted a steady expansion of American trade in the region.

Roberts was born in Portsmouth, New Hampshire, on June 29, 1784.

See also: Jackson, Andrew

References and Further Reading

Bowers, David. *The Rare Silver Dollars Dated 1804 and the Exciting Adventures of Edmund Roberts*. Wolfeboro, NH: Bowers and Merena Galleries, Inc., 1999.

Roberts, Edmund. *Embassy to the Eastern Courts of Cochin-China, Siam, and Muscat; in the U.S. Sloop-of-War Peacock, David Geisinger, Commander, during the Years 1832–3–4*. Wilmington, DE: Scholarly Resources Inc., 1972.

Roberts, Edmund, and W. S. W. Ruschenberger. *Two Yankee Diplomats in 1830s Siam*. Bangkok: Orchid Press, 2002.

Steve Roane

ROCHEFORT, CAPTAIN JOSEPH J. (MAY 12, 1900–JULY 20, 1976)

Captain Joseph John Rochefort, born May 12, 1900, in Dayton, Ohio, and died July 20, 1976, in Torrance, California, was one of the founders of U.S. naval crypt-analysis and helped alert (1942) Admiral Chester W. Nimitz to the Japanese attack on Midway Island. Rochefort rose from the enlisted (1918) ranks (a "mustang") and was commissioned (1919) following graduation from the Stevens Institute of Technology. His acumen for solving puzzles, noted while serving on the USS *Arizona* (1925), led to his posting (October 1925) to the then single-person code-breaking bureau. Rochefort headed the Office of Naval Communications (1926–1927); returned to sea (1927–1929); studied the Japanese language while posted to the United States Tokyo Embassy (1929–1932); was posted to the Office of Naval Intelligence (OIC, 1932–1936); was reassigned to the Eleventh Naval District, San Diego (1936–1938); and was the intelligence officer for USS *Indianapolis* Scouting Force in the Pacific (1938–1941) before assuming command (1941) of the Combat Intelligence (Comint) Unit Station Hypo, Pearl Harbor, Hawaii.

Rochefort's staff helped break the Japanese Navy's JN-25 code following the Pearl Harbor attack (December 7, 1941), and the derivative intelligence led to the Battle of the Coral Sea (May 7–8, 1942) and uncovered an impending target designated by the Japanese as AF, posited by Rochefort's staff as Midway and by the OIC's OP-20-G as the Aleutian Islands. Hypo's Jasper Holmes suggested that Midway report a broken freshwater condenser in a compromised cipher and the Japanese informed the AF attack task force to load additional water desalinization equipment. Nimitz used this information to set the Battle of Midway (June 3–6, 1942) ambush, sinking four Japanese carriers to the U.S.'s one (USS *Yorktown*) and bringing the opposing naval forces into rough parity.

Though Rochefort's intelligence changed the course of the war and demonstrated the importance of intelligence in modern warfare, infighting between the director of naval intelligence and the director of naval communications led to his eventual transfer to the Pacific Strategic Intelligence Group in Washington (1942–1946). He retired (1947), was reactivated (1950) for the Korean War, and retired again (1953). He consulted for the movie *Tora, Tora, Tora* (1970), but he died before the release of the movie *Midway* (1976) with Hal Holbrook appearing as Rochefort.

He was posthumously awarded the National Defense Service Medal (1986) and was inducted (2000) into the National Security Administration's Honor Hall of Fame.

See also: American Intelligence, World War II; Midway, Battle of; Pearl Harbor; PURPLE

References and Further Reading

Layton, Rear Admiral Edwin T. *And I Was There: Breaking the Secrets—Pearl Harbor and Midway.* Old Saybrook, CT: William S. Konecky Associates, Inc., 2001.

Prange, Gordon W., Donald M. Goldstein, and Katherine V. Dillon. *Miracle at Midway,* reprint ed. New York: Penguin, 1983.

Richard M. "Rich" Edwards

ROCKEFELLER COMMISSION

Officially known as the U.S. President's Commission on CIA Activities Within the United States, the Rockefeller Commission was established by President Gerald Ford on January 4, 1975, in response to a series of articles that appeared in the *New York Times*, written by Seymour Hersh, on CIA illegal domestic activities including surreptitious mail openings, engaging in surveillance of domestic dissidents, and experimentation with mind control drugs (Project MKULTRA).

In his memoirs Ford stated that he established the commission in the hope that it would prevent crippling investigations into the CIA by congressional committees. Ford placed Vice President Nelson Rockefeller in charge of the commission. Rockefeller had served as governor of New York from 1959 until his appointment as vice president under Ford, following Richard Nixon's resignation and Ford's elevation to the presidency. Earlier in his career Rockefeller had served on the President's Foreign Intelligence Advisory Board. Commission members included Ronald Reagan, Douglas Dillon, and Lane Kirkland.

The Rockefeller Commission submitted its report to President Ford in June 1975. It identified 10 significant areas of investigation: (1) mail intercepts; (2) intelligence community coordination; (3) Operation CHAOS; (4) involvement of the CIA in improper activities for the White House (including Watergate); (5) domestic activities of the Directorate of Operations; (6) domestic activities of the Directorate of Science and Technology; (7) CIA relationships with other federal, state, and local agencies; (8) protection of the Agency against threats of violence; (9) other investigations by the Office of Security; and (10) allegations concerning the assassination of President John Kennedy.

In addition, the Rockefeller Commission gathered evidence on the CIA's involvement with organized crime in assassination plots against foreign leaders, most notably

Cuba's Fidel Castro and the Dominican Republic's Rafael Trujillo. In doing so it also examined the possible role of Cuban involvement in Kennedy's death. Their study was not completed by the time the Commission completed its report and all of the data collected was given to the White House.

Ford's hopes that the Rockefeller Commission would silence potential criticism of the CIA went unrealized. The Church Committee was established by the Senate on January 27, 1975, and the House of Representatives set up its own committee on February 19, 1975. It was first chaired by Lucien Nedzi and then by Otis Pike. The Commission's largely supportive report also had little impact on softening the findings of either the Church or Pike Committees.

See also: Central Intelligence Agency; Church Committee; Colby, William Egan; Ford Administration and Intelligence; Pike Committee

References and Further Reading

Haines, Gerald K. "Looking for a Rogue Elephant: The Pike Committee Investigations and the CIA," *Studies in Intelligence* (Winter 1998–1999), 81–92.

Olmsted, Kathryn S. *Challenging the Secret Government.* Chapel Hill, NC: University of North Carolina Press, 1996.

Rockefeller Commission. Report to the President by the Commission on CIA Activities Within the United States, June 1975 History-Matters. http://history-matters.com/archive/church/rockcomm/contents.htm. (accessed September 2007).

Glenn P. Hastedt

ROE, AUSTIN
(MARCH 2, 1749–NOVEMBER 29, 1830)

Austin Roe was a courier in the Culper Ring, an American spy network in New York and on Long Island during the War of American Independence. Roe was born on March 2, 1749, in Drowned Meadow, New York. He joined the Culper spy group in 1778, when Major Benjamin Tallmadge organized it at the behest of General George Washington. His job was to carry intelligence about the enemy from Robert Townsend (Culper Junior) in New York City to Abraham Woodhull (Culper Senior) in Setauket, Long Island. Woodhull then had Caleb Brewster carry the information by rowboat across Long Island Sound to Tallmadge in Connecticut.

Repeatedly during the war, Roe made the round-trip of 110 miles through territory infested with British soldiers, carrying documents on his return that were invaluable to Washington but endangered his own and his colleagues' lives. He died on November 29, 1830, in Patchogue, New York.

See also: Brewster, Caleb; Culper Ring; Tallmadge, Major Benjamin; Townsend, Robert; Woodhull, Abraham

References and Further Reading

Ford, Corey. *A Peculiar Service.* Boston: Little, Brown and Company, 1965.

Groth, Lynn. *The Culper Spy Ring.* Philadelphia: Westminster Press, 1969.

Pennypacker, Morton. *General Washington's Spies on Long Island and in New York*. Brooklyn, NY: Long Island Historical Society, 1939.

Paul David Nelson

ROOM, THE

The Room as a private U.S. intelligence service. In 1927 a group of prominent East Coast businessmen, bankers, attorneys, and philanthropists began meeting together to share intelligence on world events. The initial group included Vincent Astor, son of John Jacob Astor IV, Kermit Roosevelt, son of President Theodore Roosevelt, journalist Marshall Field III, naturalist Suydam Cutting, and philanthropist Duncan Ellsworth. New recruits included investment banker Winthrop Aldrich, publisher Nelson Doubleday, landlord and socialite William Rhinelander Stewart, Chief Justice of the New York Court of Special Sessions Frederic Kernochan, and diplomat and future OSS agent David K. E. Bruce. Members met monthly in a Manhattan apartment at 34 East 62nd Street to discuss world events and to share information gleaned from their extensive travels and networks of global contacts. Members also occasionally invited outsiders to share stories of their travels, including Admiral Richard E. Byrd and British intelligence officer and novelist Somerset Maugham.

In 1932 the members of the Room began sharing their discoveries with their social peer, Franklin D. Roosevelt. Astor and Kermit Roosevelt became the primary conduits for information into the White House. Frequently these reports were verbally communicated during fishing outings on Astor's yacht, the *Nourmahal*. Other written reports remain in the Franklin Roosevelt Papers in the FDR Library.

Because of the connections of the membership, most of the information produced by the Room involved foreign banking and business practices. Aldrich, for example, used his position as chairman of the board of Chase National Bank to monitor the financial activities of the Amtorg Corporation, which controlled all Soviet trade, and allegedly espionage, within the United States.

The wealth of members also allowed them to travel extensively to collect information. In 1937 Astor and Kermit Roosevelt sailed the *Nourmahal* around the Japanese-mandated islands in the Pacific recording the location of Japanese radio stations, fortifications, and military personnel. With the outbreak of war, the members of the Room scattered in a variety of wartime endeavors. Many, however, including Kermit Roosevelt, Henry Field, and David Bruce, remained involved in intelligence activities including the OSS and the army's Military Intelligence Division.

See also: Astor, Captain William Vincent; Roosevelt, Franklin Delano; Roosevelt, Kermit

References and Further Reading

Dorwart, Jeffrey. "The Roosevelt-Astor Espionage Ring," *New York Journal of History* 62 (1961), 307–322.

Persico, Joseph. *Roosevelt's Secret War: FDR and World War II Espionage*. New York: Random House, 2002.

Peter F. Coogan

ROOM 40

Considered to be the most among the most innovative and significant code-breaking operations of World War I, Room 40 is the location and name of the British Royal Navy Admiralty's establishment in Whitehall, which began operations at the onset of World War I. Among the successes enjoyed by the cryptanalysts of Room 40 was the ability to read practically all of Germany's naval and diplomatic communications traffic.

Many of the staff hired to work within the Room 40 establishment were noted scholars, and faculty with expertise in German from the Royal Naval Colleges of Dartmouth and Osborne. Their first success came with the capture of a code book that was retrieved from the blown-up German cruiser ship *Magdenburg* in August 1914.

Perhaps one of the most startling and decisive Room 40 code-breaking efforts of World War I dealt with the deciphering of the January 1917 Zimmermann Telegram. Arthur Zimmermann was the German Foreign Minister, who attempted, through his ambassador in Mexico, to convince Mexico to engage in a war against the United States. The actual encrypted message read as follows: "We make Mexico a proposal of alliance . . . [with] an understanding on our part that Mexico is to reconquer the lost territory in Texas, New Mexico and Arizona. The settlement in detail is left to you. Arthur Zimmermann." Those in Room 40 deciphered a total of 1,000 code groups in several weeks. This code-breaking effort resulted in significant change to U.S. foreign policy.

Among the consumers of encrypted products coming from Room 40 was Sir Winston Churchill who, in November 1914, issued specific instructions for the careful handling of all intercepted telegrams. Realizing the significance and capability of Room 40, Churchill himself drafted instructions for handling all intercepted telegrams, and to see them all himself.

The code-breaking operations of Room 40 continued well beyond World War I and into World War II.

See also: Zimmermann Telegram

References and Further Reading

Beesly, Patrick. *Room 40: British Naval Intelligence 1914–1918*. New York: Harcourt Brace Jovanovich, 1982.

The First World War—The Zimmermann Telegram. http://www.channel4.com/history/microsites/F/firstworldwar/cont_cracking_3.html.

Khan, David. *The Reader of Gentlemen's Mail: Herbert O. Yardley and the Birth of American Codebreaking*. New Haven, CT: Yale University Press, 2004.

Polmar, Norman, and Thomas B. Allen. *The Spy Book: The Encyclopedia of Espionage*. New York: Random House, 2004.

David Jimenez

ROOSEVELT, FRANKLIN DELANO (JANUARY 30, 1882–APRIL 12, 1945)

The only U.S. president ever to serve more than two terms, Franklin Delano Roosevelt was elected to office in 1932 and was reelected three more times before he died near the end of World War II. In domestic politics Roosevelt was a reformer credited with securing the passage of the New Deal legislation and helping guide the United States out of the Great Depression. In foreign affairs he helped move the United States from a policy of neutrality and isolationism into one of global involvement and leadership.

Born on January 30, 1882, Roosevelt spent his early years at the family estate in Hyde Park, New York, and later attended Harvard and Colombia Universities. In 1905 he married Eleanor Roosevelt, a distant cousin and niece of Theodore Roosevelt. A Democrat, Roosevelt entered into the field of electoral politics in 1910 by winning a seat in the New York Senate in a heavily Republican district. His political star rose rapidly on the national scene, coming to serve in the Wilson administration as assistant secretary of the navy and as the party's vice presidential candidate in 1920 only to be undercut by polio in 1921. Roosevelt recovered his health to the point where in 1928 he was elected governor of New York. Four years later he was elected president.

Roosevelt initially did little to challenge the isolationist consensus in the United States. During his first term his major foreign policy imitative was the Good Neighbor Policy. As part of it in December 1933 he signed he Montevideo Convention on the Rights and Duties of States which pledged the United States not to intervene in Latin American affairs, something the poor state of the U.S. economy virtually precluded in any case.

In his second term Roosevelt sought to move the United States away from isolationism. To this end he entered into secret talks with France on how to bypass U.S. neutrality legislation. Once war broke out in 1939, Roosevelt also entered into talks with Great Britain. In 1940 he prodded Congress into establishing a peacetime draft and called for the United States to become the "arsenal of democracy." In 1941 this translated into the establishment of the Lend-Lease program.

The Japanese attack on Pearl Harbor transformed the domestic political climate in which Roosevelt operated laying the foundation for post–World War II internationalism in U.S. foreign policy. During the war Roosevelt helped oversee a centralization of U.S. military planning and organization. Among its most concrete manifestations were the creation of a de facto Joint Chiefs of Staff and setting up the Office of Strategic Services (OSS). This organization was charged with gathering and analyzing intelligence as well as conducting covert operations and engaging in espionage. Col. William Donovan was placed in charge of the OSS. As Roosevelt's personal agent he had been instrumental in meeting with the British leaders and promoting a centralized intelligence service for the United States. Roosevelt's actions laid the foundation for the creation of the Central Intelligence Agency and the unification of the military services under a secretary of defense in a Department of Defense.

See also: Donovan, Major General William Joseph; Office of Strategic Services; Pearl Harbor; Stephenson, Sir William Samuel

References and Further Reading

Perisco, Joseph, *Roosevelt's Secret War: FDR and World War II Espionage*. New York: Random House, 2002.

Smith, R. Harris. *OSS: The Secret History of America's First Central Intelligence Agency*. Berkeley, CA: University of California, 1972.

Troy, Thomas. *Wild Bill and Intrepid: Donovan and Stephenson and the Origins of the CIA*. New Haven, CT: Yale University Press, 1996.

Glenn P. Hastedt

ROOSEVELT, KERMIT
(FEBRUARY 16, 1916–JUNE 8, 2000)

Kermit "Kim" Roosevelt, Jr., was the Central Intelligence Agency (CIA) agent who directed Operation Ajax, an Anglo-American covert operation in 1953 that overthrew the democratically elected government in Iran of Prime Minister Mohammed Mossadegh and restored Shah Mohammad Reza Pahlavi to the throne. Operation Ajax was the first time the CIA orchestrated a covert action to overthrow a democratically elected government. The success of Operation Ajax emboldened the CIA to carry out similar operations in Guatemala (1954) and Cuba (1961).

Roosevelt was born in Buenos Aires, Argentina, on February 16, 1916. He was the eldest son of Kermit Roosevelt, the son of former president Theodore Roosevelt. After completing his education at Harvard University, Roosevelt joined the Office of Strategic Services (OSS), the precursor of the CIA. During World War II, he worked and traveled in the Middle East. After the war, Roosevelt returned to teach at Harvard University. In 1950, Frank Wisner recruited Roosevelt to work in the Office of Policy Coordination, the espionage branch of the CIA.

In 1951, Mossadegh was elected prime minister of Iran. In 1952, he nationalized without compensation the British-owned Anglo-Iranian Oil Company (AIOC). At the same time, Mossadegh began to favor socialist legislation and show greater tolerance toward the pro-Soviet Tudeh Party. In 1953, CIA Director Allen W. Dulles, in collusion with British government officials, authorized Roosevelt to spend $1 million to fund pro-monarchy forces in Iran. On August 3, Roosevelt told the Shah that the United States was willing to fund an insurrection, especially within the military, against Mossadegh. The resulting chaos between Mossadegh supporters and U.S.-funded insurgents convinced the Shah to flee the country on August 16. Nevertheless, on August 19, Mossadegh was arrested by pro-U.S. forces and the Shah returned home. As a condition of restoring the AIOC to the British, the U.S. government insisted that the AIOC's monopoly on oil production in Iran was over. Thereafter, five U.S. and two European oil companies were also allowed to operate in Iran.

In 1958, Roosevelt left the CIA to work for the Gulf Oil Company, eventually becoming a vice president. In 1970, he became a consultant for U.S. companies doing business in the Middle East. In 1979, he published his recollections of Mossadegh's overthrow in *Counter Coup: The Struggle for the Control of Iran*. Roosevelt argued that the U.S. operation was needed to keep Communism out of Iran. Roosevelt died on June 8, 2000.

See also; Ajax, Operation; Central Intelligence Agency; Dulles, Allen Welsh; Office of Strategic Services

References and Further Reading

Roosevelt, Kermit. *Countercoup: The Struggle for the Control of Iran*. New York: McGraw-Hill, 1979.

Zabih, Sepehr. *The Mossadegh Era: Roots of the Iranian Revolution*. Chicago: Lake View Press, 1986.

Michael R. Hall

ROSENBERG, JULIUS AND ETHEL
(JULIUS: MAY 12, 1918–JUNE 19, 1953;
ETHEL: SEPTEMBER 28, 1915–JUNE 19, 1953)

The penetration of the Manhattan Project during World War II was a spectacular espionage coup by the Soviet Union. Most likely it accelerated the development of a Soviet atom bomb by 18 months, which had profound repercussions on the foreign policies of both the Soviet Union and the United States. Although physicists such as Klaus Fuchs and Theodore Hall transmitted more vital information to the Soviets than the small spy ring gathered around Julius Rosenberg, it was the arrest, trial, and execution of the Rosenbergs that was indelibly etched into the history of espionage during the early cold war. They were convicted for committing what Federal Bureau of Investigation (FBI) Director J. Edgar Hoover termed "the crime of the century," and their death sentence for espionage in peacetime was unprecedented in U.S, history.

Julius Rosenberg, the son of Polish immigrants, Harry and Sophie, was born in East Harlem, New York, on May 12, 1918. With one older brother and three sisters he was the youngest in the family. Bar Mitzvahed at 13 and educated at Hebrew schools until 16, he was passionately devoted to Judaism until politicized on the streets of Lower East Side by radical orators during the Great Depression. After several local rabbis refused to participate in the campaign against the conviction of the Scottsboro Boys, a cause célèbre of socialists in the early 1930s, Julius exchanged Judaism for Marxism, the Torah for the Daily Worker. In 1934 he enrolled in electrical engineering at the tuition-free College of the City of New York. He was a central figure in a close-knit and influential group of engineering students who were members of the Young Communist League, some of whom he later recruited into Soviet espionage. He became a passionate supporter of the Republican cause in the Spanish civil war. In December 1936, at the age of 18, he met the 21-year-old Ethel Greenglass, whom he married three years later on June 18, 1939.

Ethel was the only daughter and eldest child of Tessie and Barnet Greenglass, Jewish immigrants from, respectively, Austria and Russia. She was born on September 28, 1915, in an overcrowded tenement at 64 Sheriff Street on New York's Lower East Side. David, whose incriminating testimony contributed to her execution in 1953, was born seven years later. Her early life was impoverished and her relationship with her mother was embittered. However, her school experiences at Seward Park High, especially in music, language, and acting, were positive. She graduated in June 1931 and briefly embraced the world of amateur theatre and singing. After completing a secretarial course, Ethel was employed by the National New York Packing and Shipping Company from February 1932 until September 1935. This position both widened her horizons and exposed her to the Communist Party. She joined the Shipping Clerks' Union strike committee, was fired from her job. and successfully challenged her employer with wrongful dismissal under the National Labor Relations Act. The year 1936 found her singing at demonstrations and local political events organized by the Communist-dominated Workers' Alliance of America; at one of these, a benefit concert for the International Seamen's Union, she met for the first time her future husband.

By the time of the Nazi-Soviet Pact, which the now-married Rosenbergs both supported, Julius's political convictions had solidified; on December 12, 1939, he formally

Ethel and Julius Rosenberg ride to separate jails on March 29, 1951, after being convicted of espionage. The trial of the Rosenbergs for conspiracy to commit espionage took place in New York City from March 6–29, 1951, at the height of the red scare. (AP/Wide World Photos)

joined Branch 16B of the American Communist Party (CPUSA). In 1940 the FBI established files on each. During World War II, she worked in the United States Department of Commerce and he as a civilian inspector for the Army Signal Corps. Based on FBI information, he attended army loyalty hearings in 1941 and, foreshadowing his response 10 years later, denied under oath that he had any interest in or involvement with Communism. He was not dismissed until February 9, 1945, when unequivocal evidence of his past membership of the CPUSA resurfaced.

In 1943, the year their first son, Michael, was born, Julius had the first of 50 meetings with Alexander Feklisov, a Soviet intelligence officer, and commenced providing classified information. He also commenced running an active espionage operation. Amongst others, he recruited his brother-in-law, David Greenglass who, since August 1944, worked at the Los Alamos weapons research laboratories as a machinist. Greenglass supplied him with sketches, drawn from memory, of a high-explosive lens mold being developed by Manhattan Project scientists. According to Greenglass' testimony in 1951, but recanted by him in 2001, his sister typed up his notes, intended for transmission to Moscow, on a portable Remington typewriter. Ethel was now a full-time volunteer secretary for a Communist front organization, the East Side Defense Council. From 1946, Julius, whose code name had been changed from "Antenna" to "Liberal" in November 1944, ran a small, unsuccessful machine workshop, G and R Engineering, with Greenglass. The Rosenbergs now lived in Knickerbocker Village in the Lower East Side and Ethel immersed herself, with difficulty, in motherhood. Their second son, Robert, was born in May 1947.

On June 17, 1950, the FBI arrested Julius Rosenberg after interrelated confessions by Klaus Fuchs, Harry Gold, and David Greenglass. Three weeks later, on August 11, Ethel was also arrested. On March 6, 1951, in the federal courthouse at Foley Square, Manhattan, the Rosenbergs and Morton Sobell were tried on the charge of conspiracy to commit espionage. They were alleged to have played central roles in a plot to procure classified information on U.S. atomic bomb development for the benefit of the Soviet

Union. They were charged with conspiracy rather than espionage or treason because the United States and the Soviet Union were wartime allies at the time information was being passed to the Russians. The principal prosecution witness against the Rosenbergs was David Greenglass. He stated that his sister had typed notes which were given to Harry Gold, who would then turn them over to Anatoly Yakovlev, a senior NKVD case officer. He had agreed to testify on condition that his wife, Ruth, would not be charged and that his sentence would be mitigated. The trial was both protracted and controversial, and it polarized the United States. To some the Rosenbergs personified the threat of atomic espionage and reinforced fears of Communist subversion; to others they were unjust victims of McCarthyism and anti-Semitism.

The trial was preceded by a series of sensational events that fuelled anti-Communist hysteria and provided the Rosenberg trial with a dramatic context: the detonation of an atom bomb by the Soviet Union in September 1949, the loss of China to the Red Army in October, the conviction of Alger Hiss in January 1950, the Wheeling speech by Joseph McCarthy in February, the sentencing of Klaus Fuchs in March and, significantly—for it intruded upon the judgment of Judge Irving R. Kaufman—the outbreak of the Korean War in June. Because the charge was conspiracy, hearsay evidence (normally ruled invalid in sworn testimony) was permitted; this made it easier for the prosecution to secure a conviction. On the other hand, the top-secret decrypted VENONA cables, which clearly implicated Julius and supported the testimony of Gold and Greenglass, were not made available to the court. From these the FBI was also aware of Ethel's minor, accessory role in the espionage ring and, along with Justice Department officials and the prosecuting attorney, Irving Saypol, was opposed to the imposition of the death sentence upon her. Both Rosenbergs persistently denied either any involvement in espionage or any ties to the CPUSA, while the CPUSA distanced itself from the efforts of the National Committee to Secure Justice in the Rosenberg Case.

On April 5, 1951, Judge Kaufman imposed a double death sentence. The severity of the sentence contrasts to that imposed by British courts on Alan Nunn May and Klaus Fuchs who passed far more vital atomic information to the Soviet Union and who were jailed for, respectively, 10 and 14 years. Kaufman wrongly judged Ethel to be a "full-fledged partner" in espionage, just as he wrongly insisted that the Rosenbergs had put the atomic bomb in the hands of the Russians—which was "worse than murder"—and that they were responsible for 50,000 Korean War casualties. J. Edgar Hoover believed that Ethel would succumb to the threat of the electric chair and persuade Julius to confess and identify his espionage confederates. The Rosenbergs knew a confession would save their lives and prevent their two young sons from being orphaned. Yet they admitted nothing and defiantly protested their innocence until the end.

The Rosenbergs remained on death row for 26 months whilst lawyers appealed and international outrage intensified. The appeals process spent itself, President Eisenhower refused to grant clemency, and the White House was picketed. On June 19, 1953, one newspaper headline read "Spies Fry Tonight." Ten thousand sympathizers gathered in Union Square and waited, emotionally, for the countdown. At 8.00 P.M. in Sing Sing prison, New York, Julius and Ethel Rosenberg were electrocuted. Ethel's death was difficult: the first minute-long jolt of electricity failed to kill her and she was given two more jolts before being pronounced dead. She was 37 years old; Julius was 35 years old. Until recently, their sons continued to proclaim their innocence.

With the declassification of the VENONA documents and the publication of Feklisov's memoirs, this position—unlike the appropriateness of the death penalty—is no longer a source of debate.

See also: Atomic Spy Ring, Feklisov, Alexandre; Fuchs, Emil Julius Klaus; Gold, Harry; Greenglass, David; Hall, Theodore Alvin; Hiss, Alger; McCarthy, Joseph; Nunn May, Alan

References and Further Reading

Carmichael, Virginia. *Framing History: The Rosenberg Story and the Cold War*. Minneapolis: University of Minnesota Press, 1993.

Feklisov, Alexander, and Sergei Kostin. *The Man Behind the Rosenbergs*. New York: Enigma Books, 2001.

Garber, Marjorie, and Rebecca L. Walkovwitz (eds.). *Secret Agents: The Rosenberg Case, McCarthyism, and Fifties America*. New York: Routledge, 1995.

Meeropol, Michael (ed.). *The Rosenberg Letters: A Complete Edition of the Prison Correspondence of Ethel and Julius Rosenberg*. New York: Garland, 1994.

Radosh, Ronald, and Joyce Milton. *The Rosenberg File: A Search for the Truth*. New York: Holt, Rinehart and Winston, 1983.

Roberts, Sam. *The Brother: The Untold Story of Atomic Spy David Greenglass and How He Sent His Sister, Ethel Rosenberg, to the Electric Chair*. New York: Random House, 2001.

Phillip Deery

ROSITZKE, HARRY
(FEBRUARY 25, 1911–NOVEMBER 4, 2002)

Born in Brooklyn, New York, on February 25, 1911, Harry August Rositzke held important positions within the U.S. intelligence establishment during World War II and the cold war. Rositzke graduated from Union College in 1931 and received his PhD in Germanic philology from Harvard University in 1935. After completing his PhD, he taught English at Harvard University, the University of Omaha, and the University of Rochester. At the outbreak of World War II, Rositzke enlisted in the U.S. Army, where he attained the rank of major. In 1944, he was transferred to the Office of Strategic Services (OSS).

In 1947, Rositzke joined the newly created Central Intelligence Agency (CIA) as a member of the Office of Special Operations, which was responsible for clandestine intelligence activities. In May 1952, he was appointed chief of Soviet operations in Munich, West Germany. Here, he was responsible for agent operations in the Soviet Union, agent recruitment, and counterespionage. Rositzke was appointed CIA chief of station in New Delhi, India, in 1957 and charged with conducting operations against Soviet and Chinese intelligence services. In 1962, he was reassigned to Washington DC, where he was responsible for intelligence operations targeting Soviet and East European officials in the United States and coordinating operations against Communist parties abroad. He remained at this position until his retirement in 1970.

Following his retirement, Rositzke moved to his farm in Middleburg, Virginia. He subsequently authored a number of books on the subject of intelligence. Rositzke died of pneumonia on November 4, 2002, in Warrenton, Virginia.

See also: Central Intelligence Agency; Office of Strategic Services

References and Further Reading

Richelson, Jeffrey. *A Century of Spies: Intelligence in the Twentieth Century.* New York: Oxford University Press, 1995.

Rositzke, Harry. *The CIA's Secret Operations: Espionage, Counterespionage and Covert Action.* New York: Reader's Digest Press, 1977.

Rositzke, Harry. *The KGB: The Eyes of Russia.* New York: Doubleday & Co., 1981.

Derek A. Bentley

ROWAN, LIEUTENANT ANDREW SUMMERS

Lieutenant Andrew Summers Rowan was a U.S. Army officer sent to make contact with Cuban rebels before the Spanish-American War. Rowan graduated from West Point in 1881 and became a staff officer. In 1897, Rowan published a book about Cuba and was considered one of the army's leading experts on the island. As tensions between Spain and the United States began to lead to war, General Nelson Miles took charge of planning an attack on Cuba. Fearing decimation by tropical diseases, Miles decided to emphasize the supply of Cuban rebel forces instead of a large U.S. expeditionary force.

Rowan's expertise won him an important role in Miles' planning. On April 9, 1898, Rowan was dispatched to enter Cuba and establish contact with the island's guerrilla insurgents. On May 1, Rowan located the rebel general Calixto García. Rowan then smuggled three Cuban diplomats back to the United States. Rowan's mission was vital in establishing links between the Cuban rebels and the United States, and provided General Miles with invaluable intelligence. Rowan was awarded the Distinguished Service Cross.

Rowan's success was immortalized in Elbert Hubbard's 1899 essay "A Message to Garcia," which held Rowan up to a generation of schoolchildren as the epitome of dutiful perseverance. After the Spanish-American War, Rowan served in the Philippines, fighting the anti-American independence movement. He left the army a few years later and lived in retirement for over 30 years.

See also: Spanish-American War

References and Further Reading

Brooks, Nancy Growald (ed.). *West Point in the Making of America, 1802–1918.* National Museum of American History, 2003. http://americanhistory.si.edu/westpoint.

Rowan, Andrew Summers, and Marathon Montrose Ramsey. *The Island of Cuba: A Descriptive and Historical Account of the "Great Antilla."* New York: Henry Holt and Company, 1897.

Trask, David F. *The War With Spain in 1898.* Lincoln, NE: University of Nebraska Press, 1981.

James L. Erwin

RUSSIAN FEDERAL SECURITY SERVICE

In November 1991 following an unsuccessful coup against Soviet leader Mikhail Gorbachev in which some of its members participated the Committee for State Security (KGB) was dismantled. The KGB was the Soviet Union's premier intelligence organization carrying out a wide range of security, police, and intelligence functions. With its dissolution, these functions were distributed among a number of different agencies. Its domestic security tasks including counterintelligence, border security, internal security, counterterrorism, and surveillance were assigned to a newly established Federal Counterintelligence Service (FSK). In 1995 the FSK was renamed the Federal Security Service (FSB). A comparison is often made between the FSB and the combined missions of the Federal Bureau of Investigation, Secret Service, National Security Agency, Homeland Security, and the Drug Enforcement Administration in the United States.

In 1998 Russian President Boris Yeltsin appointed career KGB official Vladimir Putin to head the FSB. Putin's later rise to the presidency of Russia along with the prevalent position that FSB officials hold in the Russian government has caused many to argue that it is the driving force in Russian politics today. Under Putin FSB funding reportedly increased by 40 percent in 2006 and 78 percent of the "top 1000" political leaders in Russia are said to have worked for the FSB or its predecessors. In some eyes the FSB is more powerful politically than the KGB because the KGB was responsible to a strong central Communist party.

Following this line of argument many link the FSB to attacks on a series of attacks conducted against Putin's opponents. Two of his leading critics, Anna Stepanova Politovskaya and Alexander Litvinenko, were killed in 2006. Politovskaya was a journalist who covered Russia's war in Chechnya and Litvinenko was a former KGB official writing an expose on FSB abuses. In addition a number of high-profile scientists who opposed the regime have been arrested and sentenced to long prison terms on espionage charges or accusations of illegally export, high-technology products out of Russia. The same is true of investigative journalists who have sought to highlight ecological problems in Russia.

The FSB is also asserted to have played a central role in building up support for the Chechnya War as well as helping to provoke it. During the war the FSB reportedly assassinated several Chechen leaders during the Chechnya War. Some also hold it responsible for terrorist incidents such as the hostage crisis at a Moscow Theater and the bombings of a marketplace in Astrakham. The FSB is said to have arranged these incidents in order to build up support for Putin and the war against Chechnya. Lending support to these arguments is the fact that those making these arguments such as Politovskaya and Boris Stomakhim were targeted for reprisals.

See also: GRU (Main Intelligence Directorate); KGB (Komitet Gosudarstvennoi Bezopasnosti); NKVD (Narodnyj Komissariat Vnutrennikh Del—Peoples Commissariat for Internal Affairs)

References and Further Reading

Felshintsky, Yuri, Alexander Litvinenko and Geoffrey Andrews. *Blowing Up Russia: Terror from Within*. New York: Encounter Books, 2007.

Knight, Amy. *Spies without Cloaks: The KGB Successors*. Princeton, NJ: Princeton University Press, 1994.

Satter, David. *Darkness at Dawn: The Rise of the Russian Criminal State*. New Haven, CT: Yale University Press, 2003.

Glenn P. Hastedt

S

SABERI, ROXANA
(APRIL 26, 1977–)

Roxana Saberi is a U.S.-Iranian national who was convicted by Branch 28 of the Iranian Revolutionary Council of espionage on behalf of the United States in April 2009. A journalist, she was first arrested in January 2009 for buying wine which is illegal in the Islamic Republic of Iran. She was next charged with working as a journalist without a valid press card. The charge of espionage was added on April 8.

Saberi had worked in Iran as a journalist from 2003 to 2006. She initially worked for Feature Story News, an independent news broadcast service. Her reports were carried on PBS, NPR, and Fox News in addition to many non-U.S. news outlets. In June 2003, less than six months after it began operation, Feature Story News was closed and her press credentials were revoked by the Iranian government. Saberi was able to obtain a new set of press credentials and began work for the BBC. In late 2006 these credentials were again rescinded. She continued to live in Iran researching a book and providing occasional reports to NPR and ABC Radio.

Saberi has maintained her innocence and no evidence of her reported espionage was made public before or during her trial. An appeals court reduced her eight-year prison sentence to a suspended two-year sentence. Saberi was released on May 9, 2009.

See also: Post–Cold War Intelligence

References and Further Reading

Adams, James. *The New Spies: Exploring the Frontiers of Espionage*. New York: Hutchinson, 1994.
Fathi, Nazila. "American Journalist Stands Trial in Iran," *New York Times* (April 14, 2009).

Glenn P. Hastedt

SACKETT, NATHANIEL
(APRIL 10, 1732–JULY 28, 1805)

Nathaniel Sackett was a spymaster in New York from 1776 to 1777. Sackett, a merchant in Fishkill, New York, helped organize his local committee of safety and became a member from Dutchess County of the New York Provincial Convention in 1776. On September 21, 1776, the convention appointed him to its newly formed Committee for Detecting and Defeating Conspiracies; he had direct responsibility for supervising its intelligence activities and the militia units arresting those suspected of "disaffection." In February 1777 on the recommendation of William Duer, then chairman of the committee, General Washington authorized Sackett to form an organized intelligence network for the region. Washington promised him $50 per month for his "care and trouble" and $500 per month for intelligence expenditures. Sackettt's ring collected information on British recruitment in the Hudson Valley and also conveyed information from British-occupied Long Island across the Long Island Sound to Connecticut and from there to the army in New York. Sackett developed a system for disguising agents as enemy sympathizers with realistic cover stories and placing them behind British lines, and outlined his various new forms of spycraft in a letter to Washington of April 7, 1777. However, Washington complained Sackett failed to relay reliable intelligence in a timely manner and dismissed him after an abortive mission. Sackett was later a sutler for the Continental Army. In 1785 he failed to persuade Congress to create a new state in the Ohio Valley and in 1789 to receive a federal political appointment from Washington.

See also: American Revolution and Intelligence

References and Further Reading

"Minutes of the Committee and of the First Commission for Detecting and Defeating Conspiracies in the State of New York December 11, 1776–September 23, 1778," *New York Historical Society Collections*, LVII and LVIII.

Morris, Richard B. *John Jay: The Making of a Revolutionary—Unpublished Papers, 1745–1780*. New York: Harper & Row, 1975.

Philander D. Chase, Frank E. Grizzard, et al. (eds.). *The Papers of George Washington: Revolutionary War Series*. Volumes 7-9. Charlottesville, VA: University of Virginia Press, 1985.

Rose, Alexander. *Washington's Spies: The Story of America's First Spy Ring*. New York: Bantam Dell, 2006.

Elizabeth M. Nuxoll

SANFORD, HENRY
(JUNE 13, 1832–MAY 21, 1891)

Henry Shelton Sanford was U.S. minister to Belgium and headed the Secret Service in Europe. During the Civil War, he organized agent networks to track Confederate procurement, conducted "grey" propaganda operations, and engaged in covert economic warfare.

Born in Woodbury, Connecticut, on June 13, 1823, Sanford received a law degree in Heidelberg and served as an American diplomat. Joining the Republican Party in 1860, he befriended Senator William H. Seward. After Seward became secretary of state, Sanford went to Belgium as American minister in April 1861.

Seward instructed Sanford to counter Confederate activities in Europe. By October 1861 Sanford had recruited agents in London, Liverpool, Paris, and Antwerp. Besides personal informants, Sanford paid private detectives, including the famous English detective Ignatius Pollaky to collect intelligence on Confederate agents. Sanford's principal opponent was Confederate Navy Captain James Bulloch, who obtained two raiders, the *Florida* and the *Alabama*, despite Sanford's efforts.

Sanford paid to place unattributed stories in the French-language press and enlisted a journalist of the Parisian *Opinion Nationale*. He preempted Confederate purchases of war material, once cornering the market on salt-peter to deny the Confederacy a key gunpowder ingredient.

Sanford's operations angered Charles Adams, American minister to Great Britain, who accused Sanford of "poaching" in his territory. Seward's deputy in November 1861 instructed Sanford to turn his agents in England over to Freeman Morse and Thomas Dudley, American consuls in London and Liverpool. Sanford then concentrated his efforts in Belgium and Paris, where his intelligence blocked the sailing of Confederate raiders fitted out in France. Sanford remained Seward's conduit for funding secret service operations throughout Europe.

Sanford remained minister to Belgium until 1869. He later bought land in Florida and founded the city of Sanford. Sanford died on May 21, 1891, in Healing Springs, Virginia.

See also: Secret Service; Wood, William P.

References and Further Reading

Fry, Joseph A. *Henry S. Sanford: Diplomacy and Business in Nineteenth-Century America*. Reno, NV: University of Nevada Press, 1982.

Molloy, Leo T. *Henry Shelton Sanford: 1823–1891; A Biography*. Derby, CT: Private Printing, 1952.

Register: Henry Shelton Sanford Papers at the General Sanford Memorial Library, Sanford, Florida. Nashville, TN: Tennessee State Library and Archives, 1960.

Jackson L. Sigler

SATELLITES

For the duration of the cold war, the United States used various airborne methods to collect intelligence over the Soviet Union, the Warsaw Pac, and China. Having found political, technical, and mechanical issues with the use of balloons and aircraft, the United States moved to the use of satellites in the late 1950s. By the end of the 1960s, the United States used specifically designed satellites for collecting a wide variety of electronic, signals, communication, and political intelligence throughout the world. Satellites became one of the primary intelligence collection platforms used by the United States during the cold war, and remain a vital and valuable tool in the intelligence community.

The history of the development of U.S. intelligence-gathering satellites began in October 1945 when the U.S. Navy contracted with North American Aviation and

An Aerospace Audiovisual Service crew of videographers and photographers set up an Inmarsat satellite transmitter on the sand during Operation Desert Storm in Saudi Arabia. (Courtesy U.S. Department of Defense)

the Guggenheim National Aeronautical Laboratory to assess the technical feasibility of building satellites. Although the report from North American Aviation and Guggenheim Aeronautical Lab provided positive feedback on the technological feasibility of producing a satellite, the navy scoffed at the estimated cost of five to eight million dollars for the satellite. To assist in alleviating the cost of producing a satellite, Commander Harvey Hall of the navy's Bureau of Aeronautics proposed a joint navy and army air force program to air force Generals H. J. Kerr, H. W. McLellan, and W. L. Richardson. The air force generals agreed to present the program to the air force's director of research and development, Major General Curtis E. LeMay. Lemay rejected the joint research project and instead asked a burgeoning think tank within the Douglas Aircraft Company, known as Project RAND, to produce a satellite feasibility study for the air force. On May 2, 1946, the engineers from Project RAND presented their report, "Preliminary Designs of an Experimental World Circling Spaceship" to the air force.

Within the report, Louis Ridenour, an engineer at the Douglas Aircraft Company and a member of the Project RAND team, outlined the military significance and application of satellites for the air force. According to Ridenour, satellites could provide reconnaissance, navigation, intelligence gathering, communication, and weather data functions for the air force and other military services. From these initial findings, the air force expressed interest in the future use of satellites, but wanted more studies and research into the technology and application of future satellite systems.

In the interim, between the findings of Project RAND (1946) and the next satellite study (1951), the army air force achieved independent status and evolved into the

United States Air Force (USAF) and the small think tank within the Douglas Aircraft Corporation broke away and became the RAND Corporation. By the end of the 1940s the air force, army, and navy were all interested in the future use of satellites for intelligence and military purposes, with the air force taking the lead in the development of satellites.

In the first half of the 1950s, the RAND Corporation continued to refine the use and application of satellites for military use. In April 1951, USAF authorized RAND to produce further studies on the feasibility and technological capabilities of satellites. Known as Project FEEDBACK, this project became the foundation for the first U.S. military intelligence-gathering satellites.

The air force's Air Research and Defense Command (ARDC) ran the satellite program initially known as Project 1115, and later as Weapons System 117L (WS-117L). WS-117L had several components to it. The air force's initial plan identified the WS-117L program as a series of satellite systems designed to collect continuous photographic, video, and infrared intelligence over enemy territory. Theses system evolved into separate and distinct intelligence-gathering platforms. The photographic and video program evolved into the CORONA satellite program, while the infrared detection satellite system developed as the Missile Defense Alarm system (MIDAS). Together, these two satellites provided the United States with a robust capability to keep track of a wide variety of photo-optic strategic intelligence. Beyond the use of satellites for the collection of visual and heat signatures, the air force, navy, and army worked toward the development of better satellite systems that could provide additional intelligence gathering capabilities.

Beyond the development of CORONA and MIDAS, the United States developed a full spectrum of satellite systems designed to collect communication, signal, electronic, weather, and geodetic intelligence from space. After the Soviet Union's launch of Sputnik on October 4, 1957, Eisenhower supported the development of satellites for intelligence-gathering missions. The air force no longer had a monopoly of satellite development; the army and navy developed systems, as did the newly created National Aeronautics and Space Administration (NASA). The proliferation of satellite systems for civilian, military, and intelligence-gathering operations flourished in the decades to come.

Future U.S. presidents, from John F. Kennedy to George W. Bush, maintained and used intelligence-gathering satellites for a wide variety of national security missions. Beyond the use of satellites for the collection of photographic intelligence, the U.S. government also developed satellites for electronic, oceanic, nuclear explosion detection, and meteorological intelligence-gathering missions between 1960 and present day. Electronic reconnaissance satellites, also known as Ferets, were designed in the late 1950s as U.S. aircraft used to collect electronic signatures became increasingly susceptible to air-to-air and surface-to-air interception. Feret satellites were able to eavesdrop on communications and electromagnetic emissions from enemy air defense systems and radar stations. These systems provided U.S. military commanders and presidents with intelligence that advanced the understanding of data collected from photoreconnaissance satellites. Furthermore, the U.S. government also used Feret satellites to collect telemetry data from missile tests done by the Soviet Union and China. Often the U.S. government and its allies used the collected electronic data in conjunction with photographs to produce a more complete picture of the enemy's strategic systems.

To keep track of activity on the world's oceans, the U.S. Navy, in conjunction with the Applied Physics Laboratory at John Hopkins University, developed the TRANSIT and ANNA navigation satellites starting in 1960 as a means to provide a more accurate navigation system for U.S. Navy ships. As these systems evolved beyond navigation beacons in the 1960s, 1970s, and 1980s, they became more sophisticated in their abilities to locate and track surface vessels and submarines through both active and passive measures. During the cold war, knowing the location of the Soviet Union's surface ships and submarines became vital intelligence in the planning of national security and strategic policy of the United States. Although the details of the early TRANSIT and ANNA navigations satellites are declassified, the U.S. government has maintained tight security on the release of information and details about ocean reconnaissance satellites.

A third series of intelligence-gathering satellites used by the United States detected nuclear explosions worldwide. The VELA nuclear detection satellite program evolved out of the MIDAS program during the Eisenhower era. The Advanced Research Projects Agency (ARPA), an organization within the Department of Defense that worked on the application of advanced technologies for military applications, developed the program between 1959 and 1963. The United States launched the first VELA satellites in October 1963, with the follow-on launch of additional sets of satellites in July 1964 and July 1965. The United States superseded the initial series of VELA satellites with advanced models in the three-year period between 1967 and 1970.

The VELA hotel satellite program provided the U.S. government with a consistent and reliable platform that detected nuclear detonations throughout the globe. In addition to providing vital strategic intelligence, the VELA program also provided verification that signatories to the October 1963 Nuclear Test Ban Agreement, which banned the testing of nuclear weapons in the atmosphere, outer space, and under water, did not violate the terms of the international agreement. The VELA satellite program provides insights into the dual-use capability of intelligence-gathering satellites. Although the satellites provided valuable data on nuclear detonations, the U.S. government also used them as peaceful sentries designed to maintain the integrity of the Nuclear Test Ban agreement.

The final class of intelligence-gathering satellites, weather reconnaissance, is probably the most common system known. The engineers from the Douglas Corporation first identified weather data collection as a potential mission for satellites in their initial report in 1946. Taking over research from the military services in 1958, NASA built the Television Infrared Observation System (TIROS) as a satellite designed to collect weather data from space. First launched in 1962, NASA continually refined the program from its first launch. Presently, NASA and the National Oceanic and Atmospheric Administration (NOAA) maintain derivatives from the original TIROS satellite that still orbits in space and broadcasts weather data back to earth. The images can be seen by watching a nightly news weather segment.

In addition to the TIROS satellite system, NASA also developed the NIMBUS weather satellite in 1964. NASA, and later NOAA, used NIMBUS satellites for the collection of data on atmospheric temperatures, sea-surface temperature, and sea and ice coverage. The data supplied by NIMBUS provided additional atmospheric and sea-state data that NASA and NOAA could combine with the data collected by TIROS to provide a better forecast of atmospheric and meteorological conditions. Although often overlooked as vital military and intelligence assets, weather satellites provide the U.S. military with a constant stream of data that is vital in the planning and execution of a wide variety of missions. Unlike the other categories of intelligence-gathering satellites, the public can easily see the data collected by weather reconnaissance satellites and the U.S. government openly acknowledges their existence.

The satellite functions first identified in 1946 by the engineers of the Douglas Aircraft Company framed the use and application of satellites for the collection of photographic, electronic, oceanographic, nuclear detection, and meteorological intelligence for the duration of the cold war. Despite the end of the cold war, intelligence-gathering satellites remain a vital asset in the military, political, and diplomatic actions of the United States. Although the U.S. government maintains tight security in the operations and capability of many of these space-based systems, the commitment to the use of satellites for intelligence-gathering missions has become an entrenched element of the U.S. national security system.

See also: Aerial Surveillance; Balloons; Central Intelligence Agency; CHALET; CORONA; Eisenhower Administration and Intelligence; Ferret; GENETRIX; Johnson Administration and Intelligence; Kennedy Administration and Intelligence; KEYHOLE—SIGINT Satellites; MAGNUM; Open Skies Proposal; Overflight Operation; U-2 Incident

References and Further Reading

Baucom, Donald R. *Origins of SDI, 1944–1983*. Lawrence, KS: University Press of Kansas, 1992.

Burrows, William E. E. *Deep Black: Space Espionage and National Security*. New York: Random House, 1986.

Day, Dwayne A., John M. Logsdon, and Brain Latell (eds.). *Eye in the Sky: The Story of the CORONA Spy Satellite*. Washington, DC: Smithsonian Institution Press, 1998.

Friedman, Norman. *Seapower and Space: From the Dawn of the Missile Age to Net-Centric Warfare*. Annapolis, MD: Naval Institute Press, 2000.

Peebles, Curtis. *The CORONA Project: America's First Spy Satellite*. Annapolis, MD: Naval Institute Press, 1997.

Richelson, Jeffrey T. *America's Space Sentinels: DSP Satellites and National Security*. Lawrence, KS: University Press of Kansas, 1999.

Spires, David N. *Beyond Horizons: A Half Century of Air Force Leadership in Space*. Maxwell Air Force Base: Air University Press, 1998.

Stares, Paul B. *The Militarization of Space: U.S. Policy 1945–1984*. Ithaca, NY: Cornell University Press, 1985.

Taubman, Philip. *Secret Empire: Eisenhower, the CIA, and the Hidden Story of America's Space Espionage*. New York: Simon & Schuster, 2003.

Sean N. Kalic

SCHLESINGER, ARTHUR M., JR. (OCTOBER 15, 1917–FEBRUARY 28, 2007)

Arthur Meier Schlesinger, Jr., U.S. journalist, writer, social critic, and historian, was born on October 15, 1917, in Columbus, Ohio. His father, Arthur M. Schlesinger, was a well-known and respected historian. During his youth, Schlesinger, Jr., excelled academically and was admitted to Harvard University.

The year following his graduation from Harvard, Schlesinger had his senior thesis published in 1939, titled *Orestes A. Brownson: A Pilgrim's Progress*. The publication garnered him immediate attention and even praise. Soon after however, Schlesinger was hired by the federal Office of War Information in 1942. While there, he worked on the United States' positive propaganda campaign until he was transferred to the Office of Strategic Services (OSS), the predecessor of the Central Intelligence Agency, in 1943. He served with the office until the conclusion of the war, returning to journalism and writing in 1945.

In 1946, Schlesinger became a history professor at Harvard University, where he stayed until 1961. While at Harvard, he found time to finish and to compose many prize-winning works, including *Age of Jackson* and *Age of Roosevelt*. Soon after in 1947, he was one of the founders of Americans for Democratic Action, a liberal organization formed in support of the Democratic Party. While still at Harvard, he served as an assist to John F. Kennedy during his presidential campaign.

After Kennedy's election, Schlesinger was appointed as his advisor for Latin American affairs. With his access to the Kennedy White House, he was able to compose one of his most famous works, *A Thousand Days*, a study of Kennedy's time in power. It was published in 1965 and it was awarded the Pulitzer Prize for biography.

Schlesinger went back to teaching in 1966, joining the faculty at the City University of New York. He continued writing, authoring many more titles. He is respected for his scholarship, his two Pulitzer Prizes, and adamant support for liberalism and the Great Society.

See also: Office of Strategic Services

References and Further Reading

Schlesinger, Arthur M., Jr. *A Life in the 20th Century: Innocent Beginnings 1917–1950*. Norwalk, CT: Easton Press, 2001.

Smith, Bradley. *The Shadow Warriors: OSS and the Origins of the CIA*. New York: Basic Books, 1983.

Arthur Holst

SCHLESINGER, JAMES RODNEY (FEBRUARY 15, 1929–)

James Schlesinger was the ninth Director of Central Intelligence (DCI). He served from February 2, 1973, to July 2, 1973. Born in New York City, Schlesinger earned a PhD in economics from Harvard and taught at the University of Virginia prior to moving to the Rand Corporation. From there he moved to the Bureau of the Budget, now the Office of Management and Budget, where he rose to the position of assistant director. Immediately prior to becoming DCI, Schlesinger served as chairman of the Atomic Energy Commission.

Schlesinger came to the Central Intelligence Agency (CIA) with clearly defined views on the intelligence community. While serving in OMB he authored a 47-page report, commonly referred to as the Schlesinger Report, which called for streamlining and centralizing the management of intelligence. It concluded that too often operators and program managers in intelligence collection rather than the intelligence customers were determining collection priorities, and that much unproductive duplication of collection efforts existed. One of its recommendations was creating the position of Director of National Intelligence, leaving the DCI to concentrate on management of the CIA. Upon becoming DCI, Schlesinger moved quickly to bring about his desired reforms. Convinced that there was too much deadwood and too many "old boys" from the days of the Office of Strategic Services (OSS) still working in the CIA, he forced the retirement of some 1,400 CIA officials. Over 100 were members of the Clandestine Service. Additionally, Schlesinger renamed the Directorate of Plans the Directorate of Operations and subordinated the overt collection system to the clandestine services. He set in motion steps to abolish the Office of National Estimates. And, in a symbolic move he replaced the old "Bureau of Public Works" sign that marked the entrance to the CIA from the George Washington Parkway with one identifying it as the CIA. Days before stepping down as DCI Schlesinger gave instructions for all current and past CIA employees to come forward with any information they might have about past or ongoing illegal activities being carried out by the CIA. These instructions were the foundation for the "family jewels" study that his successor, William Colby, presented to Congress in its investigations of CIA illegalities. Schlesinger reforms made him among the least popular DCIs. So too did the fact that his appointment was regarded as an overt attempt by President Richard Nixon to gain managerial control over the CIA and the intelligence community. Some at the time referred to his appointment as "Nixon's revenge."

Schlesinger went from DCI to secretary of defense where he served from 1973 to 1975. Following that he became the first secretary of energy, holding that position from 1977 to 1979. Schlesinger returned to government service in 1983 as a member of the President's Commission on Strategic Forces.

See also: Central Intelligence Agency; Director of Central Intelligence; Schlesinger Report

References and Further Reading

Andrew, Christopher. *For the President's Eyes Only: Secret Intelligence and the American Presidency from Washington to Bush*. New York: HarperCollins, 1995.

Laqueur, Walter. *A World of Secrets: The Uses and Limits of Intelligence*. New York: Basic Books, 1985.

Ranelagh, John. *The Rise and Decline of the CIA*. Revised and updated. New York: Touchstone, 1987.

Glenn P. Hastedt

SCHLESINGER REPORT

The Schlesinger Report was commissioned in 1971 by President Richard Nixon. Long obscured by more famous investigations into the operation of the intelligence community, such as those by the Church and Pike Committees and the Rockefeller Commission, the Schlesinger Commission has recently come into renewed attention with recent publication of its report.

James Schlesinger was the assistant director of the Office of the Management and Budget in Nixon's administration. A concern for the inability of the intelligence community to effectively coordinate its activities in producing intelligence analytical products had long been a concern of those receiving intelligence. To this was now added a concern for controlling the spiraling costs of intelligence that followed on its increased reliance on sophisticated technology to supplement, if not supplant, human intelligence-gathering efforts. Still another impetus for the Schlesinger study was the suspicion and distrust of the Central Intelligence Agency (CIA) that Nixon brought with him to the White House in 1969. He along with his national security advisor, Henry Kissinger, saw its members as having a political agenda that was at odds with theirs and unsupportive of the policies they sought to advance.

In his report Schlesinger argued that structural problems lay at the heart of the intelligence community's problems. It had been created in an era in which collection capabilities were smaller and cheaper, the conflicts between tactical and strategic intelligence less pronounced, and the coordination challenges facing the Director of Central Intelligence far fewer in number making it possible for this individual to simultaneously head the CIA and the intelligence community. To remedy this situation the Schlesinger Report recommended separating these two positions and as part of this separation creating the position of Director of National Intelligence to control the budgets and operations of the major intelligence collection agencies. Within the Defense Department, where much of the technology-driven growth had taken place, the Schlesinger Report called for creating a Director of Defense Intelligence who would direct and control all Defense intelligence resources. Third, the Report called for redrawing the functional boundaries between intelligence agencies in an effort to rationalize the collection and production of intelligence.

The reform proposals of the Schlesinger Report were in many respects ahead of its time. The Nixon administration found them too far reaching and, soon absorbed by Watergate, it did not pursue them with vigor. Congress would soon become the driving force behind intelligence reform and bring a different agenda with it. The report nonetheless remains significant for focusing attention on managerial and structural issues in intelligence reform.

See also: Church Committee; Defense Department Intelligence; Director of National Intelligence; Nixon Administration and Intelligence; Pike Committee; Schlesinger, James Rodney

References and Further Reading

"A Review of the Intelligence Community," March 10, 1971, Document 229 in Department of State, *Foreign Relations of the United States, 1969–1976, Volume II, Organization and Management of U.S. Foreign Policy, 1969–1972*, pp. 492–516. Washington, DC: Government Printing Office, 2006.

Warner, Michael. "Reading the Riot Act: The Schlesinger Report, 1971," *Intelligence and National Security* 24 (2009), 387–417.

Glenn P. Hastedt

SCHOOL OF THE AMERICAS

From 1946 to 2000, the School of the Americas was the U.S. Army's principal Spanish-language training facility for Latin American military personnel. In 1946, the School of the Americas originated at Fort Amador, Panama Canal Zone, as the Latin American Training Center-Ground Division. By 1950, the training center had moved to Fort Gulick, Panama Canal Zone, and been renamed the U.S. Army Caribbean School. Initially, the primary purpose of the School of the Americas was to train Latin American military personnel how to use advanced weapons and artillery systems that the United States was selling to Latin American nations. A secondary goal was to instruct the Latin Americans in nation-building skills. In the aftermath of Fidel Castro's successful 1959 Cuban Revolution, however, the school's curriculum was greatly expanded to include counterinsurgency training to combat Communist insurgencies in Latin America. To reflect the school's hemispheric role, the institution was renamed the U.S. Army School of the Americas. Under the provisions of the Panama treaty signed in 1977, the School of the Americas left the Panama Canal Zone and moved to Fort Benning, Georgia, in 1984.

Since its inception, more than 63,000 soldiers, officers, civilians, and noncommissioned officers from 22 Latin American nations and the United States have trained at the School of the Americas. The presence of the School of the Americas in Georgia brought the institution to the attention of human rights activists. Critics of the School of the Americas, who allege that the institution trained the Latin American military personnel responsible for human rights abuses committed by Latin American military dictatorships during the 1970s and 1980s, argue that U.S. Army training manuals recommended torture, false arrest, and the use of truth serum. Human rights activists point out that former Panamanian dictator Manuel Noriega; El Salvador's Roberto D'Aubuisson; and Argentina's General Leopoldo Galtieri, who was largely responsible for Argentina's Dirty War which resulted in the disappearance of thousands of civilians, were trained at the School of the Americas. School of the Americas officials, however, contend that only about 300 graduates of the institution have ever been accused of human rights violations. They argue that no school should be held accountable for the actions of some of its graduates. Following a decade of intense criticism by liberals, the army temporarily closed the School of the Americas in December 2000.

In January 2001, a new institution, the Western Hemisphere Institute for Security Cooperation (WHINSEC), opened at Fort Benning. WHINSEC uses the same facilities as the School of the Americas and offers many of the same courses. The new institution, which includes a human rights component in every class, contends that the courses at WHINSEC foster knowledge, cooperation, democratic values, respect for human rights, and understanding of U.S. traditions. Since it reopened in 2001, the largest number of students have come from Chile. Currently, the cost to operate WHINSEC is about $6 million.

See also: Cold War Intelligence

References and Further Reading

Gill, Lesley. *The School of the Americas: Military Training and Political Violence in the Americas.* Durham, NC: Duke University Press, 2004.

Thomas, Kenneth H., Jr. *Fort Benning.* Mt. Pleasant, SC: Arcadia Publishing, 2003.

Michael R. Hall

SCOWCROFT, LIEUTENANT GENERAL BRENT (MARCH 19, 1925–)

Brent Scowcroft was born on March 19, 1925. He served in various capacities in government, including national security advisor during the Gerald Ford and the George H. W. Bush administrations. In topics ranging from the Soviet Union to the Middle East, he has resisted ideas which he believes are overly optimistic and threaten to lull the United States into a false sense of security.

A West Point graduate, his military career lasted 29 years and rose to lieutenant general. He served as professor of Russian history at West Point and also as head of the Political Science Department at the Air Force Academy. He was a member of the President's Special Review Board (called the Tower Commission), which investigated President Reagan's management style in the wake of the Iran-contra scandal. He mentored Sovietologist Condoleezza Rice, who later served as national security advisor and then as secretary of state. Scowcroft later sat on the boards of several corporations and nonprofit organizations.

He chaired the Scowcroft Commission in the early 1980s. The Commission was established to make suggestions about strategic issues, especially regarding the controversy surrounding deployment of the MX missile. The Commission's findings sought to create a middle ground, but the Commission's report was upstaged by President Reagan's announcement on March 23, 1983, of a space-based missile defense research program later dubbed "Star Wars" by the media.

Unwilling to endanger U.S. security through excessive optimism, Scowcroft was skeptical of many appraisals, which were often later shown to be overly simplistic. As national security advisor to Gerald Ford, Scowcroft applauded Ford's courage in deciding to keep marines in South Vietnam—rather than to immediately remove all U.S. personnel from the country—to facilitate the evacuation of Vietnamese fleeing Communist takeover in 1975 after the U.S. pullout two years earlier.

As national security advisor under George H. W. Bush, he viewed an optimistic prediction, NSR 3, made by the National Security Council regarding the Soviet transformation away from Communism to be a "big disappointment." Although pleased with the CIA's ability to gather information (particularly in its use of satellites), Scowcroft noted its inability to predict Soviet policy intentions and a lack of high-value intelligence sources from within the Kremlin.

In 2002, he argued against the impending campaign against Saddam Hussein of Iraq, writing that the campaign would distract the United States from its focus against terrorism. He emphasized the importance of "enthusiastic international cooperation, especially on intelligence" to combat terrorism.

See also: Bush, George H. W., Administration and Intelligence; Ford Administration and Intelligence; Reagan Administration and Intelligence; Scowcroft Commission

References and Further Reading

Arbel, David, and Ran Edelist. *Western Intelligence and the Collapse of the Soviet Union: 1980–1990: Ten Years that did not Shake the World.* London, Frank Cass, 2003.

Fitzgerald, Frances. *Way Out There in the Blue: Reagan, Star Wars, and the End of the Cold War.* New York: Simon & Schuster, 2000.

Nicholas M. Sambaluk

SCOWCROFT COMMISSION

In the aftermath of the 9/11 terrorist attacks the Bush administration found it politically necessary to set up a commission to investigate the factors that led to the surprise attack. As the 9/11 Commission neared the completion of its report, the Bush administration turned its attention to a report by retired General Brent Scowrcoft. Four months before 9/11 President George Bush had commissioned two studies of the intelligence community. One chaired by Scowcroft and the other by Director of Central Intelligence (DCI) George Tenet. After 9/11 Tenet's inquiry ended its work without issuing a report but Scowcroft continued his work. In March 2002 he issued his report and according to press reports its recommendations included giving a single person managerial authority over all members of the intelligence community and removing the three largest intelligence agencies (the National Security Agency, the National Reconnaissance Agency, and the National Imagery and Mapping Agency) from the control of the Department of Defense.

The Scowcroft Commission Report (formally, The 2001 Presidential Commission on Intelligence Reform) received little attention at the time from the White House but was now being reexamined as a means of preempting the 9/11 Commission's reform proposals. In the end, instead of calling for a Director of National Intelligence, the administration settled for issuing an executive order that strengthened the DCI's power over the intelligence budget. The Report remains classified.

At the time he wrote this report Scowrcoft was the president of the Scowcroft Group, an international business consulting firm. He was a retired air force officer who had risen to the rank of lieutenant general. A protégé of Henry Kissinger, Scowcroft had served in Richard Nixon's administration as a military assistant to the president and as deputy assistant to the president for national security affairs. He went on to hold the position of national security advisor under Presidents Gerald Ford and George H. W. Bush. After leaving government service, Scowcroft was appointed to several presidential commissions. Among the most notable were the President's Special Review Board (the Tower Commission) that investigated the Iran-Contra Affair and the Defense Policy Review Board. Scowcroft was an outspoken critic of the George W. Bush administration's policies leading up to the start of the Iraq War and its occupation policies after the war.

See also: Iran-Contra Affair; National Commission on Terrorist Attacks on the United States (The 9/11 Commission); National Security Advisor; September 11, 2001; Tenet, George

References and Further Reading

Kitts, Kenneth. *Presidential Commissions and National Security: The Politics of Damage Control.* Boulder, CO: Lynne Reinner, 2006.

U.S. National Commission on Terrorist Attacks Upon the United States. *The 9/11 Commission Report*. Washington, DC: Government Printing Office, 2004.

Glenn P. Hastedt

SCRANAGE, SHARON
(1955–)

Sharon Scranage was the first person convicted under the Intelligence Identities Protection Act that was passed in 1982. At the time of her arrest, Scranage was a Central Intelligence Agency (CIA) employee working as an operations support assistant in Ghana. There, she passed along classified information to her boyfriend, Michael Soussoudis, who was a Ghanaian intelligence officer, first cousin of Ghana's leader and had permanent residence status in the United States. Included in the information she passed to him were the identities of Ghanaians working as espionage agents in Ghana for the United States.

Scranage was identified as a security threat when, upon coming back to the United States in 1985, she failed a polygraph test. Scranage agreed to cooperate with intelligence officials as evidence mounted of her activities, leading to the arrest of Soussoudis who was sentenced to 20 years in prison. He was exchanged for Ghanaian agents that had been arrested for spying on behalf of the United States after Scranage was indicted. Scrange was sentenced to five years in prison with this sentence later being shortened to two years.

See also: Central Intelligence Agency; Cold War Intelligence

References and Further Reading

Richelson, Jeffrey. *A Century of Spies: Intelligence in the Twentieth Century*. New York: Oxford University Press, 1995.

Source Watch Online. "Covert Agent Identity Protection Act," http://www.sourcewatch.org/wiki.phtml?title=Covert_Agent_Identity_Protection_Act (accessed January 12, 2006).

Glenn P. Hastedt

SEBOLD, WILLIAM G.
(MARCH 10, 1899–1970)

William G. Sebold was a double agent who was recruited to spy against the United States by Nazi Germany in World War II but in reality worked with the Federal Bureau of Investigation (FBI) to identify and arrest Nazi agents working in the United States as part of the Duquesne Spy Ring.

Sebold was born in Germany in 1899 and, after serving in the German army in World War I, he left to take jobs with aircraft plants in the United States and South America. He became a naturalized U.S. citizen on February 10, 1936. In 1939 Sebold returned to Germany for a lengthy family visit. Adolph Hitler was now in power. In September of that year Sebold was approached by someone identifying himself as "Dr. Gassner," who questioned him about U.S. military plans and equipment. Gassner also sought to convince Sebold to spy for Germany when he returned to the United States. Fearing for the safety of his family in Germany, Sebold agreed and underwent training in the use of secret codes, microphotography, and transmitting information. On February 4, 1940, Sebold returned to the United States using the alias Harry Sawyer and the code name "Tramp."

Not long after his meeting with Gassner, Sebold's U.S. passport was stolen. He went to the American embassy to obtain a new one and informed officials there about his contacts with German intelligence officials. Sebold also indicated a willingness to work with U.S. officials. As a result, when Sebold arrived in New York City the FBI helped set him up in a business office in Manhattan and a shortwave radio transmitting station on Long Island. Nazi agents were tape-recorded and videotaped in their meetings with Sebold in his office.

Over a period of 16 months, Sebold was able to help the FBI collect massive amounts of information on Nazi spies operating in the United States, Mexico, and South America. On June 24, 1941, the FBI moved to close down the Duquesne Spy Ring. Nineteen members of the spy ring pled guilty. On December 13, 1941, the 14 that pled not guilty were convicted. On January 2, 1942, the 33 members of this spy were sentenced to over 300 years in prison. The leader of the spy ring, Frederick Joubert Duquesne, received a sentence of 18 years on espionage charges and a $2,000 fine for violating the Registration Act.

After the trial ended, Sebold disappeared as the government relocated him and gave him a new identity.

See also: American Intelligence, World War II; Federal Bureau of Investigation (FBI)

References and Further Reading

Jeffrey-Jones, Rhodri. *The FBI: A History*. New Haven, CT: Yale University Press, 2007.

Kahn, David. *Hitler's Spies: German Military Intelligence in World War II*. New York: Macmillan, 1978.

Glenn P. Hastedt

SECRET COMMITTEE OF THE CONTINENTAL CONGRESS

The Secret Committee of the Continental Congress was charged with secretly importing military supplies during the American Revolution. The Second Continental Congress created the controversial Secret Committee on September 18, 1775, to procure military supplies at a time when most private trade was banned by Continental nonimportation and nonexportation regulations. Early in the Revolution the term *secret committee* was also applied to certain other congressional administrative committees, particularly the Committee of Secret Correspondence, and to some similar local committees. Such committees handled matters that had to be kept secret from the public and, at least in matters of detail, from the legislature itself, particularly military procurement, foreign affairs, and intelligence issues.

Initially, the Secret Committee secretly contracted with trusted well-connected merchants to ship commodities or bills of exchange abroad and invest the proceeds in needed supplies—not only arms and ammunition, but medicines, uniforms, blankets, sail cloth, tent cloth, supplies for allied Indians, and salt. The Committee also purchased munitions privately imported and issued permits for exports of equivalent value. Congressmen from Pennsylvania, New York, and New England dominated the Committee; several also became Secret Committee agents or contractors.

Once Congress opened American ports to foreign trade in March 1776, the committee employed special agents on a commission basis. At that time Robert Morris of Philadelphia became committee chairman and chief domestic agent. Often, for security reasons and to reduce the inflated prices charged the government, Morris disguised committee ventures as private operations of his firm, Willing, Morris and Company. Such procedures aroused suspicion that he juggled public and private ventures to his own advantage.

Silas Deane, sent abroad by the Committee of Secret Correspondence in 1776 to begin negotiating aid and an alliance with France, also represented Secret Committee contractors; his commercial mission was to provide cover for his diplomatic one. Other Secret Committee agents included William Bingham and Stephen Ceronio in the West Indies, and in Europe, William Lee, John Ross, and Thomas Morris. Rivalries and jurisdictional conflicts among the various agents contributed to the Deane-Lee affair, the procurement scandal that embroiled Congress from 1778 to 1779.

Within the United States the continental agents who handled marine affairs also acted for the Secret Committee, receiving cargoes, delivering them to appropriate military agencies, and remitting goods or funds to pay for them. The most important agents were John Langdon (New Hampshire), John Bradford (Massachusetts), Nathaniel Shaw, Jr. (Connecticut), Joseph Hewes (North Carolina), John Dorsius (South Carolina), and John Wereat (Georgia). Agents conducted both public and private business, including privateering. Their private affairs benefited from the scale of operations, prestige, and connections their public role gave them. The public gained the access to mercantile experience and to the private credit of their agents.

The intensifying British naval blockade in 1776 prevented the continued arrival of Secret Committee cargoes in the Delaware and Chesapeake Bay regions, and the departure of shipments of tobacco and grain and other provisions. Rice, indigo, and other commodities were therefore shipped from North Carolina, South Carolina, and Georgia to the West Indies and sold there or transferred to neutral ships for transport to Europe. Goods acquired in France, Holland, Germany, and elsewhere generally also arrived via the West Indies, especially from St. Eustatius, Martinique, and Hispaniola. After 1776, imports landed in Massachusetts or New Hampshire or in the southernmost states. Because the Secret Committee had greater success receiving supplies than in paying for them, the government was deeply in debt to its agents and their suppliers by the time the Commercial Committee replaced the Secret Committee in July 1777. By that time cargoes American diplomats obtained through secret foreign aid replaced Secret Committee commercial ventures as the chief source of supplies. Lost, stranded, and scattered cargoes and records protracted settlement of Secret Committee accounts. The unsettled accounts and charges of malfeasance raised primarily by the Lees of Virginia long shadowed the careers of those associated with the Secret Committee.

See also; American Intelligence; Committee on Secret Correspondence; Deane, Silas

References and Further Reading

Alberts, Robert C. *The Golden Voyage: The Life and Times of William Bingham, 1752–1804.* Boston: Houghton Mifflin Company, 1969.

Ferguson, E. James. *The Power of the Purse: A History of American Public Finance, 1776–1790.* Chapel Hill, NC: University of North Carolina Press, 1961.

Nuxoll, Elizabeth Miles. *Congress and the Munitions Merchants: The Secret Committee of Trade during the American Revolution, 1775–1777.* New York: Garland Publishing, Inc., 1985.

Ver Steeg, Clarence L. *Robert Morris, Revolutionary Financier, With an Analysis of His Earlier Career.* Philadelphia: University of Pennsylvania Press, 1954.

Elizabeth M. Nuxoll

SECRET SERVICE

The U.S. Secret Service is charged by law and by executive orders with two essential missions—provide physical protection and conduct criminal investigations into certain kinds of crimes. The first mission is to provide physical protection. Most of the other threats, such as counterfeiting or computer fraud, are threats to the integrity of the American financial system.

In 1894 the Secret Service began an informal role as protector of the president when it began work as an agency protecting President Grover Cleveland. In the years following the assassination of President William McKinley in 1901, the Secret Service was assigned the responsibility for protecting presidents.

In the twentieth century, threats against presidents, the attack on President Harry S. Truman (1951), the assassination of President John F. Kennedy (1963), and later of his brother, Robert Kennedy, led to Secret Service protection by act of Congress for presidents, presidential candidates, their families, as well as others such as individuals who are in the order of succession to the office of the president. Foreign heads of state and their spouses have also been placed under Secret Service protection by Congress when these persons are visiting the United States.

In 1997 Congress passed the Presidential Threat Protection Act (Public Law 106–544). It authorizes the Secret Service to participate in the planning, coordination, and implementation of security operations at special events of national significance ("National Special Security Event" NSSA). The president makes the final decision as to what is a NSSA. Events such as the G-8 meeting at Sea Island, Georgia, in 2004 have been so designated.

During election campaigns major presidential and vice presidential candidates and their spouses are given Secret Service protection within 120 days of the presidential general election. After presidential elections the Secret Service protects presidents-elect and vice-presidents elect. The families of these individuals are also assigned Secret Service agents for their protection.

Former presidents' spouses for their lifetimes, even after the death of the former president, are assigned Secret Service protection. However, if the spouse of a late president or vice president remarries then the protection is removed. The children of former presidents are also give protection until they reach age 16. In 1997 Congress

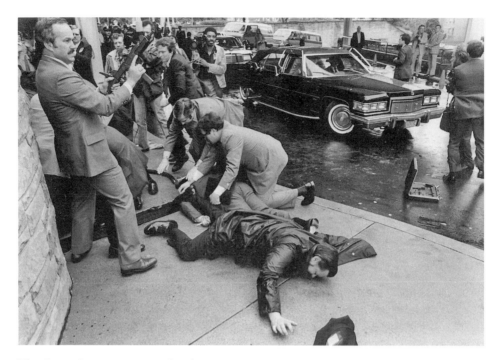

The Secret Service moves in after the assassination attempt on President Ronald Reagan on March 30, 1981. The Secret Service is a security agency, under the Department of Homeland Security since 2003, that is responsible for the safety of the president, the vice president, and their families. (Ronald Reagan Library)

acted to limit the Secret Service protection given former presidents and vice presidents to 10 years after they left office.

Events can be designated National Special Security Events. If the secretary of the Department of Homeland Security gives an event this designation then it will be protected by Secret Service agents. The president of the United States may issue executive orders that designate individuals for Secret Service protection.

In 2002 Congress adopted Public Law 107-296, which established the Department of Homeland Security. The act transferred the U.S. Secret Service from the Department of the Treasury to the new Department of Homeland Security on March 1, 2003. Since joining the Department of Homeland Security, the Secret Service has developed a Secret Service Strategic Plan for meeting future challenges.

The work of protection performed by the Secret Service is sensitive, so the agency does not discuss the ways and means of its duties. Operations to keep protectees safe include using advanced technology and other resources to develop a security plan. In the security plan will be assessments of the role and vulnerabilities of critical infrastructures as well as other elements.

The Secret Service conducts protective visits in advance of the arrival of protectees. The protective visits conduct site surveys, assessments of local manpower, equipment, hospitals, evacuation routes, fire, rescue, and other available public service personnel. These are also alerted as to their likely role during a visit. A command post is set up which acts as the communications center for protective activities. It coordinates the network of support for the members of the detail working close to the protectee. After a protective visit, an after-action report is developed in which agents analyze every step of the protective operation. A record is made of any unusual incidents and then suggestions are made for improvements for the future.

For the Secret Service protective research is the key to effective security operations. Agents and specialists conduct protective research in order to evaluate information received from law enforcement, intelligence agencies, and other sources. The intelligence is about individuals or groups that pose a threat to protectees. Any communications received at the White House, whether letters, e-mails, or public comments that can be understood as a physical threat to protectees, is evaluated. The work of coordination protection information is conducted around the clock every day.

In 1998 the National Threat Assessment Center (NTAC) was created as an institution that could provide the intelligence to assess threats. The NTAC's research into attacks on public officials, public figures, and in the public school has provided information that is specific and is the foundation for clear knowledge of the person or persons who are most likely to become a threat. Its research is currently being extended to other areas of law enforcement such as stalking.

Among the NTAC's research projects has been the Exceptional Case Study Project (ECSP). Findings have been that assassins are rarely mentally ill; instead they have a range of motives on a variety of issues. Therefore no assassin "profile" exists. Instead what we have is a common is a set of attack behaviors. These include the ability to act in a dangerous manner such as getting weapons, scouting several targets before action, expressing threats, or other behaviors.

Based upon its findings, the Secret Service now seeks to manage subjects who may pose a threat. And it is engaged in ongoing protection research.

See also: Baker, Lafayette; Sanford, Henry; Wood, William P.

References and Further Reading

Holden, Henry M. *To Be a U.S. Secret Service Agent*. St. Paul, MN: Zenith, 2006.

Melanson, Philip H., and Peter F. Stevens. *The Secret Service: The Hidden History of an Enigmatic Agency*. New York: Carroll & Graf Publishers, 2004.

Petro, Joseph, and Jeffrey Robinson. *Standing Next to History: An Agent's Life Inside the Secret Service*. New York: Thomas Dunne Books, 2005.

Secret Service: http://www.secretservice.gov/index.shtml.

Andrew J. Waskey

SECRET SERVICE FUND

The Secret Service Fund, also known as the Contingency Fund of Foreign Intercourse, helped to establish the idea of the president's prerogative in foreign relations. Despite congressional debate over the fund as a resource for intelligence activities, Congress allowed the president to withhold information regarding Secret Service expenditures. And presidents would use the Secret Service Fund for covert operations, including peacetime efforts to foment violent revolutions against foreign countries.

Remembering the importance of secret agents for the American cause in the Revolutionary War, George Washington in his first annual message as president requested a discretionary fund that would give the chief executive the financial resources for covert operations. Washington, like other leaders of the founding generation, believed secret agents were crucial for achieving some foreign-policy objectives. Indeed, secret agents could be employed in a wide range of overseas missions, including intelligence gathering and other clandestine operations.

Enacted as law on July 1, 1790, the Secret Service Fund by its third year of existence had grown to $1 million, which was 12 percent of the federal budget. And the act that created the fund did not require the president to state how the money was spent. President Washington soon used executive agents in a variety of missions, including a secret effort to ransom American hostages being held by the Barbary states of North Africa, as well as to play off Great Britain and Spain against each other to gain the use of the Mississippi River from Spain and to obtain a more extensive trade treaty with Britain.

From the end of the Washington administration to the creation of the Central Intelligence Agency in 1947, the Secret Service Fund continued to be a vehicle for covert operations in war and peace. Later examples of presidential use of the fund included James Madison's effort to overthrow Spanish authority in East and West Florida, Andrew Jackson's effort to acquire Texas and to negotiate commercial treaties with Asian countries, and Benjamin Harrison's support for the overthrow of the Hawaiian monarchy.

See also: Jackson, Andrew

References and Further Reading

Andrew, Christopher. *For the President's Eyes Only: Secret Intelligence and the American Presidency from Washington to Bush.* New York: HarperCollins, 1995.

Corwin, Edwin S. *The President's Control of Foreign Relations.* Princeton, NJ: Princeton University Press, 1917.

Jeffrey-Jones, Rhodri. *American Espionage: From Secret Service to CIA.* New York: Free Press, 1977.

Knott, Stephen F. *Secret and Sanctioned: Covert Operations and the American Presidency.* New York: Oxford University Press, 1996.

Miller, Nathan. *Spying for America: The Hidden History of U.S. Intelligence.* New York: Dell Publishing, 1989.

Wriston, Henry Merritt. *Executive Agents in American Foreign Relations.* Baltimore, MD: The Johns Hopkins University Press, 1929.

Steven E. Siry

SEDITION ACT, 1918

The Sedition Act of 1918 adopted by Congress on May 16, 1918, was an extension of the Espionage Act of 1917. The Espionage Act adopted shortly after the American entry into the war was the result of public outcry over the Black Tom explosion on July 29, 1916. German espionage agents sabotaged a huge ammunition depot on a spit of land jutting from New Jersey into New York Harbor. The explosion killed two night watchmen and dramatically destroyed huge quantities of war material destined for the Allies fighting in Europe.

The United States was at the time neutral; however, the German spies had used anti-British Irish immigrants in order to gather information on the facility. That immigrant Americans had been recruited by foreign agents had kindled political suspicions of foreigners and set off an obsession with the "enemy within." The Espionage Act was the first attempt aimed at protecting Americans from foreign spies. It made it a crime to interfere with the operation of the armed forces of the United States. The act also created some new internal security machinery, including a Justice Department agency called the Bureau of Investigation.

The Sedition Act of 1918 extended the Espionage Act to make it a crime to speak out against the government. President Woodrow Wilson had sought the act because he feared widespread dissent which would be a hindrance to American victory.

The law sought to restrict the freedom of speech of Americans in wartime by preventing subversive activities. Wilson was concerned about the effects that "subversive activity" might have. The Easter Rising in Ireland (1916) and Russian Revolution (1917) were products of subversive activities from the government's point of view.

The Sedition Act forbade during time of war interfering with the war effort by disrupting operations of the armed forces. It outlawed acting in concert with others and joining groups to teach or plan to disrupt the government's conduct of the war. In addition it forbade sending subversive literature through the mails. It gave the postmaster general the duty to refuse to deliver subversive literature.

The goal of the act was to prevent agitators who were concealed agents of foreign powers or merely agents of an ideology that was hostile to the war effort from acting. Most of those prosecuted under the Espionage and Sedition Acts were socialists such as Eugene Debs, pacifists, or others who were opposed to the war. Some were given lengthy jail sentences. The Supreme Court upheld the act in *Schenck vs. United States* (1919). However, both laws were repealed in 1921 and most of those convicted were pardoned. Portions of the Espionage Act are now spread across the federal code in a variety of places.

See also: Espionage Act, 1917

References and Further Reading

Kohn, Stephen M. *American Political Prisoners: Prosecutions under the Espionage and Sedition Acts.* Westport, CT: Praeger, 1994.

Manz, William H. *Civil Liberties in Wartime: Legislative Histories of the Espionage Act of 1917 and the Act of 1918.* Buffalo, NY: W. S. Hein, 2007.

Andrew J. Waskey

SENATE SELECT COMMITTEE ON INTELLIGENCE (SSCI)

The Senate Select Committee on Intelligence (usually abbreviated SSCI) was established in 1976 after the investigations of the Church Committee indicated that Congress had not effectively overseen the work of U.S. intelligence agencies that had been involved in abuses in regard to domestic surveillance and covert actions overseas.

As a select committee, SSCI consists of members named by the Senate majority and minority leaders; prior to 2004 members were limited to eight years on SSCI but, responding to recommendations of the 9/11 Commission, the Senate removed the limitation.

A principal responsibility of SSCI is preparation of intelligence authorization bills that are subsequently voted on by the entire Senate. These bills authorize the activities of the Office of the Director of National Intelligence and the major national intelligence agencies—the Central Intelligence Agency (CIA), the Defense Intelligence Agency (DIA), the National Security Agency (NSA), etc.

SSCI is also responsible for the oversight of intelligence activities conducted by national intelligence agencies such as the CIA, DIA, and NSA. Unlike the situation in the House of Representatives, however, the tactical intelligence activities of the military services are overseen not by the intelligence committee but by the armed services committee (although there is informal coordination). Oversight involves hearings, investigations, and the publication of reports to assess whether the executive branch is faithfully executing the relevant statutes. Oversight may lead the Senate to amend existing laws and to encourage or pressure the administration to modify its policies. SSCI's publications are posted on its Web site: http://intelligence.senate.gov/.

The Senate is responsible under the Constitution for receiving nominations to key positions and for providing its advice and consent before the nominees can take office. For senior intelligence positions, including that of the Director of National Intelligence (DNI), the names of nominees are forwarded to SSCI for consideration which often takes the form of public hearings. Subsequently, SSCI will send the nomination to the entire Senate for its consideration.

See also: Church Committee; House Permanent Select Committee on Intelligence (HPSCI); Pike Committee

References and Further Reading

Smist, Frank J., Jr. *Congress Oversees the United States Intelligence Community, 1947–1994*, 2nd ed. Knoxville, TN: University of Tennessee Press, 1994.

Snider, L. Britt. *Sharing Secrets with Lawmakers: Congress as a User of Intelligence*. Washington, DC: Central Intelligence Agency, Center for the Study of Intelligence, 1997.

U.S. Senate. Select Committee on Intelligence. *Legislative Oversight of Intelligence Activities: The U.S. Experience*. 103rd Congress, 2nd session. 1994. Senate Print 103–88.

Richard A. Best, Jr.

SEPTEMBER 11, 2001

The U.S. Intelligence Community's failure to provide advance warning of the attacks on the World Trade Center and the Pentagon on September 11, 2001, was quickly characterized as a major intelligence failure. That conclusion, however, was modified by subsequent research and analysis. There was no doubt a failure to provide tactical warning that would have led to the arrest of the hijackers prior to their boarding the ill-fated aircraft, but in retrospect it was concluded that the failure resulted in large measure from the inability of government analysts to have perceived the linkages between international terrorist groups and a few obscure foreign young men traveling and taking classes in the United States.

Intelligence agencies were well aware of the goals of the al-Qaeda terrorist group; the role of its leader, Osama bin Laden; and its previous successes in attacking U.S. embassies in Kenya and Tanzania in 1998 and the USS *Cole* in October 2000. In mid-summer of 2001 analysts warned of the likelihood of an imminent attack (although an overseas location was deemed most likely); as then-Director of Central Intelligence George Tenet has said, the "system was blinking red." Government analysts had not, however, combined their understanding of the threat from al-Qaeda with the scraps of available information about the 19 individuals who had traveled to the United States beginning in early 2000. They did not "connect the dots."

Why this was the case has been analyzed at great length by the two congressional intelligence committees, the National Commission on Terrorist Attacks Upon the United States (the 9/11 Commission), and the Commission on Intelligence Capabilities of the United States Regarding Weapons of Mass Destruction (the WMD Commission). In general, assessments focus on the existence of separate worlds of intelligence and law enforcement that did not cooperate effectively. Analysts in the respective communities were unable, because of legal restrictions, regulations, and customary bureaucratic practice, to share information on potential terrorist attacks in the United States. Intelligence agencies focused their attentions overseas. Law enforcement agencies were responsible for monitoring suspicious behavior in the United States. The morass of statutes and regulations that governed any exchanges of information had effectively resulted in a wall between the two sets of agencies. In practice, all agencies were required by law and regulation to avoid collecting information on U.S. persons unless there was probable cause that they had committed a crime or were about to. This limited their ability to monitor the men who would commit the terrorist attacks of September 2001. It has to be recognized, however, that even had there had been far more information and had it been better shared, a discernable pattern may not have emerged. Suicidal terrorists are difficult to stop under any circumstances.

A number of other factors contributed to the inability to prevent the 9/11 attacks. U.S. intelligence agencies had failed to place agents in terrorist groups—a daunting challenge but one that may not have received adequate attention before 9/11. There were also too few linguists to translate the masses of information that had been collected.

The main response by the U.S. government to 9/11 was to tear down the walls that had prevented sharing law enforcement and intelligence information. The USA Patriot Act was quickly enacted in October 2001, followed by the establishment of the Department of Homeland Security in 2002, and the Intelligence Reform and Terrorism Prevention Act of 2004 which was the most far-reaching reorganization of the intelligence community since the National Security Act of 1947.

After 9/11, U.S. executive branch agencies devoted considerable effort to ensuring that information is exchanged and analyzed with the National Counterterrorism Center becoming the focus of the effort. Further attacks on the 9/11 scale have not reoccurred but to what extent this success results from changed analytical and collection practices cannot be determined. There are, moreover, persisting concerns that collecting more information in the United States and combining it with intelligence from abroad may ultimately threaten civil liberties by exposing innocent individuals to pervasive government scrutiny.

See also: Director of National Intelligence; Homeland Security, Department of; Intelligence Community; National Commission on Terrorist Attacks on the United States (The 9/11 Commission); National Security Act; USA Patriot Act

References and Further Reading

Posner, Gerald. *Why America Slept: The Failure to Prevent 9/11*. New York: Random House. 2003.

Senate Select Committee on Intelligence and House Permanent Select Committee on Intelligence. *Joint Inquiry into Intelligence Community Activities Before and After the Terrorist Attack of September 11, 2001*. 107th Congress, 2nd session. Senate Report No. 107–351; House Report 107–792. 2002.

U.S. Commission on the Intelligence Capabilities of the United States Regarding Weapons of Mass Destruction. *Report to the President of the United States*. Washington, DC: Government Printing Office, 2005.

U.S. National Commission on Terrorist Attacks Upon the United States. *The 9/11 Commission Report*. Washington, DC: Government Printing Office. 2004.

Richard A. Best, Jr.

SESSIONS, WILLIAM STEELE
(MAY 27, 1930–)

William Steele Sessions, a famous attorney and former director of the FBI, was born in Fort Smith, Arkansas, on May 27, 1930. He attended Northeast High School in Kansas City, Missouri, from which he graduated in 1948.

Upon graduation, he signed up for the U.S. Air Force and received a commission in October 1952. On active duty until three years later, Sessions found time to pursue his studies as well and he was able to complete his undergraduate degree from Baylor University in 1956. A student of law, he went on to receive his LLB in 1958.

Following the completion of his studies, Sessions began his legal career as an attorney for a firm located in Waco, Texas. He remained there from 1958 until 1969 and quickly became a partner. During his time there, he had accrued some fame and was appointed to chief of the Government Operation Section of the Criminal Division of the U.S. Department of Justice in 1969. Sessions only stayed in Washington, DC, for roughly two years before becoming a U.S. attorney, assigned back to the western district of Texas in 1971. He was appointed to be U.S. district judge for the same district in 1974, going on to become the chief judge in 1980. Meanwhile, he participated on the Board of the Federal Judicial Center in Washington.

Sessions had a good reputation throughout the legal field and the federal government. In 1987, he was selected by President Ronald Reagan to lead the FBI.

He was sworn into power on November 2, 1987, succeeding William H. Webster. Sessions was known for his work to improve diversity at the FBI. His time as director, however, was riddled by two major FBI standoffs at Ruby Ridge, Montana, and at the Branch Dividian compound in Waco, Texas. During the Ruby Ridge standoff, an FBI sniper killed an unarmed woman at the scene in 1992. Later, the storming of the Branch Davidian compound on February 28, 1993, was decried by many as unnecessarily confrontational and violent. Meanwhile, numerous issues arose within the FBI's crime laboratory.

Following Bill Clinton's inauguration as president, Sessions was fired on July 19, 1993, amid a controversy about using federal money for his trips and improvements to his home. He was succeeded by Louis Freeh. Sessions returned to Texas and remained active in politics there, participating in a lobby to reduce gun crime. He remains a member of the U.S. Bar Association and still denies any misuse of federal money or fraud while FBI director.

See also: Federal Bureau of Investigation (FBI)

References and Further Reading

Andrew, Christopher. *For the President's Eyes Only: Secret Intelligence and the American Presidency from Washington to Bush.* New York: HarperCollins, 1995.
Freeh, Louis. *My FBI: Bringing Down the Mafia, Investigating Bill Clinton, and Fighting the War on Terror.* New York: St. Martin's, 2006.
Jeffrey-Jones, Rhodri. *The FBI: A History.* New Haven, CT: Yale University Press, 2007.

Glenn P. Hastedt

SHAABAN, SHAABAN HAFIZ AHMAD ALI

Shaaban Hafiz Ahmad Ali Shaaban is believed be a Palestinian who was born in Jordan and who once lived in Russia where he may have received intelligence training from the KGB. Shaaban is one of at least one dozen identities adopted by Shaaban, including Shaaban Hafed and Joe H. Brown. He possessed five passports and several Social Security numbers. He came to the United States around 1993 and later obtained U.S. citizenship.

Beginning in 2002 and continuing into 2003, Shaaban acted as an agent for the Iraqi government. In that capacity he agreed to travel to Baghdad in late 2002 to sell the names of U.S. intelligence agents and operatives to Iraq for $3 million. He also sought to gain Iraqi support for a pro-Iraq television station in the United States, tried to get Iraq to sign an agreement whereby he would provide volunteers to act as human shields to protect the Iraqi infrastructure during war, and broadcasted messages supporting the Iraqi government on Iraqi media calling upon listeners to forcibly resist the United States and those who opposed Iraq.

U.S. law requires that anyone who agrees to act as an agent of a foreign government must register with the attorney general. Shaaban never registered. His travel to Iraq was in violation of the International Emergency Powers Act (IEEPA) that banned any type of travel and any transactions with Iraq that were not approved by the attorney general. These restrictions were put in place by President George H. W. Bush after Iraq invaded Kuwait and remained at least partially in place until President George W. Bush rescinded them in July 2004.

Shaaban was arrested in March 2005. He went on trial in January 2006 and was acting as a foreign agent without notification, violation of the Iraqi Sanctions under the IEEPA, and unlawful procurement of naturalization. The jury did not convict him of the charge of offering to sell secrets to Iraq. He was sentenced to 160 months. Shabaan is serving his prison time in a super-maximum security prison in Florence, Colorado. Commentators note that this location is typically reserved for more severe cases of espionage such as that by Robert Hanssen, who is also serving his time there.

Shabaan acted as his own counsel during the trial. He argued that the government was confusing him with a twin brother. Both were CIA agents and the brother was now dead. Another brother testified that Shabaan did not have a twin. Shabaan did not call anyone from the CIA to testify in his defense.

See also: Post–Cold War Intelligence

References and Further Reading

Adams, James. *The New Spies: Exploring the Frontiers of Espionage.* New York: Hutchinson, 1994.

Herbig, Katherine. *Changes in Espionage by Americans.* Monterey, CA: Defense Personnel Research Center, 2008.

Glenn P. Hastedt

SHACKLEY, THEODORE G., JR.
(JULY 16, 1927–DECEMBER 9, 2002)

Theodore G. Shackley, Jr., was a longtime Central Intelligence Agency covert action specialist who rose to the position of associate deputy director for operations in 1976 under Director of Central intelligence (DCI) George H. W. Bush. This position put him in charge of CIA covert operations. Shackely reportedly had aspirations to become DCI but failed to obtain this position due to opposition from Carter administration officials.

Ted Shackley joined the CIA in the early 1950s after having served in Army Counter Intelligence. His first major posting was as station chief in Miami where he headed up the CIA's post–Bay of Pigs covert action campaign against Fidel Castro. JMWAVE, as the operation was known, included some 2,000 Cuban agents and 200 CIA officers. From Miami, Shackley went to Southeast Asia. He became station chief in Laos in 1966 where he directed the Hmong against the Viet Cong. In 1968 he was transferred to Vietnam where he played a central role in the controversial Phoenix Program that was designed to neutralize the Viet Cong but instead engaged in widespread indiscriminate violence that neutralized its effectiveness. From Vietnam, Shackley became head of the CIA's Western Hemisphere Division where he participated in the CIA plan to remove Salvadore Allende from power in Chile. This posting also put him in direct conflict with Philip Agee, a CIA officer who was writing a highly critical account of the agency.

Shackley left the agency under a cloud of controversy stemming from his association with Edwin Wilson, a CIA agent, who was involved in an arms sales project with Libya. In 1984 DCI William Casey sought out his help in obtaining the freedom of William Buckley, a CIA diplomat and CIA station chief, who was being held hostage in Beirut by Hezbollah guerrillas. Efforts to free Buckley ultimately led to the Iran-Contra crisis. Central to the plans formulated by Oliver North and others was the use of dummy companies and foreign bank accounts to hide money obtained from arms sales to Iran that would be sent to support the Contras in Nicaragua. From his days in Laos, Shackley was well connected with such companies. His involvement came to light when in October 1986 a cargo plane flying supplies to the Contras was shot down. Information from the pilot who had worked for Air America, a CIA front company, pointed to the involvement of the CIA and led investigators to longtime associates of Shackley whom he had recruited to help him in the weapons-for-hostages project.

See also: Casey, William; Castro, Fidel; Central Intelligence Agency; Iran-Contra Affair; JMWAVE

References and Further Reading

Corson, William. *Armies of Ignorance. The Rise of the American Intelligence Empire.* New York: Dial, 1977.

Shackley, Theodore. *The Third Option: An American View of Counterinsurgency Operations.* New York: Reader's Digest Press, 1981.

Glenn P. Hastedt

SHALER, WILLIAM
(1778–MARCH 29, 1833)

William Shaler was an American diplomat and agent who served in various posts throughout Latin America and supervised an invasion of Spanish Texas by Mexican revolutionaries.

Shaler, orphaned at 13, became a ship's captain and traded throughout Latin America. A friend of Madison's Secretary of State Robert Smith, Shaler was appointed as an agent to observe and report on the Mexican port of Veracruz. He arrived in Havana in 1810 and was denied permission to go on to Mexico. While in Cuba, Shaler colluded with Cuban rebels and was arrested by the Spanish authorities. In December of 1811, Shaler returned to New Orleans. There, he met José Gutiérrez, a former blacksmith who held a commission in the revolutionary army of Hidalgo. Gutiérrez was determined to eject the Spanish from the Americas, and gained the ear of the U.S. government. Madison's administration sent Gutiérrez to the border, and allowed him to gather an army. At the same time, it officially denied any support for the filibuster and attached Shaler to Gutiérrez's expedition as a minder.

In August of 1812, the Gutiérrez expedition—composed largely of American frontiersmen—crossed into Spanish Texas. The invasion stalled at La Bahia, where Gutiérrez's advance force was besieged for four months. On March 2, 1813, Gutiérrez's commander Samuel Kemper (a veteran of anti-Spanish intrigues in West Florida) decisively defeated the Spanish outside San Antonio. On April 6, Gutiérrez declared Texas independent. His administration was incompetent and brutal, and by the end of the summer, he had lost his army and his brief independence. Shaler, who never crossed the border, was ordered to abandon the expedition by President Madison.

After the expedition, Shaler was sent to Europe to represent the United States in conferences following the Napoleonic Wars. He then spent 12 years as U.S. consul at Algiers before returning to Havana, where he died of cholera in 1833.

See also: Early Republic and Espionage

References and Further Reading

Nichols, Roy F. "William Shaler: New England Apostle of Rational Liberty," *The New England Quarterly* 9 (1936), 71–96.

Owsley, Frank Jr., and Gene A. Smith. *Filibusters and Expansionists: Jeffersonian Manifest Destiny, 1800–1821.* Tuscaloosa, AL: University of Alabama Press, 1997.

Warren, Harris Gaylord. *The Sword Was Their Passport: A History of American Filibustering in the Mexican Revolution.* Baton Rouge, LA: Louisiana State University Press, 1943.

James L. Erwin

SHAMROCK, PROJECT

Project SHAMROCK was a domestic intelligence-gathering operation in the United States that ran secretly from 1945 to 1975. At its height, some 150,000 messages per month were being analyzed by the National Security Agency (NSA). Senator Frank Church (D-Idaho), chair of the Senate Select Committee on Intelligence when Project SHAMROCK was terminated, characterized it as perhaps the largest government interception program ever targeted against Americans.

Project SHAMROCK was set up by the Armed Forces Security Agency, the predecessor of the NSA. It collected and analyzed all telegraphic data entering into or leaving the United States. Access to this information required the participation and acquiescence of the major international cable companies: RCA Global, ITT, and Western Union. Reportedly they pressed officials in Washington for assurances that they would not be subject to criminal prosecution and lawsuits. In receipt of such assurances these companies cooperated and apparently never inquired about what was done with the information they provided.

The initial focus of Project SHAMROCK was limited to a small NSA watch list. At first this information was passed along in the form of microfilm copies of all transmissions passing through their offices. Technological developments such as magnetic tapes and then computer keyword scanning programs gradually made it possible to gather more and more information on more and more people. NSA's watch list, now known as Project MINARET, grew accordingly. Project SHAMROCK grew to such proportions that in 1966 a front company (identified in documents by the code name "LPMEDLEY") was set up in New York near the offices of the three cable companies to facilitate the analysis of intercepted material.

A confluence of factors came together in the early 1970s that led to the termination of Project SHAMROCK. In 1972 the Supreme Court ruled in the *Keith* case (*U.S. vs. U.S. District Court*) that a warrant was necessary to place wiretaps on Americans who did not have a significant connection to a foreign power. The *Keith* decision did not in and of itself put an end to the existence of NSA watch lists or intercepts. Federal Bureau of Intelligence Director Clarence Kelly, for example, argued that *Keith* did not apply to NSA electronic surveillance. Political impetus for ending Project SHAMROCK came from the joining of *Keith* with the beginning of the Watergate saga and the appointment of General Lew Allen, Jr., to the position of NSA director. With the NSA now coming under increasing public scrutiny by Congress for its involvement in domestic intelligence gathering activities, Allen suspended Project SHAMROCK in May 1975 in an effort to protect the agency from even greater damage. The official rationale given was that it was no longer an effective intelligence-gathering program. Secretary of Defense James Schlesinger formally ordered it terminated on May 15, 1975.

One of the major consequences of the congressional investigation into Project SHAMROCK was the passage of the 1978 Foreign Intelligence Surveillance Act and the establishment of the Foreign Intelligence Surveillance Court. This secret court was created to hear requests from the U.S. government to put in place electronic surveillance devices on American citizens.

See also: Church Committee; MINARET, Project; National Security Agency

References and Further Reading

Bamford, James. *Body of Secrets: Anatomy of the Ultra Secret National Security Agency*. New York: Anchor, 2002.

United States Senate. Select Committee to Study Government Operations with Respect to Intelligence Activities, *Final Report, Book II, Intelligence Activities and the Rights of Americans*. Washington, DC: U.S. Government Printing Office, April 26, 1976.

Glenn P. Hastedt

SHEINWOLD, ALFRED
(JANUARY 26, 1912–MARCH 8, 1997)

Alfred Sheinwold was a bridge expert and newspaper columnist who worked for the OSS during World War II, using his talents in mathematics as the chief coder and cipher expert. Born in England, Sheinwold moved with his family to Brooklyn, New York, at the age of nine. He graduated from City College in 1933, and then worked as a writer for Ely Culbertson, a leading authority on bridge, being editor of the magazine *The Bridge World* from 1934 until 1963, often writing under the pseudonym Saxon Fairwood. This name was derived from "Saxon" for the Anglo-Saxon King Alfred, and "Fair Wood" as a translation from the German "Schein Wald."

During World War II, Sheinwold was used to crack codes for the OSS, with his knowledge of applied mathematics being particularly useful, as well as his ability to speak several languages. His tasks involved working through garbled messages, and also ensure that the OSS codes could not be compromised. After the war Sheinwold helped develop, with Edgar Kaplan, the Kaplan-Sheinwold bidding system used in Bridge, and was on the U.S. Bridge Team as captain of the team in the controversial match in Bermuda in 1975 when two Italian players were accused of using illegal signals. Sheinwold wanted to withdraw from the game, but was overruled by other officials. He wrote 13 books on bridge, with his *Five Weeks to Winning Bridge* selling millions of copies. Sheinwold, who lived in Los Angeles, was also an authority on backgammon.

See also: American Intelligence, World War II; Office of Strategic Services

References and Further Reading

Kahn, David. *The Code-Breakers*. New York: Macmillan, 1967.
Smith, Bradley F. *The Shadow Warriors: OSS and the Origins of the CIA*. New York: Basic Books, 1983.

Justin Corfield

SHEVCHENKO, ARKADY
(1930–1998)

In 1978 Arkady Shevchenko became the highest-ranking Soviet diplomat to defect to the West. Born in the Ukrainian Soviet Socialist Republic on October 11, 1930, Shevchenko joined the Soviet foreign service in 1956. Two years later he was temporarily posted to New York City as part of the Soviet delegation to the United Nations (UN). He returned to the United Nations on a permanent posting in 1963, where he remained until 1970. At that time he was made an advisor to Andrei Gromyko. Shevchenko returned to the UN again in 1973 when he became under secretary general, the second highest position at the UN.

Shevchenko claims to have become disillusioned with the Soviet system in the early years of détente. In 1975 he approached the Central Intelligence Agency (CIA) about defecting but was convinced to become an agent in place supplying the CIA with information about Soviet political and strategic thinking as well as the identities of many agents. In March 1978 he was recalled to Moscow for consultations. By now Shevchenko was aware that Soviet authorities suspected him of being a spy and he feared the consequences of returning to the Soviet Union. Accordingly, he contacted the CIA and demanded asylum. One of those who formally debriefed him for the CIA was Aldrich Ames, who was himself a Soviet spy.

His wife chose not to defect with him and returned to Moscow. Two months later she died apparently by committing suicide. Shevchenko remained in the United States for the rest of his life and became an American citizen. His later life was punctuated by problems with alcoholism and charges that the CIA provided him with prostitutes.

See also: Central Intelligence Agency; Cold War Intelligence; KGB (Komitet Gosudarstvennoi Bezopasnosti)

References and Further Reading

Charlton, Michael. *The Eagle and the Small Birds. Crisis in the Soviet Empire: From Yalta to Solidarity*. London: British Broadcasting Corporation, 1984.
Shevchenko, Arkady N. *Breaking With Moscow*. New York: Alfred A. Knopf, 1985.

Glenn P. Hastedt

SHU, QUANG-SHENG

Dr. Quang-Sheng Shu pled guilty on November 17, 2008, to charges that in December 2003 he violated the U.S. Arms Export Control Act by providing the People's Republic of China (PRC) with a document on the construction of a cryogenic fueling system for space launch vehicles without first obtaining an export license or written approval from the State Department. He also was charged with offering bribes to Chinese government officials in hopes of obtaining contracts from the PRC for his firm and an allied French company. These actions, U.S. authorities argued, put U.S. national security at risk.

Shu, 68, was sentenced to more than four years in federal prison in April 2009. He had faced the possibility of a 10-year prison term. In arguing for a reduced sentence, his defense attorney argued that most of the information Shu gave was publicly available. Also, most of his attempted bribes were unsuccessful.

Shu holds a PhD in physics. Born in China, he came to the United States in 1990 and is a naturalized U.S. citizen and at the time of his arrest was president and treasurer of AMAC International, located in Newport News, Virginia. Before this he worked for Northrup-Gruman in Seattle, Washington. AMAC did contract work for the Department of Energy and the National Aeronautics and Space Administration (NASA).

This case is one of more than a dozen cases involving China that have been prosecuted by U.S. authorities over the past several years.

See also: China, Intelligence Operations of; Industrial Espionage; Post–Cold War Intelligence

References and Further Reading

Fialka, John J. *War by Other Means: Economic Espionage in America*. New York: W. W. Norton, 1999.

Lewis, Jonathan E. *Spy Capitalism: ITEK and the CIA*. New Haven, CT: Yale University Press, 2002.

Nasheri, Hedieh, et al. *Economic Espionage and Industrial Spying*. Cambridge, MA: Cambridge University Press, 2004.

Glenn P. Hastedt

SIGNALS INTELLIGENCE SERVICE

Established in 1930, the Signals Intelligence Service (SIS) was an attempt to streamline and make more effective the U.S. Army's code-breaking capabilities. In the early stages of World War I, the United States was the target of intelligence operations of both Britain and Germany. Both warring nations wanted to know the position of the neutral nation. British code breakers had intercepted and deciphered the famous Zimmermann Telegram—Germany's offer of support and territorial spoils to Mexico if it declared war on the United States. American military leaders quickly realized the strategic and diplomatic value of cryptology.

When the United States entered the world war in 1917, its primary intelligence concerns were supporting possible combat operations in France. The United States began a "special relationship" with the British intelligence community and also created its own

U.S. signals intelligence (SIGINT) with a code and cipher unit. The unit was under the direction of Herbert Yardley. After the war, Yardley's interception and code-breaking efforts were maintained, and designated the Cipher Bureau. Better known as the "Black Chamber," it was funded by both the State and War Departments. Yardley's Black Chamber achieved success when it broke Japanese diplomatic codes during the Washington Naval Disarmament Conference (1921–1922). Yardley's unit managed to provide the U.S. delegation with exact details of Japan's naval limits negotiation position. The United States successfully kept Japanese naval expansion under control, thereby slowing down her imperialistic appetite. However, postwar isolationism saw support for the Black Chamber diminish. In 1929, Secretary of State Henry L. Stimson ordered the program to be shut down.

In 1930, however, the U.S. Army enlarged and consolidated its efforts with the establishment of the Signal Intelligence Service (SIS). The division was started by William F. Friedman and three former mathematics teachers, Frank Rowlett, Abraham Sinkov, and Solomon Kullback. In the mid-1930s Friedman's division cracked Japanese diplomatic messages encrypted by the "Red Machine" (began operations in the early 1930s). In 1938, the Japanese foreign ministry, seeking to protect top-secret messages, introduced a more formidable and secure device, the "Purple Machine." In response, Friedman reorganized his small staff by adding more mathematicians, cryptanalysts, and linguists in order to construct his own Purple Machine. The result was MAGIC, the code word applied to the solution of Japanese diplomatic messages that were encrypted by the Purple Machine.

In early 1941, Friedman and SIS managed to re-create several duplicate copies of the machine that broke the Japanese code. By the end of the year eight machines were built—four stayed in Washington, DC, where the army and navy each used two, three were given to the British, and one was sent to intelligence headquarters of General Douglas MacArthur in the Philippines.

MAGIC made available to American intelligence agencies a staggering amount of diplomatic communications between Tokyo and all of its consular and embassy representatives throughout the world. Although MAGIC played a far greater role in terms of gathering diplomatic information, it was central to U.S. victories at the battle of Midway and elsewhere in the Pacific. MAGIC also provided the United States with details respecting Hitler's planned invasion of the Soviet Union in the spring of 1941 and, later, in May 1944, when Japanese ambassador to Germany, Hiroshi Oshima, informed Tokyo that Hitler was convinced that the main Allied invasion of France would take place near Calis rather than Normandy.

During the war, SIS was renamed the Signal Security Service in 1942. It also began intercepting Soviet messages from New York City. The project was given the code name "VENONA." By 1945 some 200,000 Soviet messages had been deciphered. On December 20, 1946, cryptanalyst Meredith Gardner revealed the existence of a Soviet espionage ring at the Los Alamos National Laboratory. On September 15, 1945, the U.S. Army Signal Security Agency was renamed the Army Security Agency. The 1947 National Security Act, passed by Congress in a growing fear of cold war tensions, created a civilian organization, the Central Intelligence Agency, to handle foreign intelligence. In 1952, the National Security Agency was created to oversee all matters related to gathering and interpreting intelligence information.

See also: Army Intelligence; Black Chamber; MAGIC; VENONA; Yardley, Herbert; Zimmermann Telegram

References and Further Reading

Bidwell, Bruce. *History of the Military Intelligence Division, Department of the Army General Staff*. Frederick, MD: University Publications of America, 1986.

Kahn, David. *The Codebreakers: The Comprehensive History of Secret Communication from Ancient Times to the Internet*. New York: Charles Scribner & Sons, 1996.

Kahn, David. *The Reader of Gentlemen's Mail: Herbert O. Yardley and the Birth of American Codebreaking*. New Haven, CT: Yale University Press, 2004.

Lowenthal, Mark. *Intelligence: From Secrets to Policy*. Washington, DC: Congressional Quarterly Press, 2003.

Lowenthal, Mark. *U.S. Intelligence: Evolution and Anatomy*, 2nd ed. Westport, CT: Praeger, 1992.

Watson, Bruce, Susan M. Watson, and Gerald Hopple (eds.). *United States Intelligence: An Encyclopedia*. New York: Garland, 1990.

West, Nigel. *The SIGINT Secrets: The Signals Intelligence War, 1900 to Today*. New York: Avon Books, 1988.

Charles F. Howlett

SILICON VALLEY AS AN INTELLIGENCE TARGET

Located in the Santa Clara Valley in Northern California, Silicon Valley has been the center of semiconductor and computer technology since the early 1970s. The area was named for the silicon chips designed and manufactured there, but the area has been a military and technological hub since the 1930s. In 1933 the Naval Air Station Moffett Field opened to house the airship USS *Macon*. In 1939 the National Advisory Committee for Aeronautics (NACA), the precursor to the National Aeronautics and Space Administration (NASA), was opened on Moffett Field. Renamed NASA Ames in 1958, it is a prime research facility for theoretical aeronautics, aircraft research, wind tunnel research, and simulation technology. Major technology firms, such as Lockheed, opened in the area to serve the U.S. Navy and later the U.S. Air Force.

In 1960 the Air Force Satellite Test Center opened in Sunnyvale, California. Located near Moffett Field and built on land purchased from Lockheed, the Test Center was the primary base of operations for the tracking and control of military intelligence satellites. Known locally as the "Blue Cube," the facility was part of a network of satellite tracking centers around the world. In 1987, concerns over the facility's vulnerability to foreign intelligence agencies and fears that Sunnyvale would be "Ground Zero" in a nuclear attack, the air force established a new satellite center in Colorado Springs, Colorado, called the Consolidated Space Operations Center. The Satellite Test Center (renamed Onizuka Air Force Base after the *Challenger* crash), remained open as a backup facility, but is slated for closure by 2011.

In Silicon Valley an added dimension to corporate espionage is the military's reliance on semiconductor chips. Since the early 1970s, corporate espionage, chip theft, and chip counterfeiting have directly impacted the U.S. government, military, and NASA. Counterfeit chips were discovered in the space shuttle and stolen chips made their way into the hands of Soviets and their allies.

In the 1970s and 1980s James Durward Harper and Ruby Louise Schuler passed stolen classified documents to the KGB through Polish agents. Both Harper and Schuler had been employed by Silicon Valley companies working on national security projects. Between October 1979 and June 1980 Harper passed research and development designs to the Poles for the Minuteman Ballistic Missile Defense Project. The documents had been obtained by Schuler from Systems Control, Inc., in Palo Alto. Harper was sentenced to life in prison and Schuler died of cirrhosis of the liver in 1983.

In another case, Anatoli Maluta, a Russian-born naturalized U.S. citizen, who had served in the U.S. Air Force as a mechanic and intelligence linguist, was sentenced to five years in prison for his part in a the shipment of electronic components to the Soviet Union through a West German entrepreneur, Werner Bruchhausen. Although the U.S. government and semiconductor chip manufacturers strive to maintain strict security controls, the desire for acquisition of high technology and the financial and strategic rewards for that technology continues to make Silicon Valley the target of corporate and military espionage.

See also: Industrial Espionage; Post–Cold War Intelligence

References and Further Reading

Halamka, John D. Espionage in the Silicon Valley. Berkeley, CA: Sybex, 1984. http://www.moffettfieldmuseum.org/

NASA Ames. http://www.nasa.gov/centers/ames/history/history.html.

Nasheri, Hedieh, et al. *Economic Espionage and Industrial Spying*. Cambridge, MD: Cambridge University Press, 2004.

Katie Simonton

SKULL AND BONES SOCIETY

The Skull and Bones Society, a secret organization located at Yale University in New Haven, Connecticut, was created by William Huntington Russell in December 1830. The society is also known as Chapter 322 and the Brotherhood of Death. It is one of the most prestigious and powerful, yet secretive societies in the United States.

William Huntington Russell went to study in Germany from 1830 to 1831 where he came into contact with a multitude of powerful student societies. While there, he was initiated into one of these secret societies that he in turn brought back with him to the United States. The next year in 1832, he worked along with Alphonso Taft to create Skull and Bones at Yale University.

Since the first induction in 1832, 15 rising juniors a year are initiated by the outgoing seniors. Little is known about the initiation, but it has been claimed that every inductee receives $15,000 and a watch. Certainly, it is not like any other organization or fraternity. Members and alumni of Skull and Bones remain committed to the society well after their graduation, creating an extremely powerful network.

Officially, the society is known as the Russell Trust Association which owns the chapter house at 64 High Street at Yale University and a private retreat known as Deer Island located in the Saint Lawrence River. Many conspiracy theories and published research papers deal with the Skull and Bones Society. Nothing conclusive has been established except for a somewhat overwhelming about of political power its members have come to possess. Claims have been that there are real skeletons in the chapter house, that members are forced to reveal information so they do not break with the group out of fear of blackmail, and that it is an active chapter of an international organization.

Nevertheless, Skull and Bones members are found throughout the U.S. political scene. Famous members include George W. Bush, John Kerry, William Taft, George H. W. Bush, Prescott Bush, and William F. Buckley, Jr.

See also: Buckley, William Frank, Jr.; Bush, George Herbert Walker

References and Further Reading

Millegan, Kris (ed.). *Fleshing Out Skull & Bones*. Walterville, OR: Trine Day, 2003.

Robbins, Alexandra. *Secrets of the Tomb: Skull and Bones, the Ivy League, and the Hidden Paths of Power*. New York: Little, Brown, 2002.

Sora, Steven. *Secret Societies of America's Elite: From Knights Templar to Skull and Bones*. New York: Destiny Books, 2003.

Arthur Holst

SMEDLEY, AGNES
(FEBRUARY 23, 1892–MAY 6, 1950)

Agnes was a journalist and author, well known for her books and articles on China and on the Far East. Agnes Smedley was born February 23, 1892, in Campground, Sullivan County, Missouri, and was largely self-educated. After an early marriage that ended in divorce and various menial jobs, she moved to New York City, probably the winter between 1916 and 1917, where she was accused of "aiding German espionage" from her involvement with an Indian revolutionary movement financed by the German government as a means of damaging Great Britain, then at war with Germany, by undermining British imperial rule in India. Smedley was arrested for violating U.S. neutrality laws but she was not brought to trial and was released. She went to Berlin in the 1920s where she became active in the Communist movement. She visited Moscow in 1921 to attend a meeting of Indian revolutionaries and then went to China in 1928, the year after she published her semi-autobiographical novel, *Daughter of Earth* (1927). Smedley began her journalist career as the correspondent for the *Frankfurter Zeitung*, working out of Shanghai.

As a Communist sympathizer, Smedley's associations eventually got her involved in intelligence activity. It started when she befriended Richard Sorge, who worked for GRU, Soviet military intelligence; he used her apartment for clandestine radio transmissions and she introduced Sorge to her friend Ozaki Hozumi, who became his principal Japanese collaborator.

Hozumi was her first recruit for Sorge's spy ring but Sorge generally stayed in the background until Smedley identified a candidate for his espionage ring. Others in Smedley's Shanghai circle included Sonia, another top Soviet spy, and Roger Hollis, a future head of the British Security Service (MI-5). When Sorge moved from China to Japan in 1933, Smedley went to the Soviet Union for medical treatment. At the same time, she wrote about her experiences in *Chinese Destinies*, published in 1933, followed a year later by *China's Red Army Marches*. In 1935, Smedley returned to China where she was a publicist and a field worker for the Chinese Red Cross Medical Corps and a special correspondent for the *Manchester Guardian* while she continued to send intelligence material to Moscow and attempted to influence people with her idealistic and rather naive views of Communism. Two important admirers were Sir Archibald Clark-Kerr (Lord Inverchapel), British ambassador to China in the late 1930s and later British ambassador to the United States where his views seemingly confused the issue of American policy toward China after the war, and Joseph Stilwell, later the commanding officer of U.S. forces in Burma and China.

Two more books, *China Fights Back: An American Woman with the Eighth Route Army* (1938) and *Battle Hymn of China* (1943), which praised the Communist forces in China, were heavily compiled from information covertly supplied by Chinese Communist Party (CCP) agents that gave Smedley's writing a certain notoriety since these contacts allowed her access to information and to incidents that she might otherwise might not have had. In 1941, she returned to the United States. In a November 1943 radio program, "Author Meets Critic," Smedley attacked the United States and Great Britain as largely responsible for the backward conditions in China. The Federal Bureau of Investigation began to investigate her activities as a suspected Communist and after the war, Major General Charles Willoughby, Douglas MacArthur's chief intelligence officer, exposed Smedley as a key member of the Communist conspiracy in the Far East in an official report completed in 1947 and released in Washington, DC, two years later. Smedley wrote to President Truman to ask him to force MacArthur to apologize to her or to waive the general's immunity so that he could be sued for libel. The Department of the Army issued a retraction: "The [intelligence] division has no proof to back up the spy charges. The report was based on information from the Japanese police and should have said so. While there may be evidence in existence to substantiate the allegations, it is not in our hands."

After this, Smedley chose not to appear at public events with some of her friends, fearing that they would suffer from guilt by association, but other people outright rejected her. Still, several journalists defended her and former Secretary of the Interior Harold L. Ickes wrote: "No one who knows Miss Smedley would ever suspect that this courageous and intelligent American citizen has stooped to be so low as to be a spy for any country, even for her own to which she is deeply attached." However, documents found in Soviet archives after the fall of the Soviet Union found that she was, in fact, working for Communist International and for the Soviet intelligence service. Smedley died on May 6, 1950, in Oxford, England; her ashes were placed in Peking's National Memorial Cemetery of Revolutionary Martyrs.

See also: Federal Bureau of Investigation (FBI); GRU (Main Intelligence Directorate); Sorge, Richard

References and Further Reading

MacKinnon, Janice R., and Stephen R. MacKinnon. *Agnes Smedley: The Life and Times of an American Radical*. Berkeley, CA: University of California Press, 1988.

Price, Ruth. *The Lives of Agnes Smedley*. Cambridge, UK: Oxford University, 2005.

Willoughby, Charles A. *Shanghai Conspiracy; The Sorge Spy Ring, Moscow, Shanghai, Tokyo, San Francisco*. New York: Dutton, 1952.

Martin J. Manning

SMERSH

SMERSH was a Soviet military counterintelligence organization operating from 1943 to 1946. In 1943, Soviet General Secretary Joseph Stalin moved military counterintelligence operations from the Commissariat of Security to the Commissariat of Defense, creating the Chief Directorate Counterintelligence of the People's Commissariat of Defense. The new directorate was given the alias, SMERSH, an acronym for *Smert' Shpionam* or "Death to Spies." SMERSH ultimately would play a critical role in the Soviet success during World War II through monitoring loyalty in all ranks of the Red Army, performing counterintelligence operations against Nazi Germany, and eliminating partisan movements and consolidating Soviet dominance in Eastern Europe.

The precise date of and rationale for SMERSH's formation is unclear. What is clear, however, was the general inability of the Red Army's political officers to manage the continual wave of defection and desertion from 1941 through the winter of 1943. The severity and impact of desertion in the Red Army resulted in Stalin's July 1942 order of "Not One Step Backward," threatening the execution of those seen as cowards. Regardless, SMERSH's formation was the culmination of the growing importance of counterintelligence at every level of Soviet society in the early years of World War II.

Following the appointment of Viktor Abakumov (1894–1954) as head of SMERSH on April 19, 1943, counterintelligence officers were trained and placed throughout the rank and file of the Red Army. One immediate priority of SMERSH was to restore discipline and loyalty throughout the Soviet military. The primary tactic of infiltrating all aspects of the Red Army was recruiting agents to a tertiary level, resulting in as many as two million Soviet soldiers serving as informants. Military tribunals, with SMERSH cooperation, ordered the execution of more than 140,000 soldiers and sent hundreds of thousands more to punishment battalions. Further, SMERSH was responsible for the surveillance of captured senior officers during their detention.

In addition to controlling desertion and subversion within the ranks of the Red Army, SMERSH played a key role in counterintelligence operations. SMERSH activities resulted in the capture of thousands of German spies who provided accurate information on German intelligence priorities. More importantly, however, was the ability of SMERSH to recruit captured Germans to serve as double agents, providing positive information to the Soviets while disseminating false information to the German high command.

Although SMERSH played a critical role from 1943 to 1945 in the success of the Soviet Union against Nazi Germany, perhaps the longest-lasting impact of SMERSH's activities was in quashing partisan movements and consolidating local Communist Party rule in occupied territories. Following victory in Eastern Europe, SMERSH played an active role in the elimination of Nazi sympathizers throughout the region. Networks of agents were established in the Baltic republics, Ukraine, and Poland to crack down on anti-Soviet partisan movements, resulting in hundreds of thousands of deportations. Finally, high-level SMERSH officials closely worked with Moscow imposed intelligence services in Eastern Europe, establishing an essential instrument in controlling the Soviet Union's new satellite states. After the conclusion of hostilities in 1946, SMERSH was reincorporated into the Commissariat of State Security.

See also: KGB (Komitet Gosudarstvennoi Bezopasnosti); NKVD (Narodnyj Komissariat Vnutrennikh Del—Peoples Commissariat for Internal Affairs)

References and Further Reading

Parrish, Michael. *The Lesser Terror: Soviet State Security, 1939–1953*. Westport, CT: Praeger, 1996.

Pringle, Robert W. "SMERSH: Military Counterintelligence and Stalin's Control of the USSR," *International Journal and Counterintelligence* 21 (2008), 122–134.

Stephan, Robert W. *Stalin's Secret War: Soviet Counterintelligence against the Nazis, 1941–1945*. Lawrence, KS: University of Kansas Press, 2004.

Jonathan H. L'Hommedieu

SMITH, GENERAL WALTER BEDELL (OCTOBER 5, 1895–AUGUST 9, 1961)

General Walter Bedell Smith was the fourth Director of Central Intelligence (DCI), serving from October 7, 1950, to February 9, 1953. Smith was born in Indianapolis and briefly attended Butler University. Prior to his appointment as DCI, Smith held a series of important military and diplomatic posts. During World War II he served as chief of staff of the Allied forces in North Africa and the Mediterranean and as chief of staff to General Dwight Eisenhower. After the war Smith was ambassador to the Soviet Union from 1946 to 1949. Upon leaving the Central Intelligence Agency (CIA), Smith took the position of undersecretary of state.

Smith is considered to be among the most important and best DCIs. He is characterized as a bright, hard driving, and energetic administrator whose rank and stature demanded the respect of those in and out of the CIA. Smith is credited with vigorously weeding out unqualified individuals, recruiting highly qualified top-level administrators, and putting into place an organizational structure that remained largely unchanged for some two decades. Key organizational reforms affected both the analytic and operational sides of the CIA. On the analytic side, Smith broke up the Office of Reports and Estimates (ORE). Under his predecessor, Rear Admiral Roscoe H. Hillenkoetter, the CIA had come to focus heavily on current intelligence. It had not succeeded in producing coordinated national intelligence estimates but instead seemed to drift from task to task producing background papers, country studies, and surveys. In its place Smith set up the Office of National Estimates (ONE) to produce national intelligence estimates. He also renamed the ORE the Office of Research and Reports to carry out research projects. Its most important subunit was the Economic Research Area that focused on Soviet economic, military, and strategic issues.

Smith also engineered an important reorganization on the operational side of the CIA. The central issue here was resolving a growing tension between the Office of

Policy Coordination (OPC) and the Office of Special Operations (OSO). The Office of Special Projects, the immediate forerunner of the OPC, was set up through National Security Council (NSC) Directive 10/2. It sought to provide policy makers with a small, covert action capability that would undertake occasional projects. Formally lodged within the CIA, policy guidance for the OPC came from the State Department and the Defense Department. Once in place, however, the OPC quickly expanded the size and scope of its activities so that it was regularly engaged in operations on a global scale. Also existing within the CIA was the OSO. It had been created by DCI Lt. General Hoyt S. Vandenberg to house the espionage and counterespionage units of the Office of Strategic Services. OPC and OSO operated independently out of American embassies and engaged in competition for foreign agents. They also were in conflict over the true purpose of clandestine activity: gathering intelligence or conducting operations. Smith moved slowly to bring order to their competition. First, they were both placed under the direction of Allen Dulles, who was appointed deputy director for plans in January 1951. The next year, in August, they were formally unified as the Directorate of Plans.

See also: Central Intelligence Agency; Director of Central Intelligence; Office of National Estimates; Office of Policy Coordination; Office of Special Operations

References and Further Reading

Andrew, Christopher. *For the President's Eyes Only: Secret Intelligence and the American Presidency from Washington to Bush.* New York: HarperCollins, 1995.

Cline, Ray. *Secrets, Spies and Scholars: The Essential CIA.* Washington, DC: Acropolis, 1976.

Karalekas, Anne. *History of the Central Intelligence Agency.* Laguna Hills: Aegean Park Press, 1977.

Ranelagh, John. *The Rise and Decline of the CIA.* Revised and updated. New York: Touchstone, 1987.

Glenn P. Hastedt

SNEPP, FRANK W.
(MAY 3, 1943–)

Frank Snepp is a journalist and former chief analyst of North Vietnamese strategy for the Central Intelligence Agency (CIA) in Saigon during the Vietnam War.

Recruited by the CIA out of Columbia University's School of International Affairs in 1968, Snepp worked on NATO and European security matters for the Agency until he was handpicked for duty at the CIA's station in Saigon in 1969. Doubling as an analyst and counterintelligence officer, his duties included preparation of strategic estimates of NVA forces, coordination of agent networks, and interrogation of captured NVA and Viet Cong. In April 1975, he was one of the last CIA officers to be evacuated by helicopter off the Embassy roof as the Communist forces closed on Saigon.

Upon his return to the United States, Snepp was awarded the Intelligence Medal for Merit for his service in Vietnam, but he was upset at the CIA's unwillingness to rescue Vietnamese left behind when the Americans pulled out. He became further disillusioned with the Agency's refusal to acknowledge the mistakes it had made in Vietnam.

Unable to prompt any internal after-action review, Snepp resigned in 1976 to write *Decent Interval*, his memoir that describes his perception of the shortcomings of the CIA's performance in Vietnam, particularly during the fall of Saigon in 1975. The CIA sued because Snepp had not received prior permission to publish from the CIA Publications Review Board. In a landmark First Amendment decision, the U.S. Supreme Court held that because Snepp had failed to seek official clearance for his memoirs, he created the "appearance" of a breakdown of discipline within the CIA and had "irreparably harmed" national security. Snepp, who had enlisted the aid of the American Civil Liberties Union is his defense, was placed under a lifetime gag order preventing him forever writing again without CIA permission, and forced him to surrender all profits from the book.

In 2001, Snepp published another book that chronicled his battle with the CIA and the Supreme Court over free speech and the publication of his earlier memoir.

See also: Central Intelligence Agency; Cold War Intelligence; Vietnam War and Intelligence Operations

References and Further Reading

Snepp, Frank. *Decent Interval: An Insider's Account of Saigon's Indecent End Told by the CIA's Chief Strategy Analyst in Vietnam*, New York: Random House, 1977.

Snepp, Frank. *Irreparable Harm: A Firsthand Account of How One Agent Took on the CIA in an Epic Battle Over Free Speech*. Lawrence, KS: University Press of Kansas, 2001.

James H. Willbanks

SOBELL, MORTON (APRIL 11, 1917–JUNE 19, 1953)

Morton Sobell was arrested for espionage in 1950 and tried along with Julius and Ethel Rosenberg as part of the Atomic Spy Ring, although later evidence indicates that he was not part of this conspiracy. All three pled innocent to charges of espionage. Along with the Rosenbergs, he was convicted of spying for the Soviet Union in 1951. Unlike the Rosenbergs, who were sentenced to death and executed on June 19, 1953, Sobell was sentenced to 30 years in prison. He was paroled in 1969.

Sobell was born on April 11, 1917, in New York City to Russian-born parents who had immigrated to the United States. Sobell graduated from college with a degree in electrical engineering in 1938 and went to work for the Bureau of Naval Ordnance the following year. He resigned in 1940 in order to obtain a masters degree in electrical engineering from Michigan State. From there his career took him into the private sector with electric companies in New York. These positions gave him access to classified information.

In his youth Sobell was friends with Julius Rosenberg and Max Elitcher and was believed to have been active in the American Communist Party. He worked summers from 1934 to 1938 at Camp Unity, which was suspected of being under the control of Communists. Sobell and Elichter roomed together in Washington, DC, in 1939 when Elichter claims that Sobell recruited him to join the Communist Party.

Along with his family, Sobell fled hurriedly to Mexico on June 22, 1950, telling his employer he needed a break from work. Mexico City had become a popular destination for those suspected of being a Communist or fearful of being called to testify before the House Un-American Activities Committee. From Mexico Sobell tried unsuccessfully to flee to Europe. Mexican authorities seized him and forcibly returned him to the United States on August 18, 1950.

Sobell did not testify at his trial. Instead, he invoked his Fifth Amendment rights. Sobell asserted that he was innocent, claiming that he fled to Mexico because he had lied about his membership in the Communist Party. No evidence of his involvement in developing the atomic bomb was presented at his trial and at first Sobell was not even charged with a particular crime. The prosecution built its case around the testimony of Elichter that Sobell had obtained secret information while working for General Electric. Sobell appealed his conviction on the grounds that Elichter had provided hearsay evidence and that he had been kidnapped. The appeal was rejected.

See also: Atomic Spy Ring; Rosenberg, Julius and Ethel

References and Further Reading

Garber, Marjorie, and Rebecca L. Walkovwitz (eds.). *Secret Agents: The Rosenberg Case, McCarthyism, and Fifties America.* New York: Routledge, 1995.
Sobell, Morton. *On Doing Time.* New York: Scribner's, 1974.

Glenn P. Hastedt

SONS OF LIBERTY (AMERICAN REVOLUTION)

The Sons of Liberty were a radical vanguard of American colonists opposed to Britain in the decade from 1765 to 1775, many of whom were espionage agents in the War of American Independence. The first stirrings of the Sons of Liberty came in 1765. At that time, societies were organized to oppose the Stamp Act, which was designed to levy direct taxes upon American colonists. The name Sons of Liberty came from a comment by Colonel Issac Barré, a radical English politician of the 1760s, in a speech in the House of Commons during debates on the Stamp duties. Charles Townshend, Chancellor of the Exchequer, had spoken in favor of the tax, and Barré had risen to declare (in a flight of fervid oratory) that the Americans, hardy sons of liberty, would find it an intolerable violation of their rights as Englishmen.

At first the Sons of Liberty were an unfocused, unorganized group of individuals. Gradually they came together in defiance of the British claim to the right to levy whatever taxes on Americans that were deemed appropriate, without the colonists having any say in the matter. Among the rank and file, the Sons of Liberty were mostly mechanics, artisans, and shopkeepers of the middling and lower sorts, who adopted symbols such as the Liberty Tree in Boston, where meetings were held, and medallions that they wore around their necks. They also adopted headwear such as liberty caps or hats with the number 45 attached, to show their support for John Wilkes, who had criticized King George III in *The North Briton*, Number 45, in April 1763. In Boston, they were organized and led by the Loyal Nine, who came from the upper ranks of society, men like Samuel Adams and John Hancock. In New York they were likewise led mostly by the upper sort.

The Sons of Liberty used various means to protest against British taxes and persuade the American people to join them. Often they resorted to propaganda. They made great displays of rituals, menacing or otherwise, such as burning public figures in effigy, threatening the use of tar and feathers, raucous parades, or public meetings. They also used violence, destroying the property of offending public officials. Not a few patriotic Americans were disgusted by these excesses, but they also felt that British officials had brought these humiliations upon themselves.

The Sons of Liberty remained a vanguard of revolution until 1775. Afterward, many of them joined in the fighting, or in political groups such as the committees of correspondence and safety. Some, such as Paul Revere, became active espionage agents for the patriot cause, contributing their part to the ultimate independence of the United States.

See also: American Revolution; Revere, Paul

References and Further Reading

Dawson, Henry B. *The Sons of Liberty in New York*. New York: Arno Press, 1969.
Pencak, William. *War, Politics, and Revolution in Provincial Massachusetts*. Boston: Northeastern University Press, 1981.
Shaw, Peter. *American Patriots and the Rituals of Revolution*. Cambridge, MA:Harvard University Press, 1981.

Paul David Nelson

SONS OF LIBERTY (CIVIL WAR)

During the Civil War, a Copperhead secret society known as the Knights of the Golden Circle was reorganized as the Order of the Sons of Liberty, which attacked President Abraham Lincoln's conduct of the war and sought reunion through peaceful means. In February 1864, the organization elected Clement L. Vallandigham, who was a former Ohio congressman, as its supreme commander. Attending various Democratic conventions throughout the North, Vallandigham attempted to rekindle peace negotiations between the Union and Confederacy by denouncing the Civil War as an unnecessary conflict and called for an immediate end of hostilities. Republicans dismissed his actions and noted that the Sons of Liberty represented a pro-Confederate conspiracy.

In 1864, Union detectives uncovered a plot in which members of the Sons of Liberty residing in the Midwest were planning an insurrection designed to detach their states from the Union. Once free, the states would negotiate a separate peace with the Confederacy. The Lincoln administration regarded this plot as the Northwest Conspiracy.

The Sons of Liberty collaborated with Canadian-based Confederate agents led by Thomas H. Hines, who engaged in sabotage operations against the North. They attempted to capture the USS *Michigan*, a gunboat operating on Lake Erie, and liberate Confederate prisoners housed at Camp Douglas in Chicago and Johnson's Island near Sandusky, Ohio. However, War Department detectives were able to infiltrate the organization's security. The operatives arrested the northern sympathizers, warned officers aboard the *Michigan* about the scheme, and increased the number of Union soldiers stationed at the prisoners of war camps.

Although the initial activities of the Sons of Liberty ended in disaster, federal officials warned Northern governors to remain cautious of other potential plots. Believing that the Sons of Liberty was a powerful organization armed to commit treasonable actions, Union authorities sent out additional agents to uncover the various plots linked with the group.

In July 1864, members of the secret society planned uprisings in Chicago and New York. Prior to the scheduled rebellions, Confederate soldiers arrived in the cities to assist the Sons of Liberty. Both insurrections proved unsuccessful because federal authorities and military leaders arrested thousands of conspirators and captured a cache of arms. By the end of 1864, the Sons of Liberty's activities in the Midwest collapsed because some members believed that they could overthrow the Lincoln administration through political measures instead of insurrection.

See also: Civil War Intelligence; Northwest Conspiracy

References and Further Reading

Gray, Wood. *The Hidden Civil War: The Story of the Copperheads*. New York: Viking Press, 1942.

Klement, Frank L. *The Limits of Dissent: Clement L. Vallandigham and the Civil War*. Lexington, KY: University Press of Kentucky, 1970.

McPherson, James. *Battle Cry of Freedom: The Civil War Era*. New York: Oxford University Press, 1988.

Kevin M. Brady

SORGE, RICHARD (OCTOBER 4, 1895–NOVEMBER 7, 1944)

Richard Sorge was probably the most successful Soviet spy in history. Sorge was born in 1895 in the Russian Caucasus region where his father was working as an oil engineer. Among the first books he read in his youth was a copy of *Das Kapital*, which had been given to him by his paternal grandfather who for a time had served as a private secretary to Karl Marx.

A German citizen, Sorge served in the German army in World War I where he was twice wounded. By 1920 he was a committed Communist and an early member of the German Communist Party and a spy for the People's Commissariat for State Security (NKVD). Threatened with arrest by the German police, he fled to Moscow where he was schooled in spy craft and then was sent back to Germany to settle in Frankfurt where he was to develop a spy ring. In 1925 he went to Moscow and was given membership in the Party by Party leaders.

In 1930 Sorge was transferred to the Foreign Military Directorate (GRU) and was sent to Shanghai. His assignment was to develop a spy ring that provided intelligence on the Chinese Nationalists.

In November of 1930 he met Agnes Smedley and Hotsumi Ozaki. From Ozaki's contacts he was able to gather accurate intelligence on China. However, with the Japanese invasion of China he was recalled to Moscow and given the assignment of developing intelligence on Japan and its intentions of war against the Soviet Union.

Sorge then was given the code name "Ramsey." He returned to Germany where he pretended to undergo a conversion to Nazism. Posted to Tokyo as a journalist, he developed a spy ring that delivered accurate intelligence to Moscow. He became a close friend of many in the German embassy. He delivered to Stalin the details of Operation Barbarossa, the Nazi invasion of the Soviet Union, but Stalin considered the intelligence to be a British disinformation operation.

In October of 1941 Sorge's end began when his spy ring in Tokyo was captured. He was hanged November 7, 1944, at Sugamo Prison. In 1964 he was declared a Hero of the Soviet Union.

See also: GRU (Main Intelligence Directorate); Smedley, Agnes

References and Further Reading

Prange, Gordon W., Donald M. Goldstein, and Katherine V. Dillon. *Target Tokyo: The Story of the Sorge Spy Ring.* New York: McGraw-Hill, 1984.
Whymant, Robert. *Stalin's Spy: Richard Sorge and the Tokyo Espionage Ring.* New York: St. Martin's Press, 1998.

Andrew J. Waskey

SOUERS, REAR ADMIRAL SIDNEY WILLIAM (MARCH 30, 1882–JANUARY 14, 1973)

Rear Admiral Sidney W. Souers served as the first Director of Central Intelligence (DCI). He was born in Dayton, Ohio, and graduated from Miami University (Ohio) in 1914. During World War II, Souers rose to the rank of rear admiral and the position of deputy chief of naval intelligence. In June 1945 Secretary of the Navy James Forrestal tasked Ferdinand Eberstadt, a personal friend and investment banker, with the job of examining the question of military unification. Eberstadt's report went beyond the question of unifying the War and Navy Departments and examined a wide range of national security issues. One of its recommendations was the creation of a National Security Council. The section on intelligence, authored by Souers, called for the establishment of a Central Intelligence Group (CIG) headed by a Director of Central Intelligence. The CIG would play a coordinating and synthesizing role in the production of intelligence rather than a managerial one. Once created, it did, however, receive authority to engage in the covert collection of intelligence. On January 22, 1946, President Harry S. Truman acted upon the recommendations of the Eberstadt Report and issued a presidential directive creating a National Intelligence Authority that was to plan, coordinate, and develop the U.S. intelligence effort. Under it was the CIG, headed by the DCI.

Souers served as DCI from January 23, 1946, to June 10, 1946. He had agreed to take the position for a limited period of time with the objective of seeing to it that the CIG's basic organizational structure was put into place. The existing intelligence units within the national security bureaucracy were not inclined to cooperate with the CIG in the production of intelligence. They frequently denied it resources and withheld intelligence. For his part, Souers was not inclined to challenge their position. Souers met less resistance in developing the CIG's covert intelligence collection mission. The primary assets were unwanted remnants of the World War II Office of Strategic Services (OSS), the Foreign Broadcast Information Service that monitored foreign radio programs and the Domestic Contact Service that debriefed Americans about what they had seen and heard when they had been abroad.

Souers was not a career officer but a successful businessman who had joined the reserves. After six months in the position he resigned to return to private life in Missouri. Souers, a friend of President Truman, returned to government service in 1947 when he took the position of executive secretary of the National Security Council. He held this position until 1950.

See also: Central Intelligence Agency; Director of Central Intelligence; Eberstadt Report; Office of Strategic Services

References and Further Reading

Andrew, Christopher. *For the President's Eyes Only: Secret Intelligence and the American Presidency from Washington to Bush*. New York: HarperCollins, 1995.

Cline, Ray. *Secrets, Spies and Scholars: The Essential CIA*. Washington, DC: Acropolis, 1976.

Karalekas, Anne. *History of the Central Intelligence Agency*. Laguna Hills: Aegean Park Press, 1977.

Ranelagh, John. *The Rise and Decline of the CIA*. Revised and updated. New York: Touchstone, 1987.

Glenn P. Hastedt

SPANISH-AMERICAN WAR

U.S. intelligence and espionage during the Spanish-American War contributed significantly to a rapid American victory. The Office of Naval Intelligence (ONI) and the army's Military Intelligence Division (MID), established during the 1880s, were America's first formal, permanent intelligence agencies. In 1898, U.S. military attachés in American embassies in Europe created spy networks and orchestrated reconnaissance missions to ascertain the strength and location of the Spanish navy. The U.S. Secret Service, which had been established in the closing days of the Civil War, dispersed a Spanish spy network based in Montreal, Canada. The most successful and significant U.S. intelligence and espionage activities during the war, however, involved Key West–based U.S. military officer Martin Luther Hellings, who had recruited Domingo Villaverde, a Western Union telegraph officer in Havana, Cuba, to intercept communications between Spanish officials in Spain and Cuba. Not realizing that their telegraph office in Havana had been compromised, at the beginning of the war Spanish officials agreed to keep the telegraph cable linking Key West and the rest of the United States to Cuba and the rest of the Caribbean.

Before the outbreak of the Spanish-American War, ONI and MID officers openly collected information in Europe. After April 1898, however, these officers initiated espionage. The Spanish government was assembling two fleets: one, led by Pascual Cevera, was being formed in the Cape Verde Islands for deployment to Cuba; and the other, led by Manuel Cámara, was being formed in Cádiz for deployment to the Philippines. The United States was especially interested in the location of the Cape Verde fleet. William S. Sims, the U.S. naval attaché in Paris, France, directed his spy network, which stretched from Port Said, Egypt, to the Canary Islands, to verify the

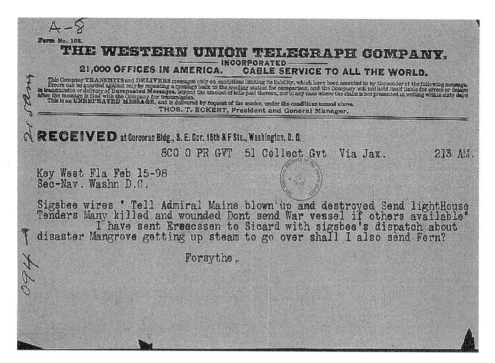

A Western Union telegram delivered to Secretary of the Navy Benjamin Tracy announcing the news of the sinking of the battleship USS *Maine* off Havana on February 15, 1898. This unexpected incident led to U.S. military involvement in what became the Spanish-American War over colonial influence in Cuba and the Philippines. (National Archives)

location of Spain's Atlantic fleet. Although Sims even had spies working in Cádiz, he was unable to verify the location of the Cape Verde fleet. Since the U.S. Atlantic fleet had been deployed to blockade Cuba, Americans living along the Atlantic seaboard were justifiably nervous. Unbeknownst to U.S. officials, however, the most important information regarding Cevera's fleet was not its location, but rather its condition. Spanish officials ordered Cevara, whose ships were in a state of disrepair, to depart the Cape Verde Islands without sufficient coal, ammunition, and supplies.

Meanwhile, Spanish officials, after leaving Washington, DC, just days before the outbreak of the war, attempted to establish an intelligence and espionage network in Montreal, Canada. Given the proximity of Montreal to the St. Lawrence River and Montreal's large Roman Catholic population, the Spaniards were convinced that they had found the ideal location for their spy network. Secret Service agents, led by John Wilkie, however, were able to disrupt the Spanish attempts at intelligence gathering and espionage. George Downing, the first agent recruited by the Spaniards, was captured in Washington, DC, when he tried to post a letter containing valuable military secrets.

The activities of Martin Hellings, the manager of the Western Union telegraph office in Key West, Florida, proved to be the most significant example of intelligence and information gathering, both before and during the war. Hellings, who was eventually commissioned as a captain in the U.S. Volunteer Signal Corps, was the principal agent for Charles D. Sigsbee, the commander of the battleship *Maine*, which had been stationed in Key West since December, 1897. Using Domingo Villaverde, his contact in the Western Union telegraph office in the Governor's Palace in Havana, Hellings was able to pass valuable information about developments in Cuba to Sigsbee. Late in the evening on February 15, 1898, Villaverde cabled Hellings that the *Maine*, which had been sent to Havana on January 25, 1898, had exploded and was sinking off the coast of Havana. Within one hour, President William McKinley knew of the explosion, which caused the death of 268 Americans. A U.S. Naval Court of Inquiry, which quickly, and perhaps erroneously, claimed that the Spaniards were responsible for the explosion, increased prowar sentiment among the American public. On April 22, the U.S. Navy blockaded Cuba in an attempt to end Spanish control of the island. At the same time, the U.S. government ordered George Dewey's Pacific fleet to destroy Spain's Pacific fleet in the Philippines. Dewey, who lacked information about the Spanish Pacific fleet, ordered his aide, F. B. Upham, to pose as a civilian and interview sailors from ships arriving in Hong Kong from Manila. Dewey learned that the Spanish Pacific fleet was weak and unprepared for an attack.

On May 19, 1898, Cevera's Cape Verde fleet, which only consisted of six ships, steamed into the port of Santiago, Cuba. Cevera's fleet had passed undetected through the American blockade, which was concentrated on the western part of the island, especially around Havana and Cienfuegos, where U.S. officials had expected Cevera to arrive. Once in the harbor of Santiago, Cevera's fleet was not longer visible from the Caribbean. Although Cevera's fleet was weak, unable to break the American blockade of Cuba, and posed no significant threat to the U.S. Atlantic seaboard, the U.S. government, which did not even know the location of Cevera's fleet, did not know this. ONI and MID agents in Europe had been unable to ascertain either the location or the strength of the Cape Verde fleet. After going ashore in Santiago, Cevera telegraphed his location to the Spanish governor-general in Havana. Villaverde immediately telegraphed Hellings the location of the Cape Verde fleet. Within a few hours of Villaverde's message, the U.S. Navy had blockaded the port of Santiago. Unwilling to allow the United States to capture the Cape Verde fleet, Spanish officials ordered Cevera to run the blockade. On July 3, 1898, after a brief sea battle, the entire Cape Verde fleet was destroyed. News of the destruction of Cevera's fleet convinced Spanish officials to recall Cámara's fleet, which was on the way to Manila to confront the blockade of Manila harbor imposed by Dewey's fleet. Within a few weeks, the Spanish government sued for peace and the Spanish-American War was over.

See also: Military Intelligence Division; Office of Naval Intelligence; Villaverde, Domingo

References and Further Reading

Bradford, James C. (ed.). *Crucible of Empire: The Spanish-American War and Its Aftermath.* Annapolis, MD: Naval Institute Press, 1992.

Jeffrey-Jones, Rhodri. *Cloak and Dollar: A History of American Secret Intelligence.* New Haven, CT: Yale University Press, 2002.

O'Toole, George J. A. *The Spanish War: An American Epic.* New York: Norton, 1984.

Michael R. Hall

SPANISH CONSPIRACY

The Spanish Conspiracy involved attempts by Spain in the decade after the War of American Independence to create a buffer state west of the Allegheny Mountains between Spanish territory and the eastern United States. In 1783, the Madrid court was not sympathetic with the new American republic. It disputed the claim of the United States to the trans-Appalachian region and maintained military posts on American soil at Natchez and other places. It asserted sovereignty over Indian tribes east of the Mississippi River, in the present states of Mississippi and Alabama, and made treaties of alliance with them. It also contested American claims to free commercial navigation on the Mississippi River to the port of New Orleans. These issues came to a crisis in 1784, when Spain, which saw little reason to make concessions to the weak American Confederation, declared that henceforth the Mississippi River would be closed to American shipping.

Looking to the future, however, Spain feared that the exploding population in the American West would eventually overcome any paper barriers upon Mississippi navigation and would even put pressures upon the Spanish southwest. In 1785, Spain sent Diego de Gardoqui to New York to curry favor with Secretary of State John Jay. Yielding to Gardoqui's ministrations, Jay urged Congress to accept a treaty that ceded American demands for free Mississippi shipping in return for a commercial treaty with Spain. No such treaty could pass muster in Congress, and so the Jay-Gardoqui negotiations ended futilely in 1787.

Thereupon Gardoqui stepped up intrigues with a small group of American westerners who were willing to ignore the American government, withdraw from the United States, and make their own commercial treaty with Spain. This Spanish Conspiracy included John Brown, James White, John Sevier, and James Robertson. The archconspirator was General James Wilkinson, a Kentuckian, who in 1787 became a paid agent of Spanish officials in Louisiana and took a secret oath of allegiance to the King of Spain. In the next few years, he worked mightily to get his Kentucky neighbors to set up an independent western country. Cooler heads in Kentucky and Tennessee stymied his and the other secessionists' efforts, and after ratification of the Constitution of 1787 both were soon admitted to the Union as states. All talk of secession ended with the implementation of the treaty of San Lorenzo (Pinckney's Treaty) in 1795. In that document Spain recognized U.S. western boundaries, granted free navigation of the Mississippi River, and ceded control of the Indians east of the river to the United States.

See also: Early Republic and Espionage

References and Further Reading

Bemis, Samuel Flagg. *Pinckney's Treaty: A Study of America's Advantage from Europe's Distress, 1783–1800*. Baltimore, MD: Johns Hopkins University Press, 1926.

Green, Thomas Marshall. *The Spanish Conspiracy: A Review of Early Spanish Movements in the Southwest*. Cincinnati, OH: R. Clarke and Company, 1891.

Jacobs, James Ripley. *Tarnished Warrior: Major-General James Wilkinson*. New York: Macmillan, 1938.

Whitaker, A. P. *The Spanish-American Frontier, 1783–1795: The Westward Movement and the Spanish Retreat in the Mississippi Valley*. Boston: Houghton Mifflin, 1927.

Paul David Nelson

SPANN, JOHNNY MICHAEL (MARCH 1, 1969–NOVEMBER 25, 2001)

Johnny Michael "Mike" Spann, a paramilitary operative of the Central Intelligence Agency's (CIA) Special Activities Division, was the first American to die on the field of battle in Afghanistan following the attacks of September 11. Born on March 1, 1969, Spann grew up in Winnfield, Alabama, and by high school had decided that he would serve in the military and then become an agent with either the FBI or the CIA. After graduating with a degree in criminal justice from Auburn University in 1991, he joined the Marine Corps, where he spent most of his seven years as an artillery officer. In June 1999, after his stint in the military, he joined the CIA, which set him on course for his tragic demise in the war on terrorism.

His death on November 25, 2001, during a Taliban prison revolt at the Qala Jangi fortress in Mazar-i-Sharif shortly followed his interrogation of the "American Taliban," John Walker Lindh. Part of an American contingent (three CIA operatives, a dozen Green Berets, and two air force bomb guiders) attached to a Northern Alliance faction led by the warlord Abdul Rashid Dostum, Spann had been in the country six weeks gathering intelligence in the search for Osama bin Laden.

Spann's interrogation of Lindh, conducted about two hours prior to the 400-man uprising, was recorded on videotape and later aired on the major American television networks. The tape shows Spann and another CIA operative, Dave Tyson, questioning the prisoner whom they thought was from Ireland. Lindh remained silent, prompting some to later accuse him of treason for not warning about the pending revolt. Although Lindh has maintained that he was not privy to any plans for an uprising, others remain unconvinced. The 79th CIA agent to die in the line of duty, Spann was buried at Arlington National Cemetery on December 10, 2001.

See also: Central Intelligence Agency; Post–Cold War Intelligence; Terrorist Groups and Intelligence

References and Further Reading

Kukis, Mark. *"My Heart Became Attached": The Strange Journey of John Walker Lindh.* Washington, DC: Brassey's, 2003.

Mahoney, Richard D. *Getting Away with Murder: The Real Story behind American Taliban John Walker Lindh and What the U.S. Government Had to Hide.* New York: Arcade Publishers, 2004.

Roger Chapman

SPECIAL ACTIVITIES DIVISION—CIA

The Special Activities Division is a section within the CIA responsible for conducting covert paramilitary operations. One of the advantages of such a group is in providing U.S. policy makers with increased flexibility, mobility, and speed all cloaked within the oftentimes necessity of official deniability. Although SAD personnel are largely recruited from within the U.S. military special operations community, SAD officers wear nothing to identify themselves as agents of the United States. Missions of the Special Activities Division require a "finding" or presidential approval.

In addition to drawing from special operation forces units such as Army Delta, Seal Team Six (now called Naval Development Group), Marine Recon, or Air Force Special Operations, CIA SAD also draws from colleges and other organizations whose members may have specific skill sets or knowledge useful to SAD objectives and tasks. Recruits and existing members receive training in various locations. These include CIA's Special Training Center (STC), Camp Peary—referred to as "The Farm," located in Virginia, a civilian organization, known as G8, and various other privately owned "black ops" training centers throughout the United States. Members of the Special Activities Division also receive specialized training at the Defense Department's Harvey Point Defense Testing Activity, outside Hertford, North Carolina. SAD training includes paramilitary and conventional espionage tradecraft.

The forerunner to the CIA, SAD was the Office of Strategic Services (OSS), whose paramilitary operations were performed during World War II. After the establishment of the Central Intelligence Agency in 1947, these units were called the Paramilitary Group (PG) and were contained within the Military Support Program (MSP). It was in 1999 that the Director of Central Intelligence, George Tenet renamed the unit the Special Operations Group—Special Activities Division (SOG-SAD).

The division has also been referred to as the Special Activities Group or SAG. SAD has a permanent base of personnel referred to as the Special Activities Staff of about two hundred personnel. The SAS consists of mostly hardened, experienced, and extremely skilled former and retired U.S. military. As requirements arise and tasks are assigned, SAD has the capability to draw on a larger group of some three hundred operators constructing special mission units designed for the region and the task at hand.

Generally, SAD operates in small teams usually consisting of 6 to 12 individuals and unlike U.S. military special operations teams, at times, includes women. The units operate in areas throughout the globe, in remote areas or urban, and often behind enemy lines. These missions include espionage, counterintelligence, sabotage, hostage rescue, assassination, recruiting, and training of friendly forces, ex-filtration and infiltration transportation, and protection.

The history of the covert paramilitary capability within CIA began in earnest with American involvement in the Korean War (1950–1953). During World War II, General Douglas MacArthur had refused entry into the Pacific theater of OSS operatives and, as a result, by the beginning of hostilities on the Korean peninsula, the CIA was limited in its Asian capabilities. Despite this, the appointment of Bedell Smith as DCI in October 1950 and OSS veteran Allen Dulles as his operations lieutenant, covert CIA capabilities expanded rapidly. Smith created the Deputy Directorate for Plans (DDP) with the word "plans" serving as a euphemism for covert action and special units were housed within the Office of Policy Coordination (OPC).

During the Korean War, CIA paramilitary groups developed evasion and escape routes for downed U.S. flyers and trained more than one thousand Korean guerrillas to fight behind enemy lines. They also operated two fishing fleets posing as black marketeers and established clandestine civil air transport to support U.S. operations.

In Vietnam, one year after the end of the Korean War, CIA operations veteran Lucien Conein formed squads of anti-Communist Vietnamese to organize guerrillas, abduct or assassinate officials, and establish espionage networks. The CIA had argued that conventional military tactics would be ineffective in South Vietnam and it would be in the interests of the United States to confine itself to running counterinsurgency operations. This counterinsurgency policy included the Phoenix Program, a covert campaign designed to uproot the Vietcong's rural structure and to target South Vietnam's Communist political organization.

During the Soviet invasion of Afghanistan, which lasted from 1979 to 1989, covert CIA operatives provided weaponry and support to the Afghans who fought the Communists. At one point, 300,000 fundamentalist Afghan warriors carried weapons provided by the CIA, including one of the most deadly and effective against Soviet aircraft—Stinger shoulder-held surface-to-air missiles.

After the terrorist attacks on the United States on September 11, 2001, SAD officers were among the first on the ground leading the attack that subsequently forced the Taliban from power and removed Afghanistan as a safe haven for the architects of the terror attacks in the United States—al-Qaeda.

See also: Camp Peary; Central Intelligence Agency; Office of Policy Coordination; Office of Strategic Services; Terrorist Groups and Intelligence; Vietnam War and Intelligence Operations

References and Further Reading

Best Richard A., and Andrew Feickert. *Special Operations Forces (SOF) and CIA Paramilitary Operations: Issues for Congress*. Washington, DC: Library of Congress, Congressional Research Service, CRS Report, January 4, 2005.

Kibbe, Jennifer D. "The Rise of the Shadow Warriors," *Foreign Affairs* 83: (2004), 102–115.

Schroen, Gary C. *First In: An Insider's Account of How the CIA Spearheaded the War on Terrorism in Afghanistan*. New York: Presidio Press, 2005.

Woodward, Bob. *VEIL: The Secret Wars of the CIA, 1981–1987*. New York: Simon & Schuster, 1987.

Woodward, Bob. "Secret CIA Units Playing a Central Combat Role," *Washington Post* (November 18, 2001), A1.

James Brian McNabb

SPECIAL BRANCH

The Special Branch, a division of Scotland Yard, has played a role in surveillance, protection, and counterespionage in the United Kingdom since the late nineteenth century. Known originally as the Special Irish Branch, the unit was founded in 1883 in response to a bombing campaign launched by Irish separatists. Since that time, the Special Branch has been involved in conducting surveillance at British ports, gathering intelligence about political extremists and potential terrorists, protecting government ministers and visiting dignitaries, and assisting other government agencies (most notably Britain's domestic Security Service, MI-5) in combating threats to British security. In October 2006 the Special Branch, which included approximately 600 officers, merged with the Anti-Terrorist Branch to form a new Counter Terrorism Command (SO15). The Branch has since continued its role in intelligence gathering, both in London and throughout the United Kingdom.

The Special Irish Branch was launched in March 1883 as part of a coordinated response to Fenian terrorism in England. In the space of less than two years, radical Irish separatists had detonated bombs throughout London and several other English cities. The Special Irish Branch worked in cooperation with the port police, the Royal Irish Constabulary, a network of informers throughout mainland Britain, and the rest of Scotland Yard to quash the Fenian dynamite campaign.

With the Fenian threat at least temporarily diminished by 1885, the anti-Fenian surveillance system was partially dismantled. Nevertheless, the Special Irish Branch continued to function, though the word "Irish" was dropped from the name. For the next two decades, the Special Branch directed its intelligence-gathering efforts against potentially "subversive" organizations including trade unions and suffragist groups. Special Branch officers also offered protection to government ministers, visiting dignitaries, and members of the royal family.

Following the 1909 creation of Britain's Secret Service Bureau, and throughout World War I, the Special Branch worked closely with the home department responsible for counterespionage (the forerunner of MI-5) to investigate rumors of German spy rings operating in England. After the war, Special Branch detectives continued to conduct surveillance at the behest of MI-5, only now the targets were political extremists and suspected Communists, rather than German spies.

Since the end of the cold war, the main role of the Special Branch has been to assist the internal Security Service, known as MI-5, in combating terrorism, although it has continued to play a role in maintaining public order as well. In 2006, the Special Branch was restructured and subsumed under the new Counter Terrorism Command.

See also: MI-5 (The Security Service); MI-6 (Secret Intelligence Service)

References and Further Reading

Allason, Rupert. *The Branch: A History of the Metropolitan Police Special Branch, 1883–1983.* London: Secker & Warburg, 1983.

Andrew, Christopher. *Her Majesty's Secret Service: The Making of the British Intelligence Community.* New York: Viking, 1985.

"Guidelines on Special Branch Work in the United Kingdom (2004)", http://www.statewatch.org/news/2004/mar/special-branch.pdf.

Thurlow, Richard. *The Secret State: British Internal Security in the Twentieth Century.* London: Blackwell, 1994.

Kathleen Ruppert

SPECIAL COLLECTION SERVICE NSA-CIA

The Special Collection Service is a super-secret joint NSA-CIA organization conducting high-risk close surveillance deploying the most advanced technology to listen and transmit. The Special Collection Service (SCS) is officially unacknowledged as an intelligence unit and, consequently, has no acknowledged facilities or personnel.

It is believed that SCS maintains operational stations within selected U.S. embassies as well as other clandestine locations. While SCS deploys exceptionally sophisticated electronic listening equipment, it is also a covert-entry organization conducting what is often referred to as "black bag operations."

In covert entries, SCS personnel break into facilities to plant "bugs," install signal capture devices, defeat communication security or COMSEC equipment, steal passwords, copy encryption tokens, and gather information less readily available to other means of collection. Often, long-distance signals intelligence is incapable of obtaining necessary information as the target may be using low-powered signals which may not be obtainable from satellite distances. This creates a requirement for close-in collection techniques.

From 1947 until 1977, the Central Intelligence Agency (CIA) and military intelligence units that eventually evolved into the National Security Agency (NSA), ran relatively independent and, at times, overlapping signals and communications intelligence surveillance operations. After the Vietnam War, increased public and congressional scrutiny of the U.S. intelligence community led to efforts to streamline duplicative activities.

Becoming director of the NSA in July 1977, Vice Admiral Bobby R. Inman collaborated with OSO Chief Barry Kelly in leading the effort in creating a joint unit. In 1978, congressional oversight required the CIA to discontinue SIGINT activities and to work more closely with the NSA. Towards this, and using the power of the purse, Congress effectively cut off signals intelligence-gathering funds for the CIA.

The joint collection enterprise established was initially headed by an official from the CIA serving a two-year term and his or her deputy would be selected from the NSA. After two years, an NSA official was expected to take the top slot with a CIA representative serving as his deputy. Thus, an alternating leadership between both agencies was established in the newly created SCS. The first SCS director was CIA's Roy Burk with Bill Black of the NSA serving as his deputy.

The first years following the SCS's creation did not proceed without difficulty as the leadership of the CIA was reluctant to embrace this newly mandated joint organization. Traditionally, close-in surveillance had been the province of CIA's Division D, an elite group of fewer than one hundred personnel. During the initial years following the SCS start-up, NSA employees were not, as was the case in CIA, routinely poly-graphed. Other difficulties arose as CIA leaders were reluctant to courier documents to NSA's College Park, Maryland, headquarters. This forced SCS Director Burk to send a cleared secretary.

During the cold war, the primary targets of the SCS were the communications of hostile military organizations and governments. Reportedly, many sensitive sites in Eastern Europe, then members of the Soviet-led Warsaw Pact, were successfully penetrated and valuable intelligence generated by SCS efforts. SCS expertise and skills used advanced technology as well as simple ideas. For instance, during the late 1970s electronic experts had discovered the fact that a standard telephone's microphone, even while "hung up," transmitted largely unnoticeable impulses through the telephone wires. These impulses could then be exploited as they were isolated and converted to sound. As a result every telephone in every room and office became a listening device without requiring physical intrusion. Later, with the advance of technology, collectors could direct a small invisible beam at windows from the outside and after bouncing the signal off the glance pick it up at a receiver and transmitter located hundreds of feet away.

The core of SCS operations is based on special collections elements of two- to three-man teams which are embedded in U.S. embassies abroad. This often means 12-hour shifts spent in windowless three-room suites using state-of-the-art technology. However advances and the proliferation of high-tech equipment have created new difficulties for special collection. For example, advances in micro-wave transmissions, which SCS intercepted with relative ease, have given way to fiber-optic cables which allows for far more circuits and at far greater distances. With advances in increased bandwidth, these systems transmit enormous volumes of information and data. Without direct access to the cables, collection efforts become increasingly problematic.

In the first decade of the twenty-first century, it became apparent that the American reliance on satellites had come at a cost of HUMINT and close-in surveillance intelligence. The rising need to be on the ground and collect intelligence led to a necessary increase in importance of the missions of SCS personnel.

See also: Central Intelligence Agency; National Security Agency

References and Further Reading

Bamford, James. *The Puzzle Palace: Inside the National Security Agency, America's Most Secret Intelligence Organization*. Boston, MA: Houghton Mifflin Co., 1982.

Eyeball Series. "Eyeballing the CIA/NSA Special Collection Service," http://www.eyeball-series.org/scs-eyeball.htm.

Richelson, Jeffrey T. *The Wizards of Langley: Inside the CIA's Directorate of Science and Technology*. Boulder, CO: Westview Press, 2002.

Trento, Joseph J. *The Secret History of the CIA*. Reprint ed. New York: Avalon, 2005.

Woodward, Bob. *VEIL: The Secret Wars of the CIA, 1981–1987*. New York: Simon & Schuster, 1987.

James Brian McNabb

SPECIAL GROUP

This was the term used to refer to two different National Security Council subcommittees that oversaw covert action plans in the 1950s and 1960s. Originally it referred to the 5412 Committee that took its name from the National Security Council Directive issued in the Eisenhower administration that created it. The Special Group became a short-hand term used to describe this committee. Later it became more formally used to describe the committee in the Kennedy administration following the failed Bay of Pigs operation against Cuba. Its name was again changed by National Security Action Memorandum 303 of June 2, 1964, to the 303 Committee. No change in membership or duties accompanied this change in terminology. During its existence, the Special Group and 303 Committee approved 163 covert operations in the Kennedy administration and 142 covert action plans in the Johnson administration through February 1967. The focus here is on the Special Group as it operated during these two administrations.

After the Bay of Pigs, Kennedy commissioned a postmortem study chaired by General Maxwell Taylor. That report recommended strengthening the management and direction of covert action undertakings. Kennedy acted on that report by introducing a series of changes. One procedural change established criteria for determining which covert action programs required Special Committee approval. In 1963 programs costing over $25,000 and holding significant political risk to the United States and the potential for exposure had to come before the Special Group.

At the organizational level he created two additional NSC subcommittees to complement the work of the Special Group. The first, the Special Group (Counterinsurgency), was charged with supervising large paramilitary operations. It was created on January 18, 1962, when Kennedy issued National Security Action Memorandum 124. Special Group (Counterinsurgency) was chaired by Maxwell Taylor as the military representative of the president, the attorney general, the chair of the Joint Chiefs of Staff, the Director of Central Intelligence, the deputy undersecretary of state for political affairs, the deputy secretary of state, the president's special assistant for national security affairs, and the administrator of the agency for international development. Its mission was to ensure that U.S. resources were being used with maximum effectiveness to deal with subversion, and other forms of indirect aggression against friendly countries. The situations in Thailand, Vietnam, and Laos were specially mentioned as areas of concern in the founding document. Iran and Indonesia were two other countries the Special Group (Counterinsurgency) directed its attention to.

The Special Group (Counterinsurgency) was terminated by National Security Action Memorandum 341, signed by President Lyndon Johnson on March 2, 1966. Johnson took this action in response to a recommendation by Taylor that this unit be made into an agency supporting the secretary of state who should be given responsibility for coordinating interdepartmental countersubversion policies. Accordingly, Johnson set up a Senior Interdepartmental Group chaired by an undersecretary of state for this purpose.

The second group Kennedy created to assist the Special Group was the Special Group (Augmented). It carried over the existing membership of the Special Group (the special assistant to the president for national security, the deputy undersecretary of state for political affairs, the deputy secretary of defense, the Director of Central Intelligence, and the chair of the Joint Chiefs of Staff) along with Attorney General Robert Kennedy and General Taylor as chair. From November 1961 until October 1962 the Special Group (Augmented) was responsible for supervising Operation Mongoose.

Also known as the Cuban Project, Operation Mongoose consisted of a series of covert operations, including assassination designed to remove Fidel Castro from power in Cuba. After the failed Bay of Pigs operation, Robert Kennedy had become a strident force within the administration pushing for such action, hence his inclusion in Special Group (Augmented). Operation Mongoose was led by Air Force General Edward Lansdale and CIA officer William Harvey King. Operation Mongoose was suspended on October 30, 1962, with the advent of the Cuban Missile Crisis.

See also: Bay of Pigs; 5412 Committee; Johnson Administration and Intelligence; Kennedy Administration and Intelligence; Landsale; Edward Geary; Mongoose, Operation

References and Further Reading

Bohning, Don. *The Castro Obsession: U.S. Covert Operations Against Cuba, 1959–1965.* Washington, DC, Potomac Books, 2005.

Kornbluh, Peter, ed. *Bay of Pigs Declassified: The Secret CIA Report on the Invasion of Cuba.* New York: Free Press, 1998.

Glenn P. Hastedt

SPECIAL OPERATIONS EXECUTIVE (SOE)

After withdrawing from continental Western Europe in the summer of 1940, Britain set out to reorganize irregular warfare tools. The goal of the resulting SOE was, as Churchill put it: "to set Europe ablaze." The SOE became the model for the U.S. Office of Strategic Services (OSS), and continued to organize resistance movements and conduct clandestine operations behind enemy lines throughout World War II.

On July 19 1940, the autonomous SOE was established from existing organizations like the Military Research Intelligence of the War Office, and Section D of the Secret Intelligence Service under the Foreign Office. Important tasks became smuggling weapons, explosives, and saboteurs behind enemy lines; encourage sedition and intelligence-gathering; and facilitating escape routes for agents and allied POWs. But, just as important, was to bolster moral, both in Britain and the occupied countries.

SOE HQ was located on 64th Bakerstreet, London, and the research department at Aston House. In addition there were various training facilities all over Great Britain. Initially, SOE was also intended as a "stay behind" army—a core from which a resistance movement could be built in case of a German invasion of Britain. Its first chief was Sir Frank Nelson, and from April 2, 1942, Sir Charles Hambro. In August 1943, the latter resigned over a cabinet decision to coordinate the SOE's activities with the army, and was replaced by Major General Colin Gubbins.

The SOE's field organization was divided into geographic sections. The F and RF section dominated operations in France; the latter engaged most available free French agents. Both sections fielded about 600 operatives during the German occupation, whose most notable contribution were preparations for the Normandy landings in 1944. The SOE in the Netherlands was infiltrated by the Germans due to slack security routines but networks were rebuilt towards the end of 1943, and they contributed to the Allied campaign of 1944 and 1945. Section T, operating in neighboring Belgium, saw their country more quickly liberated following the outbreak from Normandy, but it played an important role in enabling the Allies to secure the Antwerpen harbor facilities intact. The SOE found it difficult to build up an organization in Nazi Germany and satellites such as Hungary and Romania. In fellow axis state Italy, few efforts were made to build up assets until Mussolini's regime had collapsed in 1943. In Czechoslovakia, the most famous SOE operation was the assassination of deputy chief of the SS, Reinhard Heydrich, on May 27 1942. Poland was more difficult to access from Britain, but some weapons reached the non-Communist Armia Krajowa (Home army).

The Scandinavian Section covered occupied Demark and Norway, and among its single most important achievements were the evacuation of Danish Jews and the sabotage of heavy water production in Norway which made the development of a German nuclear bomb even more difficult. Agents along the Norwegian coast also tracked German naval movements, an important asset in the battle of the Atlantic. Sabotage activity in general helped nurture Hitler's fear of an invasion in the North, ensuring that many troops and other resources went into defensive preparations. In the Balkans, the SOE not only faced the forces of Axis occupation, but also found themselves entangled in bitter infighting between Nationalist and Communist resistance groups. In Yugoslavia, they chose Jozip Broz "Tito's" partisans as it was the most effective and reliable ally in the country, as was fellow Communist Enver Hoxha in Albania.

In Greece initial cooperation between Communist ELAS and republican EDES resistance movements led to the famous 1942 Operation Harling, blowing up the Gorgopotamos Railway Viaduct. In 1943, open conflict broke out between the groups, followed by an armistice in 1943. Civil war flared up immediately following German withdrawal in 1944, in which the SOE actively participated, securing Athens and Pireus on behalf of the republicans. The SOE also carried out operations in the North African and East Asian theaters of war.

In 1946, the war was over and the Labour government under Prime Minister Clement Atlee saw no reason to continue the service. The SOE was disbanded and the MI-6 absorbed most of its functions.

See also: MI-6 (Secret Intelligence Service)

References and Further Reading

Foot, M. R. D. *An Outline History of the Special Operations Executive*. London: British Broadcasting Corporation, 1984.
Mackenzie, William. *The Secret History of SOE—Special Operations Executive 1940–1945*. London: St. Ermin's Press, 2000.
Wylie, Neville (ed.). *The Politics of Strategic and Clandestine War: Special Operations Executive, 1940–1946*. London: Routledge, 2007.

Frode Lindgjerdet

SPECIAL OPERATIONS FORCES

SOF, the acronym for Special Operations Forces, consists of highly versatile military, paramilitary, and/or civilian personnel, all of which specialize in covert tactics and utilize unorthodox methods. These elite units conduct clandestine missions involving infiltration, intelligence gathering, rescue, insurgency, counterinsurgency, counternarcotics, and counterterrorism. Referred to as the "silent professionals" because much of their work is classified, SOF troops are often rapidly deployed to troubled spots with little visibility.

In short, SOF engages in special operations (special ops). According to the Department of Defense (DOD), in its official dictionary of military terms (2004), special ops are "operations conducted in hostile, denied, or politically sensitive environments to achieve military, diplomatic, informational, and/or economic objectives employing military capabilities for which there is no broad conventional force requirement."

Both the Central Intelligence Agency and the U.S. military rely on SOF to conduct special ops. It is estimated that of the Central Intelligence Agency's (CIA) 22,000 full-time employees, approximately 5,000 work for the Directorate of Operations (DO), its SOF wing. The DO's Special Operations Group (SOG), a paramilitary unit, has several hundred members. In 2004 about 2 percent of the American military were serving in SOF units, approximately 34,000 active and 15,000 reserve personnel. SOF military personnel are sometimes assigned to the CIA and vice versa.

The history of modern SOF can be traced back to the Strategic Services Unit of the Pentagon, formed following World War II after President Truman disbanded the Office of Strategic Services. The unit, which was renamed the Office of Special

Operations (OSO), came under the Central Intelligence Group, the predecessor of today's CIA. In June 1948, with the creation of the Office of Policy Coordination (OPC), a special organization committed itself to carrying out political activities, psychological warfare, and paramilitary operations, the latter including sabotage, countersabotage, and guerilla-type missions. In August 1952 the OPC and the OSO merged as the Directorate of Plans (DP), which oversaw the Special Activities Division. In 1973, with the Vietnam War waning, the DP became the DO and was downsized.

The Special Activities Division of the CIA was behind many clandestine activities over the years, including operations in Guatemala (1954), the Far East (1950s–1960s), Cuba (the Bay of Pigs, 1961), Laos and Cambodia (beginning in 1962), South America (1960s–1990s), Central America (1980s), Afghanistan (1980s), and Bosnia and Kosovo (1990s). During the Reagan administration the reputation of CIA covert operations was sullied due to the Iran-Contra scandal, leading to a virtual dismantling of the SOG. After a two-decade decline, however, the SOG began a rebuilding period, which was accelerated following the attacks of September 11. Divided into ground, maritime, and air branches, the SOG is a military separate and apart from the DOD. The first fatality in the war on terrorism was a SOG officer, Johnny "Mike" Spann, who was killed in Afghanistan in November 2001 while on the hunt for Osama bin Laden.

In the American military special ops units are a part of the four service branches and include, among others, Special Forces, Rangers, and Delta Force (U.S. Army); SEALs, Special Boat Squadrons, and SEAL Delivery Vehicle Teams (U.S. Navy); Force Reconnaissance (U.S. Marines); and the 16th Special Operations Wing and combat control teams (U.S. Air Force).

The military's modern SOF units date back to April 10, 1952, with the founding of the Psychological Warfare Center at Fort Bragg, North Carolina. Personnel from the 1st Special Forces Group, activated in Okinawa in 1957, were the first American military advisers sent to Vietnam. In July 1959 12 Special Forces teams, initially maintaining a "civilian" identity, were sent to Laos to train the Laotian army. In 1961 Special Forces were authorized to wear the green beret, thereafter becoming popularly known as the Green Berets. The SEALs (an acronym for SEa, Air, and Land) were commissioned in 1962 and saw much action in the rivers and coastal waterways of Vietnam. SEALs, arguably the most elite of the SOF family, trace their lineage back to the underwater demolition teams of World War II and today are a combination of frogman, paratrooper, and commando. During the 1980s the CIA relied on Special Forces and SEALs for its mission to train the Contras in Nicaragua.

SOF was neglected following the Vietnam War, although two Army Ranger battalions were activated in 1974. Also, on November 19, 1977, the army formed an antiterrorist squad, Special Forces Operational Detachment—Delta, headed by Colonel Charlie A. Beckwith. This latter unit, commonly known as Delta Force, was inspired in part due to the terrorist attacks at the Olympic Games in Munich in 1972. Despite the creation of these new SOF units, resources were limited, especially since top Pentagon officials maintained a bias preference for conventional forces. Most significantly, Delta Force and the Rangers were not provided with adequate transportation support for infiltration and exfiltration, which became apparent after the breakdown of helicopters during the failed Iran rescue mission of April 1980.

After the fiery debacle in the Iranian desert, DOD began administrative reform. Unfortunately, not enough was done in time for Operation URGENT FURY, the October 1983 invasion of Grenada. Delta Force, the Rangers, and the SEALs were sent in harm's way with inadequate transportation delivery. Finally, on June 1, 1987, the Pentagon activated the United States Special Operations Command (USSOCOM), headquartered at MacDill Air Force Base in Tampa, Florida, to give SOF units a unified command and improved support. This revamping was in place in time for Operation JUST CAUSE in Panama (1988–1989), of which 4,500 of the 27,000 U.S. troops were SOF personnel. During the first Gulf War, Operation DESERT STORM (1990–1991), approximately 9,000 SOF personnel were deployed, greater than any previous conflict. Of the deployed SOF units in 2004, 80 percent were in Afghanistan and Iraq.

The trend, following the recommendation of the 9/11 Commission Report, is for all paramilitary clandestine and covert operations to be placed under USSOCOM. However, since September 11 there has been an expansion of the CIA's special operations, leading to a turf war between the Pentagon and Langley.

See also: Army Intelligence; Central Intelligence Agency; Defense Department Intelligence; Iraq War; Marine Corps Intelligence; National Commission on Terrorist Attacks on the United States (The 9/11 Commission); Navy Intelligence; Office of Policy Coordination; Office of Special Operations; Persian Gulf War; Spann, Johnny Michael; Strategic Services Unit

References and Further Reading

Clancy, Tom, General Carl Stiner, and Tony Koltz. *Shadow Warriors: Inside the Special Forces.* New York: G.P. Putnam's Sons, 2002.

Landau, Alan M., Frieda W. Landau, Terry Griswold, D. M. Giangreco, and Hans Halberstadt. *U.S. Special Forces.* Ann Arbor, MI: Lowe and B. Hould Publishers, 1999.

Lang, Walter N. *The World's Elite Forces: The Men, Weapons and Operations in the War Against Terrorism.* New York: Salamander Books, 1987.

Marquis, Susan L. *Unconventional Warfare: Rebuilding U.S. Special Operations Forces.* Washington, DC: Brookings Institution Press, 1997.

Prados, John. *Presidents' Secret Wars: CIA and Pentagon Operations since World War II.* New York: William Morrow, 1986.

Roger Chapman

SPETSNAZ

Spetsnaz is a generic Russian term for "troops of special purpose," which has come to mean "Russian special forces" in English. During the cold war, Spetsnaz units were raised by the GRU, the intelligence directorate of the Soviet General Staff. By the 1980s, these special purpose forces numbered approximately 30,000. There was usually one Spetsnaz company (approximately 135 strong) in each army, one Spetsnaz regiment in each of the three Soviet theaters of operation; one Spetsnaz brigade in each of the four Soviet fleets, and an independent Spetsnaz brigade in most military districts of the USSR. There were also special Spetsnaz intelligence detachments in each front and fleet.

The existence of Spetsnaz troops was a closely guarded secret within the Warsaw Pact and individual troops were not allowed to admit membership; army Spetsnaz wore standard airborne uniforms and insignia, whereas naval Spetsnaz wore naval infantry uniforms and insignia.

Spetsnaz troops were deployed in Eastern Europe in order to carry out strategic reconnaissance and sabotage missions against NATO force during the final days prior to war breaking out and in war itself. These wartime tasks would include deep reconnaissance of strategic targets, the destruction of strategically important command-control-and-communications facilities, the destruction of strategic weapons delivery systems, demolition of important bridges and transportation routes, and the snatching or assassination of important military and political leaders. Many of these missions would be carried out before the enemy could react and some even before the war had actually broken out.

During the 1970s and 1980s, special operations troops became increasingly the vogue in various ministries of the then Soviet Union. Therefore, similar bodies with similar missions were set up by different parts of the same ministry, particularly within the Committee for State Security (KGB) and the Ministry of Internal Affairs (MVD). These special troops went under the generic title of *Spetsgruppe* and were paramilitary forces that received special training and indoctrination for a variety of missions. Many of these units served in a variety of roles in the war in Afghanistan and, more recently, in conflicts within the Russian Federation, particularly in operations against insurgents in Chechnya.

Special Group Alpha was set up by the KGB's Seventh Directorate in 1974 and appears to have been inspired by the British SAS and U.S. 1st Special Forces Operational Detachment-D (Delta) as a counterterrorist and hostage-rescue group. It is generally believed that Special Group A was the unit that attacked the presidential palace in Kabul, Afghanistan, on December 28, 1980, and murdered President Hafizullah Amin and his family. This unit is now controlled by the Federal Security Service (FSB), which its equivalent to the U.S. Federal Bureau of Investigation. It is believed that Alpha Group was involved in the Beslan school hostage crisis on September 3, 2004, and was criticized for the use of excessive deadly force, which resulted in hostage casualties.

The First Chief Administration of the KGB established an organization known as *Spetsgruppa Vympel*, whose mission was to fulfill the KGB's wartime role of assassination and snatching. After the collapse of the Soviet Union, this group was transferred to the MVD but is now under the FSB with primary responsibility for hostage rescue and countersabotage. In the last mission, they are responsible for defending against possible terrorist attacks involving nuclear plants, hydroelectric dams, and other key industrial facilities.

The Ministry of Internal Affairs also has at least two groups of special troops known as the *Omon* (Black Berets), which were originally raised to provide additional security and (if necessary) hostage rescue at the 1980 Moscow Olympics. Since then they have been used for counterterrorist activities and defeating armed criminals, and are currently involved in campaigns against drug cultivation.

Also included in this category of forces is the *GROM* Security Company, which is a quasi-private organization working under exclusive contract to the federal government.

GROM (the Russian word for "thunder" and with no relationship to the Polish group of the same name) is manned by former troops of the various KGB special forces and provides security for selected government personnel and buildings, as well as for certain trains and aircraft.

The last group that falls within this category is Speznaz UIN, a group of special-purpose troops on assignment with the Ministry of Justice. This group is responsible for the suppression of mass disorders and revolts in prisons, rescue of hostages seized in prisons, and other situations that threaten discipline and order in prisons or other incarceration facilities.

Spetsnaz-like forces can also be found in a few countries of the former Soviet Union, such as Belarus, Ukraine, and Georgia.

See also: KGB (Komitet Gosudarstvennoi Bezopasnosti)

References and Further Reading

Adams, James. *Secret Armies: Inside the American, Soviet, and European Special Forces.* Westminster, MD: Bantam, 1989.

Suvorov, Viktor. *Spetznaz: The Inside Story of the Soviet Special Forces.* New York: W.W. Norton, 1988.

James H. Willbanks

SR-71

The SR-71 (Strategic Response-71) was a U.S. Air Force reconnaissance aircraft that flew from 1964 to 1998. A total of 32 aircraft were built. Twelve were lost through accidents. None were shot down by the enemy. According to folklore, the SR-71's ability to elude the enemy was due to its invisibility to radar. Nicknamed the "blackbird" for its dark blue coloring, the SR-71 was said to be invisible to radar. In reality the SR-71 was visible on radar for hundreds of miles. What made the SR-71 able to elude the enemy was its great speed. Able to operate at Mach 3, it could accelerate when detected and outrun threats.

The SR-71 was built by Lockheed as a black or secret project at its famous Skunk Works unit. Clarence "Kelly" Johnson, who had played a central role in designing the A-12 Oxcart reconnaissance aircraft for the Central Intelligence Agency, also was instrumental in building the SR-71. The existence of the SR-71 was made public by President Lyndon Johnson during the 1964 presidential campaign. Johnson was under attack from Republican candidate Barry Goldwater for failing to keep pace with Soviet strategic advances. Disclosure of the SR-71 was meant to counter this criticism.

The A-12 first flew in 1962. Design work on the SR-71 began in February 1963. The first test flight took place in December 1964 and the SR-71 became operational in January 1966. Most heavily used in Southeast Asia, SR-71's initially averaged one sortie per week. As the U.S. involvement in Vietnam deepened, so too did the SR-71's flight time. In 1972 they averaged almost one per day.

The SR-71 was retired twice. The first time came in 1989. A combination of cost concerns and shifting air force priorities led to this decision. Satellites were cheaper than reconnaissance aircraft and the air force was more interested in developing the

B-1 Lancer and upgrading the B-52. The SR-71 was reactivated at congressional insistence in 1993 when evidence surfaced that North Korea was pursuing a nuclear bomb and fears rose about the political stability of the Middle East. The air force remained uncommitted to the SR-71 and in 1996 once again proposed its deactivation. Congress continued funding the SR-71 but this money was line item vetoed by President Clinton. The SR-71 was retired for a second and final time in 1998.

See also: Air Force Intelligence; Powers, Francis Gary; U-2 Incident

References and Further Reading

Crickmore, Paul F. *Lockheed SR-71: The Secret Missions Exposed*. Oxford, UK: Osprey, 1993.

Jenkins, Dennis R. *Lockheed SR-71/YF-12 Blackbirds*. WarbirdTech Series Volume 10. North Branch, MN: Specialty Press, 1997.

Glenn P. Hastedt

SS (SCHUTZ STAFFEL)

The SS (Schutz Staffel or protection squad) was a powerful and lethal military and security organization in the Third Reich. The SS's intelligence and security organization, the SD (Sicherheitsdienst or security service), was created in 1932 by Reinhard Heydrich and focused on political intelligence. The SD infiltrated the United States before and during World War II, and the Federal Bureau of Investigation (FBI) tracked and infiltrated several Nazi spy rings. During the war, agents from the Office of Strategic Services (OSS), the precursor to the CIA, also successfully penetrated the SD in Nazi Germany.

The SS was an elite guard first formed to protect Hitler in 1925, but it soon morphed into the Nazis' special security force. In 1929, Heinrich Himmler became the leader of the SS. In need of an intelligence organization, the SD was created in 1931 under Himmler's direct authority and the SD became the SS's official intelligence organization in 1932. After the Nazis took control of Germany in 1933, the SD's overall power created a police state.

In 1936, Himmler was appointed chief of German police. He fused the SS with Germany's police force or the Sipo, composed of the Gestapo (secret police) and the Kripo (criminal police). This gave Himmler legal control of all police forces. In 1939, Himmler merged the SD with the Sipo to create the RSHA, or Reich Security Administration. In 1944, the Abwehr, Germany's military intelligence organization, was placed under the jurisdiction of the RSHA and thus SS-controlled.

In 1934, Heydrich created SD's foreign intelligence branch, or Department VI. This department was ordered to discover actual or potential enemies of the Nazi leadership and defuse any threats. Walter Schellenberg became head of Department VI in 1941. Civilian foreign intelligence gathering fell under the SD Ausland (outside of Germany) department. Department D focused on espionage in the American sphere. In 1937, Himmler ordered the Gestapo to create a spy network in the United States and several agents came. Guenther Rumrich instigated several espionage operations, including one to obtain 50 blank passports. Kurt Frederick Ludwig, aka Joe K., operated a widespread spy ring, delivering classified and secret American information to Berlin.

German-born American citizen William Sebold agreed to spy for the Gestapo in the United States, but became a U.S. counterspy instead. In 1944, German intelligence launched Operation Magpie, a last attempt to infiltrate the United States. This ill-fated mission involved Erich Gimpel and an American-born man named William Curtis Colepaugh.

Despite lack of funding and support by the U.S. Congress, the FBI ruthlessly tracked the Gestapo's presence in the United States, overthrowing several potentially disastrous schemes, including a kidnapping plot in 1938 to abduct an American general and the destruction of several spy rings. In June 1938, the U.S. Justice Department indicted 18 people on charges of espionage, leading to a sensational trial that drew attention to the vast Nazi spy network in the United States.

The OSS was the SD's main adversary during World War II, and they successfully infiltrated the SD in Nazi Germany. The Ruppert Mission involved a White Russian émigré named Youri Vinogradov whose penetration of the inner workings of the SD proved invaluable after the war's end.

In 1942, Himmler declared that RSHA would direct the Final Solution in all aspects and jurisdiction. The SS and the SD oversaw the concentration camp system and committed several atrocities during the Holocaust. At the end of the war, the SS and SD were classified as criminal organizations and their members were tried as criminals at Nuremberg.

See also: Abwehr; American Intelligence, World War II; Duquesne Spy Ring; Federal Bureau of Investigation (FBI); Office of Strategic Services; Sebold, William G.

References and Further Reading

Breuer, William. *Hitler's Undercover War: The Nazi Espionage Invasion of the U.S.A.* New York: St. Martin's, 1989.

Browder, George C. *Hitler's Enforcers: The Gestapo and the SS Security Service in the Nazi Revolution.* New York: Oxford University Press, 1996.

Farago, Ladislas. *The Game of the Foxes: The Untold Story of German Espionage in the United States and Great Britain During World War II.* New York: David McKay Company, Inc., 1971.

Kahn, David. *Hitler's Spies: German Military Intelligence in World War II.* New York: Macmillan, 1978.

Persico, Joseph E. *Piercing the Reich: The Penetration of Nazi Germany by American Secret Agents during World War II.* New York: Barnes and Noble Books, 2000.

Melissa A. Marsh

ST. ALBANS RAID

On October 19, 1864, 21 Confederate soldiers, under the command of Lieutenant Bennet Young, carried out a successful raid on the town of St. Albans, Vermont. The goals of the raid were to secure funds for the Confederate war effort and to draw Union troops away from the South. Launched from Canadian soil, this was the northernmost engagement of the Civil War and led to friction between Great Britain and the Union.

Lieutenant Bennett Young had escaped to Canada from a Union prisoner of war camp in the spring of 1864. He received a commission from the Confederate government to attempt the release of other Confederate prisoners. Two such attempts failed, but Young was allowed to lead a raid on a Union town to steal money for the Confederate war effort. He entered Vermont alone and selected St. Albans for the operation. Some Confederates joined him and, together, passing themselves off as travelers, they reconnoitered the town, located its four banks and stables, and planned the robberies and escape routes. The remaining Confederate soldiers arrived in twos and threes by different routes and trains, found rooms in a number of local hotels, and waited.

At 3 o'clock in the afternoon on October 19, the 21 men assembled and then entered the four St. Albans' banks and the stable. Shocked residents were forced into the town square. The Confederates garnered $208,000 and then escaped to Canada on stolen horses. The raid was well planned and casualties low, with one St. Albans man killed and a number wounded.

Thirteen of the soldiers, including Young, were apprehended in Canada. American authorities considered entering Canada to retrieve the raiders, but this would have violated British neutrality. Instead, the United States demanded their extradition, but Great Britain allowed the Canadian courts to try the raiders. Young and his men were released by the Canadians on technicalities, and soon journeyed to the Confederacy with the stolen money. Canada, however, agreed to reimburse St. Albans for the lost money and paid the amount equal to that found on the captured raiders, $50,000.

See also: Civil War Intelligence

References and Further Reading

Kinchen, Oscar A. *Daredevils of the Confederate Army: The Story of the St. Albans Raiders.* Boston: Christopher Publishing House, 1959.
Van Doren Stern, Philip. *Secret Missions of the Civil War.* New York: Wings Books, 1990.

Richard M. Mickle

STASI

STASI, the East German Ministry for State Security (Ministerium für Staatssicherheit, or MfS) was responsible for domestic surveillance, foreign intelligence, and counterespionage. Created February 8, 1950, only months after the foundation of the German Democratic Republic (GDR) in 1949, the STASI was modeled on the Cheka, the Soviet secret police founded by Felix Dzerzhinsky in 1917. For over four decades, the STASI served as "The Sword and the Shield" of the GDR's ruling Communists' Party, the Socialist Unity Party (Sozialistische Einheitspartei Deutschlands, or SED). The STASI was the integral instrument of the SED against its enemies at home and abroad in its global struggle against capitalism. One of the most efficient and pervasive secret services in history, the STASI used a network of personal informers and extensive postal and telephone monitoring to conduct a blanket surveillance of East Germany society. It exercised almost complete control over the population of East Germany. In many regards, the STASI functioned as a state within a state. During its existence, the STASI had three chairmen: Wilhelm Zasser (1950–1953), Ernest Wollheber (1953–1957), and Erich Mielke (1957–1989).

When the Berlin wall fell in 1989, the STASI had over 91,100 full-time staff, half employed in its central apparatus in East Berlin (Normannenstrasse 22 in Lichtenberg) and the rest in the 15 Regional Administrations (Bezirkverwaltungen, or BVs), the 211 District Service Units (Kreisdienststellen, or KDs), and 7 so-called "Objects" (Objekte, or major complexes, such as the nuclear power station in Greifswald and the technical university in Dresden). In addition to the full-time staff, the STASI had over 175,000 informants (known as IMs, for Inoffizielle Mitarbeiter, or unofficial collaborators) within the GDR's general population of 16.4 million. Organizationally, the regional administrative units of the STASI corresponded to those of the SED and GDR.

East German espionage was carried out by the STASI'S foreign intelligence wing, the Hauptverwaltung Aufklärung, or HVA. Marcus Wolf was appointed chief of the HVA in 1957, a position he held until 1985. The HVA's reputation was based on its ability to infiltrate the West German government, while at the same time proving almost impervious to Western infiltration. Most infamously, Guenther Guillaume, an East German agent, became the personal assistant to Chancellor Willy Brandt, a situation which eventually forced Brandt to resign in 1977. During the Honecker years (1971–1989), the HVA's first priority was to impede the "imperialistic" role of the United States, and its security service, the Central Intelligence Agency, from endangering the German Democratic Republic and its Warsaw Pact allies. In theory, the HVA operated in all areas of the world where the United States and its North Atlantic Treaty Organization (NATO) allies were active. In practice, however, the HVA concentrated its activities against the Federal Republic of Germany, since the FRG was NATO's strategic bridgehead against the Warsaw Pact (and the leading economic power in Europe). One of the HVA's primary concerns was circumventing the scientific and technical embargo employed against the GDR by the United States and its allies.

Counterespionage was the provenance of the department within the MfS known as the Second Main Directorate, headed by Lt. General Guenther Kratsch. This directorate employed 2,350 full-time agents, half of whom were stationed in Berlin in 1989. The STASI viewed every U.S. diplomat as a potential spy, bugging their apartments and often subjecting them to round-the-clock surveillance. Mielke had directed the entire MfS staff to cooperate with the Second Main Directorate when it required assistance. East Germans who had contact with U.S. diplomatic personnel were vetted and also placed under surveillance.

With the opening of the Berlin Wall on the night of November 9, 1989, the SED ceded its monopoly on power, and also its dependence upon its "Sword and Shield." On the evening of January 12, 1990, several thousand protestors stormed STASI headquarters and ransacked the building, looking for personal files. Initially, STASI files remained sealed because the German government feared that they would have a divisive effect on reunification efforts. Under the auspices of the Gauck Authority, the agency responsible for STASI documents, many STASI records were eventually opened.

See also: Gehlen Organization; German Democratic Republic and Intelligence

References and Further Reading

Childs, David, and Richard Popplewell. *The STASI: East German Intelligence and Secret Service.* London: MacMillan Press, LTD, 1996.

Dennis, Mike. *The STASI: Myth and Reality*. Harlow: Pearson/Longman, 2003.

Giesek, Jens. *Mielke-Konzern: Die Geschichte der STASI 1945–1990*. Stuttgart: Deutsche Verlags-Anstalt, 2001.

Wendell G. Johnson

STATE DEPARTMENT INTELLIGENCE

The United Stated Department of State, along with the Treasury Department and the War Department (now Defense), were the first departments created at the beginning of the Republic. The Department of State has the responsibility of conducting diplomacy for the United States. It operates under the authority of the Congress and

U.S. ambassador to the United Nations, Henry Cabot Lodge, shows the Security Council a listening device which he said the Soviet authorities had managed to plant in the office of U.S. Ambassador Llewellyn Thompson in Moscow. The device, a wooden carving of the Great Seal of the United States, was hollow and contained a hidden microphone. (AP/Wide World Photos)

the supervision of the president of the United States through the secretary of the State Department.

Most intelligence work in the United States is done by the military or by special agencies such as the Central Intelligence Agency or the National Security Agency; however, there are several civilian agencies such as the Departments of Transportation, Energy, Commerce, and State that do some intelligence work. The State Department is involved with intelligence in a number of ways. It seeks political intelligence as a matter of course in which it gathers on all countries with which the United States has relations. It also is engaged in counterintelligence to protect the political secrets of the United States on such matters as delicate negations or on the long-range policy goals.

After President Harry Truman abolished the Office of Strategic Services (OSS) at the end of World War II, its research and analysis functions were transferred to the State Department where they were conducted by a unit called the Interim Research and Intelligence Service. Between 1946 and 1957 the unit's name was changed twice and it underwent several reorganizations. Finally the unit was stabilized as the Bureau of Intelligence and Research (INR). With a staff that grew to 360 people, it analyzed intelligence data from open and especially diplomatic sources. It also performed functions that were related to operations, and acted as a liaison between the intelligence community and the goals of American foreign policy.

The Bureau of Intelligence and Research is a contributor to the National Intelligence Estimates (NIEs) and to the Special Estimates (SEs). It also prepares a variety of intelligence products. One of these in the secretary of state's Morning Summary, which is a briefing paper that keeps the secretary and others informed of intelligence estimates of current events of importance to American foreign policy. In addition, the INR writes regional and other intelligence summaries. It also prepares single subject Intelligence Research Reports.

The director of the Bureau of Intelligence and Research also hold the title of assistant secretary of state for Intelligence and Research. He or she reports directly to the secretary of state.

Supporting the assistant secretary is the principle deputy assistant secretary who handles current intelligence. Also part of the intelligence personnel are the staff associated with the work, and the Office of the Executive Director. There are other units doing intelligence work that report to the principle deputy. These include the head of the Office of Publications, the deputy assistant secretary for Analysis, and the deputy assistant secretary for Intelligence Policy. Subordinate to the latter two officers are over a dozen officers that conduct specific intelligence functions.

The deputy assistant secretary for analysis supervises offices that cover six geographic regions. They are Africa, East Asia and the Pacific, Inter-American Affairs, the Near East and South Asia, Russia and Eurasia, and Europe and Canada. These offices keep up with current events in their respective regions. The staff is very knowledgeable about the people, the culture, and all aspects of the politics of their region. The staff might be called upon to give a detailed report on some aspect or upon general conditions and specifics about key political actors in their region.

The deputy assistant secretary for analysis is in charge of developing long-range analytical studies. In addition, the secretary for analysis is the supervisor for the Office of Economic Analysis; the Office of Geographer and Global Issues; the External Research

Staff; and the Office of Analysis for Strategic, Proliferation, and Military Affairs; and the Office of Analysis for Terrorism, Narcotics and Crime.

The External Research Staff issues contracts for projects that the INR cannot do. The Office of Economic Analysis writes reports on current issues involving economic concerns. The reports may also be on long-term issues of concern to policy makers. The reports may involve the economic policies of foreign countries; trade issues; economic conditions; international economic issues such as the value and flow of currencies, food, population growth and migrations; energy supplies and prices; as well as the economic relations between other countries and the United States.

The Office of Strategic, Proliferation, and Military Affairs studies the nuclear capability and intentions of the Russians, Chinese, Pakistanis, and other nuclear powers. It also issue reports on those countries seeking to develop a nuclear weapons program and those that have already done so but which have kept their success secret and unacknowledged.

The deputy assistant secretary for intelligence policy supervises the Office of Intelligence Coordination, the Office of Intelligence Liaison, the Office of Administrative Liaison, and the Office of Intelligence Resources. It works with the Federal Bureau of Investigation (FBI) and other members of the intelligence community.

The Bureau for International Narcotics and Law Enforcement Affairs, Counterterrorism Office, and the Bureau of Diplomatic Security deal with issues and events in foreign countries that may involve violence. It is also the duty of the State Department to expel persons with diplomatic immunity who have been caught spying inside of the United States. For example, when FBI Special Agent Robert Hanssen was arrested on February 18, 2001, four Russians handlers with whom he had worked as a spy were declared persona non grata.

See also: Foreign Broadcast Information Service, U.S. (FBIS); Intelligence Community; Office of Strategic Services

References and Further Reading

Barnes, William H., and John Heath Morgan. *The Foreign Service of the United States: Origins, Development, and Functions.* Westport, CT: Greenwood Press, 1979.

Lowenthal, Mark M. *Intelligence: From Secrets to Policy.* 4th ed. Washington, DC: CQ Press, 2008.

O'Donnell, Patrick K. *Operatives, Spies and Saboteurs: The Unknown Story of the Men and Women of WWII's OSS.* New York: Free Press, 2004.

Richelson, Jeffrey T. *The U.S. Intelligence Community*, 5th edition. Boulder, CO: Westview Press, 2008.

Andrew J. Waskey

STAY-BEHIND

Secret anti-Communist NATO networks in Western Europe run by the U.S. Central Intelligence Agency (CIA) and British Secret Intelligence Service (MI-6) in cooperation with numerous European military intelligence services, discovered in 1990, were known as stay-behind networks. In case of a Soviet invasion of Western Europe, an international stay-behind network was designed to fight as secret North Atlantic

Treaty Organization (NATO) guerrillas behind enemy lines on Soviet-occupied territory. In order to be able to function independently of regular national armies, the stay-behind network was trained in secret warfare by U.S. and British Special Forces and controlled secret arms caches across Western Europe containing guns, explosives, hand grenades, and other small arms. The top-secret network, discovered only in 1990, operated outside democratic control and in some countries was accused of having been linked to acts of torture, terror, and coup d'états in the absence of a Soviet invasion.

During World War II, British Prime Minister Winston Churchill set up a secret army under the code name "Special Operations Executive" (SOE). Its task was to clandestinely parachute behind enemy lines into German-controlled territory and to cooperate with resistance movements and covert action operatives of various anti-German intelligence services, including the U.S. Office of Strategic Services (OSS).

After World War II, British and U.S. military strategists feared an invasion and occupation of Western Europe by the Soviet Union and decided that a secret guerrilla and resistance movement should be set up on the model of the SOE. CIA and MI-6 were given the task to secretly contact reliable persons within the military intelligence services of all countries of Western Europe. Within the CIA the Office of Policy Coordination (OPC), responsible for covert action operations and headed by Frank Wisner, was given the sensitive task. Former CIA Director William Colby later called it "a major program" of the CIA, designed to have top-secret armed soldiers in Western Europe "ready to be called into action as sabotage and espionage forces when the time came."

In cooperation with European military secret services, stay-behind armies were set up by the CIA and MI-6 in the NATO countries of Germany, France, Italy, Greece, Spain, Portugal, Turkey, Belgium, Luxemburg, Holland, Denmark, and Norway, as well as in the officially neutral countries Sweden, Switzerland, Finland, and Austria. U.S. Special Forces, including the Green Berets, and British Special Forces, including the Special Air Services (SAS), trained the stay-behind soldiers in the techniques of secret warfare. NATO's Supreme Headquarters Allied Powers Europe (SHAPE), together with the U.S. Pentagon, coordinated and supervised the stay-behinds through two secret committees: The Allied Clandestine Committee (ACC), and the Clandestine Planning Committee (CPC). International exercises were being held on a regular basis.

In order to limit the potential danger caused to the network through exposure, information was distributed on a strict "need to know basis" within the networks and during international exercises. Different stay-behinds operated under different code names, such as "Gladio" (Italy), "ROC" (Norway), "P26" (Switzerland), "Counter-Guerrilla" (Turkey), or "SDRA8" (Belgium).

In almost all countries national parliaments remained ignorant of the existence of the secret armies throughout the cold war. This led parliamentarians to conclude that the stay-behind networks were illegal and incompatible with national constitutions as they operated beyond checks and balances and with virtually no democratic oversight. In Belgium, Italy and Switzerland parliamentary investigations led to the demobilization of the respective secret armies. The EU parliament passed a resolution on the stay-behind networks on November 22, 1990, sharply criticizing NATO for having set up military structures which for decades operated beyond democratic control.

In some countries elements of the stay-behind networks were accused to have been linked to torture (Turkey), coup d'états (Greece), terror (Italy), assassinations (Spain), and militant political struggle (France). NATO, according to some interpretations, feared that European Communist Parties, strong above all in France and Italy during the cold war, might weaken the defense alliance from within, and therefore used unorthodox warfare and stay-behind assets to confront that challenge. The CIA, MI-6, and NATO refused to comment.

In 1990, acting Italian Prime Minister Giulio Andreotti for the first time officially confirmed the existence of the international stay-behind network; the European press concluded that the "story seems straight from the pages of a political thriller." Although stay-behind data was hardly covered in the U.S. press, European newspapers argued that the stay-behind networks were "the best-kept, and most damaging, political-military secret since World War II."

Please note: The entry "Operation Gladio" or "Gladio" in the Encyclopaedia should guide the reader directly to the entry "Stay-Behind," because many people know the topic under the keyword "Gladio" only.

See also: Central Intelligence Agency; MI-6 (Secret Intelligence Service); Special Operations Forces

References and Further Reading

Colby, William. *Honourable Men: My Life in the CIA*. New York: Simon & Schuster, 1978.
Ganser, Daniele. *NATO's Secret Armies. Operations Gladio and Terrorism in Western Europe*. London: Frank Cass, 2005.

Daniele Ganser

STEPHENSON, SIR WILLIAM SAMUEL (JANUARY 25, 1897–JANUARY 31, 1989)

A Canadian, Sir William Stephenson was instrumental in establishing the Office of Strategic Services (OSS), the forerunner of the Central Intelligence Agency. He did so covertly working for British intelligence under the guise of the British Security Coordination Office in New York City. This office, which he headed, was charged with conducting a propaganda campaign and secret diplomacy in the United States to bring it into the war, as well as engaging in a full range of intelligence operations against Nazi targets in the Western Hemisphere. Stephenson had served with honor in World War I as a fighter pilot. In one encounter Stephenson's plane was shot down and he was imprisoned in a prisoner-of-war camp from which he escaped.

After the war Stephenson became a millionaire from his patenting of a machine that made it possible for the radio transmission of photographs. From there he expanded into a number of other business ventures, including steel mills. When World War II broke out he used this knowledge to help British intelligence and took part in a failed sabotage mission. British intelligence next asked him to serve as a liaison with American officials in order to ferret out German espionage and sabotage programs in the United States. When his efforts to work with Federal Bureau of Investigation Director J. Edgar Hoover produced few positive results, Stephenson turned his attention to one of President Franklin Roosevelt's many confidants, William "Wild Bill" Donovan.

He accompanied Donovan on a trip to London in 1940. Donovan was evaluating the strategic situation in Europe and the Mediterranean for Roosevelt. Bad weather delayed the flight from Bermuda for eight days and Stephenson used the time to press his case for a centralized civilian intelligence agency that would engage in covert action, espionage, and analysis. Donovan proved to be far more receptive to Stephenson's message than had Hoover and he produced a report for Roosevelt urging the creation of such an organization. Donovan's proposal led to the creation first of the Office of the Coordinator of Information and then the OSS. Stephenson worked closely with these bodies in order to provide them with the necessary skills to carry out their missions and to ensure that their activities were consistent with British objectives. At war's end Stephenson went back into private business. He was knighted in 1945 and also received the U.S. Medal of Merit.

See also: Donovan, Major General William Joseph; Office of Strategic Services

References and Further Reading

Stevenson, William. *A Man Called Intrepid*. New York: Ballantine, 1976.
Troy, Thomas. *Wild Bill and Intrepid: Donovan, Stephenson, and the Origins of the CIA*. New Haven, CT: Yale University Press, 1996.

Glenn P. Hastedt

STRAIGHT, MICHAEL WHITNEY (SEPTEMBER 1, 1916–JANUARY 4, 2004)

Michael Whitney Straight was a member of a wealthy American family. He was to be an American student at Cambridge University in the mid-1930s when he was recruited by Anthony Blunt as an agent for the Soviet Committee for State Security (KGB). The Cambridge group was composed mainly of homosexuals according to his biography, *After Long Silence* (1983).

On December 28, 1936, John Cornford, a close friend of Straight, was killed while fighting in the Spanish civil war with a Communist unit. Following the instructions of Anthony Burgess, who was relaying KGB orders, Straight broke with the Communists and returned to the United States. He was to later claim that that was the end of his work with the KGB. However, the break is believed to have been a pretense because he returned to the United States to become an agent of influence and an agent provocateur.

In 1963 Straight applied for a job with the federal government. Fearing that a background check by the Federal Bureau of Investigation (FBI) would reveal his secret past, he made a full disclosure of his espionage activities. He named Anthony Blunt and others as members of the Cambridge spy ring.

Straight worked in the Roosevelt and Nixon administrations. He headed various private organizations, and was editor of *The New Republic*. His claim that he was only a agent for the KGB while at Cambridge have been seriously questioned because of files released in Moscow after the collapse of the Soviet Union, the testimony of other KGB agents and by evidence gathered by the FBI.

See also: Blunt, Anthony; Federal Bureau of Investigation (FBI); KGB (Komitet Gosudarstvennoi Bezopasnosti)

References and Further Reading

Perry, Roland. *Last of the Cold War Spies: The Life of Michael Straight, the Only American in Britain's Cambridge Spy Ring*. Cambridge, MA: Da Capo Press, 2005.
Straight, Michael. *After Long Silence*. New York: Norton, 1983.

Andrew J. Waskey

STRATEGIC SERVICES UNIT

The Strategic Services Unit was the operational arm of the Office of Strategic Services (OSS), which was transferred to the Department of War after World War II. On September 20, 1945, President Harry S. Truman issued Executive Order 9621, effective on October 1, disbanding the OSS, the wartime U.S. intelligence, espionage, and sabotage agency. The OSS, except for the Research and Analysis Branch, which was transferred to the Department of State, was placed under the authority of the Department of War and renamed the Strategic Services Unit (SSU). Brigadier General John Magruder, deputy director for intelligence of the OSS, was designated as the director of the SSU. Although the SSU cut its personnel and budget for special operations and paramilitary functions that were not necessary in peacetime, it still played a very important role. Assistant Secretary of War John J. McCloy directed Magruder to retain the secret intelligence capability that the OSS had developed during the war.

On January 22, 1946, President Truman issued a directive that created the National Intelligence Authority (NIA) comprising of the secretaries of state, war, and navy and the president's personal representative. He also established under the NIA the post of Director of Central Intelligence (DCI) and the Central Intelligence Group (CIG), the immediate predecessor organization of the Central Intelligence Agency. As the U.S. postwar intelligence system gradually emerged, Magruder insisted that the SSU should be incorporated by the CIG as the basis of clandestine intelligence procurement during peacetime. DCI Sidney William Souers, accepting Magruder's assertion, established a committee, named the Fortier Committee, after its Chairman Colonel Louis J. Fortier, to study the disposition of the SSU. That committee essentially approved Magruders' insistence and recommended that the CIG should take over the SSU.

The NIA authorized DCI Hoyt Sanford Vandenberg, who succeeded Souers on June 10, 1946, to conduct all federal espionage and counterespionage outside the U.S. Vandenberg followed this instruction and established the Office of Special Operations in the CIG on July 11, 1946. The SSU was absorbed by the office and became the nucleus of American secret intelligence and counterintelligence activities. The SSU was officially abolished on October 19, 1946.

See also: Central Intelligence Agency; Central Intelligence Group; National Intelligence Authority; Office of Special Operations; Office of Strategic Services

References and Further Reading

Darling, Arthur B. *The Central Intelligence Agency: An Instrument of Government to 1950.* University Park, PA: The Pennsylvania State University Press, 1990.

Rudgers, David F. *Creating the Secret State: The Origins of the Central Intelligence Agency, 1943–1947.* Lawrence, KS: University of Kansas Press, 2000.

Troy, Thomas F. *Donovan and the CIA: A History of the Establishment of the Central Intelligence Agency.* Frederick, MD: University Publications of America, 1981.

Warner, Michael. "Salvage and Liquidation: The Creation of the Central Intelligence Group," *Studies in Intelligence* 39 (1996), 11–20.

Naoki Ohno

STRONG, MAJOR GENERAL KENNETH W. D. (1900–1982)

Kenneth W. D. Strong was the head of British intelligence working for General Dwight Eisenhower in World War II, later writing his memoirs on how efforts were made to get U.S. and British intelligence to work together during the war.

Kenneth William Dobson Strong was born on September 9, 1900, and educated at Montrose Academy, Glenalmond, and the Royal Military College at Sandhurst. He was commissioned as second lieutenant in the Royal Scots Fusiliers. In 1935 he was a member of the Saar Force and held a number of positions in Germany, France, Italy, and Spain, learning to speak German, French, Italian, and Spanish, qualifying as an interpreter in all four languages.

In 1942 Strong was appointed to be head of intelligence of the Home Forces and then attached to the forces of Eisenhower in North Africa in early 1943. At the end of 1943 when Eisenhower became supreme commander of Allied forces in Europe, he asked whether Strong could be seconded as his chief intelligence officer. This request was turned down by General Sir Alan Brooke, chief of the Imperial General Staff, whereupon Eisenhower approached Churchill who agreed. This saw Strong serving in Sicily, Italy, France, and then Germany.

From 1945 until 1947 Strong was director general of the Political Intelligence Department at the British Foreign Office, and from 1948 until 1964 was first director of the Joint Intelligence Bureau at the Ministry of Defence. He was the first director-general of Intelligence at the Ministry of Defence from 1964 until his retirement from the security services two years later, whereupon he became a director of Philip Hill Investment Trust and Eagle Star Insurance.

See also: American Intelligence, World War II

References and Further Reading

Brown, Anthony Cave. *The Secret Servant: The Life of Sir Stewart Menzies, Churchill's Spymaster.* London: Michael Joseph, 1988.

Eisenhower, David. *Eisenhower: At War, 1943–1945.* New York: Random House, 1986.

Strong, Sir Kenneth. *Intelligence at the Top: The Recollections of a British Intelligence Officer.* Garden City, NY: Doubleday, 1968.

Justin Corfield

STUDEMAN, ADMIRAL WILLIAM O.
(JANUARY 16, 1940–)

Admiral William O. Studeman served as director of the National Security Agency (NSA) from August 1988 to April 1992, a period that included Operations Desert Storm and Desert Shield. He assumed this position after having served from 1985 to 1988 as Director of Naval Intelligence. At NSA, Studeman replaced Army Lieutenant General William E. Odom, who had a stormy tenure as director. At NSA Odom is credited with being an innovative manager and as one who took steps to improve bilateral cooperation between NSA and the Central Intelligence Agency (CIA) and cared about community wide management issues.

Upon leaving NSA, Studeman became Deputy Director of Central Intelligence. He held this position from April 9, 1992, to July 3, 1995. Twice during this period he became acting director of Central Intelligence. The first time was from January 21 to February 5, 1993, following the departure of Robert Gates, and the second time from January 11 to May 9, 1995, following the departure of R. James Woolsey.

Studeman was born on January 16, 1940, in Brownsville, Texas. He graduated in 1962 from the University of the South and went on to receive a graduate degree from George Washington University and attended both the Naval War College and National War College. He began his naval career in 1963 when he was commissioned an ensign. He would rise through the ranks and become commanding officer at the Navy Operational Intelligence Center in 1982.

Studeman retired from the navy in 1995. In retirement Studeman entered private business as a consultant and executive. He served as vice president and deputy general manager for intelligence and information superiority of Northrop Grumman Mission Systems. On February 6, 2004, President George W. Bush appointed Studeman to the Commission on Intelligence Capabilities of the United States Regarding Weapons of Mass Destruction.

See also: National Security Agency

References and Further Reading

Bamford, James. *Body of Secrets: Anatomy of the Ultra Secret National Security Agency.* New York: Anchor, 2002.

Garthoff, Douglas. *Directors of Central Intelligence as Leaders of the U.S. Intelligence Community, 1946–2005.* Washington, DC; Center for the Study of Intelligence, Central Intelligence Agency, 2005.

Glenn P. Hastedt

STUDIES AND OBSERVATION GROUP

The Studies and Observation Group was a covert joint service (U.S. Army, Navy, Air Force, and Marine Corps) unconventional warfare task force that conducted highly secret operations and covert intelligence gathering throughout Southeast Asia during the Vietnam War.

MACV Special Operations Group (SOG) was established on January 24, 1964, as a subordinate command under the direction of the special assistant for Counterinsurgency and Special Activities (SACSA) at the Pentagon. SOG was charged with conducting covert operations against North Vietnam, Laos, and Cambodia, which had formerly been controlled by the Central Intelligence Agency (CIA). The name of the organization, which had been meant to serve as a cover for its covert nature, was changed to Studies and Observation Group in late 1964 because the original name was too close to the unit's actual mission.

As a counterpart to SOG, the South Vietnamese established the Special Exploitation Service in 1964; this was later renamed the Strategic Technical Service early in 1965, and the Strategic Technical Directorate (STD) late in 1967.

SOG headquarters was in Saigon, but the organization used bases scattered throughout South Vietnam and, from 1966 onward, at Nakhon Phanom in Thailand.

SOG was commanded by U.S. Army colonels from Special Forces. Colonel Clyde Russell became the first commander of SOG in January 1964. The task force consisted of about 2,000 U.S. personnel, including Special Forces–qualified army personnel, Air Force 90th Special Operations Wing personnel, Navy SEALs, and Marine Corps force recon personnel. The organization also included 8,000 indigenous South Vietnamese and Montagnard troops.

SOG was divided into a number of different groups: (1) Psychological Studies Group, operating out of Hue and Tay Ninh, made false radio broadcasts from powerful transmitters; (2) Air Studies Group, complete with UH-1F "Green Hornet" and H-34 helicopters, a C-130 squadron, and a C-123 squadron, specialized in dropping and recovering special intelligence groups into Laos, Cambodia, and North Vietnam; (3) Maritime Studies Group concentrated its efforts on commando raids along the North Vietnamese coast and in the Mekong Delta; and (4) Ground Studies Group, which carried out the greatest number of missions, including ambushes and raids, monitoring the location of American POWs, assassinations, kidnapping, rescue of airmen downed in enemy territory, long-range reconnaissance patrols, training and dispatching agents into North Vietnam, and harassment and booby-trapping of enemy infiltration routes and ammunition supply facilities along the Ho Chi Minh Trail in Laos and Cambodia.

In 1968, SOG reorganized its ground strike elements into three field commands: Command and Control Central (CCC) in Kontum, Command and Control North (CCN) in Da Nang, and Command and Control South (CCS) in Ban Me Thuot. CCC was responsible for classified unconventional warfare operations throughout the tri-border region of Laos, Cambodia, and Vietnam. CCN was responsible for special unconventional warfare missions into Laos and North Vietnam. CCS was responsible for clandestine unconventional warfare operations inside VC-dominated South Vietnam and throughout Cambodia.

In March 1971, MACV-SOG's CCN, CCC, and CCS were redesignated as Elements 1, 2, and 3, respectively, of MACV Advisory Team 158, charged with advising the South Vietnamese Strategic Technical Directorate. MACV-SOG was deactivated on April 30, 1972; MACV-SOG personnel earned a total of six Medals of Honor during the fighting in Southeast Asia.

See also: Vietnam War and Intelligence Operations

References and Further Reading

Conboy, Kenneth, and Dale Andrade. *Spies and Commandos: How America Lost the Secret War in North Vietnam*. Lawrence, KS: University Press of Kansas, 2001.

Plaster, John L. *SOG: The Secret Wars of America's Commandos in Vietnam*. New York: Simon & Schuster, 1997.

Shultz, Richard H., Jr. *The Secret War Against Hanoi*. New York: Harper Collins, 1999.

Simpson, Charles M. *Inside the Green Berets: The First Thirty Years*. Novato, CA: Presidio Press, 1983.

Singlaub, John, and Malcolm McConnell. *Hazardous Duty*. New York: Simon & Schuster, 1991.

Stanton, Shelby. *Green Berets at War*. Novato, CA: Presidio Press, 1985.

Veith, George. *Code Name Bright Light*. New York: Free Press, 1998.

James H. Willbanks

SUN-TZU
(544BC–496BC)

Sun Wu tzu is believed to have been a general and the author of *The Art of War*, written during the Period of the Warring States. Recent Chinese archeology has recovered a great many ancient books including a complete copy of *The Art of War* and previously unknown additional chapters.

Sun-tzu describes intelligence work in Chapter 13 of *The Art of War*. For Sun-tzu, intelligence is what wins battles and wars. He identifies five kinds of spies who should be working simultaneously to secure a full knowledge of the enemy. The five kinds of spies are "local spies," "internal spies," "double agents," "expendable spies," and "living spies."

Native agents are spies recruited from among the people of the kingdom being opposed. They spy quite often for money. Internal agents are spies recruited from among the officials of the kingdom being opposed. They are willing to commit treason because they have been passed over for promotion, punished for wrong doing, or have some other kind of grievance. They are usually kept loyal with money. They can provide detailed intelligence on what is happening in the councils of the kingdom. They can also act as agents of influence. Double agents are enemy spies who have agreed to spy against their own country. Turning them into double agents is often easily done by bribery. Expendable agents are sent out as decoys or with disinformation. When caught, they usually give up the false information, believing it to be true and are then executed. Living agents are those who successfully complete their mission and then return alive to report.

See also: American Intelligence, World War I; American Intelligence, World War II; Civil War Intelligence; Cold War Intelligence; Early Republic and Espionage; Post–Cold War Intelligence; Spanish-American War; Terrorist Groups and Intelligence; Vietnam War and Intelligence Operations

References and Further Reading

Andrew, Christopher, and Jeremy Noakes. *Intelligence and International Relations, 1900–1945*. Exeter, UK: University of Exeter, 1987.

Sun-tzu. *The Art of War*. Translated by Samuel B. Griffith. Oxford: Oxford University, 1963.

Andrew J. Waskey

SURETE GENERALE

Currently, the French intelligence community is divided into two branches: one military and the other civilian. Responsibility for the internal security of France has been assigned to the national gendarmerie and the national police force. The national gendarmerie (military police under the supervision of the Ministry for Defense) is a military police force. It polices about the roughly half of the population of France that lives in the countryside and in small towns. Although administratively a part of the French armed forces, it is operationally attached to the Ministry of the Interior.

Civilian security is the responsibility of the Judicial Police (Direction Centrale Police Judiciaire, DCPJ). The main responsibility of the DCPJ is to combat criminal activity inside of France, including threats to national security.

French police agencies were reorganized in 1966 and even more radically in 1995. One motive for the reorganization was the need to overcome the bitter legacy of mistrust from World War II in which the Vichy cooperated with the Nazis and the Resistance fought against them. The cold war and the war in Algeria had only worsened tensions. Today the goal is to organize to meet the needs of domestic and political intelligence especially to combat terrorism.

The La Sûreté Nationale is the former name of the Direction Générale de la Police Nationale (National Police). It operates under the authority of the Ministry of the Interior and exercises general law enforcement in the cities and large towns. Within the National Police, specialized groups engage in security operations. The Central Headquarters for Surveillance of the Territory (Direction de la Surveillance du Territoire) gathers intelligence on organizations located outside of France that are potential security risks.

The General Intelligence Central Service (Direction Centrale des Renseignenments Généreaux), or RG, is the main counterintelligence agency. It combats threats posed by organizations or individuals located inside of France. The director of the RG reports to the Minister of the Interior. The Direction de la Surveillance du Territoire (DST) is a directorate of the French National Police. It conducts both intelligence and counterintelligence operations. Much of its work is economic counterintelligence that seeks to prevent the theft of French technology.

The National Police can trace its history to the Comité De Sûreté Générale, which was created by the National Convention as a tool of French Revolutionary justice in 1792. It was used by the Committee of Public Safety during the Reign of Terror. Napoleon took control of police forces and used them for his own purposes. His successors followed suit. Among their activities were keeping a cabinet B (list of people to be arrested in time of war) and a cabinet noire in the French post office reading private correspondences.

See also: Cold War Intelligence

References and Further Reading

Polisar, Patti. *Inside France's DGSE: The General Directorate for External Security*. New York: The Rosen Publishing Group, 2003.

Porch, Douglas. *The French Secret Services: A History of French Intelligence from the Dreyfus Affair to the Gulf War*. New York: Farrar, Straus and Giroux, 1995.

Andrew J. Waskey

SUVOROV, VICTOR
(APRIL 20, 1947–)

Pseudonym of Vladimir Rezun, Victor Suvorov was a major in Soviet Military Intelligence (GRU), prominent defector, and author of several books on Soviet intelligence and World War II. Suvorov received his nickname in the army because of his reputation as a know-it-all; the original, Field Marshal Alexander V. Suvorov (1729–1800) is regarded as one of Russia's greatest military commanders. Suvorov spent most of his career providing support for intelligence operations, although he was occasionally given the opportunity for more serious work such as recruiting agents. In 1978 Suvorov became involved in a scandal at his embassy; fearing that he was to be recalled to Moscow, he defected to Great Britain. Suvorov published *Inside the Aquarium* in 1985; the title refers to the glass and steel headquarters of the GRU called the *aquarium* by its inhabitants, a selective account of his career notable for its relentless championing of the GRU at the expense of the KGB. Suvorov is most famous for his revisionist historical writings such as *Icebreaker*, published in 1990, which reject the traditional viewpoint that the Nazi invasion of Russia caught the Soviet army in a critical state of confusion and disarray. Instead, Suvorov claims that the Red Army was in a high state of preparedness, organized in an offensive posture, and poised to strike into Western Europe. Stalin, Suvorov suggests, hoped to create the conditions for European-wide revolutions, defeat a weakened Germany, and dominate all of continental Europe. Only Hitler's premature invasion, catching the Red Army in an offensive rather than defensive posture, thwarted Stalin's plans. Most historians reject Suvorov's claims, citing the disastrous effects of the purges on the military command structure, the poor moral of the troops, and the inability of the army to properly organize itself as the reasons for the early German victories.

See also: GRU (Main Intelligence Directorate)

References and Further Reading

Suvorov, Victor. *Icebreaker*. London: Hamish Hamilton, 1990.
Suvorov, Victor. *Inside the Aquarium*. New York: MacMillan, 1985.

Vernon L. Pedersen

T

TALLMADGE, MAJOR BENJAMIN (FEBRUARY 25, 1754–MARCH 7, 1835)

Major Benjamin Tallmadge was intelligence chief for General George Washington during the War of American Independence. Born on February 25, 1754, in Setauket, Long Island, New York, Tallmadge was educated at Yale College. In 1776 he enlisted as a lieutenant in Colonel John Chester's Connecticut regiment, and rose to the rank of major in the Continental Light Dragoons. General George Washington chose him in 1778 to head American military intelligence services and spy on the British army in New York City and on Long Island.

To affect this service, Tallmadge organized the Culper Spy Ring, recruiting childhood friends from Setauket. Robert Townsend (Culper Junior) a merchant and society reporter for James Rivington's *Royal Gazette* gathered information in the city. Austin Roe carried this unsifted evidence to Abraham Woodhull (Culper Senior) at Setauket. Woodhull digested it and passed it to Caleb Brewster, who conveyed it by whaleboat across Long Island Sound to Tallmadge at Fairfield, Connecticut. Tallmadge then dispatched it by dragoon couriers to Washington's headquarters at New Windsor, New York.

Tallmadge and his spies provided Washington with valuable information on enemy troop movements, numbers, and morale. In 1780 they warned Washington of an impending British attack on Rhode Island, and allowed him to foil it. Also in 1780 Tallmadge helped capture the British spy, John André. He died on March 7, 1835, in Litchfield, Connecticut.

See also: American Revolution and Intelligence; André, Major John; Rivington, James; Woodhull, Abraham

References and Further Reading

Hall, Charles Swain. *Benjamin Tallmadge: Revolutionary Soldier and American Businessman.* New York: Columbia University Press, 1943.

Pennypacker, Morton. *General Washington's Spies on Long Island and in New York.* Brooklyn, NY: Long Island Historical Society, 1939.

Tallmadge, Benjamin. *Memoir of Col. Benjamin Tallmadge, Prepared by Himself, at the Request of His Children.* New York: T. Holman, 1858.

Paul David Nelson

TALLEYRAND-PÉRIGORD, CHARLES MAURICE DE (FEBRUARY 2, 1754–MAY 17, 1838)

Talleyrand was a French diplomat who served under Napoleon Bonaparte. Born February 2, 1754, in Paris, France, he pursued a career in religion because a childhood foot injury prevented him from joining the military service. In 1789, Talleyrand was appointed bishop of Autun.

Elected to the Estates-General in 1789, he favored a constitutional monarchy and signed the Declaration of Rights. Three years later, Talleyrand was elected president of the National Assembly, where he gained popular support for proposing that the government take control of church property to pay for the nation's debts. His actions caused Pope Pious VI to excommunicate him from the Catholic Church.

In 1792, Talleyrand traveled to England on a diplomatic mission to avert war between the two nations. While aboard, the French Revolution took a radical turn and he was exiled as a royalist supporter. After remaining in England for two years, he fled to the United States.

In September 1796, Talleyrand returned to France. The following year he became Minister of Foreign Affairs. During the XYZ Affair, Talleyrand demanded a bribe and a loan from American commissioners Charles C. Pinckney, John Marshall, and Elbridge Gerry to open negotiations regarding French privateers seizing American merchant vessels.

Allying himself with Napoleon Bonaparte, Talleyrand assisted in overthrowing the directory and replacing it with the consulate. By 1803, Napoleon had lost interest in establishing an American empire, so Talleyrand negotiated with American diplomats James Monroe and Robert Livingston to sell the entire Louisiana Territory to the United States for $15 million.

In 1807, Talleyrand resigned as foreign minister and came to oppose Napoleon's conquests as injurious to France and European peace. Following the abdication of Napoleon in 1814, Talleyrand was instrumental in the restoration of the Bourbons to the French throne. Serving as one of the chief French negotiators at the Congress of Vienna in 1815, he reestablished France's 1792 boundaries.

After 1815, the Bourbon court excluded Talleyrand from public affairs. By 1830, he supported the establishment of a constitutional monarchy under Louis Philippe. Under the new regime, Talleyrand served as ambassador of Great Britain from 1830 until 1834. Talleyrand died on May 17, 1838.

See also: Early Republic and Espionage; XYZ Affair

References and Further Reading

Bernard, Jack F. *Talleyrand: A Biography*. New York: Putnam, 1973.

Brinton, Crane. *The Lives of Talleyrand*. New York: Norton, 1936.

McCabe, Joseph. *Talleyrand: A Biographical Study*. London: Hutchinson and Co., 1906.

Kevin M. Brady

TAYLOR, CAPTAIN DANIEL M.

Captain Daniel M. Taylor helped pioneer organized military intelligence in the United States. He served as the first effective head of the Military Intelligence Division. In the years after the U.S. Civil War, logistical constraints continued to insulate the United States from any possible European invasion. Nevertheless, Canada (under British control) was a potential springboard for invasion.

In 1885, U.S.-British relations were severely strained over disputes about fishing rights and the position of the Alaskan boundary. Both nations seized vessels of the other nation before the crisis was ended by arbitration. During the crisis, Brigadier General R. C. Drum, adjutant to the secretary of war, wanted information about the potential enemy, but because the United States still lacked a General Staff, little was readily available. The Division of Military Information was organized under Major William Volkmar to collect information on Canada.

Captain Daniel M. Taylor, an ordinance officer, was moved to Drum's office in April 1886 and in August he was selected for a reconnaissance mission of the Canadian border. Traveling in an indirect route from Washington, DC, to Canada through the Great Lakes, he examined the Welland Canal, and the cities of Kingston, Ottawa, Montreal, and Quebec. Taylor's report came in October. It recommended that, in the event of war, the United States should capture Canadian canals rather than destroy them and antagonize the local inhabitants. He also urged that more reconnaissance be made, particularly on the Pacific coast.

His report impressed his superiors, and when the War Department established a more autonomous Military Information Division (MID) on April 12, 1889, Taylor was selected to lead it. As the head of MID until 1892, he worked to implement his suggestions.

See also: Army Intelligence; Civil War Intelligence; Early Republic and Espionage

References and Further Reading

Angevine, Robert G. "Mapping the Northern Frontier: Canada and the Origins of the U.S. Army's Military Information Division, 1885–1898," *Intelligence and National Security* 16:3 (2001), 121–145.

Bethel, Elizabeth. "The Military Information Division: Origin of the Intelligence Division," *Military Affairs* 11:1 (1947), 17–24.

Bidwell, Bruce W. *History of the Military Intelligence Division, Division of the Army General Staff. 1.* Frederick, MD: University Publications of America, 1986.

Nicholas M. Sambaluk

TELEVISION—ESPIONAGE SHOWS ON

In the mid- to late-twentieth century, Americans became fascinated with the secret agent; this is evident by the vast number of television shows and movies depicting espionage and those involved in it. Espionage shows began on television in the early 1950s during the Red Scare and McCarthyism; however, the spy craze actually hit television sets in the early 1960s and held on tightly until the late 1960s to early 1970s. The craze faded in the mid-1970s and 1980s but made a strong reemergence at the very end of twentieth century and into the twenty-first century.

Many of the predecessors to the spy shows of the 1950s and beyond came from radio shows or books. Radio spy shows date back to the 1930s. Espionage found a new media with the advent of the television into Americans' homes. The earliest espionage shows debuted in 1951 with *Doorway to Danger* (also known as *Door with No Name*), *Dangerous Assignment*, and *Foreign Intrigue*. None of those, however, matched the success of *I Led 3 Lives*.

I Led 3 Lives ran from 1953 to 1956 and was based on the life of Herbert Philbrick. Philbrick was a FBI agent who had infiltrated the American Communist Party and was leading essentially three lives: citizen, FBI agent, and Communist. Philbrick's book, by the same title released in 1952, inspired the television show. The FBI supported *I Led 3 Lives* and was even said to be highly regarded by J. Edgar Hoover.

I Led 3 Lives was part of a genre called documentary melodrama which consisted of mixing fact with fiction. This genre describes most early spy shows. *I Led 3 Lives* not only served as anti-Communist propaganda but also reinforced gender roles similar to the other sitcoms of the time that were also set in suburbia.

In the late 1950s spy shows were still visible on television (*Behind Closed Doors* and *World of Giants*) but were unsuccessful at obtaining an audience. It was not until the first James Bond film, *Dr. No*, was released in 1962 that audiences everywhere would be intrigued by the exciting and mysterious lifestyles of spies.

British author Ian Fleming created the first Bond novel in 1953 entitled *Casino Royale*. His novels, and the films that resulted from them, inspired the spy genre that many are familiar with today. This genre started in the 1960s with the first major spy series, *The Man from United Network Command for Law and Enforcement*, or commonly known as *The Man from U.N.C.L.E.*

The Man from U.N.C.L.E., which ran from 1964 to 1968, was about two agents, Napoleon Solo and Illya Kuryakin, trying to stop the organization THRUSH from achieving world domination. It teams a Westerner and a Russian who join forces to stop a common enemy, which was daring considering it was during the cold war. Ian Fleming came up with the title character's name but was later prohibited from further involvement due to legal issues (a villain in *Goldfinger*, a Bond movie in production, was named Solo as well). *The Man from U.N.C.L.E.* was not a big hit from the start but after it took off it become a cultural phenomenon. It even had a spin-off *The Girl from U.N.C.L.E.* *The Girl from U.N.C.L.E.* could not match the success of its predecessor and only lasted one season (1966).

I Spy, which debuted in 1965, was a hip spy show about two undercover agents—one disguised as a tennis player and the other his trainer played by Robert Culp and Bill Cosby, respectively. In the midst of the civil rights movement, *I Spy* showcased an

Don Adams (Maxwell Smart) stars in the popular comedic spy television show *Get Smart*. (Photofest)

African-American in a leading role equal to that of his white costar. This drew such controversy that several markets in the South refused to air the premiere episode. *I Spy* went on to have a three-year run.

Some felt this spy craze was getting too intense and needed some humor. *Get Smart* did just that in 1965. *Get Smart* was a parody of the whole spy genre. It ran from 1965 to 1969 on NBC and was picked up for one last season in 1970 by CBS. The opposite of James Bond, clumsy Agent 86 (also known as Maxwell Smart, played by Don Adams), is paired up with Agent 99 (Barbara Feldon). Both are operatives of "Control," a top-secret counterspy agency located in Washington, DC whose mission it was to stop the evil forces of Kaos, an organization whose goal was to foment worldwide unrest and revolution. This show would feature silly gadgets such as the shoe phone that Agent 86 would use to communicate with the Chief (Ed Platt) to poke fun at the shows that seriously used sophisticated gadgets to achieve their goals. It not only poked fun at the spy genre but even at the government. Some of the plotlines and events of the show became so realistic that they were investigated by government agents. Mel Brooks, a writer for the series, feels that the show was such a success because of the way authority was portrayed; in a very comedic way at a time when authority was being questioned.

Westerns were immensely popular at this time so why not incorporate aspects of both espionage shows and Westerns to make a television show. The result of this combination was *The Wild Wild West* (1965–1969). *The Wild Wild West* featured two Secret Service agents, James West (Robert Conrad) and Artemus Gordon (Ross Martin). They took their orders from Ulysses S. Grant, the president of the United States, and scuffled with villains in the American frontier.

Mission: Impossible (1966–1973) was different from any other show on TV at the time, with its suspenseful intricate plots. It won numerous Emmy Awards and ran for seven seasons on CBS, making it the longest-running spy series on American television. Characters and actors on *Mission: Impossible* were constantly changing and each mission relied heavily on teamwork (as opposed to the movies by the same released in the late twentieth century and early twenty-first century with Tom Cruise as the lead character that focused on individualism, action, and high-tech gadgets).

The very British import *The Avengers* debuted on American television in 1966. It featured two secret agents John Steed (Patrick Macnee), with his trademark bowler hat and umbrella, and Diana Rigg as Emma Peel (1966–1967). Diana Rigg was neither the first nor the last to fulfill the role of Steed's partner; the show went through several costars throughout its run. An attempt was made to revive the success of *The Avengers* in the 1970s with the short-lived *The New Avengers* (1976–1977).

Espionage shows in the 1970s and 1980s were not innovative but rather used old formats and updated the technology or reunited stars from the original shows. In the 1990s, however, there was a shift to the unexplainable. TV science fiction programs became popular and many elements from that genre merged into the spy genre creating spy-fi. An example of this merge would be *The X-Files*.

The X-Files featured Dana Scully (Gillian Anderson) and Fox Mulder (David Duchovny) as two FBI agents investigating cases of phenomena, such as aliens and mutants. *The X-Files* enjoyed a successful nine-year run starting in 1993 and has created a cult following. This illustrates that women were featured in more active roles in 1990s spy shows. Another example could be *La Femme Nikita* (also known as simply *Nikita*), which aired from 1997 to 2001 and featured Peta Wilson as Nikita, secret agent and assassin.

Espionage shows made a strong comeback in the opening of the twenty-first century. In the 2001 fall season three new spy shows appeared on three different networks; *Alias* on ABC, *24* on Fox, and *The Agency* on CBS. This reemergence of spy mania coincided, ironically, with the September 11 attacks on the United States.

Alias centers on Sydney Bristow (Jennifer Garner), a college student turned spy for a "secret" CIA organization. She finds out that the organization is not part of the CIA at all but rather an enemy of the CIA. Sydney then becomes a double agent. *Alias* had a strong following and lasted until May 2006.

As of early 2007, *24* was starting its sixth season. Jack Bauer (Kiefer Sutherland) is part of an elite CIA organization whose mission is to stop terrorism. With an interesting format, each season of *24* covers a 24-hour period. Twenty-four has received numerous nominations and has won countless awards including a Golden Globe in 2003 for Best Television Series-Drama, and an Emmy for Outstanding Drama Series in 2006. *The Agency* (CBS) produced a breakthrough of sorts when for the first time the CIA allowed scenes for the series to be partially filmed on its premises. *The Agency* attempted to deal with CIA agents and terrorism in a realistic way. It was also meant to portray the CIA in a positive light. *The Agency*, despite its potential, could not meet the success of either *Alias* or *24*. The fantasy elements of *Alias* and the unusual format of *24* edged out the realism of *The Agency*, which ended its run in 2003.

Espionage television shows continue to fascinate American audiences. With reruns and the popularity of television series becoming available on DVDs, new generations are now discovering the older spy shows such as *Get Smart* and *I Spy*. Espionage on television continues to evolve with the times. It is clear, however, that spy shows have become embedded in American popular culture.

See also: American Communist Party; Central Intelligence Agency; CHAOS; Federal Bureau of Investigation (FBI); Fiction—Spy Novels; Hoover, J. Edgar; Movies, Spies in

References and Further Reading

Biederman, Danny. *The Incredible World of Spy-Fi: Wild and Crazy Spy Gadgets, Props, and Artifacts from TV and the Movies.* San Francisco: Chronicle Books, 2004.

Britton, Wesley. *Beyond Bond: Spies in Fiction and Film.* Westport, CT: Praeger Publishers, 2005.

Britton, Wesley. *Spy Television.* Westport, CT: Praeger Publishers, 2004.

Kackman, Michael. *Citizen Spy: Television, Espionage and Cold War Culture.* Minneapolis: University of Minnesota Press, 2005.

Lisanti, Tom, and Louis Paul. *Film Fatales: Women in Espionage Films and Television, 1962–1973.* Jefferson, NC: McFarland & Co., 2002.

Miller, Toby. *Spyscreen: Espionage on Film and TV from the 1930s to the late 1960s.* Oxford: Oxford University Press, 2003.

Vanessa de los Reyes

TENENBAUM, DAVID

David Tenenbaum was an engineer employed by the U.S. Army Tank-Automotive and Armaments Command. From July 1992 to February 1997 he was investigated by the Federal Bureau of Investigation (FBI) on six different allegations of having provided Israel with classified information over a 10-year period. In February 1998 the U.S. Attorney's Office declined to bring charges against Tenenbaum because of insufficient evidence. Nonetheless, based on the results of a polygraph test, Tenenbaum lost access to classified information in 1997 and his security clearance was revoked in February 2000 because of these allegations. In 2003 his personnel security clearance was restored and upgraded.

Tenenbaum maintained that he was singled out for suspicion and unfair treatment, including a fabricated confession and harassment of himself and his family due to his religion. In October 1998 Tenenbaum initiated legal action against the U.S. Army, asserting that he was the subject of irregular and unequal treatment by army and Defense Investigative Service employees. The case was dismissed because the relevant evidence was classified as secret and could not be revealed. In January 2000 Tenenbaum again brought suit against the army, arguing that his civil rights had been violated. This case was also dismissed on the basis of the non-justiciability of security clearance remedies regarding the alleged civil rights violations.

Subsequently, in March 2006 Senator Carl Levin (D-MI) requested an investigation into the handling of Tenenbaum's case by the Office of the Inspector General in the Department of Defense. Its 55-page report produced in July 2008 found that Tenenbaum was the subject of inappropriate treatment by army and Defense Investigative Service officials who failed to follow established policies and procedures for conducting personnel security investigations and counterintelligence allegations. The report also concluded that Tenenbaum's religion was a factor that led to the inappropriate behavior stating that "but for Mr. Tenenbaum's religion, the investigations would likely have taken a different course." The actions taken by the government were defined as fitting a definition of discrimination. The inspector general's report was limited in scope to reviewing the actions of Defense Department officials and did not examine the actions of FBI or Justice Department officials.

See also: Federal Bureau of Investigation (FBI); Post–Cold War Intelligence

References and Further Reading

Inspector General, Department of Defense. *Review of the Case of Mr. David Tenenbaum, Department of the Army Employee.* July 13, 2008.

Raviv, Dan, and Yossi Melman. *Every Prince a Spy: The Complete History of Israel's Intelligence Community.* Boston: Houghton Mifflin, 1990.

Glenn P. Hastedt

TENET, GEORGE
(JANUARY 5, 1953–)

George Tenet was the 18th Director of Central Intelligence (DCI). He served under Bill Clinton and George W. Bush from July 11, 1997, to July 11, 2004. Prior to that Tenet served as acting director of Central Intelligence and Deputy Director of Intelligence. Tenet was born in Flushing, New York, and graduated with a masters in international affairs from Columbia University in 1978. Upon graduation, he went to work for the American Hellenic Institute in Washington, DC. Both of his parents were Greek immigrants and in a Greek-American lobbying organization. In 1982 Tenet became a legislative aide to Senator John Heinz (R-PA) with responsibility for national security issues, among others. After three years in this position he moved on to become a staff member of the Senate Select Committee on Intelligence and served as staff director from 1988 to 1993. Tenet was a member of President Bill Clinton's national security transition team and held the position of special assistant to the president and Senior Direct for Intelligence Programs, National Security Council in the new administration. It was from this position that he was appointed Deputy Director of Intelligence.

Tenet is described as a Washington insider, someone who throughout his career was capable of working with both Republicans and Democrats. He developed a strong loyalty to those he worked with whether they were senators, intelligence professionals, or the president. He was a member of the "war cabinet" and briefed the president personally almost every day on intelligence matters. His loyalty to the president shown when he took public responsibility for the questionable intelligence used in justifying the Iraq War.

As DCI, Tenet expressed an initial desire to return the Central Intelligence Agency (CIA) to its core missions. He sought to move away from risky covert operations and paramilitary undertakings. Tenet reemphasized human intelligence collection, increasing by tenfold the number of CIA officers undergoing training to be case officers and work in clandestine collection operations. This does not mean he ignored other areas of intelligence collection. Tenet worked to establish a centralized Measures and Signature Intelligence (MASINT) organization within the Defense Intelligence Agency.

He also merged the Community Open Source Program Office into the Foreign Broadcast Information Service. Finally, Tenet wanted the CIA to focus on its warning function and to move away from soft intelligence questions and back to military-oriented ones. Tenet did not ignore other areas of intelligence collection.

Tenet's tenure as DCI was dominated by the events leading up to and following the terrorist attacks of 9/11. A complex and often contradictory pattern emerges here. Tenet began to focus on Osama bin Laden as a serious national security threat to the United States in 1999. Some came to characterize it as an obsession. Yet, the CIA's institutional response never reached that depth of concern or produced an equivalent level of activity directed at terrorism. Tenet was often cautious in presenting intelligence on bin Laden and Iraq, noting on occasion that it came from a "single thread," meaning that there was no collaborative intelligence. Yet as movement toward war with Iraq intensified he would present intelligence as solid, "a slam dunk," that he would later acknowledge was not accurate and that some of his human intelligence sources had fabricated information and that the CIA should have done a better job assessing its accuracy and reliability.

See also; Bin Laden, Osama; Bush, George W., Administration and Intelligence; Clinton Administration and Intelligence; Post–Cold War Intelligence; September 11, 2001; Terrorist Groups and Intelligence

References and Further Reading
Coll, Steve. *Ghost Wars: The Secret History of the CIA, Afghanistan, and Bin Laden, from the Soviet Invasion to September 10, 2001.* New York: Penguin, 2004.

Garthoff, Douglas. *Directors of Central Intelligence as Leaders of the U.S. Intelligence Community 1946–2005.* Washington, DC: Center for the Study of Intelligence, Central Intelligence Agency, 2005.

Tenet, George. *At the Center of the Storm: My Years at the CIA.* New York: HarperCollins, 2007.

Woodward, Bob. *Bush at War.* New York: Simon & Schuster, 2002.

Glenn P. Hastedt

TERRORIST GROUPS AND INTELLIGENCE

Terrorist groups present a unique intelligence challenge for many reasons, not the least of which is identifying who is a terrorist. In 2003 the United States had at least six different terrorist lists. They included "Foreign Terrorist Organizations," "State-Sponsors of Terrorism," "Special Designated Terrorists," "Specially Designated Global Terrorists," "Specially Designated Nationals and Blocked Persons," and "Terrorist Exclusion List."

Looking beyond their identification, the structure of terrorist groups presents a fundamental intelligence challenge. Unlike states or even international organizations and nongovernmental agencies, terrorist groups lack a clearly defined center of gravity against which to target one's intelligence resources. In place of the clearly defined organizations and routines of governments, one finds a much more fluid structure and modus operandi. This is fully evident in the changes that have taken place in organization and

President George W. Bush is joined by (l–r) Senator Patrick Leahy (with camera), Senator Harry Reid, and Representative James Sensenbrenner as he signs the antiterrorism bill at a White House ceremony on October 26, 2001. (AP/Wide World Photos)

operation of al-Qaeda since 9/11. At the time it was common to equate Osama bin Laden with the head of a hostile government who was directing his country's assets against the United States. Today his role seems far different, more of an enabler and symbolic source of energy than a commanding general. Al-Qaeda is less a central controlling organization than a loosely connected ring of concentric circles. Beyond the core of al-Qaeda central lies a second ring composed of al-Qaeda affiliates who receive training and guidance from the center but operate independently. In a third ring are al-Qaeda locals. Finally in the outermost ring are found homegrown radicals with no direct connection to al-Qaeda but are drawn to it by its ideology and resentment of the West. Each ring presents intelligence with different challenges and opportunities, with the furthest removed rings being the easiest to target for information but also offering the least amount of information on the actions and plans of al-Qaeda per se.

A related challenge for intelligence is identifying the goals of terrorist groups. Terrorism per se is an instrument of policy. It is not limited to any one goal. Knowing that an organization is a terrorist group thus says little about the purposes to which its power will be put. Today's terrorism is the fourth wave of modern global international terrorism. The first, anarchist wave of terrorism began in Russia in the 1880s. A second anti-colonial wave began in the 1920s to be replaced by a third new left wave of terrorism in the 1960s. The current religious wave of terrorism commenced in 1979 and speculation exists that it will run its course by 2025 when still another wave of terrorism will replace it. Thus, unlike most states, terrorist organizations have relatively short lives. They cannot be permanently infiltrated with agents. Monitoring their behavior may allow officials to disrupt their behavior but it will not alert these same officials to the onset of a new wave of terrorism or even the emergence of new groups in an ongoing wave. The situation is complicated even further by the category of state-supported terrorist groups. These groups are seen as allied with states such as Iran and can be viewed as instruments of their foreign policy. As one moves to more self-sufficient and independent terrorist groups this linkage grows weaker. States and terrorist groups now may be allies of convenience but a symmetry of interests cannot be assumed.

The intelligence challenge in dealing with terrorism is heavily dependent on the strategy adopted by policy makers in responding to it. A "war on terrorism" puts intelligence agencies in a context in which the military is the lead instrument of policy. Defining the terrorist threat as a criminal activity moves intelligence into the realm of supporting police work. In each case tactical and strategic intelligence is needed but where the first approach emphasizes intelligence to defeat terrorists, the second definition of the problem stresses intelligence in the context of obeying the rule of law. In a military context everyone is a potential terrorist. In a criminal justice context a clear distinction exists between criminals and others.

The activity of terrorist groups also complicates the intelligence challenge by its blurring of the boundary between domestic and foreign policy. Historically policy makers and citizens have been far more willing to act aggressively to outsiders than they are to their own citizens. Accordingly the techniques used to obtain information abroad have been far more expansive than those used at home. When this distinction is ignored intelligence agencies often become the target of political repercussions when the crisis has passed. This has occurred more than once in the history of U.S. intelligence. In the 1970s revelations about mail openings, electronic surveillance, and the infiltration of antigovernment organizations caused a political outcry and led to passing a series of intelligence reforms. After 9/11 the Bush administration engaged in a warrantless electronic surveillance operation targeted on Americans. Additionally it endorsed the use of a series of harsh interrogation techniques such as waterboarding against non-Americans suspected of being terrorists or supporting terrorism that many held to be acts of torture. As with the 1970s, revelations that the CIA engaged in assassinations these interrogation techniques violated American's image of themselves and produced a backlash.

A final factor complicating intelligence work against terrorist groups is not unique to this particular problem. It lies in the attitude that policy makers have to intelligence. Surprise is not taken as an inherent aspect of international politics. It is something that can be prevented. This view finds expression in the phrase "connecting the dots," implying that if only intelligence had collected the proper information and analyzed it correctly the incident would not have occurred. In doing so they fail to appreciate the extent to which terrorism is a mystery with many possible solutions as opposed to a puzzle with a picture solution known to all before the pieces are assembled into a whole.

See also: Bin Laden, Osama; Bush, George W., Administration and Intelligence; Clinton Administration and Intelligence; National Commission on Terrorist Attacks on the United States (The 9/11 Commission); Post–Cold War Intelligence; September 11, 2001; Special Operations Forces

References and Further Reading

Cronin, Audrey. *The 'FTO List' and Congress: Sanctioning Designated Foreign Terrorist Organizations*. Congressional Research Service Report for Congress RL32120. Washington, DC: Congressional Research Service, October 21, 2003.

Pillar, Paul. "Intelligence," in Audrey Cronin and James Ludes (eds.), *Attacking Terrorism: Elements of a Grand Strategy*, pp. 115–139. Washington, DC: Georgetown University Press, 2004.

Stevenson, Jonathan. "Demilitarizing the War on Terror," *Survival* 48 (2006), 37–54.
"Terrorism Index," *Foreign Policy* 155 (2006), 48–55.

Glenn P. Hastedt

THEREMIN, LEON
(AUGUST 28, 1896–NOVEMBER 3, 1993)

Leon Theremin was born Lev Sergryevich Termen. His studies in electronics led to a pioneering career in music that was overshadowed by Soviet demands for espionage efforts. Drafted into the Russian military during World War I, Theremin was fortunate to be sent to the Petrograd Officers Electro-Technical School as a result of his scientific talents. After the Bolshevik revolution, Lenin noticed these talents. Lenin supported Theremin's invention of the Theremin, a musical instrument named for himself. Most popular in the 1920s, the Theremin helped pioneer electronic music.

Theremin was allowed to leave USSR to travel to the United States, ostensibly a brief visit to demonstrate his new instrument, but actually to also conduct espionage. His stay lasted from 1927 until 1938. Briefly ahead of his competitors in developing television, he was handicapped by Stalin's myopic interest in technology being harnessed as secret weapons. In the 1930s he faced increasing financial worries as his developments failed to garner sufficient investments. Throughout his life, he also pursued a number of romantic interests.

Jan Berzin, his spy contact while outside the USSR, was murdered in Stalin's Purge as a Fascist. Theremin returned to the USSR and was also arrested shortly before the signing of the August 1939 Nazi-Soviet Pact on the same charge. Imprisoned at the Butyrky gold mine manned by slave laborers, he barely survived until being transferred to Central Design Bureau Number 29 (TsKB-29), an NKVD prison for slave labor scientists. He labored at TsKB-29 from 1947 until 1964, first as a slave laborer and later as an employee.

Some of his most notable projects were a bug hidden in the Great Seal in the Spaso House (residence of the American ambassador to USSR). Undetected from 1945 until 1952, the United States announced the existence of the bug in 1960. Under the supervision of the brutal security chief Lavrenti Beria, Theremin also applied a listening system using the reverberations of windows to spy on Josef Stalin. In 1990, Theremin joined the Communist Party.

See also: Cold War Intelligence; NKVD (Narodnyj Komissariat Vnutrennikh Del— Peoples Commissariat for Internal Affairs)

References and Further Reading

Epstein, Edward Jay. *Deception: The Invisible War Between the KGB and the CIA*. New York: Allen, 1989.
Glinsky, Albert. *Theremin: Ether Music and Espionage*. Chicago: University of Illinois Press, 2000.

Nicholas M. Sambaluk

TOWNSEND, ROBERT
(NOVEMBER 25, 1753–MARCH 7, 1828)

Member of the Culper Spy Ring in New York and on Long Island during the War of American Independence. Townsend was born on November 25, 1753, at Oyster Bay, Long Island, New York. In 1775, he declared for the patriot cause and three years later was recruited by Major Benjamin Tallmadge into an espionage network being organized at the behest of General George Washington. The spy net was located in New York City and on Long Island, to observe British military operations. Townsend (Culper Junior) was a key member in the city. Acting as a society reporter for James Rivington's newspaper and also the owner of a dry goods store, he had access to information from British officers without rousing suspicion.

Once he had collected intelligence, Townsend inscribed documents in code and passed them to a courier, Austin Roe, who rode with them to Setauket on Long Island. There Roe passed the documents to Abraham Woodhull (Culper Senior), who evaluated the information. Woodhull passed the important evidence to Caleb Brewster, who conveyed it in a whaleboat across Long Island Sound to Fairfield, Connecticut. There the material was collected by Tallmadge, who dispatched it by dragoon couriers to Washington at New Windsor, New York.

Throughout the war, Townsend and his allies lived in peril of being found out and hanged. They never were, and so provided Washington with much valuable information. Townsend died on March 7, 1828, at Oyster Bay.

See also: Culper Ring; Rivington, James; Roe, Austin; Woodhull, Abraham

References and Further Reading

Groth, Lynn. *The Culper Spy Ring*. Philadelphia: Westminster Press, 1969.

Pennypacker, Morton. *General Washington's Spies on Long Island and in New York*. Brooklyn, NY: Long Island Historical Society, 1939.

Pennypacker, Morton. *The Two Spies, Nathan Hale and Robert Townsend*. Boston: Houghton Mifflin Company, 1930.

Paul David Nelson

TREHOLT, ARNE
(DECEMBER 13, 1942–)

Arne Treholt was a Norwegian government official and Labour party politician arrested in 1984 and sentenced to 20 years for treason and spying on behalf of the Soviet Union and Iraq. Treholt was pardoned in 1992.

Treholt worked as a journalist before he became personal secretary to the Minister of Trade in 1973 and parliamentary secretary from 1976 to 1979. Treholt later served as counsellor for the Norwegian ambassador to the United Nations and at the time of his arrest he was chief of the press section of the Norwegian Foreign Ministry. Despite the ongoing investigation aided by the Federal Bureau of Investigation, he was requested to sign up for courses at the Norwegian National Defense College during this posting.

In the late 1970s, the national security police suspected that Treholt had irregular foreign contacts, later disclosed as being Iraqi and Soviet agents. In 1984 he was arrested en route to Vienna to meet his Committee for State Security (KGB) contact Genadij Titov, carrying a briefcase containing classified documents.

As many social democrats of his generation, his views on the cold war was at odds with that of official North Atlantic Treaty Organization (NATO) policy. His stated motive for his actions was to lessen east-west tension through disclosing information that would ease Soviet insecurity. On the other hand, large sums of money were confiscated following his conviction as paybacks for material delivered to the Soviets. In the aftermath, the harshness of his sentence remains contested, as it is disputed how damaging his contacts with the Soviets were and if he ever passed on any sensitive material to the KGB, whose archives remain closed.

See also: KGB (Komitet Gosudarstvennoi Bezopasnosti)

References and Further Reading

Treholt, Arne. *Alene* (*Alone*). Oslo: Cappelen, 1985.
Treholt, Arne. *Gråsoner* (*Grey Areas*). Oslo: Gyldendal, 2004.

Frode Lindgjerdet

TROFIMOFF, COLONEL GEORGE (1927–)

Retired U.S. Army Colonel George Trofimoff, age 74, was arrested for espionage on behalf of the Soviet Union on July 14, 2000. He began spying in 1969 and continued until 1994. It is estimated that he received about 90,000 DM (German marks) for the information he provided. Trofimoff was convicted of espionage on June 26, 2001, and was sentenced to life imprisonment on September 27, 2001. He is the highest-ranking military officer charged with espionage. Trofimoff was awarded the Order of the Red Banner by the Soviet Union for his espionage.

Trofimoff was born in Germany in 1927 where his Russian parents had immigrated to. He joined the U.S. Army in 1948 and became a naturalized American citizen in 1951. After leaving active duty, Trofimoff joined the army reserves and retired with the rank of colonel in 1987. From 1959 to 1994 he worked for the army as a civilian in military intelligence. Trofimoff was chief of the Army Element in Nuremburg Joint Interrogation Center from 1968 to 1994. In this position he had access to all classified information and documents produced by the Army Element. These included information provided by East European defectors, lists of current intelligence information required by the United States, intelligence priority rankings, Soviet and Warsaw Pact Order of Battle documents, and Collection Support Briefs which detailed the current chemical and biological warfare threat posed by the Warsaw Pact. Trofimoff would steal these documents and photograph them.

Trofimoff was recruited as a spy in 1969 by a close childhood friend, Igor Susemihl, who was a KGB agent under the cover of a Russian Orthodox priest. During his career, Susemihl served in such positions as archbishop of Vienna, Baden, and Bavaria. He died in 1999. At the time Trofimoff had just recently been promoted to chief of the

Army Element. Among the code names used by Trofimoff were "Antey," "Markiz," and "Konsul."

Trofimoff came under suspicion as a result of information provided by KGB archivist Vasili Mitrokhim who defected to the Great Britain in 1992. Both Trofimoff and Susemihl were arrested by German authorities under suspicion of espionage in December 1999 but the case was dropped because of the statute of limitations period within which the alleged spying took place had expired. Trofimoff's arrest and conviction in the U.S. came after a lengthy investigation by the Federal Bureau of Investigation (FBI). It included a false flag operation in which Trofimoff accepted payment from an FBI agent posing as a Russian agent, and six hours of videotaped conversations between Trofimoff and the FBI agent in which he pledged his loyalty to the Moscow.

See also: Federal Bureau of Investigation (FBI); KGB (Komitet Gosudarstvennoi Bezopasnosti)

References and Further Reading

Byers, Andy. *The Imperfect Spy*. St. Petersburg, FL: Vanamere Press, 2005.

Epstein, Edward Jay. *Deception: The Invisible War Between the KGB and the CIA*. New York: Allen, 1989.

Glenn P. Hastedt

TRUMAN ADMINISTRATION AND INTELLIGENCE

Harry S. Truman was president from 1945 to 1953. It was during his administration that the basic organizational features of the contemporary American intelligence community took shape. In his presidency, Rear Admiral Sidney W. Souers, Lt. General Hoyt S. Vandenberg, Roscoe Hillenkoetter, and General Walter Bedell Smith all served as Directors of Central Intelligence.

Truman became president upon the death of Franklin D. Roosevelt, with virtually no previous exposure to intelligence and little familiarity with foreign policy. He was not informed about work on the atomic bomb until his first cabinet meeting as president and received his first briefing on Ultra a few days later. In fact, Truman's first major decision involving intelligence dealt with the future signals intelligence (SIGINT). In September 1945 Truman agreed to continue the wartime practice of collaborating with the British on SIGINT and established the Army Security Agency (ASA) to centralize the administration of all military communications and cryptanalysis. Truman did not hold espionage and counterespionage activities in the same high regard he did SIGINT. Shortly after this decision he moved to disband the Office of Strategic Services (OSS). Created during World War II, the OSS had little political support in Washington for maintaining its existence. OSS Director William Donovan tried unsuccessfully to plead his case for a permanent postwar intelligence organization to Truman and on September 20, 1945, Truman issued Executive Order 9621 ending its existence and splitting its espionage and counterespionage functions between the State Department and the army.

Truman's lack of experience and interest in intelligence matters was reflected in the manner in which the intelligence bureaucracy operated in his administration.

Truman was not interested in intelligence forecasts or estimates. What he sought was a filtering device to reduce the flow of intelligence to him and present him with a manageable flow of information. The system he set up did not allow for this to happen. Instead, absent a central intelligence organization, old rivalries between intelligence bureaucracies resurfaced. To rectify this situation Truman first supported the creation of a National Intelligence Authority and a Central Intelligence Group. The former was to coordinate all national intelligence activities, whereas the latter was to analyze information collected by others. Soon it was apparent that this organizational structure was also deficient and, as part of the 1947 National Security Act, the Central Intelligence Agency (CIA) was created.

Changes also continued to take place in the organization of SIGINT. Conflict between the army and navy led to the creation in 1949 of an Armed Forces Security Agency (AFSA) to coordinate military SIGINT and an Armed Forces Security Agency Community (AFSAC) to oversee its operation. This change did not, however, prevent American officials from being caught off guard by North Korea's attack on South Korea. Years of bureaucratic infighting, limited SIGINT resources and an underappreciation of the situation on the Korean peninsula by American officials had taken its toll. A June 13, 1952, report issued by the Brownwell Committee again took up the matter of SIGINT coordination and management. It recommended that AFSAC be abolished with authority for SIGINT going to a new organization, the National Security Agency (NSA), to replace AFSA. Truman signed a secret executive order creating the NSA on November 4, 1952.

Although Truman publicly proclaimed little interest or support for covert action, it was in his administration and with his support that the CIA began to engage in it. The first such operation he authorized came on November 14, 1947, when NSC 1/1 authorized covert action to prevent a Communist victory in the upcoming Italian election. Subsequent NSC directives signed by Truman would expand and solidify the organizational base for CIA covert actions and the range of activity engaged in.

Truman had a complex relationship with the Federal Bureau of Investigation (FBI) and its head J. Edgar Hoover. Although often critical of Hoover, Truman, nonetheless, relied upon him for information on the personal behavior of critics of his administration and those he suspected of leaking information to the media. Truman also was not particularly responsive to Hoover's warnings about Communist espionage in the United States and he only reluctantly agreed to allow the FBI to conduct loyalty investigations of government employees. Surprisingly, Truman's lack of a vigorous response to the mounting evidence of Soviet espionage and the high-profile investigations by the House Un-American Activities Committee into the activities of Wittaker Chambers and Alger Hiss did not cost him politically as he unexpectedly won the 1948 presidential election.

See also: Armed Forces Security Agency; Central Intelligence Agency; Central Intelligence Group; Chambers, Whittaker; Hillenkoetter, Rear Admiral Roscoe Henry; Hiss, Alger; National Intelligence Authority; National Security Act; National Security Agency; Office of Strategic Services; Smith, General Walter Bedell; Souers, Rear Admiral Sidney William; Ultra; Vandenberg, General Hoyt Sanford

References and Further Reading

Andrew, Christopher. *For the President's Eyes Only: Secret Intelligence and the American Presidency from Washington to Bush.* New York: HarperCollins, 1995.

Karalekas, Anne. *History of the Central Intelligence Agency.* Laguna Hills: Aegean Park Press, 1977.

Kessler, Ronald. *The Bureau: The Secret History of the FBI.* New York: St. Martin's Press, 2002.

Ranelagh, John. *The Rise and Decline of the CIA.* Revised and updated. New York: Touchstone, 1987.

Glenn P. Hastedt

TSOU, DOUGLAS
(1924–)

Douglas Tsou, a former Federal Bureau of Investigation (FBI) official, was convicted of espionage on October 4, 1991, and sentenced to a 10-year prison term on January 2, 2002. He was the first person convicted of spying for Taiwan. In his defense Tsou claimed that the information he gave to Taiwan was not secret since his offer to become a spy was declined. At his trial, prosecutors argued that Tsou had in fact given a great deal of information to Taiwan over the years. Loyalty to Taiwan is seen as having been the primary motive behind his act of espionage.

Tsou was born in China in 1924 and fled to Taiwan following the Communist's 1949 victory in the Chinese civil war. He moved to the United States in 1969 and became a naturalized citizen in 1977. He worked as a Chinese translator for the FBI from 1980 to 1986, at which time he was dismissed. While stationed in Houston, Texas, Tsou wrote a handwritten letter to Y. C. Chen, the Houston director of Taiwan's Coordination Council for North American Affairs, identifying an individual who was an intelligence officer for the People's Republic of China. This individual had approached the FBI about becoming a double agent and was in the process of being evaluated for that role. Tsou was arrested on February 11, 1988.

According to the FBI, there was no indication that Taiwan had solicited this particular piece of information from Tsou and that it cooperated in the investigation.

See also: Post–Cold War Intelligence

References and Further Reading

Adams, James. *The New Spies: Exploring the Frontiers of Espionage.* New York: Hutchinson, 1994.

Richelson, Jeffrey. *A Century of Spies: Intelligence in the Twentieth Century.* New York: Oxford University Press, 1995.

Glenn P. Hastedt

TU-20/TU-95 BEAR

The Tupolev Tu-95 "Bear" is the best-known long-range reconnaissance and espionage aircraft of the Soviet Union and later Russia. Although fielded as the Tu-20, the aircraft is known as the Tu-95, its original designation. The Soviet Union introduced the Tu-95 in 1955 as a strategic bomber. The innovative plane boasted four turboprops at a time when jet engines were emerging as the main propulsion system for military aircraft. Each turboprop engine carried a set of counter-rotating propellers, providing the aircraft with a maximum speed of over 900 kilometers per hour and a cruising speed of over 400 kilometers per hour. Reconnaissance/espionage versions of the Tu-95 could fly over 13,000 kilometers while on missions. Although any Tu-95 could be utilized for visual reconnaissance, the Soviet Union utilized at least four variants of the Tu-95 as specific reconnaissance/espionage aircraft. The Tu-95 Bear C carried two radomes for Electronics Intelligence (ELINT) gathering, whereas the Tu-95 Bear D had a chin radome. The Tu-95 Bear D reconnaissance version, often referred to as the Tu-95RTS, flew its first operational mission in 1966. The aircraft of this variant did not have bomb bays and were utilized strictly for reconnaissance. The Tu-95 Bear E was the photo reconnaissance version of the Bear. This variant was produced by converting Tu-95M bombers and adding a photographic package to the bomb bay area. The Bear F, also known as the Tu-142, is a maritime variant of the aircraft and utilized also for long-range reconnaissance. Throughout the cold war, Tu-95 reconnaissance aircraft operated from bases in the Soviet Union as well as overseas locations including Angola, Cuba, Ethiopia, Guinea, Libya, Mozambique, and Vietnam. Bear reconnaissance aircraft regularly flew in the vicinity of the United States, Canada, and NATO countries to gather intelligence, test defensive reaction times, and record radar and radio frequencies. Bears flying from Angola reportedly tracked the British fleet sailing to the Falklands in 1982. The last surviving aircraft of the Tu-95 series are scheduled to remain in service with Russia through 2015.

See also: Aerial Surveillance; Cold War Intelligence

References and Further Reading

Gordon, Yefim. *Tupolev Tu-95/-142*. Arlington, TX: Polygon Press, 2005.
Gordon, Yefim, and Vladimir Rigmant with Jay Miller. *Tupolev Tu95/Tu-142 "Bear."* Arlington, TX: Aerofax, 2007.
Gunston, Bill. *An Illustrated Guide to the Modern Soviet Air Force.* New York: ARCO, 1982.

Terry M. Mays

TUB PLOT CONSPIRACY

At the height of the Quasi-War with France, the Tub Plot was an alleged French scheme to incite a Southern slave revolt and possibly bring down the U.S. government. In January 1799, Secretary of State Pickering, a Federalist, learned that a Danish ship, the *Minerva*, was sailing to Charleston, South Carolina. On board was Matthew Salmon, a mulatto and an alleged agent of the French Executive Directory, who supposedly had been sent with documents that were hidden in tubs with false bottoms. The documents would prove that the French intended to dismantle the U.S. government. Unhappy with Jay's Treaty in 1794 between the United States and Great Britain, France began attacking American ships. France believed the treaty violated the 1778 American alliance with France during the American Revolution. In 1797,

President John Adams sent a diplomatic team to Paris to negotiate peace, but French Minister Talleyrand offered to negotiate only if the United States paid a bribe (now known as the XYZ Affair). This insult nearly caused the United States to declare war with France. Americans were aware of recent French reconnaissance activities in the United States, especially the western exploits of French General Victor Collot along the Mississippi River. Highly suspicious of the French and their supporters in the Republican Party, Federalists in Congress increased military spending and passed new legislation, including the 1798 Alien and Sedition Acts, in order to protect the nation. Federalists feared the French would seize back control of the Louisiana Territory from the Spanish and perhaps lead U.S. Southern slaves to revolt. When Pickering learned of Matthew Salmon's journey towards the southern US, therefore, he believed the plot to be true and warned South Carolina leaders, who then arrested Salmon and his four companions when their boat arrived in February 1799. Before Federalists could celebrate however, they learned Salmon and his traveling companions were not French spies, but were enemies of the French Directory and were destined for Haiti. The questionable documents proved France's intent to retake the island, not start a U.S. slave revolt. The Tub plot was not the evidence against France for which some Federalists had hoped, but it did illustrate how tensions with France had deeply divided the nation.

See also: Early Republic and Espionage; XYZ Affair

References and Further Reading

Clarfield, Gerard H. *Timothy Pickering and American Diplomacy 1795–1800*. Colombia, MO: University of Missouri Press, 1969.

Collot, V. "General Collot's Plan for a Reconnaissance of the Ohio and Mississippi Valleys, 1796," *The William and Mary Quarterly* 9 (1952), 512–520.

DeConde, Alexander. *The Quasi-War, the Politics and Diplomacy of the Undeclared War with France 1797–1801*. New York: Charles Scribner's Sons, 1966.

Hickey, Donald R. "America's Response to the Slave Revolt in Haiti, 1791–1806." *Journal of the Early Republic* 2 (1982), 361–379.

Miller, John C. *Crisis in Freedom: The Alien and Sedition Acts*. Boston: Little, Brown, 1951.

Cynthia A. Boyle

TUBMAN, HARRIET
(1820/21–MARCH 10, 1913)

Underground Railroad operative during the 1850s, Tubman was also a spy and a scout for the Union army during the American Civil War. Born in Dorchester County, Maryland, Tubman escaped Southern slavery in 1849 but returned repeatedly to secretly bring other slaves north. Once the Civil War began in 1861, Tubman first assisted the Union army at Fort Monroe, Virginia, caring for refugee slaves. In May 1862, the army escorted Tubman to Port Royal, South Carolina, where she nursed soldiers and contraband slaves along the occupied coast. Soon the Union army, aware of her prior work, realized she could glean information from the surrounding countryside. Tubman organized a local spy ring, impressively transmitting information, by memory, on Confederate strength to her superiors. In June 1863, Tubman led 150 black soldiers in a successful raid up the Combahee River. They rescued 750 slaves, burned stores of cotton and rice, and destroyed several plantations. Colonel James Montgomery praised her, writing, " . . . a most remarkable woman, and invaluable as a scout." Within a few weeks, Tubman nursed soldiers of the 54th Massachusetts regiment after the Battle of Fort Wagner. In 1864 she returned home to Auburn, New York, a hero. Tubman began receiving a military pension in 1899 in recognition of her service. She died March 10, 1913, in Auburn, and was honored with a military funeral.

See also: Civil War Intelligence; Confederate Signal and Secret Service Bureau

References and Further Reading

Clinton, Catherine. *Harriet Tubman, The Road to Freedom*. New York: Little, Brown, 2004.

Larson, Kate Clifford. *Bound for the Promised Land: Harriet Tubman, Portrait of an American Hero*. New York: Ballantine Books, 2004.

Markle, Donald E. *Spies and Spymasters of the Civil War*, Revised and expanded. New York: Hippocrene Books, 2004.

Cynthia A. Boyle

TURNER, ADMIRAL STANSFIELD (DECEMBER 1, 1923–)

Admiral Stansfield Turner was the twelfth Director of Central Intelligence (DCI). He served from February 24, 1977, to January 20, 1981. Born in Highland Park, Illinois, Turner graduated from the Naval Academy in 1946 and went on to become a Rhodes Scholar. Turner assumed the position of DCI with no background in intelligence. Rather, he approached the position from a managerial perspective which reflected his career background. Turner had served as director of the Systems Analysis Division in the Office of the Chief of Naval Operations and as commander of the Second Fleet. He had also served as the president of the U.S. Naval War College. Turner achieved the rank of admiral in 1975.

Turner was not President Jimmy Carter's first or second choice for DCI. Theodore Sorensen, an aide to President John Kenney, was nominated for the position but withdrew when it became known that he requested noncombat status as a conscientious objector when he registered for the draft and that in writing Kennedy's biography he had used classified material without permission. Carter then turned to Army Chief of Staff General Bernard Rogers who turned down the position. Carter and Turner had been classmates at the Naval Academy but not close friends.

Turner had a tension-filled relationship with intelligence professionals during his tenure as DCI. He quickly came to be viewed as a political director along the lines of James Schlesinger; that is, he was put into the Central Intelligence Agency (CIA) in order to bring it more firmly under White House control. Because he was the most informed DCI yet on technology matters Turner also was somewhat of a threat to the organizational culture of the CIA. He regarded human intelligence as outmoded and saw technology as the key to the future of espionage. Together these perspectives on intelligence led Turner to take a number of highly controversial initiatives. First, he introduced the concept of National Intelligence Topics. These was a set of 59 prioritized intelligence questions that were to guide collection and analysis. This was not the first time such a system had been put forward. Two earlier attempts were Key Intelligence Questions (KIQ) and Priority National Intelligence Objectives (PNIOs). It does not appear that this attempt at prioritization worked significantly better than the previous ones. Second, Turner continued and accelerated Schlesinger's purge of the clandestine service. In what is referred to as the Halloween Massacre, Turner abolished 800 positions there and retired approximately 200 covert operators. Third, he sought to gain administrative control over the intelligence community by seeking day-to-day and budgetary control over the National Reconnaissance Office and the National Security Agency, and creating the National Intelligence Tasking Center. Fourth, Turner believed that intelligence on economics and other nonmilitary matters was as important to the president as military intelligence. Finally, he instituted a number of administrative reforms designed to help him achieve his reforms. He surrounded himself with former naval staffers and made heavy use of the polygraph in evaluating employees.

Turner enjoyed only limited as DCI. His initiatives were resisted from within by intelligence professionals. He also never achieved a close working relationship with President Carter. National Security Advisor Zbigniew Brzezinski insisted on presenting intelligence briefings to the president. Turner became the public scapegoat for such intelligence failures as the seizure of the American embassy in Iran and the "discovery" of a Russian brigade in Cuba.

See also: Carter Administration and Intelligence; Central Intelligence Agency; Director of Central Intelligence

References and Further Reading

Andrew, Christopher. *For the President's Eyes Only: Secret Intelligence and the American Presidency from Washington to Bush*. New York: HarperCollins, 1995.

Laqueur, Walter. *A World of Secrets: The Uses and Limits of Intelligence*. New York: Basic Books, 1985.

Ranelagh, John. *The Rise and Decline of the CIA*. Revised and updated. New York: Touchstone, 1987.

Turner, Stansfield. *Secrecy and Democracy: The CIA in Transition*. London: Sidgwick & Jackson, 1985.

Glenn P. Hastedt

U

U-2 INCIDENT

The U-2 incident centered on the Soviet shootdown of a U-2 spy plane some 1,200 miles into Soviet territory on the eve of a U.S.-Soviet summit conference. Initially the United States denied Soviet charges of espionage only to be confronted with irrefutable evidence in the form of its pilot, Francis Gary Powers. The shootdown occurred on May 1, 1960, two weeks before a scheduled U.S.-Soviet summit conference between Soviet leader Nikita Khrushchev and President Dwight Eisenhower. The summit was to deal with Berlin which had emerged as the primary point of U.S-Soviet cold war confrontation in Europe. At the summit meeting Khrushchev demanded an apology for the U-2 over flight. When none was forthcoming he left the meeting, returning an element of tension and distrust into U.S.-Soviet relations that both Eisenhower and Khrushchev had hoped to overcome through earlier summit meetings and as symbolized by the Spirit of Camp David.

U-2 overflights over Soviet territory had been going on since 1956. They were valued for the information they provided the Central Intelligence Agency about Soviet military capabilities. Especially valuable was the information about its nuclear missile program. U-2 overflights were also used to obtain information about the 1957 Suez crisis after France and Great Britain stopped providing the United States with information about their activities.

It appears that on this particular flight Francis Gary Powers had engine, parachuted to earth and was captured. The initial story put forward by the Eisenhower administration on June 3 was that a NASA research plane studying weather patterns had crashed over Turkey. On June 5, Khrushchev announced that an American plane had been shot down after violating Russian air space. The State Department now stated that a civilian weather plane had probably strayed over Soviet airspace accidentally. Khrushchev then produced pictures of Gary Francis Powers, photo reconnaissance

Nikita Khruschev examines equipment found among the wreckage of the American U-2 spy plane piloted by Francis Gary Powers. (Library of Congress)

equipment, and pictures of Soviet military installations. The State Department then acknowledged that the plane "probably" was on an intelligence operation.

Eisenhower then took responsibility for the mission, asserting that the U-2 flight was necessary to avert another Pearl Harbor. Eisenhower's statement appears to have undercut Khrushchev's standing within the Soviet Politburo giving hard-liners who opposed the ongoing thaw in U.S.-Soviet relations an opening to undermine the Paris summit.

See also: Aerial Surveillance; Cold War Intelligence; Eisenhower Administration and Intelligence; Powers, Francis Gary; SR-71

References and Further Reading

Powers, Francis Gary. *Operation Overflight: The U-2 Pilot Tells his Story for the First Time.* New York: Holt, Rinehart and Winston, 1970.
Redlow, Gregory, and Donald Welzenbach. *The CIA and the U-2 Program 1954–1974* Washington, DC: The Center for the Study of Intelligence, 1974.

Glenn P. Hastedt

UKUSA

The United Kingdom-United States of America Communications Intelligence Agreement (UKUSA) remains classified, but it is variously dated from 1947 or 1948. Its still-secret provisions probably extended wartime US-UK intelligence-sharing arrangements which focused on interception of Axis Powers' secret diplomatic and military communications. These World War II-era agreements included the May 1943 bilateral British-United States Communications Intelligence Agreement (BRUSA), which governed US-UK cooperation in signals interception, decryption, and analysis. The postwar UKUSA agreement is likely a series of operational agreements and memoranda of understanding developed by the United States and Britain since the end of World War II and in the early postwar period, when strategic concerns in both Washington and London shifted from their principle wartime enemies Japan and Germany to the Communist-led Soviet Union, its new allies in Eastern Europe, and their supporters in Asia and Africa.

The original agreements formalized under UKUSA provided for a rough division of labor between the United States and Britain, assigning each primary responsibility for communications intelligence monitoring, deciphering, and analysis in specific geographical regions. It is believed that Britain assumed special responsibility, monitoring communication originating in Eastern Europe, the Near and Middle East, Africa, and parts of South Asia and the Far East, whereas the United States focused upon the Soviet Union, China, and parts of Southeast Asia, as well as North, Central, and South America.

The UKUSA agreement partnered the United Kingdom's Government Communications Headquarters (GCHQ), the World War II era British code-breaking agency based at Cheltenham in Gloucestershire, with the U.S. Communications Intelligence Board. This Board operated as a representative of U.S. civilian agencies and the U.S Armed Forces Security Agency (AFSA) which included relevant wings of the U.S. National Security Agency and the US Air Force. Both the Board and AFSA were absorbed into the US National Security Agency which was formally established in November 1952, and inherited all U.S. responsibilities under UKUSA.

UKUSA provided for the allocation of signals interception resources by the US and Britain, and outlined protocols for the exchange of raw and processed data as well as analyses and interpretive material. The agreement also seems to have included arrangements for sharing technical data on monitoring and decoding systems and for personnel visits, and placements at both agency administrative headquarters and at operational sites worldwide. In the late 1940s Canada, Australia, and New Zealand were admitted into selected parts of UKUSA exchanges and became known as "Second Party" states. Subsequently a new tier of "Third Party" sates was created within the UKUSA structure. Typically providing only operational sites for NSA and/or GCHQ equipment and personnel, and receiving very limited intelligence output from monitoring activities, these 'Third Party' countries are thought to include Japan, Denmark, Greece, Norway, Turkey, South Korea, and perhaps others. With changing technologies the UKUSA agreement has doubtless been amended many times since the late 1940s, and evidently remains in force.

The best-known UKUSA intelligence-gathering project is ECHELON which involves that interception of email, fax, telex, and telephone communications. UKUSA enjoyed particular successes in obtaining information from Third World locations where communication security measures were not as advanced as in the Soviet Union.

Controversy has come to surround the UKUSA agreement on a number of counts. One concern is that the United States was using the UKUSA system as a pretext and means of eavesdropping on its own citizens without obtaining warrants. A second concern is that the United States was using the system to spy on its allies. Third, some see it as a vehicle for economic or industrial espionage.

See also: ECHELON

References and Further Reading

Aid, Matthew M. "The National Security Agency and the Cold War," *Intelligence and National Security* 16 (2001), 27–66.

Aldrich, Richard J. *The Hidden Hand: Britain, America and Cold War Secret Intelligence.* London: John Murray, 2001.

Keefe, Patrick Radden. *Chatter: Dispatches from the Secret World of Global Eavesdropping.* New York: Random House, 2005.

Laura M. Calkins

ULTRA

The decryption network, employed by British intelligence, headquartered in Bletchley Park, deciphered the German Enigma machines during World War II. Through the infiltration of German cryptography, the Allies gained an advantage over the Nazis that would culminate in their final victory.

The German inventor, Arthur Scherbius, conceived of a cryptographic machine in 1918, which was given the name "Enigma" in 1923 from a promotional pamphlet. Although a commercial failure, Enigma became useful to governments for its ciphering and deciphering capabilities.

Enigma was a most sophisticated cipher system. The commercial version resembled a typewriter with a German keyboard that contained only letters. The secret to Enigma was its cipher drums, or rotor system. Above the keyboard was a panel of "glow-lamps" with the same arrangement of letters. Above the lamp board were five disks, which made up the scrambling unit. Two outside disks were fixed into the machine. The other three disks could be rotated around and be arranged in different sequences. Through the use of these rotors, one letter could be substituted for another. The military version contained a plug board or "commutator," which resembled a telephone switchboard. Thus, if the letter A on the commutator were plugged to "Z," then when the operator typed the letter A, the letter "Z" would be inputted. It took two people to operate an Enigma—one to operate the keyboard and another to operate the radio. A message entered into the Enigma would become coded, based on whatever setting was chosen, as it was sent. When a message was received, it would be fed into the Enigma at the right setting and would be transformed into text. Scherbius's Enigma became a formidable weapon in the field of espionage.

The German government in the 1920s and 1930s realized the potential of Enigma. The Germans saw in Enigma opportunity for secrecy in military operations. The German navy first employed a commercial version of Enigma in 1926, followed by the army in 1928. The military version was introduced in 1930, and by 1934, the Nazis used Enigma as its primary cipher system that was adopted by the military and intelligence operations. By 1939, 40,000 Enigmas were in use in Germany. Throughout the war, the Germans continually updated and refined Enigma, confident that it could never be deciphered.

Work on deciphering the Enigma began with the Poles, although their contribution to the creation of Ultra and the defeat of Nazi Germany would not be known until three decades after the end of World War II. In 1929, the Cipher Bureau of the Polish

A German Enigma cipher machine, used by the German military in World War II to encrypt communications. (Hulton|Getty Images)

government selected Marian Rejewski, Jerzy Rozycki, and Henryk Zygalski who studied cryptology at Poznan University to decipher German cryptograms. By 1932, the Polish government acquired an Enigma from the French, which was stolen by Hans Thilo-Schmidt who worked in the German army's Cipher Center.

After calculating the astronomical number of possible permutations, Rajewski, Rozycki, and Zygalski collaborated toward analyzing the sequences necessary to decipher messages, while keeping abreast with the changes the Germans had made, creating the Polish version, the "Bomba." The Poles shared their information with the French and the British, who would build upon their contribution.

After Britain declared war on Germany, the Government Code and Cypher School, which became the Government Communications Headquarters, commenced at Bletchley Park, located at the midpoint between Oxford and Cambridge Universities, consisting of a diverse group of academics, mathematicians, linguists, and chess players, who were to form an elite group of cryptanalysts, whose numbers were to peak at 10,000 before the end of the war. This group that gathered at Bletchley Park was to be part of a vast intelligence network devoted to intercepting and decryption of German signals transmissions, the analysis and translation of ciphers, and the distribution of information to Allied military commanders. Among this group, mathematicians Alan Turing and Gordon Welchman, who studied the Polish Bomba machine to make Britain catch up in the cryptology war, created the British version in 1940 known as the "Bombe." Although it was one thing to discover the intricacies of Enigma, what was equally important was the analysis of the information deciphered and distributing it to the proper channels.

The task of analyzing and making useful application of the Enigma decryptions fell to Group Captain F. W. Winterbotham, an intelligence officer at Bletchley Park. His experience as a prisoner of war during World War I allowed him to speak German fluently. During the 1930s, he was engaged in espionage activities, taking information on foreign air forces and extracting information from within the Nazi government itself. When the war with Germany began, Winterbotham realized the importance of not only distributing the Enigma decrypts, but also maintaining their security.

To that end, he proposed combining and consolidating all translation and analysis of the decrypts at Bletchley Park while distributing the processed intelligence through MI-6, through units of trained radio and cryptographical personnel known as special liaison units (SLU). The army, navy, and air force would participate in the intelligence gathering and distribution. The Royal Navy, resisted however, as he expected. Winterbotham dubbed this system of intelligence gathering and distribution "Ultra" because the nature of the work was "ultra-secret." As the war continued, this intelligence network grew and expanded, particularly in the number of German translators. The SLUs were employed at all areas where British and, later, American land and air forces operated.

Ultra was crucial in the European theater of the World War II. Ultra was instrumental during the Battle of Britain by intercepting codes by the German air force. Where Ultra was most valuable was the Battle of the Atlantic. As in World War I, German submarines threatened British communications and supply lines. "Wolf Packs" of German U-boats patrolled the North Atlantic waiting for supply ships to destroy. The cryptographers at Bletchley Park worked feverishly to decode the German naval Enigma ciphers, which differed from those used by the army and air force by using eight rotors instead of five. Their luck changed in May of 1941 when the British captured an Enigma from U-110, which contained an intact Enigma and its accompanying codebook.

Throughout the war, there was a race between the Germans and Bletchley Park in keeping ahead of one another, as the Germans continually made improvements on the Enigma and as Bletchley Park raced to keep abreast of such improvements. After 1943, Bletchley Park gained the upper hand and narrowly neutralized the U-boat threat. The value of Ultra culminated in 1944 as it helped coordinate what would become Operation Overlord, the success of which assured Allied military victory.

See also: American Intelligence, World War II

References and Further Reading

Andrew, Christopher, and Jeremy Noakes. *Intelligence and International Relations 1900–1945*. Exeter, UK: University of Exeter, 1987.

Gannon, James. *Stealing Secrets, Telling Lies: How Spies and Codebreakers helped Shape the Twentieth Century*. Washington, DC: Brassey's, 2001.

Parker, Johnson. *Secrets of a Century: The Influence of Espionage and Secret Agreements*. Lanaham, MD: University Press of America, Inc., 2004.

Richelson, Jeffrey T. *A Century of Spies: Intelligence in the Twentieth Century*. Oxford: Oxford University Press, 1995.

Dino E. Buenviaje

UNDERSECRETARY OF DEFENSE FOR INTELLIGENCE

On March 11, 2003, the first undersecretary of defense for intelligence ever, Stephen Cambone, was put into power. In this rather new post, the undersecretary is responsible for providing the secretary of defense and his colleagues with advice, new initiatives and policies, and budgeting recommendations. Not only must the undersecretary respond to the intelligence needs and requests of the secretary of defense, but must also coordinate with the National Security Agency, the National Imagery and Mapping Agency, the Defense Intelligence Agency, and the Nation Reconnaissance Office. Additionally, the undersecretary must work closely with the Direction of Central Intelligence in order to meet the demands and needs of his post.

Created in the aftermath of September 11, 2001, and the resulting reorganizations and reforms, the undersecretary has a staff of over 100 in the office. The office has four major areas of concentration: ensuring intelligence information arrives at the front lines in a timely fashion, preparing for the future of military intelligence, developing military security and counterintelligence, and program budgeting in perspective of military and intelligence benefits. Notably, the undersecretary and his staff are not charged with any type of intelligence collection or analysis. As a result, the office concentrates almost solely on efficient dissemination of the latest intelligence information and working to guarantee that the latest information is sent out in the future.

In order to stay on top of intelligence advances, the office is very forward-looking. One of its concentration areas relates to reforming itself daily in order to best meet its mission. Additionally, one of the office's programs involves directing the military space-based intelligence satellites.

See also: Defense Department Intelligence; Intelligence Community; September 11, 2001

References and Further Reading

Federation of American Scientists Online. "Establishment of the Under Secretary of Defense for Intelligence," http://www.fas.org/irp/congress/2002_cr/usdint.html (accessed January 12, 2006).

Department of Defense, "Office of the Secretary of Defense," http://www.defenselink.mil/osd/ (accessed January 13, 2006).

Arthur Holst

USA PATRIOT ACT

Officially known as the Uniting and Strengthening America by Providing Appropriate Tools Required to Intercept and Obstruct Terrorism Act, the USA Patriot Act was adopted by Congress on October 25, 2001, and signed into law the following day by President George W. Bush.

Three hundred and forty-two pages in length, the USA Patriot Act emerged as the Bush administration's immediate legislative response to the September 11, 2001, terrorist attacks on the World Trade Center and the Pentagon. Its intent is to provide law enforcement officials with an enhanced ability to investigate and prosecute terrorism. One of its provisions expands the definition of engaged in terrorist activity to include providing support for groups that the individual "knew or should have known were terrorist organization." Among its primary targets are the monetary transactions and electronic communications employed by terrorists. Financial institutions and

President George W. Bush signs the USA Patriot Act during a ceremony at the White House on October 26, 2001. The law was passed in response to the terrorist attacks of September 11, 2001, and gives intelligence and law enforcement agencies unprecedented authority to conduct terror investigations. (White House)

agents must now provide additional verifiable information about their customers. The USA Patriot Act also expands the list of toxins that are classified as dangerous and requires background checks of scientists who work with them. As further evidence of the Act's scope, waste-hauling companies must now provide background checks for divers transporting hazardous material. It permits the attorney general to arrest and detain foreign suspects in the United States for seven days without filing charges.

One of the most important set of provisions in the USA Patriot Act affects the conduct of intelligence in the United States. Intelligence surveillance is now permitted when foreign intelligence is a "significant purpose" rather than "the purpose" of the undertaking. The Act broadens the authority of the government to contract for terrorist information with individuals once placed off limits because of human rights violations or other transgressions. Included in this listing is (1) the ability of the Federal Bureau of Investigation (FBI) to obtain and review medical, mental health, financial, and educational records without court orders or producing evidence of criminal activity, (2) the ability of the Central Intelligence Agency to designate priority targets in the United States for surveillance thus freeing it from the requirement to operate outside the country, (3) the ability of federal agents to obtain search warrants and search private property without telling the owner and, (4) the ability to use search warrants to read opened voice mail messages and electronic mail from Internet providers rather than obtain a wiretap order. The USA Patriot Act also contains a number of directives intended to promote intelligence sharing and cooperation among intelligence agencies. Included here is the prompt disclosure of information obtained in a criminal investigation and the establishment of a virtual translation center within the intelligence community.

Both many of the provisions of the USA Patriot Act and the speed with which it was passed concern many onlookers. The legislation was passed so quickly that there were no committee reports or votes taken thus denying law enforcement officials and outside experts the opportunity to comment on its provisions. Furthermore, the absence of typical committee hearings deprived implementers and legal officials insight into the congressional intent in passing the USA Patriot Act. Its key provisions were worked out in negotiations between Attorney General John Ashcroft, Senator Patrick Leahy (D-Vermont) and Senator Orrin Hatch (R-Utah). A particularly controversial provision calls for increasing the national DNA database to include not only samples from convicted terrorists but also "any crime of violence." The crimes to be included in this database have been debated since its controversial creation in October 1998. Also controversial is the extended time that aliens suspected of being involved in acts of terrorism may be detained without having charges filed against them. As noted above the USA Patriot Act permits them to be held for seven days. The Bush administration had sought the power to do so for an indefinite period of time.

Numerous controversies arose in the years following the passage of the USA Patriot Act. One point of contention involved its effectiveness. According to Attorney General John Ashcroft in his 2004 Justice Department report 368 individuals had been criminally charged in terrorism investigations with 195 resulting in guilty pleas or convictions. President George W. Bush placed the number at over 400 in a 2005 speech and claimed over one-half had resulted in convictions or guilty pleas. A 2005 Washington Post study, however, concluded that of 180 people on a Justice Department list only 39 had been convicted or pleaded guilty and many of those did so to relatively minor crimes.

The USA Patriot Act also ran into difficulty in the courts. In 2005 a federal judge ruled against actions taken by the FBI under terms of the Act. At issue was the ability of the FBI to impose an automatic and permanent ban on any public discourse of its investigations. In this case the FBI sought to prevent the names of librarians who had received an FBI demand for records from the becoming public.

Finally, 16 provisions of the USA Patriot Act contained sunset provisions, causing them to expire on December 31, 2005, unless renewed in follow-up legislation. Most of these provisions relate to the ability of intelligence services and the FBI to conduct searches and obtain access to communications without a warrant or public disclosure. In June 2005 the House passed a bill that would have taken away the FBI's power to seize library, bookstore, and hotel records for terrorism investigations. President Bush threatened to veto that bill if it passed. In the aftermath of the London subway attacks the House passed a bill more to the liking of the Bush administration. A Senate committee, however, passed a bill containing such prohibitions.

See also: Bush, George W., Administration and Intelligence; Federal Bureau of Investigation (FBI); September 11, 2001

References and Further Reading

U.S. National Commission on Terrorist Attacks Upon the United States, *The 9/11 Commission Report*. Washington, DC: Government Printing Office. 2004.
USA Patriot Act. House Resolution 3166. United States Congress, 24 October 2001.

Glenn P. Hastedt

V

VAN DEMAN, RALPH
(SEPTEMBER 3, 1865–JANUARY 22, 1952)

Known as the "father of U.S. military intelligence," Ralph Van Deman was born on September 3, 1865, in Delaware, Ohio, and graduated from Ohio Wesleyan University and Harvard University. After attending law school, and enrolling in medical school, Van Deman was commissioned as second lieutenant in the infantry. He then went to Miami University Medical School in Cincinnati, Ohio, graduating in 1893 and entering the army as a surgeon. There he met Arthur Wagner who was appointed head of the Military Information Division of the War Department. Wagner hired him and Ralph Van Deman moved to Washington, DC.

In the U.S. capital, Van Deman had the task of collating information on the military strengths and weaknesses of Spain in Cuba, the Philippines, and Puerto Rico. In charge of the White House war map room, after the war he went to Cuba and Puerto Rico where he collected more information, then being assigned to the Philippines where he was appointed aide to Brigadier-General Robert Patterson Hughes. In 1901 he was promoted to captain and transferred to the Bureau of Insurgent Records in Manila, which he turned into the Philippine Military Information Division, recruiting agents to run a counterintelligence branch.

Returning to the United States in 1902, Van Deman was posted to California and then Minnesota. In 1904 he was one of the four officers selected to form the first class of the Army War College. Graduating in 1906, Van Deman went to China to reconnoiter the new defenses around Beijing, which had been rebuilt after the end of the Boxer Uprising. Back in Washington, he was appointed chief of the Mapping Section in the Second Division of the U.S. General Staff. Returning to the Philippines, he used it as a base for mapping routes of communications in China, leading to Japanese protests.

In 1915 Major Van Deman returned to the War College Division and managed to convince the War Department to establish its own military intelligence section. This was created on May 3, 1917, with Van Deman, promoted to colonel, in charge. This was to play a crucial role in World War I, at the end of which the division employed 282 officers and 1,159 civilians. In spite of this, Van Deman always felt that he did not have enough agents to fully protect the United States from internal sabotage, as well as provide agents for the war effort in Europe.

Going to France in 1918, Van Deman was appointed in charge of security at the Paris Peace Conference held at Versailles. Briefly deputy chief of MID, he returned to the army in 1920, taking up another appointment in the Philippines. He was eventually promoted to brigadier-general and retired in September 1929. In retirement he used his contacts to compile his own files on suspected foreign agents in the United States. Appointed as a consultant on intelligence matters in World War II, he died on January 22, 1952, in San Diego. His wife, Irene (née Kingscombe), flew with Wilbur Wright in 1909, being the first American woman to fly.

See also: Taylor, Captain Daniel M.

References and Further Reading

Kahn, David. *The Reader of Gentlemen's Mail: Herbert O. Yardley and the Birth of American Codebreaking*. New Haven, CT: Yale University Press, 2004.

Weber, Ralph E. *Final Memoranda of Major General Ralph H. Van Deman*. Willimington, DE: Scholarly Resources, 1988.

Justin Corfield

VANDENBERG, LIEUTENANT GENERAL HOYT SANFORD (JANUARY 24, 1899–APRIL 2, 1954)

Lieutenant General Hoyt S. Vandenberg served as the second Director of Central Intelligence (DCI) from June 10, 1946, to May 1, 1947. Born in Milwaukee, Wisconsin, he graduated from West Point in 1923 and was a former head of army intelligence; Vandenberg was ambitious and well connected. He was recommended for the DCI position by outgoing DCI Sidney Souers and he was the nephew of the powerful Republican Senator Arthur Vandenberg who sat on the Foreign Relations Committee and had been a staunch isolationist before Pearl Harbor but was now a convert to the internationalist cause. Vandenberg saw the post of DCI as a temporary one. His ultimate career objective was to become chief of staff of the soon-to-be-independent air force. He achieved this goal in 1948 and held this position until 1953.

Like his predecessor, Vandenberg found the established intelligence units resistive to any efforts by the Central Intelligence Group (CIG) to develop its analysis mission of coordinating and disseminating reports on intelligence matters. His major successes in this area were in expanding its analytical staff and the production of current intelligence. In August 1946 the Office of Reports and Estimates was established. It was under Vandenberg's tenure as DCI that the first National Intelligence Estimate on the Soviet Union was produced. These moves were in part a reaction to the June 1946 official expansion of the CIG's mission to include independent analysis. At that time the National Intelligence Authority that had been established by President Harry Truman through a presidential directive in January 1946 directed it to conduct research and analysis "not being presently performed" by other departments. Vandenberg also followed Souers' precedent of acquiring unwanted parts of the Office of Strategic Services (OSS). Where Souers had focused on building the CIG's overt collection capabilities, Vandenberg strengthened its covert capabilities through the bureaucratic acquisition of SI (espionage) and X-2 (counterespionage) from the army's Strategic Services Unit. He combined them into an Office of Special Operations. Significantly, there had been no mention of a covert or clandestine collection mission for CIG in any of its founding documents. But when the National Security Act of 1947 was passed and replaced the CIG with the Central Intelligence Agency and authorized it to carry out such missions, an organizational ability to do so already existed.

See also: Central Intelligence Agency; Central Intelligence Group; Director of Central Intelligence; National Intelligence Estimates; Office of Special Operations; Office of Strategic Services

References and Further Reading

Andrew, Christopher. *For the President's Eyes Only: Secret Intelligence and the American Presidency from Washington to Bush.* New York: HarperCollins, 1995.

Karalekas, Anne. *History of the Central Intelligence Agency.* Laguna Hills: Aegean Park Press, 1977.

Ranelagh, John. *The Rise and Decline of the CIA.* Revised and updated. New York: Touchstone, 1987.

Glenn P. Hastedt

VAN LEW, ELIZABETH (OCTOBER 25, 1818–SEPTEMBER 25, 1900)

Elizabeth "Crazy Bet" Van Lew was a spy for the Union, operating out of Richmond, Virginia. She was the daughter of a prominent family which had a magnificent mansion near the James River in Richmond on Church Hill. Eliza had been educated at a finishing school in Philadelphia. She returned to Richmond as an abolitionist. She continued to maintain an extensive correspondence with friends in the North.

After Eliza's father died she persuaded her mother to free the family slaves. Her outspoken views opposing slavery became widely known. With the start of the war she decided that she would do what she could to help Union prisoners kept on Belle Island located in the middle of the James River and other prison camps. Her aid to Union prisoners was not appreciated by the people of Richmond. However, her aid put her in contact with men who had military intelligence about the Confederacy.

In 1863 Eliza began to send reports to Union General George Henry Sharpe, head of the Bureau of Military Intelligence. At first reluctant to put any credence into her reports he soon saw the value of her intelligence. Constantly watched, she put her reports in code. Boarders in her home were asked by authorities to watch her for suspicious activities. Temperamental by nature, she exaggerated her behavior to appear to be somewhat crazy.

The reports were smuggled out of Richmond by servants or slaves. Her greatest achievement was to plant an agent in the home of Jefferson Davis. She arranged for a former slave, Mary Elizabeth Bowser, who had been educated in Philadelphia at a Quaker school, to be hired as a maid. Pretending to be illiterate, Bowser used her photographic memory to steal numerous battle plans and other information. The intelligence reports that Van Lew sent also included drawings of military interest.

In 1864 Eliza aided the escape of some Union prisoners from Belle Island. After their escape they were provided with civilian clothes to enable them to blend into the local population until they could make a move to reach Union lines. When Richmond fell she was provided protection by the Union army. She was an outcast for the remainder of her life.

See also: Civil War Intelligence

References and Further Reading

Markle, Donald. *Spies and Spymasters of the Civil War*. New York: Hippocrene Books, 1994.

Ryan, David D. (ed.). *A Yankee Spy in Richmond: The Civil War Diary of "Crazy Bet" Van Lew*. Mechanicsburg, PA: Stackpole Books, 2001.

Andrew J. Waskey

VENONA

VENONA is the code name given to a secret operation to decode wartime communications between the Soviet Union and its diplomatic and military officials in Washington, DC. At first referred to as BRIDE, VENONA existed from 1943 to 1985. It became public in 1995 when three thousand decoded messages were released. Although the original intent of the VENONA transcripts was to obtain insight into Joseph Stalin's World War II intentions toward Nazi Germany, they instead provided U.S. intelligence officials with information on the scope of Soviet espionage activities within the United States and Great Britain as well as the identities of several key agents.

Soviet diplomatic communications to and from the United States were available to U.S. intelligence officials because wartime censorship policies required commercial international cable companies to provide the government with copies of all incoming and outgoing messages. In 1943 the Army Security Agency began to examine these cables in hopes of breaking the Soviet code. Since the Soviet Union used a one-time pad to encrypt its messages this was a daunting task. No two messages would use the same code. The first breakthrough occurred in October 1943 when an analyst examined 10,000 messages and found that Soviet intelligence officials had become careless and rather than use new codes with each message, the same code had been used multiple times. There were at least seven cases of a duplicate key being used. Progress in deciphering Soviet messages was further aided by plain-text versions of messages obtained by the Federal Bureau of Investigation and a copy of the NKVD codebook purchased in 1944 by William Donovan, head of the Office of Strategic Services.

By 1946 Meredith Gardner was able to decipher portions of enough messages to confirm that the Soviet Union had placed spies inside of the Manhattan Project and the Los Alamos labs. Among those Soviet spies operating in the United States whose identities were uncovered as a result of VENONA were Alger Hiss, Klaus Fuchs, David Greenglass, and Ethel and Julius Rosenberg. VENONA transcripts also established that at least eight Russian agents were operating in Great Britain. In time they would be identified as Donald Maclean, Guy Burgess, Kim Philby, and Anthony Blunt.

Soviet intelligence was aware of VENONA by 1948. Some speculate it knew about VENONA as early as 1945. In 1945 or 1946 Soviet intelligence recruited an Army Security Agency cipher clerk William Weisband as a spy and he informed the Soviet Union of its existence two years later. Weisband's espionage was not discovered until 1950 and by then the damage had been done as the Soviet Union changed its procedures for encrypting communications effectively placing an end point on the period in time where VENONA could be used decipher Soviet communications. Weisband was not the only Soviet spy aware of VENONA. In 1949 Kim Philby, who spied for the Soviet Union in Great Britain, was posted in Washington as the British SIS liaison officer with the Central Intelligence Agency. In this capacity Philby observed first hand as Gardner worked to decipher Soviet wartime communications. It is speculated that armed with this knowledge Philby alerted another Soviet spy British diplomat Donald Maclean of his impending arrest thus allowing him to escape to the Soviet Union.

See also: Blunt, Anthony; Burgess, Guy Francis De Moncy; Central Intelligence Agency; Fuchs, Emil Julius Klaus; Greenglass, David; Hiss, Alger; MacLean, Donald Duart; MI-6 (Secret Intelligence Service); NKVD (Narodnyj Komissariat Vnutrennikh Del—Peoples Commissariat for Internal Affairs); Office of Strategic Services; Philby, Harold Adrian Russell "Kim"; Rosenberg, Julius and Ethel; White, Harry

References and Further Reading

Center for Cryptological History, National Security Agency. *Introductory History of VENONA and Guide to the Translations*. Fort George G. Mead, MD: National Security Agency, 1995.

Haynes, John Earl, and Harvey Klehr. *VENONA: Decoding Soviet Espionage in America*. New Haven, CT: Yale University Press, 1999.

Glenn P. Hastedt

VETTERLEIN, KURT E.

A German engineer, Kurt Vetterlein ran a radio intercept station on the Dutch coast and was involved in recording and decrypting telephone communications between Franklin Roosevelt and British Prime Minister Winston Churchill during World War II.

Kurt E. Vetterlein was a chief engineer working in the German telephone and telegraph system, and in the summer of 1941 was assigned to see whether he could monitor trans-Atlantic communications which, in the case of many telephone calls, went by wireless. The idea was that of Wilhelm Ohnesorge, head of the German telephone system, and Vetterlein was sent to the Netherlands with machinery to investigate what was feasible. With research and intuition, he managed to replicate the Bell A-3 system. This was the system used for scrambling radio-telephone conversations and involved changing frequencies regularly, making it hard to decode messages. For this reason it was thought to be possible for the British prime minister and U.S. president to talk confidentially without anybody being able to listen in.

The German interception system, known as the Forschungsstelle ("Research Post"), was set up in a secluded former youth hostel at Eindhoven, in the Netherlands. There, from March 1, 1942, Vetterlein started to rotate the giant antenna. Within a week he had some success and Ohnesorge was able to report to Hitler that he was able to intercept telephone traffic between Britain and the United States, and had "succeeded in rendering conversations, that had been made intelligible, intelligible again at the instant of reception."

It was not long before technicians working under Vetterlein's direction were intercepting up to 60 telephone calls a day between Allied leaders who were all using the A-3 model, and the transcripts were available to Hitler within hours. On July 29, 1943, General Alfred Jodl, chief of military operations, was able to give Hitler a transcript of a conversation between Churchill and Roosevelt about Italy which showed that some Italians had been negotiating with the Allies. This made Hitler send 20 divisions to Italy and when he was given the transcript of Roosevelt and Churchill making military plans for Italy, he was able to redeploy his troops.

Vetterlein also was able to listen in to conversations from General Mark Clark, Anthony Eden, Lord Halifax, Averell Harriman, Harry Hopkins, Lord Keynes, and many others. However, he had to move this listening station from Eindhoven when it appeared that the place could be susceptible to commando attacks. An improvement in the A-3 system in late 1943 made it impossible for Vetterlein to listen in to any more messages.

See also: American Intelligence, World War II

References and Further Reading

Kahn, David. *Hitler's Spies: German Military Intelligence in World War II*. New York: Macmillan, 1978.

Persico, Joseph. *Roosevelt's Secret War: FDR and World War II Espionage*. New York: Random House, 2002.

Justin Corfield

VICTORICA, MARIA VON KRETSCHMANN DE (1878–AUGUST 12, 1920)

Maria von Kretschmann de Victorica was a German spy captured in the United States during World War I. Born in 1878 in Germany, her parents were the Baron Hans von Kretschmann, a Prussian general to whom Marshall Bazaine relinquished his sword at Metz in 1870 and Countess Jennie von Gustedt, daughter of a Prussian diplomat and kinswoman of the Kaiserin.

Like her older sister, Amalie, who is better known as the feminist Socialist Lily Braun, Victorica studied foreign languages and reading and writing from various governesses and tutors. She earned degrees from the University of Heidelberg, the University of Berlin, and the Swiss University at Zurich where she studied political economy and linguistics. Unusually clever and having a facility for languages, De Victorica was described as blonde, graceful, stately, and having a gracious manner.

Around 1910, Col. Walther Nicolai recruited her to the German High Command where her attributes and intelligence were useful. De Victorica used various aliases including Baroness Maria Kretschmann, Mlle. Marie de Vussiere, Baroness con Retchmann, Miss Clarks, and Frau Maria Kretschmann.

She married three times, first to an Argentinean who died soon after the marriage, leaving her with an Argentinean passport; second, to Professor Otto Eckmann of Heidelberg University; and last to Manuel Gustave de Victorica, a Chilean whom she married in October or November of 1914, in order to procure neutral citizenship.

De Victorica first came to the notice of British intelligence in 1914, most likely after returning from missions to Russia. She spent two years in Great Britain, likely working with Sinn Fein to provoke Irish rebellion and was rumored to be involved in the plot to blow up the HMS *Hampshire*, the vessel British Secretary of War Lord Horatio Kitchener, was aboard off the Orkenys.

She arrived in the United States in January 1917, a few weeks before the United States declared war on Germany, on the Norwegian liner *Bergensfjord* as an agent of the Propaganda Division of the German Foreign Office. She was also on a special mission for the German Admiralty. Soon after her arrival in the United States, she deposited a check for $35,000 at the banking firm of Schulz & Ruckgraber. She stayed at fashionable hotels like the Hotel Knickerbocker, Waldorf-Astoria and worked under the direction of Carl Roediger (aka Herman Wessels), who headed the German spy ring in the United States. His main objective was stirring up Irish sentiment against England in the United States to bring the country more in line with Germany.

De Victorica's duties under Roediger included spreading propaganda among Sinn Fein members in the United States and importing explosives to the country. One of her directives was inducing young Sinn Fein loyalists to enlist in the British navy and place bombs on naval vessels. When her original idea to import explosives inside children's toys did not work out, tetra was packed inside religious statuary imported from Switzerland, which was then distributed to saboteurs in the United States.

Her silk mufflers were not a fashionable accessory, but were saturated with a secret ink chemical. When she soaked them in water and wrung them out, the liquid collected was used to write coded messages back to Germany. Once received, the messages were revealed by using a vinegar and iodine mixture. The Secret Ink Bureau of the U.S. Cipher Bureau (MI-8), better known as the Black Chamber, finally discovered the solution and decoded her messages.

Arrested on April 27, 1918, on a presidential warrant, she was indicted by federal court on June 1918 under the Espionage Acts and accused of conspiring to bomb American and British ships, to destroy docks and piers in this country, to organize a messenger system for the conveyance of information obtained here by German spies, and to interfere with the output and transportation of munitions of war.

In February 1919, she testified in the trial of Jeremiah A. O'Leary. She appeared in court in expensive clothing, described as a coat of sable with a muff to match, two cluster rings of diamonds, and a ring set with a large emerald. She testified to being a drug addict—she took morphine in decreasing doses for the past 20 years—and receiving treatment from Bellevue Hospital, the Florence Crittendon Home, and Waverly House, all places she was confined after her arrest.

In March 1919 de Victorica was acquitted and was released from custody in September 1919. She lived in a Catholic convent outside New York City until a week before her death, when she petitioned the U.S. District Court to return to Germany.

See also: American Intelligence, World War I; Black Chamber

References and Further Reading

Hoehling, A. A. *Women Who Spied*. New York: Dodd, Mead & Company, 1967.

Ind, Alison. *A Short History of Espionage*. New York: David McKay, 1963.

"Maria Kretschmann de Victoria," in M. H. Mahoney (ed.), *Women in Espionage: A Biographical Dictionary*, pp. 69–71. Santa Barbara, CA: ABC-CLIO, 1993.

Rebecca Tolley-Stokes

VIETNAM WAR AND INTELLIGENCE OPERATIONS

The U.S. involvement in Vietnam spanned the terms of six presidents. The first president to have to deal with Vietnam was Harry Truman. Initially his views on Indochina resembled those held during World War II by Franklin Roosevelt who was sympathetic to Ho Chi Minh's efforts to establish independent states in the region and unsympathetic to French attempts to reestablish their colonial holdings. A founding member of the French Communist Party, Ho Chi Min had established himself as a valuable ally against Japan. As such, in 1947 Truman resisted French requests for aid and urged them to end the war against Ho Chi Minh. His position soon changed and by 1952 the United States was providing France with $30 million in aid to defeat him. Ho was now the enemy. The key factor in Truman's change of heart was the need to secure French participation in a European Defense System, something it would not do without U.S. support in Vietnam.

The Eisenhower administration continued and expanded this policy of financial aid but would go no further. In 1954, with its troops facing defeat at the hands of the Communists at Dien Bien Phu, they called for U.S. military support. Eisenhower refused and the French presence in the region officially ended later that year at the Geneva Peace Talks. It was agreed here that the Communists would withdraw its forces north of the 17th parallel and pro-French forces would move to the South. Elections were to be held in 1956 to determine who would rule a united Vietnam. The United States did not sign this agreement but pledged not to disrupt it. But, in fact it did. The United States created the South East Asia Treaty Organization and extended its security provisions to "the free people of Vietnam." It also supported the South Vietnamese government's decision not to hold an election in 1956. At that point Ho Chi Minh and the Communists announced their determination to reunite Vietnam by force.

Under Eisenhower the U.S. military presence in Vietnam had begun to take form. One thousand military advisors were in the country. Under John Kennedy combat troops began to arrive. The Taylor-Rostow Report had called for introducing 8,000 soldiers to save the South Vietnamese government. The logic of this move directed the

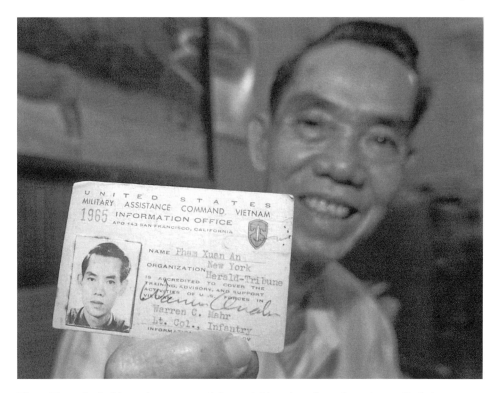

Pham Xuan An holds up his press card from 1965 in this photo from 2000. He led a remarkable and perilous double life as a Communist spy and a respected reporter for Western news organizations during the Vietnam War. (AP/Wide World Photos)

United States away from a guerrilla war strategy that sought to gain political control of the population to a military strategy designed to eliminate the enemy. Under Lyndon Johnson this military presence escalated dramatically. The United States retaliated for a February 1965 attack on Pleiku with a massive sustained bombing campaign against North Vietnam known as Operation Rolling Thunder. By June 1965, 200,000 U.S. troops were in Vietnam and the military was projecting a need for 600,000 troops by 1967. This buildup was marked by a dramatic extension of presidential war powers through the Gulf of Tonkin Resolution, which followed an attack upon two U.S. intelligence ships of the North Vietnamese coast. Passed overwhelmingly by the Senate, the Gulf of Tonkin Resolution authorized the president to take "all necessary measures" to repel an armed attack on U.S. forces. The events behind this incident continue to be debated.

Richard Nixon came to the presidency following the January 1968 Tet Offensive. A nationwide military attack by North Vietnamese forces was defeated by U.S. forces but its political impact was to create a sense of defeat in the U.S. public. Johnson did not seek reelection. Nixon's solution to the Vietnam problem was Vietnamization, a strategy which called for South Vietnam to do the bulk of the fighting, permitting the United States to gradually withdraw. The weakness of this strategy was that it could only succeed if North Vietnam did not engage South Vietnam forces before they were capable of holding their own in battle. To buy time, Nixon expanded the war with an expanded bombing campaign against North Vietnam and the invading Cambodia and Laos to eliminate sanctuaries.

Peace talks began in earnest in 1969 but made little progress. Once again Nixon stepped up the bombing of North Vietnam. When talks resumed, progress was forthcoming and on January 23, 1973, a peace treaty was signed. Gerald Ford was in office when South Vietnam fell in 1975. What started as a normal military engagement ended in a rout and on April 30, 1975, South Vietnam surrendered unconditionally.

Not surprisingly, the U.S. intelligence community's involvement in Vietnam is just as long as its political and military involvement. In 1945 the Office of Strategic Services (OSS) established a liaison team to work with Ho Chi Minh against the Japanese. In this capacity it trained hundreds of Vietminh guerrillas and nursed Ho back to health after he became seriously ill. After World War II ended, OSS teams reentered Vietnam in search of information and to protect American prisoners of war. By Dien Bien Phu the OSS and Ho Chi Minh were on opposite sides. Although Eisenhower did not send U.S. forces to support the French, he did permit Civil Air Transport, a secretly owned Central Intelligence Agency (CIA) firm, to provide it with air support.

To bolster the new post–Geneva Agreement South Vietnamese government, the United States sent a CIA team to provide it with advice and frustrate North Vietnamese efforts to establish a strong political base in the North by sabotaging its transportation networks. Col. Edward Lansdale, who had already helped the Pilipino government beat back a Communist insurgency, was placed in charge of this mission that operated out of the U.S. embassy under the cover of the Saigon Military Mission. Later, under the leadership of Chief of Station and future Director of Central Intelligence William Colby, U.S. covert operations in South Vietnam would extend to efforts to mobilize the Montagnards and other ethnic minorities against the Vietcong through the creation of Civilian Irregular Defense Groups.

In the late 1960s, under the leadership of Robert Komer and with Colby's support, a new covert initiative was undertaken. Operation Phoenix sought to centralize the different counterintelligence operations being conducted in South Vietnam. It encouraged the South Vietnamese to turn in Communists and their sympathizers who were then interrogated. Although its defenders cite Operation Phoenix as the source of important information, its detractors cite the abuses that occurred in the arrest of South Vietnamese citizens and the interrogation tactics used. It was terminated in 1971. Operation Phoenix was part of a larger program known as the Civil Operations and Revolutionary Development Support (CORDS) program that had as its goal the separation of the people from the Viet Minh by providing for better security and living conditions.

Intelligence-gathering activities occurred on land, sea, and air. A prime example of land intelligence was Operation Muscle Shoals. This program involved planting by air drops Unattended Ground Sensors along key passage ways such as the Ho Chi Minh Trail. The sensors detected the movement of people and vehicles. This information was picked up by monitoring aircraft that could be used to trigger an air strike or provide contextual information about troop and resupply patterns. Sea intelligence is best represented by the presence of U.S. naval ships such as the USS *Maddux* and *C. Turner Joy* off of the North Vietnamese coast. These were the two vessels attacked by the North Vietnamese that led to the Gulf of Tonkin Resolution. Their presence was compromised by Operation DESOTO, an ongoing U.S. covert program against North Vietnam. Air reconnaissance largely was employed for purposes of identifying potential targets and carrying out post-attack damage assessments. The air force also employed Remotely Piloted Vehicles and high-altitude SR-71s to engage in reconnaissance over North Vietnam.

Intelligence analytical products also became areas of great controversy. Among the most intense disputes was that on the Order of Battle. Two intelligence battles were fought. One was within the CIA where Sam Adams convinced superiors that the Defense Department's numbers greatly underestimated the enemy's true strength and therefore understated the number of U.S. forces that would be needed to defeat it. Once Adams' position triumphed, the second battle began between the CIA and the military led by the Defense Intelligence Agency. In the end the CIA acquiesced to the military's numbers, numbers that the scale of the Tet Offensive proved to be wrong. Adams' charges became the focal point of a CBS news story that accused General William Westmoreland of deliberately falsifying the Order of Battle numbers. Westmoreland unsuccessfully sued CBS for libel.

Finally, the United States was also the target of intelligence-gathering activities by North Vietnam. The most prominent case involves Pham Xuan An, who was a Vietnamese journalist. He worked for a number of Western news agencies and publications during the Vietnam War while also in the employ of the Communist Party Central Office for South Vietnam's H.63 military intelligence network. His contacts included Lansdale as well as such well-known authors of books on Vietnam as David Halberstam, Neil Sheehan, and Stanley Karnow.

See also: Adams, Sam; Central Intelligence Agency; Colby, William Egan; Defense Intelligence Agency; DESOTO, Operation; Journalists, Espionage and; Lansdale, Edward Geary; Office of Strategic Services; SR-71; Xuan An, Pham

References and Further Reading

Adams, Sam. "Vietnam Cover-up: Playing War with Numbers," *Harper's* 250 (975), 41–44, 62–73.

Halberstam, David. *The Best and the Brightest*. New York: Random House, 1969.

Sheehan, Neil. *A Bright Shining Lie: John Paul Vann and America in Vietnam*. New York: Random House, 1988.

Snepp, Frank. *Decent Interval*. New York: Random House, 1977.

Wirtz, James. "Intelligence to Please? The Order of Battle Controversy During the Vietnam War," *Political Science Quarterly* 106 (1991), 239–263.

Glenn P. Hastedt

VILLAVERDE, DOMINGO

Domingo Villaverde was a Cuban telegraph operator in the governor-general's palace in Havana, Cuba, during the Spanish-American War. Key West–based U.S. military officer and Western Union employee, Martin Luther Hellings recruited Havana-based Western Union employee Villaverde to intercept communications between Spanish officials in Spain and Cuba. Not realizing that their telegraph office in Havana had been compromised, at the beginning of the war Spanish officials agreed to keep the telegraph cable linking Key West and the rest of the United States to Cuba and the rest of the Caribbean. Villaverde's intelligence and espionage activities, therefore, contributed significantly to a rapid American victory.

Villaverde's first major contribution to intelligence gathering for the United States took place on the evening of February 15, 1898. Villaverde promptly reported the explosion that sank the battleship Maine. Villaverde's greatest feat, however, occurred on May 18, 1898, when he intercepted a message from Pascual Cevera, the admiral of Spain's Cape Verde fleet that had recently arrived in Santiago, Cuba, to the Spanish governor-general in Havana. Within days, the U.S. Navy, which had been unable to locate Cevera's fleet, was able to blockade Cevera's fleet in the port of Santiago, which led to the destruction of the Cape Verde fleet on July 3, 1898. Within a few weeks, the Spanish government sued for peace and the Spanish-American War was over.

Hellins and Villaverde never received any awards or citations for their actions. Nor did either of the men ever write their memoirs. Throughout the war, Villaverde's identity was a closely guarded secret. After the war, Villaverde left his job at the telegraph office.

See also: Spanish-American War

References and Further Reading

Bradford, James C. (ed.). *Crucible of Empire: The Spanish-American War and Its Aftermath.* Annapolis, MD: Naval Institute Press, 1992.
O'Toole, George J. A. *The Spanish War: An American Epic.* New York: Norton, 1984.

Michael R. Hall

VON PAPEN, FRANZ JOSEPH HERMANN MICHAEL MARIA (OCTOBER 29, 1879–MAY 2, 1969)

German politician and diplomat, von Papen was born into a wealthy, minor noble family on October 29, 1879, in Werl, Germany. He started out as a professional soldier, becoming the military attaché at the German embassies in Washington, DC, and Mexico City in 1913.

At the beginning of World War I, he, along with the German naval attaché Karl Boy-Ed, organized an espionage and sabotage network in the United States in an attempt to impede American economic aid to the Entente powers. Von Papen also reported on the shipping of war material to the Entente. Von Papen spent millions of dollars on his espionage activity, including the purchasing of several American businesses as cover for his operations. His plots included the making and planting of bombs on munitions ships, and the unsuccessful attempts to blow up the Canadian Pacific railway bridge linking Vanceboro, Maine, and Halifax, Nova Scotia, and the Canadian Welland Canal connecting lakes Ontario and Erie near Buffalo.

For their spy activities, the U.S. government demanded the recall of von Papen and Boy-Ed on December 1, 1915; both returned to Germany with diplomatic immunity. The British, however, seized von Papen's papers and released details of his missions.

Von Papen then served on the Western Front before being assigned to Palestine on the Turkish front.

After the war, von Papen entered German politics and served as a deputy in the Reichstag. He briefly served as German chancellor in 1932 and vice chancellor under Adolf Hitler before being appointed ambassador to Austria (1934–1938). He actively worked for German annexation of Austria after which he became ambassador to Turkey (1939–1944), where he focused on espionage and attempts to keep it neutral during World War II. After the war, the Allies put him on trial at the Nuremberg War Trials, where he was acquitted. He died on May 2, 1969, in Obersasbach, West Germany.

See also: American Intelligence, World War I

References and Further Reading

Austrian and German papers found in possession of Mr. James F. J. Archibald, Falmouth, August 30, 1915. London: H. M. Stationery Office, Harrison and Sons, printers, 1915.

Sayers, Michael, and Albert E. Kahn. *Sabotage! The Secret War Against America.* New York: Harper & Brothers, 1942.

Witcover, Jules. *Sabotage at Black Tom: Imperial Germany's Secret War in America 1914–1917.* Chapel Hill, NC: Algonquin Books, 1989.

Gregory C. Ference

VOSKA, EMANUEL VICTOR
(NOVEMBER 14, 1875–APRIL 1, 1960)

A Czech nationalist, Voska was born on November 14, 1875, in Kutná Hora, Bohemia. He immigrated to the United States in 1894, becoming a successful businessman.

In June 1914, he traveled to Prague, where he discussed with his friend Professor Thomas G. Masaryk, founder and president of Czechoslovakia, possible Czech national statehood in anticipation of World War I. After returning to the United States Voska unified various Czech-American associations into the Bohemian National Alliance while organizing its anti-Austro-Hungarian activity. He also created a secret courier service between the foreign and domestic elements of the Czecho-Slovak independence movement, informing American government officials about it, and acted as a go-between for Masaryk and President Woodrow Wilson. In 1915, Voska established a spy network in the United States consisting of émigré Czechs and Slovaks to uncover espionage and other activity by German and Austro-Hungarian agents and diplomats against American neutrality and the Entente powers.

After the United States entered the war, he joined the U.S. Army as a captain, becoming the liaison between it and the Czecho-Slovak Legions, a military unit consisting of noncitizen Czechs and Slovaks. From 1918 to 1919, he directed the Central European press section for the American general staff, and acted as an advisor to the American delegation to the Versailles peace conference.

In 1919, he moved to Czechoslovakia, leaving in 1939 for the United States after the Nazis annexed the country. From 1941 to 1945, he was an American press officer in Turkey where he worked on espionage and for the reestablishment of Czechoslovakia.

After World War II, Voska returned to Czechoslovakia where the Communists imprisoned him from 1950 to 1960, releasing him shortly before he died in Prague on April 1, 1960.

See also: American Intelligence, World War I

References and Further Reading

Kalvoda, Josef. *The Genesis of Czechoslovakia*. Boulder, CO: East European Monographs, 1986.

Masaryk, Thomas G. *The Making of a State*. London: G. Allen & Unwin, 1927.

Voska, Emanuel Victor, and Will Irwin. *Spy and Counterspy*. New York: Doubleday, Doran & Co., 1940.

Gregory C. Ference

W

WAGNER, MAJOR ARTHUR L. (MARCH 16, 1853–1905)

The head of the Military Intelligence Division during the Spanish-American War, Arthur Wagner was the author of the first serious U.S. work on intelligence. Arthur Lockwood Wagner was born on March 16, 1853, in Ottawa, Illinois, the son of Joseph H. Wagner and Matilda (née Hapeman), and graduated from West Point in 1875, gaining a commission as second lieutenant. He served in the fighting against the Sioux in 1876 and 1877 and in the Ute campaigns of 1880 and 1881, becoming a professor of military science and tactics in Gainesville, Florida. He served as an instructor at Fort Leavenworth, Kansas, from November 1886 until 1897, after which he was appointed to be in charge of the newly formed Military Information Division of the War Department in Washington, DC. He served on the staff of Major General Nelson A. Miles during the Spanish-American War, in Cuba with Major-General Henry Lawton until the surrender of Santiago, and then returning to serve with Miles in Puerto Rico. He was then posted to the Philippines where he remained until 1902. He was a colonel in the adjutant general's department in Chicago when he died in 1905.

In 1884 Wagner had written an essay on "The Military Necessities of the United States and the Best Provisions for Meeting Them," which won him the Gold Medal of the Military Service Institution of the United States. His other books included *The Campaign of Königgrätz* (1889), his acclaimed *The Service of Security and Information* (1893), *Organization and Tactics* (1895), and *A Catechism of Outpost Duty* (1896).

See also: Spanish-American War

References and Further Reading

Bradford, James C. (ed.). *Crucible of Empire: The Spanish-American War and Its Aftermath.* Annapolis, MD: Naval Institute Press, 1992.

Brereton, T. R. *Educating the U.S. Army: Arthur L. Wagner and Reform 1875–1905.* Lincoln, NE: University of Nebraska Press, 2000.

Justin Corfield

WALKER SPY RING

Exposed in 1985, the Walker Spy Ring gained the infamous title of being the most damaging espionage ring in recent U.S. history. It was initiated and run by John Anthony Walker for 18 years.

John A. Walker (chief warrant officer, retired) had recruited his son, Michael Lance Walker (yeoman third class, serving); his brother, Arthur James Walker (lieutenant commander, retired working for a defense contractor); and friend, Jerry Alfred Whitworth (senior chief radioman, retired) to supply classified documents to sell to the Soviets.

John started supplying documents to the Soviets in 1967, at a time when he was facing financial ruin (used family savings on a bar venture). At the time he was a watch officer in the communications section at Operations Headquarters of the U.S. Atlantic Fleet. He had special access to secret communications and the keylists and manuals to cryptographic machines, which were the backbone of the National Security Agency's communication system, used to decipher naval communiqué.

John often wondered how easy it would be to steal documents and sell them. In late 1967, he walked into the Soviet embassy in Washington, DC, and offered his services for payment. He was to receive between $2,000 and $4,000 a month with "bonuses" if he could supply specifically asked for material. Procedures were explained as to where they would meet (mainly Vienna) and how the dead drops were to be conducted.

John's main source of information to the Soviets was the keylists and technical manuals of cryptographic machines, allowing the Soviets to monitor the U.S. Navy and its operations. He also passed on information on the Sound Surveillance System (SOSUS), which incorporated the laying of communication cables on the Continental Shelf to monitor the movements of Soviet submarines.

John started living the high life, but was never questioned as to where he got the extra cash. His work began to suffer and a performance review stated it was unsatisfactory. He decided to transfer and in 1968, was assigned to the Radioman School at The Naval Training Center in San Diego. The documents supplied from here were situation summaries of naval operations worldwide. It was here in 1970 that he met Jerry Whitworth who was a new instructor at the center.

In 1971, John was assigned to the USS *Niagara Falls* where he was the Classified Material System (CMS) custodian, with top-secret communiqué access and in charge of cryptographic machines. John also stole documents on how the navy tracked Soviet submarines and was reportedly paid $30,000 for this.

Retiring in 1976 John was concerned that the Soviets would not consider him useful anymore without direct access to classified material. He set about recruiting for his spy ring, knowing those he was going to "target" would find the money irresistible. Hence he was convinced that all he approached would gladly join. This was not the case when he asked his daughters, Laura and Cynthia, and his half-brother, Gary Walker.

During subsequent years, John joined and operated several businesses, notably the two investigative firms that dealt with industrial espionage and insurance fraud, which were used as a means of laundering his spy money. Meanwhile, Jerry started having financial difficulties after leaving the navy in 1974 for the third time. While on holiday he met with John who talked him into reenlisting with the promise he would make a lot of money spying for a foreign power (convinced Jerry that it was an ally—Israel). Jerry reenlisted and trained in satellite communications at a time when the U.S. Navy was upgrading its communication systems to include the launch of "spy-proof" satellites. Jerry was supplying information on the latest technology.

Jerry was assigned as the senior radioman and the CMS custodian in 1975 and 1976 at the new communications station on Diego Garcia that would house the important cryptographic machines. He supplied film containing images of classified messages and keylists. He was then assigned, in 1976, to the USS *Constellation*, with access to classified communiqué.

In 1978 Jerry decided to transfer to the USS *Niagara Falls* and become the CMS custodian and the information gathered gave the Soviets the "complete" set of technical manuals for the cryptographic machines. When the ship was decommissioned he was assigned to the Telecommunications Center at Alameda, California, as the CMS custodian. Jerry was becoming bored, and scared of being caught. He wanted to retire both from the navy and the spy ring but was persuaded to continue for at least three months for an extra one off payment ($50,000). By 1980 the documents were delivered. Jerry actually remained in the navy and was assigned to the USS *Enterprise* at the time when war games were being played off the Soviet coast and was able to provide operational plans and progress reports on them.

Arthur retired from the navy in 1973 and, in and out of employment, opened up a business with John as the financial backer in 1975. The company installed radios and stereo equipment into new cars. Before long Arthur was in financial difficulties, and the business went bankrupt. Arthur then secured a position with VSE Corporation, a defense contractor and it wasn't long before John was insisting that he supply documents for the Soviets. Arthur, feeling obliged to John, complied with his wishes, and by 1980 he was providing information on the amphibious fleet that the U.S. Navy was working on as well as documents outlining the procedures for "damage control" of the command ship USS *Blue Ridge*.

Michael in the meantime was in and out of trouble with the law, drinking heavily, and using drugs (especially after the divorce of his parents). Barbara couldn't handle him anymore, so he went to live with John in 1980. Michael went out with John on a few insurance investigations and learned how to use antisurveillance techniques. John saw the potential and encouraged Michael to join the navy. Michael, always after his father's approval, agreed and enlisted in 1982.

When Michael returned from his first posting aboard USS *America* he told John that he had clearance to view classified information. John indicated that payment would be made if Michael supplied top-secret information to him. Michael's second assignment was in the operations room on USS *Nimitz*, and thus began Michaels' stealing of mission documents, including those dealing with the missile defense system being used. He would hide the documents in his quarters before giving them to John when on shore leave. When arrested in 1985 he had a cache of stolen documents in his quarters.

It was not until late 1984/early 1985 that the FBI was aware that such a group existed. It was a combination of two events that led to its downfall. Jerry, who wanted to retire, and knowing that John would disapprove, decided to anonymously write to the Federal Bureau of Investigation (FBI) stating his involvement in a spy ring and that they should investigate. After requesting immunity and having limited correspondence, he decided not to continue and go against John. At the same time, Barbara, John's bitter ex-wife (he refused to pay money that was owed) contacted the FBI and turned John in. Laura also gave evidence and the FBI began surveillance in late 1984. Barbara was questioned several times, even undergoing a polygraph. She spoke of the other members; therefore, the agents working on the case were able to connect Jerry to the letters received.

It was not until May 1985 that the FBI arrested John, after he left documents at a dead drop just outside of Rockville, Maryland. The 129 documents found at the drop were from Michael. When the agents searched John's motel room they found documents and personal correspondence that implicated the other members.

Michael was placed in custody on board the USS *Nimitz* and, after confessing, flown back to the United States and arrested for espionage. Arthur was questioned at his home but it was not until he implicated himself in front of a grand jury that he was arrested. Jerry was also questioned at his home but, after searching it, there was nothing substantial to hold him, so he was placed under surveillance. It was a fingerprint on secret documents and John implicating him that led to his arrest.

John was sentenced to two life sentences plus 100 years, to be served concurrently. Jerry received 365 years plus a fine of $410,000 for tax avoidance on his spy earnings. His sentence was the most severe because it was judged that the material he supplied was the most damaging to the security of the United States. Arthur was fined $250,000 and sentenced to life in prison. Michael received a 25-year sentence.

It was estimated that the Walker Spy Ring handed over more than one million pieces of classified documents to the Soviets, making it the most traitorous organization in the history of the U.S. Navy.

See also: Federal Bureau of Intelligence (FBI); Year of the Spy, 1985

References and Further Reading

Bennett, R. M. *Espionage: Spies and Secrets*. London: Virgin Books, 2002.

Blum, H. *I Pledge Allegiance ... The True Story of the Walkers: An American Spy Family*. London: Weidenfeld and Nicholson, 1987.

Earley, P. *Family of Spies: Inside the John Walker Spy Ring*. New York: Bantam Books, 1988.

Polmar, Norman, and Thomas B. Allen. *Spy Book, The Encyclopedia of Espionage*,. New York: Random House, 2004.

Shelley Allsop

WATERBOARDING

Waterboarding is an interrogation technique in which an individual is strapped down and water poured over their cloth-covered face, creating the sensation of drowning. Dating back to at least the Spanish inquisition, waterboarding was been a reoccurring phenomenon during international and domestic wars. The CIA has acknowledged that it engaged in waterboarding in 2002 and 2003 but no longer does so. Three suspected members of al-Qaeda were identified as the targets of this interrogation tactic: Abu Zubaydah, Khalid Sheikh Mohammed, and Abd al-Rahim al-Nashiri. Additionally, one CIA contract employee, David Passaro, was convicted for his role in the death of a detainee that he was questioning in Afghanistan. Passaro was sentenced to eight years and four months in jail.

Experts disagree about both the value of the information obtained in this manner and its legality. The U.S. military in the past defined it as illegal. During the Spanish-American War, President Theodore Roosevelt court-martialed a general for permitting his troops to use it. After the conclusion of World War II, the United States sentenced a Japanese officer to 15 years of hard labor for waterboarding a U.S. civilian. During Vietnam a soldier was court-martialed for waterboarding.

In late April and early May 2004 CBS News and the *New Yorker* magazine published reports of torture at Abu Ghraib prison. Subsequent newspaper stories indicated that allegations of torture were not restricted to Iraq, Abu Ghraib, or the conduct of Iraqi interrogators and may have originated at Guantanamo Bay. The interrogation stories revealed that CIA interrogators had "used graduated levels of force" against Khalid Shaikh Mohammed, "including a technique known as "water boarding." The article noted that such techniques were controversial but had been authorized by a "secret set of rules adopted by the Bush administration shortly after the 9/11 attacks and endorsed by the Justice Department."

Evidence suggests that the officials within the CIA had early doubts about the legality of waterboarding as an interrogation technique, as did officials in the State Department and Federal Bureau of Investigation. In spring 2004 the CIA's inspector general issued a warning that the interrogation procedures approved in 2002 might violate international agreements on torture. Further controversy arose when in December 2007 it was revealed that the CIA had begun taping interrogations of al-Qaeda members in 2002 and destroyed those tapes 2005.

In its public comments Bush administration officials insisted that the United States did not engage in torture, referring to waterboarding and other techniques as "enhanced interrogation" tools. They also asserted that the president had the power to authorize its use because of his commander-in-chief powers and that the Geneva Convention on the Treatment of Prisoners of War did not apply to these detainees. In December 2007 and February 2008 the House and Senate passed the 2008 Intelligence Authorization Bill prohibiting the use of waterboarding. President Bush vetoed the bill in March 2008 and the House failed to override the veto.

See also: Bush, George W., Administration and Intelligence; Post–Cold War Intelligence; Renditions; September 11, 2001

References and Further Reading

McCoy, Alfred. *A Question of torture: CIA Interrogation, from the Cold War to the War on Terror.* New York: Metropolitan Books, 2006.

Paust, Jordan. *Beyond the Law: The Bush Administration's Unlawful Responses in the War on Terror.* Cambridge, MD: Cambridge University Press, 2007.

Welch, Michael. *Scapegoats of September 11th: Hate Crimes and State Crimes in the War on Terror.* New Brunswick: Rutgers University Press, 2006.

Glenn P. Hastedt

WATERGATE

Encompassing a time period spanning from 1972 to 1975, the "Watergate scandal" consumed the political energies of the Nixon administration, led to the voting of articles of impeachment against President Richard Nixon, and ultimately his resignation. Watergate had multiple dimensions. It was the site of an illegal break-in, the focus of congressional impeachment hearings, and a presidential cover-up. Although never involved in the Watergate scandal, the Central Intelligence Agency (CIA) was indirectly linked to its origins and played a more direct role in its critical end game.

The Watergate break-in occurred on June 17, 1972, when five individuals were arrested for breaking into the headquarters of the Democratic National Committee which was located in the Watergate hotel in Washington, DC. Arrested were Bernard Barker, Virgilio Gonzalez, Eugenio Martinez, James W. McCord, Jr., and Frank Sturgis. This was actually their third break-in attempt into these offices. They had broken in three weeks earlier and left wiretaps and other listening devices that were not working properly. This break-in was to fix them as well as photograph additional documents.

Many of the individuals involved in the plot had ties to the CIA or other intelligence agencies. L. Gordon Liddy, once employed by the Federal Bureau of Investigation (FBI) had proposed the operation in February. He was supported by E. Howard Hunt, who earlier had worked for the CIA. Among those caught at the Watergate with intelligence ties were James W. McCord, Jr., an ex-CIA who worked for the Committee to Re-elect the President and was put in charge of installing the electronic listening devices, and Bernard Barker who had been recruited by the CIA when he was a Cuban policemen.

This was not the first burglary engineered by Liddy and Hunt. Earlier they had been recruited by Egil "Bud" Krogh who worked for John Ehrlichman, Nixon's assistant to the president for domestic affairs, to be part of a "plumbers" unit that would break in to Daniel Ellsberg's psychiatrist's office. Ellsberg was a Defense Department official who was responsible for leaking the "Pentagon Papers" and was a principal target of Nixon's anger over perceived disloyalty within the government. That operation had accomplished little and after the plumbers were terminated Liddy and Hunt had gone to work for the Committee to Re-elect the President that was chaired by Attorney General John Mitchell who approved Liddy's Watergate break-in plan.

After the break-in, Nixon approved a cover-up plan put forward by his Chief of Staff H. R. Haldeman to hide the White House's involvement in the Watergate break-in. At its core was a CIA request to the FBI to halt its investigation into the Watergate break-in because of national security concerns. The CIA was seen as likely to respond positively to this request because of its desire to avoid the negative publicity that would come to it due to Hunt's previous ties to the CIA and as well as the ill-fated 1961 Bay of Pigs invasion. Haldeman met with Director of Central Intelligence (DCI) Richard Helms and his assistant General Vernon Walters. Walters would later testify that he was to go to FBI Acting Director L. Patrick Gray and cite an ongoing CIA operation in Mexico as the national security operation to be protected. Helms and Walters showed little interest in the plan and in the end refused to block the FBI's investigation into Watergate when Gray made a formal request for such a statement.

Richard Nixon boards a helicopter after resigning the presidency on August 9, 1974. Oddly, he flashes his trademark "V for Victory" sign at this moment of disgrace. (National Archives)

For his decision Helms was removed as DCI and replaced by James Schlesinger. Helms became ambassador to Iran.

Nixon's June 23 conversation with Haldeman had been recorded on tape, along with many others in the president's office. It would become the "smoking gun" that documented Nixon's personal involvement in the cover-up. The tape became public in August 1974. The previous month the House Judiciary Committee voted three articles of impeachment against the president for obstruction of justice, abuse of power, and contempt of Congress. With the release of this tape, the ten congresspeople who had voted against all three articles of impeachment now indicated they would switch their vote when the matter went to the full House. Evidence also pointed to sufficient votes in the Senate to convict him. Armed with this information, President Nixon announced on August 8, 1974, that he would resign as president the following day.

See also: Central Intelligence Agency; Ellsberg, Daniel; Federal Bureau of Investigation (FBI); Gray, L. Patrick, III; Nixon Administration and Intelligence

References and Further Reading

Bernstein, Carl, and Bob Woodward. *All the President's Men.* New York: Simon & Schuster, 1974.
White, Theodore. *Breach of Faith: The Fall of Richard Nixon.* New York: Antheneum, 1975.

Glenn P. Hastedt

WEBSTER, TIMOTHY
(MARCH 12, 1822–APRIL 29, 1862)

One of the greatest of the Pinkerton agents, Timothy Webster completed several important undercover assignments, including the thwarting of a plot to assassinate Abraham Lincoln in 1861. He was captured in Richmond, Virginia, in 1862 and executed.

In 1853, Webster left the New York City police to work for the Pinkerton Agency. At the outset of the Civil War, Webster accompanied Pinkerton to Washington, DC. He helped to scout the route used by Lincoln to enter the city for his inauguration, and then infiltrated a militia group in Baltimore that planned to assassinate Lincoln before he was sworn in.

In the summer of 1861, Webster was dispatched to Louisville to judge the level of secessionist activity in Kentucky. He gathered a great deal of information and came under Confederate surveillance. Webster evaded his pursuers and returned north. He was then sent to Baltimore. He was recognized as a Pinkerton agent, but bluffed his way out of it. In September, he was sworn into a secessionist conspiracy and used his contacts to arrest the entire group. The next month, he went undercover with a group of Maryland volunteers into the South and surveyed Richmond. Over the next few months, he reported the smuggling ring that moved him south, stole papers intended for the Confederate Secretary of War Judah Benjamin, and met Benjamin himself. In January of 1862, he came down with a severe attack of rheumatism and was stranded in Richmond.

When Webster failed to report, Pinkerton sent agents to find him. They aroused suspicion immediately—they were recognized by someone whose house they'd searched in Washington. The two Pinkerton agents were arrested, but escaped. Recaptured, one of them betrayed Webster in return for a pardon. Webster was sentenced to death. Despite appeals from Pinkerton and the U.S. Army, Webster was executed on April 29, 1862, barely able to walk to the scaffold.

See also: Pinkerton, Allan

References and Further Reading

Axelrod, Alan. *The War Between the Spies: A History of Espionage During the American Civil War.* New York: Atlantic Monthly Press, 1992.

Fishel, Edwin C. *The Secret War for the Union: The Untold Story of Military Intelligence in the Civil War.* Boston: Houghton Mifflin, 1996.

Pinkerton, Allan. *Spy of the Rebellion: Being a True History of the Spy System of the United States During the Late Rebellion, Revealing Many Secrets of the War.* Lincoln, NE: University of Nebraska Press, 1989.

James L. Erwin

WEBSTER, WILLIAM HEDGECOCK (MARCH 6, 1924–)

William Webster served as the 14th Director of Central Intelligence (DCI) from March 6, 1987, to August 31, 1991. Born in St. Louis, Missouri, Webster received his law degree from Washington University (St. Louis) in 1949. He served in the navy in World War II and the Korean War. In between stints in private law practice, Webster was U.S. attorney for Missouri's Eastern District from 1960 to 1961. He was first appointed to the judiciary in 1970 as a judge for the U.S. District Court in that same region. From there he went on to serve on the U.S. District Court of Appeals (Eighth Circuit).

President Jimmy Carter selected Webster from that position to become director of the Federal Bureau of Investigation (FBI) in 1978. At the time the FBI was still reeling from revelations of wrongdoing during J. Edgar Hoover's long tenure as director.

Hoover's successor, Clarence Kelly, had been unable to restore public confidence in the FBI and Carter turned to Webster on the recommendation of Attorney General Griffin Bell. At the FBI, Webster quickly established a reputation as a skilled administrator. He made the training program more sophisticated and increased the diversity of the FBI. Webster also reoriented the FBI's activities in the direction of prosecuting spies in an effort to deter espionage. Among the high-profile spies caught while he served as director were John Walker, Jonathan Jay Pollard, and Ronald Pelton.

On March 3, 1987, President Ronald Reagan nominated Webster to become DCI. Just as with his nomination to serve as director of the FBI, Webster was brought in to restore the image of an organization tarnished by scandal. Under DCI William Casey the Central Intelligence Agency (CIA) engaged in a number of controversial quasi-covert actions in support of the Contras in Nicaragua. Details of the Iran-Contra deal had recently come to light, forcing the administration to establish an independent commission, the Tower Commission, to assess responsibility for the arms-for-hostages exchange that lay at the heart of the Iran-Contra deal. Deputy Director of Central Intelligence Robert Gates was too closely linked to this undertaking to take over the position of DCI after Casey's death. After three others turned down the post, Reagan turned to Webster.

Webster maintained his reputation as an able administrator as DCI. His lack of background in intelligence and foreign policy, however, hampered his effectiveness. Also, unlike Casey he did not have cabinet rank. Webster became the target of criticism for the CIA's failure to produce intelligence on Iraq's invasion of Kuwait and the George H. W. Bush administration's failed effort to oust Panama's Manuel Noriega. He took steps to increase the FBI's counterterrorism capability following the kidnapping of Italian Prime Minster Aldo Moro by instructing the FBI training academy to place added emphasis on this terrorism. Webster returned to private law practice after resigning. In 2001 he served on a special commission to investigate security problems in the United States. The commission was established after Philip Hanssen was arrested for espionage. It concluded that a widespread inattention to security matters existed within the FBI.

See also: Carter Administration and Intelligence; Central Intelligence Agency; Director of Central Intelligence; Federal Bureau of Investigation (FBI); Reagan Administration and Intelligence

References and Further Reading

Garthoff, Douglas. *Directors of Central Intelligence as Leaders of the U.S. Intelligence Community, 1946–2005*. Washington, DC; Center for the Study of Intelligence, Central Intelligence Agency, 2005.

Kessler, Ronald. *The Bureau: The Secret History of the FBI*. New York: St. Martin's Press, 2002.

Glenn P. Hastedt

WELCH, RICHARD
(1929–DECEMBER 23, 1975)

Richard Skeffington Welch was a Central Intelligence Agency (CIA) clandestine officer who was killed by a leftist Greek group known as the Revolutionary Organization of November 17 in Athens, Greece, outside of his residence on

December 23, 1975. His death became the focal point of a major controversy over what limits, if any, should be placed on the growing body of anti-CIA literature that was prevalent at the time, much of it written by CIA officials who left the agency in protest over U.S. foreign policy.

Particular attention focused on Phillip Agee who had written several anti-CIA tracks in which he revealed the identities of numerous CIA officials, including Welch's. The best known of these was *Counterspy*. Others argue that although it was true that Welch's position as station chief had been compromised by such revelations, poor trade craft was also responsible. Welch lived in the same residence as had previous station chiefs and a review of the credentials held by U.S. diplomats made it relatively easy to identify CIA personnel. So commonplace was knowledge of his real identity that bus tours would point out his residence.

Welch had joined the CIA after graduating from Harvard in 1951 and was the 32nd officer to be assassinated. His killers were later convicted of a number of politically motivated assassinations, although they were not charged with Welch's death due to the statute of limitations in the case. Welch's death led Congress to pass the Intelligence Identities Protection Act of 1982. He is buried in Arlington National Cemetery.

See also: Agee, Philip; Central Intelligence Agency; Intelligence Identities Protection Act of 1982; Plame, Valerie Elise

References and Further Reading

Prados, John. *Safe for Democracy: The Secret Wars of the CIA*. Chicago: Ivan R. Dee Publisher, 2006.

Rositzke, Harry. *The CIA's Secret Operations: Espionage, Counterespionage and Covert Action*. New York: Reader's Digest Press, 1977.

Glenn P. Hastedt

WELLINGTON HOUSE

Officially established as the War Propaganda Bureau, Wellington House got its name from the apartment block in which it was headquartered. Its efforts were directed toward neutral nations, especially the United States. It operated from 1914 until American involvement in 1917. Wellington House worked with material given to it by the British government, but efforts were to conceal the fact that official sources had originated its material. Canadian author Sir Gilbert Parker steered British propaganda in the United States.

C. F. G. Masterman led its operations. Wellington House concentrated on publicizing accounts which were believed at the time to be true rather than to spread sensationalized rumors. John Buchan succeeded Masterman, and their mutual respect for one another averted tumult which might have emerged from the change in leadership. Nevertheless, Buchan's view of human nature was darker than that of his predecessor, and he worked for greater utilization of mass propaganda.

Although Wellington House primarily used pamphlets, diverse other types of material included free copy offered to American newspapers, picture postcards, maps, cartoons, and illustrations. It also produced a number of propaganda films. Notable was *Britain Prepared*, released in December 1915, and *The Battle of the Somme*, released in August 1916. *Britain Prepared* was a creation of Wellington House. It garnered success and publicity and sparked naval interest in creating films.

Most of *The Battle of the Somme* consisted of genuine battle footage, but some segments were simulated, and this was not reported to the viewers. The film was a success, garnering 30,000 pounds for military charities. It showed the dead (both real and reenacted), and the film's success has been attributed to the fact that this flouted contemporary conventions in photography.

Efforts for Wellington House to coordinate propaganda efforts with the British Foreign Office and War Office were hampered by rivalries between the departments. The presence of multiple propaganda bodies detracted from the overall ability to coordinate Britain's propaganda effort. Between January 1916 and February 1917, Wellington House was brought under the Foreign Office.

Under Buchan, Wellington House's staff grew, and so its output. At the close of 1917, British propaganda was transformed. Wellington House's work focused on building sympathy in the neutral United States toward Britain, but by this time the United States was in the war on Britain's side. A paper shortage contributed to a dramatic fall in the output of pamphlets. British propaganda was directed to begin targeting German civilians as well as German troops.

Secret during American neutrality, Wellington House was replaced by the British Bureau of Information upon U.S. entry into the war. After the war ended in 1918, Britain dismantled the propaganda machine which it had constructed.

See also: American Intelligence, World War I

References and Further Reading

Calder, Robert. *Beware the British Serpent: The Role of Writers in British Propaganda in the United States, 1939–1945*. London: McGill-Queen's University Press, 2004.

Messinger, Gary S. *British Propaganda and the State in the First World War*. Manchester: Manchester University Press, 1992.

Sanders, Michael, and Philip M. Taylor. *British Propaganda during the First World War, 1914–18*. London, 1982.

Sanders, Michael. "Wellington House and British Propaganda During the First World War," *The Historical Journal* 18:1 (1975), 119–146.

Nicholas M. Sambaluk

WENTWORTH, PAUL
(?–NOVEMBER 1793)

American loyalist spy for Britain during the War of American Independence. Wentworth was born probably on the island of Barbados; his birth date is unknown. He inherited a rich sugar plantation in Surinam and in 1764 employed Dr. Edward Bancroft as his plantation physician. He moved to London, speculated in stocks, and entertained Benjamin Franklin. In 1770, he joined the New Hampshire council and two years later became a British spy, with a salary of 500 pounds. He resigned from the council in 1774 and, during the War of American Independence, began reporting to William Eden, undersecretary of state and head of the British secret service.

Wentworth was assigned to Paris, with the duty of spying on Americans Benjamin Franklin and Silas Deane, who were seeking French recognition and a treaty of alliance. He recruited Bancroft, who was employed by Deane as an agent and clerk, to become a double agent. Throughout 1777, Wentworth worked mightily to thwart a French-American alliance. He believed that American leaders such as Franklin could be bribed with titles and money, but Franklin spurned his enticements. The French, aware of his activities, worked quickly to affect the French-American treaty of 1778.

Wentworth continued his espionage efforts until the end of the war, but with decreasing effectiveness. In 1780, he was elected to Parliament, and he continued to speculate in stocks. Ten years later he retired to his plantation in Surinam; he died in November 1793.

See also: American Revolution and Intelligence; Bancroft, Dr. Edward; Deane, Silas; Eden, William; Franklin, Benjamin

References and Further Reading

Bakeless, Catherine, and John Bakeless. *Spies of the Revolution*. Philadelphia: Lippincott, 1962.
Bemis, Samuel Flagg. "British Secret Service and the French-American Alliance," *American Historical Review* 29 (1923–1924), 474–495.
Van Doren, Carl. *Secret History of the American Revolution*. New York: Viking Press,1941.

Paul David Nelson

WEST, NIGEL
(NOVEMBER 8, 1951–)

Nigel West is the pen name of spy novel writer Rupert William Simon Allason. His spy novels weave tales of espionage that are so credible that many of his readers believe that he is the unofficial historian of the British Secret Service. He is also the author of numerous nonfiction military history books that examine security and intelligence issues. In addition to being an author, West was also the Conservative Party member of Parliament for Torbay in Devon from 1987 to 1997. In 1997, he lost his seat to Liberal Democrat Adrian Sanders by a margin of 12 votes.

West was born on November 8, 1951, in London, England. He was raised a Roman Catholic by his Irish mother and went to school at the Benedictine Academy. West worked as a researcher for authors Ronald Seth (1935–1975) and Richard Deacon (1951–), who had been the foreign editor of *The Sunday Times*. West eventually joined the BBC and contributed to the *Spy!* and *Escape* series. His first book, co-authored with Deacon in 1980, was the basis of *Spy!* British counterintelligence expert Arthur Martin of the British Security Service (MI-5), West's mentor, allowed West to publish numerous works of fiction and nonfiction that have helped many to understand espionage history. His books include: *The Third Secret: The CIA, Solidarity, and the KGB*; *VENONA: The Greatest Secret of the Cold War*; *Crown Jewels: The British Secrets at the Heart of the KGB Archives*; *MI5: British Security Service Operations, 1909–1945*;

The Secret War for the Falklands; and *Molehunt: The Hunt for the Soviet Spy inside MI5*. He is also the European editor of the *World Intelligence Report* and the *International Journal of Intelligence and Counterintelligence*. In addition, West has been a frequent (and popular) guest lecturer on Queen Elizabeth II.

See also: Fiction—Spy Novels

References and Further Reading

West, Nigel. *The Crown Jewels: The British Secrets at the Heart of the KGB Files*. New Haven, CT: Yale University Press, 1999.

West, Nigel. *Molehunt: Searching for Spies in MI5*. New York: William Morrow & Company, 1989.

Michael R. Hall

WHALEN, LIEUTENANT COLONEL WILLIAM H.

William H. Whalen, a U.S. Army lieutenant colonel, served as an advisor to the Joint Chiefs of Staff in 1959 and betrayed the United States for approximately $400,000. Whalen joined the army in October 1940 and after World War II began to receive intelligence assignments. He was assigned to the executive officer in the army's Executive Office Staff, Intelligence (OACSI) in 1948. From 1951 to 1952, Whalen served as a plans and policy officer with the Army Security Agency. The importance of his intelligence assignments continued to grow and by 1959 he was assigned to the Joint Chiefs of Staff's Intelligence Objectives Agency (JIOA) as first deputy chief and subsequently chief. In March 1959, Whalen met Colonel Sergei A. Edemski, the Soviet military attaché in Washington, and agreed to trade classified documents for cash.

Whalen supplied the Soviet Military Intelligence (GRU) through Edemski and later Mikahil A. Shumaev, a Soviet intelligence officer, with details on nuclear weapons capabilities and potential targets. He also supplied 17 manuals that contained operational plans for U.S. Air Force units in both war and peace. Most importantly, Whalen provided American intelligence estimates of Soviet military capabilities. On July 4, 1960, Whalen suffered a heart attack, which forced him into retirement in February 1960. His retirement did not end his attempts at espionage in 1962 and 1963, but prevented him from attaining any more vital information. Dimitri Polyakov, one of the CIA's greatest spies during the 1960s, 1970s, and 1980s, whose code name was "Top Hat," revealed Whalen as a spy. He claimed that Whalen had given the Soviets enough vital to information to allow them a victory in the event of an outright conflict. Whalen was indicted on charges of conspiracy as an agent of the Soviet Union on July 12, 1966. Whalen was given a 15-year sentence and died in prison.

See also: Cold War Intelligence; GRU (Main Intelligence Directorate)

References and Further Reading

Epstein, Edward Jay. *Deception: The Invisible War Between the KGB and the CIA*. New York: Allen, 1989.

Minnick, Wendell L. *Spies and Provocateurs: A Worldwide Encyclopedia of Persons Conducting Espionage and Covert Action, 1946–1991.* Jefferson, NC: McFarland, 1992.

Lazarus F. O'Sako

WHITE, HARRY DEXTER
(OCTOBER 9, 1892–AUGUST 16, 1948)

Born in Boston on October 9, 1892, to Lithuanian Jewish immigrants, Harry Dexter White became the highest-ranking government official accused of espionage on behalf of the Soviet Union. White, who held a PhD in economics from Harvard University, pursued an academic career until 1934 when he went to work for the Treasury Department. White's progressive, anti-Fascist political views brought him to the attention of Harold Ware, a veteran member of the Communist Party, who recruited White as a member of a group of government employees dedicated to advancing the cause of socialism and adding the Soviet Union. Unlike most of the members of the Ware Group, White never joined the Communist Party but his sympathy for the Soviet Union allowed him to easily step from influencing government to practicing espionage when Josef Peters, the Hungarian-born director of the Communist Party's underground apparatus, took charge of the group after Ware's death in an auto accident. White rose rapidly in the Treasury Department, eventually becoming assistant to Secretary Henry Morgenthau and one of the architects of the Bretton Woods agreements on postwar economic policy.

Although formally a part of the espionage apparatus overseen by close friend Gregory Silvermaster, White often met directly with Soviet intelligence officers. They remembered him as a nervous agent, fearing political scandal, who once proposed having meetings while driving around in his car. White actively promoted the careers of other Soviet agents and made his most valuable contributions to the Soviets during the 1940s by passing along information on American monetary policy and plans for postwar Germany. He derailed loans to the Nationalist government in China while promoting generous loans to the Soviet Union and cost the United States billions in inflation when he arranged for the Soviets to receive their own copies of the plates for printing German occupation currency. Named by both Whittaker Chambers and Elizabeth Bentley as a Soviet agent, White was summoned before the House Committee on Un-American Activities in 1948 where he defended himself in dramatic speech claiming that a man holding the views he held could never be a Communist. White died of a heart attack on August 16, just days after his testimony. Regarded for years as an innocent victim of anticommunism, White's role as a Soviet source was confirmed by the release of the VENONA files where he appears, under the code name "Jurist," in over a dozen messages.

See also: VENONA

References and Further Reading

Craig, R. Bruce. *Treasonable Doubt: The Harry Dexter White Spy Case.* Lawrence, KA: University Press of Kansas, 2004.

Weinstein, Allen, and Alexander Vassilev. *The Haunted Wood: Soviet Espionage in American—The Stalin Era*. New York: Random House, 1999.

Vernon L. Pedersen

WHITNEY, LIEUTENANT HENRY H. (1866–1949)

Henry H. Whitney was a lieutenant in the Military Intelligence Division during the Spanish-American War. Whitney surveyed Puerto Rico before the American invasion of that island in 1898.

Philip C. Hanna served as consul at San Juan before the Spanish-American War. Shortly after the outbreak of hostilities, Hanna urged that Puerto Rico be invaded. He suggested that the Puerto Ricans would rise up and assist the United States. Hanna urged this again, but nothing was done before the destruction of the Spanish fleet.

After the Spanish fleet's defeat at the hands of the U.S. Caribbean Squadron, Lt. Henry H. Whitney of the U.S. Army's Military Intelligence Division was ordered in May of 1898 to go to Puerto Rico and survey the island in preparation for its invasion. Somehow, word of his mission was leaked to the newspapers, and Spanish authorities were waiting to arrest him at Ponce. Whitney eluded capture; he had signed on as a stoker for the trip to Puerto Rico and was covered in coal dust. Once ashore, Whitney presented himself as H. W. Elias, an officer in the British Merchant Marine.

Whitney reconnoitered much of the island, assuming various disguises and identities as he switched ships. His fluency in six languages was a vital part of these disguises. Whitney returned to the United States in June and presented a number of maps and careful notes. His intelligence was vital to the American landing in Puerto Rico. Whitney was awarded the Distinguished Service Cross and served in the U.S. Army for another three decades before retiring as a brigadier general.

See also: Spanish-American War

References and Further Reading

Arlington National Cemetery. Henry Howard Whitney, Brigadier General, United States Army, 2005. http://www.arlingtoncemetery.net/hhwhitney.htm.

Flores Román, Milagros. "A Spy Named Whitney," *Cultural Resource Management* 21 (1998), 34–35.

O'Toole, G. J. A. *The Spanish War: An American Epic*. New York: Norton, 1984.

Trask, David F. *The War With Spain in 1898*. Lincoln, NE: University of Nebraska Press, 1981.

James L. Erwin

WILLOUGHBY, MAJOR GENERAL CHARLES A. (MARCH 8, 1892–OCTOBER 15, 1972)

Major General Charles Willoughby was General Douglas MacArthur's Intelligence Chief from 1941 to 1951. Born March 8, 1892, in Heidelberg, Germany, Karl Weidenbach moved to the United States, became an American citizen, and changed his name to Charles Willoughby. He enlisted in the U.S. Army and was commissioned in 1916. He transferred to the Army Air Corps in 1917 and commanded the American Aviation School. In 1923 he was assigned to the Military Intelligence Division, serving as attaché in Venezuela, Colombia, and Ecuador.

General Douglas MacArthur named him assistant chief of staff for intelligence of U.S. forces in the Far East on October 17, 1941. In June 1942 he was promoted to brigadier general and named assistant chief of staff for intelligence for the entire Southwest Pacific Area. Willoughby controlled American Army Intelligence in the Pacific, largely excluding the Office of Strategic Services (OSS). He created the Allied Intelligence Bureau (AIB) to use indigenous resources to collect intelligence and carry out sabotage. This group included the famous "coastwatchers," and the Allied Translator and Interpreter Section (ATIS, which translated captured and decrypted Japanese documents).

With the end of World War II, Willoughby shifted his attentions to gathering information about domestic and foreign Communists. His primary targets included Canadian diplomat Herbert Norman and American journalist Agnes Smedley, whom Willoughby accused of being a critical link in Richard Sorge's Soviet spy chain. Critics charged that this infatuation with Soviet spies led him to neglect his primary responsibilities for military intelligence, resulting in American failure to anticipate neither the North Korean invasion of the South nor the Chinese Communist intervention.

With MacArthur's dismissal on April 10, 1951, Willoughby retired. He continued to play a prominent role in anti-Communist activities in the United States until his death in 1972.

See also: Central Bureau; Coastwatchers; Office of Strategic Services; Smedley, Agnes; Sorge, Richard

References and Further Reading

Moore, Jeffrey. *Spies for Nimitz: Joint Military Intelligence in the Pacific War.* Annapolis, MD: Naval Institute Press, 2004.

Schaller, Michael. *Douglas MacArthur: The Far Eastern General.* New York: Oxford University Press, 1989.

Yu, Maochin. *OSS in China: Prelude to Cold War.* New Haven, CT: Yale University Press, 1996.

Peter F. Coogan

WILSON, EDWIN P.
(1928–)

Edwin P. Wilson was a former Central Intelligence Agency (CIA) officer who was convicted of illegally selling weapons to Libya in 1983. During his career with the CIA and later with naval intelligence, Wilson operated a number of dummy companies that dealt in arms sales, served as a conduit for information to the CIA, and a vehicle for CIA covert operations. As a result of these business activities Wilson amassed $21.8 million from arms sales to Libya alone. Wilson appealed the verdict, arguing that the CIA had lied about the extent of its involvement with Wilson after his retirement.

In 2003 a judge vacated the decision and he was released from Allenwood Federal Prison Camp on September 14, 2004.

Wilson was born in 1928 and joined the marines in 1953. In 1956 he was discharged and he started working for the CIA, remaining with them for 15 years. His primary assignment with the CIA was to establish front companies through which the CIA could conduct business. Former CIA agents were key partners in many of these firms. One of the most successful was Consultants International. After he left the CIA, Wilson began to operate in a similar capacity and using the same firms for a secret naval intelligence unit, Task Force 157. He continued in this capacity until 1976.

In September 1976 a former CIA employee alerted the Federal Bureau of Investigation (FBI) to the likelihood that a U.S. firm operated by Wilson was engaging in arms sales with Libya. Such dealings were illegal at the time because of economic sanctions placed on Libya by the United States. The following year the *Washington Post* ran a story about how Wilson had smuggled 500,000 explosive timers in Libya in summer 1976. The CIA's inspector general's office began an investigation into Wilson's activities two days after the article appeared. The CIA suspended its investigation at the request of the FBI. During its internal investigation Wilson was supported by Ted Shackley and Thomas Clines, CIA officials and business partners in his front companies.

In 1980 a grand jury indicted Wilson for shipping explosives to Libya. He was not convicted but went into self-imposed exile in Libya which would not extradite him. He did, however, meet with a U.S. official in Italy in 1981 where he provided them with information on Libya's nuclear program, assassination teams, and Americans assisting or taking bribes from the Libyan government. Unhappy and fearing for his safety in Libya, Wilson was convinced in June 1982 to leave Libya and go to the Dominican Republic. When he arrived he was captured and sent to New York where he was arrested. On July 19, 1982, he was indicted for conspiring to ship plastic explosives to Libya, falsifying a ships export declaration, exporting explosives without a license, and transporting explosives by aircraft. On February 5, 1983, Wilson was convicted on all counts. He was sentenced to 17 years in jail and fined $145,000.

During the trial Wilson argued in his defense that he was at least implicitly acting under the direction and authority of the CIA and that he had engaged in eight other projects for the CIA since his official retirement in 1976, including gathering intelligence on Soviet military operations in Libya. The CIA denied that with one exception it had had any contact with him. Wilson unsuccessfully appealed the verdict. Years later his lawyer, a former CIA official, was able to document some 80 contacts between Wilson and the CIA and the decision was overturned.

See also: Central Intelligence Agency; Federal Bureau of Investigation (FBI)

References and Further Reading

Goulden, Joseph C., with Alexander Raffio. *Death Merchant: The Rise and Fall of Edwin P. Wilson*. New York: Simon & Shuster, 1984.

Maas, Peter. *Manhunt: The Incredible Pursuit of a CIA Agent Turned Terrorist*. New York: Penguin, 1987.

Glenn P. Hastedt

WISEMAN, SIR WILLIAM
(FEBRUARY 1, 1885–JUNE 17, 1962)

Sir William Wiseman, a British intelligence officer, had the task of liaising with the United States during World War I, becoming a confidant of Colonel Edward M. House, the close adviser to Woodrow Wilson.

William George Eden Wiseman was born on February 1, 1885, the eldest son of Sir William Wiseman, 9th Baronet, who had annexed the Pacific island of Tongareva in 1888. A month before his eight birthday, at the death of his father, William inherited the baronetcy that was created in 1628. He was educated at Winchester College and Jesus College, Cambridge, where he was a member of the university boxing team. He tried his hand as a journalist and then traveled in Canada and the United States where he built up some business interests. Just before the outbreak of World War I, Wiseman joined the artillery, and when war started, he served as a captain in the 6th (Service) Battalion.

After being injured in a gas attack, Wiseman was appointed intelligence officer attached to the British embassy in Washington, DC. In 1916 he was asked by the British ambassador, Sir Cecil Spring Rice, to communicate with Colonel House and he soon became an intermediary between House and the British government. *The intimate papers of Colonel House*, published from 1926 to 1928, make many references to him, showing his importance at the time. The British politician Lord Reading commented that "Wiseman is well named."

One of the operations run by Wiseman concerned an attempt to support the Kerensky government in Russia in May 1917. To this end Wiseman contacted a family friend, the writer W. Somerset Maugham, and persuaded him to go to Petrograd with $150,000—half provided by Colonel House, and the other half from British sources. Many of the adventures that Maugham had during this venture appeared in his Ashenden short stories, with one of the people who worked with him, Tomas Masaryk, ending up as president of Czechoslovakia from 1918 to 1935. During the Peace Conference at Versailles at the end of World War I, Wiseman, by then a lieutenant colonel, was placed on the staff of military intelligence, and chief adviser on American affairs to the British delegation.

After the Treaty of Versailles, Wiseman moved to the United States and became a partner in the New York banking house of Kuhn, Loeb and Company. He became chairman of the committee in the United States of the Dollar Exports Council, and was described as having been, for many years, one of the most prominent British residents in the United States. He died on June 17, 1962, at a New York Hospital.

See also: American Intelligence, World War I

References and Further Reading

Andrew, Christopher. *For the President's Eyes Only: Secret Intelligence and the American Presidency from Washington to Bush*. New York: HarperCollins, 1995.

Andrew, Christopher. *Her Majesty's Secret Service: The Making of the British Intelligence Community*. New York: Viking, 1985.

Justin Corfield

WISNER, FRANK GARDINER
(1910–OCTOBER 29, 1965)

Frank G. Wisner oversaw the early development of the Central Intelligence Agency's (CIA) covert action capabilities. Born in Laurel, Mississippi, in 1910, Wisner was educated at Woodberry Forest School in Orange and the University of Virginia. He enlisted in the U.S. Navy six months prior to the Japanese attack on Pearl Harbor. After working in the navy's censor's office, Wisner obtained a transfer to the Office of Strategic Services (OSS).

In June 1944, the OSS sent Wisner to Turkey on his first assignment. In August, he was transferred to Romania, where his principal responsibility was to spy on the Soviet Union. Although most U.S. officials still considered Stalin an ally during World War II, Wisner's experiences in Romania convinced him that conflict with the Soviet Union was imminent. Henceforth, he became increasingly involved in anti-Soviet policy initiatives.

In 1947, Undersecretary of State Dean Acheson recruited Wisner into the State Department's Office of Occupied Territories. On June 18, 1948, National Security Council Directive 10/2 established the Office of Special Projects and Wisner was appointed its first director. Soon renamed the Office of Policy Coordination (OPC), this organization became the covert operations branch of the CIA.

In August 1952, the OPC was merged with the CIA's espionage branch to form the Directorate of Plans (DPP). Wisner was appointed to head the DPP. As deputy director for plans, Wisner oversaw operations that resulted in the overthrow of Iranian Prime Minister Mohammed Mossadegh in 1953 and of Jacobo Arbenz in Guatemala in 1954. In December 1956, Wisner suffered a mental breakdown and was diagnosed as a manic depressive. He was institutionalized at the Sheppard-Pratt Institute in Baltimore, Maryland, where he was subjected to electroshock therapy, until 1958.

Too ill to return to the DPP, Wisner was appointed CIA chief of station in London in 1959. In April 1962, the CIA recalled Wisner to Washington. Soon afterward he agreed to retire from the agency. On October 29, 1965, Wisner committed suicide using one of his son's shotguns. He was buried at Arlington National Cemetery.

See also: AJAX, Operation; Central Intelligence Agency; Cold War Intelligence; Office of Strategic Services

References and Further Reading

Montague, Ludwell Lee. *General Walter Bedell Smith as Director of Central Intelligence, October 1950–February 1953.* University Park, PA: The Pennsylvania State University Press, 1992.

Richelson, Jeffrey T. *A Century of Spies: Intelligence in the Twentieth Century.* New York: Oxford University Press, 1995.

Thomas, Evan. *The Very Best Men: Four Who Dared: The Early Years of the CIA.* New York: Simon and Schuster, 1995.

Derek A. Bentley

WITZKE, LOTHAR
(1895–)

A German agent and saboteur in the United States during World War I, Lothar Wotzke was the only German spy sentenced to death in the United States during the war. Born in Posen, Germany, both of Lothar Witzke's parents were born in Russian Poland. Lothar joined the Germany navy and served on the *Dresden*, surviving the sinking of the ship in the Pacific, and being interned in Valparaiso, Chile. He escaped in 1916 and went to the United States where he was involved in an attempt to destroy munitions at Black Tom Island, New York, on July 30, 1916. He then worked in Mexico and was sent back into the United States in 1918. Leaving Mexico in civilian clothes and assuming the identity of Pablo Waberski, a Russian Pole, he was arrested by the customs officials after he left the Central Hotel at Nogales, Mexico, and entered into Arizona. A cipher message in his luggage, decoded by U.S. military intelligence, confirmed him as a spy.

The U.S. Army put Witzke on trial at a secret court-martial on the charge of spying at the American Army encampment where he was held after his arrest, and he was found guilty and sentenced to be executed. There were stays of execution and on January, 5, 1920, the U.S. Census records Witzke living at the Fort San Antonio Army Post, Texas. Later that year President Woodrow Wilson commuted his sentence to life imprisonment. This was partly because the case, according to commentators, should have been held before civilian authorities. Three years later, Witzke rescued several fellow prisoners in a fire which broke out after a boiler exploded, and was freed. He returned to Germany and was awarded two Iron Cross medals. He later moved to Venezuela where he worked for an oil company, and then worked for the Hamburg-America steamship line in China.

See also: American Intelligence, World War I

References and Further Reading

Landau, Henry. *The Enemy Within: The Inside Story of German Sabotage in America*. New York: Putnam's, 1937.

Witcover, Jules. *Sabotage at Black Tom: Imperial Germany's Secret War in America, 1914–1917*. Chapel Hill, NC: Algonquin Books, 1989.

Justin Corfield

WOLF, MARKUS JOHANNES
(JANUARY 19, 1923–NOVEMBER 9, 2006)

Johannes Markus Wolf was an East German spymaster. Wolf was born on January 19, 1923, in Hechingen, Germany. The Jewish background and Communist Party membership of Wolf's father forced the family to flee first to Switzerland, and then to the Soviet Union after Hitler's rise to power. In Moscow, he attended the German Karl Liebknecht School before graduating at a Russian high school. He started studying aeronautical engineering when the Nazis invaded the Soviet Union in 1941. Evacuated to central Asia, he joined the Comintern in Bashkiria, where he learned how to use various weapons, explosive devices, propaganda techniques, and other espionage methods.

After the war Wolf worked in a Berlin radio station in the Soviet Zone, and covered the Nuremberg War Trials. In 1951, he helped to establish the East German foreign intelligence network, later called die Hauptverwaltung Aufklärung (HVA), a branch of the secret police or STASI. The following year he became its head, personally supervising many of his 4,000 agents in various activities such as disguises, forgeries, safe houses, surveillance, blackmail, planting listening devices, stealing secrets, and clandestine meetings. He also served as a link between East Germany and various terrorist organizations worldwide, including the PLO.

Known as the "man without a face" since he was rarely photographed, he perfected using sex as an espionage tool. His "Romeo spies," East German males using identities of people killed during wartime bombings on Dresden, seduced secretaries who had access to classified information, including Dagmar Kahlig-Schheffler, who later worked in the office of West German Chancellor Helmut Schmidt. He also established brothels in East Berlin to trap unsuspecting Westerners to work for him. He succeeded in infiltrating NATO headquarters and the highest levels of politics, business, and government of West Germany by planting moles with the most famous being Günter Guillaume, a top aide to West German Chancellor Willy Brandt, upon whose unmasking caused Brandt to resign in 1974.

Wolf retired in 1986, but as a supporter of the policies of Soviet leader Mikhail Gorbachev, he advocated change in East Germany along the lines of glasnost and perestroika in the Soviet Union. In 1993, after the fall of the Berlin Wall in 1989 and German reunification in 1990, Wolf was arrested and convicted of treason and spying charges, receiving a six-year sentence. It was later overturned, but in 1997, he received a two-year suspended sentence for lesser crimes.

See also: Cold War Intelligence; German Democratic Republic—and U.S. Intelligence; STASI

References and Further Reading

Colitt, Leslie. *Spymaster: The Real Life of Karla, His Moles, and the East German Secret Police.* Reading, MA: Addison Wesley, 1995.

Whitney, Craig R. *Spy Trader: East Germany's Devil's Advocate and the Darkest Secrets of the Cold War.* New York: New York Times Books, 1993.

Wolf, Markus, with Anne McElvoy. *Man Without a Face: The Autobiography of Communism's Greatest Spymaster.* New York: Public Affairs, 1999.

Gregory C. Ference

WOOD, WILLIAM P.
(MARCH 11, 1820–MARCH 20, 1903)

William P. Wood was the first person appointed to run the United States Secret Service. The Department came in to being on July 5, 1865, with Wood being appointed by Treasury Secretary Hugh McCulloch. William Wood had served in the army during the Mexican American War and prior to his appointment as head of the Secret Service he had been commandant of the old Capital Prison. The Old Capital Prison was on the site that is the U.S. Supreme Court's home today.

Wood served as a cavalry officer in the Mexican American War; during the U.S. Civil War, Wood once again served in the cavalry. Wood collected intelligence for the Union army, including missions that took him behind enemy lines; he was also credited with rescuing prisoners. Wood's exploits earned him a reputation in the South as a daring soldier. Wood was also recruited during the war to help the Treasury Department to track down Peter McCartney and other notorious counterfeiters and forgers that were operating in the United States at the time.

The Secret Service had 10 agents when the office was created in 1865. Part of the staff that Wood hired was former forgers and counterfeiters to help Wood and his agents learn to identify counterfeit currency and other financial documents. Once the Secret Service was established, Wood and his agents relentlessly pursued counterfeiters. Under Wood's leadership, the Secret Service captured over 200 counterfeiters between 1865 and 1869. Wood resigned his post as chief of the Secret Service after he tracked down William E. Brock and tried to collect the reward offered for Brock's capture. Wood received $5,000 of the $20,000 reward and spent the rest of his life trying to get the remaining reward from the Treasury Department.

See also: Sanford, Henry; Secret Service

References and Further Reading

Melanson, Philip H., and Peter F. Stevens. *The Secret Service: The Hidden History of an Enigmatic Agency.* New York: Carroll & Graf Publishers, 2004.

Mogelever, Jacob. *Death to Traitors: the Story of General Lafayette C. Baker, Lincoln's Forgotten Secret Service Chief.* Garden City, NY: Doubleday, 1960.

Steven F. Marin

WOODHULL, ABRAHAM (OCTOBER 7, 1750–JANUARY 23, 1826)

Abraham Woodhull was a member of the Culper Spy Ring in New York and on Long Island during the War of American Independence. Woodhull was born on October 7, 1750, in Setauket, Long Island, New York. When the Culper Spy Ring was organized in 1778 by Major Benjamin Tallmadge at the behest of General George Washington, Woodhull (Culper Senior) was put in charge of day-to-day operations. Additionally, he risked his life many times by collecting information in New York City and on western Long Island.

As a rule, the Culper Ring operated by an agreed-upon set of procedures. Robert Townsend (Culper Junior) gathered intelligence in the city, which he transcribed in encoded documents. Austin Roe conveyed these to Setauket, where he leased a pasture and barn from Woodhull and kept cattle as a pretense for being in the vicinity. He deposited his dispatches in a secret box, tended his cattle, and departed. Woodhull then collected the documents, evaluated them, and determined which needed to be sent forward to Washington's headquarters. These he gave to Caleb Brewster, who carried them by whaleboat across Long Island Sound to Tallmadge in Connecticut. Finally, Tallmadge dispatched the information by a series of mounted dragoons to Washington in New Windsor, New York.

Woodhull's health was precarious and not improved by his constant fear of being discovered. But he, and his spy colleagues, survived the war without mishap. In later years Woodhull became judge of Suffolk County and died on January 23, 1826, at Setauket.

See also: Brewster, Caleb; Culper Ring; Roe, Austin; Tallmadge, Major Benjamin; Townsend, Robert

References and Further Reading

Ford, Corey. *A Peculiar Service*. Boston: Little, Brown & Company, 1965.

Groth, Lynn. *The Culper Spy Ring*. Philadelphia: Westminster Press, 1969.

Pennypacker, Morton. *General Washington's Spies on Long Island and in New York*. Brooklyn, NY: Long Island Historical Society, 1939.

Paul David Nelson

WOOLSEY, R. JAMES, JR. (SEPTEMBER 21, 1941–)

R. James Woolsey was the 16th Director of Central Intelligence (DCI). He held that position from February 5, 1993, to January 10, 1995. Woolsey was born in Tulsa, Oklahoma, and received his law degree from Yale University. Prior to obtaining that degree, he was a Rhodes Scholar. Prior to becoming DCI Woolsey served as a captain in the army and as a program analyst in the office of the secretary of defense. From there he went on to serve on the National Security Council Staff and as a member of the Strategic Arms Limitation Talks I (SALT I) delegation. Later he was Delegate-at-Large to the U.S.-Soviet Strategic Arms Limitation Talks (START) and ambassador and U.S. representative to the negotiations on Conventional Armed Forces in Europe. In addition to these positions, Woolsey served as undersecretary of the navy and on several presidential commissions, most notably the President's Commission on Strategic Forces (1983–1984) and the President's Commission on Defense Management (1985–1986). In 1993 Woolsey chaired a panel that investigated the state of American imagery intelligence. Complaints had risen about its performance during the recently concluded Persian Gulf War. A consensus had developed that the National Reconnaissance Office was too decentralized and that its different units often worked at cross purposes. Woolsey's panel was charged with finding ways to consolidate and streamline its performance. Published reports suggest that his report was well received by the White House and the intelligence community.

Woolsey's tenure as DCI coincided with the ending of the cold war and budget cuts for the intelligence community. This is in spite of the fact that he told senators during his confirmation hearing that although the cold war dragon [the Soviet Union] had been slain, the United States now faced a world populated by a jungle filled with dangerous poisonous snakes. Woolsey also labored under the handicap of serving a president, Bill Clinton, who had little interest in foreign policy matters or intelligence. Their relationship is described as having been distant, with Woolsey unable to gain regular access to the president. He did not have a private meeting with Clinton during the president's first year in office. At the CIA, Woolsey alienated many with his combative style, his penchant for viewing his role as DCI through the lens of domestic politics rather than as a presidential advisor, and his emphasis on technical means of collecting intelligence over human intelligence. Ultimately, Woolsey's effectiveness as DCI was undermined and his resignation all but forced by revelations that Aldrich Ames, who began working in the Central Intelligence Agency's Directorate of Operations in 1968, had been spying for the Soviet Union since 1985. He was not arrested until 1994. Upon his retirement, Woolsey returned to the law firm of Shea and Gardner for whom he began working in 1973.

See also: Central Intelligence Agency; Director of Central Intelligence

References and Further Reading

Garthoff, Douglas. *Directors of Central Intelligence as Leaders of the U.S. Intelligence Community 1946–2005*. Washington, DC: Center for the Study of Intelligence, Central Intelligence Agency, 2005.

Prados, John. *Safe for Democracy: The Secret Wars of the CIA*. Chicago: Ivan R. Dee Publisher 2006.

Glenn P. Hastedt

WRIGHT, PETER
(AUGUST 9, 1916–APRIL 27, 1995)

Peter Wright, a former British Security Service (MI-5) intelligence agent and author, was born on August 9, 1916, in Chesterfield, England. His father was one of the innovators of signals intelligence which was an important part of the Allied victory in World War I. Like his father, Wright excelled in the intelligence field, although he did not break into the sector until after the Great Depression.

The start of World War II marked Wright's transition from working as an agricultural laborer to being hired by the Admiralty's Research Laboratory. While there, according to his own account, he worked with the Central Intelligence Agency (CIA). Following his work with the CIA, he was hired by the British MI5.

Most of what is known about Wright's intelligence work comes from his highly controversial autobiography and novel, *Spycatcher*. Since the book contained what many within the UK government considered confidential information, it was delayed in its publication starting in 1985. Ultimately, the British government could delay the publication at home, but could not prevent it abroad. *Spycatcher* was finally printed on October 13, 1988, in the United Kingdom, only after having been a best seller in the United States and Australia.

According to his account, Wright worked with the CIA to investigate a strange listening device which had been discovered on a gift from the Kremlin to the U.S. ambassador to the Soviet Union in 1952. He solved the mystery, discovering that the device could be read if targeted by a microwave beam which would reflect back information.

Thanks to his discovery, he was then promoted to the MI-5, where he worked on Egyptian ciphering machines in 1956, remote detection technology in 1958, and French ciphering machines in 1960. His most controversial claim is his book relates to a supposed mole hunt within MI-5, during which he claims that his boss, Sir Roger Hillis, was a traitor. Additionally, he claimed that Secret Intelligence Service (MI-6) had actually attempted to assassinate Egyptian leader Abdel Nasser during the Suez Canal crisis.

Wright retired as Senior Director from MI-5 in 1976, using his acquired fortune to buy a ranch in Tanzania. He died there on April 27, 1995.

See also: MI-5 (The Security Service)

References and Further Reading

BBC News Online. "On this day: 1988—British Government Loses Spycatcher Battle," http://news.bbc.co.uk/onthisday/hi/dates/stories/october/13/newsid_2532000/2532583.stm (accessed October 26, 2005).

Wright, Peter. *Spycatcher*. New York: Viking, 1987.

Arthur Holst

WYNNE, GREVILLE MAYNARD
(MARCH 19, 1919–FEBRUARY 28, 1990)

Greville Maynard Wynne was a British intelligence officer, working with Soviet double agents. Arrested by the Soviets in 1961 and exchanged in 1964. Trained as an engineer at Nottingham University, he set up a business as a machinery salesman after the war. In 1959 he assisted in the defection of Soviet intelligence officer Major Kuznov.

In 1960, Soviet officer Oleg Penkovsky decided to offer his services to the Western powers of the cold war. The Americans rejected him, fearing a trap. The British, however, accepted his offer. Penkovsky's work with scientific exchanges with the West, and Wynne's business selling electrical machinery in Eastern Europe, provided a perfect cover. During their cooperation, which lasted from April 1961 to October 1962, Western intelligence required data on Soviet missile development, troop movements, locations of military headquarters; identities of Committee for State Security (KGB) officers, as well as confidential economic and political information.

Moscow suspected a mole, and Soviet double agents, William H. Whalen, Jack Dunlap, and George Blake, assisted in exposing Penkovsky, as well as their Secret Intelligence Service (MI-6) contacts with the British embassy in Moscow. Upon questioning, Penkovsky revealed Wynne's name, and the latter were subsequently arrested in Budapest and taken to Moscow where he stood trial in May 1963. Wynne denied being any more than a courier, lured into service by British intelligence. Whereas Penkovsky was shot for treason, Wynne got sentenced to eight years, parts to be served in labor camps.

In 1964, Wynne was exchanged for Soviet agent Gordon A. Lonesdale, and came out from detention in the infamous Lubljanka Prison emaciated and mentally distressed. Wynne later went on to publish memoirs, much to his former superiors' dismay and also figured in BBC television documentaries on espionage.

See also: Lonsdale, Gordon Arnold; MI-6 (Secret Intelligence Service); Penkovsky, Oleg Vladimirovich

References and Further Reading

West, Nigel. *Seven Spies Who Changed the World*. London: Secker & Warburg, 1991.

Wynne, Greville Maynard. *The Man from Moscow the Story of Wynne & Penkovsky*. London: Hutchinson, 1967.

Wynne, Greville Maynard. *The Man from Odessa*. London: Granada, 1983.

Frode Lindgjerdet

X

XUAN AN, PHAM
(SEPTEMBER 12, 1927–SEPTEMBER 20, 2006)

Pham Xuan An was a Vietnamese journalist who worked for a number of Western news agencies and publications during the Vietnam War, including Reuters and *Time*, while simultaneously serving as a spy in the Communist Party Central Office for South Vietnam's H.63 military intelligence network. Born September 12, 1927, in Binh Hoa, Dong Nai province, Vietnam, An joined the Communist Party in 1953. He was selected by his party superior, Mai Chi Tho, brother of Le Duc Tho, who later negotiated the Paris Peace Accords with Henry Kissinger, for intelligence work and given the alias "Tran Van Trung."

After a brief service as a noncommissioned officer in the South Vietnamese army, An's proficiency in English helped him to obtain positions with the operations staff of the Military Assistance Advisory Group (MAAG), predecessor of the Military Assistance Command Vietnam (MACV), which was building up the new military. His position enabled him to begin building what would become an extensive network among both the future leaders of the Saigon regime and their American advisors from the Central Intelligence Agency (CIA), including Major General Edward Lansdale and Lieutenant Colonel Lucien Conein. Lansdale arranged for an Asia Foundation scholarship that enabled An to study journalism at Orange Coast College in Costa Mesa, California, from 1957 to 1959, and interned with the *Sacramento Bee*.

Returning to Vietnam, An worked for number of publications, primarily Reuters (1960–1964) and *Time* (1964–1975), becoming at the latter the first Vietnamese to be full-time staff correspondent for any major American publication. Among the leading foreign journalists covering the expanding conflict for whom he became a trusted source were David Halberstam and Neil Sheehan of the *New York Times*, Stanley Karnow and Frank McCulloch of *Time*, Morley Safer of CBS News, and Bob Shaplen of the *New Yorker*. (The extent to which An's role as a Communist agent influenced the reporting of the journalists who relied on his briefings for their understanding of Vietnamese culture and politics remains much disputed.)

Because his American education and contacts presumably vouched for his loyalty, he was brought in to advise Tran Kim Tuyen when the latter began setting up South Vietnam's Central Intelligence Office (CIO) under the tutelage of then CIA Station Chief William Colby in 1960.

Although his broad network of contacts and wide access to American and South Vietnamese military and political officials enabled him to supply the Vietnamese Communist leadership with a steady stream of documents which he copied. His most significant contribution is deemed to have been the extensive strategic assessments which he wrote in invisible ink and had smuggled out of Saigon through the Cu Chi tunnel network and then dispatched north via the Ho Chi Minh Trail. Although An considered himself above all a strategic intelligence analyst, he has been described as the "greatest spy" of the Vietnam War—in fact, he delivered to his handlers almost every important military and civilian operational plan during the conflict.

After the unification of Vietnam in 1975, An was named a "Hero of the People's Armed Forces" and publicly assumed his military rank of lieutenant colonel, eventually rising to the rank of major general, one of only two Vietnamese intelligence officers to ever achieve that distinction. It was also revealed that during the Vietnam War, An had been secretly awarded the coveted Liberation Exploit Medal no less than four times: for his contributions to the Communist victory at the Battle of Ap Bac (1963), for his warning to Hanoi that the United States would introduce ground troops along with suggested tactical countermeasures (1964–1965), for his role in planning the Tet Offensive (1968), and for his contributions to the final campaign against South Vietnam (1974–1975).

An continued working as a senior analyst for Vietnam's General Department of Intelligence until shortly before his death on September 20, 2006, in Ho Chi Minh City, the former Saigon.

See also: Cold War Intelligence; Vietnam War and Intelligence Operations

References and Further Reading

Berman, Larry. *Perfect Spy: The Incredible Double Life of Pham Xuan An, Time Magazine Reporter and Vietnamese Communist Agent*. New York: HarperCollins, 2007.

Hoang Hai Van, and Tan Tu. *Pham Xuan An: A General of the Secret Service*. Hanoi: The Gioi Publishers, 2003.

Safer, Morley. *Flashbacks: On Returning to Vietnam*. New York: Random House, 1990.

J. Peter Pham

XYZ AFFAIR

The XYZ affair refers to a French attempt to secure bribes from the U.S. government in order to resolve maritime disputes. The scandal stemmed from the French government's reaction to Jay's Treaty, a 1794 commercial agreement between Great Britain and the United States. Believing that the United States had conceded too much to the British, and also that the treaty's terms betrayed the Franco-American alliance of 1778, the French government began to attack American commercial vessels at sea. The Directory, France's governmental body, also refused to acknowledge the appointment of Charles Pinckney, the new American ambassador, thus setting the two nations on the verge of war.

In a speech to a special session of Congress on May 16, 1797, President John Adams addressed the French crisis. He stated that the Directory's actions treated the United States "neither as allies nor as friends, nor as a sovereign state." Adams declared his intention to expand the military in preparation for a potential conflict with France. He also promised further negotiations with the provoking nation.

To begin peace negotiations with the Directory, Adams sent John Marshall and Elbridge Gerry to join Charles Pinckney in France. In October 1797 an agent working for Charles Maurice de Talleyrand, the French foreign minister, approached the envoy. This agent, Monsieur Hottinguer, told them that Adams' May speech had offended the Directory, and that the Americans would not be formally received until they met the minister's demands. These included disavowing Adams' offensive comments, making a loan to France, and paying a bribe of approximately $250,000 to Talleyrand.

The envoy's refusal to assuage the French minister brought a second agent, Monsieur Bellamy, to inform them that a meeting with the directors would lead to a fair treaty. Any meeting however would have to be preceded by a bribe to Talleyrand; as another agent, Monsieur Hubbard, informed the Americans: bribes were indispensable in Paris. For a lesser bribe, the French later offered Marshall and Pinckney safe passage home for further instructions. They ultimately refused it though when a fourth agent, Monsieur Hauteval, told them that the French would not cease their attacks on American shipping vessels in the interval.

Talleyrand had been vainly attempting to prolong the negotiations, believing that inaction would delay any potential intervention by the American military. In January 1798, the commissioners wrote to Adams that there was no hope of being officially received, and that their mission had failed. The president denounced the arrogance of the Directory, and believed that its conduct required an immediate declaration of war from Congress. Until that time however, the country would remain in a state of undeclared war.

In April 1798, the House voted that before any further discussion of war could continue, the envoy's original dispatches had to be released. Having assured the French agents of their anonymity, the commissioners named them only as Messrs. W, X, Y, and Z in the original dispatches. The resulting congressional debate over American retaliation never led to a formal declaration of war, and thus the XYZ Affair set the United States in a state of "Quasi-War" with France.

See also: Early Republic and Espionage; Talleyrand-Périgord, Charles Maurice de

References and Further Reading

O'Toole, George J. A. *Honorable Treachery: A History of Intelligence, Espionage, and Covert Action from the American Revolution to the CIA.* New York: Atlantic Monthly Press, 1991.

Stinchcombe, Walter. *The XYZ Affair.* Westport, CT: Greenwood Press, 1980.

Matthew C. Cain

Y

YARDLEY, HERBERT
(APRIL 13, 1889–AUGUST 7, 1958)

Herbert Osborne Yardley was a cryptanalyst who organized and directed the United States' first code-breaking efforts. Yardley was born in Worthington, Indiana, in 1889 to Mary Emma and Robert Kirkbride Yardley. After graduating from high school in 1907, Yardley worked with his father, who was the stationmaster and telegrapher for the local railroad. In 1912, he passed the civil service exam and was hired as a government telegrapher. Yardley began his career in code-breaking as a code clerk in the U.S. State Department. In addition, he accepted a Signal Corps Reserve commission and served as a cryptanalysis officer with the American Expeditionary Forces in France during World War II.

Concerned over the U.S. government's weak codes, Yardley responded by writing a hundred-page "Solution of American Diplomatic Codes," thus initiating a complete change in the U.S. code system. Yardley convinced the head of military intelligence that he could also break other country's codes and in 1912 he initiated a code-breaking operation within the U.S. State Department that came to be known as Black Chamber. In June 1917, Yardley became head of the newly created eighth section of military intelligence (MI-8). Although MI-8 had no real successes in World War I, the U.S. Army and the State Department continued to jointly fund MI-8 after the war.

Code-named "The Cipher Bureau" and disguised as a commercial code company that produced codes for businesses, MI-8 had the mission of breaking the diplomatic codes of several foreign countries. In 1921, Yardley and his staff decrypted the codes used by Japanese negotiators at the Washington Naval Conference. The information the Cipher Bureau provided the American delegation was instrumental in getting the Japanese to agree to a 5:3 ratio of battle ships instead of the 10:7 ratio the Japanese wanted.

In 1929, the State Department stopped operation of MI-8 due to Secretary of State Henry Stimson's absolute dislike for the covert operation of breaking other nation's codes. In 1931, Yardley published his memoirs, *The American Black Chamber*, which revealed the work of MI-8. It became an international bestseller. As a result of Yardley's publication, both the U.S. and Japanese governments completely changed their code systems. Due to the vague wording of espionage laws at that time, the government was unable to ever prosecute Yardley. During World War II, Yardley helped the Nationalists in China break Japanese codes and helped the Canadian government establish an office for cryptanalysis. Despite never being trusted by the U.S. government again, Yardley obtained a place in the National Security Agency Hall of Honor in 1999. Yardley died on August 7, 1958, of a stroke. He is buried in Arlington National Cemetery.

See also: American Intelligence, World War I; American Intelligence, World War II; Black Chamber

References and Further Reading

Gaines, Helen Fouché. *Cryptanalysis: A Study of Ciphers and their Solutions*. Mineola, NY: Dover Publications, 1939.

Kahn, David. *The Reader of Gentlemen's Mail: Herbert O. Yardley and the Birth of American Codebreaking*. New Haven, CT: Yale University Press, 2004.

Yardley, Herbert O. *The American Black Chamber*. Annapolis, MD: Naval Institute Press, 1931.

Charlene T. Overturf

YEAR OF THE SPY, 1985

The year 1985, coined by the U.S. media as the "Year of the Spy," saw three major cases that commanded the attention of the public—Edward Lee Howard, Ronald W. Pelton, and the Walker Family Spy Ring.

Edward Lee Howard had a colorful career path before joining the Central Intelligence Agency (CIA). After graduating from university, Howard worked for a while with Exxon Corporation in Ireland before joining the Peace Corps working in Columbia. He left the Peace Corp in 1975 to join the U.S. Agency for International Development in Peru as an analyst with top-security clearance. The year 1979 saw Howard back in the United States working with an environmental firm while waiting to hear the results of his application to join the CIA.

The CIA was aware of Howard's heavy drinking and drug use; they were still willing to accept him because of his level of education, extensive overseas experience, and the fact he was trilingual. Howard began his trainee year in 1980 and on completion was assigned as an intelligence officer in the Directorate of Operations which runs the CIA's secret services. Excelling in countersurveillance tactics, he was assigned in 1982 to the East German/Soviet Union section of the European division. Soon after, Howard and his wife (trained in counterintelligence as well), were asked to fill a vacancy in the Soviet Union division. They trained in all the techniques and procedures pertaining to the Soviet Union, including information on the CIA agents situated in Moscow.

As part of CIA security, Howard had to pass a polygraph and unfortunately it was found that he had been less than honest concerning his addictions, therefore deemed unsuitable for the service and in May 1983 he was dismissed from the CIA.

Extremely angry and devastated by his dismissal, he moved his family to New Mexico where he found work as an economic analyst. Howard decided to contact the Soviet embassy in Washington, DC, where it was arranged for him to fly to Vienna and meet with KGB agents. Trips were made between 1984 and 1985 where Howard received payments for information on the identification of the CIA operatives working in Moscow.

Howard was identified indirectly by the Soviet defector Vitaly Yurchenko, who knew that an agent by the code name "Robert" had trained and was assigned to Moscow before being suddenly dumped. This gelled with setbacks in Moscow at the time for example; Howard was attributed with a major operation being uncovered, American diplomats being expelled, and a Russian stealth technology researcher, Adolf Tolkachev, being convicted of espionage and sentenced to death.

Howard was placed under FBI surveillance but because of his training he evaded and avoided capture. He left the United States and moved from country to country across Europe, just ahead of the agents, before walking into the Soviet embassy in Budapest to defect. He was granted political asylum in 1986 and given Soviet citizenship. Living in Moscow, he worked as a consultant until his death in 2002.

Howard was given the infamous title of being the first American spy to defect to the Soviet Union.

Ronald W. Pelton, fluent in Russian, joined the U.S. Air Force in 1960 and trained as a signals intelligence officer, before being assigned to Pakistan to eavesdrop on the Soviets. Discharged in 1964, he joined the National Security Agency (NSA) in 1965 as a communications and intelligence analyst, with access to top-secret information. Facing bankruptcy and fearing this would jeopardize his security clearance he resigned in 1979.

In and out of employment, with finances at rock bottom, he walked into the Soviet embassy in 1980 and offered his services. During routine surveillance of the embassy, the FBI noticed a figure enter but not exit, and the report amounted to nothing.

Pelton sold highly classified material, including a program coded "Ivy Bells," which outlined the usage of U.S. submarines to tap into an underwater communications cable linking Soviet naval bases; this included technical and command procedures on the exact locations of the listening devices. This was especially relevant to the KGB as at the time the U.S. intelligence community was undergoing an extensive and expensive upgrade. He was allegedly paid over $35,000 between the years 1980 and 1983.

Like Howard, Pelton was exposed by the Soviet defector, Vitaly Yurchenko, who described a former NSA employee who had met with the KGB. The FBI then remembered the surveillance of 1980 and made the connection to Pelton. Surveillance was ordered but no incriminating evidence was turned up until he was asked to view the tape. Boasting of a photographic memory, and thinking they were going to enlist him as double agent, Pelton told of the secrets he had sold for payment.

He was arrested and put on trial but due to the sensitive nature of the information divulged to the Soviets, none of it was referred to by name. It was deemed too high a risk for the security of the United States. He was found guilty of espionage and sentenced to three concurrent life sentences.

The Walker Family Spy Ring was headed by John Anthony Walker (chief warrant officer, retired). It included his son, Michael Lance Walker (yeoman third class); his brother, Arthur James Walker (lieutenant commander, retired, working for a defense contractor); and his friend, Jerry Alfred Whitworth (senior chief radioman, retired). The men were lured into spying with promises of financial security and safety from detection as John would act as the courier (he no longer had access to classified material).

Arthur provided information on defense plans and control manuals relating to navy amphibious craft. Michael provided information on signal communiqué and missile defense. When he was arrested on the USS *Nimitz*, a hidden cache of documents was found. Whitworth however, provided the most damaging information on satellite and cryptographic communications.

The FBI only realized there were others involved when John was arrested in 1985, following a tip-off from his former wife. Documents in his procession contained personal letters which implicated the involvement of the others. It was estimated that John A. Walker and the spy ring had sold over one million pieces of top-secret information between the years 1967 and 1985.

John was sentenced to life imprisonment, and Michael was given a 25-year sentence. Arthur was given life in prison and fined $250,000 and Jerry Whitworth was sentenced to 365 years in prison and fined $410,000 for not declaring his spy money.

The Walker Family Spy Ring caused damage to the security of the U.S. naval intelligence structure. The uncovering of the spy ring caused the intelligence community to investigate its security procedures, which in turn led to further arrests for espionage against the United States.

See also: Central Intelligence Agency; Federal Bureau of Investigation (FBI); Howard, Edward Lee; KGB (Komitet Gosudarstvennoi Bezopasnosti); Pelton, Ronald W.; Walker Spy Ring

References and Further Reading

Bennett, R. M. *Espionage: Spies and Secrets*. London: Virgin Books Ltd., 2002.

Earley, P. *Family of Spies: Inside the John Walker Spy Ring*. New York: Bantam Books, 1988.

Polmar, Norman, and Thomas B. Allen. *The Spy Book: The Encyclopedia of Espionage*, New York: Random House, 2004.

Shelley Allsop

YOSHIKAWA, TAKEO (MARCH 7, 1912–FEBRUARY 20, 1993)

Takeo Yoshikawa was a Japanese spy in Hawaii before the Pearl Harbor attack. Born on March 7, 1912, in Ehime Prefecture, Takeo Yoshikawa graduated from the Japanese Naval Academy in 1933. He then became ensign on reserve for health reasons and worked as a temporary employee at the Naval General Staff.

In March 1941, Yoshikawa, under the alias Tadashi Morimura, was sent to the Japanese Consulate-General in Honolulu. He was ostensibly a first secretary. His duty was, in fact, to watch the weather conditions of Pearl Harbor, to spy on the U.S. military facilities, and the movements of the U.S. Pacific Fleet. His reports were sent to Tokyo and used for the planning of the Pearl Harbor attack.

Although there is a divergence of views as to what degree the United States knew about Yoshikawa's activities, the United States broke the code of Japanese diplomatic communications and got hold of the instructions Tokyo sent to Honolulu. They, however, were not enough for the United States to be assured of the Japanese raid on Pearl Harbor. After the attack, Yoshikawa was interned in Arizona by the U.S. authorities. He was repatriated in 1942. After the war, he returned to Ehime and lived as a private citizen. He died on February 20, 1993.

See also: Pearl Harbor

References and Further Reading

Prange, Gordon W. *At Dawn We Slept: The Untold Story of Pearl Harbor.* New York: McGraw-Hill, 1981.

Stinnet, Robert. *Day of Deceit: The Truth about FDR and Pearl Harbor.* New York: Free Press, 1999.

Yoshikawa, Takeo. *Higashi no Kaze Ame: Shinjuwan Supai no Kaisou* [*East Wind Rain: Reminiscence of a Pearl Harbor Spy*]. Tokyo: Kodansha, 1963.

Naoki Ohno

YURCHENKO, VITALY SERGEYEVICH (MAY 2, 1936–)

Vitaly Yurchenko was a 25-year KGB veteran who defected to the United States in September 1985 and provided it with valuable intelligence about Soviet spies operating in the United States and threats to key American agents operating in the Soviet Union. That same year, in November, he redefected to the Soviet Union. Debate continues as to whether Yurchenko was a legitimate defector or a Soviet provocateur.

After serving in the Soviet navy, Yurchenko joined the KGB's Armed Forces Counterintelligence Directorate in 1960. He rose quickly through the ranks, becoming a prominent and well-placed KGB official. From 1975 to 1980 he was in charge of clandestine operations in the United States and Canada. Following that he became chief of the KGB's counterintelligence directorate for five years where his primary responsibility was finding foreign agents operating inside the KGB. After this tour ended in 1985 he was put in charge of KGB officials operating under legal cover in the United States and Canada.

In July 1985 Yurchenko attended a conference of scientists in Rome and in August U.S. intelligence knew of his interest in defecting. His reasons for defecting appear to have consisted of a generalized sense of frustration with the Soviet system and to be reunited with a former mistress, the wife of a Soviet government official now stationed in Canada.

Yurchenko immediately provided the Central Intelligence Agency (CIA) with critical information. He told them that Oleg Gordievsky, a key British agent inside the KGB, was about to be arrested. The British acted quickly and were able to get Gordievsky out of the Soviet Union. Yurchenko also provided information that led to the identification of Edward Lee Howard, a former CIA employee, and Ronald Pelton, a National Security Agency official, as Soviet spies. Howard managed to flee to the Soviet Union before he was caught. Pelton was arrested for espionage. After providing the CIA with his information, Yurchenko became less cooperative and offered little additional information. He appears to have become increasingly dissatisfied with his life even though the CIA had offered him a furnished home, $1 million, and an annual salary of $60,000. The CIA arranged a meeting with his mistress that did not go well. She refused his suggestion that she should also defect and join him.

On November 2, 1985, at dinner in a Georgetown restaurant with his CIA protector, Yurchenko excused himself to go to the bathroom. He proceeded to climb out the window and walk to the Soviet embassy. Two days later he held a press conference claiming that he had been kidnapped by the CIA in Rome and heavily drugged during his interrogations. On November 6, he returned to Moscow.

Two general theories exist on his defection and redefection and the fact that the Soviet Union allowed him to live. One holds that his first defection was a rouse designed to protect a valuable Soviet mole within the American intelligence community by sacrificing Howard and Pelton. A second holds that he was a legitimate defector and that his case was mishandled by the CIA. Like many defectors, Yurchenko had second doubts. The CIA did little to reassure him. His defection was leaked to the press and became public knowledge, making him feel as if he were a pawn in a bigger game of espionage rather than important in his own right. The CIA severely limited his ability to interact with others, keeping him largely isolated. And, the CIA treated him with little respect. The protector sent to have dinner with him the night he defected did not speak Russian and had no knowledge to speak of about the Soviet Union.

See also: Central Intelligence Agency; Gordievsky, Oleg; Howard, Edward Lee; KGB (Komitet Gosudarstvennoi Bezopasnosti); National Security Agency; Pelton, Ronald W.

References and Further Reading

Brook-Sheppard, Gordon. *The Storm Birds. Soviet Post War Defectors: The Dramatic True Stories 1945–1985.* New York: Henry Holt, 1989.

Kessler, Ronald. *Escape from the CIA: How the CIA Won and Lost the Most Important KGB Spy Ever to Defect to the U.S.* New York: Pocket Books, 1991.

Richelson, Jeffrey. *A Century of Spies: Intelligence in the Twentieth Century.* New York: Oxford University Press, 1995.

Glenn P. Hastedt

Z

ZARUBIN, VASSILIY MIKHAILOVICH (1894–1972)

Vassiliy Mikhailovich Zarubin was a Soviet intelligence director in the United States during World War II, and one of the most important spies ever to reside on American soil.

Vassiliy Zarubin was born in Podolsk, near Moscow, in 1894. He had only two years of formal education, then worked as a sales clerk and continued to read. He fought in World War I, was wounded in 1917, and received treatment in Voronezh. During the Russian Civil War, Zarubin served the Red Army in Siberia and East Asia. By 1923 he headed the economic section of the OGPU (State Political Directorate and predecessor to the Committee for State Security—KGB) in Vladivostok.

Zarubin moved to the organization's foreign section in 1925, assigned to China for a year. Before returning to that country, he did illegal work in Finland, Denmark, Germany, and France. In the spring of 1941 he was back in China, near a ranking German advisor to Chiang Kai-shek. There he learned of Germany's impending attack on the USSR.

After an audience with Soviet leader Joseph Stalin, Zarubin was dispatched to the embassy in the United States, nominally as Vassiliy Zubilin, its third secretary. In reality however, Zarubin was deputy head of the People's Commissariat for State Security's (NKVD) Foreign Intelligence Directorate (Upravlenie). The network he oversaw stole atomic research secrets, which greatly aided the Soviet Union during the cold war.

On August 7, 1943, Federal Bureau of Investigation (FBI) Director J. Edgar Hoover received a Russian-language letter from a disgruntled rival who revealed Zarubin's existence, his real name and that his wife, Elizabeth, was also running an American network. The anonymous writer also named nine more ranking agents in the United States and Canada, and revealed that Zarubin had had some role in the 1940 massacre of thousands of Poles in the Katyn forest. By 1944 the U.S. government had confirmed enough to declare Zarubin and his wife persona non grata.

He returned to the Soviet Union and was appointed a vice chief of foreign intelligence. He received the regime's highest awards: two Orders of Lenin, two Orders of the Red Banner, and one Order of the Red Star. Zarubin resigned for "health" reasons in 1948—when anti-Semitic purges resumed late in Stalin's life.

See also, American Intelligence, World War II; Federal Bureau of Investigation; KGB (Komitet Gosudarstvennoi Bezopasnosti)

References and Further Reading

Benson, Robert Louis, and Michael Warner (eds.). *VENONA: Soviet Espionage and the American Response, 1939–1957*. Washington, DC: National Security Agency and Central Intelligence Agency, 1996

Haynes, John Earl and Harvey Klehr. *VENONA: Decoding Soviet Espionage in America*. New Haven, CT: Yale University Press, 1999.

Ryan, James G. "Socialist Triumph as a Family Value: Earl Browder and Soviet Espionage," in *American Communist History* Vol. I, No. 2, pp. 125–142, 2002.

Weinstein, Allen, and Alexander Vassiliev. *The Haunted Wood: Soviet Espionage in America—The Stalin Era*. New York: Random House, 1999.

"Zarubin, Vassiliy Mikhailovich," in *Entsiklopedicheskiy Slovar' Rossiyskikh Spetssluzhb: Razveka I Kontrrazvedka v Litsakh*, pp. 188–189. [Encyclopedic Dictionary of the Russian Special Services: Personalities of Intelligence and Counterintelligence.] Moscow: Russian World, 2002.

James G. Ryan

ZASLAVSKY, ALEXANDER AND ILYA

Brothers Alexander and Ilya Zaslavsky, who held dual U.S. and Russian citizenship, were charged by Russian officials with industrial espionage in March 2008 after they allegedly sought to obtain classified information for foreign energy companies. They were arrested after meeting with a representative from a major Russian energy company. Ilya Zaslavsky worked in Russia for a joint venture between three Russian billionaires and the British energy firm BP. Alexander Zaslavsky was employed by the British Council a culture and arts organization that is financed by the British government and whose Russian offices were recently closed as a result of allegations that it operated illegally and was a front for spies.

In conducting its investigations the Russian Federal Security Service (FSB) stated that it found material evidence of espionage including copied reports and analytical documents, along with business cards from foreign defense officials and Central Intelligence Agency officials. BP denied allegations that it was involved in espionage. Speculation existed that the arrests were part of a move by the Russian government to force the Russian partners in the joint venture to sell its share in a major gas file to Gazprom which Russian President Dmitry Medvedev once ran.

See also: Industrial Espionage

References and Further Reading

Cook, Joseph Lee, and Earleen H. Cook. *Industrial Spying and Espionage*. Monticello, IL: Vance Bibliographies, 1985.

Fialka, John J. *War by Other Means: Economic Espionage in America*. New York: W. W. Norton, 1999.

Glenn P. Hastedt

ZENIT SATELLITE RECONNAISSANCE

From August 1960 to May 1972 the United States conducted a series of highly successful photoreconnaissance satellite missions under the code name "Corona." They provided detailed pictures of Chinese and Soviet military developments as well as intelligence on the June 1967 Six Day War in the Middle East, the construction of the Berlin Wall, and Sino-Soviet border clashes.

The Soviet Union's response to Corona was the Zenit satellite reconnaissance program, which had its genesis in a January 30, 1956 governmental decree authorizing the development of an artificial satellite called Object D. After several years of trial and error the Soviets finally achieved successful space imagery photos from the Zenit 2-Kosmos 7 mission for August 8, 1962. On March 10, 1964, the Soviet Ministry of Defense declared Zenit 2's space reconnaissance capability operational, although this capability was not limited to the satellite itself. Zenit satellites were initially launched from Tyuratam or Baikonaur in what is now Kazakhstan, but beginning in 1966 the rockets carrying these satellites were launched from Plesetsk in northern Russia.

These satellites initially remained in orbit for 8 to 12 days, although their orbital lifetimes would gradually increase. Consequently, the Soviets needed to launch many more of these satellites than the United States did, and they averaged 30 to 35 launches per year during the early 1970s, whereas the United States was averaging 6 to 10 launches annually. A key reason for the short lifespan of the Zenit satellites was their inability to eject individual film rolls to aircraft anywhere on Earth, in contrast with Corona. Zenit satellites and imagery had to be brought down within Soviet territory.

Zenit's data was used by numerous organizations within the Soviet military, including its military intelligence service, the GRU, whose Satellite Intelligence Directorate interpreted and analyzed space photos. Additional Soviet photoreconnaissance users during this period included the Topographical Directorate of the Armed Forces General Staff and the Strategic Rocket Forces Commanding Staff. Topographical Directorate responsibilities included military mapping, and Intelligence Department responsibilities included using Zenit information for precision ICBM targeting. The Soviets also sought to disguise their military space missions by mixing military and civilian satellites and failed probes as part of the Kosmos program, which constituted approximately 95 percent of Soviet space missions at this time.

The Zenit program did not have a clear end in the early 1970s like Corona but has probably evolved into current Russian military space satellite programs such as the Kobalt, Yenisey, Strela–3, and GLONASS systems.

See also: CORONA

References and Further Reading

Burrows, William E. *Deep Black: Space Espionage and National Security.* New York: Random House, 1986.

Day, Dwayne A., John M. Logsdon, and Brain Latell (eds.). *Eye in the Sky: The Story of the CORONA Spy Satellite.* Washington DC: Smithsonian Institution Press, 1998.

Glenn P. Hastedt

ZEPPELIN, OPERATION

This operation was a deception plan drawn up by the Allies and was to have been an amphibious landing in the eastern Mediterranean, particularly on the Mediterranean island of Crete, on the coast of Western Greece, or the Black Sea coast of Romania. Drawn up in the period just before the Normandy Invasion, its purpose was to confuse and distract the Germans.

The planning of Operation Zeppelin involved the Americans, the British, and the Russians with hints that the Allies might be involved in an operation on any of seven spots, the main three being Crete, the western coast of Greece from the Ionian islands, or the Black Sea coast of Romania, or even Bulgaria, involving a joint operation between the British and the Red Army. Other possible landing sites were identified as the Peloponese peninsula, the southernmost part of mainland Greece; Albania; the Dalmatian coast of Yugoslavia; or the Pola and Istrian peninsula at the head of the Adriatic. Information was leaked that this might take place in mid-March 1944, at the same time as a renewed Soviet land offensive.

In February 1944 the plan was formalized with the idea of it taking place on the full moon, which was on March 23. It would involve a series of landings on Crete, the Peloponese peninsula, in Albania and Dalmatia (then part of the pro-German Republic of Croatia). However, as the date approached, planners came up with some technical problems, postponing the operation until late May. These were then modified again with attacks on Albania, Dalmatia, and parts of Greece scheduled for mid-June.

The planning involved the Polish III Corps in southern Italy being prepared for an amphibious landing at the strategic Albanian port of Durrës, from where they would try to take Tirana. It would coincide with attacks on Dalmatia and Istria, coordinated with the partisans of Marshal Tito, the British having ended their support for the Royalist Chetniks of Mihailovic. Tito was against the involvement of Polish soldiers, as he saw that a postwar Poland might try to exert its power in the Balkans. The British, however, were unable to pretend to use other troops and were also not able to tell Tito that Zeppelin was merely a deception to prevent the Axis redeploying their forces to France. With D-Day, Zeppelin was seen to have been bogus, and on October 17, 1944, Albanian partisans, without help from the Allies, captured Tirana.

See also: American Intelligence, World War I

References and Further Reading

Brown, Anthony Cave. *Bodyguard of Lies.* London: HarperCollins, 1975.

O'Toole, G. J. A. *The Encyclopedia of American Intelligence and Espionage. From the Revolutionary War to the Present.* New York: Facts on File, 1988.

Justin Corfield

ZIMMERMANN TELEGRAM

The Zimmermann Telegram represented a secret effort by the German government to recruit Mexico, and indirectly Japan, as allies in any future war between the United States and Germany. When war began in Europe in August 1914, Germany searched for ways to provoke a military conflict between the United States and Mexico, which was experiencing revolution and civil war at the time. A U.S.-Mexican conflict would interrupt the movement of war supplies and make U.S. intervention in the European war more difficult.

Germany had cultivated ties with revolutionary leader Francisco "Pancho" Villa but had to switch to his revolutionary rival, Venustiano Carranza, who by 1916 represented the only viable German hope for interrupting the flow of U.S. arms to Europe. To offset U.S. influence, Carranza sought closer commercial relations with Germany and German assistance in upgrading the Mexican armed forces. He even offered to let German submarines operate out of Mexican bases.

It was in this context that the Zimmermann Telegram appeared. Arthur Zimmermann, Germany's foreign secretary, assumed that the resumption of unrestricted submarine warfare would probably lead to U.S. entry into the war. In order to limit the U.S. contribution to the European war effort, Zimmermann hoped to spark a military conflict between Mexico and the United States.

On January 16, 1917, Zimmermann outlined his plan in a coded telegram to the German ambassador in Mexico, Heinrich von Eckardt. In the telegram Zimmermann indicated that Germany would renew unrestricted submarine warfare on February 1, 1917. The ambassador was to propose a military alliance with Mexico in the event of U.S. entry into the war. Germany would provide "generous financial support" and aid Mexico in recovering the "lost territory" of Texas, New Mexico, and Arizona. Eckardt was also directed to suggest to President Carranza that Mexico encourage Japan to join in the military alliance against the United States.

Officials in the German Foreign Office worried about the impact on U.S. neutrality if the contents of the telegram became known. Their concerns proved justified. British intelligence had broken the German code and had intercepted the telegram in Mexico. The British did not immediately turn over the telegram to U.S. officials or publicize it because they did not want it known that they had broken the German code. The British also hoped that the renewal of unrestricted submarine warfare would be enough to bring the United States into the war. When the United States broke relations with Germany but did not declare war, the British turned the decoded telegram over to U.S. officials on February 24. President Wilson later authorized the release of the telegram to the U.S. press, which published it under sensational headlines on March 1.

When the telegram was released, the Carranza administration denied that it had ever been offered an alliance by Germany and also refused to break relations with Germany, despite U.S. pressure. Later, in a secret meeting with Ambassador Eckardt, Carranza officially turned down the offer of an alliance but held open an alliance as a future possibility.

U.S. officials at the time and historians since have attributed considerable significance to the Zimmermann Telegram in the U.S. decision to enter the war in April 1917. Despite the diplomatic uproar over the telegram, the telegram did not produce a change in Mexico's proclaimed policy of neutrality. Even after the telegram fiasco, Germany made another secret offer of a military alliance with Mexico which Carranza turned down in August 1917. The German secret service moved its North American headquarters to Mexico after U.S. entry into the war. Germany even prepared—but never used—a base for submarines on Mexico's gulf coast. Although the Zimmermann Telegram shocked the U.S. public, it in fact represented the latest in a series of covert German attempts to embroil Mexico and the United States in a military conflict.

See also: American Intelligence, World War I

References and Further Reading

Coerver, Don M., and Linda B. Hall. *Texas and the Mexican Revolution: A Study in State and National Border Policy, 1910–1920*. San Antonio: Trinity University Press, 1984.

Katz, Friedrich. *The Secret War in Mexico: Europe, the United States and the Mexican Revolution*. Chicago: University of Chicago Press, 1981.

Tuchman, Barbara W. *The Zimmermann Telegram*. New York: Viking Press, 1958.

Don M. Coerver

Glossary

A-2: The intelligence staff section of the U.S. Army Air Corps.

acoustic intelligence: (ACINT) is intelligence gathered from auditory phenomena. It is generally collected undersea by ships, submarines, or sensors. It is a subcategory of Measurements and Signals Intelligence (MASINT).

agent: This term has two different meanings. When used to refer to the FBI, an agent is a professional law enforcement official. When it is used in the context of CIA clandestine operations, an agent refers to the person recruited by the CIA to engage in spying. It does not refer to the CIA official.

Agent 711: The code name given to George Washington during the American Revolution.

Agent Tom: The Soviet code name assigned to Kim Philby.

analytical intelligence: Information becomes intelligence only after it has been analyzed, subjected to systematic examination, and evaluated. Analytical intelligence may take several forms including basic intelligence, current intelligence, and estimative intelligence.

aquarium: The nickname for the main military intelligence (GRU) headquarters in Moscow. It takes its name from its basic structure as a glass-encased nine-story tower.

ARGON: The code name given to a series of mapping satellites that included CORONA and LANYARD.

aunt minnies: Refers to commercial photographs or photos taken by tourists and journalists that are used by intelligence agencies to fill in gaps in existing photographic coverage.

basic intelligence: This is factual and fundamental intelligence about another state. It is relatively unchanging and constitutes a type of encyclopedic background picture that can be built upon by intelligence analysts.

BfV: The Federal Office for the Protection of the Constitution was the West German counterintelligence organization set up with the help of the United States and Great Britain. It continues to operate in Germany today.

Big Bird: The code name given to a series of low-orbit KH-9 satellite launches from 1971 to 1986. It was also known as HEXAGON.

Black Bag Job: A covert entry operation that generally involved illegally breaking and entering into a location in order to obtain information. It was practiced by the FBI from 1942 to 1967. J. Edgar Hoover ordered its termination the previous year.

Black Chamber: Exists as a generic term that applies to code-breaking operations. It dates back at least to the late sixteenth century when King Henry IV of France employed agents to secretly read correspondence.

BLUEBELL: Human intelligence collection plan during the Korean War in which North Korean families and refugees were sent back to North Korea in order to provide the United States with information.

BND: The West German Federal Intelligence Agency, formed with American and British help, that was built on the network of spies run by Richard Gehlen for the Nazi Germany government against the Soviet Union.

BODYGUARD: The code name given to the overall deception plan for the Allied invasion of Europe in 1944.

Cambridge Five: One of many phrases used to describe the Soviet spy ring operating in Great Britain during World War II and the early 1950s. Its members were Kim Philby, Donald Maclean, Guy Burgess, Anthony Blunt, and John Cairncross. It is also commonly referred to as the Cambridge Spy Ring.

Camp Swampy: Slang phrase used to identify Camp Peary, the CIA training center.

CARNIVORE: A commercially available software system used by the FBI to monitor e-mails that was established during the Clinton administration.

CHALET: Also known as CHALET/VORTEX this is the code name given to a series of signals intelligence earth orbit satellites. The first and only known CHALET flight was in 1978. VORTEX flights took place in 1979, 1981, 1984, 1988, and 1989.

CHAOS: A domestic spying operation run by the CIA. Authorized by President Lyndon Johnson, it was expanded under President Richard Nixon. A primary target was the antiwar movement especially student groups, radical Black Power organizations, and women's groups for peace.

CIA: Central Intelligence Agency.

CIO: Central Imagery Office.

ciphers: A cipher is a system of secret writing that utilizes a prearranged scheme to prevent its detection and comprehension.

clandestine collection: A secret collection of intelligence. It is contrasted with the overt collection of intelligence whereby intelligence is collected through publicly available means.

coastwatchers: Refers to Australian and New Zealand agents who observed Japanese military movements in the Southwest Pacific during World War II.

code talkers: Refers to Native Americans who used native languages as codes for voice transmissions on tactical intelligence matters for the marines during World War I and World War II. It is generally associated with Navajos but this was not exclusively the case.

codes: Codes refer to symbols that have a predetermined meaning and are used for secrecy in transmitting a message.

COINTELPRO: Stands for Counter Intelligence Program. It was run by the FBI between 1956 and 1971. In theory directed at infiltrating and disrupting subversive groups, but it came to be used against a wide range of groups that had no connections with foreign powers and whose only crimes were opposition to existing governmental policies.

COLDFEET: Intelligence collection project designed to acquire Soviet acoustic intelligence from abandoned drift stations in the Arctic.

collection: The acquisition of information in any manner. Information may be collected through direct observation, liaison with official agencies, public sources, or through clandestine means.

combat intelligence: Consists of knowledge of the enemy, weather, and geographical features required by a commander in the planning and conduct of combat operations.

Committee of Secret Correspondence: Identified by some as the United States' first intelligence agency. It was established by the Continental Congress to, among other things, hire secret agents, conduct covert operations, create a code and cipher system, and acquire foreign intelligence.

communications intelligence: Also referred to as COMINT, it is a subcategory of signals intelligence that focuses on the acquisition of intelligence by intercepting voice communications from foreign states.

CORONA: The first U.S. photo reconnaissance satellite, also identified as Discoverer, it possessed both a mapping and intelligence-gathering capability. It operated from August 1960 to May 1972. Its existence was declassified in 1995.

COS: Chief of Station.

counterespionage: More broadly this is often referred to as counterintelligence. Two tasks are involved. First, the protection of one's own secrets. Second, the neutralization and apprehension of spies who are employed by foreign powers.

counterintelligence: This is an overarching category of activity that includes counterespionage. Counterintelligence is intelligence gathered against espionage, other intelligence activities, sabotage, or assassination conducted by a hostile foreign power or group.

covert action: This is clandestine activity designed to affect a situation in another country. The key to success is that the identity of the sponsoring country or organization is not revealed. Covert action is different from clandestine collection which seeks to acquire information but not to influence events in the target state.

cryptanalysis: This is the science of translating secret messages into plain text. It may operate either deductively or inductively. In the former, the analysis hinges on the detection of patterns that allow analysts to move from reoccurring combinations to more unique ones. Inductive analysis is based on hunches as to possible words in the message that produce leads as to the meaning of the message. Cryptanalysis generally is treated as an applied science where cryptography is abstract and theoretical in nature.

cryptography: This is the abstract science of secret writing. Mathematical equations are often used for establishing its basic parameters and translation rules.

current intelligence: A category of analytical intelligence that stresses up to date information that is of immediate interest to policy makers.

cyber espionage: A new and growing concern to intelligence officials, cyber espionage is the act of obtaining secrets from individuals, groups, organizations, and governments by exploiting weaknesses in the Internet, software, or computers.

damage assessment: This refers to an evaluation of the impact of a compromise in security that results in the loss of secret information. The assessment includes both a judgment regarding the benefits gained by an adversary and the impact on one's own collection capabilities, and ways to prevent its reoccurrence.

data mining: The process of trying to uncover otherwise hidden patterns and relationships among large quantities of data that are otherwise not readily apparent.

dead drops: This is a method of exchanging intelligence, instructions, and money between a spy and his or her handler. Dead drops are exchanges that do not involve actual physical contact between the two. Rather, a location is chosen for the exchange and a signal used to indicate that material has been put in place to be picked up. Dead drops are seen as the safest way of making an exchange.

defector: A defector is an individual in the employ of a foreign government who is either induced to come over to one's side or does so voluntarily.

DESOTO: A long-standing naval patrol operation conducted in international waters off the coast of North Vietnam designed to acquire electronic intelligence. Two ships involved in it, the C. *Turner Joy* and *Maddox* became entangled in the Gulf of Tonkin incident.

DHS: Department of Homeland Security.

DIA: Defense Intelligence Agency.

Director of Central Intelligence: From its inception until the creation of the Director of National Intelligence, the Director of Central Intelligence was simultaneously the head of the CIA and the intelligence community was a whole.

Director of National Intelligence: The statutory head of the intelligence community. Frequently proposed in studies of the intelligence community, the political impetus for creating it was the 9/11 terrorist attacks.

directorates: Administrative units. They form the main organizational subdivisions with the CIA.

dirty tricks: A catch-all phrase used to describe activities undertaken as part of a covert action plan. Dirty tricks are designed to disrupt a target's ability to perform some important function. Espionage is important to dirty tricks because it may provide information about a target's vulnerabilities.

disinformation: Also known as Black Propaganda, it is deliberately spread false or misleading information designed to weaken an adversary's defensive capabilities.

DOD: Department of Defense.

Double-Cross System: Also known as the XX system. It was the British military intelligence's antiespionage, deception, and counterintelligence operation directed with great effect at Nazi Germany.

ECHELON: Refers to a signals intelligence collection operation that was run by the National Security Agency (NSA) with the cooperation of British, Canadian, and Australian officials as part of the UKUSA agreement. It had the effect of allowing the NSA to circumvent bans on spying on Americans.

economic espionage: This refers to espionage directed at acquiring foreign economic intelligence. It targets both governments and private businesses. Of interest are such items as production methods, financial and taxation systems, research and development projects, dual-use technologies, and government contracts.

electronic intelligence: Often identified as intelligence that is obtained from communications between machines as opposed to humans. More exactly it is technical and geolocational intelligence derived from foreign noncommunications electromagnetic radiations emanating from sources other than nuclear detonations or radioactive sources.

electronic surveillance: Refers to activities to obtain information through electronic means without the individual targeted being aware of the collection effort. Common techniques include wiretapping, bugging, use of a pen register, closed circuit and photographic taping, and the use of wired agents and informers.

electro-optical intelligence: Involves the collection of data from the portion of the electromagnetic spectrum of wavelengths that contains ultraviolet radiation, visible light, and infrared radiation. When analyzed, such information can reveal the location and movements of humans and heat-generating machinery as well as distinguish between the exhaust of a missile and that of a commercial aircraft.

espionage: Also referred to as spying, it is the secret collection of information; often referred today under the heading of clandestine collection. It may be carried out either through technical means or by agents who infiltrate key organizations in order to acquire documents, photographs, or other material of value.

executive action: A colloquial term used by the CIA in the 1950s and 1960s when referring to assassination attempts.

false flag: Refers to a situation in which a government, individual, group, or organization adopts a false identity in order to shield the true purpose behind its actions. Used by intelligence organizations to obtain information that would otherwise be denied it.

Family Jewels: A list of illegal and questionable CIA activities produced by the CIA itself at the request of Director of Central Intelligence James Schlesinger as he sought to determine the extent of CIA involvement in these types of activities. The list of 300 entries became the centerpiece for congressional investigations of the CIA n the 1970s.

Farm, the: Slang phrase used for Camp Peary, the CIA's longtime training center.

FBI: Federal Bureau of Investigation.

ferret: Electronic intelligence satellites whose primary function was to gather information from microwave, radar, radio, and voice transmissions.

fifth man: All accounts agree on the first four members of the Cambridge Spy Ring (Philby, Maclean, Blunt, and Burgess). Disagreement exists on the identity and even existence of the fifth member. Cairncross now is generally considered to be the fifth man.

Firm, the: Slang term used to identify the CIA.

FISA: Foreign Intelligence Surveillance Act.

Foreign instrumentation signals intelligence: Also referred to as FISINT, it is technical information obtained through the intercept of electromagnetic emissions that accompany the testing and operational use of military systems.

FORTITUDE: The deception operation used to misguide German forces as to the location of the British landing that took place at Normandy. It was divided into Fortitude North (Norway) and Fortitude South (Pais de Calle).

FSB: Russian Federal Security Service is the current-day successor to the KGB, Cheka, and NKVD.

FSK: Russian Federal Counterintelligence Service was the immediate successor to the KGB, which was disbanded in 1991 following the coup attempt against Mikhail Gorbachev. It existed from 1991 to 1995 and was replaced by the FSB.

G-2: U.S. Army General Staff Intelligence Division.

GAMBIT: A U.S. photoreconnaissance KH-7 system used from July 1963 to June 1967. The program remains classified but many of its photos were released to the public in 2002.

GENETRIX: A 1950s U.S. intelligence that sent balloons over the Soviet Union in an attempt to obtain photographic intelligence.

GOLD: U.S. code name for the operation to obtain information from a tunnel under Berlin that gave access to Soviet communication lines. It was compromised from the start by the involvement of Soviet spy George Blake. Known by the British as Operation Stopwatch.

GRU: The Foreign Military Intelligence Directorate of the General Staff of the Armed Forces of the Russian Federation. Formerly the main military intelligence directorate of the Red Army.

Halloween Massacre: The mass firing of some 820 CIA employees in 1977 carried out by DCI Stansfield Turner who argued that budget cuts and a need to change the organizational culture of the CIA away from covert action to intelligence analysis was needed.

handler: This refers to the intelligence official who manages a spy. The handler is the spy's point of contact with the intelligence organization he or she is working for.

HTLINGUAL: A clandestine operation intercepting mail destined for the Soviet Union and China that was in place from 1952 until 1973.

human intelligence: Also referred to as HUMINT, intelligence derived from information collected and provided by human sources. These sources may be friendly or hostile. They may or may not know the purpose of the interpersonal communications taking place.

imagery intelligence: Formerly identified as photo intelligence imagery intelligence (IMINT), it is intelligence gathered from photography, infrared sensors, and synthetic aperture radar. It may be collected by planes or satellites.

information: Also referred to as raw intelligence. It is unanalyzed data that has been collected but has not yet been evaluated for its reliability, validity, and meaning.

information security: Protecting information and information systems from unauthorized modification, destruction, disruption, or use. Often equated with protection of computer systems.

intelligence: Intelligence is evaluated information. Until information has been assessed for its reliability and validity and then evaluated for its significance, it remains raw data. One of the major fallacies of intelligence is that facts are self-interpreting or "speak for themselves."

intelligence community: The intelligence community consists of those national security bureaucracies in the United States that are involved in the collection, analysis, and dissemination of intelligence. It is headed by the Director of National Intelligence. The most prominent members of the intelligence community include the CIA, National Security Agency, the Defense Intelligence Agency, the Department of Homeland Security, the FBI, and the Bureau of Intelligence and Research within the State Department. One of the major problems facing the intelligence community is the effective coordination of action. Each of these organizations has its own bureaucratic culture and set of values as well as a unique sense of mission and purpose.

intelligence cycle: This refers to the functional stages by which information is acquired, turned into intelligence, and made available to policy makers. Typically the steps involved are described as tasking, collection, processing and evaluation, reporting, and feedback.

intelligence estimates: Formal and informal documents produced by the intelligence analysts that provide policy makers with insights needed to understand situations, anticipate the actions of the others, and formulate their own policy. The most formal of these documents is the National Intelligence Estimate.

intelligence oversight: The process of ensuring the accountability of intelligence agencies. It may be exercised internally through inspector general offices, in the executive branch through presidential review and advisory boards, in Congress through congressional committees, and by special review groups.

Intrepid: The code name for Sir William Stephenson, a Canadian businessman who was the senior British intelligence operative in the United States during World War II and worked closely with Col. William Donovan in setting up the Office of Strategic Services.

IVY BELLS: A joint operation by the U.S. Navy and the National Security Agency to tap into a submerged Soviet communications cable in the Sea of Okhotsk.

JEDBURGH: World War II intelligence operation that air-dropped teams into occupied Nazi territory in order to help local resistance forces as well as engage in sabotage and guerrilla warfare. It was run by the British Special Operations Executive and the American Office of Strategic Services.

JENNIFER: The code name for a largely failed 1974 project undertaken by the CIA to raise a sunken Soviet submarine, Project (E-20th) Glomar Explorer.

JICs: Joint Intelligence Centers.

JMWAVE: The code name for the U.S. intelligence operation center in Miami that from 1961 to 1962 was responsible for directing intelligence gathering and covert action plans against Cuba.

KEYHOLE: A digital-imaging satellite the size of a school bus that operates in an egg-shaped elliptical orbit of the earth. It delivers high-resolution pictures in real time to ground stations and has infrared heat sensors. Keyhole 1 (KH -1) was known as CORONA. During the Iraq War, three KH-11 satellites helped provide hourly coverage.

KGB: The Committee for State Security was the premier Soviet intelligence agency during the Cold War. It broke off from the Ministry for State Security (MGB) in 1954 and was terminated in 1991. Most recently it was replaced by the Russian Federal Security Service (FSB).

KMSOURDOUGH: A CIA mail intercept operation run from 1969 to 1971.

MAGIC: The code name for information obtained by breaking the Japanese Purple cipher during World War II that allowed the United States to read Japan's most important diplomatic messages.

materials intelligence: Also known as MASINT, it is intelligence collected from the analysis of gas, liquid, or solid samples. It is important for evaluating nuclear, chemical, and biological threats as well as assessing environmental and public health conditions

measurement and signature intelligence: Also identified as MASINT, it constitutes an umbrella category of collection means that fall outside of the other major collection disciplines of human intelligence, signals intelligence, technological intelligence, open source intelligence, and imagery intelligence.

medical intelligence: Also identified as MEDINT, it is intelligence obtained from foreign medical, bioscientific, and environmental information that is important for purposes of strategic planning and assessing the foreign medical capabilities of military and civilian sectors.

MI: Military Intelligence.

MI-5: British Security Service responsible for counterintelligence operations.

MI-6: British Secret Intelligence Service that serves as its foreign intelligence agency.

MI-8: The cryptographic section of the Military Intelligence Division. Later popularized and equated with the Black Chamber.

MICE: Acronym for the four primary recruitment tools used to get someone to engage in espionage: money, ideology, compromise, and ego.

MINARET: An electronic communications intercept program operated by the National Security Agency between 1967 and 1973. Working off of a watch list of foreign individuals and organizations, over 3,900 reports on Americans were issued.

MKULTRA: CIA Technical Services Division program for mind-control drugs from 1953 to 1964.

MOCKINGBIRD: A clandestine CIA operation to enlist journalists in promoting the image of the CIA and protecting it from criticism. Journalists were also used as sources of information and as covers for CIA operatives abroad.

mole: A spy who has been secretly placed within an adversary's intelligence service or other important national security organization. The mole may be quiet or inactive for a long period of time before becoming active and providing intelligence.

MSIC: Missile and Space Intelligence Center.

National Clandestine Service: Today serves as the principal U.S. agency for conducting human intelligence. It was created by absorbing the CIA's Directorate of Operations and coordinates the human intelligence collection activities of other members of the intelligence community.

NCTC: National Counter Terrorism Center.

NFIB: National Foreign Intelligence Board.

NGA: National Geospatial Intelligence Agency.

NIE: National Intelligence Estimate.

NIMA: National Imagery and Mapping Agency.

NIO: National Intelligence Officer.

NKVD: Peoples Commissariat for Internal Affairs. It was the Soviet secret police during the Stalinst period. It ran the gulag system and the main directorate for state security which became the KGB.

NMIC: National Maritime Intelligence Center.

NRO: National Reconnaissance Office.

NSA: National Security Agency.

NSC: National Security Council.

noise: In gathering information, intelligence agencies must distinguish between signals and noise. Signals are valid indicators of an adversary's intentions or capabilities. Noise is the clutter of irrelevant background information that surrounds any activity. It can be seen as similar to the "static" one encounters in trying to tune in a distant radio station.

ONI: Office of Naval Intelligence.

open-source intelligence: Information may be collected from a variety of sources. Open-source information refers to information that is obtained from public sources. Its collection requires no deception or espionage. Open sources include the Internet, newspapers, journals, speeches, and government documents. Clandestine collection is the other broadly defined means of collecting information.

operational intelligence: This is intelligence that is required for planning and conducting campaigns and major operations to accomplish strategic objectives within theaters or areas of operations.

OSS: Office of Strategic Services.

OTA: Office of Terrorism Analysis.

photographic intelligence: The analyzed and evaluated product of photographic products.

polygraph test: This is commonly referred to as a lie detector test. It is used to establish the truthfulness, loyalty, and reliability of an individual. Polygraph tests are not used uniformly throughout the national security bureaucracies and, when used, successful spies are known to have passed polygraph tests. Many consider the most useful way to look at a polygraph is as a deterrent to spying rather than a device that can catch spies.

proprietary: Front companies that appear to be legitimate business enterprises but are owned and operated by an intelligence organization and used as cover for espionage or to service ongoing covert operations. Air America is a frequently cited CIA example and Amtorg is an often-cited Russian example.

PURPLE: The code name given to the Japanese cipher machine used during World War II to transmit sensitive Japanese diplomatic messages. Broken by U.S. cryptanalysts, the information obtained from it was designed as MAGIC.

radar intelligence: Also known as RADINT, it is intelligence obtained from the collection of radar which uses electromagnetic waves to identify the range, direction, altitude, and, if relevant, the speed of moving and stationary objects. Radar is an acronym for radio detection and ranging.

reconnaissance: The act of scouting or actively seeking out information.

secret information: This is a security designation given to information that if disclosed could reasonably be expected to cause serious harm to national security.

SHAMROCK: Carried out by the Armed Forces Security Agency and then the National Security Agency, Operation Shamrock examined incoming and outgoing communications handled by Western Union. At its height 150,000 messages a month were looked at.

signals intelligence: This is often referred to as SIGINT. Signals intelligence is intelligence derived from signal intercepts coming from communications intelligence, electronic intelligence, and foreign instrumentation signals intelligence regardless of how it is transmitted.

skunk works: A generic phrase that refers to a small group of individuals assigned to work on a special project with a great deal of autonomy. It was the term used to describe Lockheed Martin's Advanced Development Programs unit that was responsible for developing a number of reconnaissance aircraft such as the U-2 and SR -71.

spy ring: A spy ring is a group of spies that are organized around a central individual or work closely with one another in obtaining secret information.

strategic intelligence: This is a category of analytical intelligence that focuses on information related to an adversary's strategic forces. Typically, this involves forces with a nuclear capability. Strategic intelligence encompasses both information about weapons systems and military doctrine.

surveillance: Surveillance is the process of shadowing, observing, and monitoring the actions of an individual who is suspected of being engaged in espionage. Surveillance may take place through human or technical means.

tasking: The first stage in the intelligence cycle. Tasking is the process by which intelligence needs are identified.

technical intelligence: This is intelligence about the military weapons and equipment used by other states.

technological espionage: This form of espionage involves the collection of information through scientific and technical means such as by monitoring or intercepting foreign commercial or military communications, satellite transmissions, and weapons telemetry. It is contrasted with human espionage or spying.

telemetry intelligence: Also known as TELINT, it is a subcategory of Foreign Instrumentation Signals Intelligence. It is the process of capturing the continuous set of signals sent back by remotely monitored devices. The most important of these have been missiles and the telemetry can be used to its throw weight and performance capabilities.

UKUSA: A post–World War II signals intelligence-sharing agreement between the United States and Great Britain that includes participation by Canada, New Zealand, and Australia.

Ultra: Code name for the British breaking of the Axis codes in World War II. The principle source of this information came from being able to read communications sent on the German cipher machine code-named Enigma.

VENONA: A secret cooperative project begun in 1943 between U.S. and British intelligence to cryptoanalyze messages sent by Soviet intelligence agencies during World War II. Details of the project were not officially released until 1995, although the program was ended in 1980. Information obtained through VENONA has shed light on a number of controversial espionage cases.

walk-in: This refers to a spy who volunteers his or her services to an adversary's intelligence organization. This is the opposite of a spy who is singled out and recruited by an intelligence organization.

X-2: The counterespionage branch of the Office of Strategic Services (OSS). It was absorbed by the War Department when the OSS was disbanded after World War II and later came to be housed in the CIA.

Year of Intelligence: Term used to refer to 1975 when the Rockefeller Commission as well as the Church and Pike Congressional Committees investigated the CIA for abuses and failures.

Year of the Spy: Term used to refer to 1985 when several spy cases made headlines, most famously those involving the Pelton, Pollard, Howard, and Walker families.

Bibliography

Books/Chapters/Journal Articles

Abel, Richard. *Americanizing the Movies and "Movie-Mad" Audience: 1910–1914*. Berkeley, CA: University of California Press, 2006.

Abernathy, Thomas Perkins. *The Burr Conspiracy*. New York: Oxford University Press, 1954.

Abraham, Spencer. *Energy Security for America: Speeches and Editorials*. Washington, DC: United States Government Printing Office, 2002.

Abtey, Jacques. *La Guerre secrete de Joséphine Baker* (*The Secret War of Josephine Baker*). Paris & Havana: Editions Sibony, 1948.

Ackerman, Kenneth. *Young J. Edgar Hoover, the Red Scare, and the Assault on Civil Liberties*. New York: Carroll and Craf, 2007.

Adams, Charles Francis, Jr. *Charles Francis Adams*. Boston: Houghton Mifflin, 1900.

Adams, James. *The New Spies: Exploring the Frontiers of Espionage*. New York: Hutchinson, 1994.

Adams, James. *Secret Armies: Inside the American, Soviet, and European Special Forces*. Westminster, MD: Bantam, 1989.

Adams, Sam. "Vietnam Cover-up: Playing War with Numbers," *Harper's* 250, 1500 (1975), 41–44, 62–73.

Adams, Samuel A. *War of Numbers: An Intelligence Memoir*. South Royalton, VT: Steerforth Press, 1994.

Agee, Philip. *Inside the Company*. New York: Bantam, 1975.

Agee, Philip. *On the Run*. Secaucus, NJ: Lyle Stuart, Inc., 1987.

Agee, Philip, et al. "Who We Are." *Covert Action Information Bulletin* 1 (1978), 3.

Agee, Philip, and Warner Poelchau. *White Paper on Whitewash: Philip Agee on the CIA and El Salvador*. New York: Deep Cover Books, 1981.

Aid, Matthew M. "The National Security Agency and the Cold War." *Intelligence and National Security* 16 (2001), 27–66.

Alberts, Robert C. *The Golden Voyage: The Life and Times of William Bingham, 1752–1804.* Boston: Houghton Mifflin, 1969.

Albright, Joseph, and Marcia Kunstel. *Bombshell: The Secret Story of America's Unknown American Spy Conspiracy.* New York: Random House, 1997.

Aldrich, Richard J. *The Hidden Hand: Britain, America, and Cold War Secret Intelligence.* New York: The Overlook Press, 2001.

Allason, Rupert. *The Branch: A History of the Metropolitan Police Special Branch, 1883–1983.* London: Secker & Warburg, 1983.

Allen, Deane, and Brain Shellum (eds.). *Defense Intelligence Agency: At the Creation, 1961–1965.* Washington, DC: DIA History Office, Defense Intelligence Agency, 2002.

Allen, Louis. "Japanese Intelligence Systems," *Journal of Contemporary History* 22:4 (1987), 547–562.

Allen, Thomas, and Norman Polmar. *Merchants of Treason, America's Secrets for Sale.* New York: Delacorte Press, 1988.

Ambrose, Stephen. *Ike's Spies: Eisenhower and the Espionage Establishment.* Garden City, NY: Doubleday, 1981.

Ameringer, Charles. *U.S. Foreign Intelligence: The Secret Side of American History.* Lexington, MA: Lexington Books, 1990.

Andrade, Dale. *Ashes to Ashes: The Phoenix Program and the Vietnam War.* Lexington, MA: Lexington Books, 1990.

Andrew, Christopher. "British Intelligence and the Breach with Russia in 1927." *The Historical Journal* 24:4 (1982), 957–964.

Andrew, Christopher. *For the President's Eyes Only: Secret Intelligence and the American Presidency from Washington to Bush.* New York: HarperCollins, 1995.

Andrew, Christopher. *Her Majesty's Secret Service: The Making of the British Intelligence Community.* New York: Viking, 1985.

Andrew, Christopher, and Jeremy Noakes. *Intelligence and International Relations, 1900–1945.* Exeter, UK: University of Exeter Press, 1987.

Andrew, Christopher, and Oleg Gordievsky. *KGB: The Inside Story of Its Foreign Operations from Lenin to Gorbachev.* New York: HarperCollins, 1990.

Andrew, Christopher, and Oleg Gordievsky (eds.). *Comdrade Kryuchkov's Instructions: Top Secret Files on KGB Foreign Operations, 1975–1985.* Stanford: Stanford University Press, 1993.

Andrew, Christopher, and Vasili Mitrokhin. *The Mitrokhin Archive: The KGB in Europe and the West.* London: Penguin Press, 1999.

Andrew, Christopher, and Vasili Mitrokhin. *The Sword and the Shield: The Mitrokhin Archive and the Secret History of the KGB.* New York: Basic Books, 2000.

Andrew, Christopher, and Vasili Mitrokhin. *The World Going Our Way: The KGB and the Battle for the Third World.* New York: Basic Books, 2005.

Andryszewski, Tricia. *The Amazing Life of Moe Berg.* Brookfield, CT: The Millbrook Press, 1996.

Angevine, Robert. "Mapping the Northern Frontier: Canada and the Origins of the U.S. Army's Military Information Division, 1885–1898," *Intelligence and National Security* 16:3 (2001), 121–145.

Arbel, David, and Ran Edelist. *Western Intelligence and the Collapse of the Soviet Union: 1980–1990: Ten Years That Did Not Shake the World.* London: Frank Cass, 2003.

Armstrong, Robert, and Janet Shenk. *El Salvador: The Face of Revolution*. Boston: South End Press, 1998.

Aron, Paul. *Unsolved Mysteries of American History: An Eye-Opening Journey through 500 Years of Discoveries, Disappearances and Baffling Events*. New York: John Wiley & Sons, Inc., 1997.

Aronoff, Myron Joel. *The Spy Novels of John Le Carre: Balancing Ethics and Politics*. London: Palgrave Macmillian, 1998.

Ashley, Clarence Ashley. *Spymaster*. Gretna, LA: Pelican Publishing Company, 2004.

Augur, Helen. *The Secret War of Independence*. New York: Duell, Sloan and Peirce, 1955.

Axelrod, Alan. *The War Between the Spies: A History of Espionage During the American Civil War*. New York: Atlantic Monthly Press, 1992.

Babington-Smith, Constance. *Evidence in Camera: The Story of Photographic Intelligence in World War Two*. London: Chatto and Windus, 1958.

Babcock, Charles R. "FBI Discloses How Soviet Spy Switched Sides." *Washington Post* (March 4, 1980), A1.

Bakeless, John. *Spies of the Confederacy*. Philadelphia: J.B. Lippincott, 1970.

Bakeless, John. *Turncoats, Traitors, and Heroes*. New York: J.B. Lippincott Company, 1960.

Baker, Josephine, and Jo Bouillon. *Josephine*. Translated from French by Mariana Fitzpatrick. New York: Paragon House, 1988.

Bakeless, Katherine, and John Bakeless. *Spies of the Revolution*. Philadelphia: Lippincott, 1962.

Balfour, Sebastian. *Castro*. New York: Longman, 2003.

Ballendorf, Dirk A. and Merrill L. Bartlett. *Pete Ellis: An Amphibious Warfare Prophet 1880–1923*. Annapolis, MD: Naval Institute Press, 1996.

Bamford, James. *Body of Secrets: Anatomy of the Ultra Secret National Security Agency: From the Cold War through the Dawn of a New Century*. New York: Knopf, 2001.

Bamford, James. *The Puzzle Palace: Inside the National Security Agency, America's Most Secret Intelligence Organization*. New York: Penguin, 2001.

Barker, Rodney. *Dancing with the Devil: Sex, Espionage and the U.S. Marines: The Clayton Lonestreet Story*. New York: Simon & Schuster, 1996.

Barnes, Trevor. "The Secret Cold War: The CIA and American Foreign Policy in Europe, 1946–1956. Part I," *The Historical Journal* 24 (1981), 399–415.

Barnes, Trevor. "The Secret Cold War: The CIA and American Foreign Policy in Europe 1946–1956. Part II," *The Historical Journal* 25 (1982), 649–670.

Barnes, William H., and John Heath Morgan. *The Foreign Service of the United States: Origins, Development, and Functions*. Westport, CT: Greenwood Press, 1979.

Barrnett, Harvey. *Tale of the Scorpion*. Sydney, Australia: Macmillan, 1988.

Bartlett, Merrill, L. *Assault from the Sea: Essays on the History of Amphibious Warfare*. Annapolis, MD: Naval Institute Press, 1993.

Bates, David Homer. *Lincoln in the Telegraph Office: Recollections of the United States Military Telegraph Corps During the Civil War*. New York: The Century Co., 1907.

Bates, David Homer. *The Telegraph Goes to War: The Personal Diary of David Homer Bates, Lincoln's Telegraph Operator*. Edited by Donald E. Markle. Hamilton, NY: Edmonston, 2003.

Baucom, Donald. *Origins of SDI, 1944–1983*. Lawrence: University Press of Kansas, 1992.

Bearden, Milt, and James Risen. *The Main Enemy: The Inside Story of the CIA's Final Showdown with the KGB*. New York: Random House, 2003.

Bechloss, Michael. *Mayday: Eisenhower, Khrushchev, and the U-2 Affair*. New York: Harper and Row, 1986.

Beckman, Bengt. *Codebreakers: Arne Beurling and the Swedish Crypto Program During World War II*. Stockholm: American Mathematical Society, 1962.

Beesly, Patrick. *Room 40: British Naval Intelligence 1914–1918*. New York: Harcourt Brace Jovanovich, 1982.

Bemis, Samuel Flagg. "British Secret Service and the French-American Alliance," *American Historical Review* 29 (1923–1924), 474–495.

Bemis, Samuel Flagg. *The Diplomacy of the American Revolution*. Bloomington, IN: Indiana University Press, 1957.

Bemis, Samuel Flagg. *Jay's Treaty: A Study in Commerce and Diplomacy*. New York: Macmillan, 1924.

Bemis, Samuel Flagg. *Pinckney's Treaty: A Study of America's Advantage from Europe's Distress, 1783–1800*. Baltimore: Johns Hopkins University Press, 1926.

Bendictson, L. "The Restoration of Obliterated Passages and of Secret Writing in Diplomatic Missives," *Franco-American Review* 1 (1937), 243–256.

Bennett, R. M. *Espionage: Spies and Secrets*. London: Virgin Books, 2002.

Benson, Robert Louis, and Michael Warner (eds.). *Venona: Soviet Espionage and the American Response, 1939–1957*. Washington, DC: National Security Agency and Central Intelligence Agency, 1996.

Bentley, Elizabeth T. *Out of Bondage*. London: R. Hart-Davis, 1952.

Beria, Sergo. *Beria, My Father: Inside Stalin's Kremlin*. Edited by Thom Francosie. Translated by Brian Pearce. London: Duckworth, 2001.

Berkin, Carol. *Revolutionary Mothers: Women in the Struggle for America's Independence*. New York: Alfred A. Knopf, 2005.

Berman, Larry. *Perfect Spy: The Incredible Double Life of Pham Xuan An, Time Magazine Reporter and Vietnamese Communist Agent*. New York: HarperCollins, 2007.

Bernard, Jack F. *Talleyrand: A Biography*. New York: Putnam, 1973.

Berner, Brad. *The Spanish-American War*. Lanham, MD: Scarecrow Press, 1998.

Bernikow, Louise. *Abel*. New York: Ballantine Books, 1982.

Bernstein, Carl, and Bob Woodward. *All the President's Men*. New York: Simon & Schuster, 1974.

Beschloss, Michael R. *MAYDAY: Eisenhower, Khrushchev, and the U-2 Affair*. New York: Harper & Row, 1986.

Best, Richard A. *U.S. Intelligence and Policymaking: The Iraq Experience*. Congressional Research Service, December 2, 2005. CRS Report No. RS21696.

Best, Richard A., and Andrew Feickert. *Special Operations Forces (SOF) and CIA Paramilitary Operations: Issues for Congress*. Washington, DC: Library of Congress, Congressional Research Service, CRS Report, January 4, 2005

Bethel, Elizabeth. "The Military Information Division: Origin of the Intelligence Division," *Military Affairs* 11:1 (1947), 17–24.

Betts, Richard. *Enemies of Intelligence*. New York: Columbia University Press, 2007.

Beymer, William Gilmore. *Scouts and Spies of the Civil War*. Lincoln, NE: University of Nebraska Press, 2003.

Bialoguski, Michael. *The Petrov Story*. Melbourne, Australia: William Heinemann, 1955.

Bidwell, Bruce. *History of the Military Intelligence Division, Department of the Army General Staff*. Frederick, MD: University Publications of America, 1986.

Biederman, Danny. *The Incredible World of Spy-Fi: Wild and Crazy Spy Gadgets, Props and Artifacts from TV and the Movies*. San Francisco: Chronicle Books, 2004.

Bird, Kai. *The Color of Truth: McGeorge Bundy and William Bundy: Brothers in Arms*. New York: Simon & Schuster, Inc., 1998.

Bissell, Richard Melvin, Jr., with Jonathan Lewis and Francis Pudlo. *Reflections of a Cold Warrior: From Yalta to the Bay of Pigs*. New Haven, CT: Yale University Press, 1996.

Bittman, Ladislav. *The KGB and Soviet Disinformation: An Insiders View*. London: Pergamon, 1972.

Black, Ian, and Benny Morris. *Israel's Secret Wars: The Untold Story of Israeli Intelligence*. London: Hamish Hamilton, 1991.

Blackman, Ann. *Wild Rose: Rose O'Neale Greenhow, Civil War Spy*. New York: Random House, 2005.

Blake, George. *No Other Choice: An Autobiography*. New York: Simon & Schuster, 1990.

Blum, H. *I Pledge Allegiance ... The True Story of the Walkers: An American Spy Family*. London: Weidenfeld and Nicholson, 1987.

Boatner, Mark M. *Encyclopedia of the American Revolution*. Mechanicsburg, PA: Stackpole Books, 1966.

Bodansky, Yossef. *Bin Laden: The Man Who Declared War on America*. New York: Forum, 1999.

Bohning, Don. *The Castro Obsession: U.S. Covert Operations Against Cuba, 1959–1965*. Washington, DC: Potomac Books, 2005.

Boni, William, and Dr. Gerald L. Kovacich. *Netspionage: The Global Threat to Information*. Boston: Butterworth-Heinemann, 2000.

Booth, Alan R. "The Development of the Espionage Film," in Wesley K. Wark (ed.), *Spy Fiction, Spy Films, and Real Intelligence*. Portland, OR: Frank Cass & Co., 1991.

Booth, Nicholas. *Zigzag: The Incredible Wartime Exploits of Double Agent Eddie Chapman*. New York: Arcade Publication, 2007.

Born, Hans, Loch Johnson, and Ian Leigh (eds.). *Who's Watching the Spies? Establishing Intelligence Service Accountability*. Washington, DC: Potomac Books, 2005.

Borosage, Robert, and John Marks (eds.). *The CIA File*. New York: Grossman Publishers, Inc., 1976.

Borovik, Genrikh Avitezerovich, and Phillip Knightley. *Philby Files: The Secret Life of a Master Spy*. Boston: Little, Brown & Co., 1994.

Bouzereau, Laurent. *The Art of Bond: From Storyboard to Screen: The Creative Process Behind the James Bond Phenomenon*. New York: Abrams, 2006.

Bowman, M. E. "The 'Worst Spy': Perceptions of Espionage," *American Intelligence Journal* 18 (1998), 57–62.

Boyd, Belle. *Belle Boyd in Camp and Prison*. Baton Rouge, LA: Louisiana State University Press, 1998.

Boyd, Carl. *The Extraordinary Envoy: General Hiroshi Oshima and Diplomacy in the Third Reich, 1934–1939.* Washington, DC: University Press of America, 1982.

Boyd, Carl. *Hitler's Japanese Confidant: General Oshima Hiroshi and MAGIC Intelligence, 1941–1945.* Lawrence, KS: University Press of Kansas, 1993.

Boyd, Julian P. "Silas Deane: Death by a Kindly Teacher of Treason," *William and Mary Quarterly* 16 (1959), 167–187, 319–342, 515–550.

Boylan, Brian Richard. *Benedict Arnold: The Dark Eagle.* New York: Norton, 1973.

Boyle, Andrew. *The Climate of Treason.* London: Hodder and Stoughton, 1980.

Boyle, Walter. *Beyond the Wild Blue: A History of the United States Air Force, 1947–1997.* New York: St. Martin's, 1997.

Bradford, James C. (ed.). *Crucible of Empire: The Spanish-American War and Its Aftermath.* Annapolis, MD: Naval Institute Press, 1992.

Brandt, Clare. *The Man in the Mirror: A Life of Benedict Arnold.* New York: Random House, 1994.

Brandt, Ed. *The Last Voyage of the USS Pueblo.* New York: Norton, 1969.

Brandt, Nat. *The Man Who Tried to Burn New York.* Syracuse, N.Y.: Syracuse University Press, 1986.

Breckinridge, Scott. *CIA and the Cold War: A Memoir.* Westport, CT: Praeger, 1993.

Breckinridge, Scott. *The CIA and the U.S. Intelligence System.* Boulder, CO: Westview Press, 1986.

Breitman, Richard, Norman J. W. Goda, Timothy Naftali, and Robert Wolfe. *U.S. Intelligence and the Nazis.* New York: Cambridge University Press, 2005.

Brereton, T. R. *Educating the U.S. Army: Arthur L. Wagner and Reform 1875–1905.* Lincoln, NE: University of Nebraska Press, 2000.

Breuer, William. *Hitler's Undercover War: The Nazi Epionage Invasion of the U.S.A.* New York: St. Martin's, 1989.

Brewin, Bob, and Sydney Shaw. *Vietnam on Trial: Westmoreland vs. CBS.* New York: Atheneum, 1987.

Brinton, Crane. *The Lives of Talleyrand.* New York: Norton, 1936.

Britton, Wesley. *Beyond Bond: Spies in Fiction and Film.* Westport, CT: Praeger, 2005.

Britton, Wesley. *Onscreen and Undercover: The Ultimate Book of Movie Espionage.* Westport, CT: Praeger, 2006.

Britton, Wesley. *Spies in Fiction and Film.* Westport, CT: Praeger, 2004.

Britton, Wesley. *Spy Television.* Westport, CT: Praeger, 2004.

Brook-Shepard, Gordon. *The Storm Petrels: The Flight of the First Soviet Defectors.* New York: Harcourt Brace Jovanovich, 1977.

Brook-Shepard, Gordon. *The Storm Birds. Soviet Post War Defectors: The Dramatic True Stories, 1945–1985.* New York: Henry Holt, 1989.

Brookhiser, Richard. *America's First Dynasty: The Adamses 1735–1918.* New York: Free Press, 2002.

Broughton, James M., and Roger J. Sandilands. "Politics and the Attack on FDR's Economists: From the Grand Alliance to the Cold War," *Intelligence and National Security* 18 (2003), 73–99.

Browder, George. *Hitler's Enforcers: The Gestapo and the SS Security Service in the Nazi Revolution.* New York: Oxford University Press, 1996.

Brown, Anthony Cave. *Bodyguard of Lies.* London: HarperCollins, 1975.

Brown, Anthony Cave. *The Secret Servant: The Life of Sir Stewart Menzies, Churchill's Spymaster*. London: Michael Joseph, 1988.

Brown, Anthony Cave. *The Secret War Report of the OSS*. New York: Berkley, 1976.

Brown, Anthony Cave. *Wild Bill Donovan: The Last Hero*. London: Michael Joseph, 1982.

Brown, J. Willard. *The Signal Corps, U.S.A. in the War of Rebellion*. Boston: U.S. Veteran Signal Corps Association, 1896.

Brown, Paul. "Report on the IRR File on the Red Orchestra," *The U.S. National Archives & Records Administration*. http://www.archives.gov/iwg/research-papers/red-orchestra-irr-file.html (accessed December 21, 2006).

Brownell, George. *The Origin and Development of the National Security Agency*. Laguna Hills, CA: Aegean Press, 1988.

Brugioni, Dino. *Eyeball to Eyeball: The Inside Story of the Cuban Missile Crisis*. New York: Random House, 1991.

Bryce, Lord James. *Report of the Committee on Alleged German Outages Appointed by His Britannic Majesty's Government*. London: Wellington House, 1915.

Brysac, Shareen Blair. *Resisting Hitler: Mildred Harnack and the Red Orchestra*. Oxford: Oxford University Press, 2000.

Bucher, Lloyd M., with Mark Rascovich. *Bucher: My Story*. New York: Doubleday, 1970.

Buitenhuis, Peter. *The Great War of Words: British, American, and Canadian Propaganda and Fiction*. Vancouver: University of British Columbia Press, 1987.

Bulloch, James D. *The Secret Service of the Confederate States in Europe: or, How the Confederate Cruisers Were Equipped*. New York: The Modern Library, 2001. (Originally published: New York: G.P. Putnam's Sons, 1884.)

Bulloch, John, and Henry Miller. *Spy Ring: The Full Story of the Naval Secrets Case*. London: Secker & Warburg, 1961.

Burleson, Clyde, W. *The Jennifer Project*. Englewood Cliffs, N.J.: Prentice Hall, 1977.

Burnes, John P. *MI5*. London: Pocket Essentials, 2007.

Burns, Thomas S. *The Secret War for the Ocean Depths: Soviet-American Rivalry for the Mastery of the Seas*. New York: Rawson Associates, 1978.

Burrows, William E. *By Any Means Necessary: America's Secret Air War in the Cold War*. New York: Farrar, Strauss, and Giroux, 2001.

Burrows, William E. *Deep Black: Space Espionage and National Security*. New York: Random House, 1986.

Burt, Alfred Leroy. *The United States, Great Britain and British North America for the Revolution to the Establishment of Peace after the War of 1812*. New York: Russell and Russell, 1961.

Byers, Andy. *The Imperfect Spy*. St. Petersburg, FL: Vanamere Press, 2005.

Bywater, Hector C. *The Great Pacific War: A History of the American-Japanese Campaign of 1931–1933*. Boston: Houghton Mifflin, 1925.

Bywater, Hector C. *Sea Power in the Pacific: A Study of the American-Japanese Naval Problem*. Boston: Houghton Mifflin, 1921.

Bywater, Hector C., and H. C. Ferraby. *Strategic Intelligence: Memoirs of Naval Secret Service*. New York: Richard R. Smith, 1931.

Cahn, Anne Hessing. *Killing Détente: The Right Attacks the CIA*. University Park, PA: The Pennsylvania University Press, 1998.

Cain, Frank. *The Australian Security Intelligence Organization: An Unofficial History.* London: Frank Cass, 1994.

Calder, Robert. *Beware the British Serpent: The Role of Writers in British Propaganda in the United States, 1939–1945.* London: McGill-Queen's University Press, 2004.

Caldwalder, John. "Operation Coldfeet: An Investigation of the Abandoned Soviet Arctic Drift Station NP 8," *ONI Review* 17 (1962), 344–355.

Caldwell, Oliver J. *A Secret War: Americans in China 1944–1945.* Carbondale, IL: Southern Illinois University Press, 1972.

Calhoon, Robert M. *The Loyalists in the American Revolution, 1760–1781.* New York: Harcourt Brace Jovanovich, 1965.

Calloway, Colin. *The Scratch of a Pen, 1763 and the Transformation of North America.* Oxford: Oxford University Press, 2006.

Cameron, William. "Balloons." In David and Jeanne Heidler (eds.). *The Encyclopedia of the American Civil War.* Vol. I, 163–167. Santa Barbara, CA: ABC-CLIO, 2000.

Carlisle, Rodney. *Encyclopedia of Intelligence and Counterintelligence.* 2 vols. Armonk, NY: Sharpe Reference, 2005.

Carmichael, Virginia. *Framing History: The Rosenberg Story and the Cold War.* Minneapolis: University of Minnesota Press, 1993.

Carter, John J. *Covert Operations as a Tool of Presidential Foreign Policy in American History from 1800 to 1920: Foreign Policy in the Shadows.* Lewiston, New York: Edwin Mellen Press, 2000.

Carter, Miranda. *Anthony Blunt: His Lives.* New York: Farrar, Straus & Giroux, 2002.

Caruso, A. Brooke. *The Mexican Spy Company: United States Covert Operations in Mexico, 1845–1848.* Jefferson, NC: McFarland & Co., 1991.

Casey, William, and Peter Forbath. *Honorable Men: My Life in the CIA.* New York: Simon & Shuster, 1978.

Caute, David. *The Great Fear: The Anti-Communist Purge under Truman and Eisenhower.* New York: Simon & Schuster, 1978.

Cave Brown, Anthony. *Wild Bill Donovan: The Last American Hero.* New York: Time Books, 1982.

Cawelti, John G., and Bruce A. Rosenberg. *The Spy Story.* Chicago: University of Chicago Press, 1987.

Cecil, Robert. *A Divided Life: A Personal Portrait of the Spy Donald MacLean.* New York: HarperCollins, 1989.

Center for Cryptological History, National Security Agency. *Introductory History of VENONA and Guide to the Translations.* Fort George G. Mead, MD: National Security Agency, 1995.

Central Intelligence Agency. "Black Dispatches: Black American Contributions to Union Intelligence During the Civil War." https://www.cia.gov/library/center -for-the-study-of-intelligence/csi-publications/books-and-monographs/black -dispatches/index.html (accessed January 12, 2007).

Central Intelligence Agency. "Intelligence in the Civil War," 2005 http://fas.org/irp/ cia/product/civilwar.pdf.

Central Intelligence Agency. *Intelligence in the War of Independence.* Washington, DC: Public Affairs, Central Intelligence Agency, 1997.

Chadwick, French Ensor. *The Relations of the United States and Spain: The Spanish-American War*. New York: Charles Scribner's Sons, 1911.

Chafee, Zechariah. *Free Speech in the United States*. Cambridge, MA: Harvard University Press, 1941.

Chalou, George (ed.). *The Secrets of War: The Office of Strategic Services in World War II*. Washington, DC: National Archives and Records Administration, 1992.

Chambers, Whittaker. *Witness*. New York: Regnery Gateway, 1952.

Chang, Laurence, and Peter Kornbluh (eds.). *The Cuban Missile Crisis, 1962: A National Security Archive Documents Reader*. New York: New Press, 1998.

Charlton, Michael. *The Eagle and the Small Birds. Crisis in the Soviet Empire: From Yalta to Solidarity*. London: British Broadcasting Corporation, 1984.

Childs, David, and Richard Popplewell. *The STASI: East German Intelligence and Secret Service*. London: MacMillan Press, LTD, 1996.

Chomsky, Noam, and Edward S. Herman. *After the Cataclysm*. Sydney, Australia: Hale & Iremonger, 1980.

Clancy, Tom, General Carl Stiner, and Tony Koltz. *Shadow Warriors: Inside the Special Forces*. New York: G.P. Putnam's Sons, 2002.

Clarfeld, Gerald. *Timothy Pickering and American Diplomacy 1795–1800*. Colombia, MO: University of Missouri Press, 1969.

Clark, Ronald William. *The Man Who Broke Purple: The Life of Colonel William F. Friedman, Who Deciphered the Japanese Code in World War II*. Boston: Little, Brown & Co., 1977.

Clarke, Comer. *The War Within*. London: World Distributors, 1961.

Clarke, Richard, A. *Against All Enemies: Inside America's War on Terror*. New York: Free Press, 2004.

Clarke, Richard A. (ed.). *Defeating the Jihadists: A Blueprint for Action*. New York: Century Foundation Press, 2004.

Clarke, Richard A., and Rand Beers. *The Forgotten Homeland: A Century Foundation Task Force Report*. New York: Century Foundation Press, 2006.

Clemens, Martin. *Alone on Guadalcanal: A Coastwatcher's Story*, new ed. Xenia, OH: Bluejacket Books, 2004.

Cleroux, Richard. *Official Secrets: The Story Behind the Canadian Security Intelligence Service*. Scarborough, Canada: McGraw-Hill Ryerson Limited, 1990.

Clifford, Clark, with Richard Holbrooke. *Counsel to the President*. New York: Random House, 1991.

Cline, Ray. *Secrets, Spies and Scholars: The Essential CIA*. Washington, DC: Acropolis, 1976.

Clinton, Catherine. *Harriet Tubman, the Road to Freedom*. New York: Little, Brown, 2004.

Clinton, Sir Henry. *The American Rebellion: Sir Henry Clinton's Narrative of His Campaigns, 1775–1782*. Edited by William B. Wilcox. New Haven, CT: Yale University Press, 1954.

Clough, Bryan. *State Secrets: The Kent-Wolcott Affair*. East Sussex: Hideaway Books, 2005.

Codman, John. *Arnold Expedition to Quebec*. New York: Macmillan, 1901.

Coerver, Don M., and Linda B. Hall. *Texas and the Mexican Revolution: A Study in State and National Border Policy, 1910–1920*. San Antonio, TX: Trinity University Press, 1984.

Coggins, Jack. *Arms and Equipment of the Civil War*. Wilmington, NC: Broadfoot Publishing, 1990.

Colby, William, and Peter Forbath. *Honorable Men: My Life in the CIA*. New York: Simon & Schuster, 1978.

Colby, William, and James McCargar. *Lost Victory: A Firsthand Account of America's Sixteen-Year Involvement in Vietnam*. Chicago: Contemporary Books, 1989.

Cole, D. J. *The Imperfect Spy*. London: Robert Hale Ltd., 1999.

Colitt, Leslie. *Spymaster: The Real Life of Karla, His Moles, and the East German Secret Police*. Reading, MA: Addison Wesley, 1995.

Coll, Steven. *Ghost Wars: The Secret History of the CIA, Afghanistan, and Bin Laden, from the Soviet Invasion to September 10, 2001*. New York: Penguin, 2004.

Collier, Simon. *A History of Chile, 1808–2002*. London: Cambridge University Press, 2004.

Collot, V. "General Collot's Plan for a Reconnaissance of the Ohio and Mississippi Valleys, 1796," *The William and Mary Quarterly*, 9 (1952), 512–520.

Conboy, Kenneth. *Shadow War: The CIA's Secret War in Laos*. Boulder, CO: Paladin Press, 1995.

Conboy, Kenneth, and James Morrison, *The CIA's Secret War in Tibet*. Lawrence: University Press of Kansas, 2002.

Conboy, Kenneth, and Dale Andrade. *Spies and Commandos: How America Lost the Secret War in North Vietnam*. Lawrence, KS: University Press of Kansas, 2001.

Cook, Joseph Lee, and Earleen H. Cook. *Industrial Spying and Espionage*. Monticello, IL: Vance Bibliographies, 1985.

Cookridge, E. H. *Gehlen: Spy of the Century*. New York: Random House, 1971.

Cooper, James Fenimore. *The Spy: A Tale of Neutral Ground*. Hammondsworth: Penguin Books, 1997.

Cornell, Jean Gay. *Ralph Bunche*. Champaign, IL: Garrard Publishing Co., 1976.

Corson, William. *Armies of Ignorance. The Rise of the American Intelligence Empire*. New York: Dial, 1977.

Corson, William, Susan B. Trento, and Joseph Trento. *Widows: The Explosive Truth Behind 25 Years of Western Intelligence Disasters*. London: MacDonald and Company, 1989.

Corwin, Edwin S. *The President's Control of Foreign Relations*. Princeton, NJ: Princeton University Press, 1917.

Costello, John. *Days of Infamy: MacArthur, Roosevelt, Churchill—The Shocking Truth Revealed*. New York: Pocket Books, 1994.

Costello, John. *Mask of Treachery: Spies, Lies, Buggery and Betrayal: The First Documented Dossier on Anthony Blunt's Cambridge Spy Ring*. Lanham, MD: Rowman & Littlefield Publishers, 1991.

Costello, John, and Oleg Tsarev. *Deadly Illusions: The KGB Orlov Dossier Reveals Stalin's Master Spy*. New York: Crown Books, 1993.

Cothren, Marion. *Pigeon Heroes: Birds of War and Messengers of Peace*. New York: Coward-McCann, 1944.

Cox, Issac. "The American Intervention in West Florida," *The American Historical Review* 17:2 (1912), 290–311.

Craig, R. Bruce. *Treasonable Doubt: The Harry Dexter White Spy Case*. Lawrence, KA: University Press of Kansas, 2004.

Craig, William. *The Fall of Japan*. London: History Book Club, 1968.

Crary, Catherine S. "The Tory and the Spy: The Double Life of James Rivington," *William & Mary Quarterly* 16 (1959), 61–72.

Cray, Edward. *General of the Army: George C. Marshall, Soldier and Statesman*. New York: Cooper Square Press, 1990.

Crenshaw, Ollinger. "The Knights of the Golden Circle: The Career of George Bickley," *American Historical Review* 47 (1941), 23–50.

Crickmore, Paul F. *Lockheed SR-71: The Secret Missions Exposed*. Oxford, UK: Osprey, 1993.

Critchfield, James H. *Auftrag Pullach: Die Organization Gehlen 1948–1956*. Deutscher Militärverlag: Berlin, 1969.

Croffut, W. A. (ed.). *Fifty Years in Camp and Field: Diary of Major-General Ethan Allen Hitchcock*. New York: Putnam's Sons, 1909.

Cronin, Audrey. *The 'FTO List' and Congress: Sanctioning Designated Foreign Terrorist Organizations*. Congressional Research Service Report for Congress RL32120. Washington, DC: Congressional Research Service, Octobber 21, 2003.

Cronin, Audrey, and James Lutes (eds.). *Attacking Terrorism: Elements of a Grand Strategy*. Washington, DC: Georgetown University Press, 2004.

Cross, Robert E. *Sailor in the White House: The Seafaring Life of FDR*. Annapolis, MD: Naval Institute Press, 2003.

Cruickshank, Charles. *Deception in World War II*. Oxford, UK: Oxford University Press, 1979.

Currey, Cecil B. *Edward Lansdale: The Unquiet American*. Boston: Houghton Mifflin, 1988.

Cusik, James. *The Other War of 1812: The Patriot War and the American Invasion of Spanish East Florida*. Gainsville, FL: University of Florida Press, 2003.

Daniel, Donald C., and Katherine L. Herbig (eds.). *Strategic Military Deception*. Elmsford, NY: Pergamon Press, 1982.

Darling, Arthur B. *The Central Intelligence Agency: An Instrument of Government to 1950*. University Park, PA: Pennsylvania State University Press, 1990.

Davis, Jack. *Sherman Kent and the Profession of Intelligence Analysis*. Washington, DC: Central Intelligence Agency, The Sherman Kent Center for Intelligence Analysis Occasional Paper 1, 2002.

Davis, William C. *The Pirates Laffite: The Treacherous World of the Corsairs of the Gulf*. Orlando, FL: Harcourt, 2005.

Dawidoff, Nicholas. *The Catcher Was a Spy: The Mysterious Life of Moe Berg*. New York: Vintage Books, 1995.

Dawson, Henry B. *The Sons of Liberty in New York*. New York: Arno Press, 1969.

Day, Dwayne, John M. Logsdon and Brian Latell (eds.). *Eye in the Sky: The Story of the CORONA Spy Satellites*. Washington, DC: Smithsonian Institution Press, 1998.

Deacon, Richard. *A History of the Japanese Secret Service*. London: Frederick Muller, 1982.

Deacon, Richard. *Kempei Tai: A History of the Japanese Secret Service*. New York: Beaufort Books, 1983.

Deacon, Richard. *The Silent War: A History of Western Naval Intelligence*. New York: Hippocrene Books, 1978.

Deane Papers, The. New-York Historical Society, Collections, 1886–1890. 5 vols. New York: The Society, 1887–1891.

DeBenedetti, Charles. "A CIA Analysis of the Anti-Vietnam War Movement," *Peace and Change* 9 (1983), 31–42.

DeConde, Alexander. *The Quasi-War, the Politics and Diplomacy of the Undeclared War with France, 1797–1801.* New York: Charles Scribner's Sons, 1966.

Defense Intelligence Agency. *Defense Intelligence Agency, 35 Years, a Brief History.* Washington, DC: The Defense Intelligence Agency, 1996.

Delattre, Lucas. *Betraying Hitler; The Story of Fritz Kolbe: The Most Important Spy of the Second World War.* London: Atlantic Monthly Press, 2005.

Dennis, Mike. *The STASI: Myth and Reality.* Harlow: Pearson/Longman, 2003.

Denniston, Alastair. "The Government Code and Cypher School Between the Wars," *Intelligence and National Security* 1 (1986), 48–70.

Der Auslandsnachrichtendienst Deutschlands. Bundesnachrichten-dienst Öffentlichkeitsarbeit: Berlin, 2005.

Destler, I. M. "National Security II: The Rise of the Assistant," in Hugh Heclo and Lester Salamon (eds.), *The Illusion of Presidential Government*, pp. 263–286. Boulder, CO: Westview, 1981.

Die Präsidenten des Bundesnachrichtendienstes. Bundes-nachrichtendienst Öffentlichkeitsarbeit: Berlin, 2006.

Dignan, Don K. "The Hindu Conspiracy in Anglo-American Relations during World War I," *Pacific Historical Review* (1971), 57–77.

Doherty, Thomas. *Cold War, Cool Medium: Television, McCarthyism and American Culture.* New York: Columbia University Press, 2005.

Donaldson, Scott, in collaboration with R. H. Winnik. *Archibald MacLeish: An American Life.* Boston: Houghton Mifflin, 1992.

Donner, Frank. *The Age of Surveillance: The Aims and Methods of America's Political Intelligence System.* New York: Vintage, 1981.

Dorland, Gil. *Legacy of Discord—Voices of the Vietnam War Era.* Washington, DC: Brassey's, 2001.

Dorwart, Jeffrey. *The Office of Naval Intelligence.* Annapolis, MD: Naval Institute Press, 1979.

Dorwart, Jeffrey. "The Roosevelt-Astor Espionage Ring," *New York Journal of History* 62 (1981), 307–322.

Draper, Theodore. *A Very Thin Line: The Iran Contra Affairs.* New York: Touchstone, 1992.

Dreux, William. *No Bridges Blown.* Notre Dame, IN: University of Notre Dame Press, 1971.

Dreyfuss, Robert. "TECHINT: The NSA, the NRO, and NIMA," in Craig Eisendrath (ed.), *National InSecurity: U.S. Intelligence After the Cold War*, pp. 149–171. Philadelphia: Temple University Press, 2000.

Duberman, Martin B. *Charles Francis Adams 1807–1886.* Boston: Houghton Mifflin, 1961.

Duffies, Whitfield, and Susan Landau. *Privacy on the Line: the Politics of Wiretapping and Encryption.* Cambridge, MA: MIT Press, 1998.

Dujmovic, Nicholas. "Extraordinary Fidelity: Two CIA Prisoners in China, 1952–73," *Studies in Intelligence* 50 (2006), 21–36.

Dull, Jonathan. *A Diplomatic History of the American Revolution*. New Haven, CT: Yale University Press, 1985.

Dulles, Allen. *The Craft of Intelligence*. Westport: Greenwood Press, 1977.

Dunham, Mikel. *Buddha's Warriors*. Los Angeles: J.P. Tarcher, 2004.

Durand, John. *New Materials for the History of the American Revolution Taken from Documents in the French Archive*. New York: H. Holt and Company, 1889.

Early, P. *Family of Spies: Inside the John Walker Spy Ring*. New York: Bantam Books, 1988.

Ebon, Martin. *The Andropov File: The Life and Ideas of Yuri V. Andropov, General Secretary of the Communist Party of the Soviet Union*. New York: McGraw-Hill, 1983.

Ebon, Martin. *KGB: Death and Rebirth*. New York: Praeger, 1990.

Eftimiades, Nicholas. *Chinese Intelligence Operations*. New York: Taylor Francis, 1994.

Elkins, Stanley, and Eric McKitrick. *The Age of Federalism: The American Republic, 1788–1800*. New York: Oxford University Press, 1993.

Ellis, Edward Robb. *The Epic of New York City*. New York: Carroll and Graf, 2005.

Elphick, Peter. *Far Eastern File: The Intelligence War in the Far East, 1930–1945*. London: Hodder and Stoughton, 1997.

Englemann, Larry. *Tears Before the Rain: An Oral History of the Fall of South Vietnam*. New York: Oxford University Press, 1990.

English, George Bethune. *A Narrative of the Expedition to Dongola and Sennaar*. Boston: Wells and Lilly, 1823.

Ennes, James M., Jr. *Assault on the Liberty: The True Story of the Israeli Attack on an American Intelligence Ship*. New York: Random House, 1979.

Epstein, Edward Jay, *Deception: The Invisible War Between the KGB and the CIA*. New York: Allen, 1989.

Epstein, Edward Jay, *Dossier: The Secret History of Armand Hammer*. New York: Carroll & Graf Publishers, 1996.

Evans, Charles M. *War of the Aeronauts: The History of Ballooning in the Civil War*. Mechanicsburg, PA: Stackpole Books, 2002.

50 Jahre BND. Bundesnachrichtendienst. Bundesnachrichtendienst Öffentlichkeitsarbeit: Pullach, 2006.

Farago, Ladislas. *The Broken Seal: 'Operation Magic' and the Secret Road to Pearl Harbor*. New York: Bantam, 1968.

Farago, Ladislas. *The Game of the Foxes: The Untold Story of German espionage in the United States and Great Britain During World War II*. New York: David McKay Company, 1971.

Farson, A. Stewart. "Is Canadian Intelligence Being Re-Invented?" *Canadian Foreign Policy* 6 (1999), 49–83.

Federation of American Scientists Online. "National Foreign Intelligence Board," http://www.fas.org/irp/offdocs/dcid3-1.htm (accessed January 2, 2006).

Fehner, Terrence R., and Hack M. Hall. *Department of Energy, 1977–1994: A Summary History*. Oak Ridge, TN: Office of Scientific and Technical Information, 1994.

Feis, William. *Grant's Secret Service: The Intelligence War from Belmont to Appomattox*. Lincoln, NE: University of Nebraska Press, 2002.

Feis, William. "'Lee's Army is Really Whipped': Grant and Intelligence Assessment from the Wilderness to Cold Harbor," *North & South* 7:4 (2004), 28–37.

Feis, William B. "Intelligence Activities," in Steven E. Woodworth (ed.), *The American Civil War: A Handbook of Literature and Research*, pp. 419–432. Westport, CT: Greenwood Press, 1996.

Feklisov, Alexander, and Sergei Kostin. *The Man Behind the Rosenbergs: Memoirs of the KGB Spymaster Who Also Controlled Klaus Fuchs and Helped Resolve the Cuban Missile Crisis*. New York: Enigma Books, 2001.

Feldt, Eric Agustus. *The Coastwatchers*. New York: Ballantine Books, 1966.

Felshintsky, Yuri, Alexander Litvinenko, and Geoffrey Andrews. *Blowing Up Russia: Terror from Within*. New York: Encounter Books, 2007.

Ferguson, E. James. *The Power of the Purse: A History of American Public Finance, 1776–1790*. Chapel Hill, NC: University of North Carolina Press, 1961.

Fialka, John J. *War by Other Means: Economic Espionage in America*. New York: W. W. Norton, 1999.

Finley, James, P. (ed.). *U.S. Army Military Intelligence History: A Sourcebook*. Fort Huachaca, AZ: U.S. Army Intelligence Center, 1995.

Finnegan, John Patrick. *Military Intelligence: An Army Lineage Series*. Center of Military History, United States Army. Washington, DC: US Government Printing Office, 1998.

Fishel, Edwin C. "The Mythology of Civil War Intelligence," *Civil War History* 10 (1964), 344–367.

Fishel, Edwin C. "Myths That Never Die," *International Journal of Intelligence and Counterintelligence* 2 (1988), 27–58.

Fishel, Edwin C. *The Secret War for the Union: The Untold Story of Military Intelligence in the Civil War*. Boston: Houghton Mifflin, 1996.

Fitch, Noel. R. *Appetite for Life: The Biography of Julia Child*. New York: Anchor Books, 1997.

Fitzgerald, Frances. *Way Out There in the Blue: Reagan, Star Wars, and the End of the Cold War*. New York: Simon & Schuster, 2000.

Fleming, Thomas. "The Northwest Conspiracy," in Robert Cowley (ed.), *What Ifs? Of American History*, pp. 103–125. New York: Berkley Books, 2003.

Fletcher, Katy. "Evolution of the Modern American Spy Novel," *Journal of Contemporary History* 22:2 (1987), 319–331.

Flexner, James Thomas. *The Traitor and the Spy: Benedict Arnold and John André*. 1953. Reprint. Syracuse, NY: Syracuse University Press, 1992.

Flory, Harriette. "The Arcos Raid and the Rupture of Anglo-Soviet Relations, 1927," *Journal of Contemporary History* 12 (1977), 707–723.

Foerstel, Herbert N. *Freedom of Information and the Right to Know: The Origins and Applications of the Freedom of Information Act*. Westport, CT: Greenwood Press, 1999.

Foot, M. R. D. *An Outline History of the Special Operations Executive*. London: British Broadcasting Corporation, 1984.

Ford, Corey. *A Peculiar Service*. Boston: Little, Brown & Company, 1965.

Ford, Harold P. *An Honorable Man: William Colby: Retrospect*. https://www.cia.gov/library/center-for-the-study-of-intelligence/csi-publications/csi-studies/studies/97unclass/colby.html.

Ford, Kirk. *OSS and the Yugoslav Resistance, 1943–1945*. College Station, TX: Texas A&M Press, 1992.

Ford, Roger. *Steel from the Sky: The Jedburgh Raiders, France, 1944*. London: Weidenfeld & Nicholson, 2004.

Foreman, Grant. *A Traveler in Indian Territory: The Journal of Ethan Allen Hitchock, late Major-General in the United States Army*. Norman OK: University of Oklahoma Press, 1996.

Fowler, Will. *Barbarossa: The First 7 Days*. Havertown, PA: Casemate, 2004.

Franklin, Charles. *The Great Spies*. New York: Hart Publishing, 1967.

Frazier, Joseph. *Alfred I. Dupont: The Man & His Family*. New York: Random House Value Publishing, 1992.

Freedman, Lawrence. "The CIA and the Soviet Threat: The Politicalization of Estimates, 1966–1977," *Intelligence and National Security* 12 (1997), 122–142.

Freedman, Lawrence, and Efraim Karsh (eds.). *The Gulf Conflict, 1990–1991*. Princeton, NJ: Princeton University Press, 1993.

Freeh, Louis. *My FBI: Bringing Down the Mafia, Investigating Bill Clinton, and Fighting the War on Terror*. New York: St. Martin's Press, 2006.

Frei, Eduardo Montalva. *The Mandate of History and Chile's Future*. Athans, OH: Ohio University Press, 1977.

French, Allen. *The First Year of the American Revolution*. Boston: Houghton Mifflin, 1934.

French, Allen. *General Gage's Informers: New Material upon Lexington and Concord, Benjamin Thompson as Loyalist and the Treachery of Benjamin Church*. Ann Arbor, MI: University of Michigan Press, 1932.

Fried, Albert. *McCarthyism, the Great American Red Scare: A Documentary History*. New York: Oxford University Press, 1997.

Friedman, G. *America's Secret War: Inside the Hidden Worldwide Struggle Between the United States and Its Enemies*. London: Little Brown, 2004.

Friedman, Norman. *Seapower and Space: From the Dawn of the Missile Age to Net-Centric Warfare*. Annapolis, MD: Naval Institute Press, 2000.

Frost, Mike, and Michael Gratton. *Spyworld: Inside the Canadian and American Intelligence Establishments*. Toronto: Doubleday Canada Limited, 1994.

Frye, William. *Marshall: Citizen Soldier*. Indianapolis, IN: Bobbs-Merrill, 1947.

Fursenko, Aleksandr, and Timothy Naftali. *"One Hell of a Gamble": Khrushchev, Castro, and Kennedy, 1958–1964*. New York: W.W. Norton, 1997.

Furst, Alan. *Dark Voyage*. New York: Random House, 2004.

Furst, Alan. *Night Soldiers*. Boston: Houghton Mifflin, 1988.

Furst, Alan. *Red Gold*. New York: Random House, 1999.

Furst, Alan. *The World at Night*. New York: Random House, 1996.

Gaines, Helen Fouche. *Cryptanalysis: A Study of Ciphers and their Solutions*. Mineola, NY: Dover Publications, 1939.

Gann, Ernest. *The Black Watch: The Men Who Fly America's Secret Spy Planes*. New York: Random House, 1989.

Gannon, James. *Stealing Secrets, Telling Lies: How Spies and Codebreakers Helped Shape the Twentieth Century*. Washington, DC: Brassey's, 2001.

Ganser, Daniele. *NATO's Secret Armies: Operations Gladio and Terrorism in Western Europe*. London: Frank Cass, 2005.

Garber, Marjorie, and Rebecca Walkovwitz (eds.). *Secret Agents: The Rosenberg Case, McCarthyism, and Fifties America*. New York: Routledge, 1995.

Garrison, Jim. *On the Trail of the Assassins: My Investigation and Prosecution of the Murder of President Kennedy*. New York: Sheridan Square Press, 1988.

Garthoff, Douglas. *Directors of Central Intelligence as Leaders of the U.S. Intelligence Community, 1946–2005*. Washington, DC: Central Intelligence Agency, Center for the Study of Intelligence, 2005.

Garthoff, Raymond. "Polyakov's Run," *The Bulletin of the Atomic Scientists* 56 (2000), 37–40.

Gates, Robert M. *From the Shadows: The Ultimate Insider's Story of Five Presidents and How They Won the Cold War*. New York: Simon & Schuster, 1997.

Gazur, Edward P. *Alexander Orlov: The FBI's KGB General*. New York: Caroll & Graf Publishers, 2002.

Gehlen, Reinhard. *Der Dienst-Erinnerungen 1942–1971*. Hase & Koehler: Mainz, 1971.

Gehlen, Reinhard. *The Service: The Memoirs of General Reinhard Gehlen*. New York: World Publishing, 1972.

George, Roger Z., and James B. Bruce (eds.). *Analyzing Intelligence*. Washington, DC: Georgetown University Press, 2008.

German Campaign in Russia: Planning and Operations (1940–1942). Washington, DC: U.S. Army, Center of Military History, 1955.

Gervasi, Frank. *Big Government: The Meaning and Purpose of the Hoover Commission Report*. New York: Whittlesey House, 1949.

Gibney, Frank (ed.). *The Penkovsky Papers: The Russian Who Spied for the West*. London: Collins, 1965.

Giesek, Jens.*Mielke-Konzern: Die Geschichte der Stasi 1945–1990*. Stuttgart: Deutsche Verlags-Anstalt, 2001.

Gill, Lesley. *The School of the Americas: Military Training and Political Violence in the Americas*. Durham, NC: Duke University Press, 2004.

Gilmore, Allison B. *You Can't Fight Tanks with Bayonets: Psychological Warfare against the Japanese Army in the Southwest Pacific*. Lincoln, NE: University of Nebraska Press, 1998.

Gimbel, John. "U.S. Policy and German Scientists: The Early Cold War," *Political Science Quarterly* 101 (1986), 433–451.

Gimpel, Erich. *Spy for Germany*. London: Hale, 1957.

Gisevius, Hans B. *To the Bitter End*. Boston: Houghton Mifflin, 1947.

Glantz, David. *Soviet Military Deception in the Second World War*. London: Frank Cass, 1989.

Glantz, David. *Soviet Military Intelligence in War*. London: Frank Cass, 1990.

Glick, Brian. *War at Home: Covert Action Against American Activists and What We Can Do About It*. Boston: South End Press, 1989.

Glinksy, Albert. *Theremin: Ether Music and Espionage*. Chicago: University of Illinois Press, 2000.

Godson, Roy (ed.). *Intelligence Requirements for the 1980's: Clandestine Collection*. Washington, DC: National Strategy Information Center, 1982.

Godson, Roy (ed.). *Intelligence Requirements for the 1980's: Counter-Intelligence*. Washington, DC: National Strategy Information Center, 1980.

Godson, Roy (ed.). *Intelligence Requirements for the 1980's: Domestic Intelligence.* Washington, DC: National Strategy Information Center, 1986.

Goldberg, Arthur J. *The Defenses of Freedom: The Public Papers of Arthur J. Goldberg,* 1st ed. Daniel Patrick Moynihan (ed.). New York: Harper & Row, 1966.

Goldstein, Kalman. "Silas Deane's Preparation for Rascality," *The Historian* 43 (1890–1981), 75–97.

Gordievsky, Oleg. *Next Stop Execution: The Autobiography of Oleg Gordievsky.* London: Macmillan, 1995.

Gordon, Yefim. *Tupolev Tu-95/-142.* Arlington, TX: Polygon Press, 2005.

Gordon, Yefim, and Vladimir Rigmant with Jay Miller. *Tupolev Tu95/Tu-142 "Bear."* Arlington, TX: Aerofax, 2007.

Gould, Jonathan S. *The OSS and the London "Free Germans."* CIA Online Library: https://www.cia.gov/library/center-for-the-study-of-intelligence (accessed October 15, 2007)

Goulden, Joseph C., with Alexander Raffio. *Death Merchant: The Rise and Fall of Edwin P. Wilson.* New York: Simon & Shuster, 1984.

Granatstein, J. L., and David Stafford. *Spy Wars: Espionage and Canada from Gouzenko to Glasnost.* Toronto: Key Porter, 1990.

Grant, Gordon R. *Barbarossa: The German Campaign in Russia: Planning and Operations, 1940–1942.* Victoria, BC: Tafford Publishing, 2006.

Gray, Stephen. *Ghost Plane.* New York: St. Martin's, 2006.

Gray, Wood. *The Hidden Civil War: The Story of the Copperheads.* New York: Viking Press, 1942.

Greene, Graham. *A Sort of Life.* London: Brodely Head, 1971.

Green, Thomas Marshall. *The Spanish Conspiracy: A Review of Early Spanish Movements in the Southwest.* Cincinnati, OH: R. Clarke and Company, 1891.

Greenhow, Rose O'Neal. *My Imprisonment and the First Year of Abolition Rule in Washington.* London: Richard Bentley, 1863.

Gresh, Lois H., and Robert Weinberg. *The Science of James Bond: From Bullets to Bowler Hat to Boat Jumps, the Real Technology Behind 007's Fabulous Films.* New York: John Wiley & Sons, 2006.

Gribble, Leonard. *Famous Feats of Espionage.* London: Arthur Baker Limited, 1972.

Griffith, John. "The Official Secrets Act, 1989," *Journal of Law and Society* 16.2 (1989), 273–290.

Griffith, Robert. *The Politics of Feat: Joseph R. McCarthy and the Senate.* University of Amherst: Massachusetts Press, 1970.

Griffith, Samuel B., translator. *Sun-Tzu: The Art of War.* Oxford, UK: Oxford University Press, 1971.

Grisold, Terry, and D. M. Giangreco. *Delta, America's Elite Counterterrorist Force.* Osceola, WI: MBI Publishing Company, 1992.

Groh, Lynn. *The Culper Spy Ring.* Philadelphia: Westminster Press, 1969.

Grose, Peter. *Gentleman Spy: The Life of Allen Dulles.* Boston: Houghton Mifflin, 1994.

Groves, Leslie M. *Now It Can Be Told.* New York: Harper, 1962.

Gruber, Helmut. *Soviet Russia Masters the Comintern: International Communism in the Era of Stalin's Ascendancy.* Garden City, NY: Anchor Press/Doubleday, 1974.

"Guidelines on Special Branch Work in the United Kingdom (2004)." http://www .statewatch.org/news/2004/mar/special-branch.pdf.

Guisnel, Jean. *CYBERWARS: Espionage on the Internet*. Translation from the French by Gui Masai. New York: Perseus Books, 1997.

Gunn, Geoff, and Jeff Lee. *Cambodia Watching Down Under*. Bangkok: Chulalongkorn University Press, 1991.

Gunston, Bill. *An Illustrated Guide to Spy Planes and Electronic Warfare*. New York: Arco Publishers, 1983.

Gunston, Bill. *An Illustrated Guide to the Modern Soviet Air Force*. New York: ARCO, 1982.

Gutjahr, Melanie. *The Intelligence Archipelago: The Community's Struggle to Reform in the Globalized Era*. Washington, DC: Center for Strategic Intelligence Research, Join Military Intelligence College, 2005.

Haines, Gerald K. "Looking for a Rogue Elephant: The Pike Committee Investigations and the CIA," *Studies in Intelligence* (Winter 1998–1999), 81–92.

Haines, Gerald K., and Robert Leggett (eds.). *Watching the Bear: Essays on CIA's Analysis of the Soviet Union*. Washington, DC: Central Intelligence Agency, 2003.

Halamka, John D. Espionage in the Silicon Valley. Berkeley, CA: Sybex, 1984. http:// www.moffettfieldmuseum.org/.

Halberstam, David. *The Best and the Brightest*. New York: Random House, 1969.

Halberstam, David. *War in a Time of Peace: Bush, Clinton and the Generals*. New York: Touchstone, 2001.

Halevy, Efraim. *Man in the Shadows: Inside the Middle East Crisis with a Man Who Led the Mossad*. New York: St. Martin's Press, 2006.

Hall, Charles Swain. *Benjamin Tallmadge: Revolutionary Soldier and American Business-man*. New York: Columbia University Press, 1943.

Halperin, Morton H., et al. (eds.). *The Lawless State*. New York: Penguin, 1976.

Halpern, Samuel, and Hayden Peake. "Did Angleton (1917–1987) Jail Nosenko?," *International Journal of Intelligence and Counterintelligence* 3 (1989), 457–464.

Hamilton, Dwight. *Inside Canadian Intelligence: Exposing the New Realities of Espionage and International Terrorism*. Toronto, Canada: Dundurn Press, 2006.

Hammond, Paul Y. *Organizing for Defense: The American Military Establishment in the Twentieth Century*. Princeton, NJ: Princeton University Press, 1961.

Hamon, Joseph. *Le Chevalier de Bonvouloir*. Paris: Jouve, 1953.

Hamrick, S. J. *Deceiving the Deceivers: Kim Philby, Donald Maclean, and Guy Burgess*. New Haven, CT: Yale University Press, 2004.

Handel, Michael. *Strategic and Operational Deception in the Second World War*. London: Frank Cass, 1987.

Handel, Michael (ed.). *Leaders and Intelligence*. London: Frank Cass, 1988.

Hartgrove, J. Dane (ed.). *Covert Warfare Vol 8. The OSS-NKVD Relationship, 1943–1945*. New York: Garland, 1989.

Harr, John. *The Professional Diplomat*. Princeton, NJ: Princeton University Press, 1969.

Hasketh, Roger. *Fortitude: The D-Day Deception Campaign*. London: St. Ermin's Press, 1999.

Hastedt, Glenn. "Creation of the Department of Homeland Security," in Ralph Carter (ed.), *Contemporary Cases in U.S. Foreign Policy*, 2nd ed. Washington, DC: CQ Press, 2005.

Hastedt, Glenn. "Washington Politics, Intelligence, and the Struggle Against Global Terrorism," in Loch K. Johnson (ed.), *Strategic Intelligence: Counterintelligence and Counterterrorism*, volume 4. Westport, CT: Praeger, 2007.

Haugestad, Arne. *Kappefall-Et varslet justismord, (Fall of a Robe—An Announced Misscarriage of Justice)*. Oslo: Aschehoug, 2004.

Hayden, Sterling. *Wanderer*. New York: Bantam, 1964.

Haydock, Michael. *City Under Siege: The Berlin Blockade and Airlift, 1948–1949*. Washington, DC: Batsford Brassey Publishing Inc., 1999.

Haydon, F. Stansbury. *Aeronautics in the Union and Confederate Armies with a Survey of Military Aeronautics to 1861*. Baltimore: The Johns Hopkins University Press, 1941.

Hayes, Carlton. *Wartime Mission to Spain*. London: Macmillan, 1945.

Haynes, John E. and Harvey Klehr. *Early Cold War Spies: The Espionage Trials That Shaped American Politics*. New York: Cambridge University Press, 2006.

Haynes, John E. and Harvey Klehr. *VENONA: Decoding Soviet Espionage in America*. New Haven, CT: Yale University Press, 1999.

Heaps, Leo. *Hugh Hambleton, Spy*. Toronto: Methuen, 1981.

Helgerson, John L. *Getting to Know the President: CIA Briefings of Presidential Candidates, 1952–1992*. Washington, DC: Central Intelligence Agency, Center for the Study of Intelligence, 1995.

Henrickson, Ryan. *The Clinton Wars: The Constitution, Congress, and War Powers*. Nashville, TN: Vanderbilt University Press, 2002.

Hensler, Alistair. "Canadian Intelligence: An Insider's Perspective," *Canadian Foreign Policy* 6 (1999), 127–132.

Herbig, Katherine. *Changes in Espionage by Americans*. Monterey, CA: Defense Personnel Research Center, 2008.

Herken, Greg. *Cardinal Choices: Presidential Science Advising from the Atomic Bomb to SDI*. Oxford: Oxford University Press, 1992.

Herken, Greg. *The Winning Weapon: The Atomic Bomb in the Cold War, 1945–1950*. Princeton, NJ: Princeton University Press, 1981.

Herman, Arthur. *Joseph McCarthy: Reexamining the Life and Legacy of America's Most Hated Senator*. New York: Free Press, 2000.

Herman, Michael. *Intelligence Power in Peace and War*. New York: Cambridge University Press, 1996.

Hersh, Seymour. *The Target Is Destroyed*. London: Farber, 1986.

Hewlett, Richard, and Oscar Anderson. *A History of the United States Atomic Energy Commission*. University Park, PA: Pennsylvania University Press, 1962.

Hickey, Donald. "America's Response to the Slave Revolt in Haiti, 1791–1806." *Journal of the Early Republic* 2:4 (1982), 361–379.

Hinckle, Warren, and William Turner. *Deadly Secrets: The CIA-Mafia War Against Castro and the Assassination of J.F.K.* New York: Thunder's Mouth Press, 1992.

Hinsley, F. H., and C. A. G. Simpkins. *British Intelligence in the Second World War, Volume 4, Security and Counter-Intelligence*. London: H.M. Stationary Office, 1990.

Hinsley, F. H., and Alan Stripp. *Code Breakers: The Inside Story of Bletchley Park*. NY: Oxford University Press, 1994.

Hinsley, F. H. et al. *British Intelligence in the Second World War*, 5 vols. London: Cambridge University Press, 1993.

Historical Manuscripts Commission. *Report on American Manuscripts in the Royal Institution of Great Britain*, 4 vols. London: H.M. Stationary Office, 1904–1909.

Hitchcock, Ethan Allen. W. A. Croffut (ed.). *Fifty Years in Camp and Field: Diary of Major-General Ethan Allen Hitchcock, U.S.A.* New York: G.P. Putnam's Sons, 1909.

Hitchcock, Walter T. (ed.). *The Intelligence Revolution, a Historical Perspective.* Washington, DC: Office of Air Force History, 1988.

Hoang Hai Van, and Tan Tu. *Pham Xuan An: A General of the Secret Service.* Hanoi: The Gioi Publishers, 2003.

Hodgson, Godfrey. *Woodrow Wilson's Right Hand, the Life of Colonel Edward M. House.* New Haven, CT: Yale University Press, 2006.

Hoehling, A. A. *Women Who Spied.* New York: Dodd, Mead & Company, 1967.

Hoffman, Tod. *Le Carre's Landscape.* Montreal, Canada: McGill-Queens University Press, 2001.

Holbrook, James. *Potsdam Mission.* Carmel, IN: Cork Hill Press, 2005.

Holden, Henry M. *To Be a U.S. Secret Service Agent.* St. Paul, MN: Zenith, 2006.

Holzman, Michael. *James Jesus Angleton, the CIA, and the Craft of Counterintelligence.* Amherst, MA: University of Massachusetts Press, 2008.

Honan, William H. *Visions of Infamy: The Untold Story of How Journalist Hector C. Bywater Devised the Plans That Led to Pearl Harbor.* New York: St. Martin's, 1991.

Hood, William. *Mole: The True Story of the First Russian Intelligence Officer Recruited by the CIA.* New York: Norton, 1982.

Hooper, David. *Official Secrets: The Use and Abuse of the Act.* London: Secker & Warburg, 1987.

Hoover Commission Report on the Organization of the Executive Branch of Government. New York: McGraw Hill, 1949.

Hopple, Gerald, and Bruce Watson (eds.). *The Military Intelligence Community.* Boulder, CO: Westview Press, 1986.

Hougan, Jim. *Secret Agenda.* New York: Random House, 1984.

House, Edward M., arranged by Charles Seymour. *The Intimate Papers of Colonel House*, two volumes. Boston: Houghton-Mifflin, 1926–1928.

Houston, Lawrence R. "The CIA's Legislative Base," *International Journal of Intelligence and Counterintelligence* 5 (1992), 411–415.

Hoveyda, Fereydoun. *The Fall of the Shah.* Translated by Roger Liddell. New York: Wyndham Books, 1980.

Howard, Edward, Lee. *Safe House: The Compelling Memoirs of the Only CIA Spy to Seek Asylum in Russia.* Bethesda, MD: National Press Books, 1995.

Howe, Russell Warren. *Mata Hari: The True Story.* New York: Dodd, Mead, 1986.

Huber, Thomas M. *Pastel: Deception in the Invasion of Japan.* Fort Leavenworth, KS: Combat Studies Institute, U.S. Army Command And General Staff College, 1988.

Hunt, Linda. *Secret Agenda: The United States Government, Nazi Scientists, and Project Paperclip, 1945–1990.* New York: St. Martin's Press, 1991.

Huse, Caleb. *The Supplies for the Confederate Army: How They Were Obtained in Europe and Paid For.* Boston: T.R. Marvin and Son, 1904.

Hyde, H. Montgomery. *The Atom Bomb Spies.* London: Hamish Hamilton, 1980.

Hyde, H. *George Blake, Superspy*. London: Constable, 1987.

Ind, Allison. *Allied Intelligence Bureau*. New York: David McKay Company, 1958.

Ind, Allison. *A Short History of Espionage*. New York: David McKay, 1963.

Inderfurth, Karl, and Loch Johnson (eds.). *Decisions of the Highest Order: Perspectives on the National Security Council*. Pacific Grove, CA: Brooks/Cole, 1988.

Inderfurth, Karl F., and Loch K. Johnson (eds.). *Fateful Decisions: Inside the National Security Council*. New York: Oxford University Press, 2004.

Innis, Brian. *The Book of Spies*. London: Bancroft, 1966.

Isaacson, Walter. *Kissinger. A Biography*. London: Faber and Faber, 1992.

Jackson, Robert. *High Cold War: Strategic Air Reconnaissance and the Electronic Intelligence War*. Newbury Park, CA: Haynes North America, 1998.

Jacobs, James Ripley. *Tarnished Warrior: Major-General James Wilkinson*. New York: Macmillan, 1938.

James, Coy Hilton. *Silas Deane—Patriot or Traitor?* East Lansing, MI: Michigan State University Press, 1975.

James, Marquis. *Alfred I. DuPont: The Family Rebel*. New York: Bobbs-Merrill, 1941.

Jeffrey-Jones, Rhodri. *American Espionage: From Secret Service to CIA*. New York: Free Press, 1977.

Jeffrey-Jones, Rhodri. *The CIA and American Democracy*, 2nd ed. New Haven, CT: Yale University Press, 1998.

Jeffrey-Jones, Rhodri. *Cloak and Dollar: A History of American Secret Intelligence*. New Haven, CT: Yale University Press, 2002.

Jeffrey-Jones, Rhodri. *The FBI: A History*. New Haven, CT: Yale University Press, 2007.

Jeffrey-Jones, Rhodri. "The Montreal Spy Ring of 1898 and the Origins of 'Domestic' Surveillance in the United States." *Canadian Review of American Studies* 5 (Fall 1974), 119–334.

Jeffrey-Jones, Rhodri, and Andrew Lownie (eds.). *North American Spies*. Pittsburg: University of Pittsburgh Press, 1991.

Jenkins, Dennis R. *Lockheed SR-71/YF-12 Blackbirds*. WarbirdTech Series Volume 10. North Branch, MN: Specialty Press, 1997.

Jensen, Joan M. "The 'Hindu Conspiracy': A Reassessment," *Pacific Historical Review* 48 (1979), 65–83.

Johnson, Clarence Leonard (Kelly), and Maggie Smith. *Kelly—More than My Share of It All*. Washington, DC: Smithsonian Institution Press, 1985.

Johnson, Donald. *The Challenge to American Freedoms: World War I and the Rise of the American Civil Liberties Union*. Lexington, KY: University of Kentucky Press, 1963.

Johnson, Loch K. *America's Secret War: The CIA in a Democratic Society*. New York: Oxford University Press, 1989.

Johnson, Loch K. "Congressional Supervision of America's Secret Agencies: The Experience and Legacy of the Church Committee," *Public Administration Review* 64:1 (2004), 3–14.

Johnson, Loch K. "Legislative Reform of Intelligence Policy," *Polity* 17:3 (1985), 549–573.

Johnson, Loch K. *A Season of Inquiry: The Senate Intelligence Investigation*. Lexington, KY: University Press of Kentucky, 1985.

Johnson, Loch K. *Secret Agencies: U.S. Intelligence in a Hostile World*. New Haven, CT: Yale University Press, 1996.

Johnson, Loch K., and James Wirtz (eds.). *Strategic Intelligence: Windows Into a Secret World: An Anthology*. Los Angeles: Roxbury, 2005.

Johnston, Henry Phelps. *Nathan Hale: 1776*. New York: Private Printing, 1901.

Joint Committee on Atomic Energy. *Soviet Atomic Espionage*. Amsterdam: Fredonia Books, 2001.

Judis, John B. *William F. Buckley Jr.: Patron Saint of the Conservatives*. New York: Simon & Schuster, 2001.

Juretzko, Norbert and Dietl, Wilhelm. *Im Visier: ein Ex-Agent enthüllt die Machenschaften des BND*. München: Heyne, 2006.

Kackman, Michael. *Citizen Spy: Television, Espionage and the Cold War Culture*. Minneapolis: University of Minnesota Press, 2005.

Kahn, David. "The Black Code," *MHQ: Quarterly Journal of Military History* 18 (2005), 36–43.

Kahn, David. *The Codebreakers: The Comprehensive History of Secret Communications from Ancient Times to the Internet*. New York: Charles Scribner & Sons, 1996.

Kahn, David. *Hitler's Spies: German Military Intelligence in World War II*. New York: Macmillan, 1978.

Kahn, David. *The Reader of Gentlemen's Mail: Herbert O. Yardley and the Birth of American Codebreaking*. New Haven, CT: Yale University Press, 2004.

Kahn, David. *Seizing the Enigma: The Race to Break the German U-Boat Codes, 1939–1943*. Boston: Houghton Mifflin, 1990.

Kalugin, Oleg (with Fen Montaigne). *The First Directorate: My 32 Years in Intelligence and Espionage Against the West*. New York: St. Martin's Press, 1994.

Kalvoda, Josef. *The Genesis of Czechoslovakia*. Boulder, CO: East European Monographs, 1986.

Kaplan, Lawrence S. *Colonies into Nation: American Diplomacy, 1763–1801*. New York: Macmillan, 19972.

Karalekas, Anne. *History of the Central Intelligence Agency*. Laguna Hills: Aegean Park Press, 1977.

Katz, Barry. *Foreign Intelligence: Research and Analysis in the Office of Strategic Services, 1942–1945*. Cambridge, MA: Harvard University Press, 1989.

Katz, Friedrich. *The Secret War in Mexico: Europe, the United States and the Mexican Revolution*. Chicago: University of Chicago Press, 1981.

Kauffman, Louis, Barbara Fitzgerald, and Tom Sewell. *Moe Berg: Athlete, Scholar, Spy*. Boston: Little, Brown and Company, 1974.

Kazichkin, Valdimir. *Inside the KGB: My Life in Soviet Espionage*. London: Andre Deutsch, 1990.

Keay, Julia. *The Spy Who Never Was: The Life and Loves of Mata Hari*. London: Michael Joseph, 1987.

Keefe, Patrick Radden. *Chatter: Dispatches from the Secret World of Global Eavesdropping*. New York: Random House, 2005.

Keegan, John. *Intelligence in War: Knowledge of the Enemy from Napoleon to Al-Qaeda*. New York: Vintage, 2004.

Kennedy, David M. *Over Here: The First World War and American Society*. New York: Oxford University Press, 1980.

Kent, Sherman. "The First Year of the Office of National Estimates: The Directorship of William L. Langer," in Donald Steury (ed.), *Sherman Kent and the Board of National Estimates*, pp. 143–156. Washington, DC: Center for the Study of Intelligence, 1994.

Kent, Sherman. *Strategic Intelligence for American World Policy*. Princeton, N.J. Princeton University Press, 1949.

Kern, Gary. *A Death in Washington: Walter G. Krivitsky and the Stalin Terror*. New York: Enigma Books, 2004.

Kesaris, Paul (ed.). *The Rote Kapelle: The CIA's History of Soviet Intelligence and Espionage Networks in Western Europe, 1936–1945*. Westport, CT: Greenwood Publishing, 1979.

Kessler, Lauren. *Clever Girl: Elizabeth Bentley, the Spy Who Ushered in the McCarthy Era*. New York: HarperCollins, 2003.

Kessler, Ronald. *The Bureau: The Secret History of the FBI*. New York: St. Martin's Press, 2002.

Kessler, Ronald. *The CIA at War: Inside the Secret Campaign Against Terror*. New York: St Martin's Press, 2004.

Kessler, Ronald. *Escape from the CIA: How the CIA Won and Lost the Most Important KGB Spy Ever to Defect to the U.S.* New York: Pocket Books, 1991.

Kessler, Ronald. *Inside the CIA: Revealing the Secrets of the World's Most Powerful Spy Agency*. New York: Simon & Schuster, 1992.

Kessler, Ronald. *Moscow Station: How the KGB Penetrated the American Embassy*. New York: Charles Scriber's Sons, 1989.

Kessler, Ronald. *Spy vs. Spy: Stalking Soviet Spies in America*. New York: Scribner's, 1988.

Kettl, Donald. *System Under Stress: Homeland Security and American Politics*. Washington, DC: CQ Press, 2004.

Khrushchev, Sergi. "The Day We Shot Down the U-2," *American Heritage* 51 (September 2000), 36–49.

Kibbe, Jennifer D. "The Rise of the Shadow Warriors," *Foreign Affairs* 83: (2004). 102–115.

Killian, James R., Jr. *Sputnik, Scientists, and Eisenhower: A Memoir of the First Special Assistant to the President for Science and Technology*. Cambridge, MA: The MIT Press, 1977.

Kinchen, Oscar A. *Confederate Operations in Canada and the North North; a little-known phase of the American Civil War*. North Quincy, MA: The Christopher Publishing House, 1970.

Kinchen, Oscar A. *Daredevils of the Confederate Army: The Story of the St. Albans Raiders*. Boston: Christopher Publishing House, 1959.

Kinzer, Stephen. *All the Shah's Men: An American Coup and the Roots of Middle East Terror*. Hoboken, NJ: John Wiley & Sons, 2003.

Kirkpatrick, Lyman B., Jr. *The Real CIA: An Insider's View of the Strengths and Weaknesses of Our Government's Most Important Agency*. New York: Macmillan, 1968.

Kissinger, Henry. *The White House Years*. Boston: Little, Brown, 1979.

Kissinger, Henry. *Years of Upheaval*. Boston: Little, Brown, 1982.

Kite, Elizabeth S. *Beaumarchais and the War of Independence*. 2 vols. Boston: Gorham Press, 1918.

Kitts, Kenneth. *Presidential Commissions and National Security: the Politics of Damage Control.* Boulder, CO: Lynne Reinner, 2006.

Klass, Philip. *Secret Sentries in Space.* New York: Random House, 1971.

Klehr, Harvey, John Earl Haynes, and Fridrikh Igorevich Firsov (eds.). *The Secret World of American Communism.* New Haven, CT: Yale University Press, 1995.

Klehr, Harvey, and Ronald Radosh. *The Amerasia Spy Case: Prelude to McCarthyism.* Chapel Hill, NC: The University of North Carolina Press, 1996.

Klein, Milton M. "John Jay and the Revolution." *New York History* 51 (2000), 19–30.

Klement, Frank. *The Limits of Dissent: Clement L. Vallandigham and the Civil War.* Lexington, KY: University of Kentucky Press, 1970.

Knaus, John Kenneth. *Orphans of the Cold War: America and the Tibetan Struggle for Survival.* New York: Public Affairs, 1999.

Knight, Amy. *Beria: Stalin's First Lieutenant.* Princeton, NJ: Princeton University Press, 1993.

Knight, Amy. *Spies without Cloaks: The KGB Successors.* Princeton, NJ: Princeton University Press, 1994.

Knightly, Philip. *Master Spy: The Story of Kim Philby.* New York: Knopf, 1989.

Knott, Stephen. *Secret and Sanctioned: Covert Operations and the American Presidency.* New York: Oxford University Press, 1996.

Koch, Stuart (ed.). *Selected Estimates on the Soviet Union, 1950–1969.* Washington, DC: Center for the Study of Intelligence, Central Intelligence Agency, 1993.

Kohn, Stephen M. *American Political Prisoners: Prosecutions under the Espionage and Sedition Acts.* Westport, CT: Praeger, 1994.

Kornbluh, Peter (ed.). *Bay of Pigs Declassified: The Secret CIA Repor on the Invasion of Cuba.* New York: Free Press, 1998.

Kreis, John (ed.). *Piercing the Fog, Intelligence and Army Air Operations in World War II.* Washington, DC: Air Force History and Museums Program, 1996.

Krepon, Michael, and Amy Smithson (eds.). *Open Skies, Arms Control, and Cooperative Security.* New York: St. Martins, 1992.

Krivitsky, Walter. *In Stalin's Secret Service.* New York: Enigma, 2000.

Kukis, Mark. *"My Heart Became Attached:" The Strange Journey of John Walker Lindh.* Washington, DC: Brassey's, 2003.

Labaree, Leonard W., Benjamin B. Wilcox, et al. (eds.). *The Papers of Benjamin Franklin.* Volumes 22 and 27. New Haven, CT: Yale University Press, 1959.

Laird, Thomas. *Into Tibet: The CIA's First Atomic Spy and His Secret Expedition to Lhasa.* New York: Grove Press, 2002.

Lamphere, Robert J., and Tom Shachtman. *The FBI-KGB War: A Special Agent's Story,* New York: Random House, 1986.

Landau, Alan M., Frieda W. Landau, Terry Griswold, D. M.Giangreco, and Hans Halberstadt. *U.S. Special Forces.* Ann Arbor, MI: Lowe and B. Hould Publishers, 1999.

Landau, Henry. *The Enemy Within: The Inside Story of German Sabotage in America.* New York: Putnam's, 1937.

Lang, Walter N. *The World's Elite Forces: The Men, Weapons and Operations in the War Against Terrorism.* London: Salamander Books, 1987.

Langer, William L. *In and Out of the Ivory Tower.* New York: N. Watson Academic Publications, 1977.

Lanning, Michael Lee. *Senseless Secrets: The Failures of U.S. Military Intelligence*. New York: Barnes & Noble, 1996.

Lansdale, Edward. *In the Midst of Wars: An American's Mission to Southeast Asia*. New York: Harper & Row, 1972.

Laqueur, Walter. *A World of Secrets: The Uses and Limits of Intelligence*. New York: Basic Books, 1985.

Larson, Kate Clifford. *Bound for the Promised Land: Harriet Tubman, Portrait of an American Hero*. New York: Ballantine Books, 2004.

Lasby, Clarence G. *Project Paperclip: German Scientists and the Cold War*. New York: Atheneum, 1971.

Lashmar, Paul. *Spy Flights of the Cold War*. Annapolis, MD: Naval Institute Press, 1996.

Lathrop, Charles E. (ed.). "Journalists, Businessmen, & Clergy," in *The Literary Spy: The Ultimate Source for Quotations on Espionage & Intelligence*, pp. 219–224. New Haven, CT: Yale University Press, 2004.

Lawson, John. "The 'Remarkable Mystery' of James Rivington, 'Spy,'" *Journalism Quarterly* 35 (1958), 317–323, 394.

Layton, Rear Admiral Edwin T. *And I Was There: Breaking the Secrets—Pearl Harbor and Midway*. Old Saybrook, CT: William S. Konecky Associates, Inc., 2001.

Leary, William. *Perilous Missions: Civil Air Transport and CIA Covert Operations in Asia*. Tuscaloosa: University of Alabama Press, 1984.

Leary, William, and Leonard LeSchack. *Project Coldfeet: Secret Mission to a Soviet Ice Station*. Annapolis, MD: Naval Institute Press, 1996.

Lee, Wen Ho, and Helen Zia. *My Country Versus Me: The First-Hand Account by the Los Alamos Scientist Who Was Falsely Accused of Being a Spy*. New York: Hyperion, 2003.

Lefebrve, Stephane. "The Case of Donald Keyser and Taiwan's National Security Bureau," *The International Journal of Intelligence and CounterIntelligence* 20 (2007), 512–526.

Lefkowitz, Arthur. *George Washington's Indispensable Men: The 32 Aides-de-Camp Who Helped Win American Independence*. Mechanicsburg, PA: Stackpole Books, 2003.

Lehrer, Eli. "The Homeland Security Bureaucracy," *The Public Interest* 156 (2004), 71–85.

Leman-Langlois, Stephane and Jean-Paul Brodeur. "Terrorism Old and New: Counterterrorism in Canada," *Police Practice and Research* 6:2 (2005), 121–140.

Leonard, Elizabeth. *All the Darling of the Soldier: Women of the Civil War Armies*. New York: W.W. Norton, 1999.

Leonard, Raymond. *Secret Soldiers of the Revolution: Soviet Military Intelligence, 1918–1933*. Westport, CT: Greenwood Press, 1999.

Lerner, Mitchell B. *The Pueblo Incident: A Spy Ship and the Failure of American Foreign Policy*. Lawrence, KS: University of Kansas Press, 2003.

Lester, Malcolm. *Anthony Merry Redivivus, a Reappraisal of the British Minister to the United States, 1803–6*. Charlottesville: University Press of Virginia, 1978.

Leverkuehn, Paul. *German Military Intelligence*. London: Weidenfeld & Nicolson, 1954.

Lewin, Ronald. *The American Magic: Codes, Ciphers, and the Defeat of Japan*. New York: Farrar, Straus and Giroux, 1982.

Lewis, Jonathan E. *Spy Capitalism: ITEK and the CIA*. New Haven, CT: Yale University Press, 2002.

Liang, Qiao, and Wang Xiangsui. *Unrestricted Warfare*. Translation from the Chinese by FBIS. Beijing: PLA Literature and Publishing House, 1999.

Lilly, James. *China Hands*. New York: Public Affairs, 2004.

Lindsey, Robert. *The Falcon and the Snowman: A True Story of Friendship and Espionage*. New York: Simon & Schuster, 1979.

Lindsey, Robert. *The Flight of the Falcon: The True Story of the Manhunt for America's Most Wanted Spy*. New York: Pocket Books, 1983.

Lisanti, Tom, and Louis Paul. *Film Fatales: Women in Espionage Films and Television, 1962–1973*. Jefferson, NC: McFarland and Co., 2002.

Long, Duncan. *Defeating Industrial Spies*. Port Townsend, WA: Loompanice Unlimited, 1991.

Lonsdale, Gordon. *Spy: The Memoirs of Gordon Lonsdale*. London: Mayflower-Dell, 1966.

Lord, Carnes. *The Presidency and the Management of National Security*. New York: Free Press, 1988.

Lord, Walter. *Lonely Vigil: Coastwatchers of the Solomons*. New ed. Annapolis, Naval Institute Press, 2006.

Lord, Walter, and A. B. Feuer. *Coast Watching in World War II: Operations Against the Japanese in the Solomon Islands, 1941–1943*. Mechanicsburg, PA: Stackpole Books, 2006.

Lough, Loree. *Nathan Hale: Revolutionary Hero*. Philadelphia: Chelsea House Publishers, 2000.

Lowenthal, John. "VENONA and Alger Hiss," *Intelligence and National Security* 15 (2000), 98–130.

Lowenthal, Mark. *Intelligence: From Secrets to Policy*, 4th ed. Washington, DC: Congressional Quarterly Press, 1978/2003/2006/2009.

Lowenthal, Mark. *The National Security Council: Organizational History*. Washington, DC: Congressional Quarterly Press, 1978.

Lowenthal, Mark. *U.S. Intelligence: Evolution and Anatomy*, 2nd ed. Westport, CT: Praeger, 1992.

Lowenthal, Mark. *The U.S. Intelligence Community: An Annotated Bibliography*. New York: Garland, 1994.

Lycett, Andrew. *Ian Fleming: The Man Behind James Bond*. Atlanta: Turner Publishing, 1995.

Lyon, Verne. "Domestic Surveillance: The History of Operation CHAOS," *Covert Action Information Bulletin* (Summer 1990). http://www.serendipity.li/cia/lyon.

Maas, Peter. *Manhunt: The Incredible Pursuit of a CIA Agent Turned Terrorist*. New York: Penguin, 1987.

Macdonald, Bill. *The True Intrepid: Sir William Stephenson and the Unknown Agents*. Vancouver: Raincoast Books, 2001.

Macintyre, Ben. *Agent Zigzag: A True Story of Nazi Espionage, Love and Betrayal*. New York: Harmony Books, 2007.

Mackenzie, Angus. *Secrets: The CIA War at Home*. Berkeley, CA: University of California Press, 1997.

Mackenzie, William. *The Secret History of SOE—Special Operations Executive 1940–1945.* London: St. Ermin's Press, 2000.

MacKinnon, Janice R., and Stephen R. Mackinnon. *Agnes Smedley: The Life and Times of an American Radical.* Berkeley, CA: University of California Press, 1988.

Macksey, Kenneth. *The Searchers: Radio Intercepts in Two World Wars.* London: Cassell, 2003.

Maddrell, Paul. "The Western Secret Services, the East German Ministry of State Security, and the Building of the Berlin Wall," *Intelligence and National Security* 21 (2006), 829–847.

Mahoney, M. H. (ed.). *Women in Espionage: A Biographical Dictionary.* Santa Barbara, CA: ABC-CLIO, 1993.

Mahoney, Richard D. *Getting Away with Murder: The Real Story behind American Taliban John Walker Lindh and What the U.S. Government Had to Hide.* New York: Arcade Publishers, 2004.

Malone, John E. *Top Secret Missions.* Oxford, UK: Trafford Publishing, 2006.

Mangold, Tom. *Cold Warrior, James Jesus Angleton: The CIA's Master Spy Hunter.* New York: Touchstone, Simon & Schuster, 1991.

Manne, Robert. *The Petrov Affair: Politics and Espionage.* Sydney, Australia: Pergamon, 1987.

Manz, William H. *Civil Liberties in Wartime: Legislative Histories of the Espionage Act of 1917 and the Act of 1918.* Buffalo, NY: W. S. Hein, 2007.

Marchetti, Victor, and John D. Marks. *The CIA and the Cult of Intelligence.* New York: Dell, 1974.

Mark, Eduard. "Who Was VENONA's Ales? Cryptanalysis and the Hiss Case," *Intelligence and National Security* 18 (2003), 45–72.

Markle, Donald. *Spies and Spymasters of the Civil War.* Revised and expanded. New York: Hippocrene Books, 2004.

Marquis, Susan L. *Unconventional Warfare: Rebuilding U.S. Special Operations Forces.* Washington, DC: Brookings Institution Press, 1997.

Marshall, George C. *General Marshall's Report—The Winning of the War in Europe and the Pacific.* Washington, DC: War Department, 1945.

Marshall, Max (ed.). *The Story of the U.S. Army Signals Corps.* New York: Franklin Watts, 1965.

Martin, David C. *Wilderness of Mirrors.* New York: Ballantine, 1981.

Masaryk, Thomas G. *The Making of a State.* London: G. Allen & Unwin, 1927.

Masterman, John C. *The Double-Cross System: The Incredible True Story of How Nazi Spies were Turned into Double Agents.* New Haven, CT: Yale University Press, 1972.

Masterson, William H. *William Blount.* Baton Rouge: Louisiana University Press, 1954.

Matthias, Willard. *America's Strategic Blunders: Intelligence Analysis and National Security Policy, 1936–1991.* University Park, PA: Penn State Press, 2001.

Mauch, Christof. *The Shadow War against Hitler: The Covert Operations of America's Wartime Secret Intelligence Service.* Translated by Jeremiah Riemer. New York: Columbia University Press, 2002.

Mavis, Paul. *The Espionage Filmography: United States Releases, 1989 Through 1999.* McFarland, 2006.

May, Robert E. *Manifest Destiny's Underworld: Filibustering in Antebellum America*. Chapel Hill, NC: University of North Carolina Press, 2002.

May, Robert E. *The Southern Dream of a Caribbean Empire, 1854–1861*. Baton Rouge, LA: Louisiana State University Press, 1973.

Mazarr, Michael, et al. *Desert Storm: The Gulf War and What We Learned*. Boulder, CO: Westview, 1993.

McCabe, Joseph. *Talleyrand: A Biographical Study*. London: Hutchinson and Co., 1906.

McCarthy, James P. *The Air Force*. Westport, CT: Hugh Lauter Levin Associates, 2002.

McClintock, Michael. *Instruments of Statecraft: U.S. Guerrilla Warfare, Counterinsurgency and Counterterrorism, 1940–1990*. New York: Pantheon Books, 1990.

McCormick, Donald. *17F: The Life of Ian Fleming*. London: Peter Owen, 1993.

McCouch, Grayson M. P. " 'Naming Names': Unauthorized Disclosure of Intelligence Agents' Identities," *Stanford Law Review* 33 (1981), 693–712.

McCoy, Alfred. *The Politics of Heroin in Southeast Asia*. New York: Harper & Row, 1972.

McDonald, Forrest. *Alexander Hamilton, a Biography*. New York: W.W. Norton & Company, 1979.

McGarvey, Patrick. *The CIA: The Myth and the Madness*. Baltimore: Penguin, 1972.

McIntosh, Elizabeth. *Sisterhood of Spies: The Women of the OSS*. Annapolis, MD: Naval Institute Press, 1998.

McKnight, David. *Australia's Spies and Their Secrets*. Sydney, Australia: Allen & Unwin, 1994.

McPherson, James. *Battle Cry of Freedom: The Civil War Era*. New York: Oxford University Press, 1988.

Meadows, William C. *The Comanche Code Talkers of World War II*. Austin: University of Texas Press, 2003.

Medvedev, Zhores. *Andropov*. New York: Penguin, 1984.

Meeropol, Michael (ed.). *The Rosenberg Letters: A Complete Edition of the Prison Correspondence of Ethel and Julius Rosenberg*. New York: Garland, 1994.

Meeropol, Michael and Robert Meeropol. We are Your Sons: The Legacy of Ethel and Julius Roxenberg. Boston: Houghton Mifflin, 1975.

Melanson, Philip H., and Peter F. Stevens. *The Secret Service: The Hidden History of an Enigmatic Agency*. New York: Carroll & Graf Publishers, 2004.

Melton, Buckner F., Jr. *The First Impeachment: The Constitution's Framers and the Case of Senator William Blount*. Macon, GA: Mercer University Press, 1998.

Melvin, David Skene, and Ann Skene Melvin. *Crime, Detective, Espionage, Mystery and Thriller Fiction and Film: A Comprehensive Bibliography of Critical Writing through 1979*. Westport, CT: Greenwood Press, 1980.

Melzer, Richard. *Breakdown: How the Secret of the Atomic Bomb Was Stolen*. Santa Fe, NM: Sunstone Press, 1999.

Mendez, Antonio. *The Master of Disguise: My Secret Life in the CIA*. New York: William Morrow & Co., 1999.

Mendez, Antonio. *Spy Dust: Two Masters of Disguise Reveal the Tools and Operations that Helped Win the Cold War*. New York: Atria, 2002.

Merry, Bruce. *Anatomy of the Spy Thriller*. Dublin: Gill and Macmillan, 1977.

Messinger, Gary. *British Propaganda and the State in the First World War*. Manchester: Manchester University Press, 1992.

Meyer, Cord. *Facing Reality: From World Federalism to the CIA*. New York: Harper & Row, 1980.

Meyer, Karl E., and Tad Sulc. *The Cuban Invasion: The Chronicle of a Disaster*. New York: Praeger, 1968.

Millegan, Kris (ed.). *Fleshing Out Skull & Bones*. Walterville, OR: Trine Day, 2003.

Miller, Jay. *Lockheed Martin's Skunk Works*, rev. ed. Leicester, England: Midland Publishers, 1995.

Miller, John C. *Alexander Hamilton and the Growth of the New Nation*. New Brunswick, NJ: Transaction Books, 2004.

Miller, John C. *Crisis in Freedom: The Alien and Sedition Acts*. Boston: Little, Brown, 1951.

Miller, Melanie. *Envoy to the Terror: Gouverneur Morris and the French Revolution*. Dulles, VA: Potomac Books, 2005.

Miller, Nathan. *Spying for America: The Hidden History of U.S. Intelligence*. New York: Dell Publishing, 1990.

Miller, Toby. *Spyscreen: Espionage on Film and TV from the 1930s to the late 1960s*. Oxford: Oxford University Press, 2003.

Millett, Allan R. *Semper Fidelis: The History of the United States Marine Corps*, rev. ed. New York: The Free Press, 1991.

Minnick, Wendell L. *Spies and Provocateurs: A Worldwide Encyclopedia of Persons Conducting Espionage and Covert Action, 1946–1991*. Jefferson, NC: McFarland, 1992.

"Minutes of the Committee and of the First Commission for Detecting and Defeating Conspiracies in the State of New York December 11, 1776–September 23, 1778," *New York Historical Society Collections*, LVII and LVIII.

Mitchell, Marcia, and Thomas Mitchell. *The Spy Who Seduced America: The Judith Coplon Story*. Montpellier, VT: Invisible Cities Press, 2002.

Mitchell, Marcia, and Thomas Mitchell. *The Spy Who Tried to Stop War: Katherine Gunn and the Secret Plot to Sanction the Iraq Invasion*. London: PoliPoint Press, 2008.

Mitford, Jessica. *A Fine Old Conflict*. New York: Alfred A. Knopf, 1977.

Modin, Yuri. *My 5 Cambridge Friends: Burgess, MacLean, Philby, Blunt and Cairncross by Their KGB Controller*. Trans. by Anthony Roberts. Darby, PA: DIANE Publishing Co., 2000.

Mogelever, Jacob. *Death to Traitors: the Story of General Lafayette C. Baker, Lincoln's Forgotten Secret Service Chief*. Garden City, NY: Doubleday, 1960.

Monaghan, Frank. *John Jay: Defender of Liberty*. New York: Bobbs-Merrill, 1935.

Montague, Ludwell Lee. *General Walter Bedell Smith as Director of Central Intelligence, October 1950–February 1953*. University Park, PA: The Pennsylvania State University Press, 1992.

Moon, Tom. *This Grim and Savage Game: The OSS and U.S. Covert Operations in WW II*. Cambridge, MA: Da Capo Press, 2000.

Moore, Jeffrey. *Spies for Nimitz: Joint Military Intelligence in the Pacific War*. Annapolis, MD: Naval Institute Press, 2004.

Morris, Richard B. *John Jay: The Making of a Revolutionary—Unpublished Papers, 1745–1780*. New York: Harper & Row, 1975.

Morris, Richard B. *John Jay: The Winning of the Peace—Unpublished Papers, 1780–1784*. New York: Harper & Row, 1980.

Morris, Richard B. *The Peacemakers: The Great Powers and American Independence*. New York: Harper and Row, 1965.

Mosley, Leonard. *A Biography of Eleanor, Allen and Foster and Their Family Network*. New York: Dial Press, 1978.

Moss, Norman. *Klaus Fuchs: The Man Who Stole the Atom Bomb*. New York: St. Martins, 1987.

Muffeo, Steven E. *Most Secret and Confidential: Intelligence in the Age of Nelson*. Annapolis, MD: Naval Institute Press, 2000.

Mulligan, Timothy P. "Spies, Ciphers and 'Zitadelle': Intelligence and the Battle of Kursk, 1943," *Journal of Contemporary History* 22 (1987), 235–260.

Murphy, Brenda. *The Butcher of Lyon: The Story of Infamous Nazi Klaus Barbie*. New York: Empire Books, 1983.

Murphy, David. *What Stalin Knew: The Enigma of Barbarossa*. New Haven, CT: Yale University Press, 2006.

Murphy, David, Sergei Kondrashev, and George Bailey. *Battleground Berlin: CIA vs. KGB in the Cold War*. New Haven, CT: Yale University Press, 1999.

9/11 Commission Report: The Final Report of the National Commission on Terrorist Attacks on the United States. New York: Norton, 2004.

Naimack, Norman. *The Russians in Germany: A History of the Soviet Zone of Occupation, 1945–1949*. Cambridge, MA: Harvard University Press, 1995.

Nasheri, Hedieh, et al. *Economic Espionage and Industrial Spying*. Cambridge, MA: Cambridge University Press, 2004.

Neilson, Keith. *Britain, Soviet Russia and the Collapse of the Versailles Order, 1919–1939*. Cambridge, MA: Cambridge University Press, 2006.

Nelson, Anna K. "President Truman and the Evolution of the National Security Council," *Journal of American History* 71 (1985), 360–78.

Nelson, Michael. *War of the Black Heavens: The Battles of Western Broadcasting in the Cold War*. Syracuse: Syracuse University Press, 1997.

Nelson, Paul David. *General Sir Guy Carleton, Lord Dorchester: Soldier-Statesman of Early British Canada*. Madison, NJ: Farleigh Dickinson University Press, 2000.

Nelson, Paul David. *William Tryon and the Course of Empire: A Life in British Imperial Service*. Chapel Hill, NC: University of North Carolina Press, 1990.

Nesbit, Roy Conyers. *Eyes of the RAF: A History of Photo-Reconnaissance*. London: Sutton, 1996.

Nichols, Roy F. "William Shaler: New England Apostle of Rational Liberty," *The New England Quarterly* 9 (1936), 71–96.

Norman, E. Herbert. "The Genyosha: A Study of the Origins of Japanese Imperialism," *Pacific Affairs* 17 (1944), 262–284.

North, Oliver. *Under Fire: An American Story*. London: Fontana, 1992.

Nuxoll, Elizabeth Miles. *Congress and the Munitions Merchants: The Secret Committee of Trade during the American Revolution, 1775–1777*. New York: Garland Publishing, Inc., 1985.

Odom, William. *Fixing Intelligence: For a More Secure America*. New Haven, CT: Yale University Press, 2003.

O'Donnell, Patrick K. *Operatives, Spies and Saboteurs: The Unknown Story of the Men and Women of WWII's OSS.* New York: Free Press, 2004.

Olmsted, Kathryn S. *Challenging the Secret Government.* Chapel Hill, NC: University of North Carolina Press, 1996.

Olmsted, Kathryn S. *Red Spy Queen: A Biography of Elizabeth Bentley.* Chapel Hill, NC: University of North Carolina Press, 2002.

O'Reilly, Kenneth. *Hoover and the Un-Americans: the FBI, HUAC, and the Red Menace.* Philadelphia: Temple University Press, 1983.

Oren, Michael B. "The USS Liberty: Case Closed," *Azure* (2000), 74–98.

Oseth, John. *Regulating U.S. Intelligence Operations.* Lexington, KY: University of Kentucky Press, 1985.

O'Toole, G. J. A. *Honorable Treachery. A History of U.S. Intelligence, Espionage, and Covert Action from the American Revolution to the CIA.* New York: Atlantic Monthly Press, 1991.

O'Toole, G. J. A. *The Spanish War: An American Epic.* New York: Norton, 1984.

Owen, David, and Antonio Mendez. *Hidden Secrets: The Complete History of Espionage and the Technology Used to Support It.* Toronto: Firefly Books, 2002.

Owsley, Frank, Jr., and Gene A. Smith. *Filibusters and Expansionists, Jeffersonian Manifest Destiny, 1800–1821.* Tuscaloosa: The University of Alabama Press, 1997.

Pacepa, Ion Mihai. *Red Horizons: The True Story of Nicolae and Elena Ceausescus' Crimes, Lifestyles, and Corruption.* Washington, DC: Regnery Gateway, 1990.

Packard, Wyman H. *A Century of U.S. Naval Intelligence.* Washington, DC: Department of the Navy, 1996.

Paltsits, Victor Hugo. "The Use of Invisible Ink for Secret Writing during the American Revolution," *The Bulletin of the New York State Library* 39 (1935), 361–365.

Parker, James E., Jr. *Covert Ops: The CIA's Secret War in Laos.* New York: St. Martins, 1995.

Parker, Johnson. *Secrets of a Century: The Influence of Espionage and Secret Agreements.* Lanaham, MD: University Press of America, Inc., 2004.

Parrish, Michael. *The Lesser Terror: Soviet State Security, 1939–1953.* Westport, CT: Praeger, 1996.

Parrish, Thomas. *Berlin in the Balance: The Blockade, The Airlift, The First Major Battle of the Cold War.* Reading, MA: Perseus Books, 1998.

Pash, Boris. *The Alsos Mission.* New York: Charter Books, 1969.

Patrick, Rembert W. *Florida Fiasco: Rampart Rebels on the Georgia-Florida Border, 1810–1815.* Athens, GA: University of Georgia Press, 1954.

Paust, Jordan. *Beyond the Law: The Bush Administration's Unlawful Responses in the War on Terror.* Cambridge, MA: Cambridge University Press, 2007.

Payne, Robert. *The Marshall Story.* New York: Prentice Hall, 1951.

Payne, Ronald. *Mossad: Israel's Most Secret Service.* New York: Bantam, 1990.

Pearson, John. *The Life of Ian Fleming.* New York: McGraw Hill, 1966.

Peebles, Curtis. *The CORONA Project: America's First Spy Satellite.* Annapolis: Naval Institute Press, 1997.

Peis, Gunter. *The Mirror of Deception: How Britain Turned the Nazi Spy Machine Against Itself.* London: Weidenfeld and Nicholson, 1976.

Pemberton, William E. *Exit with Honor: The Life and Presidency of Ronald Reagan.* New York: M.E. Sharpe, 1997.

Pencak, William. *War, Politics, and Revolution in Provincial Massachusetts.* Boston: Northeastern University Press, 1981.

Penkovsky, Oleg. *The Penkovsky Papers.* St. John's Place, London, England: Collins, 1965.

Pennypacker, Morton. *General Washington's Spies on Long Island and in New York.* Brooklyn, NY: Long Island Historical Society, 1939.

Pennypacker, Morton. *The Two Spies: Nathan Hale and Robert Townsend.* Boston: Houghton Mifflin, 1930.

Perrault, Gilles. *Red Orchestra.* New York: Knopf Publishing Group, 1989.

Perry, Mark. *Eclipse: The Last Days of the CIA.* New York: William Morrow, 1992.

Perry, Mark. *Four Stars: The Joint Chiefs in the Post Cold War Era.* New York: Houghton Mifflin, 1989.

Perry, Roland. *Last of the Cold War Spies: The Life of Michael Straight, the only American in Britain's Cambridge Spy Ring.* Cambridge, MA: Da Capo Press, 2005.

Perry, Roland. *Casey, William (1913–1987): The Lives and Secret Lives of William Casey.* Toronto: Penguin Books of Canada, 1991.

Perry, Roland. *Roosevelt's Secret War: FDR and World War II Espionage.* New York: Random House, 2002.

Perry, Roland. *Piercing the Reich: The Penetration of Nazi Germany by American Secret Agents during World War II.* New York: Barnes and Noble Books, 2000

Perry, Roland. *Casey: From the OSS to the CIA.* New York: Viking Press, 1990.

Peterson, H. C. and Gilbert C. Fite. *Opponents of War, 1917–1918.* Seattle: University of Washington Press, 1968.

Petro, Joseph, and Jeffrey Robinson. *Standing Next to History: An Agent's Life Inside the Secret Service.* New York: Thomas Dunne Books, 2005.

Philander, D. Chase, Frank E. Grizzard, et al. (eds.). *The Papers of George Washington: Revolutionary War Series.* Volumes 7–9. Charlottesville, VA: University of Virginia Press, 1985.

Philby, Kim. *My Silent War: The Autobiography of a Spy.* New York: Random House, 2002.

Philby (Filbi), Rufina, Mikhail Lybimov, and Hayden B. Peake. *The Private Life of Kim Philby: The Moscow Years.* New York: Fromm International, 2000.

Philips, David Atlee. *The Night Watch: 25 Years of Peculiar Service.* New York: Antheneum, 1977.

Pike Committee Report. *The Village Voice* (February 16, 1975) 1.

Pilat, Oliver. *The Atom Spies.* New York: Putnam, 1952.

Pillar, Paul. "Intelligence," in Audrey Cronin and James Ludes (eds.), *Attacking Terrorism: Elements of a Grand Strategy,* pp. 115–139. Washington, DC: Georgetown University Press, 2004.

Pillar, Paul. "Intelligence, Policy and the War in Iraq," *Foreign Affairs* 85 (2006), 15–28.

Pincher, Chapman. *Too Secret Too Long.* New York: St. Martins, 1984.

Pincher, Chapman. *Traitors: The Anatomy of Treason.* New York: St. Martins, 1987.

Pinkerton, Allan. *Spy of the Rebellion: Being a True History of the Spy System of the United States During the Late Rebellion, Revealing Many Secrets of the War.* Lincoln, NE: University of Nebraska Press, 1989.

Plame, Valerie. *Fair Game*. New York: Simon & Schuster, 2007.

Plaster, John. *SOG: The Secret Wars of America's Commandos in Vietnam*. New York: Simon & Schuster, 1997.

Pleshakov, Constantine. *Stalin's Folly: The Tragic First Ten Days of WWII on the Eastern Front*. Boston: Houghton Mifflin, 2006.

Plowman, Matthew E. "Irish Republicans and the Indo-German Conspiracy of World War I," *New Hibernia Review* 7 (2003), 80–105.

Plum, William Rattle. *The military telegraph during the Civil War in the United States*. New York: Arno Press, 1974.

Pocock, Chris. *The U-2 Spyplane: Toward the Unknown: A New History of the Early Years*. Atglen, PA: Schiffer Military History, 2000.

Pogue, Forrest C. *George C. Marshall*. 4 vols. New York: Viking Press, 1963–1987.

Polenberg, Richard. *Fightinq Faiths: The Abrams Case, the Supreme Court, and Free Speech*. Ithaca, NY: Cornell University Press, 1987.

Polisar, Patti. *Inside France's DGSE: The General Directorate for External Security*. New York: The Rosen Publishing Group, 2003.

Pollard, Vincent Kelly. *Globalization, Democratization and Asian Leadership: Power Sharing, Foreign Policy and Society*. Aldershot, UK: Ashgate Publishing, Ltd., 2004.

Polmar, Norman. *Spyplane: The U-2 History Declassified*. Osceola, WI: MBI Publishing Company, 2001.

Polmar, Norman, and Thomas B. Allen. *The Spy Book: The Encyclopedia of Espionage*. New York: Random House, 2004.

Ponsonby, Arthur. *Falsehood in Wartime: Containing an Assortment of Lies Circulated Throughout the Nations During the Great War*. Sudbury, UK: Bloomfield, 1991.

Popplewell, Richard. "The Surveillance of Indian 'Seditionists' in North America, 1905–1915," *Intelligence and International Relations, 1900–1945* (1987), 49–75.

Porch, Douglas. *The French Secret Service: From the Dryfus Affair to the Gulf War*. New York: Farrar, Strauss, and Giroux, 1995.

Posner, Gerald. *Case Closed: Lee Harvey Oswald and the Assassination of JFK*. New York: Random House, 1993.

Posner, Gerald. *Why America Slept: The Failure to Prevent 9/11*. New York: Random House, 2003.

Potter, E. B. (ed.). *Sea Power: A Naval History*, 2nd ed. Annapolis, MD: Naval Institute Press, 1981.

Potts, Louis W. *Arthur Lee: A Virtuous Revolutionary*. Baton Rogue, LA: Louisiana State University Press, 1981.

Powell, Bill. *Treason: How a Russian Spy Led an American Journalist to a U.S. Double Agent*. New York: Simon & Schuster, 2002.

Powers, Gary Francis, and Curt Gentry. *Operation Overflight: A Memory of the U-2 Incident*. New York: Holt, Rinehart and Winston, 1970.

Powers, Richard. *Secrecy and Power: The Life of J. Edgar Hoover*. New York: Free Press, 1986.

Powers, Thomas. *Heisenberg's War: The Secret History of the German Bomb*. Cambridge, MA: Da Capo Press, 2000.

Powers, Thomas. *Intelligence Wars: American Secret History from Hitler to al-Qaeda*. New York: Review Books, 2002.

Powers, Thomas. *The Man Who Kept Secrets Richard Helms and the CIA*. New Yok: Alfred A. Knopf, Inc., 1979.

Powys-Lybbe, Ursula. *The Eye of Intelligence*. London: William Kimber, 1983.

Prados, John. *Combined Fleet Decoded: The Secret History of American Intelligence and the Japanese Navy in World War II*. New York: Random House, 1995.

Prados, John. *Keepers of the Keys: A History of the National Security Council from Truman to Bush*. New York: William Morrow, 1991.

Prados, John. *Lost Crusader: The Secret Wars of CIA Director William Colby*. New York: Oxford University Press, 2003.

Prados, John. *Presidents' Secret Wars: CIA and Pentagon Operations since World War II*. New York: William Morrow, 1986.

Prados, John. *Safe for Democracy: The Secret Wars of the CIA*. Chicago: Ivan R. Dee Publisher, 2006.

Prados, John. *The Soviet Estimate: U.S. Intelligence Analysis and Soviet Strategic Forces*. Princeton: Princeton University Press, 1986.

Prange, Gordon W. *At Dawn We Slept: The Untold Story of Pearl Harbor*. New York: McGraw-Hill, 1981.

Prange, Gordon W., Donald M. Goldstein, and Katherine V. Dillon. *Miracle at Midway*, reprint ed. New York: Penguin, 1983.

Prange, Gordon W., Donald M. Goldstein, and Katherine V. *Target Tokyo: The Story of the Sorge Spy Ring*. New York: McGraw-Hill, 1984.

President's Special Review Board [The Tower Commission Report]. New York: Times Books, 1987.

Preston, William, Jr. *Aliens and Dissenters: Federal Suppression of Radicals, 1903–1933*. New York: Harper & Row, 1966.

Price, Ruth. *The Lives of Agnes Smedley*. Cambridge, UK: Oxford University Press, 2005.

Priestman, Martin. *The Cambridge Companion to Crime Fiction*. Cambridge, MA: Cambridge University Press, 2003.

Pringle, Robert W. "SMERSH: Military Counterintelligence and Stalin's Control of the USSR," *International Journal and Counterintelligence* 21 (2008), 122–134.

Prouty, L. Fletcher. *The Secret Team: The CIA and its Allies in Control of the United States and the World*. Englewood Cliffs, NJ: Prentice Hall, 1973.

Public Affairs Reports, *The WMD Mirage: Iraq's Decade of Deception and America's False Premise for War*. New York: Public Affairs, 2005.

Pujol, Juan. *Operation Garbo*. New York: Random House, 1985.

Radosh, Ronald, and Joyce Milton. *The Rosenberg File: A Search for the Truth*. New York: Holt, Rinehart & Winston, 1983.

Rafalko, Frank. *Counterintelligence Reader: American Revolution to World War II*. Washington, DC: National Intelligence Center, 2004.

Raines, Rebecca Robbins. *Getting the Message Through, a Branch History of the U.S. Army Signal Corps*. Washington, DC: Center of Military History, 1996.

Ramage, James A. *Gray Ghost: The Life of Col. John Singleton Mosby*. Lexington, KY: University Press of Kentucky, 1999.

Ramsey, John Fraser. *Anglo-French Relations 1763–1770: A Study of Choseul's Foreign Policy*. Berkeley, CA: University of California Press, 1939.

Ranelagh, John. *The CIA: A History*. London: BBC Books, 1992.

Ranelagh, John. *The Rise and Decline of the CIA*. Revised and updated. New York: Touchstone, 1987.

Ranlet, Philip. *The New York Loyalists*. Knoxville, TN: University of Tennessee Press, 1986.

Ransom, Harry Howe. *The Intelligence Establishment*. Cambridge, MA: Harvard University Press, 1970.

Rashed, Zenab Esmat. *The Peace of Paris 1763*. Liverpool: University Press, 1951.

Raviv, Dan, and Yossi Melman. *Every Prince a Spy: The Complete History of Israel's Intelligence Community*. Boston: Houghton Mifflin, 1990.

Read, Anthony. *Operation Lucy, Most Secret Spy Ring of the Second World War*. London: Hodder & Stoughton, 1980.

Read, Anthony, and David Fisher. *Colonel Z: The Life and Times of a Master of Spies*. London: Hodder & Stoughton, 1984.

Redlow, Gregory, and Donald Welzenbach, *The CIA and the U-2 Program 1954–1974* Washington, DC: The Center for the Study of Intelligence, 1974.

Reese, Mary Ellen. *General Reinhard Gehlen: The CIA Connection*. Fairfax, VA: George Mason University Press, 1990.

Reeve, Simon. *The New Jackels: Ramzi, Yousef. Osama bin Laden and the Future of Terrorism*. Boston: Northeastern University Press, 1999.

Regis, Ed. *The Biology of Doom: America's Secret Germ Warfare Project*. New York: Owl Books, 2000.

Reich, Robert C. "Re-examining the Team A-Team B Exercise," *International Journal of Intelligence and Counterintelligence* 3 (1989), 387–403.

Reilly, Sydney. *Britain's Master Spy: The Adventures of Sidney Reilly, an Autobiography*. New York: Carroll & Graf, 1986.

Reuben, William A. *The Atom Spy Hoax*. New York: Action Books, 1960.

Revere, Paul. *Paul Revere's Accounts of His Famous Ride*. With an Introduction by Edmund S. Morgan. Boston: Massachusetts Historical Society, 1976.

Rhodes, Richard. *The Making of the Atomic Bomb*. Reprint ed. New York: Simon & Schuster, 1995.

Rich, Ben R., and Leo Janos. *Skunk Works: A Personal Memoir of My Years at Lockheed*. Boston: Little, Brown, 1994.

Richardson, Doug. *Modern Spyplanes*. New York: Salamander Books, 1990.

Richelson, Jeffrey. *American Espionage and the Soviet Target*. New York: Quill, 1987.

Richelson, Jeffrey. *America's Space Sentinels: DSP Satellites and National Security*. Lawrence, KS: University of Kansas Press, 1999.

Richelson, Jeffrey. *A Century of Spies: Intelligence in the Twentieth Century*. New York: Oxford University Press, 1995.

Richelson, Jeffrey. *The U.S. Intelligence Community*, 5th ed. Boulder, CO: Westview, 2008.

Richelson, Jeffrey. *The Wizards of Langley: Inside the CIA's Directorate of Science and Technology*. Boulder, CO: Westview, 2002.

Ricks, Thomas. *Fiasco: The American Military Adventure in Iraq*. New York: Penguin, 2006.

Riebling, Mark. *Wedge: The Secret War between the FBI and the CIA*. New York: Alfred A. Knopf, 1994.

Riggs, Alvin R. *The Nine Lives of Arthur Lee, Virginia Patriot*. Edited by Edward M. Jones. Williamsburg, VA: Independence Bicentennial Commission, 1976.

Ringe, Donald. *James Fenimore Cooper*. Boston: Twayne, 1988.

Ritcheson, Charles R. *Aftermath of Revolution: British Policy Towards the United States, 1783–1795*. Dallas, TX: Southern Methodist University Press, 1969.

Roberts, Sam. *The Brother: The Untold Story of Atomic Spy David Greenglass and How He Sent His Sister, Ethel Rosenberg, to the Electric Chair*. New York: Random House, 2001.

Robbins, Alexandra. *Secrets of the Tomb: Skull and Bones, the Ivy League, and the Hidden Paths of Power*. New York: Little, Brown, 2002.

Robbins, Christopher. *Air America*. New York: Putnam, 1990.

Rogers, Ann. *Secrecy and Power in the British State: A History of the Official Secrets Act*. London: Pluto Press, 1997.

Romerstein, Herbert, and Eric Breindel. *The VENONA Secrets. Exposing Soviet Espionage and America's Traitors*. Washington, DC: Regnery Publishing, 2001.

Ronnie, Art. Counterfeit Hero: Fritz Duquesne, Adventurer and Spy. Annapolis, MD: Naval Institute Press, 1995.

Root, Jean Christie. *Nathan Hale*. New York: The MacMillan Company, 1915.

Roosevelt, Kermit. *Countercoup: The Struggle for the Control of Iran*. New York: McGraw-Hill, 1979.

Rose, Alexander. *Washington's Spies: The Story of America's First Spy Ring*. New York: Bantam Dell, 2006.

Rose, Phyllis. *Jazz Cleopatra*. London: Vintage, 1991.

Rose, P. K. "The Civil War: Black American Contributions to Union Intelligence," *Studies in Intelligence*, (1998–1999), 73–80.

Rosen, Philip. *The Canadian Security Intelligence Service*. Ottawa, Canada: Parliament Research Branch, Library of Parliament, 2000.

Rosenberg, Bruce. *The Neutral Ground: The Andre Affair and the Background of Cooper's "The Spy."* Westport, CT: Greenwood Press, 1994.

Rositzke, Harry. *The CIA's Secret Operations: Espionage, Counterespionage and Covert Action*. New York: Reader's Digest Press, 1977.

Rositzke, Harry. *The KGB: The Eyes of Russia*. New York: Doubleday & Co., 1981.

Ross, Ishbel. *Rebel Rose: Life of Rose O'Neale Greenhow, Confederate Spy*. New York: Harper & Brothers, Publishers, 1954.

Ross, Joel N. *Double Cross Blind*. New York: Doubleday, 2005.

Rowan, Andrew Summers, and Marathon Montrose Ramsey. *The Island of Cuba: A Descriptive and Historical Account of the "Great Antilla."* New York: Henry Holt and Company, 1897.

Royal, Robert. "The (Mis)Guided Dream of Graham Green," *First Things: A Monthly Journal of Religion and Public Life* (Nov. 1999), 16.

Rudgers, David F. *Creating the Secret State: The Origins of the Central Intelligence Agency, 1943–1947*. Lawrence, KS: University of Kansas Press, 2000.

Ruffner, Kevin (ed.). *CORONA: America's First Satellite Program*. Washington, DC: Central Intelligence Agency, Center for the Study of Intelligence, 1995.

Ruffner, Kevin (ed.). *Forging an Intelligence Partnership: CIA and the Origins of the BND, 1945–1949*, vol 1. CIA History Staff, Center for Study of Intelligence, 1999.

Russell, David Lee. *The American Revolution in the Southern Colonies*. Jefferson, NC: McFarland & Co., 2000.

Russell, Dick. *The Man Who Knew Too Much*. New York: Avalon Books, 2003.

Rustmann, F. W., Jr. *CIA, Inc.: Espionage and the Craft of Business Intelligence*. Washington, DC: Brassey's Inc, 2002.

Ryan, Cornelius. *The Longest Day: June 6th, 1944. D-Day*. London: Victor Gollancz, 1960.

Ryan, David D. (ed.). *A Yankee Spy in Richmond: The Civil War Diary of "Crazy Bet" Van Lew*. Mechanicsburg, PA: Stackpole Books, 2001.

Ryan, James G., "Socialist Triumph as a Family Value: Earl Browder and Soviet Espionage," in *American Communist History* Vol. I, No. 2, pp. 125–142. 2002.

Sable, Martin Howard. *Industrial Espionage and Trade Secrets*. New York: Haworth Press, 1985.

Safer, Morley. *Flashbacks: On Returning to Vietnam*. New York: Random House, 1990.

Sample, Robert (ed.). *Four Days in November: the Original Coverage [by the New York Times] of the John F. Kennedy Assassination*. New York: St. Martins, 2003.

Sanders, Michael. "Wellington House and British Propaganda During the First World War," *The Historical Journal* 18:1 (1975), 119–146.

Sanders, Michael, and Philip M. Taylor. *British Propaganda During the First World War*. London: Macmillan, 1982.

Sandilands, Roger J. "Guilt by Association: Lauchlin Currie's Alleged Involvement with Washington Economists in Soviet Espionage," *History of Political Economy* 32 (2000), 473–515.

Sandilands, Roger J. *The Life and Political Economy of Lauchlin Currie*. Durham, NC: Duke University Press, 1990.

Santella, Andrew. *Navajo Code Talkers*. Mankato, MN: Compass Point Books, 2004.

Sapolsky, Harvey. *Science and the Navy: The History of the Office of Naval Research*. Princeton, NJ: Princeton University Press, 1990.

Satter, David. *Darkness at Dawn: The Rise of the Russian Criminal State*. New Haven, CT: Yale University Press, 2003.

Saunders, Frank Stonor. *The Cultural Cold War*. New York: Norton, 2000.

Sawatsky, John. *Gouzenko: The Untold Story*. Toronto: Macmillan, 1984.

Sawyer, Ralph. *The Tao of Spycraft: Intelligence in Theory and Practice*. Boulder, CO: Westview, 2004.

Sayers, Michael, and Albert E. Kahn. *Sabotage! The Secret War Against America*. New York: Harper & Brothers, 1942.

Scarborough, Ruth. *Belle Boyd: Siren of the South*. Macon, GA: Mercer University Press, 1997.

Schecter, Jerold, and Leona Schecter. *Sacred Secrets: How Soviet Intelligence Operations Changes American History*. Washington, DC: Brassey's Inc, 2002.

Scheips, Paul J. (ed.). *Military Signals Communications*. 2 vols. New York: Arno Press, 1980.

Schiller, Lawrence. *Into the Mirror: The Life Story of Masterspy Robert Hanssen*. New York: HarperCollins, 2001.

Schlesinger, Arthur M., Jr. *A Life in the 20th Century: Innocent Beginnings 1917–1950*. Norwalk, CT: Easton Press, 2001.

Schlesinger, Arthur M., Jr. *Robert Kennedy and His Times*. Boston: Houghton Mifflin, 1978.

Schmidt, Mária. *Battle of Wits*. Budapest, Hungary: Század Intézet, 2007.

Schneir, Walter and Miriam Schneir. *Invitation to an Inquest*. New York: Pantheon, 1983.

Schrecker, Ellen (Ed). *Cold War Triumphalism: The Misuse of History After the Fall of Communism*. New York: New Press, 2006.

Schroen, Gary C. *First In: An Insider's Account of How the CIA Spearheaded the War on Terrorism in Afghanistan*. New York: Presidio Press, 2005.

Schultz, Duane P. *The Dahlgren Affair: Terror and Conspiracy in the Civil War*. New York: W.W. Norton and Company, 1999.

Schumacher, Frederick Carl, Jr., and George C. Wilson. *Bridge of No Return: The Ordeal of the USS Pueblo*. New York: Harcourt, Brace, Jovanovich, 1970.

Scott, Len. "Espionage and the Cold War: Oleg Penkovsky and the Cuban Missile Crisis," *Intelligence and National Security* 14 (1999), 23–47.

Scoville, Herbert. "Is Espionage Necessary for our Security?" *Foreign Affairs* 54 (1976): 482–495.

Sebag-Montefiore, Hugh. *Enigma: The Battle for the Code*. New York: John Wylie & Sons, 2000.

Service, Robert. *Stalin. A Biography*. London: Pan McMillan, 2005.

Shackley, Theodore. *The Third Option: An American View of Counterinsurgency Operations*. New York: Readers Digest Press, 1981.

Shapley, Deborah. "Foreign Intelligence Advisory Board: A Lesson in Citizen Oversight?," *Science* 191 (March 12, 1976), 1035–1036.

Shaw, Peter. *American Patriots and the Rituals of Revolution*. Cambridge, MA: Harvard University Press, 1981.

Shawcross, William. *The Shah's Last Ride*. London: Chatto & Windus, 1989.

Sheehan, Neil. *A Bright Shining Lie: John Paul Vann and America in Vietnam*. New York: Random House, 1988.

Sherry, Norman. *The Life of Graham Greene: Volume II: 1939–1955*. New York: Penguin Books, 1994.

Shevchenko, Arkady N. *Breaking With Moscow*. New York: Alfred A. Knopf, 1985.

Shoemaker, Christopher. *Function and the NSC Staff: An Officer's Guide to the National Security Council*. Washington, DC: Government Printing Office, 1989.

Shoemaker, Christopher. *The National Security Council Staff: Counseling the Council*. Boulder, CO: Westview, 1991.

Shulsky, Abram and Gary Schmitt. *Silent Warfare: Understanding the World of Intelligence*, Washington, DC: Brassey's, 1993.

Shultz, Richard, H. Jr. *The Secret War Against Hanoi*. New York: HarperCollins, 1999.

Shultz, Richard, and Roy Godson. *Dezinformatsia, Active Measures in Soviet Strategy*. New York: Pergamon-Brassey's, 1984.

Sibley, Katherine. *Red Spies in America: Stolen Secrets and the Dawn of the Cold War*. Lawrence, KS: University Press of Kansas, 2004.

Simpson, Charles M. *Inside the Green Berets: The First Thirty Years*. Novato, CA: Presidio Press, 1983.

Sims, Jennifer, and Burton Gerber (eds.). *Transforming U.S. Intelligence*. Washington, DC: Georgetown University Press.

Singh, Simon. *The Code Book: The Science of Secrecy from Ancient Egypt to Quantum Cryptography.* New York: Anchor Books, 2000.

Singlaub, John, and Malcolm McConnell. *Hazardous Duty.* New York: Simon & Shuster, 1991.

Smist, Frank. *Congress Oversees the United States Intelligence Community, 1947–1994,* 2nd ed. Knoxville, TN: University of Tennessee Press, 1994.

Smith, Bradley F. *The Shadow Warriors: OSS and the Origins of the CIA.* New York: Basic Books, 1983.

Smith, Jack. *The Unknown CIA: My Three Decades with the Agency.* Washington, DC: Pergamonn-Brassey's, 1989.

Smith, Joseph Burkholder. *The Plot to Steal Florida: James Madison's Phony War.* New York: Arbor House, 1983.

Smith, Michael. *The Emperor's Codes: The Breaking of Japan's Secret Ciphers.* New York: Arcade Publishing, 2001.

Smith, Michael Douglas. "CIA Publications: Serving the President with Daily Intelligence," *International Journal of Intelligence and Counterintelligence* 12 (1999), 201–206.

Smith, R. Harris. *OSS: The Secret History of America's First Central Intelligence Agency.* Berkeley: University of California Press, 1972.

Smith, Richard Norton. *An Uncommon Man: The Triumph of Herbert Hoover.* New York: Simon & Schuster, 1984.

Snepp, Frank. *Decent Interval: An Insider's Account of Saigon's Indecent End Told by the CIA's Chief Strategy Analyst in Vietnam.* New York: Random House, 1977.

Snepp, Frank. *Irreparable Harm: A Firsthand Account of How One Agent Took on the CIA in an Epic Battle Over Free Speech.* Lawrence: University Press of Kansas, 2001.

Snider, Britt L. "Congressional Oversight of Intelligence After September 11," in Jennifer Sims and Burton Gerber (eds.), *Transforming Intelligence,* pp. 239–58. Washington, DC: Georgetown University Press, 2005.

Snider, Britt L. *Sharing Secrets with Lawmakers: Congress as a User of Intelligence.* Washington, DC: Central Intelligence Agency, Center for the Study of Intelligence, 1997.

Snider, Britt L. "Unlikely Shamrock: Recollections from the Church Committee's Investigation of NSA," *Studies in Intelligence* (1999/2000), 43–52.

Sobell, Morton. *On Doing Time.* New York: Scribner's, 1974.

Soley, Lawrence C., and John S. Nichols. *Clandestine Radio Broadcasting.* New York: Praeger, 1987.

Sontag, Sherry, and Christopher Drew. *Blind Man's Bluff.* New York: Public Affairs, Inc. 1998.

Sora, Steven. *Secret Societies of America's Elite: From Knights Templar to Skull and Bones.* New York: Destiny Books, 2003

Spence, Richard B. *Trust No One: The Secret Life of Sidney Reilly.* Los Angeles: Feral House, 2002.

Spencer, Warren F. *The Confederate Navy in Europe.* Tuscaloosa, AL: University of Alabama Press, 1983.

Spires, David N. *Beyond Horizons: A Half Century of Air Force Leadership in Space.* Maxwell Air Force Base: Air University Press, 1998.

Stack, Kevin P. "A Negative View of Competitive Analysis," *International Journal of Intelligence and Counterintelligence* 10 (1998), 456–464.

Stafford, David. "'Intrepid:' Myth and Reality." *Journal of Contemporary History* 22 (1987), 303–317.

Stafford, David. *The Silent Game: The Real World of Imaginary Spies*. Athens, GA: University of Georgia Press, 1991.

Stafford, David. *Spies Beneath Berlin*. New York: The Overlook Press, 2003.

Stafford, James. "Intrepid: Myth and Reality," *Journal of Contemporary History* 22 (1987), 303–317.

Stahr, Walter. *John Jay: Founding Father*. New York and London: Hambleton & London, 2005.

Stanton, Shelby. *Green Berets at War*. Novato, CA: Presidio Press, 1985.

Stares, Paul. *The Militarization of Space: U.S. Policy 1945–1984*. Ithaca, NY: Cornell University Press, 1985.

Stargardt, A. W. "The Emergence of the Asian System of Powers," *Modern Asian Studies* 23:2 (1989), 561–595.

Starnes, John. *Closely Guarded: A Life in Canadian Security and Intelligence*. Toronto, Canada: University of Toronto Press, 1998.

Starr, Stephen Z. *Colonel Grenfell's Wars: The Life of a Soldier of Fortune*. Baton Rogue: Louisiana State University Press, 1971.

Starr, Stephen Z. "Was There a Northwest Conspiracy?," *Filson Club History Quarterly* 38 (1964), 323–341.

Steele, Jonathan, and Eric Abraham. *Andropov in Power: From Komsomol to Kremlin*. Garden City, NY: Anchor Press/Doubleday, 1984.

Steers, Edward. *Blood on the Moon: The Assassination of Abraham Lincoln*. Lexington, KY: University Press of Kentucky, 2001.

Stephan, Robert W. *Stalin's Secret War: Soviet Counterintelligence against the Nazis,1941–1945*. Lawrence, KS: University of Kansas Press, 2004.

Stern, Sheldon. *Averting 'The Final Failure': John F. Kennedy and the Secret Cuban Missile Crisis Meetings*. Stanford: Stanford University Press, 2003.

Steury, Donald (ed.) *Sherman Kent and the Board of National Estimates: Collected Essays*. Washington, DC: Center for the Study of Intelligence, Central Intelligence Agency, 1994.

Steury, Donald (ed.). *On the Front Lines of the Cold War: Documents on the Intelligence War in Berlin, 1946 to 1961*. Washington, DC: Center for the Study of Intelligence, 1999.

Stevens, B. F. (ed.). *Facsimiles of Manuscripts in European Archives Relating to America, 1773–1783*. 25 vols. London: Malby & Sons, 1889–1898.

Stevenson, Jonathan. "Demilitarizing the War on Terror," *Survival* 48 (2006), 37–54.

Stevenson, William. *A Man Called Intrepid*. New York: Ballantine, 1976.

Stinchcombe, Walter. *The XYZ Affair*. Westport, CT: Greenwood Press, 1980.

Stinchcombe, William C. *The American Revolution and the French Alliance*. Syracuse, NY: Syracuse University Press, 1969.

Stinnet, Robert. *Day of Deceit: The Truth about FDR and Pearl Harbor*. New York: Free Press, 1999.

Stober, Dan, and Ian Hoffman. *A Convenient Spy: Wen Ho Lee and the Politics of Nuclear Espionage*. New York: Simon & Shuster, 2002.

Stockwell, Frank. *In Search of Enemies. A CIA Story*. New York: Norton, 1978.

Stoler, Mark A. *George C. Marshall: Solider-Statesman of the American Century*. New York: Twayne Publishers, 1989.

Stourz, Gerald. *Benjamin Franklin and American Foreign Policy*. Chicago: University of Chicago Press, 1969.

Strada, Michael J., and Harold R. Troper. *Friend or Foe?: Russians in American Film and Foreign Policy, 1933–1991*. Lanham, MD: Rowman & Littlefield Publishers, 1997.

Straight, Michael. *After Long Silence*. New York: Norton, 1983.

Strasser, Steven. *The 9/11 Investigations*. New York: Public Affairs Reports, 2004.

Strong, Kenneth. *Men of Intelligence: A Study of the Roles and Decisions of Chiefs of Intelligence from World War One to the Present Day*. New York: St. Martin's, 1972.

Strong, Sir Kenneth. *Intelligence at the Top: The Recollections of a British Intelligence Officer*. Garden City, NY: Doubleday, 1968.

Sudoplatov, Pavel et al. *Special Tasks: The Memoirs of an Unwanted Witness, a Soviet Spymaster*. New York: Little Brown, 1994.

Sullivan, John, F. *Of Spies and Lies: A CIA Lie Detector Remembers Vietnam*. Lawrence, KS: University Press of Kansas, 2002.

Sun-tzu. *The Art of War*. Translated by Samuel B. Griffith. Oxford: Oxford University, 1963.

Sutherland, Douglas. *Great Betrayal: The Definitive Story of Blunt, Philby, Burgess, and Maclean*. New York: Penguin Group, 1982.

Suvoruv, Victor. *Icebreaker*. London: Hamish Hamilton, 1990.

Suvoruv, Victor. *Inside the Aquarium*. New York: Macmillan, 1985.

Suvoruv, Victor. *Spetznaz: The Inside Story of the Soviet Special Forces*. New York: W.W. Norton, 1988.

Syjuco, Ma. Felisa A. *The Kempei Tai in the Philippines, 1941–1945*. Quezon City: New Day Publishers, 1988.

Sylves, Richard. *The Nuclear Oracles: A Political History of the General Advisory Committee of the Atomic Energy Commission, 1947–1977*. Ames, IA: Iowa State University Press, 1987.

Syrett, Harold C., and Jacob E. Cooke (eds.). *Papers of Alexander Hamilton*. 27 vols. New York: Columbia University Press, 1961–1987.

Szasz, Ferenc Morton. *British Scientists and the Manhattan Project: The Los Alamos Years*. New York: St. Martin's, 1992.

Szulc, Tad. *Fidel: A Critical Portrait*. New York: Harpers Perennial, 2000.

Taipale, K. A. "The Ear of Dionysus: Rethinking Foreign Intelligence Surveillance," *Yale Journal of Law and Technology* 9 (2007), 128–161.

Tallmadge, Benjamin. *Memoir of Col. Benjamin Tallmadge, Prepared by Himself at the Request of His Children*. New York: T. Holman, 1858.

Tanenhaus, Sam. *Whittaker Chambers*. New York: Random House, 1997.

Tarrant, V. E. *The Red Orchestra: The Soviet Spy Network inside Nazi Europe*. New York: John Wiley & Sons, 1960.

Taubman, Philip. *Secret Empire: Eisenhower, the CIA, and the Hidden Story of America's Space Espionage*. New York: Simon & Shuster, 2003.

Taylor, Robert A. "Prelude to Manifest Destiny: The United States and West Florida, 1810–1811," *Gulf Coast Historical Review* 7 (1992), 20–35.

Tenet, George. *At the Center of the Storm: My Years at the CIA.* New York: Harper-Collins, 2007.

"Terrorism Index," *Foreign Policy* 155 (2006), 48–55.

Theoharis, Athan. *From the Secret Files of J. Edgar Hoover.* Chicago: Ivan R. Dee, 1993.

Theoharis, Athan. *The Quest for Absolute Security: The Failed Relations Among U.S. Intelligence Agencies.* Chicago: Ivan R. Dee, 2007.

Theoharis, Athan. *Spying on Americans: Political Surveillance from Hoover to the Huston Plan.* Philadelphia: Temple University Press, 1978.

Theoharis, Athan, and John Stuart Cox. *Boss: J. Edgar Hoover and the Great American Inquisition.* New York: Bantam, 1990.

Thomas, David. "US Military Intelligence Analysis: Old and New Challenges," In Roger Z. George and James B. Bruce (Eds.), *Analyzing Intelligence,* pp. 138–156. Washington, DC: Georgetown University Press, 2008.

Thomas, Evan. *The Very Best Men: Four Who Dared: The Early Years of the CIA.* New York: Simon & Schuster, 1995.

Thomas, Gordon. *Gideon's Spies: The Secret History of the Mossad.* New York: St. Martin's Press, 1999.

Thomas, Gordon. *Journey Into Madness: The True Story of Secret CIA Mind Control and Medical Abuse.* New York: Bantam Books, 1989.

Thomas, Kenneth H., Jr. *Fort Benning.* Mount Pleasant, SC: Arcadia Publishing, 2003.

Thomas, Rosamund M. *Espionage and Secrecy: The Official Secrets Acts 1911–1989 of the United Kingdom.* London: Routledge, 1991.

Thornborough, Anthony M. *Spy Planes and other Reconnaissance Aircraft.* London: Arms and Armour, 1991.

Thurlow, Richard. *The Secret State: British Internal Security in the Twentieth Century.* London: Blackwell, 1994.

Thwaites, Michael. *Truth Will Out: ASIO and the Petrovs.* Sydney, Austalia: Collins, 1980.

Tidwell, William A. *April '65: Confederate Covert Action in the American Civil War.* Kent, OH: Kent State University Press, 1995.

Tidwell, William A., James O. Hall, and David Winfred Gaddy. *Come Retribution: The Confederate Secret Service and the Assassination of Lincoln.* Jackson: University Press of Mississippi, 1988.

Tillotson, Harry S. *The Beloved Spy: The Life and Loves of Major John Andre.* Caldwell, ID: Caxton Printers, 1948.

Toland, John. *The Rising Sun: The Decline and Fall of the Japanese Empire, 1936–1945.* London: Cassell & Company, 1971.

Trask, David F. *The War With Spain in 1898.* Lincoln, NE: University of Nebraska Press, 1981.

Treholt, Arne. *Alene (Alone).* Oslo: Cappelen, 1985.

Treholt, Arne. *Gråsoner (Grey Areas).* Oslo: Gyldendal, 2004.

Trento, Joseph J. *Prelude to Terror: The Rogue CIA and the Legacy of America's Private Intelligence Network.* New York: Carroll & Gaff, 2005.

Trento, Joseph J. *The Secret History of the CIA,* reprint ed. New York: Avalon Publishing Group, 2005.

Treverton, Gregory. *Reshaping National Intelligence for an Age of Information*. Cambridge: Cambridge University Press, 2001.

Treverton, Gregory F. *Reshaping Intelligence for an Age of Information*. New York: Cambridge University Press, 2001.

Triber, Jayne. *A True Republican: The Life of Paul Revere*. Amherst, MA: University of Massachusetts Press, 1998.

Troy, Thomas F. *Donovan and the CIA: A History of the Establishment of the Central Intelligence Agency*. Frederick, MD: University Publications of America, 1981.

Troy, Thomas F. *Wild Bill and Intrepid: Donovan, Stephenson and the Origins of the CIA*. New Haven, CT: Yale University Press, 1996.

Trulock, Notra, III. *Code Name Kindred Spirit: Inside the Chinese Nuclear Espionage Scandal*. New York: Encounter Books, 2002.

Trulock, Notra, III. "Intelligence and the Department of Energy: New Approaches for the 1990s," *American Intelligence Journal* 17 (1996), 17–22.

Tuchman, Barbara. *The Zimmermann Telegram*. New York: Viking Press, 1958.

Turner, Frederick J. "Documents on the Blount Conspiracy, 1795–1797," *The American Historical Review* 10 (1905), 574–606.

Turner, Stansfield. *Secrecy and Democracy: The CIA in Transition*. Boston: Houghton Mifflin, 1985.

United States. War Department. Strategic Services Unit. History Project. *War Report of the OSS*. New York: Walker, 1976.

Urban, George. *Radio Free Europe and the Pursuit of Democracy: My War within the Cold War*. New Haven, CT: Yale University Press, 1997.

Urquhart, Brian. *Ralph Bunche: An American Odyssey*. New York: W.W. Norton & Company, 1998.

Van der Aart, Dick. *Aerial Espionage: Secret Intelligence Flights by East and West*. New York: Arco/Prentice Hall, 1986.

Van Doren, Carl. *Secret History of the American Revolution*. New York: Viking Press, 1941.

Van Doren Stern, P. *Secret Missions of the Civil War*. New York: Wing Books, 1990.

Van Pelt, Lori. *Amelia Earhart: The Sky's No Limit*. New York: Tom Doherty Associates, 2005

Van Tyne, C. H. "French Aid Before the Alliance of 1778," *The American Historical Review* 31 (1925), 20–40.

Veith, George. *Code Name Bright Light*. New York: Free Press, 1998.

Ver Steeg, Clarence L. *Robert Morris, Revolutionary Financier, With an Analysis of His Earlier Career*. Philadelphia: University of Pennsylvania Press, 1954.

Vise, Thomas. *The Bureau and the Mole: The Unmasking of Robert Philip Hanssen, The Most Dangerous Double Agent in FBI History*. New York: Schwarz, 2003.

Volkman, Ernest. *Espionage: The Greatest Spy Operations of the Twentieth Century*. New York: John Wiley & Sons, Inc., 1995.

Volkman, Ernest *Spies: The Secret Agents Who Changed the Course of History*. New York: Wiley, 1997.

Voska, Emmanuel Victor, and Will Irwin. *Spy and Counterspy*. New York: Doubleday, Doran & Co., 1940.

Wagenaar, Sam. *Mata Hari: A Biography*. New York: Appleton, 1966.

Walsh, Lawrence E. *The Iran-Contra Conspiracy and Cover-up*. New York: W.W. Norton, 1998.

Walters, Vernon. *Silent Missions*. Garden City, NY: Doubleday, 1978.

Wark, Wesley. *The Ultimate Enemy: British Intelligence and Nazi Germany, 1933–1939*. London: Tauris, 1985.

Warner, Ezra T. *Generals in Gray: Lives of the Confederate Commanders*. Baton Rouge, LA: Louisiana State University Press, 1959.

Warner, Michael. *The CIA Under Harry Truman*. Washington, DC: Central Intelligence Agency, 1994.

Warner, Michael. "Reading the Riot Act: The Schlesinger Report, 1971," *Intelligence and National Security* 24 (2009), 387–417.

Warner, Michael. "Salvage and Liquidation: The Creation of the Central Intelligence Group," *Studies in Intelligence* 39 (1996), 11–20.

Warner, Michael and K. McDonald. *US Intelligence Community Reform Studies Since 1947*. Washington, DC: Strategic Management Issues Office, Center for the Study of Intelligence, 2005.

Warner, Roger. *Shooting at the Moon: The Story of America's Clandestine War in Laos*. Hanover, NH: Steerforth, 1998.

Warren, Harris Gaylord. *The Sword Was Their Passport: A History of American Filibustering in the Mexican Revolution*. Baton Rouge, LA: Louisiana State University Press, 1943.

Wasserstein, Bernard. *Secret War in Shanghai: Treachery, Subversion, and Collaboration in the Second World War*. London: Profile Books, 1998.

Watson, Bruce, Susan Watson, and Gerald Hopples (eds.). *United States Intelligence: An Encyclopedia*. New York: Garland, 1990.

Weber, Ralph E. (ed.). *Spymasters: Ten CIA Officers in Their Own Words*. Wilmington, DE: Scholarly Resources, 1999.

Weems, John Edward. *To Conquer a Peace: The War Between the United States and Mexico*. Garden City, NY: Doubleday, 1974.

Weigley, Russell F. *The American Way of War: A History of the United States Military Strategy and Policy*. Bloomington, IN: Indiana University Press, 1973.

Weigold, Marilyn. *The Long Island Sound: A History of Its People, Places, and Environment*. New York: New York University Press, 2004.

Weimer, Tim, et al. *Betrayal: The Story of Aldrich Ames, an American Spy*. New York: Random House, 1995.

Weinstein, Allen. *Perjury: The Hiss-Chambers Case*. New York: Alfred A. Knopf, 1978.

Weinstein, Allen and Alexander Vassiliev. *The Haunted Wood: Soviet Espionage in America—The Stalin Era*. New York: Random House, 1999.

Welch, Michael. *Scapegoats of September 11th: Hate Crimes and State Crimes in the War on Terror*. New Brunswick: Rutgers University Press, 2006.

Welch, Neil J., and David W. Marston. *Inside Hoover's FBI: The Top Field Chief Reports*. New York. Doubleday, 1984.

Wenger, Andreas. *Living with Peril: Eisenhower, Kennedy, and Nuclear Weapons*. Lanham, MD: Rowman & Littlefield, 1997.

West, Nigel. introduction. *British Security Coordination: The Secret History of British Intelligence in the Americas, 1940–45*. London: St. Ermin's Press, 1998.

West, Nigel. *The Circus: MI5 Operations, 1945–1972*. New York: Stein and Day, 1983.

West, Nigel. *The Crown Jewels: British Secrets at the Heart of KGB Files*. New Haven, CT: Yale University Press, 1999.

West, Nigel. *Historical Dictionary of Cold War Counterintelligence*. Lanham, MD: The Scarecrow Press, 2007.

West, Nigel. *MI5: British Security Service Operations, 1909–1945*. London: The Bodley Head, 1981.

West, Nigel. *Molehunt: Searching for Spies in MI5*. New York: William Morrow & Co., 1989.

West, Nigel. *Seven Spies Who Changed the World*. London: Secker & Warburg, 1991.

West, Nigel. *The SIGINT Secrets: The Signals Intelligence War, 1900 to Today*. New York: Avon Books, 1988.

West, Nigel. *A Thread of Deceit: Espionage Myths of the Second World War*. New York: Dell, 1986.

West, Rebecca. *The New Meaning of Treason*. New York: Viking, 1964.

Whaley, Barton. *Codeword Barbarossa*. Boston: MIT Press, 1974.

Wheelan, Joseph. *Jefferson's Vendetta, the Pursuit of Aaron Burr and the Judiciary*. New York: Carroll & Graf Publishers, 2005.

Wheeler, Tom. *Mr. Lincoln's t-mails: The Untold Story of How Abraham Lincoln Used the Telegraph to Win the Civil War*. New York: Collins, 2006.

Whitaker, A.P. *The Spanish-American Frontier, 1783–1795: The Westward Movement and the Spanish Retreat in the Mississippi Valley*. Boston: Houghton Mifflin, 1927.

Whitaker, Red, and Gary Marcuse. *Cold War Canada: The Making of a National Insecurity State, 1945–1957*. Toronto: University of Toronto Press, 1996.

White, G. Edward. *Alger Hiss' Looking-Glass Wars: The Covert Life of a Secret Spy*. New York: Oxford University Press, 2004.

White, Mark J. (ed.). *The Kennedys and Cuba: The Declassified Documentary History*. Chicago: Ivan R. Dee, 1999.

White, Theodore. *Breach of Faith: The Fall of Richard Nixon*. New York: Antheneum, 1975.

Whiting, Charles. *Gehlen: Germany's Master Spy*. New York: Ballantine Books, 1972.

Whitlam, Nicholas, and John Stubbs. *Nest of Traitors: The Petrov Affair*. Brisbane, Australia: Jacaranda, 1974.

Whitney, Craig R. *Spy Trader: East Germany's Devil's Advocate and the Darkest Secrets of the Cold War*. New York: New York Times Books, 1993.

Whitney, Craig R. *The WMD Mirage*. New York: Public Affairs, 2006.

Whymant, Robert. *Stalin's Spy: Richard Sorge and the Tokyo Espionage Ring*. New York: St. Martin's Press, 1998.

Wilford, Hugh. *The Mighty Wurlitzer: How the CIA Played America*. Cambridge: Harvard University Press, 2008.

Williams, Robert Chadwell. *Klaus Fuchs, Atom Spy*. Cambridge, MA: Harvard University Press, 1987.

Willoughby, Charles A. *Shanghai Conspiracy: The Sorge Spy Ring, Moscow, Shanghai, Tokyo, San Francisco, New York*. New York: Dutton, 1952.

Wilson, Harold S. *Confederate Industry: Manufacturers and Quartermasters in the Civil War*. Jackson, MS: University Press of Mississippi, 2002.

Winbourn, Byron. *Wen Bon: A Naval Intelligence Officer behind Japanese Lines in China in WWII*. Denton, TX: University of North Texas Press, 1994.

Winchell, Mark Royden. *William F. Buckley, Jr.* New York: Macmillan, 1984.

Winkler, Allan. *The Politics of Propaganda: The Office of War Information, 1942–1945*. New Haven and London: Yale University Press, 1978.

Winks, Robin. *Cloak and Gown: Scholars in the Secret War, 1939–1961*, 2nd ed. New Haven, CT: Yale University Press, 1996.

Winterbotham, F.W. *The Ultra Secret*. New York: Harper & Row, 1974.

Winton, John. *ULTRA at Sea: How Breaking the Nazi Code Affected Allied Naval Strategy during World War II*. New York: William Morrow, 1988.

Wires, Richard. *John P. Marquand and Mr. Moto: Spy Adventures and Detective Films*. Muncie, IN: Ball State University press, 1990.

Wirtz, James. "Intelligence to Please? The Order of Battle Controversy During the Vietnam War," *Political Science Quarterly* 106 (1991), 239–263.

Wise, Charles. "Organizing for Homeland Security," *Public Administration Review* 62 (March/April 2002), 44–57.

Wise, David. *The Bureau and the Mole: Unmasking of Robert Philip Hanssen: The Most Dangerous Double Agent in FBI History*. New York: Schwarz, 2003.

Wise, David. *Cassidy's Run: The Secret Spy War Over Nerve Gas*. New York: Random House, 2001.

Wise, David. *Molehunt: The Secret Search for Traitors that Shattered the CIA*. New York: Random House, 1992.

Wise, David. *Spy: The Inside Story of How the FBI's Robert Hanssen Betrayed America*. New York: Random House, 2003.

Wise, David. *The Spy Who Got Away: The Inside Story of Edward Lee Howard, the CIA Agent Who Betrayed His Country's Secrets and Escaped to Moscow*. New York: Random House, 1988.

Wise, Thomas. *The American Police State*. New York: Random House, 1976.

Witcover, Jules. *Sabotage at Black Tom: Imperial Germany's Secret War in America 1914–1917*. Chapel Hill, NC: Algonquin Books, 1989.

Wittlin, Tadeusz. *Commissar: The Life and Death of Lavrenty Pavlovich Beria*. New York: Macmillan, 1973.

Wohlstetter, Roberta. *Pearl Harbor: Warning and Decision*. Stanford: Stanford University Press, 1962.

Wolf, Markus, with Anne McElvoy. *Man Without a Face: The Autobiography of Communism's Greatest Spymaster*. New York: Public Affairs, 1999.

Woodward, Bob. *Bush at War*. New York: Simon & Schuster, 2002.

Woodward, Bob. *The Commanders*. New York: Simon & Schuster, 1991.

Woodward, Bob. *Plan of Attack*. New York: Simon & Schuster, 2004.

Woodward, Bob. *The Secret Man: The Story of Watergate's Deep Throat*. Waterville, ME: Thorndike Press, 2005.

Woodward, Bob. *State of Denial: Bush at War, Part III*. New York: Simon & Schuster, 2006.

Woodward, Bob. *VEIL: The Secret Wars of the CIA 1981–1987*. New York: Simon & Schuster, 1987.

Wright, Peter. *Spycatcher*. New York: Viking, 1987.

Wriston, Henry Merritt. *Executive Agents in American Foreign Relations*. Baltimore, MD: Johns Hopkins University Press, 1929.

Wrixon, Fred B. *Codes, Ciphers, & Other Cryptic & Clandestine Communications*. New York: Black Dog & Leventhal Publishers, Inc., 1998.

Wyden, Peter. *The Bay of Pigs: The Untold Story*. New York: Vintage, 1979.

Wylie, Neville (ed.). *The Politics of Strategic and Clandestine War: Special Operations Executive, 1940–1946*, London: Routledge, 2007.

Wynne, Greville. *The man from Odessa*. London: Granada, 1983.

Wynne, Greville Maynard. *The Man from Moscow the Story of Wynne & Penkovsky*. London, Hutchinson. 1967.

Yardley, Herbert O. *The American Black Chamber*. Annapolis, MD: Naval Institute Press, 1931.

Yoshikawa, Takeo. *Higashi no Kaze Ame: Shinjuwan Supai no Kaisou [East Wind Rain: Reminiscence of a Pearl Harbor Spy]*. Tokyo: Kodansha, 1963.

Youm, Kyu Ho. "The Radio and TV Marti Controversy: A Re-Examination," *Gazette* 48 (1991), 95–103.

Yu, Maochin. *OSS in China: Prelude to Cold War*. New Haven, CT: Yale University Press, 1996.

Zabih, Sepehr. *The Mossadegh Era: Roots of the Iranian Revolution*. Chicago: Lake View Press, 1986.

Zak, William, Jr. "Sixth Amendment Issues Posed by the Court-Martial of Clayton Lonetree," *American Criminal Law Review* 30 (1992), 187–214.

"Zarubin, Vassiliy Mikhailovich," in *Entsiklopedicheskiy Slovar' Rossiyskikh Spetssluzhb: Razveka I Kontrrazvedka v Litsakh* [Encyclopedic Dictionary of the Russian Special Services: Personalities of Intelligence and Counterintelligence.], pp. 188–189. Moscow: Russian World, 2002.

Zegart, Amy B. *Flawed by Design: The Evolution of the CIA, JCS, and NSC*. Stanford: Stanford University Press, 1999.

Zegart, Amy B. *Spying Blind: The CIA, the FBI and the Origins of 9/11*. Princeton: Princeton University Press, 2007.

Government Documents

"A Review of the Intelligence Community," March 10, 1971, Document 229 in Department of State, *Foreign Relations of the United States, 1969–1976, Volume II, Organization and Management of U.S. Foreign Policy, 1969–1972*, pp. 492–516. Washington, DC: Government Printing Office, 2006.

Air Force National Security Emergency Preparedness Agency (AFNSEP). "Our Mission," http://www.globalsecurity.org/military/agency/usaf/afnsep.htm (accessed January 12, 2006).

Central Intelligence Agency. "CIA Support to the US Military During the Persian Gulf War." June 16, 1997. https://www.cia.gov/library/reports/general-reports-1/gulfwar/061997/support.htm.

Central Intelligence Agency. "*Iraq's Known Uranium Holdings.*" Comprehensive Report of the Special Advisor to the DCI on Iraq's WMD, June 2004. https://www.cia.gov/library/reports/general-reports-1/iraq_wmd_2004/contents.html.

Commission on the Organization of the Executive Branch of the Government. *Intelligence Activities: A Report to the Congress.* Washington, DC: Government Printing Office, June 1955.

Committee on the National Security Organizations. *National Security Organization: A Report with Recommendations* [The Eberstadt Report]. Washington, DC: Government Printing Office, 1949.

Covert Identities Protection Act. http://en.wikisource.org/wiki/Intelligence_Identities_Protection_Act.

Defense Intelligence Agency. "A Brief History." http://www.fas.org/irp/dia/dia_history.pdf.

Estimative Products on Vietnam, 1948–1975. Washington, DC: National Intelligence Council, 2005.

Foreign Intelligence Surveillance Act. www.fas.org/irp/agency/doj/fisa

Information Circular: Homing Pigeons. Washington, DC: War Department, Office of the Chief Signal Officers 1934.

Intelligence Identities Protection Act. www.fas.org/irp/offdocs/laws/iipa.html.

Inspector General, Department of Defense. *Review of the Case of Mr. David Tenenbaum, Department of the Army Employee.* July 13, 2008.

National Archives and Records Administration. Watergate resources. http://www.archives.gov/digital_classroom/lessons/watergate_and_constitution/teaching_activities.html (December 1, 2002).

National Security Agency. "The VENONA Story," http://www.nsa.gov/public_info/declass/venona/index.shtml (accessed January 7, 2006).

Report on the Covert Activities of the Central Intelligence Agency [the Doolittle Report], September 30, 1954, http://cryptome.info/cia-doolittle/cia-doolittle.htm (accessed on August 30, 2008).

Report to the President by the Commission on CIA Activities Within the United States [Rockefeller Commission Report]. Washington, DC: Government Printing Office, 1975.

Report of the President's Commission on the Assassination of President John F. Kennedy. [The Warren Commission Report]. Washington, DC: United States Government Printing Office, 1964.

U.S. Congress. Committee on Armed Forces, House of Representatives. *Intelligence Success and Failures in Operations Desert Shield/Storm.* Washington, DC: Government Printing Office, August 18, 1993.

U.S. Congress. House. Committee on International Relations. Subcommittee on the Western Hemisphere. *Overview of Radio and Television Marti Hearings.* 108th Congress 1st Session. Washington, DC: Government Printing Office, 2003.

U.S. Congress. House Permanent Select Committee on Intelligence. *Central Intelligence Agency Information Act: Report, to accompany H.R. 5164 . . . referred jointly to the Permanent Select Committee on Intelligence and the Committee on Government Operations.* 98th Cong., 2 sess., 1984. H. Rpt 98–726, pts. 1–2. Washington, DC: GPO, 1984.

U.S. Congress. Senate. Committee on Foreign Relations. *Broadcasting to Cuba, Hearings*. 97th Congress, 2nd Session. Washington, DC: Government Printing Office, 1982–1983.

U.S. Department of Homeland Security, Homeland Security Advisory Council. *Intelligence and Information Sharing Initiative: Homeland Security Intelligence and Information Fusion*. Washington, DC: Government Printing Office, 28 April 2005.

U.S. Department of State. *Foreign Relations of the United States 1945–1950: Emergence of the Intelligence Establishment*. Washington, DC: Government Printing Office, 1996.

U.S. Navy. *Naval Doctrine Publication 2 (NDP-2): Naval Intelligence*. Washington, DC: Department of the Navy, 1994.

U.S. Navy Department. *Report to War and Navy Departments on Post War Organization for National Security*, October 22, 1945; 79th Congress, 1st Session: Senate Committee on Naval Affairs. Washington, DC: Government Printing Office, 1945.

U.S. Senate, 94th Cong. 2nd sess. *Final Report of the Select Committee to Study Government Operations with Respect to Intelligence Activities* (Church Committee Report). Washington, DC: Government Printing Office, 1975.

U.S. Senate, Select Committee to Study Governmental Operations with Respect to Intelligence Activities. "CIA Intelligence Collection About Americans: Chaos and the Office of Security," *Supplementary Detailed Staff Reports on Intelligence Activities and the Rights of Americans*. April 23, 1976. http://www.icdc.com/~paulwolf/cointelpro/churchfinalreportIIIi.htm.

U.S. Senate, Select Committee to Study Governmental Operations with Respect to Intelligence Activities. *Final Report, Book V: The Investigation of the Assassination of President John F. Kennedy: Performance of the Intelligence Agencies*. Washington, DC: Government Printing Office, April 23, 1976.

U.S. Senate, Select Committee to Study Government Operations with respect to Intelligence Activities. *Final Report, Book II, Intelligence Activities and the Rights of Americans*. Washington, DC: U.S. Government Printing Office, April 26, 1976.

USA Patriot Act, http://epic.org/privacy/terrorism/hr3162.html.

Web Addresses

Association of Former Intelligence Officers: http://www.afio.com/01_about.htm (accessed January 2, 2006).

Central Intelligence Agency: https://www.cia.gov/.

Centre for CounterIntelligence and Security Studies. "Spy Cases," http://www.cicentre.com/ (accessed July 17, 2008).

Consortium for the Study of Intelligence. "About CSI," http://www.intelligenceconsortium.org/.

Department of Defense: www.defenselink.mil.

Digital National Security Archive, http://nsarchive.chadwyck.com/marketing/index.jsp.

Electronic Privacy Information Center: http://epic.org/privacy/.

Federal Bureau of Investigation: www.fbi.gov.

Federation of American Scientists: http://www.fas.org/.

House Committee on Intelligence: www.intelligence.house/gov.

National Counterterrorism Center: http://www.nctc.gov/.

National Security Agency: www.nsa.gov.

National Security Archive: http://www.gwu.edu/~nsarchiv/.

National Security Council: http://www.whitehouse.gov/administration/eop/nsc/.

National Strategy Information Center: www.strategycenter.org/.

National Reconnaissance Office: http://www.nro.gov/.

Nautilus Institute in Australia: http://www.globalcollab.org/Nautilus/australia.

Office of Director of National Intelligence: www.dni.gov.

Official Secrets Act (UK): http://www.statutelaw.gov.uk/content.aspx?activeTextDocId
=1351839.

Radio Marti: http://www.martinoticias.com/.

Senate Select Committee on Intelligence: www.intelligence.senate.gov.

U.S. Intelligence Community: http://www.intelligence.gov/index.shtml.

Index

About the Editor

Glenn P. Hastedt is a professor of political science and justice studies at James Madison University where he teaches courses on American foreign policy and international relations. Formerly chair of the Political Science Department, he is now chair of the interdisciplinary Justice Studies Department. He received his PhD from Indiana University and began his teaching career at the State University of New York–Geneseo. Dr. Hastedt has edited two books on intelligence, *Controlling Intelligence* (Frank Cass, 1991) and *Analysis and Estimates* (Frank Cass, 1996). He is the author of *American Foreign Policy: Past, Present, Future* (Pearson Education, 8th edition, 2009) and edits the *American Foreign Policy Annual Edition* (McGraw Hill). Dr. Hastedt has published more than thirty articles and chapters, half of which address issues relating to controlling intelligence and problems of surprise in world politics. Other articles deal with presidential transitions and the changing relationship between the president and Congress. He is co-editor of *White House Studies* and a member of the editorial boards of *The Journal of Conflict Studies* and *Intelligence and National Security*. He is a past recipient of the the College of Arts and Letters Distinguished Teacher award and its Madison Scholar award.